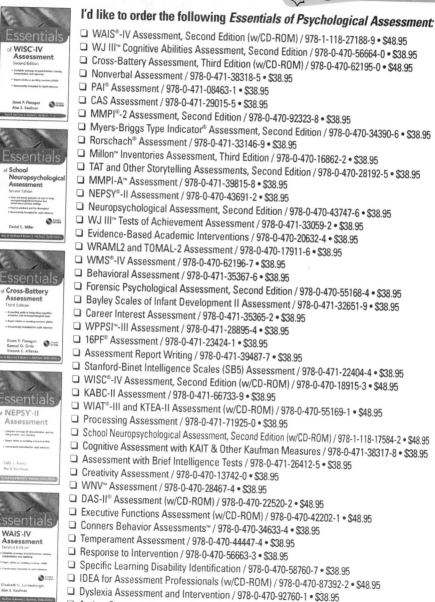

Essentials
of **Psychological Assessment** Series

ORDER FORM

Please send this order form with your payment (credit card or check) to:
John Wiley & Sons, Attn: J. Knott, 111 River Street, Hoboken, NJ 07030-5774

QUANTITY	TITLE	ISBN	PRICE
_____	_____	_____	_____
_____	_____	_____	_____
_____	_____	_____	_____
_____	_____	_____	_____
_____	_____	_____	_____

Shipping Charges:	**Surface**	**2-Day**	**1-Day**
First item	$5.00	$10.50	$17.50
Each additional item	$3.00	$3.00	$4.00

For orders greater than 15 items,
please contact Customer Care at 1-877-762-2974.

ORDER AMOUNT _____

SHIPPING CHARGES _____

SALES TAX _____

TOTAL ENCLOSED _____

NAME_____

AFFILIATION_____

ADDRESS_____

CITY/STATE/ZIP _____

TELEPHONE _____

EMAIL_____

❑ Please add me to your e-mailing list

PAYMENT METHOD:

❑ Check/Money Order   ❑ Visa   ❑ Mastercard   ❑ AmEx

Card Number _____ Exp. Date _____

Cardholder Name *(Please print)* _____

Signature _____

*Make checks payable to **John Wiley & Sons.** Credit card orders invalid if not signed.*
All orders subject to credit approval. • Prices subject to change.

To order by phone, call toll free 1-877-762-2974
To order online: www.wiley.com/essentials

WILEY

Essentials of WAIS®-IV Assessment
Second Edition

Essentials of Psychological Assessment Series
Series Editors, Alan S. Kaufman and Nadeen L. Kaufman

Essentials

of WAIS®-IV Assessment

Second Edition

Elizabeth O. Lichtenberger
Alan S. Kaufman

John Wiley & Sons, Inc.

Cover image: © Greg Kuchik/Getty Images

Cover design: John Wiley & Sons, Inc.

This book is printed on acid-free paper. ∞

Library of Congress Cataloging-in-Publication Data:
Lichtenberger, Elizabeth O.
    Essentials of WAIS-IV assessment/Elizabeth O. Lichtenberger and Alan S. Kaufman. — 2nd ed.
       p. cm. — (Essentials of psychological assessment series)
    Includes index.
    ISBN 978-1-118-27188-9 (paper/cd-rom)
  ISBN 978-1-118-43385-0 (ebk.)
  ISBN 978-1-118-42118-5 (ebk.)
  ISBN 978-1-118-41962-5 (ebk.)

Wechsler Adult Intelligence Scale, Third Edition (WAIS-III). Copyright © 1997 NCS Pearson, Inc. Reproduced with permission. All rights reserved.

Wechsler Adult Intelligence Scale, Fourth Edition (WAIS-IV). Copyright © 2008 NCS Pearson, Inc. Reproduced with permission. All rights reserved.

"Wechsler Adult Intelligence Scale" and "WAIS" are trademarks, in the US and/or other countries, of Pearson Education, Inc. or its affiliates(s).

  1. Wechsler Adult Intelligence Scale. 2. Intelligence tests. I. Kaufman, Alan S., 1944- II. Title.
     BF432.5.W4L53 2013
     153.9'3—dc23

                                                                              2012022695

Printed in the United States of America
10 9 8 7 6 5 4 3 2 1

For Nadeen, who knew me as a boy, and has been my love for 50 years.

La Bohème, Act IV

MIMI:

Sono andati? Fingevo di dormire	*Have they left us? I was pretending to sleep*
perchè volli con te sola restare.	*to be alone with you.*
Ho tante cose che ti voglio dire,	*So many things to tell you,*
o una sola,	*but really just one,*
ma grande come il mare,	*that is as huge as the ocean,*
come il mare profonda ed infinita.	*and as deep and infinite.*
Sei il mio amor e tutta la mia vita.	*You are my love and my whole life.*

RODOLFO:

O mia bella Mimi!	*My beautiful Mimi!*

MIMI:

Son bella ancora?	*Am I still beautiful?*

RODOLFO:

Bella come un'aurora.	*Beautiful as the dawn in springtime.*

A.S.K

For Hannah

Thirteen years ago, you were just a couple of weeks away from being born when I delivered the manuscript for the first edition of this book to the publisher.

In the years since then, you have grown into such a lovely young lady whom I am so proud of.

Each day you make me smile, you make me laugh, and you inspire me to be the best I can be.

Thank you for the love and joy you have brought me every day of your 13 years.

I love you.

Mom

CONTENTS

PREFACE TO THE SECOND EDITION

We published the first edition of *Essentials of WAIS-IV Assessment* in 2009, on the heels of the WAIS-IV's availability in 2008. In an excellent review of the first edition of our book, Krach (2010) noted that we did not include research findings from the literature, but relied on studies in the WAIS-IV manual because such independent research findings had not yet appeared. Krach (2010) defended our decision to publish the book in such a timely fashion, stating: "It is preferable to have the [*Essentials* book] available as soon as possible following the test's publication rather than wait the years it might take for new, independent research to be available" (p. 278). But she added: "Perhaps a second edition of the book will be published that incorporates new research findings on the psychometric quality and clinical utility of the WAIS-IV, once such research findings become available."

And that is precisely what we have done by developing the second edition of *Essentials of WAIS-IV Assessment*. A wealth of new research has become available in the few years since the publication of the first edition, and we have fully incorporated that research into the second edition. This new body of research allowed us to expand the coverage of timely topics, such as gender and ethnic differences and the role of the Flynn effect in capital punishment court cases, and to enhance our interpretive system for elderly individuals. Previously, we offered a solid interpretive system with a strong Cattell-Horn-Carroll (CHC) theoretical foundation for ages 16 to 69, but we had a less robust method of profile interpretation for ages 70 to 90. That has all changed thanks to an innovative factor-analytic investigation of the WAIS-IV (Niileksela, Reynolds, & Kaufman, 2012) that provides a five-factor CHC-based solution not only for ages 16 to 69 but for ages 70 to 90 as well. We have overhauled our system of profile interpretation to be equally powerful across the *entire* WAIS-IV age range and to emphasize that both the traditional four-factor and CHC-derived five-factor solutions are entirely *compatible* and do not reflect alternative views of the interpretive universe.

In addition, the pros and cons chapter in the first edition was written by Ron Dumont and John Willis before any published reviews were available on the test, and the WAIS-IV process interpretation chapter was written by George McCloskey prior to recent developments in clinical neuropsychology. Dumont and Willis made notable changes in their chapter to reflect the thoughtful content of several comprehensive test reviews that appeared in respected publications, such as those of Buros, and to incorporate their ongoing clinical experiences with the WAIS-IV during the past few years. McCloskey updated his chapter, with new coauthors Emily Hartz and Katherine Scipioni, to incorporate the dynamic progress that continues to accumulate in the growing field of neuropsychological processing assessment and intervention. And we have added a brand-new guest-written chapter by Tommie Cayton, Dustin Wahlstrom, and Mark Daniel, that unveils the latest WAIS-IV cutting-edge innovation: the digital version of the WAIS-IV (Q-interactive™) that allows clinicians to administer the WAIS-IV via iPad.

The most influential sources of new information, data, research, and research summaries that affected our development of the second edition of *Essentials of WAIS-IV Assessment* are the following:

- *WAIS-IV Clinical Use and Interpretation*, a 2010 edited book by Weiss, Saklofske, Coalson, and Raiford that included many innovative WAIS-IV research studies on gender, ethnicity, socioeconomic status, aging, and the Flynn effect, and that also included administration and scoring nuggets by the psychologists who developed the WAIS-IV for the test publisher.
- *Essentials of WMS-IV Assessment* (Drozdick, Holdnack, & Hilsabeck, 2011) and a special section of *Assessment* on advancing WAIS-IV and WMS-IV clinical interpretation (Frazier, 2011)—both of which offered fresh insights into the integration of the WAIS-IV and the Wechsler Memory Scale—Fourth Edition (WMS-IV). These tests were standardized together and, historically, are linked conceptually and clinically; both were developed by Wechsler and are routinely administered in tandem in neuropsychological evaluations of adults, especially the elderly. Data on integrating functional assessment with WAIS-IV in evaluating special populations was informative for groups such as adults with possible dementia (Drozdick & Cullum, 2011).
- An array of carefully crafted articles on the factor structure of the WAIS-IV that greatly enhanced the psychometric, theoretical, practical, and clinical understanding of both four-factor and five-factor solutions

(Benson, Hulac, & Kranzler, 2010; Canivez & Watkins, 2010b; Niileksela et al., 2012; Ward, Bergman, & Hebert, 2012).

- A special issue of the *Journal of Psychoeducational Assessment* devoted to the Flynn effect (Kaufman & Weiss, 2010b). Since the first edition went to press, the Flynn effect has gained national prominence in capital punishment cases around the United States. It holds the key to whether a person who committed a capital offense will live or die. Our coverage of this key societal topic in the second edition is based mainly on the diverse articles by experts on this special issue.
- Authoritative, objective, well-thought-out reviews of the WAIS-IV (Canivez, 2010; Climie & Rostad, 2011; Hartman, 2009; Schraw, 2010).
- Recent state-of-the-art edited books on intelligence (Sternberg & Kaufman, 2011) and intellectual assessment (Flanagan & Harrison, 2012) that integrate and interpret the latest research and thinking about key topics covered in the second edition of *Essentials of WAIS-IV Assessment*, such as gender differences, CHC theory, aging and intelligence, cognitive interventions with elderly individuals, historical foundations, ethnicity, cross-battery assessment, information processing approaches to test interpretation, and confirmatory factor analysis.

Our biggest disappointment in combing through the past four years of research on the WAIS-IV and adult intelligence in general was the lack of available studies with brand-new clinical samples tested on the WAIS-IV. Although some studies reported in the special section of *Assessment* devoted to the WAIS-IV and WMS-IV and in the Weiss et al. (2010) edited book involved clinical samples, the patients included in these samples overlapped substantially with patients in the samples reported in the WAIS-IV manual. Nonetheless, these new analyses on the old samples offered some fresh insights into the clinical samples that we incorporated into Chapter 8.

Despite this limitation in the clinical research conducted on the WAIS-IV, the new second edition is a thoroughly revised and updated text that incorporates the latest, most compelling research and provides clinicians with a brand-new interpretive system and CD-ROM. It also includes a timely invited chapter on the digital WAIS-IV (Q-interactive[TM]) that was written for this book before the publication of the Q-interactive[TM] platform.

Elizabeth O. Lichtenberger and
Alan S. Kaufman
June 2012

ACKNOWLEDGMENTS

We gratefully acknowledge the authors of three exceptional invited chapters that appear in the second edition of *Essentials of WAIS-IV Assessment*: George McCloskey, Emily Hartz, and Katherine Scipioni, who contributed Chapter 6 on a neuropsychological processing approach to interpreting the WAIS-IV; Ron Dumont and John Willis, who contributed Chapter 9 on the pros and cons of the WAIS-IV; and Tommie Cayton, Dustin Wahlstrom, and Mark Daniel, who contributed Chapter 11 on the brand-new Q-interactive™, a computerized approach to WAIS-IV administration. (Chapters 6 and 9 are thoughtful revisions of chapters that appeared in the first edition; Chapter 11 is new to the second edition.) We are also extremely grateful to Matt Reynolds and Chris Niileksela for conducting state-of-the-art confirmatory factor analysis of the WAIS-IV to permit interpretation of a five-factor CHC model for elderly individuals ages 70 to 90; to Larry Weiss for reading early drafts of Chapters 1 and 5 and making important contributions to these chapters; to Diane Coalson and Susie Raiford for providing us with an array of the latest articles and reviews on the WAIS-IV; to Jack Naglieri and J. J. Zhu for conducting analyses that were needed to accommodate modifications to our new interpretive system; and to Wiley's Peggy Alexander, Marquita Flemming, and Sherry Wasserman for providing the kind of amazing support and technical competence that one can only dream of from a book publisher.

In addition, we would like to acknowledge those people who were instrumental in the development of the first edition of this book: George McCloskey, for his chapter on the neuropsychological interpretation of the WAIS-IV; Ron Dumont and John Willis for carefully evaluating the WAIS-IV in their chapter on strengths and weaknesses; Clark Clipson and Shelley Lurie for providing outstanding case reports (retained in the second edition); Darielle Greenberg, James C. Kaufman, and David Loomis for their research assistance; Tim Keith and Jack Naglieri for providing important data analyses; numerous professionals at Pearson for their assistance and insights (Larry Weiss, Diane Coalson, J. J. Zhu, Susie Raiford, Jim Holdnack, Paul Williams, and Tommie Cayton); those who dedicated their time and clinical expertise to enhance the utility of the automated *WAIS-IV Data Management and Interpretive Assistant* (WAIS-IV DMIA) (Ron Dumont, John Willis, Howell Gotlieb, Richard Schere, and Steven Migalski); and Wiley's Isabel Pratt, who was vital to the success of the *Essentials* series.

One

INTRODUCTION AND OVERVIEW

INTRODUCTION

The field of assessment, particularly intellectual assessment, has grown tremendously over the past couple of decades. New tests of cognitive abilities are being developed, and older tests of intelligence are being revised to meet the needs of the professionals utilizing them. There are several good sources for reviewing major measures of cognitive ability (e.g., Flanagan & Harrison, 2012; Naglieri & Goldstein, 2009; Sattler, 2008); however, the new and revised measures multiply rapidly, and it is often difficult to keep track of new instruments, let alone know how to administer, score, and interpret them. One of the goals of this book is to provide an easy reference source for those who wish to learn essentials of the *Wechsler Adult Intelligence Scale—Fourth Edition* (WAIS-IV) in a direct, no-nonsense, systematic manner.

Essentials of WAIS-IV Assessment was developed with an easy-to-read format in mind. The topics covered in the book emphasize administration, scoring, interpretation, and application of the WAIS-IV. Each chapter includes several "Rapid Reference," "Caution," and "Don't Forget" boxes that highlight important points for easy reference. At the end of each chapter, questions are provided to help you solidify what you have read. The information provided in this book will help you to understand, in depth, the latest of the measures in the Wechsler family and will help you become a competent WAIS-IV examiner and clinician.

HISTORY AND DEVELOPMENT

The first assessment instrument developed by David Wechsler came on the scene in 1939. However, the history of intelligence testing began several decades before that, in the late 19th century, and is largely an account of the measurement of the intelligence of children or retarded adults. Sir Francis Galton (1869, 1883) studied adults and was interested in giftedness when he developed what is often considered the first comprehensive individual test of intelligence, composed of sensorimotor tasks (Kaufman, 2000b). But despite Galton's role as the father of the testing movement (Shouksmith, 1970), he did not succeed in constructing a true intelligence test. His measures of simple reaction time, strength of squeeze, or keenness of sight proved to assess sensory and motor abilities, skills that relate poorly to mental ability and that are far removed from the type of tasks that constitute contemporary intelligence tests.

BINET-SIMON SCALES

Alfred Binet and his colleagues (Binet & Henri, 1895; Binet & Simon, 1905, 1908) developed the tasks that survive to the present day in most tests of intelligence for children and adults. Binet (1890a, 1890b) mainly studied children; beginning with systematic developmental observations of his two young daughters, Madeleine and Alice, he concluded that simple tasks such as those used by Galton did not discriminate between children and adults. In 1904, the minister of public instruction in Paris appointed Binet to a committee to find a way to distinguish normal from retarded children. Fifteen years of qualitative and quantitative investigation of individual differences in children—along with considerable theorizing about mental organization and the development of a specific set of complex, high-level tests to investigate these differences— preceded the "sudden" emergence of the landmark 1905 Binet-Simon intelligence scale (Murphy, 1968).

The 1908 scale was the first to include age levels, spanning the range from 3 to 13. This important modification stemmed from Binet and Simon's unexpected discovery that their 1905 scale was useful for much more than classifying a child at one of the three levels of retardation: moron, imbecile, idiot (Matarazzo, 1972). Assessment of older adolescents and adults, however, was not built into the Binet-Simon system until the 1911 revision. That scale was extended to age 15 and included five ungraded adult tests (Kite, 1916). This extension was not conducted with the rigor that characterized the construction of tests for children, and the primary applications of the scale were for use with school-age children (Binet, 1911).

Measuring the intelligence of adults, except those known to be mentally retarded, was almost an afterthought. But Binet recognized the increased applicability of the Binet-Simon tests for various child assessment purposes just before his untimely death in 1911, when he "began to foresee numerous uses for his method in child development, in education, in medicine, and in longitudinal studies predicting different occupational histories for children of different intellectual potential" (Matarazzo, 1972, p. 42).

TERMAN'S STANFORD-BINET

Lewis Terman was one of several people in the United States who translated and adapted the Binet-Simon scale for use in the United States, publishing a "tentative" revision (Terman & Childs, 1912) four years before releasing his painstakingly developed and carefully standardized Stanford Revision and Extension of the Binet-Simon Intelligence Scale (Terman, 1916). This landmark test, soon known simply as the Stanford-Binet, squashed competing tests developed earlier by Goddard, Kuhlmann, Wallin, and Yerkes. Terman's success was undoubtedly due in part to heeding the advice of practitioners whose demand "for more and more accurate diagnoses . . . raised the whole question of the accurate placing of tests in the scale and the accurate evaluation of the responses made by the child" (Pintner & Paterson, 1925, p. 11).

Terman (1916) saw intelligence tests as useful primarily for the detection of mental deficiency or superiority in children and for the identification of "feeblemindedness" in adults. He cited numerous studies of delinquent adolescents and adult criminals, all of which pointed to the high percentage of mentally deficient juvenile delinquents, prisoners, or prostitutes, and concluded that "there is no investigator who denies the fearful role played by mental deficiency in the production of vice, crime, and delinquency" (p. 9). Terman also saw the potential for using intelligence tests with adults for determining "vocational fitness," but, again, he emphasized employing "a psychologist . . . to weed out the unfit" or to "determine the minimum 'intelligence quotient' necessary for success in each leading occupation" (p. 17).

Perhaps because of this emphasis on the assessment of children or concern with the lower end of the intelligence distribution, Terman (1916) did not use a rigorous methodology for constructing his adult-level tasks. Tests below the 14-year level were administered to a fairly representative sample of about 1,000 children and early adolescents. To extend the scale above that level, data were obtained from 30 businessmen, 50 high school students, 150 adolescent delinquents, and 150 migrating unemployed men. Based on a frequency distribution of the mental ages of a mere 62 adults (the 30 businessmen and 32 of the high school students above age 16), Terman partitioned the graph into the Mental Age (MA) categories: 13 to 15 (inferior adults), 15 to 17 (average adults), and above 17 (superior adults).

WORLD WAR I TESTS

The field of adult assessment grew rapidly with the onset of World War I, particularly after U.S. entry into the war in 1917 (Anastasi & Urbina, 1997; Vane & Motta, 1984). Psychologists saw with increasing clarity the applications of intelligence tests for selecting officers and placing enlisted men in different types of service, apart from their generation-old use for identifying the mentally unfit. Under the leadership of Robert Yerkes and the American Psychological Association, the most innovative psychologists of the day helped translate Binet's tests into a group format. Arthur Otis, Terman's student, was instrumental in leading the creative team that developed the Army Alpha, essentially a group-administered Stanford-Binet, and the Army Beta, a novel group test composed of nonverbal tasks.

Yerkes (1917) opposed Binet's age-scale approach and favored a point-scale methodology, one that advocates selection of tests of specified, important functions rather than a set of tasks that fluctuates greatly with age level and developmental stage. The Army group tests reflect a blend of Yerkes's point-scale approach and Binet's notions of the kind of skills that should be measured when assessing mental ability. The Army Alpha included the Binet-like tests of Directions or Commands, Practical Judgment, Arithmetical Problems, Synonym-Antonym, Dissarranged Sentences, Analogies, and Information. Even the Army Beta had subtests resembling Stanford-Binet tasks: Maze, Cube Analysis, Pictorial Completion, and Geometrical Construction. The Beta also included novel measures, such as Digit Symbol, Number Checking, and X-O Series (Yoakum & Yerkes, 1920). Never before or since have tests been normed and validated on samples so large; 1,726,966 men were tested (Vane & Motta, 1984).

Another intelligence scale was developed during the war, one that became an alternative for those who could not be tested validly by either the Alpha or Beta. This was the Army Performance Scale Examination, composed of tasks that would become the tools of the trade for clinical psychologists, school psychologists, and neuropsychologists into the 21st century: Picture Completion, Picture Arrangement, Digit Symbol, and Manikin and Feature Profile (Object Assembly). Except for Block Design (developed by Kohs in 1923), Army Performance Scale Examination was added to the Army battery "to prove conclusively that a man was weakminded and not merely indifferent or malingering" (Yoakum & Yerkes, 1920, p. 10).

WECHSLER'S CREATIVITY

In the mid-1930s, David Wechsler became a prominent player in the field of assessment by blending his strong clinical skills and statistical training (he studied under Charles Spearman and Karl Pearson in England) with his extensive experience in testing, gained as a World War I examiner. He assembled a test battery that comprised subtests developed primarily by Binet and World War I psychologists. His Verbal Scale was essentially a Yerkes point-scale adaptation of Stanford-Binet tasks; his Performance Scale, like other similar nonverbal batteries of the 1920s and 1930s (Cornell & Coxe, 1934; Pintner & Paterson, 1925), was a near replica of the tasks and items making up the individually administered Army Performance Scale Examination.

In essence, Wechsler took advantage of tasks developed by others for nonclinical purposes to develop a clinical test battery. He paired verbal tests that were fine-tuned to discriminate among children of different ages with nonverbal tests that were created for adult males who had flunked both the Alpha and Beta exams—nonverbal tests that were intended to distinguish between the unmotivated and the hopelessly deficient. Like Terman, Wechsler had the same access to the available tests as did other psychologists; like Terman and Binet before him, Wechsler succeeded because he was a visionary, a man able to anticipate the needs of practitioners in the field.

While others hoped intelligence tests would be psychometric tools used to subdivide retarded individuals into whatever number of categories was currently in vogue, Wechsler saw the tests as dynamic clinical instruments. While others looked concretely at intelligence tests as predictors of school success or guides to occupational choice, Wechsler looked abstractly at the tests as a mirror to the hidden personality. With the Great War over, many psychologists returned to a focus on IQ testing as a means of childhood assessment; Wechsler (1939), however, developed the first form of the Wechsler-Bellevue Intelligence Scale exclusively for adolescents and adults.

Most psychologists saw little need for nonverbal tests when assessing English-speaking individuals other than illiterates. How could it be worth 2 or 3 minutes to administer a single puzzle or block-design item when 10 or 15 verbal items could be given in the same time? Some test developers (e.g., Cornell & Coxe, 1934) felt that Performance scales might be useful for normal, English-speaking people to provide "more varied situations than are provided by verbal tests" (p. 9) and to "test the hypothesis that there is a group factor underlying general concrete ability, which is of importance in the concept of general intelligence" (p. 10).

Wechsler was less inclined to wait a generation for data to accumulate. He followed his clinical instincts and not only advocated for the administration of a standard battery of nonverbal tests to everyone but also placed the Performance Scale on an equal footing with the more respected Verbal Scale. Both scales would constitute a complete Wechsler-Bellevue battery, and each would contribute equally to the overall intelligence score.

Wechsler also had the courage to challenge the Stanford-Binet monopoly, a boldness not unlike Binet's when the French scientist created his own forum (the journal *L'Année Psychologique*) to challenge the preferred but simplistic Galton sensorimotor approach to intelligence (Kaufman, 2000b). Wechsler met the same type of resistance as Binet, who had had to wait until the French Ministry of Public Instruction "published" his Binet-Simon Scale. When Wechsler's initial efforts to find a publisher for his two-pronged intelligence test failed, he had no cabinet minister to turn to, so he took matters into his own hands. With a small team of colleagues, he standardized Form I of the Wechsler-Bellevue by himself. Realizing that stratification on socioeconomic background was more crucial than obtaining regional representation, he managed to secure a well-stratified sample from Brooklyn, New York (Kaufman, 2009).

The Psychological Corporation agreed to publish Wechsler's battery once it had been standardized, and the rest is history. Although an alternative form of the Wechsler-Bellevue Intelligence Scale (Wechsler, 1946) was no more successful than Terman and Merrill's (1937) ill-fated Form M, a subsequent downward extension of Form II of the Wechsler-Bellevue (to cover the age range 5 to 15 instead of 10 to 59) produced the wildly successful Wechsler Intelligence Scale for Children (WISC; Wechsler, 1949). Although the Wechsler scales did not initially surpass the Stanford-Binet in popularity, instead serving an apprenticeship to the master in the 1940s and 1950s, the WISC and the subsequent revision of the Wechsler-Bellevue, Form I (WAIS; Wechsler, 1955), triumphed in the 1960s. According to Kaufman: "With the increasing stress on the psychoeducational assessment of learning disabilities in the 1960s, and on neuropsychological evaluation in the 1970s, the Verbal-Performance (V-P) IQ discrepancies and subtest profiles yielded by Wechsler's scales were waiting and ready to overtake the one-score Binet" (Kaufman, 1983, p. 107).

Irony runs throughout the history of testing. Galton developed statistics to study relationships between variables—statistics that proved to be forerunners of the coefficient of correlation, later perfected by his friend Pearson (DuBois, 1970). The ultimate downfall of Galton's system of testing can be traced directly to coefficients of correlation, which were too low in some crucial (but, ironically, poorly designed) studies of the relationships among intellectual variables (Sharp, 1898–99; Wissler, 1901). Similarly, Terman succeeded with the Stanford-Binet while the Goddard-Binet (Goddard, 1911), the Herring-Binet

(Herring, 1922), and other Binet-Simon adaptations failed because Terman was sensitive to practitioners' needs. He patiently withheld a final version of his Stanford revision until he was certain that each task was placed appropriately at an age level consistent with the typical functioning of representative samples of U.S. children.

Terman continued his careful test development and standardization techniques with the first revised version of the Stanford-Binet (Terman & Merrill, 1937), but four years after his death in 1956, his legacy was devalued when the next revision of the Stanford-Binet merged Forms L and M *without a standardization* of the newly formed battery (Terman & Merrill, 1960). The following version saw a restandardization of the instrument but without a revision of the placement of tasks at each age level (Terman & Merrill, 1973). Unfortunately for the Binet, the abilities of children and adolescents had changed fairly dramatically in the course of a generation, so the 5-year level of tasks (for example) was now passed by the average 4-year-old.

Terman's methods had been ignored by his successors. The ironic outcome was that Wechsler's approach to assessment triumphed, at least in part because the editions of the Stanford-Binet in the 1960s and 1970s were beset by the same type of flaws as those of Terman's competitors in the 1910s. The fourth edition of the Stanford-Binet (Thorndike, Hagen, & Sattler, 1986) attempted to correct these problems and even adopted Wechsler's multisubtest, multiscale format; the fifth edition (Roid, 2003) is theory-based and of exceptional psychometric quality. However, these improvements in the Binet were too little and too late to reclaim the throne it had shared for decades with Wechsler's scales.

WAIS-IV AND ITS PREDECESSORS

The first in the Wechsler series of tests was the Wechsler-Bellevue Intelligence Scale (Wechsler, 1939), so named because Wechsler was the chief psychologist at Bellevue Hospital in New York City (a position he held from 1932 to 1967). That first test, followed in 1946 by Form II of the Wechsler-Bellevue, had as a key innovation the use of deviation IQs (standard scores), which were psychometrically superior to the mental age divided by chronological age (MA/CA) formula that Terman had used to compute IQ. The Don't Forget box that follows shows the history of Wechsler's scales. The WAIS-IV is the great-great-grandchild of the original 1939 Wechsler-Bellevue Form I; it is also a cousin of the WISC-IV, which traces its lineage to Form II of the Wechsler-Bellevue.

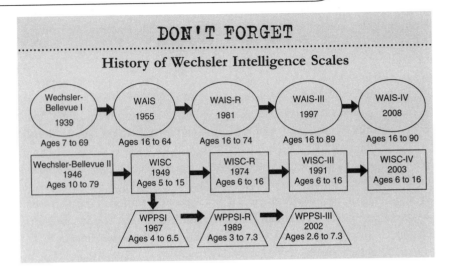

DON'T FORGET

History of Wechsler Intelligence Scales

As prodigious as Wechsler's contribution was to the assessment of children and adolescents, his impact on adult assessment might have been profound. As (Kaufman, 2010a) stated:

> For the first Stanford-Binet, Terman's (1916) adult sample was small, haphazard, and unrepresentative. . . . The Average Adult level was derived from the mental ages for 62 adults. . . . Just as incredibly, Terman and Merrill (1937) tested no one above age 18 years for the standardization sample of Forms L and M of the Stanford-Binet. . . . For the revised Stanford-Binet, "A mental age of fifteen years represents the norm for all subjects who are sixteen years of age or older." (p. 30)

Dr Wechsler was not deterred by the difficulties in identifying representative samples of adults when he developed the Wechsler-Bellevue in the 1930s for ages 7 to 70 years. . . . For all practical purposes, *Dr Wechsler developed the first real test of intelligence for adults in 1939*, even though the Binet had been used to assess the mental ability of the adult population for a generation. (pp. xiv–xv)

The development of Wechsler's tests was originally based on practical and clinical perspectives rather than on theory per se. (The origin of each of the WAIS-IV subtests is shown in Rapid Reference 1.1.) Wechsler's view of IQ tests was that they were a way to peer into an individual's personality. Years after the development of the original Wechsler scales, extensive theoretical speculations have been made about the nature and meaning of these tests and their scores, and the newest WAIS-IV subtests were developed with specific

≡ Rapid Reference 1.1

Origin of WAIS-IV Subtests

Verbal Comprehension Subtest	Source of Subtest
Similarities	Stanford-Binet
Vocabulary	Stanford-Binet
Information	Army Alpha
Comprehension	Stanford-Binet/Army Alpha

Working Memory Subtest	
Digit Span	Stanford-Binet
Arithmetic	Stanford-Binet/Army Alpha
Letter-Number Sequencing	Gold, Carpenter, Randolph, Goldberg, & Weinberger (1997)

Perceptual Reasoning Subtest	
Block Design	Kohs (1923)
Matrix Reasoning	Raven's Progressive Matrices (1938)
Visual Puzzles	Paper Form Board tasks trace back to the late 1920s (Roszkowski, 2001)
Figure Weights	Novel task developed by Paul E. Williams, PsyD (2005; pers. comm.)
Picture Completion	Army Beta/Army Performance Scale Examination

Processing Speed Subtest	
Symbol Search	Shiffrin & Schneider (1977) and S. Sternberg (1966)
Coding	Army Beta/Army Performance Scale Examination
Cancellation	Diller et al. (1974); Moran & Mefford (1959); Talland & Schwab (1964)

theory in mind. However, the original Wechsler tasks were developed without regard to theory. Nonetheless, his influence continues to reverberate. He was one of the founders of the field of clinical psychology (Wasserman, 2012); "his tests and clinical approach have changed the lives of an infinite number of children, adolescents, and adults referred for evaluation for nearly a century" (Kaufman, in press). As Matarazzo (1981) aptly stated, "Probably the work of no other psychologists, including Freud or Pavlov, has so *directly* impinged upon the lives of so many people" (p. 1542).

WECHSLER-BELLEVUE SUBTESTS THAT SURVIVE ON THE WAIS-IV

Wechsler selected tasks for the Wechsler-Bellevue from among the numerous tests available in the 1930s, many of which were developed to meet the assessment needs of World War I. Although Wechsler chose not to develop new subtests for his intelligence battery, his selection process incorporated a blend of clinical, practical, and empirical factors. His rationale for each of the nine well-known original Wechsler-Bellevue subtests that survive to the present day on the WAIS-IV is discussed in the sections that follow.[1] (Note: The WAIS-III contained three new subtests that were not part of the earlier Wechsler batteries: Letter-Number Sequencing, Symbol Search, and Matrix Reasoning. The WAIS-IV contains three additional new subtests: Visual Puzzles, Figure Weights, and Cancellation. Subtests that were not a part of the original Wechsler batteries are discussed in separate sections of this chapter and in later chapters.)

Similarities (Verbal Comprehension Index)

Wechsler (1958) noted that before the Wechsler-Bellevue (W-B), "similarities questions have been used very sparingly in the construction of previous scales . . . [despite being] one of the most reliable measures of intellectual ability" (p. 72). Wechsler felt that this omission was probably due to the belief that language and vocabulary were necessarily too crucial in determining successful performance. However,

> while a certain degree of verbal comprehension is necessary for even minimal performance, sheer word knowledge need only be a minor factor. More important is the individual's ability to perceive the common elements of the terms he or she is asked to compare and, at higher levels, his or her ability to bring them under a single concept. (Wechsler, 1958, p. 73)

A glance at the most difficult items on the W-B I, WAIS, WAIS-R, and WAIS-III Similarities subtests (fly-tree, praise-punishment) makes it evident that Wechsler was successful in his goal of increasing "the difficulty of test items without resorting to esoteric or unfamiliar words" (p. 73).

Wechsler (1958) saw several merits in the Similarities subtest: It is easy to administer, has an interest appeal for adults, has a high *g* loading, sheds light on the logical nature of the person's thinking processes, and provides other qualitative information as well. Regarding the latter point, he stressed the

---

1. Wechsler's (1958) original quotes have been modified to avoid sexist language but otherwise verbatim.

obvious difference both as to maturity and as to level of thinking between the individual who says that a banana and an orange are alike because they both have a skin, and the individual who says that they are both fruit. . . . But it is remarkable how large a percentage of adults never get beyond the superficial type of response. (Wechsler, 1958, p. 73)

Consequently, Wechsler considered his 0–1–2 scoring system to be an important innovation to allow simple discrimination between high-level and low-level responses to the same item. He also found his multipoint system helpful in providing insight into the evenness of a person's intellectual development. Whereas some individuals earn almost all 1s, others earn a mixture of 0, 1, and 2 scores. "The former are likely to bespeak individuals of consistent ability, but of a type from which no high grade of intellectual work may be expected; the latter, while erratic, have many more possibilities" (p. 74).

Vocabulary (Verbal Comprehension Index)

Contrary to lay opinion, the size of a person's vocabulary is not only an index of schooling, but also an excellent measure of general intelligence. Its excellence as a test of intelligence may stem from the fact that the number of words a person knows is at once a measure of learning ability, fund of verbal information and of the general range of the person's ideas. (Wechsler, 1958, p. 84)

The Vocabulary subtest formed an essential component of Binet's scales and the WAIS, but, surprisingly, this task, which has become prototypical of Wechsler's definition of verbal intelligence, was not a regular W-B I subtest. In deference to the objection that the word *knowledge* "is necessarily influenced by . . . educational and cultural opportunities" (p. 84), Wechsler included Vocabulary only as an alternative test during the early stages of W-B I standardization. Consequently, the W-B I was at first a 10-subtest battery, and Vocabulary was excluded from analyses of W-B I standardization data, such as factor analyses and correlations between subtest score and total score. Based on Wechsler's (1944) reconsideration of the value of Vocabulary and concomitant urging of examiners to administer it routinely, Vocabulary soon became a regular W-B I component. When the W-B II was developed, 33 of the 42 W-B I words were included in that battery's Vocabulary subtest. Since many W-B I words were therefore included in the WISC when the W-B II was revised and restandardized to become the Wechsler children's scale in 1949, Wechsler (1955) decided to include an all-new Vocabulary subtest when the W-B I was converted to the WAIS.

This lack of overlap between the W-B I Vocabulary subtest and the task of the same name on the WAIS, WAIS-R, WAIS-III, and WAIS-IV is of some concern regarding the continuity of measurement from the W-B I to its successors. Wechsler (1958) noted:

> The WAIS list contains a larger percentage of action words (verbs). The only thing that can be said so far about this difference is that while responses given to verbs are easier to score, those elicited by substantives are frequently more significant diagnostically. (pp. 84–85)

This difference in diagnostic significance is potentially important because Wechsler found Vocabulary so valuable, in part because of its qualitative aspects: "The type of word on which a subject passes or fails is always of some significance" (p. 85), yielding information about reasoning ability, degree of abstraction, cultural milieu, educational background, coherence of thought processes, and the like.

Nonetheless, Wechsler was careful to ensure that the various qualitative aspects of Vocabulary performance had a minimal impact on quantitative score:

> What counts is the number of words that a person knows. Any recognized meaning is acceptable, and there is no penalty for inelegance of language. So long as the subjects show that they know what a word means, they are credited with a passing score. (1958, p. 85)

Information (Verbal Comprehension Index)

Wechsler (1958) included a subtest designed to tap a person's range of general information, despite "the obvious objection that the amount of knowledge which a person possesses depends in no small degree upon his or her education and cultural opportunities" (p. 65). Wechsler had noted the surprising finding that the fact-oriented information test in the Army Alpha group examination had among the highest correlations with various estimates of intelligence:

> It correlated . . . much better with the total score than did the Arithmetical Reasoning, the test of Disarranged Sentences, and even the Analogies Test, all of which had generally been considered much better tests of intelligence. . . . The fact is, all objections considered, the range of a person's knowledge is generally a very good indication of his or her intellectual capacity. (1958, p. 65)

Wechsler was also struck by a variety of psychometric properties of the Army Alpha Information Test compared to other tasks (excellent distribution curve, small percentage of zero scores, lack of pile-up of maximum scores), and the long history of similar factual information tests being "the stock in trade of mental examinations, and . . . widely used by psychiatrists in estimating the intellectual level of patients" (p. 65).

Always the astute clinician, Wechsler (1958) was aware that the choice of items determined the value of the Information subtest as an effective measure of intelligence. Items must not be chosen whimsically or arbitrarily but must be developed with several important principles in mind, the most essential being that, generally, "the items should call for the sort of knowledge that average individuals with average opportunity may be able to acquire for themselves" (p. 65). Wechsler usually tried to avoid specialized and academic knowledge, historical dates, and names of famous individuals, "but there are many exceptions to the rule, and in the long run each item must be tried out separately" (p. 66). Thus, he preferred an item such as "What is the height of the average American woman?" to ones like "What is iambic tetrameter?" or "In what year was George Washington born?" but occasionally items of the latter type appeared in his Information subtest. Wechsler was especially impressed with the exceptional psychometric properties of the Army Alpha Information Test "in view of the fact that the individual items on [it] left much to be desired" (p. 65).

Although Wechsler (1958) agreed with the criticism that factual information tests depended heavily on educational and cultural opportunities, he felt that the problem "need not necessarily be a fatal or even a serious one" (p. 65). Similarly, he recognized that certain items would vary in difficulty in different locales or when administered to people of different nationalities: "Thus, 'What is the capital of Italy?' is passed almost universally by persons of Italian origin irrespective of their intellectual ability" (p. 66). Yet he was extremely fond of information, considering it "one of the most satisfactory in the battery" (p. 67).

Comprehension (Verbal Comprehension Index)

Measures of general comprehension were plentiful in tests used before the W-B I, appearing in the original Binet scale and its revisions and in such group examinations as the Army Alpha and the National Intelligence Test. However, the test in multiple-choice format, though still valuable, does not approach the contribution of the task when individuals have to compose their own responses:

> [O]ne of the most gratifying things about the general comprehension test, when given orally, is the rich clinical data which it furnishes about the subject. It is frequently of value in diagnosing psychopathic personalities, sometimes suggests the presence of schizophrenic trends (as revealed by perverse and bizarre responses) and almost always tells us something about the subject's social and cultural background. (Wechsler, 1958, p. 67)

In selecting questions for the W-B I Comprehension subtest, Wechsler (1958) borrowed some material from the Army Alpha and the Army Memoirs

(Yoakum & Yerkes, 1920) and included a few questions that were also on the old Stanford-Binet, "probably because they were borrowed from the same source" (p. 68). He was not bothered by overlap because of what he perceived to be a very small practice effect for Comprehension: "It is curious how frequently subjects persist in their original responses, even after other replies are suggested to them" (p. 68).

The WAIS Comprehension subtest was modified from its predecessor by adding two very easy items to prevent a pile-up of zero scores and by adding three proverb items "because of their reported effectiveness in eliciting paralogical and concretistic thinking" (Wechsler, 1958, p. 68). Wechsler found that the proverbs did not contribute to the subtest exactly what he had hoped; they were useful for mentally disturbed individuals,

> but "poor" answers were also common in normal subjects . . . [and] even superior subjects found the proverbs difficult. A possible reason for this is that proverbs generally express ideas so concisely that any attempt to explain them further is more likely to subtract than add to their clarity. (p. 68)

Despite the shortcomings of proverbs items, particularly the fact that they seem to measure skills that differ from prototypical general comprehension items (Kaufman, 1985), Wechsler (1981) retained the three proverbs items in the WAIS-R Comprehension subtest. Because these three items are relatively difficult (they are among the last five in the sequence), they are instrumental in distinguishing among the most superior adults regarding the abilities measured by WAIS-R Comprehension. Only two of the proverb items were retained on the WAIS-III, but the WAIS-IV includes four such items.

According to Wechsler (1958), Comprehension was termed a test of common sense on the Army Alpha, and successful performance

> seemingly depends on the possession of a certain amount of practical information and a general ability to evaluate past experience. The questions included are of a sort that average adults may have had occasion to answer for themselves at some time, or heard discussed in one form or another. They are for the most part stereotypes with a broad common base. (pp. 68–69)

Wechsler was also careful to include no questions with unusual words "so that individuals of even limited education generally have little difficulty in understanding their content" (p. 69). Comprehension scores are, however, dependent on the ability to express one's thoughts verbally.

Digit Span (Working Memory Index)

Memory Span for Digits (renamed Digit Span) combines in a single subtest two skills that subsequent research has shown to be distinct in many ways (Costa, 1975; Jensen & Figueroa, 1975): repetition of digits in the same order as they are spoken by the examiner and repetition of digits in the reverse order. Wechsler (1958) combined these two tasks for pragmatic reasons, but not theoretical ones: Each task alone had too limited a range of possible raw scores, and treating each set of items as a separate subtest would have given short-term memory too much weight in determining a person's IQ—1/6 instead of 1/11.

Wechsler was especially concerned about overweighing memory because Digit Span proved to be a relatively weak measure of general intelligence (g). He gave serious consideration to dropping the task altogether but decided to retain it for two reasons:

1. Digit Span is particularly useful at the lower ranges of intelligence; adults who cannot recall five digits forward and three backward are mentally retarded or emotionally disturbed "in 9 cases out of 10" (Wechsler, 1958, p. 71), except in cases of neurological impairment.
2. Poor performance on Digit Span is of unusual diagnostic significance, according to Wechsler, particularly for suspected brain dysfunction or concern about mental deterioration across the life span.

Digit Span also has several other advantages that may account for Wechsler's (1958) assertion that "perhaps no test has been so widely used in scales of intelligence as that of Memory Span for Digits" (p. 70): It is simple to administer and score, it measures a rather specific ability, and it is clinically valuable because of its unusual susceptibility to anxiety, inattention, distractibility, and lack of concentration. Wechsler noted that repetition of digits backward is especially impaired in individuals who have difficulty sustaining concentrated effort during problem solving. The test has been popularly "used for a long time by psychiatrists as a test of retentiveness and by psychologists in all sorts of psychological studies" (p. 70); because Wechsler retained Digit Span as a regularly administered subtest on the WAIS-R but treated it as supplementary on the WISC-R, it is evident that he saw its measurement as a more vital aspect of adult assessment than of child assessment.

The WAIS-IV provided an important innovation by adding a third section to the subtest—Digit Span Sequencing. For that section, examinees need to recall the numbers in ascending order, which (like Digits Backward) provides an excellent measure of working memory. "This change increases the role of mental manipulation and results in greater demands on working memory, relative to previous versions of Digit Span" (Drozdick, Wahlstrom, Zhu, & Weiss, 2012, p. 198).

Arithmetic (Working Memory Index)

Wechsler (1958) included a test of arithmetical reasoning in an adult intelligence battery because such tests correlate highly with general intelligence; are easily created and standardized; are deemed by most adults as "worthy of a grownup"; have been "used as a rough and ready measure of intelligence" before the advent of psychometrics; and have "long been recognized as a sign of mental alertness" (p. 69). Such tests are flawed by the impact on test scores of attention span, temporary emotional reactions, and of educational and occupational attainment. As Wechsler notes: "Clerks, engineers and businessmen usually do well on arithmetic tests, while housewives, day laborers, and illiterates are often penalized by them" (p. 69). However, he believed that the advantages of an arithmetical reasoning test far outweighed the negative aspects. He pointed out that adults "may be embarrassed by their inability to do certain problems, but they almost never look upon the questions as unfair or inconsequential" (p. 69).

He took much care in developing the specific set of items for the W-B I and the WAIS and believed that his particular approach to constructing the Arithmetic subtest was instrumental in the task's appeal to adults. Wechsler constructed items dealing with everyday, practical situations such that the solutions generally require computational skills taught in grade school or acquired "in the course of day-to-day transactions" (p. 70), and the responses avoid "verbalization or reading difficulties" (p. 69). Whereas the WISC-R and W-B I involve the reading of a few problems by the subject, all items on the WAIS, WAIS-R, WAIS-III, and WAIS-IV are read aloud by the examiner.

Bonus points for quick, perfect performance are not given to children on the WISC-R, but Wechsler considered the ability to respond rapidly to relatively difficult arithmetic problems to be a pertinent aspect of adult intelligence; bonus points are given to two items on the W-B I Arithmetic subtest, to four items on the WAIS task, to five items on WAIS-R Arithmetic, and to two items on WAIS-III Arithmetic. No bonus points are awarded on WAIS-IV Arithmetic, but only 30 seconds are allowed for each item. On the WAIS-IV, Arithmetic was modified, "to more purely reflect working memory, as opposed to verbal comprehension skills or mathematical knowledge. For example, difficult items require several successive simple mathematical steps that have to be represented in working memory instead of the complex calculations included in earlier versions" (Drozdick et al., 2012, p. 198).

Block Design (Perceptual Reasoning Index)

Kohs (1923) developed the Block Design test, which used blocks and designs that were red, white, blue, and yellow. His test was included in numerous other tests of intelligence and neuropsychological functioning before Wechsler adapted it for the W-B I. Wechsler (1958) shortened the test substantially; used designs having only two colors (although the W-B I blocks included all four colors, unlike the red and white WAIS and WAIS-III blocks); and altered the patterns that the examinee had to copy. Block Design has been shown to correlate well with various criterion measures, to be a good measure of *g*, and to be quite amenable to qualitative analysis (Wechsler, 1958). It intrigued Wechsler that those who do very well on this subtest are not necessarily the ones who treat the pattern as a gestalt; more often they are individuals who are able to break up the pattern into its component parts.

Wechsler (1958) believed that observation of individuals while they solve the problems, such as their following the entire pattern versus breaking it into small parts, provided qualitative, clinical information about their problem-solving approach, attitude, and emotional reaction that is potentially more valuable than the obtained scores. "One can often distinguish the hasty and impulsive individual from the deliberate and careful type, a subject who gives up easily or becomes disgusted, from the one who persists and keeps on working even after his time is up" (p. 80). He also felt that the Block Design subtest is most important diagnostically, particularly for persons with dementia or other types of neurological impairment. From Goldstein's (1948) perspective, those with brain damage perform poorly on Block Design because of loss of the "abstract approach," although Wechsler (1958) preferred to think that most "low scores on Block Design are due to difficulty in visual-motor organization" (p. 80).

Picture Completion (Perceptual Reasoning Index)

This subtest was commonly included in group-administered tests such as the Army Beta. A variant of this task, known as Healy Picture Completion II, which involves placing a missing piece into an uncompleted picture, was given individually in various performance scales, including the Army Performance Scale Examination; however, individual administration of Picture Completion, though conducted with the Binet scale for an identical task named Mutilated Pictures, was less common. Wechsler (1958) was unimpressed with the group-administered versions of Picture Completion because the subject had to draw in (instead of name or point to) the missing part, too few items were used, unsatisfactory items were included, and items were chosen haphazardly (a typical set of items incorporated many that were much too easy and others that were unusually difficult).

Wechsler (1958) nonetheless believed that the test's "popularity is fully deserved" (p. 77); he tried to select an appropriate set of items while recognizing the difficulty of that task. "If one chooses familiar subjects, the test becomes much too easy; if one turns to unfamiliar ones, the test ceases to be a good measure of intelligence because one unavoidably calls upon specialized knowledge" (p. 77). He thought that the W-B I set of items was generally successful, although he had to increase the subtest length by 40% when developing WAIS Picture Completion to avoid a fairly restricted range of obtained scores. Although Wechsler was critical of the group-administered Picture Completion tasks, it is still noteworthy that four of the W-B I and WAIS items were taken directly from the Army Beta test, and an additional four items were clear adaptations of Beta items (using the same pictures, with a different part missing, or the same concept).

The subtest has several psychometric assets, according to Wechsler (1958), including brief administration time, minimal practice effect even after short intervals, and good ability to assess intelligence for low-functioning individuals. Two of these claims are true, but the inconsequential practice effect is refuted by data in the *WAIS-III Manual* (Psychological Corporation, 1997) and *WAIS-IV Technical and Interpretive Manual* (Psychological Corporation, 2008), which show test-retest gains for Picture Completion to average about 2 scaled-score points over intervals of a few weeks. Limitations of the task are that subjects must be familiar with the object in order to have a fair opportunity to detect what is missing and the susceptibility of specific items to sex differences. Wechsler (1958) notes that women did better in finding the missing eyebrow in the girl's profile and that men did better in detecting the missing thread on the electric light bulb. Similarly, on the WISC-R, about two-thirds of the boys but only about one-third of the girls across the entire 6–16 age range were able to find the missing "slit" in the screw; in contrast, many more girls than boys detected the sock missing from the girl who is running.

Because a person must first have the basic perceptual and conceptual abilities to recognize and be familiar with the object pictured in each item, Wechsler (1958) saw Picture Completion as measuring "the ability of the individual to differentiate essential from non-essential details" and "to appreciate that the missing part is in some way essential either to the form or to the function of the object or picture." But because of the total dependence of the assessment of this skill on the person's easy familiarity with the content of the item, "unfamiliar, specialized and esoteric subject matter must therefore be sedulously avoided when pictures are chosen for this test" (p. 78).

Coding (Processing Speed Index)

"The Digit Symbol [Coding on WAIS-IV] or Substitution Test is one of the oldest and best established of all psychological tests. It is to be found in a large variety of intelligence scales, and its wide popularity is fully merited" (Wechsler, 1958, p. 81). The W-B I Digit Symbol subtest was taken from the Army Beta, the only change being the reduction in response time from 2 minutes to 1 1/2 minutes to avoid a pile-up of perfect scores. For the WAIS, the number of symbols to be copied was increased by about one-third, although the response time remained unchanged.

Wechsler's (1958) main concern regarding the use of Digit Symbol for assessing adult intelligence involved its potential dependency on visual acuity, motor coordination, and speed. He discounted the first two variables, except for people with specific visual or motor disabilities, but gave much consideration to the impact of speed on test performance. He was well aware that Digit Symbol performance drops dramatically with increasing age and is especially deficient for older individuals, who

do not write or handle objects as fast as younger persons, and what is perhaps equally important, they are not as easily motivated to do so. The problem, however, from the point of view of global functioning, is not merely whether the older persons are slower, but whether or not they are also "slowed up." (p. 81)

Because correlations between Digit Symbol performance and total score remain high (or at least consistent) from age 16 through old age, Wechsler concluded that older people deserve the penalty for speed, "since resulting reduction in test performance is on the whole proportional to the subject's over-all capacity at the time he is tested" (p. 81). Although neurotic individuals also have been shown to perform relatively poorly on Digit Symbol, Wechsler attributed that decrement to difficulty in concentrating and applying persistent effort, that is, "a lessened mental efficiency rather than an impairment of intellectual ability" (p. 82).

Compared to earlier Digit Symbol or Substitution tests, Wechsler saw particular advantages to the task he borrowed from the Army Beta and included on his scales: It includes sample items to ensure that examinees understand the task, and it requires copying the unfamiliar symbols, not the numbers, lessening "the advantage which individuals having facility with numbers would otherwise have" (1958, p. 82).

Optional procedures were added to the WAIS-III Digit Symbol—Coding subtest, which were developed to help examiners assess what skills (or lack thereof) may be impacting examinees' performance on the subtest. These optional procedures involve recalling shapes from memory (Pairing and Free Recall) and perceptual and graphomotor speed (Digit Symbol—Copy). However, these optional procedures were removed on WAIS-IV Coding.

WECHSLER'S LEGACY

When put into historical perspective, Wechsler made some mighty contributions to the clinical and psychometric assessment of intelligence. His insistence that every person be assessed on both Verbal and Performance scales went against the conventional wisdom of his time. Yet discrepancies between Verbal and Performance IQs (and ultimately among the four indexes that replaced the two IQs) would prove to have critical value for understanding brain functioning and theoretical distinctions between fluid and crystallized intelligence. Furthermore, Wechsler's stress on the clinical value of intelligence tests would alter the face of intellectual assessment forever, replacing the psychometric, statistical emphasis that accompanied the use and interpretation of the Stanford-Binet. Finally, Wechsler's inclusion of a multiscore subtest profile (as well as three IQs instead of one) met the needs of the emerging field of learning disabilities assessment in the 1960s, to such an extent that his scales replaced the Stanford-Binet as king of IQ during that decade. It has maintained that niche ever since for children, adolescents, and adults (Alfonso, LaRocca, Oakland, & Spanakos, 2000; Archer, Buffington-Vollum, Stredny, & Handel, 2006; Archer & Newsom, 2000; Camara, Nathan, & Puente, 2000; Rabin, Barr, & Burton, 2005).

The popularity of the adult Wechsler tests, starting with the WAIS and continuing with the WAIS-R, WAIS-III, and WAIS-IV, is remarkable and pervasive. Wechsler's adult scales are by far the first choice for measuring intelligence among clinical neuropsychologists (Rabin et al., 2005), psychologists who conduct forensic assessments (Archer et al., 2006), clinical psychologists (Camara et al., 2000), psychologists who conduct evaluations in state correctional facilities (Gallagher, Somwaru, & Ben-Porath, 1999), psychology professors who train doctoral-level students (Belter & Piotrowski, 2001), and, indeed, psychologists who conduct assessments with adults for any other reason (Groth-Marnat, 2009; Sattler & Ryan, 2009; Weiss et al., 2010). Harrison, Kaufman, Hickman, and Kaufman (1988) reported data from a survey of 402 clinical psychologists that showed 97% of these professionals utilized the WAIS or WAIS-R when administering an adult measure of intelligence. Even if the 97% figure is no longer exactly precise, the WAIS-IV has clearly continued the Wechsler tradition as being by far the most popular test of adult intelligence.

PURPOSES OF ASSESSING ADULTS AND ADOLESCENTS

As mentioned previously, adults were historically assessed because of a need to place men into the appropriate level of the military service or to determine a person's mental deficiency. Today, reasons for assessing adolescents and adults commonly include measuring cognitive potential or neurological dysfunction, obtaining clinical information, making educational or vocational placement decisions, and developing interventions for educational or vocational settings. Harrison et al. (1988) found that practitioners who assess adults most often report using intelligence tests to measure cognitive potential and to obtain clinically relevant information. About 77% of practitioners reported using intelligence tests for obtaining information about neurological functioning, and fewer than 50% reported using intelligence tests for making educational or vocational placements or interventions (Harrison et al., 1988). Camara and colleagues (2000) also reported that a large proportion of the assessment services of clinical psychologists and neuropsychologists are in the areas of intellectual/achievement assessment (20–34%) and neuropsychological assessment (13–26%).

FOUNDATIONS OF THE WAIS-IV: THEORY AND RESEARCH

Wechsler defined intelligence as "the capacity to act purposefully, to think rationally, and to deal effectively with his [or her] environment" (1944, p. 3). His concept of intelligence was that of a global entity that could also be categorized by the sum of many specific abilities. The most recent revision of Wechsler's adult intelligence scale, the WAIS-IV, has enhanced measures of more discrete domains of cognitive functioning, such as working memory and processing speed (Psychological Corporation, 2008), while continuing to provide a measure of global intelligence. Unlike the earliest Wechsler tests, the WAIS-IV also was developed with specific theoretical foundations in mind. In fact, revisions were made purposely to reflect the latest knowledge from literature in the areas of intelligence theory, adult cognitive development, and cognitive neuroscience. The theoretical constructs of fluid reasoning, working memory, and processing speed were of particular importance during the development of the WAIS-IV, just as they were in the development of the WISC-IV. Rapid Reference 1.2 defines these three theoretical constructs.

Wechsler's adult tests, from the Wechsler-Bellevue (1939) to the WAIS (1955) to the WAIS-R (1981), took the same basic form, with 6 subtests constituting the Verbal Scale, 5 making up the Performance Scale, and all 11 yielding the global

≡ Rapid Reference 1.2

Updated WAIS-IV Theoretical Foundations

Theoretical Construct	Fluid Reasoning	Working Memory	Processing Speed
Definition	Ability to process or manipulate abstractions, rules, generalizations, and logical relationships	Ability to actively maintain information in conscious awareness, perform some operation or manipulation with it, and produce a result	Ability to process information rapidly (which is dynamically related to one's ability to perform higher-order cognitive tasks)
References for the Construct	Carroll (1997); Cattell (1943, 1963); Cattell & Horn (1978); Sternberg (1995)	Beuhner, Krumm, Ziegler, & Pluecken (2006); Unsworth & Engle (2007)	Fry & Hale (1996); Kail (2000); Kail & Hall (1994); Kail & Salthouse (1994)

entity of intelligence characterized by the Full Scale IQ. The WAIS-III departed slightly from the original form by offering four separate indexes (i.e., Verbal Comprehension Index, Perceptual Organization Index, Working Memory Index, and Processing Speed Index), in addition to the Verbal, Performance, and Full Scale IQs. The WAIS-IV, like the WISC-IV, departed dramatically from the longtime Wechsler tradition by eliminating the Verbal and Performance IQs and, hence, the ever-popular V-P IQ discrepancy. The four indexes were retained in the WAIS-IV, alongside the Full Scale IQ, providing a more modern and conceptually clearer scale structure. The WAIS-IV and WISC-IV now offer the same four indexes: Verbal Comprehension (VCI), Perceptual Reasoning (PRI), Working Memory (WMI), and Processing Speed (PSI). (To achieve this synchrony, the WAIS-IV and WISC-IV Perceptual Organization Index was renamed the Perceptual Reasoning Index, and WISC-IV Freedom from Distractibility Index became the Working Memory Index.)

The focus on the four indexes in the WAIS-IV psychometric profile is a plus when it comes to understanding how to interpret individual profiles, from both a theoretical and a clinical perspective. However, this shift in focus also affects WAIS-IV Full Scale IQ (FSIQ), which is now computed from the sum of the 10 subtests that compose the four scales (3 VCI, 3 PRI, 2 WMI, and 2 PSI).

☰ *Rapid Reference 1.3*

Comparison of the Subtest Composition of the WAIS-III and WAIS-IV Full Scales

WAIS-III Full Scale Subtests	WAIS-IV Full Scale Subtests
Verbal	
Vocabulary	Vocabulary (VCI)
Similarities	Similarities (VCI)
Information	Information (VCI)
Comprehension	
Arithmetic	Arithmetic (WMI)
Digit Span	Digit Span (WMI)
Performance	
Block Design	Block Design (PRI)
Matrix Reasoning	Matrix Reasoning (PRI)
	Visual Puzzles (PRI)
Picture Completion	
Picture Arrangement	
Digit Symbol—Coding	Coding (PSI)
	Symbol Search (PSI)

Traditionally, the WAIS FSIQ has been composed of 11 subtests, 6 Verbal and 5 Performance. The end result of these changes is a WAIS-IV FSIQ that differs substantially from WAIS-III FSIQ, as shown in Rapid Reference 1.3. Of the 11 WAIS-III Full Scale subtests, only 8 are retained on the WAIS-IV Full Scale. Although this shift is not as dramatic as the change from the WISC-III to the WISC-IV Full Scale (which share only 5 of 10 subtests), it is nonetheless notable.

Although two global scores were eliminated from the WAIS-IV (Verbal and Performance IQs), one new global score was added, the optional General Ability Index (GAI). The GAI is derived from the sum of scaled scores on the three Verbal Comprehension and three Perceptual Reasoning subtests, thereby eliminating the WMI and PSI from consideration and forming a global composite composed solely of the verbal and perceptual constructs. This new global score aids examiners in interpreting test profiles and is included in our step-by-step interpretive system (see Chapter 5), just as the WISC-IV GAI is incorporated into its interpretive system (Flanagan & Kaufman, 2009).

DON'T FORGET

....

New WAIS-IV Four-Factor Structure

Verbal Indexes	Nonverbal Indexes
1. Verbal Comprehension	2. Perceptual Reasoning
3. Working Memory	4. Processing Speed

Note: The Perceptual Reasoning Index (PRI) was called the Perceptual Organization Index (POI) on the WAIS-III. This name change (on the WISC-IV as well) reflects "the increased emphasis of fluid reasoning on the WAIS-IV" (Drozdick et al., 2012, p. 198).

Description of WAIS-IV

Several issues prompted the revision of the WAIS-IV; the Manual clearly details these issues and what changes were made (Psychological Corporation, 2008, pp. 7–23). Rapid Reference 1.4 lists key features that were adapted for the Fourth Edition.

WAIS-III examiners will recognize many of the core Wechsler subtests in the WAIS-IV, but there have been several notable changes with the addition of new

≣ *Rapid Reference 1.4*

....

WAIS-IV Key Revisions

- Updated theoretical foundations
- Updated norms
- Increased developmental appropriateness
- Increased user-friendliness
- Enhanced clinical utility
- Decreased reliance on timed performance
- Enhancement of fluid reasoning measurement by adding Figure Weights and Visual Puzzles subtests
- Enhancement of working memory measurement by adding Digit Span Sequencing as the third component of Digit Span
- Strengthening the framework based on factor analysis, including state-of-the-art confirmatory factor analysis
- Statistical linkage to other measures of cognitive functioning and achievement, most notably the Wechsler Memory Scale—Fourth Edition (WMS-IV)
- Extensive testing of reliability and validity

subtests and modifications to the overall structure. (Rapid Reference 1.5 lists a description of all WAIS-IV subtests.) There are three new subtests:

1. **Visual Puzzles** (added to the Perceptual Reasoning Index; it is a visual-perceptual variation of the old Object Assembly subtest, a task that required both visual-perceptual abilities and visual-motor coordination)
2. **Figure Weights** (added to the Performance Reasoning Index as a supplemental subtest)
3. **Cancellation** (added to the Processing Speed Index as a supplemental subtest)

≡ Rapid Reference 1.5

WAIS-IV Subtest Abbreviations and Descriptions

Subtest	Abbreviation	Description
Verbal Comprehension Subtest		
Similarities	SI	The examinee is presented with two words that represent common objects or concepts and describes how they are similar.
Vocabulary	VC	For picture items, the examinee names the object presented visually. For verbal items, the examinee defines words that are presented visually and orally.
Information	IN	The examinee answers questions that address a broad range of general knowledge topics.
Comprehension	CO	The examinee answers questions based on his or her understanding of general principles and social situations.
Perceptual Reasoning Subtest		
Block Design	BD	Working within a specified time limit, the examinee views a model and a picture or a picture only and uses red-and-white blocks to recreate the design.
Matrix Reasoning	MR	The examinee views an incomplete matrix or series and selects the response option that completes the matrix or series.
Visual Puzzles[a]	VP	Working within a specified time limit, the examinee views a completed puzzle and selects three response options that, when combined, reconstruct the puzzle.

(continued)

Subtest	Abbreviation	Description
Figure Weights[a]	FW	Working within a specified time limit, the examinee views a scale with missing weight(s) and selects the response option that keeps the scale balanced.
Picture Completion[b]	PC	Working within a specified time limit, the examinee views a picture with an important part missing and identifies the missing part.
Working Memory Subtest		
Digit Span	DS	For Digit Span Forward, the examinee is read a sequence of numbers and recalls the numbers in the same order. For Digit Span Backward, the examinee is read a sequence of numbers and recalls the numbers in reverse order. For Digit Span Sequencing, the examinee is read a sequence of numbers and recalls the numbers in ascending order.
Arithmetic	AR	Working within a specified time limit, the examinee mentally solves a series of arithmetic problems.
Letter-Number Sequencing	LN	The examinee is read a sequence of numbers and letters and recalls the numbers in ascending order and the letters in alphabetical order.
Processing Speed Subtest		
Symbol Search	SS	Working within a specified time limit, the examinee scans a search group and indicates whether one of the symbols in the target group matches.
Coding	CD	Using a key, the examinee copies symbols that are paired with numbers within a specified time limit.
Cancellation[a]	CA	Working within a specified time limit, the examinee scans a structured arrangement of shapes and marks target shapes.

[a] New WAIS-IV subtest.
[b] The WAIS-IV Record Form and Manual uses PCm as the abbreviation for Picture Completion, but in this book, we use PC.

How these new subtests were created gives interesting insight into the process of test development and revision. Professionals on the Research Development (RD) Team for the WAIS-IV shared how Figure Weights and Visual Puzzles were developed for the WAIS-IV (Cancellation was developed first for the WISC-IV). Dr. Susan Raiford (personal communication, November 25, 2008) revealed:

Visual Puzzles was inspired by Object Assembly as an abstract nonmotor task that was similar. Jim Holdnack, one of the WMS-IV RDs, submitted the item type for consideration in April of 2005, and it was originally named "Puzzle Pieces." . . . As the subtest evolved we were aware of the similarities to the old Paper Form Board tests through reviews of Carroll's work and of existing measures (Quasha & Likert) published many years ago by Psychcorp. We found as we worked with the item type that difficulty could be controlled with complexity of cut and with internal cues (colors or lines), which is why the internal cues are there on the easier items and the complexity of piece cut gets greater as the items progress.

Dr. Holdnack (personal communication, November 25, 2008) continued:

The subtest was inspired from the Object Assembly subtest and the Visual Puzzles and Geometric Puzzles on NEPSY-II, although, the make-up of this test varies considerably from those subtests. Mostly, I was shooting for the items to have elements of mental construction and rotation while limiting other confounding factors such as verbalization, processing speed, and fine-motor integration.

Paul Williams, a research director at the Psychological Corporation, submitted the original Figure Weights item in 2005 (Raiford, personal communication). Dr. Williams explained (personal communication, December 1, 2008):

[T]he hard part was coming up with a way to create a relationship between the objects. I couldn't use symbols such as = +− because this would require prior knowledge. So the thought came to me that another way to symbolize > and < is by weight; which led to the idea of using a balance to create a rule or relationship between the figures. With this information a series of rules can be presented which has to be reasoned out by the examinee to balance the final scale. Susie then took it from there and did an amazing job building the items and doing the science necessary to develop the idea into a functional subtest.

Dr. Raiford (personal communication) continued:

Paul told me at the time that he intended it to be a new item type for Matrix Reasoning, but we thought we could make a whole subtest out of it, and wanted to because it seemed to be measuring quantitative reasoning, which we weren't measuring nonverbally yet. I switched the item type to a scale from the seesaws . . . because it seemed more intuitive. I also found we could get all the difficulty we needed with just two scales establishing relationships and a third scale with an empty tray.

In addition to these three new subtests, other modifications to the WAIS-III include the removal of two of Wechsler's original group of subtests from the revised test: Picture Arrangement and Object Assembly. The rationale for deleting these subtests was to lessen the motor demands of the test and to deemphasize time bonus points. When Object Assembly was originally developed, Wechsler (1958) "wanted at least one test which required putting things together into a familiar configuration" (pp. 82–83). He included Object Assembly, but only "after much hesitation" (p. 82), because of its known liabilities: relatively low reliability and predictive value, large practice effects, and low correlations with other subtests. In the development of Picture Arrangement, Wechsler selected items for his test based on "interest of content, probable appeal to subjects, ease of scoring and discriminating value" (p. 75). Yet he was never satisfied with the result, noting that "the final selection leaves much to be desired."

He spent much time and statistical analysis trying to discern which alternative responses deserved credit and even called in a team of four judges, yet the final system for assigning credit for alternative arrangements "turned out to be more or less arbitrary" (p. 76). Although bonus points were included on earlier editions of the WAIS Picture Arrangement, Wechsler (1981) reversed this trend for the WAIS-R and deemphasized speed greatly by not allowing bonus points for any of the Picture Arrangement items. Thus, Wechsler's concerns about these two subtests are consistent with The Psychological Corporation's decision to eliminate them from the WAIS-IV (and from the WISC-IV). Nonetheless, had he been alive, Wechsler undoubtedly never would have agreed to eliminate these original subtests from any version of the WAIS or WISC. He would, however, have gained solace from the fact that both Object Assembly and Picture Arrangement are included in the Wechsler Nonverbal Scale of Ability (WNV; Wechsler & Naglieri, 2006).

Further deletions from the WAIS-III to the WAIS-IV included removal of the optional procedures: Digit Symbol—Incidental Learning and Digit Symbol—Copy. However, process scores were added to the WAIS-IV Block Design, Digit Span, and Letter-Number Sequencing subtests that allow examiners to analyze errors and qualitatively interpret test performance. For example, Block Design No Time Bonus is a process score that reflects a person's performance without additional time bonus for rapid completion of items. The Digit Span task offers three process scores that reflect an examinee's performance on the separate tasks of repeating digits forward, backward, and then sequencing digits. The addition of the Digit Span Sequencing task is consistent with the test publisher's theoretical emphasis on working memory. An additional process score is offered for another Working Memory subtest, which involves the calculation of the longest Letter-Number sequence recalled. A comparison of Digit Span Sequencing and Letter-Number Sequencing will provide an auditory analog of a comparison of Trail Making A and B. Rapid Reference 1.6 describes the subtests' process analyses.

≡ Rapid Reference 1.6

Subtests with Process Analysis

Subtest	Abbreviation	Process Score	Use
Block Design			
Block Design No Time Bonus	BDN	Score reflects performance on BD without additional time bonus for rapid completion.	Useful when physical limitations, problem-solving strategies, or personality characteristics affect performance on timed tasks.
Digit Span			
Digit Span Forward	DSF	Raw scores reflect the total number of DSF trials correctly completed before discontinuing.	May help to explain variable performance on Digit Span Tasks. DSF requires immediate auditory recall, whereas DSB and DSS place demands on working memory and attention.
Digit Span Backward	DSB	Raw scores reflect the total number of DSB trials correctly completed before discontinuing.	
Digit Span Sequencing	DSS	Raw scores reflect the total number of DSS trials correctly completed before discontinuing.	

(continued)

Subtest	Abbreviation	Process Score	Use
Longest Digit Span Forward	LDSF	Raw scores reflect the number of forward digits recalled on the last trial scored 1 point.	May help to explain variable performance on DS tasks. Some examinees may arrive at their DS total raw score by inconsistently earning 1s and 0s across trials, whereas other examinees may show a pattern of consistently earning 1s until they discontinue the task.
Longest Digit Span Backward	LDSB	Raw scores reflect the number of backward digits recalled on the last trial scored 1 point.	
Longest Digit Span Sequencing	LDSS	Raw scores reflect the number of digits correctly sequenced on the last trial scored 1 point.	
Letter-Number Sequencing			
Longest Letter-Number Sequence	LLNS	Raw scores reflect the number of letters and numbers correctly sequenced on the last trial scored 1 point.	May help to explain variable performance on LN tasks. Some examinees may arrive at their LN total raw score by inconsistently earning 1s and 0s across trials, whereas other examinees may show a pattern of consistently earning 1s until they discontinue the task.

Validity of the WAIS-IV Model

With the addition of the 3 new subtests and removal of 2 subtests, the complete WAIS-IV comprises 15 subtests, although only 10 are core subtests needed to compute the 4 indexes and FSIQ. Like the WISC-IV structure, the WAIS-IV structure focuses users on the middle tier of scores—the Factor Indexes (see Figure 1.1). FSIQ and the indexes have a mean of 100 and a standard deviation of 15. Subtest scaled scores have a mean of 10 and standard deviation of 3.

Figure 1.1. WAIS-IV Structure: Three-Tier Hierarchy

Note: Shaded subtests that are bordered with dashed lines and connected to indexes with dashed lines are supplemental and contribute to the calculation of the Index score only if they have substituted for one of the core subtests.

Of the five supplemental subtests, three are normed only for ages 16 to 69: Letter-Number Sequencing (WMI), Figure Weights (PRI), and Cancellation (PSI). Comprehension (VCI) and Picture Completion (PRI) are normed for the complete 16- to 90-year range. Supplemental subtests are not included in calculation of any of the Index scores.

The *WAIS-IV Technical and Interpretive Manual* (Psychological Corporation, 2008) reports the details of several confirmatory factor analysis (CFA) studies that support the underlying four-factor structure of the WAIS-IV. For all ages, there is strong construct validity support for the four Indexes. However, at both ages 16–69 and ages 70–90, a model that allows Arithmetic to load on both the Working Memory Factor and the Verbal Comprehension Factor fits the data best. For ages 16–69, the Arithmetic subtest had a Factor loading of .75 on the Working Memory Factor and a small loading of .08 on the Verbal Comprehension Factor. For ages 70–90, the Arithmetic subtest had a loading of .48 on the Working Memory Factor and .33 on the Verbal Comprehension Factor. The Figure Weights subtest also had a split factor loading for ages 16–69, with factor loadings of .37 and .43 on the Working Memory Factor and Perceptual Reasoning Factor, respectively. The *WAIS-IV Technical and Interpretive Manual* (Psychological Corporation, 2008) also reported a different four-factor model, in which it allowed a correlated error for Digit Span and Letter-Number Sequencing and a cross-loading for Arithmetic on a *Gc* factor; these changes helped the WAIS-IV scoring model considerably.

Subsequent CFAs by Ward, Bergman, and Hebert (2012) and by Canivez and Watkins (2010a, 2010b) offered empirical support for the WAIS-IV four-factor model, but these research teams differed in the best way to interpret the data. Ward et al. (2012) modified details of the structural model based on cognitive theory (e.g., they emphasized the role of working memory on Figure Weights) and, ultimately, supported the notion that methodologists must take into consideration the "conceptual coherence and theoretical adherence in addition to statistical fit" (p. 1). Canivez and Watkins identified the four designated WAIS-IV factors, but noted that these four first-order factors accounted for relatively small amounts of variance compared to the second-order g factor; they argued "that the WAIS-IV provides strong measurement of general intelligence, and clinical interpretation should be primarily at that level" (2010b, p. 827).

It was in the spirit of alternative approaches to interpretation—both empirical and theoretical—that we offered a five-factor theory-based supplementary interpretive system in the first edition of this book. We based that alternative interpretive system on the results of CFAs of the WAIS-IV conducted by Tim Keith (personal communication, January 30, 2009). He analyzed the averaged matrix for ages 16–90 shown in the *WAIS-IV Manual* (Psychological Corporation, 2008, p. 62) and used the technique of higher-order CFA. Keith's analyses compared various models, including the Four-Factor WAIS-IV model and a Five-Factor model that is in line with the Cattell-Horn-Carroll (CHC) theory. This CHC model included Matrix Reasoning and Figure Weights on the Fluid Reasoning (Gf) Factor, along with Arithmetic. The Visual Processing (Gv) Factor included Block Design, Visual Puzzles, and Picture Completion. The Crystallized Knowledge (Gc) Factor included Similarities, Vocabulary, Comprehension, and Information. Short-Term Memory (Gsm) included Digit Span and Letter-Number Sequencing, and Processing Speed (Gs) included Coding, Symbol Search, and Cancellation. Keith reported that a CHC model with separate Gf and Gv Factors fits the data especially well. Arithmetic, though included on the WMI, is associated with the Gf factor in Keith's analysis. The loadings are shown in Figure 1.2. Note that Gf is indistinguishable from the general factor (g). Also note that Figure Weights shows a high loading (.77) on a Gf Factor.

Benson, Hulac, and Kranzler (2010) conducted CFAs of the WAIS-IV that supported Keith's five CHC factors. Benson et al. (2010) concluded from their analyses: "Results suggest that a CHC model provides a better explanation of test performance than does the WAIS–IV scoring structure" (p. 124). The authors also addressed the issue of whether CHC factor structure was invariant across ages 16–17 through 65–69. Their analyses "provide modest support for the conclusion that the WAIS–IV measures the same constructs across age groups. . . . [S]ome age differences exist, although these differences may not be large enough to be practically meaningful" (Benson et al., 2010, p. 129). Ward et al. (2012) and Weiss, Keith, Zhu, and Chen (in press) also compared five-factor CHC-based solutions to conventional four-factor WAIS-IV solutions. Ward et al. (2012) commented:

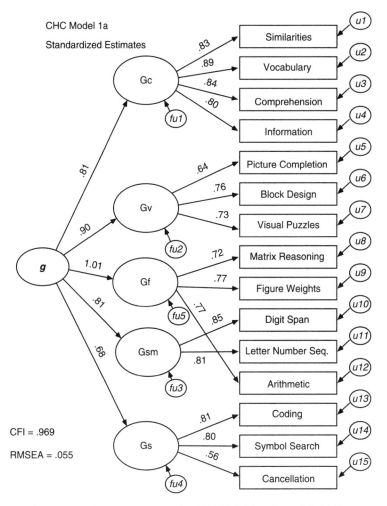

Figure 1.2. Keith's CHC Model for the WAIS-IV for Ages 16–69 Years

Note that this analysis is based on data for the total WAIS-IV sample.

Source: T. Keith, personal communication, January 30, 2009.

"The Benson et al. (2010) research is important because it is based on current taxonomic theory [, but] . . . their statistical and theoretical appraisal of the model is relatively uncritical" (p. 331). Ward et al. (2012) concluded from their sophisticated set of analyses that both four-factor and five-factor models of the WAIS-IV have merit, but they favor a four-factor model because it is more consistent with WAIS-IV Index structure, with the test's theory and constructs, with "current cognitive theory (e.g., Kane et al., 2004)" (p. 339), and with "WAIS-IV factor-analytic antecedents" (p. 339).

Weiss et al. (in press) also found empirical support for both four- and five-factor solutions, noting that the five-factor model provided a better fit. Most importantly, Weiss et al. (in press) found that the CFAs for both four and five factors were invariant for normal (N = 1,800) and clinical (N = 411) samples of adults. These authors interpret their results as providing strong validity evidence for both models and see the four-factor and CHC solutions as being complementary for normal adults as well as clinical patients. Their inclination is to begin interpretation with the four Indexes, but to consider switching to five factors if there are discrepant scores within one or more Indexes.

We have retained Keith's original analysis in Figure 1.2, based on ages 16–90, rather than limiting the analysis to ages 16–69 or reporting data from recently published studies. We continued to use Keith's data because, in the first edition of this book, we frequently referred to the CHC factors as the "Keith factors," and we will continue to do so in this edition when referring to the CHC interpretive system for ages 16–69. Moreover, the comparable WAIS-IV analysis for ages 16–69 (Benson et al., 2010, Figure 3) is nearly identical to Keith's analysis regarding the structure and factor loadings.

Benson et al. (2010) support a five-factor CHC solution; Ward et al. (2012) prefer four-factor models; Weiss et al. (in press) consider both models viable and complementary; and Canivez and Watkins (2010a, 2010b) advocate a one-factor (*g*) interpretation. We disagree emphatically with the clinical value of the *g* approach (see Chapters 4 and 5), but support *both* the four-factor and five-factor interpretive models. We believe that examiners should select whichever solution best fits their professional orientation or—on a case-by-case basis—whichever approach best fits the subtest profile for an individual referred for evaluation. For example, Keith (personal communication) concluded from his CFA analyses that "a CHC-based interpretation of the WAIS-IV is, at minimum, worth considering. I would certainly consider that interpretation if there were inconsistencies among the Perceptual Reasoning tasks, or between Arithmetic versus the Working Memory tasks."

In the previous edition of this book, we offered the four-factor solution for all ages, 16–90 years; however, we only offered the five-factor CHC solution for individuals ages 16–69 because two of the component subtests (Figure Weights and Letter-Number Sequencing) are not administered to ages 70–90 years. This limitation is no longer true for the second edition of *Essentials of WAIS-IV Assessment*. Recent CFA research produced a new CHC five-factor model for adults ages 70–90 years (Niileksela, Reynolds, & Kaufman, 2012).

Niileksala et al.'s approach rests on two main decisions: (a) to consider Arithmetic as primarily a measure of *Gf*, which has empirical support from Keith's study (see Figure 1.2) and from other CFA investigations of the WAIS-IV (Benson et al., 2010; Ward et al., 2012); and (b) to treat the three components of Digit Span (Forward, Backward, Sequencing) as separate variables in the factor analyses. The latter decision is supported by data presented in Chapters 4 and 5 of the *WAIS-IV Technical and Interpretive Manual* (Psychological Corporation, 2008): Each section of Digit Span has adequate internal consistency reliability across the age range (means of .81–.83) and for 13 clinical samples (.86–.89) (Tables 4.1 and 4.2 of WAIS-IV manual); each section has adequate stability (means of .71–.77 for four age groups, comparable to the value of .74 for Matrix Reasoning; Table 4.5 of manual); and the three parts intercorrelated .42–.53 for all ages (Table 5.1 of manual), a moderate degree of relationship that supports entering them as separate variables in CFAs (Niileksela et al., 2012). Figure 1.3 (Niileksala, personal communication, October 21, 2011) shows the new CHC structure for ages 70–90 years. As was found for the Keith CHC structure, *Gf* is indistinguishable from *g*, even though the "new" Gf factor is composed only of Matrix Reasoning and Arithmetic, and a strong *Gsm* factor emerged based on substantial loadings by all three sections of Digit Span. Notably, the *g* loading for the *Gsm* factor in the analysis for ages 70–90 (.84) is similar to the *g* loading of .81 for Keith's *Gsm* factor. The other three factors—*Gc*, *Gv*, and *Gs*—are virtually identical for ages 16–69 and 70–90, and the "fit" statistics (CFI and RMSEA) are excellent for both models (shown in Figures 1.2 and 1.3).

Although Niileksala et al. (2012) had as their main research goal the extension of the CHC model to ages 70–90, they also investigated the new model for the entire 16–90 age range and verified that this model was invariant across age groups; the factor structure, factor loadings, and "fit" statistics for ages 16–69 mirrored the values shown in Figure 1.3 for the elderly sample. These analyses provide empirical support for an alternative CHC model for ages 16–69 in those instances where examiners did not administer Figure Weights and Letter-Number Sequencing (both supplemental). The Keith CHC factors require those two subtests, but the Niileksala model does not.

The technique of CFA, championed most notably by Tim Keith and Matt Reynolds, has dramatically changed the way clinicians interpret all current measures of cognitive abilities for children and adults; for a thorough, insightful explanation of how sophisticated psychometrics has enhanced examiners' understanding of the intricacies of the patterns of strengths and weaknesses in test profiles on widely used intelligence tests, see the recent chapter by Keith and Reynolds (2012).

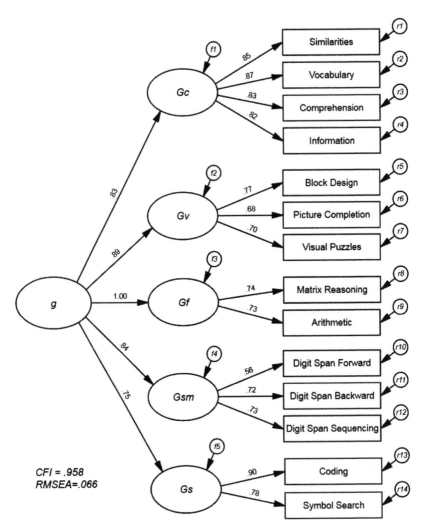

Figure 1.3. New CHC Model for the WAIS-IV for Ages 70–90 Years

Source: C. Niileksala, personal communication, October 21, 2011 (based on analyses conducted by Niileksala et al., 2012)

WAIS-IV's Relationship with the WMS-IV

The WAIS-IV was codeveloped and conormed with the Wechsler Memory Scale—Fourth Edition (WMS-IV; Wechsler, 2009b), and the two tests are commonly administered together as part of clinical, forensic, and neuropsychological evaluations, especially for older individuals (Groth-Marnat, 2009). The integration of these two Wechsler batteries as clinical and psychometric tools has been discussed insightfully by Lisa Drozdick, Jim Holdnack, and colleagues in *Essentials of WMS-IV Assessment* (Drozdick, Holdnack, & Hilsabeck, 2011) and elsewhere (Drozdick et. al, 2012; Holdnack & Drozdick, 2010; Holdnack, Zhou, Larrabee, Millis, & Salthouse, 2011; Wechsler, 2009a). Consult the complete set of articles in a special issue of *Assessment* devoted to advancing WAIS-IV and WMS-IV clinical interpretation (Frazier, 2011).

Holdnack et al. (2011) explored several different CFA models to best explain the relationship between the constructs measured by the two test batteries for ages 16–69 ($N = 900$). Variables included the 10 primary "Full Scale" WAIS-IV subtests and six WMS-IV subtests. The six WMS-IV subtests were Logical Memory (recall for a short story), Verbal Paired Associates (recall for related and unrelated word pairs), Designs (recall of spatial locations and visual details), Visual Reproduction (recall of geometric designs), Spatial Addition (ability to manipulate visual-spatial information in working memory), and Symbol Span (ability to manipulate designs in working memory). Only the delayed portions of Logical Memory, Verbal Paired Associates, Designs, and Visual Reproduction were entered into the CFA, because it is unlikely that CFA "can differentiate immediate from delayed memory functioning as this often leads to model specification errors consequent to method variance" (Holdnack et al., 2011, p. 180). They examined 13 measurement models and concluded that two were especially good and equally effective at demonstrating the interrelatedness of the WAIS-IV and WMS-IV.

The first model identified five second-order factors, along with a hierarchical first-order *g* factor; the second model extracted seven factors, but no *g* dimension (Holdnack et al., 2011). Because the empirical and conceptual support for both models is equally strong, examiners may choose to interpret whichever model is most consistent with their personal, professional, and theoretical orientation. As discussed in the following paragraphs, we favor the seven-factor solution.

The five factors in the hierarchical model were named Verbal Comprehension, Perceptual Reasoning, Processing Speed, Working Memory, and Memory. The first four correspond to the WAIS-IV Indexes; the fifth is composed of the four WMS-IV delayed recall subtests, tasks that measure primarily Long-Term Retrieval (*Glr*) and Visual Processing (*Gv*) from CHC theory (D. Flanagan, personal communication, October 21, 2011). The Working Memory factor was the only one to incorporate subtests from both batteries—Arithmetic, Digit Span, Spatial Addition, and Symbol Span.

The loadings on the first-order *g* factor ranged from .72 for Processing Speed to .94 for Working Memory (WM). This finding is consistent with the claim that:

WM comprises the functions of focusing attention, conscious rehearsal, and transformation and mental manipulation of information, while g reflects the component variance that is common to all tests of ability. The centrality of WM in individual differences in information processing leads to some cognitive theorists to equate it with g. (Colom, Rebollo, Palacios, Juan-Espinosa, & Kyllonen, 2004, p. 277)

The alternative joint CFA recommended by Holdnack et al. (2011) produced seven factors, four composed only of WAIS-IV subtests (Verbal Comprehension, Perceptual Reasoning, Processing Speed, and Auditory Working Memory) and three composed solely of WMS-IV subtests (Visual Working Memory, Auditory Memory, and Visual Memory). From CHC theory: (a) Auditory Memory measures *Glr* (specifically, the narrow abilities of meaningful memory and associative memory); (b) Visual Memory measures *Gv* (Visual Memory) with a touch of *Gsm* (Working Memory); and (c) Visual Working Memory is an amalgam of *Gv* (Visual Memory) and *Gsm* (Working Memory and Memory Span) (D. Flanagan, personal communication, October 21, 2011).

From the vantage point of CHC theory, the first model has the great disadvantage of merging *Gv* and *Glr* into a single factor, whereas the seven-factor structure does a better job of distinguishing *Gv* from *Glr*, especially when contrasting the Visual Memory and Auditory Memory factors. Furthermore, the seven-factor model also accords well with the cognitive neuroscience research and theory that underlies the WAIS-IV, including the distinction between Auditory Working Memory and Visual Working Memory, and it demonstrates the total separation of the constructs measured by the WAIS-IV and WMS-IV, providing strong empirical support for the common clinical and neuro-psychological practice of administering both test batteries as part of a comprehensive assessment. We endorse that practice and recommend that clinicians integrate the scores yielded by the two instruments by (a) internalizing the joint seven-factor structure of the WAIS-IV and WMS-IV (Holdnack et al., 2011); (b) performing some or all of the two dozen or so comparisons between the two instruments (Drozdick et al., 2011, pp. 171–172); and (c) studying the growing body of literature on joint interpretation of profiles on the two Wechsler tests (Drozdick et al., 2011; Frazier, 2011; Holdnack & Drozdick, 2010).

The case report of Jim W., a 64-year-old man referred for possible dementia (see Chapter 10), demonstrates the integration of data from the WAIS-IV and WMS-IV and provides a good illustration of the dynamic degree to which these two instruments complement each other in the diagnostic process.

WAIS-IV's Relationship with the WAIS-III

The relationship between the WAIS-IV and its predecessor, the WAIS-III, was examined in a sample of 240 adults aged 16 to 88 (Psychological Corporation, 2008). Each test was administered in a counterbalanced order with a 1- to 23-week interval (mean = 5 weeks) between the testings. The overall correlation coefficients showed that the Full Scale IQs for the WAIS-III and WAIS-IV were the most highly related (r = .94) of the global scales, followed by the Verbal Comprehension Indexes (r = .91), Working Memory Indexes (r = .87), Processing Speed Indexes (r = .86), and the Perceptual Organization/Reasoning Indexes (r = .84). Thus, despite the substantial changes from the WAIS-III to the WAIS-IV in the composition of the Full Scale (see Rapid Reference 1.3), the extremely high coefficient of .94 indicates that the construct measured by Wechsler's Full Scale has not changed at all.

As shown in Table 1.1, the average WAIS-IV Full Scale IQ was 2.9 points lower than the WAIS-III Full Scale IQ, which is the same difference the WAIS-III FSIQ was from the WAIS-R FSIQ. The difference between the two instruments on both the Working Memory Index and the Processing Speed Index is negligible (0.7 points for both), but it is more substantial for the Verbal Comprehension Index (4.3 points)

Table 1.1. Changes in Scores From the WAIS-III to the WAIS-IV

Scale	WAIS-III Mean[a]	SD	WAIS-IV Mean[a]	SD	WAIS-III—WAIS-IV Standard Score Difference	WAIS-III—WAIS-IV Correlation[b]
VCI	104.4	15.5	100.1	14.9	4.3	0.91
PRI or POI	103.7	15.3	100.3	15.5	3.4	0.84
WMI	100.0	14.5	99.3	13.7	0.7	0.78
PSI	100.8	17.2	100.1	14.9	0.7	0.86
FSIQ	102.9	15.0	100.0	15.2	2.9	0.94

[a] The values in the Mean columns are the average of the means of the two administration orders.

[b] The weighted average was obtained with Fisher's z transformation.

Note: Sample sizes ranged from 238 to 240. Correlations were computed separately for each order of administration in a counterbalanced design and corrected for the variability of the WAIS-III standardization sample (Guilford & Fruchter, 1978).

Source: Data are adapted from Table 5.5 of the *WAIS-IV Technical and Interpretive Manual* (Wechsler, 2008).

and the Perceptual Organization/Reasoning Index (3.4 points). These differences are entirely consistent with the well-known Flynn Effect (Flynn, 1987, 2007, 2009a, 2009b; Flynn & Weiss, 2007) and indicate that a person's standard scores on an old test, with outdated norms (e.g., the WAIS-III), will tend to be spuriously high. The WAIS-IV will yield scores that are a little lower than the WAIS-III, especially on the FSIQ, VCI, and PRI, but these lower scores present a more accurate estimate of the person's intellectual abilities because they are derived from contemporary standards (i.e., the most recent norms groups).

The Flynn Effect and Capital Punishment

Overall, the Flynn effect (FE) has shown that, on average, American children and adults have increased their scores on intelligence tests at the rate of 3 points per decade between the 1930s and 1990s, with gains of 5 to 8 points per decade occurring for other developed nations, such as France, The Netherlands, and Japan (Flynn, 2007, 2009b; Kaufman & Lichtenberger, 2006). The mean FSIQ difference in the WAIS-III/WAIS-IV study, which translates to a gain of 2.7 IQ points per decade (Zhou, Gregoire, & Zhu, 2010), confirms the maintenance of the FE in the United States into the first decade of the 21st century. Post-2000 data from Norway and Denmark suggest that the FE has stopped occurring in those countries and that there may even be a reverse FE (i.e., decline in IQ) taking place, especially in Denmark (Sundet, Barlaug, & Torjussen, 2004; Teasdale & Owen, 2005, 2008). However, those studies are limited by the fact that they are based solely on data from 18- to 19-year-old males; generalizations are made to entire *countries* even though the studies did not include females, children, or adults age 20 or above (Kaufman, 2010c).

Within the United States, the debate has escalated well beyond research laboratories and clinical practice (e.g., Should examiners adjust a child's IQ for the FE when diagnosing children for special education?). Now the debate has entered the arena of litigation, with a wide array of ongoing capital punishment cases in progress throughout the nation. Kaufman and Weiss (2010a) frame the current issues in their introduction to a special issue of the *Journal of Psychoeducational Assessment* devoted to the FE:

Researchers differ on why the FE occurs. Some claim that genetics is the key variable (Rodgers & Wanstrom, 2007), though most stress environmental factors such as nutrition (Colom, Lluis-Font, & Andres-Pueyo, 2005), education (Teasdale & Owen, 2005), or improvement in public health (Steen, 2009). . . . [Regardless of causality], the dispute about the scientific validity of the FE has entered the U.S. courtrooms in a big way as a burgeoning array of law cases asks whether the FE should be considered when sentencing low-functioning criminals convicted of a capital crime. Ever since the Supreme Court's decision in *Atkins v. Virginia* (2002), which stipulated that a criminal who is mentally retarded cannot be executed, whether or not to adjust IQs for the FE (i.e., by subtracting 3 points for each decade that the norms are out of date) has literally been a matter of life or death for some individuals. If a convicted criminal in a capital punishment case earned a global IQ of 73 on a test with 20-year-old norms, should that IQ be adjusted by 6 points to account for their datedness? Is the best estimate of the person's mental functioning 73 or 67? Of course, standard errors of measurement and adaptive behavior enter the equation as well, but the questions that arise from the FE are intriguing. (pp. 379–380)

The courts remain split on whether a criminal's IQ should be adjusted for the FE, with verdicts differing from state to state and from courtroom to courtroom within states. Those who argue for the FE adjustment claim that an IQ obtained on out-of-date norms is spuriously high; the downward adjustment often places a person's IQ in the range associated with Mental Retardation (Intellectual Disability), and the criminal is exempt from execution. Those who are unconvinced of the scientific validity of the FE would *not* adjust a person's IQ of, say, 75, making that criminal eligible for the death penalty. Numerous professionals have served as expert witnesses in these "Adkins" cases, such as Jack Fletcher, Alan Kaufman, Kevin McGrew, Cecil Reynolds, and James Flynn himself. Some argue for the prosecution (e.g., Hagan, Drogin, & Guilmette, 2010), others for the defense (e.g., Fletcher, Steubing, & Hughes, 2010; Reynolds, Niland, Wright, & Rosenn, 2010).

The arguments persist and are not yet resolved. The editors of the special journal issue devoted to the FE disagree about the adjustment. Weiss (2010) believes that, "the ethical position of an expert witness providing testimony is not to argue either for or against FE adjustments but to inform the court about the extant research on the topic" (p. 491). In contrast, Kaufman (2010b) states:

I respect the diversity of opinion on the topic of capital punishment, and the statistical complexity that surrounds the FE, but I am firmly in the camp with Reynolds et al. (2010), Fletcher et al. (2010), and Flynn (2006, 2007, 2009b) that IQs obtained on outdated norms should be adjusted for the FE in capital punishment cases. (p. 500)

The arguments on both sides are complex and too detailed for this book; interested readers are referred to the diverse articles in the special issue on the FE

(Kaufman & Weiss, 2010b), which is not restricted to the issue of capital punishment but covers a wide variety of topics, including causality, clinical applications, and ethical considerations (e.g., Ceci & Kanaya, 2010; Flynn, 2010; Kaufman, 2010a; McGrew, 2010; Reynolds et al., 2010; Sternberg, 2010).

In the meantime, the FE continues to be a hot topic for ongoing research investigations, and readers are encouraged to seek out state-of-the-art studies as well. For example, Zhou and colleagues (Zhou et al., 2010; Zhou, Zhu, & Weiss, 2010) conducted a particularly innovative set of analyses using data from various versions of Wechsler's scales and other tests as well. They found that: (a) males had a larger FE than females; (b) individuals with IQs of 110 and above had a notably smaller FE than those with IQs below 110; (c) adults ages 55–90 had a substantially larger FE than virtually every age group between 3–4 and 40–54 years; (d) infants and toddlers showed a *reverse* FE on the Bayley Scales, as mean cognitive scores *dropped* 6.3 points per decade from the Bayley-II to the Bayley-III standardizations.

But the main thrust of the FE research is not found in the laboratory. As Cecil Reynolds (personal communication, March 13, 2010) noted: "Whether to apply the Flynn Correction is a dire matter with implications we seldom encounter in psychology." Reynolds et al. (2010) commented on the societal responsibilities that fall, at least partly, into the hands of psychologists subsequent to *Atkins v. Virginia*: "The importance of understanding and assessing mental retardation in criminal defendants has become critical, indeed a true matter of life and death, in capital felony cases. . . . No one's life should depend on when an IQ test was normed" (pp. 477, 480).

STANDARDIZATION AND PSYCHOMETRIC PROPERTIES OF THE WAIS-IV

The standardization sample for the WAIS-IV ($N = 2,200$) was selected according to 2005 U.S. Census data and was stratified according to age, sex, race/ethnicity, geographic region, and education level. Thirteen age groups were created from a large sample of adolescents and adults, with 100 to 200 subjects in each group between ages 16–17 and 85–90.

Reliability

The average split-half reliability for the FSIQ across the 13 age groups was strong, ranging from .97 to .98 (see Rapid Reference 1.7 for split-half and test-retest reliability for all scales and subtests) (The Psychological Corporation, 2008). The Factor Indexes had average reliability coefficients ranging from .90 for

≡ Rapid Reference 1.7

Average WAIS-IV Reliability

Subtest/Composite Score	Split-Half Reliability	Test-Retest Reliability
Block Design	.87	.80
Similarities	.87	.87
Digit Span	.93	.83
Matrix Reasoning	.90	.74
Vocabulary	.94	.89
Arithmetic	.88	.83
Symbol Search	.81	.81
Visual Puzzles	.89	.74
Information	.93	.90
Coding	.86	.86
Letter-Number Sequencing	.88	.80
Figure Weights	.90	.77
Comprehension	.87	.86
Cancellation	.78	.78
Picture Completion	.84	.77
Verbal Comprehension Index	.96	.96
Perceptual Reasoning Index	.95	.87
Working Memory Index	.94	.88
Processing Speed Index	.90	.87
Full Scale IQ	.98	.96

Note: For Coding and Symbol Search, and the composite of these two (Processing Speed), only test-retest coefficients are reported because of the timed nature of the subtests.

Source: Data are from Tables 4.1 and 4.5 of the WAIS-IV Technical and Interpretive Manual (Psychological Corporation, 2008).

Processing Speed to .96 for Verbal Comprehension. Individual subtest reliabilities ranged from an average of .94 on Vocabulary to .78 on Cancellation; median values were .89 for the 10 core subtests and .87 for the 5 supplemental subtests. A subset of the standardization sample (298 adults) provided test-retest data, with an average of three weeks between testings. The results of the test-retest study showed similar reliability coefficients for the four age-group subsamples (16–29, 30–54, 55–69, and 70–90 years). Average stability coefficients across all ages were

.96 for the Full Scale IQ and Verbal Comprehension Index, .88 for the Working Memory Index, and .87 for both the Perceptual Reasoning and Processing Speed Index. The highest stability coefficient for the core subtests was .90 for Information, and the lowest was .74 for Matrix Reasoning and Visual Puzzles. Of the supplemental subtests, Comprehension had the highest stability coefficients, ranging from .86 for Comprehension to .77 for Figure Weights and Picture Completion.

Salthouse and Saklofske (2010, Table 8.4) reported reliability and stability of the WAIS-IV subtests for two broad age groups: 16–64 and 65–90. Most coefficients were within .02 of each other for the two groups. However, the following differences of .03 or greater were noted: (a) split-half reliability was *higher* for ages 65–90 than 16–64 on Information, Similarities, and Symbol Search, but was *lower* for Block Design; and (b) stability was *higher* for ages 65–90 than 16–64 on Information, Digit Span, and Picture Completion, but was lower on Matrix Reasoning and Visual Puzzles. The only truly notable differences were for the stability of Digit Span and Visual Puzzles. Digit Span had a stability coefficient of .84 for the elderly sample versus .74 for the younger group. The stability for Visual Puzzles was .72 for ages 16–64 versus an *unacceptably low value of .57 for the older sample.*

Loadings on the General Factor

General intelligence or general mental ability (Spearman, 1927) is denoted by *g*. The measurement of *g* may be done by several methods. Preliminary findings from Keith's WAIS-IV higher-order CFA (personal communications, January 30 and March 14, 2009), based on the average correlation matrix for ages 16 to 90 (Psychological Corporation, 2008, p. 62), provided the *g*-loadings reported here. These *g* loadings are the Factor loadings for each WAIS-IV subtest on the second-order general Factor that was obtained from the CFA. Factor loadings of .70 or greater are usually considered "good" measures of *g*; loadings of .50 to .69 are deemed "fair" *g* loadings; and loadings below .50 are considered poor. Rapid Reference 1.8 contains data on how well each subtest loads on the *g* factor.

Contrary to previous Wechsler scales on which measures of verbal comprehension and expression tended to yield the highest *g* loadings, the best measures of *g* on the WAIS-IV were Arithmetic and two Perceptual Reasoning tasks. Among the Verbal Comprehension subtests, only Vocabulary emerged as a good measure of *g*. The traditionally good measures, such as Comprehension, Information, and Similarities, were only fair measures, loading in the mid- to high .60s. Not surprisingly, the Processing Speed subtests were the weakest measures of *g*, but only Cancellation, with a dismal loading of .38, qualifies as a poor measure of *g*.

≡ Rapid Reference 1.8

WAIS-IV Subtests as Measures of General Ability (*g*)

	g loading	Strength as a measure of g
Arithmetic	.78	Good
Figure Weights	.77	Good
Matrix Reasoning	.73	Good
Vocabulary	.72	Good
Digit Span	.69	Fair
Block Design	.68	Fair
Comprehension	.68	Fair
Similarities	.68	Fair
Visual Puzzles	.66	Fair
Letter-Number Sequencing	.66	Fair
Information	.65	Fair
Picture Completion	.57	Fair
Coding	.55	Fair
Symbol Search	.54	Fair
Cancellation	.38	Poor

Source: T. Keith (personal communication, January 30, 2009).

Salthouse and Saklofske (2010, Figure 8.2) reported *g* loadings for the four WAIS-IV Indexes separately for two broad age groups: 16–64 and 65–90. These loadings are shown here:

Age Group	VCI	PRI	WMI	PSI
16–64	.80	.89	.82	.71
65–90	.81	.89	.95	.79

The PRI was the best measure of *g* for ages 16–64, but WMI was the best measure of *g* for elderly individuals. The PSI was the lowest for both age groups but was, nonetheless, higher for the older than the younger sample. However, Salthouse and Saklofske (2010) did not believe that the age-related fluctuations were meaningful; they concluded that the coefficients were "very similar, which suggests nearly equivalent composition of the higher-order cognitive ability factor at different ages" (p. 233). As was mentioned in the discussion of the joint CFA of WAIS-IV and WMS-IV, the strong g loadings for Working Memory are consistent with a large body of cognitive research on the topic (Colom et al., 2004).

The concept of general intelligence is one whose usefulness has been debated in the intelligence literature. Interestingly, Horn (1989) and Carroll (1993) were at the opposite poles of this debate, although their theories were merged to form CHC theory. Horn was a devout anti-g theorist, whereas Carroll had great respect for g and considered general ability to be Stratum III of his theory of intelligence. Because of their disagreements about the g construct, CHC theory focuses on Broad Abilities (Stratum II) and Narrow Abilities (Stratum I) and rarely addresses the role of g (McGrew, 2005).

From our perspective, g pertains to a practical, clinical construct that corresponds to FSIQ and, therefore, provides an overview of each person's diverse abilities. There is also evidence that the g that underlies tests of intellectual ability is closely related to the g that underlies tests of academic achievement (correlations of .77–.94 for ages 4–5 to 16–19) when intelligence and achievement are assessed by the Kaufman and Woodcock test batteries (Kaufman, Reynolds, Liu, Kaufman, & McGrew, 2012).

But we do not interpret it as a theoretical construct. Other theorists have argued otherwise (Carroll, 1993; Jensen, 1998; Spearman, 1904); even Wechsler[2] (1974) was a strong believer in g, maintaining that "[i]ntelligence is the overall capacity of individuals to understand and cope with the world around them" (p. 5). We believe that a subtest with a strong g loading should not be interpreted as one that is *the* representation of an individual's overall level of cognitive ability. Rather, as discussed in Chapters 4 and 5 on interpretation, a cognitive test assesses diverse cognitive abilities, all of which need to be understood. The person's pattern of strengths and weaknesses on the four Indexes or five Factors is far more important to interpret than FSIQ. The g loadings do represent how well psychometrically the subtests hang together as a whole but do not reflect a theoretical construct that underlies human intellect. The g loadings do offer aids to clinical interpretation by providing expectancies. For example, Arithmetic's high g loading and strong loading on the fluid reasoning Factor in Keith's CFA lead us to expect that a person will score about as well on the Arithmetic subtest as he or she scored on FSIQ and PRI. If, for example, the person scored much lower on Arithmetic than on FSIQ and PRI, that is contrary to expectations, and we would seek an explanation, such as distractibility, anxiety, poor working memory, or poor ability

---

2. Wechsler's (1974) quote has been modified to avoid sexist language but is otherwise verbatim.

to manipulate numbers. By contrast, an extremely high or low score on Cancellation is anticipated and would not cause us to think twice about it.

ETHNIC DIFFERENCES IN IQ

Differences Between Whites and African Americans

The difference of about one standard deviation in the IQs earned by Whites and African Americans, identified for numerous samples with a wide variety of tests (Hauser, 1998; Lichtenberger, Broadbooks, & Kaufman, 2000; Reynolds & Lowe, 2009), is similar to the overall findings on the WAIS-III (Heaton, Taylor, & Manly, 2003; Kaufman & Lichtenberger, 2006) and the WAIS-IV. For the WAIS-IV standardization sample ages 16–90 years, unadjusted mean Full Scale IQs of 103.2 and 88.7 were obtained for Whites ($n = 1,540$) and African Americans ($n = 260$), respectively, yielding a difference of 14.5 points. Largest Index differences occurred in fluid and visual-spatial abilities (PRI = 14.5), with smaller but notable 10- to 12-point differences emerging for verbal abilities (VCI = 11.8), working memory (WMI = 10.6), and processing speed (PSI = 10.0) (Weiss et al., 2010, Table 4.3).

However, these global differences do not come close to telling the whole story. Weiss et al. (2010) conducted an array of analyses, often ingenious and always state-of-the-art in terms of psychometrics, in an attempt to better understand ethnic difference on the WAIS-IV within a societal context (see Rapid Reference 1.9 for the key findings). In that respect, the WAIS-IV research conducted by Weiss and colleagues mirrors the important series of WISC-IV investigations that Weiss et al.

≡ Rapid Reference 1.9

....

Key Results in WAIS-IV Analyses on Differences Between Whites and African Americans (Weiss et al., 2010)

- Full Scale IQ differences varied as a direct function of birth cohort. White–African American differences were 19 points for those born between 1917 and 1942; 17 points for birth cohorts 1943–1962; 13 points for 1963–1987; and 10 points for 1988–1991 (Weiss et al., 2010, p. 123). Thus, race differences were almost twice as large for ages 65–90 years as for ages 16–19. Age trends were also noted on the WISC-IV, where race differences averaged 12 points for adolescents and 6 points for children (Prifitera, Saklofske, Weiss, & Rolfus, 2005). Nisbett (2009) reported that race differences in IQ for 12-year-olds had dropped by nearly 40% over the past three decades.

(continued)

- The IQ difference of about 15 points for adults ages 20–90 was reduced to 11 points when controlling for a variety of mediating variables—education, occupation, income, region, and gender (Weiss et al., 2010, p. 125). These findings conform to previous results with a variety of intelligence tests (Reynolds & Lowe, 2009), including the WAIS-III (Heaton et al., 2003; Kaufman & Lichtenberger, 2006).

- For adults ages 20–90, the variable of race accounted for 15% of the variance in multiple regression analysis, whereas educational attainment accounted for almost twice as much variance (29%). When occupation, income, region, and gender are added to the mix, that value increases to 35% (Weiss et al., 2010, p. 124).

(2006) reported in a groundbreaking chapter; indeed, Flanagan and Kaufman (2009) recommended reading that chapter "in its entirety to fully grasp the role of contextual factors in shaping the IQs earned by individuals from diverse ethnic groups and to be able to give 2-point responses to any questions you may be asked about SES, test bias, or ethnic differences on intelligence tests" (p. 49).

Differences Between Whites and Hispanics

For the WAIS-IV standardization sample ages 16–90 years, Weiss et al. (2010) also provided differences in scores earned by Whites and Hispanics. Unadjusted mean Full Scale IQs of 103.2 and 91.6 were obtained for Whites ($n = 1,540$) and Hispanics ($n = 289$), respectively, yielding a difference of 11.6 points. Smallest Index differences occurred in processing speed (PSI = 6.1) and fluid/visual-spatial abilities (PRI = 8.8) with the largest differences occurring on language tasks: verbal abilities (VCI = 11.5) and working memory (WMI = 10.9) (Weiss et al., 2010, Table 4.3). These Index differences mirror almost exactly data obtained on the WAIS-III (Heaton et al., 2003; Kaufman & Lichtenberger, 2006).

As with White–African American differences, Weiss et al. (2010) observed the mediating effects of age, education, and other background variables in their analyses of White-Hispanic discrepancies on the WAIS-IV, as shown in Rapid Reference 1.10.

≡ *Rapid Reference 1.10*

Key Results in WAIS-IV Analyses on Differences Between Whites and Hispanics (Weiss et al., 2010)

- Similar to the findings for Whites vs. African Americans, Full Scale IQ differences for Whites vs. Hispanics varied as an almost direct function of birth cohort. Differences were 18 points for those born between 1917 and 1942;

14 points for birth cohorts 1943–1977; 7 points for 1978–1987; and 9 points for 1988–1991 (Weiss et al., 2010, p. 123). Thus, once again, ethnic differences were almost twice as large for ages 65–90 years as for ages 16–19. These results conform to WISC-IV findings, where ethnic differences averaged 8 points for adolescents and 1 point for children (Prifitera et al., 2005).

- The IQ difference of about 12 points for adults at ages 20–90 was reduced to 6.5 points when controlling for a variety of mediating variables—education, occupation, income, region, and gender (Weiss et al., 2010, p. 125), consistent with previous analyses of adjusted White–Hispanic differences on the WAIS-III and other cognitive tests (Heaton et al., 2003; Kaufman & Lichtenberger, 2006).

- For adults ages 20–90, the variable of ethnicity (White vs. Hispanic) accounted for 11% of the variance in multiple regression analysis, whereas educational attainment accounted for about three times as much variance (31%). When occupation, income, region, and gender are added to the mix, that value increases to 37% (Weiss et al., 2010, p. 124).

OVERVIEW OF ETHNIC DIFFERENCES ON THE WAIS-IV

The results of the analyses by Weiss and his colleagues on the WISC-IV (Weiss et al., 2006) and WAIS-IV (Weiss et al., 2010) make it abundantly clear that socioeconomic status and an array of other background, behavioral, and personal variables impact a person's IQ and profile of test scores far more than the variable of ethnicity alone, and that these variables mediate the role played by ethnicity in affecting a person's IQ. Weiss and colleagues urge the interpretation of ethnic differences within a multifaceted societal context. We encourage clinicians and researchers to read these two powerful chapters on Wechsler's scales to understand the interactive and complex roles played by ethnicity, education, diverse indicators of socioeconomic status, personal beliefs, and developmental variables in shaping a person's cognitive test profile. Consult also Suzuki, Short, and Lee (2011) and *IQ Testing 101* (Kaufman, 2009) for a thorough discussion of the genetic and environmental factors that interactively affect IQ test performance.

Ultimately, we agree with Weiss et al. (2010), who state that,

racial/ethnic differences are likely to be proxies for a multitude of other variables that we are just beginning to identify and study. . . . We suggest that future researchers go beyond these easily collected proxy variables (i.e., race/ethnicity, and SES) and directly study the factors that are related to the development and maintenance of cognitive abilities both within and across culturally and linguistically diverse groups. (pp. 135–136)

COMPREHENSIVE REFERENCES ON TEST

The *WAIS-IV Administrative and Scoring Manual* (Wechsler, 2008) and the *WAIS-IV Technical and Interpretive Manual* (Psychological Corporation, 2008) currently provide the most detailed information about the WAIS-IV. These manuals review the development of the test, descriptions of each of the subtests and scales, standardization, reliability, and validity. In addition, a particularly valuable WAIS-IV reference is a book edited by professionals who were intimately involved with the development and standardization of the test: *WAIS-IV— Clinical Use and Interpretation* (Weiss, Saklofske, Coalson, & Raiford, 2010b). *Assessing Adolescent and Adult Intelligence, Third Edition* (Kaufman & Lichtenberger, 2006) provides an excellent review of the research on the WAIS, WAIS-R, and WAIS-III, much of which is still pertinent for the WAIS-IV. Rapid Reference 1.11 provides basic information on the WAIS-IV and its publisher.

Our second edition of *Essentials of WAIS-IV Assessment*, the edited book by Weiss et al. (2010b), Sattler and Ryan's (2009) *Assessment with the WAIS-IV* (2009), a recent chapter by Drozdick et al. (2012), and a special section of the June 2011 issue of

---

≡ *Rapid Reference 1.11*

Wechsler Adult Intelligence Scale—Fourth Edition

Author: David Wechsler

Publication Date: 2008

What the Test Measures: verbal comprehension, perceptual reasoning, working memory, processing speed, and general intelligence

Age Range 16–90 years

Administration Time: 10 core subtests to obtain 4 indexes = 65–90 minutes; 15 core and supplemental subtests = 85–114 minutes

Qualification of Examiners: Graduate- or professional-level training in psychological assessment

Publisher: Pearson
19500 Bulverde Road
San Antonio, TX 78259
Customer Service: (800) 211–8378
http://pearsonassess.com

Price: WAIS-IV Basic Kit Includes *Administration and Scoring Manual, Technical Manual*, 2 Stimulus Books, 25 Record Forms, 25 Response Booklet 1, 25 Response Booklet 2, Symbol Search Scoring Key, Coding Scoring Key, Cancellation Scoring Templates in a box. ISBN: 015–8980–808. $1,120.00 (in box); $1,190.00 (in hard- or soft-sided case).

Assessment (Frazier, 2011) provide the most authoritative sources for administering, scoring, interpreting, and applying WAIS-IV test profiles.

🖋 TEST YOURSELF 🖋

1. **Many of the tasks that David Wechsler used in his WAIS, WAIS-R, WAIS-III, and WAIS-IV were adapted from what sources?**

2. **Updating the WAIS-IV's theoretical foundations was achieved by considering the following theoretical constructs EXCEPT**
   a. Fluid reasoning
   b. Working memory
   c. Processing speed
   d. Phonological processing ✓

3. **What was the major structural change implemented from the WAIS-III to the WAIS-IV?** 4 indexes

4. **Which of the following WAIS-IV subtests is a CORE subtest that is used to compute FSIQ?**
   a. Visual Puzzles ✓
   b. Letter-Number Sequencing
   c. Picture Completion
   d. Comprehension
   e. Figure Weights

5. **Which subtest is NOT new to the WAIS-IV?**
   a. Visual Puzzles
   b. Figure Weights
   c. Cancellation
   d. Symbol Search ✓

6. **Which WAIS-IV subtest does NOT offer Process scores?**
   a. Digit Span
   b. Visual Puzzles ✓
   c. Block Design
   d. Letter-Number Sequencing

7. **The results of Keith's confirmatory factor analysis that supported a Five-Factor CHC model for ages 16–69 showed three WAIS-IV subtests to load highly on the fluid reasoning (*Gf*) factor. These subtests are Figure Weights, Matrix Reasoning, and**
   a. Block Design
   b. Picture Completion

(continued)

   c. Letter-Number Sequencing
   d. Similarities
   e. Arithmetic

8. **The new Five-Factor CHC model of the WAIS-IV for ages 70-90**
   a. Has strong empirical support
   b. Treats the three sections of Digit Span as separate variables
   c. Measures the same theoretical constructs from CHC theory as the Keith model
   d. Is an alternate model for ages 16–69 when examiners do not administer supplemental subtests
   e. All of the above

9. **Which index includes the subtests with the lowest loadings on the general (g) factor?**
   a. Verbal Comprehension
   b. Perceptual Reasoning
   c. Working Memory
   d. Processing Speed

10. **What term refers to the phenomenon that IQ test norms in the United States get out of date at the rate of about 3 points per decade?**
   a. Flynn Effect
   b. CFA
   c. CHC
   d. Horn Effect
   e. g theory

11. **TRUE OR FALSE? Analyses of ethnic differences on the WAIS-IV have shown that ethnicity accounts for more variance in IQ than socioeconomic status.**

Answers: 1. Army Alpha, Army Beta, Army Performance Scale Examination, and Stanford-Binet; 2. d; 3. Removal of the VIQ and PIQ; 4. a; 5. d; 6. b; 7. e; 8. e; 9. d; 10. a; 11. false.

Two

HOW TO ADMINISTER THE WAIS-IV

O ne of the strengths of a standardized test, such as the WAIS-IV, is that it is able to provide scores that represent an individual's performance compared to other individuals of about the same age. However, to obtain results that are comparable to the national norms, examiners must be careful to adhere to the same administration and scoring procedures that were used during the standardization of the test. At the same time, examiners must not be rigid and unnatural in their manner of presentation. Thus, a delicate balancing act must take place to ensure the best possible administration.

APPROPRIATE TESTING CONDITIONS

Testing Environment

The physical surroundings in which the testing takes place may vary. Some examiners may test in a school, office, clinic, nursing home, or hospital, whereas others may find it necessary to test in a home. The most important features of the testing environment are that it is quiet, free of distractions and interruptions, and comfortable for the examinee. The ideal situation would provide a room for only the examiner and the examinee, as the presence of a third person can be disruptive. A table is a necessity for testing. Because writing and drawing will be done, a smooth tabletop is ideal; however, a clipboard may provide a smooth writing surface if the table is rough. It is recommended that you sit opposite the examinee. This arrangement allows easy observation of test-taking behaviors as well as easy manipulation of all test materials by the examiner.

Testing Materials

The WAIS-IV has become less cumbersome with its manipulatives than previous versions of the Wechsler tests. Because Object Assembly and Picture

53

Arrangement were eliminated from the test battery, only Block Design requires any materials other than a stimulus book for the examiner to handle. Some materials still need to be organized, such as the *WAIS-IV Administration and Scoring Manual*, Record Form, Stimulus Booklet, pencils, and stopwatch. However, experienced Wechsler test users will breathe a sigh of relief that they no longer have to try to hide Object Assembly pieces behind a shield while trying to pick up dropped pieces off the floor as they get them out of the box. Experienced examiners also will be able to stop sweating because they cannot find number two of the five Picture Arrangement cards. Generally, the WAIS-IV materials allow an efficient, user-friendly test administration, if examiners are well rehearsed.

During the testing, only the materials necessary for the task at hand should be on the table. Visible presence of other testing materials, such as the Block Design blocks or Symbol Search booklet, may be distracting or cause anxiety. Many examiners find it useful to place unused test materials on a chair close to them but out of the examinee's view.

Position the *Manual* so that it provides a shield behind which you can place the Record Form. This setup allows you to have easy access to all of the directions but makes the record of the examinee's scores less visible. However, you should avoid being secretive.

Almost everything needed to perform the assessment is included in the WAIS-IV kit. Necessary testing materials that do not come with the WAIS-IV kit include a stopwatch, extra #2 graphite pencils without erasers, a clipboard, your own pen or pencil for recording responses, and extra paper for taking notes.

DON'T FORGET
....

Keys for Preparing to Administer the Test:

- Quiet, distraction-free room
- Table large enough for two
- Smooth writing surface

Extra needed materials not in the WAIS- IV kit:

- Two #2 pencils without erasers
- Stopwatch
- Clipboard
- Extra paper and writing implement (just in case)

RAPPORT WITH EXAMINEE

Providing a comfortable interpersonal situation for the examinee is key to obtaining the best possible administration. Throughout the assessment session, it is important to facilitate a positive rapport. The tone of conversation should be natural, pleasant, and professional. To provide this natural and smooth inter-personal interaction, it is important to be completely familiar with all of the administration and scoring procedures of the test. If you are uncertain about how a task is to be administered or are fumbling with the testing materials, this indecision will likely cause awkward pauses and take away attention from the person who is being tested. Although it is not necessary to memorize the test manual, it is extremely advantageous to be completely familiar with the details of the *Manual*, such as wording of the directions and when particular test materials should be used. Also, it is important to know exactly where to locate the needed information regarding start, stop, and timing rules.

Establishing Rapport

To facilitate building rapport at the beginning of the testing session, it is a good idea for you to provide a general introduction to the test, as was done during the collection of the standardization sample. Questions or concerns that the examinee may have should also be addressed at this time. As stated in the standard WAIS-IV instructions, some time should be spent explaining to the examinee that most test takers find some questions easy and some questions quite difficult, which helps reassure them that it is okay if they do not know every answer. Elderly individuals may voice concern about their memory or ability to maneuver objects quickly. They should be reassured that they just need to do the best they can. They also may be told that the scores they earn are always based on the test performance of other adults about their age.

Maintaining Rapport

Once the testing has begun, care should be taken to adhere to the standardized language given in the *Manual*. However, small talk and reassuring statements are also needed throughout the testing process to promote a comfortable testing environment. You must be vigilant in watching the examinee's level of fatigue, anxiety, and cooperation. Speeded tests or tests requiring fine-motor coordi-nation may be more taxing for older adults; thus, signs of fatigue should be considered, especially if testing an older person. If anything, such as loss of motivation, tiredness, or nervousness, appears to be impinging on the exam-inee's performance, you should try to insert more casual conversation between the subtests or provide more supportive statements. When providing support-ive or encouraging statements, you should be careful not to give clues regarding the correctness of an examinee's answer. Indeed, it is important *not* to give

DON'T FORGET

Keys to Positive Examiner–Examinee Rapport During Assessment

1. Effectively introduce examinee to the testing activities by using the standardized introduction provided in the WAIS-IV Administration and Scoring Manual; begin establishing rapport.
2. Interact comfortably with examinee. Don't be stilted.
3. Give eye contact. Don't bury your head in the Manual.
4. Make smooth transitions between subtests. Use some small talk.
5. Avoid small talk during a subtest.
6. Familiarize yourself ahead of time with test directions and test materials.
7. Use precise wording of questions and directions. Only the mildest of paraphrasing is occasionally acceptable.
8. Be subtle, not distracting, when using a stopwatch.

encouraging comments and feedback *only* when an examinee is doing poorly or to praise only when correct. This type of selective feedback may inadvertently give cues to individuals that they are responding correctly or incorrectly to items, based on the examiner's verbalizations. Examinees should be praised for their level of effort ("You are really working hard") or recognized for attempting items that were notably difficult ("Those were tough ones, but you're trying hard. Let's try another one.").

Breaks during testing are allowed but should be taken only between two subtests, not in the middle of a subtest. If an adult's level of motivation has been clearly lowered during a very difficult subtest, some encouraging comments plus a brief break may be warranted. If, during a challenging subtest, an examinee indicates that he or she will not go on, you may need to provide encouragement, such as "Just try your best" or "Give it your best shot." During administration of timed subtests, you will find it useful to allow examinees to have a few extra seconds past the time limit to work if they are actively involved in the task. These little tips in administration may lessen potential discouragement and will extend rapport throughout the session.

CAUTION

Appropriate Feedback and Encouragement

- Praise and encourage the examinee's level of effort.
- Be careful *not* to give feedback on whether a particular response is right or wrong.
- Give encouragement throughout items, not just when examinee is struggling.

TESTING INDIVIDUALS WITH SPECIAL NEEDS

Adults or adolescents with special needs for testing may include those who have hearing impairment, visual problems, or motor difficulties, or those who are not fluent in English. When testing such adults, special consideration needs to be taken to accommodate the particular examinee while maintaining standardized procedures to the degree possible.

It is important for you to obtain as much information as possible about the adolescent's or adult's impairment before the assessment session with the individual. You should ask a caregiver about the examinee's vision, hearing, physical condition, or any other limitations. With this information, you will be able to determine how the test procedures need to be modified. Testing should be done so that the examinee is not penalized because of sensory or motor deficits. If major modifications in the standardized procedure are made, these changes may impact test scores or invalidate the use of the norms. Clinical judgment must be used to determine whether the examinee's impairment prohibits obtaining valid scores on part or all of the test.

Modifications to the test administration to accommodate an examinee's special needs may include:

- Administering the test in American Sign Language to a deaf individual (if you are specially trained)
- Adding printed words to facilitate understanding of directions to hard-of-hearing individuals
- Administering only the Verbal Scale subtests to a blind individual
- Eliminating time limits for adolescents or adults with motor difficulties
- Extending the testing over more than one session for any adult with special needs

---

CAUTION

Modifying Standardized Procedure

- Modifications to the standardized procedure to accommodate examinees' limitations may invalidate test scores.
- Clinical judgment is key in determining what quantitative and qualitative data are interpretable from the test administration.
  - Adaptations made in the time limits allowed on speeded subtests will invalidate the use of the norms.
  - Translating the test into another language may also cause problems in interpreting the scores.

When any modification is used, such as translation into another language, problems in interpreting the scores may arise. Careful consideration must be given to determine whether using such modifications is best or whether choosing another instrument or supplemental instruments may provide the most useful information.

ADMINISTRATION CONSIDERATIONS

Starting and Discontinuing Subtests

The administration rules have been simplified from the WAIS-III to the WAIS-IV, which aids in the efficient administration of the tasks. The discontinue rules of many subtests have been reduced by at least one item (e.g., from four consecutive failures to three). The Vocabulary and Information subtests reduced their discontinue rules from six to three consecutive failures. Important rules such as when to begin and end each subtest are clearly listed both in the *Manual* and on the Record Form. The general overall rules are described here.

Many of the subtests on the WAIS-IV start at items other than 1; these subtests are clearly listed on the Record Form. This procedure allows examiners to curtail testing time for most adults, but it also enables them to administer earlier, simpler items to adults who cannot correctly answer items at the designated starting point. Examinees who are functioning at a low intellectual level will usually need to go back to these easier items. The rule employed to enable examiners to go back to easier items if the first set of items causes difficulty is called the "reverse rule." Reverse rules require administration of earlier subtest items in reverse order if a perfect score is not obtained on *either* of the first two items administered. Until the examinee obtains perfect scores on two consecutive items, this reversal procedure continues. Sample Items are not part of the reverse-sequence procedure. Figures 2.2, 2.3 and 2.4 in the *WAIS-IV Administration and Scoring Manual* show examples of how the reverse rules are applied. These Verbal Comprehension and Working Memory subtests use a reverse rule: Similarities, Vocabulary, Arithmetic, Information, and Comprehension. The Perceptual Reasoning subtests with a reverse rule are Block Design, Matrix Reasoning, Visual Puzzles, Figure Weights, and Picture Completion. Rapid Reference 2.1 summarizes the start and reverse rules for the subtests.

In contrast, the Verbal subtests that do not use a reverse rule include Digit Span and Letter-Number Sequencing. None of the Processing Speed Subtests uses reverse rules, and these subtests end when a specified time has elapsed. A summary of discontinue rules for each subtest can be found in Rapid Reference 2.2. More detail is also provided in the Subtest-by-Subtest Guide later in this chapter.

≡ Rapid Reference 2.1

Summary of Subtest Start Points and Reverse Rules

Subtest	Start Point	Reverse Rule
Block Design	Sample Item, then Item 5	Score of 0 or 1 on either Item 5 or Item 6, administer preceding items in reverse order until two consecutive perfect scores are obtained
Similarities	Sample Item, then Item 4	Score of 0 or 1 on either Item 4 or Item 5, administer preceding items in reverse order until two consecutive perfect scores are obtained
Digit Span	Forward: Item 1 Backward: Sample Item, then Item 1 Sequencing: Sample Item, then Item 1	None
Matrix Reasoning	Sample Items A and B, then Item 4	Score of 0 on either Item 4 or Item 5, administer preceding items in reverse order until two consecutive perfect scores are obtained
Vocabulary	Item 5	Score of 0 or 1 on either Item 5 or Item 6, administer preceding items in reverse order until two consecutive perfect scores are obtained
Arithmetic	Sample Item, then Item 6	Score of 0 on either Item 6 or Item 7, administer preceding items in reverse order until two consecutive perfect scores are obtained
Symbol Search	Demonstration Items, Sample Items, then Test Items	None
Visual Puzzles	Demonstration Item, Sample Item, then Item 5	Score of 0 on either Item 5 or Item 6, administer preceding items in reverse order until two consecutive perfect scores are obtained
Information	Item 3	Score of 0 on either Item 3 or Item 4, administer preceding items in reverse

Subtest	Start Point	Reverse Rule
		order until two consecutive perfect scores are obtained
Coding	Demonstration Items, Sample Items, then Test Items	None
Letter-Number Sequencing	Demonstration Item A, Sample Item A, then Item 1	None
Figure Weights	Demonstration Items A and B, Sample Item, then Item 4	Score of 0 on either Item 4 or Item 5, administer preceding items in reverse order until two consecutive perfect scores are obtained
Comprehension	Item 3	Score of 0 or 1 on either Item 3 or Item 4, administer preceding items in reverse order until two consecutive perfect scores are obtained
Cancellation	Demonstration Item A, Sample Item A, then Item 1	None
Picture Completion	Sample Item, then Item 4	Score of 0 on either Item 4 or Item 5, administer preceding items in reverse order until two consecutive perfect scores are obtained

Source: From Table 2.7 of the WAIS-IV Administration and Scoring Manual. Copyright © 2008 The Psychological Corporation. Adapted and reproduced by permission. All rights reserved.

≡ *Rapid Reference 2.2*

Summary of Subtest Discontinue Rules

Subtest	Discontinue Rule
Block Design	After 2 consecutive scores of 0
Similarities	After 3 consecutive scores of 0
Digit Span	Forward: After scores of 0 on both trials of an item
	Backward: After scores of 0 on both trials of an item
	Sequencing: After scores of 0 on both trials of an item
Matrix Reasoning	After 3 consecutive scores of 0
Vocabulary	After 3 consecutive scores of 0

Arithmetic	After 3 consecutive scores of 0
Symbol Search	After 120 seconds
Visual Puzzles	After 3 consecutive scores of 0
Information	After 3 consecutive scores of 0
Coding	After 120 seconds
Letter-Number Sequencing	After scores of 0 on all three trials of an item
Figure Weights	After 3 consecutive scores of 0
Comprehension	After 3 consecutive scores of 0
Cancellation	After 45 seconds for each item
Picture Completion	After 4 consecutive scores of 0

Source: From Table 2.7 of the *WAIS-IV Administration and Scoring Manual.* Copyright © 2008 The Psychological Corporation. Adapted and reproduced by permission. All rights reserved.

Sometimes during administration of a subtest, it may be unclear how to score a response and, therefore, whether the subtest should be discontinued. This situation occurs most frequently during the Vocabulary, Similarities, and Comprehension subtests that have some subjectivity in their scoring. If it is not possible to determine quickly whether a response is correct, it is best to continue administering further items until you are certain that the discontinue rule has been met. This procedure is safest because the scores can always be reviewed later and items that are passed after the discontinue criterion has been met can (indeed, must) be excluded from the adult's raw score on the subtest (although such successes on hard items may provide you with valuable *clinical* information). However, if upon review of the scores it is noted that items should have been administered beyond where the subtest was ended, it will be too late, and the test may be unscorable.

CAUTION

Common General Errors in Administration

- Forgetting that if the examinee gets the second item administered *partially* correct, you may have to apply the reverse rule (even though the examinee got the first item administered correct)
- Forgetting that when applying the reverse rule, you administer until two consecutive perfect scores are obtained, *including* previously administered items
- Forgetting to administer enough items to meet the discontinue rule

Recording Responses

While administering the WAIS-IV, it is crucial to write down responses for all items administered or attempted. This recording is especially important for Verbal Comprehension subtests, such as Vocabulary, Similarities, Information, and Comprehension. However, even brief verbal responses produced in Arithmetic, Digit Span, Letter-Number Sequencing, and Picture Completion are important to record. One of the most common recording errors in the administration of Wechsler intelligence scales is neglecting to record the examinee's response verbatim (Raiford, Coalson, Saklofske, & Weiss, 2010). Some examiners are tempted to write down only *a score* for a subject's response to an item, but this practice is discouraged. Irretrievable information may be lost if only a "0" or "1" is recorded. Useful clinical information and patterns in responding may be apparent when all responses are written down. When recording what an examinee says, you should try to capture most of what is said verbatim. Using abbreviations frequently helps balance the maintenance of rapport with the recording of essential information (see Rapid Reference 2.3 for a list of abbreviations). At times you will find it necessary to record your own statements. For example, if you probe to clarify an answer by saying "Tell me more about that," you should always record a "(Q)" on the Record Form directly after the response that you queried to indicate that you had to prompt the adult. When interpreting the recorded information clinically, you may then want to note whether many responses were elicited by querying or whether the examinee produced them spontaneously. It is also of clinical value to note adolescents' or adults' response to queries: Did they usually improve the quality of their answers? Did they tend not to add anything to their first responses, saying simply "Don't know"? Did they talk and talk after a query yet fail to improve their item scores?

Timing

All of the Perceptual Reasoning subtests, except Matrix Reasoning, require a stopwatch for exact timing, as do both of the Processing Speed subtests and Arithmetic on the Working Memory Index. Careful planning is necessary when administering these seven subtests so that the timing is not distracting to the examinee. The watch should be unobtrusive, but if the examinee asks whether he or she is being timed, you may want to say something like: "Yes, but you don't need to worry about that." When giving directions to these subtests, you must have your stopwatch ready to go, because properly starting the timing exactly when the examinee is told to begin is critical. Impulsive individuals, for example, may start even sooner than you would anticipate, and you must be ready to time them immediately.

≡ Rapid Reference 2.3

Abbreviations for Recording Responses

@	At
B	Both
DK	Don't know
EO	Everyone
F	Fail (examinee responded incorrectly)
INC	Incomplete (response wasn't completed within the time limit)
LL	Looks like
NR	No response
OT	Overtime
P	Pass (examinee responded correctly)
Prmt	Prompt
PC	Points correctly
PPL	People
PX	Points incorrectly
Q	Question or query
R	Are
Shd	Should
SO	Someone
ST	Something
↓	Decrease
↑	Increase
U	You
w/	With
w/o	Without
Wld	Would

DON'T FORGET

A Stopwatch Is Needed for:

- Block Design
- Arithmetic
- Symbol Search
- Visual Puzzles
- Coding
- Figure Weights
- Cancellation
- Picture Completion

Once the timing for an item has begun, it is important to remember that even if the examinee asks for clarification or repetition of the instructions, the timing is to continue. On some of the subtests, such as Block Design, the examinee may not tell you when he or she is finished (although you request that the examinee do so in the directions). Closely observe the examinees. If it appears that they have completed an item, you should ask, "Are you done?" and immediately record the time. Similarly, if you had stopped the time because you thought the examinee was done, and then the examinee continues working, be sure to restart the stopwatch and to count the entire time during which the examinee was working (which requires you to estimate the number of seconds that the stopwatch was off).

Unlike the Perceptual Reasoning subtests, strict time limits are not imposed on the Verbal Comprehension subtests. However, Raiford and colleagues (2010) suggest that 30 seconds is sufficient time for most examinees to respond. Nonetheless, the 30 seconds is a general guideline and should not be applied rigidly. If examinees continue to take long periods to respond to Verbal subtests (without a perceived benefit), you may encourage them to respond by asking, "Do you have an answer?"

Querying

At times, an examinee's response may be too vague or ambiguous to score. When such answers are given, you need to ask the examinee to clarify his or her response. The *Manual* lists responses to Vocabulary, Similarities, Comprehension, and Information items that should be queried, but these responses are only illustrative. Examiner judgment is necessary to query similar responses to ones listed in the *Manual*'s scoring system. The key is incompleteness or ambiguity. Examiners may query even responses that are *not* queried in the *Manual* if the examinee's voice or face suggests confusion or uncertainty. Bear in mind that the most common error that examiners make in administering the Wechsler scales is neglecting to query responses that should be queried (Raiford et al., 2010).

The manner in which you ask for clarification is crucial. Questioning or querying should be done with neutral statements. For example, say: "Tell me more about that" or "Explain what you mean." Be careful not to provide any hints or clues to the answer when you are querying, except when following the *Manual*'s specific queries (e.g., "Tell me another reason why child labor laws are needed."). If the examinee spontaneously produces a completely incorrect answer, you do not want to query. As mentioned earlier when discussing recording responses, queried responses should be indicated on the record form with a "Q." As a rule, it is best to query with a gentle command ("Tell me more") than with a question. The easiest response to "Can you tell me more about it?" is "No."

Repeating Items

The general rule for repeating questions or instructions is that you may do so if the examinee requests it or if the examinee does not seem to understand the task at hand. However, for Digit Span and Letter-Number Sequencing, an item trial may not be repeated, and in Arithmetic, a question may be repeated only one time. When questions are repeated, the entire verbal question, not just a portion of it, should be repeated.

Occasionally you may find that examinees are able to provide answers to more difficult items on a subtest when they responded "I don't know" to earlier, easier items. When this situation occurs, you can readminister the earlier items if you believe that an examinee knows the answers to the items. Anxiety or insecurity may have originally interfered with the subject's responses on the easier items, or the person's behaviors may have been responsible for a few quick "Don't knows" before being able to take a risk. However, you may not readminister timed items or items on the Digit Span subtest.

Teaching the Task

Sample items and the first two items administered on many of the WAIS-IV subtests are included to ensure that examinees understand what they are supposed to do to respond to the items on the subtest. These items afford the opportunity to give extra instruction if an examinee fails one of the first items in the subtest. This teaching after a failed item does not change an adolescent's or adult's score, but it does provide clarification of the directions. The underlying premise of teaching the task is that examinees should be given the opportunity to do as well as possible on items and that the items should be measuring their ability to do the task, not their ability to quickly grasp the instructions.

SUBTEST-BY-SUBTEST RULES OF ADMINISTRATION

Detailed rules for subtest-by-subtest administration are provided in the WAIS-IV *Manual* Some important reminders for competent administration of each of the subtests are presented here. This section may be used as a guide or to refresh your memory if you have already learned the details of the test. The subtests are listed in order of administration. During administration of the

DON'T FORGET

When to Teach the Task

Subtest	Demonstration Item	Sample Item	Test Item
Block Design	No	Yes	No
Similarities	No	Yes	4 & 5
Digit Span	No	Yes	No
Matrix Reasoning	No	Yes	No
Vocabulary	No	No	5 & 6
Arithmetic	No	Yes	1 & 2
Symbol Search	Yes	Yes	No
Visual Puzzles	Yes	Yes	No
Information	No	No	3 & 4
Coding	Yes	Yes	No
Letter-Number Sequencing	Yes	Yes	1 & 2
Figure Weights	Yes	Yes	No
Comprehension	No	No	3 & 4
Cancellation	Yes	Yes	No
Picture Completion	No	Yes	4 & 5

Note: Teaching the task is allowed only when specified in the directions. The table summarizes when teaching the task is acceptable; typically it is acceptable during the Demonstration Item, Sample Item, or first two items administered. Providing answers beyond what is stated in the instructions will lead to an inaccurate assessment of the examinee's abilities.

WAIS-IV, it is important to be an astute observer of an examinee's behavior. Such behavioral observations can give great insight into how to interpret a particular subtest, and patterns of behavior across many subtests may also be critical in the process of interpretation. After the rules of each subtest, key behaviors to watch for are suggested.

Block Design

This Performance subtest has many details to which the examiner needs to attend. Before administration, make sure that all of the materials are ready to be used, including a box of nine blocks, Stimulus Booklet with model forms, stopwatch, *Manual*, and Record Form. Correct positioning of the adult and the blocks is crucial to facilitate proper administration. The block model must be at a distance 7 inches away from the edge of the table, and beside the Stimulus Booklet (see Figure 3.1 in the *WAIS-IV Administration and Scoring Manual*).

An important part of this Block Design task is being able to understand the relationship between two-dimensional representations and three-dimensional representations. The first four items provide a model that is three-dimensional (in addition to the two-dimensional figure in the Stimulus Booklet) and that is then recreated by the examinee in three-dimensional space. Items 5 through 14 require the adult to perceive and visually analyze the *two*-dimensional model, and then recreate it in *three*-dimensional space. This type of problem is more complex than those that utilize three dimensions for both the model and the examinees' design. When the two-dimensional models are shown in the Stimulus Book, some of the visual cues are removed, such as the lines that distinguish one block from another. In general, the whole administration procedure is set up as a learning situation that shapes the adult from simple three-dimensional designs to complex nine-block designs depicted in pictures. In fact, the final item removes the square outline of the design such that only the red portions of the design are distinguishable from the white page on which the design is presented.

Blocks must have a variety of faces showing before each administration, so as to not bias or help the examinee. Raiford et al. (2010) have noted that examiners often forget to present the tops of the blocks in the correct manner during administration of this subtest. Careful timing is important for scoring. At times, adults may not verbalize when they have completed a design. In such instances, learn to rely on nonverbal cues to determine when to stop timing. If necessary, ask the adult if he or she is done. No credit should be awarded if it takes the examinee longer than the allowed time to complete a given Block Design item.

Lists of important Block Design rules are presented next. Important behaviors to watch for and note while administering the Block Design subtest are listed in Rapid Reference 2.4.

Start, Reverse, and Discontinue Rules
- Examinees ages 16 to 90 begin with the Sample Item and then proceed to item 5.
- If scores of 0 are obtained on either Item 5 or 6, then administer the proceeding items in reverse order until two consecutive perfect scores are obtained.
- Discontinue after two consecutive scores of 0.

Other Rules
- Begin timing after saying the last word of instructions.

- Place the Stimulus Booklet approximately 7 inches from the edge of the table, and place the model of the block design beside the Stimulus Booklet for items 1 to 4.
- Make sure the proper variety of faces of the blocks are showing before each item (i.e., some red, some white, and some red and white).
- Rotations of 30 degrees or more are considered failures. Rotations may be corrected only *once* during the subtest.
- Remember to give the extra five blocks for Item 11.
- Record responses by drawing the design of blocks made by the examinee.
- No special administration is necessary for the Block Design No Time Bonus Process score, as the score is simply calculated from the regular administration of Block Design.

═══ *Rapid Reference 2.4*

Behaviors to Note on Block Design

- Observe problem-solving styles during adults' manipulation of the blocks. Some use a trial-and-error approach, whereas others systematically examine and appear to carefully plan before moving any of the blocks.
- Observe whether the subject tends to pair up blocks and then integrates the smaller segments into the whole. On the designs requiring nine blocks, observe whether examinees work from the outside in or perhaps start in one corner and work their way around the design.
- Motor coordination and hand preference may be apparent during this task. Note whether individuals seem clumsy in their manipulation of the blocks or have hands that are noticeably trembling, or whether they move very quickly and steadily.
- Look to see whether examinees refer back to the model while they are working. This behavior could indicate visual memory ability, cautiousness, or other factors.
- Examine whether adults tend to be obsessively concerned with details (such as lining up the blocks perfectly). Such behaviors may negatively impact the examinee's speed.
- Observe how well examinees persist, especially when the task becomes more difficult and they may face frustration. Note how well they tolerate frustration.
- Look to see whether examinees lose the square shape for some designs, even if they have managed to recreate the overall pattern. This kind of response could indicate figure-ground problems.
- Note whether adults are noticeably twisting their bodies to obtain a different perspective on the model or are rotating their own designs. Such behaviors may indicate visual-perceptual difficulties.
- It is also important to note whether examinees fail to recognize that their designs look different from the models.

Similarities

The Similarities subtest is not difficult to administer. The only materials needed are the *Manual* and the Record Form. It is important to be aware of what types of answers need to be queried (those that are vague and those specifically listed in the *Manual*). When querying, you must present the question to the examinee in a neutral fashion. This verbal subtest also requires careful recording of verbal responses. A detailed description of scoring of each subtest is presented in Chapter 3 of this book, as well as in the WAIS-IV *Manual*

To succeed in Similarities, examinees must understand that abstraction is necessary. For this reason, Items 4 and 5 are teaching items on which corrective feedback is given if an examinee does not spontaneously produce a correct two-point response. These examples allow an opportunity for examinees to hear that a response involving a higher degree of abstraction is more desirable than a purely concrete response.

Lists of important queries and other Similarities rules for the Similarities subtest are presented next. Rapid Reference 2.5 lists behaviors to note on Similarities.

Start, Reverse, and Discontinue Rules
- Examinees ages 16 to 90 begin with the Sample Item and then proceed to Item 4.
- If scores of 0 or 1 are obtained on either Item 4 or 5, then administer the proceeding items in reverse order until two consecutive perfect scores are obtained.
- Discontinue after three consecutive scores of 0.

Queries
- Use neutral questions to query vague or incomplete responses.
- Query multiple responses appropriately if wrong answers are included with correct ones, or if "differences" are given.
- Do not query a string of responses; rather, score the best one if none is clearly wrong.

Other Rules
- Give an example of a two-point response if the examinee's responses to either Item 4 or Item 5 are not perfect.
- Use the general distinctions between responses scored 2, 1, or 0 (see pages 74–75 of *WAIS-IV Administration and Scoring Manual*).

≡ Rapid Reference 2.5

Behaviors to Note on Similarities

• Observe whether the adult benefits from feedback on Item 4 (if feedback was given). Adults who learn from the example given by the examiner may have flexibility, whereas those who cannot learn from the example may be more rigid or concrete.

• Observe whether the quality of response decreases as the items become more difficult.

• Length of verbal responses gives an important behavioral clue. Overly elaborate responses may suggest obsessiveness.

• Quick responses or abstract responses to easy items may indicate overlearned associations rather than high-level abstract reasoning.

Digit Span

Previous Wechsler scales, including the WAIS-III and WISC-IV, included two sections of Digit Span, the Forward and Backward series. The WAIS-IV added a third section, which requires the individual to repeat the numbers back in ascending order. Thus, WAIS-IV Digit Span is administered in three separate sections: Digit Span Forward, Digit Span Backward, and Digit Span Sequencing. However, the administration of each of these parts is quite similar. To administer this subtest, only the Record Form with the number sequences and the *Manual* are needed, along with a slow, steady voice. The key to administering this subtest is reading the series of digits at the proper rate: one digit per second. At times, some examinees will jump in and begin to respond before all of the numbers in the sequence have been read. Examinees should be encouraged to wait until the entire sequence of numbers has been read before responding. Occasionally, examinees will "chunk" the separate digits when responding. It is acceptable for an examinee to chunk 1-2-3-4 into "one-two" [pause] "three-four." However, Raiford et al. (2010) point out that if an examinee chunks their response into "twelve, thirty-four," then it is appropriate to explain to the examinee that they should repeat the digits one at a time.

Digit Span Backward and Digit Span Sequencing each provide two examples of what is required before the scored items are administered. If examinees respond correctly to the first sample, then Trial 2 of the Sample Item should be administered immediately; however, if they respond incorrectly to the first trial of the Sample Item on either the Backward or Sequencing task, provide the corrective feedback and explanation from the *Manual* before proceeding to the second trial. Careful recording of the subject's individual responses on this subtest can provide useful interpretive information.

Digit Span Forward is measuring a different aspect of memory from that of Digit Span Backward and Sequencing. The Backward and Sequencing tasks require more mental manipulation and visualization of numbers, whereas the Forward task can be done with simple rote recall. Careful attention to processing and problem-solving style can be useful for interpretation.

Lists of important Digit Span rules are presented next. Important behaviors to watch for and note while administering the Digit Span subtest are listed in Rapid Reference 2.6.

Start and Discontinue Rules
- For all ages, begin with Item 1 on the Forward Task but with the Sample Items on the Backward and Sequencing Tasks.
- There are three separate discontinue points (one for Forward, one for Backward, and one for Sequencing). For each task, discontinue after scores of 0 on both trials of an item.

General Rules
- Say the numbers at a steady rate of one per second.
- Do not "chunk" the numbers into small groups.
- Drop your voice on the last digit of each series of items.
- Remember to give the second trial of each item, whether the first trial is passed or not.
- Administer Digit Span Backward even if subject obtains a 0 on Digit Span Forward.
- Administer Digit Span Sequencing even if the examinee obtains a 0 on the Forward and Backward tasks.
- Read directions exactly; do not give extra help on Digit Span Backward or Digit Span Sequencing.

Matrix Reasoning

The Stimulus Booklet, containing two types of nonverbal reasoning tasks, the Record Form, and the *Manual* are necessary for this subtest. Two Sample Items begin Matrix Analogies. The items are included to ensure that the examinee understands what is expected in the task. The standardized procedure includes teaching the task via alternative explanation if necessary. As items become progressively more difficult, some examinees may be tempted

☰ Rapid Reference 2.6

Behaviors to Note on Digit Span

- Note whether adults are attempting to use a problem-solving strategy such as "chunking." Some examinees will use such a strategy from the beginning, and others will learn a strategy as they progress through the task.
- Note whether errors are caused by simply transposing numbers or by completely forgetting numbers.
- Attention, hearing impairment, and anxiety can impact this test; therefore, such difficulties should be noted if present.
- Watch for rapid repetition of digits or beginning to repeat the digits before you have completed the series. Such behavior may indicate impulsivity.
- Observe whether there is a pattern of failing the first trial and then correctly responding to the second trial. Such a response pattern may indicate learning or may simply be a warm-up effect.

to guess for their response. If guessing occurs, such individuals should be instructed to try to reason out the solution rather than taking random guesses. It is important to note that because there is no time limit, some examinees may take a significant amount of time to solve the problems. However, the *WAIS-IV Administration and Scoring Manual* suggests that you should encourage a response after approximately 30 seconds, if the examinee has not responded.

Lists of important Matrix Reasoning rules follow. Important behaviors to watch for and note while administering the Matrix Reasoning subtest are listed in Rapid Reference 2.7.

Start, Reverse, and Discontinue Rules
- Start administration with Samples A and B in forward order.
- Illustrate the correct response if A or B is incorrect. Provide an alternative explanation to the problem if necessary.
- Regardless of performance on Sample Items, proceed to Item 4.
- If examinee scores a 0 on either item 4 or item 5, then administer preceding items in reverse order until 2 consecutive perfect scores are obtained.

General Rules
- Point correctly to the response choices in the Stimulus Booklet when indicating from which ones the examinee may choose.
- No teaching or feedback should be given on Items 1 to 26.

≡ *Rapid Reference 2.7*

Behaviors to Note on Matrix Reasoning

- Note whether adults talk their way through the problems, using verbal mediation, or whether they are more apt to simply use mental imagery to work to the solution.
- Observe whether examinees need to touch the Stimulus Booklet to aid in their problem solving. Touching the stimuli may help some adults visualize the solution.
- Although this test is not timed, note whether adults process the information slowly, carefully, and methodically, or whether they work more quickly and impulsively.
- Observe whether examinees are distracted by inessential detail, such as color, if the solution to the problem only requires noting the shape and number of objects.
- Note whether adults attend to part of the stimuli but miss other essential parts to complete the matrix successfully.
- Make note of signs of frustration or anxiety, especially when the problems become more complex.
- Note whether examinees' problem solving includes trying each of the given possible solutions one by one, or first attempting to come up with a solution and then checking the row of choices to find the solution that they had created.

- The examinee should not be allowed to guess randomly.
- Adults who are color blind may have impaired performance on this subtest. If information about such difficulties is not offered spontaneously by the examinee, be sure to inquire whether color blindness may be affecting the responses.

Vocabulary

This subtest requires Stimulus Booklet 1 for administration of the first three picture items. Stimulus Booklet 1 is also used to present a visual list of vocabulary words as they are read aloud by the examiner for Items 4 to 30. The *Manual* and Record Form must also be used during administration. Scoring should be completed as responses are recorded, to the degree possible. As mentioned previously, it is best to continue administering items if you are unsure if a difficult-to-score response will affect the discontinue rule. Because it may be necessary to review responses after the test is over, it is critical to record the exact response of the examinee as much as possible. One of the most challenging aspects of

Vocabulary is querying vague responses appropriately. Be careful to use only *neutral* queries when prompting for more information. Scoring can also be difficult, as there is some subjectivity (see Chapter 3).

Lists of important queries and other Vocabulary rules are presented next. Important behaviors to watch for and note while administering the Vocabulary subtest are listed in Rapid Reference 2.8.

Start, Reverse, and Discontinue Rules
- Start with Item 5, unless the examinee is suspected of an intellectual disability; in that case, begin with Item 1.
- If the examinee obtains a score of 0 or 1 on either Item 5 or 6, administer the preceding items in reverse order until two consecutive perfect scores are obtained. Corrective feedback is also given after imperfect scores on Items 5 and 6.
- Discontinue after three consecutive scores of 0.

Queries
- Use neutral questions to query vague or incomplete responses.
- Query responses that are indicated in the *Manual*.
- Query responses that are similar to those in the *Manual* (scoring rules are illustrative, not exhaustive).

≡ *Rapid Reference 2.8*

Behaviors to Note on Vocabulary

- Make note of "I don't know" responses, as such responses may indicate adults with word retrieval problems who struggle with this test. Word fluency can impact an individual's performance as much as his or her word knowledge.
- Hearing difficulties may be apparent on this test. The Vocabulary words are not presented in a meaningful context (although they are presented in written as well as oral form). Because the words are presented both in visual and auditory form, hearing problems may surface for illiterate or dyslexic adults on the WAIS-IV. Note behaviors such as leaning forward during administration to hear better. Other clues to watch are indications of auditory discrimination problems ("confine" rather than "confide").
- Observe when individuals seem to jump ahead and proceed with the visually presented words, thereby disregarding the auditory stimulus. Such behavior may indicate a preference for the visual rather than auditory channel.
- Note adults who are overly verbose in their responses. They may be obsessive, inefficient in their verbal expression, or attempting to compensate for insecurity about their ability.

Other Rules
- On the Vocabulary Picture items, the examinee may respond with a marginal response, general response, a functional response, or a hand gesture. In any of these cases, further query of the response is necessary. Specific queries for each of these types of responses are listed on pages 99–100 of the *WAIS-IV Administration and Scoring Manual.*
- After the examinee understands the requirements for the verbal items, the formal directions may be omitted, and the vocabulary word may just be read.
- Use the general distinctions between responses scored 2, 1, or 0 (see pages 102–103 of the *WAIS-IV Administration and Scoring Manual*).
- Probe if the examinee responds to a word that sounds like the stimulus word but is not the word.

Arithmetic

The materials required for this test are the *Manual*, Record Form, Stimulus Booklet 1, and a stopwatch (no paper and pencil). Some examinees may exhibit frustration when they are told they may not use paper or pencil to work out the mathematical problems during this subtest. However, if they choose to write imaginary numbers in the air or on the table, this strategy is perfectly acceptable and should be noted in behavioral observations. Not allowing paper and pencil on these mathematics problems requires examinees to utilize working memory.

On two of the Arithmetic items, names from other cultures are used, and some examiners have reported that these different names are distracting to examinees (Raiford et al., 2010). However, Raiford and her colleagues explain that the names on all items were carefully selected to be a single syllable and easy to pronounce. Care was also taken to incorporate diversity into the test. If you suspect that the use of one of the names has caused an examinee to respond incorrectly, you can test-the-limits by readminstering the item with a different name at the end of the test (but the score must be based on the original response).

Lists of important Arithmetic rules are presented next. Important behaviors to watch for and note while administering the Arithmetic subtest are listed in Rapid Reference 2.9.

Start, Reverse, and Discontinue Rules
- Start administration with the Sample Item and then proceed to Item 6. However, if examinee is suspected of intellectual deficiency, then begin with Item 1 after the Sample Item is administered.

≡ Rapid Reference 2.9

Behaviors to Note on Arithmetic

- Observe examinees for signs of anxiety. Some adults who view themselves as poor at math may be more anxious during this task. Be aware of statements such as "I was never taught that in school" or "I can't do math in my head."
- Watch for signs of distractibility or poor concentration, which are usually noticeable during Arithmetic.
- Note when a subject asks for repetition of a question, as it may indicate several things, including poor hearing, inattention, or stalling for more time.
- Take note of whether examinees respond quickly and may be impulsive or are rather methodical and careful in their processing of the information.

- If examinees obtain a score of 0 on either item 6 or 7, administer the preceding items in reverse order until two consecutive perfect scores are obtained.
- Discontinue after three consecutive scores of 0.

Other Rules
- Items 1 to 5 are presented with a corresponding picture in the Stimulus Booklet.
- Repeat an Arithmetic question only once per item.
- Keep the stopwatch going even if repeating a question.
- Paper and pencil are not allowed, but an examinee can use his or her finger to "write" on the table.
- Query if an examinee provides multiple responses and you are unsure which is the examinee's intended response.

Symbol Search

Several materials are needed to administer this subtest: *Manual*, Response Booklet 1, stopwatch, and two pencils without erasers. The Scoring template will be needed to score this subtest. The directions to Symbol Search are lengthy. It is important to read them verbatim but also to maintain rapport by not burying your head in the *Manual* while doing so. Thus, become very familiar with the directions. There are both Sample and Practice Items, which are not timed. Sample Items provide an explanation and demonstration of the task for examinees. Practice Items require the examinees to attempt items that are not part of the Symbol Search score. Examinees are given immediate feedback and correction on Practice Items. You are to proceed with the task only when the examinee clearly understands the directions and is able to complete the Practice Items successfully. As examinees are completing the task, you may find it necessary to remind them that they must complete the test items in order.

Lists of important Symbol Search rules are presented next. Important behaviors to watch for and note while administering the Symbol Search subtest are listed in Rapid Reference 2.10.

Start, Reverse, and Discontinue Rules
- Start administration with the Demonstration Items followed by the Sample Items and then proceed to page 2, where the subtest Items begin.

Other Rules
- Do not proceed with the subtest unless the examinee clearly understands the task after the Demonstration and Sample Items are administered.
- Read the directions verbatim (with a minimum of paraphrasing), but do not lose rapport with the examinee.
- During administration of the Demonstration and Sample Items, point to the various symbols as you explain the directions (as advised in the *Manual*), which provides additional visual clarification of the task at hand.
- Consider a response incorrect if both a symbol and NO are marked for the same item.
- The raw score is obtained by subtracting incorrect from correct responses.

≡ *Rapid Reference 2.10*

Behaviors to Note on Symbol Search

- Note how the adult handles the pencil. Is there pressure? Is the pencil dropped? Does the examinee seem coordinated?
- Observe attention and concentration. Is the adult's focus consistent throughout the task, or does it wane as time goes on?
- Look to see whether examinees check each row of symbols only once, or if they go back and recheck the row of symbols in an item more than once. Obsessive concern with detail may be noted.
- Make note of examinees' response styles. Impulsivity and reflectivity are usually observable in this task.

Visual Puzzles

The materials needed to administer this subtest include the *Manual*, Record Form, Stimulus Booklet 1, and a stopwatch. The object of Visual Puzzles is for the examinee to view a completed puzzle and then select three response options that can be combined to reconstruct the puzzle. The examinee has from 20 to 30 seconds to complete each item. Although there are time limits for each item, it is advisable to let examinees complete their response if they have already begun selecting response options when the time limit expired. Examinees cannot receive credit for responses given in overtime, but it is good practice to allow examinees to finish responding without interruption. Giving this extra time will help foster a positive rapport and prevent undue frustration. Record the overtime responses for clinical information. Individuals who tend to respond correctly after the time limit has expired have better problem-solving skills than those who fail regardless of time limit, even if they obtain identical scaled scores.

Some examinees may appear confused after the Demonstration Item is administered. If such confusion is apparent, repeat the explanation of the task with the Demonstration Item and proceed only when the examinee understands the task. At times throughout this task, examinees may select fewer or more than the allowed three pieces to complete the puzzle. In such cases, prompt examinees to select only three pieces, or ask them to clarify which three pieces they intended for their response.

Occasionally, an examinee may ask if pieces can be "flipped" or "turned over" so that the underside would be visible. Raiford et al. (2010) suggest that in this situation you should clarify for the examinee that they cannot be flipped. However, a response that would require flipping a piece wouldn't represent the best response because it is based on the assumption that the pieces have the same design on the top and the bottom.

Lists of important Visual Puzzle rules are presented next. Important behaviors to watch for and note while administering the Visual Puzzle subtest are listed in Rapid Reference 2.11.

Start, Reverse, and Discontinue Rules
- Start with the Demonstration and Sample Items and then proceed to Item 5. However, if the examinee is suspected to have an intellectual disability, start with Item 1 after administering the Demonstration and Sample Items.
- If the examinee obtains a score of 0 on either Item 5 or 6, then administer the preceding items in reverse order until two consecutive perfect scores are obtained.
- Discontinue after three consecutive scores of 0.

Other Rules

- There is a 20-second time limit for Items 1 to 7 and a 30-second time limit for Items 8 to 26.
- Provide a "warning" of the time elapsing by saying, "Do you have an answer?" after 10 seconds on items 1 to 7 and after 20 seconds on Items 8 to 16.
- Timing should begin after the last word of the instructions is spoken or after the item is presented.
- Remember to point to the completed puzzle and across each of the response options during administration.
- Ensure that the examinee understands the task before beginning administration of the test items. If additional explanation is needed, readminister the Demonstration Item.
- Remind examinees as often as necessary that they must choose three pieces to make the puzzle.
- If more than three pieces are selected, ask examinees to clarify which three pieces were the intended responses.

⟨ *Rapid Reference 2.11*

Behaviors to Note on Visual Puzzles

- Observe whether there is verbalization during problem solving.
- Note whether the examinee studies the puzzles for a few moments before answering. Such behavior may indicate a careful, reflective style.
- Observe whether examinees visibly turn their heads or twist their bodies in attempting to rotate the pieces rather than simply mentally rotating the pieces. Such behavior may indicate difficulty with visual processing.
- Note if the examinee touches the Stimulus Booklet to aid in the visualization process. For example, some examinees try to pick up the puzzle pieces to aid in the process of mental rotation.
- Notice how the examinee handles frustration on this test. For example, a response such as "None of those responses is correct" may indicate defensiveness or avoidance. A repeated response of "I don't know" may indicate that the examinee is giving up when faced with frustration.
- Note any patterns in the errors. For example, do examinees continually pick only two rather than three pieces to complete the puzzle?
- Note patterns of spontaneously correcting oneself. Examinees who jump to a response and then correct themselves may be impulsive or uncertain of themselves.

Information

The *Manual* lists a series of short questions to be read orally in this subtest, and the Record Form is needed to record responses. The questions asked in Information were developed to tap knowledge about common events, objects, places, and people. Some examinees may ask for clarification about how to spell a word or may ask for a question to be repeated. It is acceptable to repeat a question, but the wording should not be changed whatsoever. Even if asked, the words should not be spelled or defined for the examinee, because this type of help is not part of the standardized procedure. Querying an examinee's response to gain further clarification of vague or incomplete responses is perfectly acceptable but should be done with neutral prompts.

Lists of important Information rules are presented next. Important behaviors to watch for and note while administering the Information subtest are presented in Rapid Reference 2.12.

Start, Reverse, and Discontinue Rules
- Start on Item 3 unless the examinee is suspected of intellectual disability; in that case, begin on Item 1.
- If the examinee scores 0 on either Item 3 or 4, administer items in reverse order until two perfect scores on two consecutive items are obtained. In addition, provide corrective feedback on Items 3 and 4 when one of these items is missed.
- Discontinue after three consecutive scores of 0.

General Rules
- Do not spell the words or define any words in the questions.

⚍ *Rapid Reference 2.12*

Behaviors to Note on Information

- Note whether adults may provide unnecessarily long responses. If long responses filled with excessive detail are given, it may indicate obsessiveness.
- Make note of any observable pattern in a subject's responses. Patterns of responding that include missing early, easier items and having successes on harder items may suggest anxiety, poor motivation, or retrieval difficulties.
- Observe whether items on which errors are made are those that are especially related to the examinee's cultural background, such as "Civil War" at a certain time or "Martin Luther King, Jr." Such observations should be incorporated into interpretation.

- Items can be repeated as often as necessary
- Note that Items 1, 2, 9, 19, 24, and 26 require a specific query to certain responses. These specific queries are noted in the *Manual* with an asterisk.

Coding

Many materials are needed to administer this subtest: the *Manual*, the Record Form, Response Booklet 1, a stopwatch, and two pencils without erasers. Because there are lengthy verbal directions for this subtest, and you must point to certain areas on the Response Booklet, it is highly recommended that examiners rehearse the administration multiple times. Once the examinee has gone through the Sample Items, the test can be started. Timing should be precise—allow *exactly* 120 seconds. Familiarity with your stopwatch is critical so that you do not inadvertently mistake 1:20 (i.e., one minute 20 seconds) for 120 seconds (Raiford et al., 2010). Some adults will quickly realize that the best strategy is to fill in one type of symbol at a time; however, skipping numbers is not allowed, and examinees must be corrected immediately if this unacceptable (but quite efficient) strategy is used. Be sure to record the precise symbol the subject completed when the 120 seconds elapsed.

Lists of important Coding rules are presented next. Important behaviors to watch for and note while administering the Coding subtest are listed in Rapid Reference 2.13.

Start and Discontinue Rules
- All examinees begin with the Demonstration Items, the Sample Items, and then the Test Items.
- Discontinue after 120 seconds. (There is no reverse rule.)

Other Rules
- Try not to paraphrase the directions, yet do not lose rapport with the examinee by burying your head in the *Manual*.
- While the examinee is completing the Sample Items, correct any errors immediately, as they are made.
- If necessary, remind the examinee that he or she must start at the beginning of the row and not skip any items.
- If an examinee is left-handed and partially blocks the key with his or her left hand while completing the Sample Items, place an extra Response Booklet (with the Coding subtest key visible) to the right of the examinee's Response Booklet. This arrangement will provide the examinee with an unobstructed view of the Coding key.

≡ Rapid Reference 2.13

Behaviors to Note on Coding

- Watching the eye movements of adults taking the test can be very informative. Consistent glancing back and forth from the Coding key to the response sheet may indicate a poor memory or insecurity. In contrast, someone who uses the key infrequently may have a good short-term memory and remember number-symbol pairs readily.
- Impulsivity in responding may be observed when an adult quickly but carelessly fills in symbols across the rows.
- Shaking hands, a tight grip on the pencil, or pressure on the paper when writing may indicate anxiety.
- Fatigue, boredom, or inattention may become apparent as the Coding task progresses. Noting the number of symbols copied during 30-second intervals provides helpful behavioral information.

Letter-Number Sequencing

The *Manual* and the Record Form are the only materials needed to administer this subtest. Letter-Number Sequencing provides a Demonstration Item and a Sample Item before Items 1 and 3. Be sure to administer all of these Demonstrations and Sample Items. Even if an examinee fails all of the Sample A items, the subtest is to be continued. Teaching of the task is done in stages: (1) Sample A teaches examinees to repeat numbers before letters, and (2) Sample B teaches examinees to sequence numbers and letters (Raiford et al., 2010). Thus, leaving out a sample item may negatively affect an examinee's performance. Some examinees will respond quickly and others more slowly, so you must be prepared to record each response verbatim quickly. In the directions, the examinee is asked to repeat the numbers in order first and then the letters in alphabetical order; however, the examinee will be given credit if the letters are said before the numbers, as long as they are in the correct sequence.

Lists of important Letter-Number Sequencing rules are presented next. Important behaviors to watch for and note while administering the Letter-Number Sequencing subtest are listed in Rapid Reference 2.14.

Start and Discontinue Rules
- Do not administer to examinees who are age 70 or older, except for clinical purposes; norms extend only to age 69.

- Begin administration with Demonstration Item A, Sample Item A, and then Item 1.
- Discontinue after scores of 0 on all three of the trials of an item.

General Rules
- Administer both the Demonstration A and Sample A, and also Demonstration B and Sample B, unless the examinee has met the discontinue criterion on Item 1 or 2.
- Correct the examinee during all Sample Items.
- Say each combination at a rate of one number or letter per second.
- The examinee obtains credit if letters are said before numbers, as long as they are in the correct sequence.
- No additional administration is required to obtain the Longest Letter-Number Sequence (LLNS) process score. This process score is calculated simply based on the regular administration of Letter-Number Sequencing. Chapter 3 of this book provides detail on how to calculate the LLNS score.

≡ *Rapid Reference 2.14*

Behaviors to Note on Letter-Number Sequencing

- Observe whether the examinee learns from errors made during the Sample Items. Examinees may also appear to learn from errors made within one item (i.e., miss the first trial but get the second two correct).
- Note whether adults respond by giving the numbers first and then the letters as requested, or whether the opposite pattern is produced in responses.
- Anxiety, distractibility, and concentration may impact performance on this test. Observe any behaviors that may indicate such difficulties.
- Observe and note any strategies that may be used during this task. For example, adults may keep track of numbers on one hand and letters on another. Rehearsal and chunking strategies may also be observed. Examinees who close their eyes while the items are administered (and, perhaps, while responding) are probably using a visualization strategy.
- Note whether there is a pattern in the errors, such as missing only the letters but getting all of the numbers correct. This may indicate stimulus overload.
- Note errors that may indicate hearing difficulty, such as incorrectly repeating letters that differ only slightly from the stimuli (i.e., T rather than D).

Figure Weights

The materials needed to administer this subtest include the *Administration and Scoring Manual*, Record Form, Stimulus Booklet 2, and a stopwatch. The object of Figure Weights is for the examinee to view a two-dimensional representation of a scale with missing weights and then select the response option that keeps the scale balanced. The examinee has from 20 to 40 seconds to complete each item. If examinees have begun responding but hesitate and do not complete their response before the time limit expires, allow them to complete their response to preserve rapport but do not count that response as correct if it was given after the time limit. As indicated for Visual Puzzles, it is important clinically whether a person tends to solve items correctly over time.

Examinees can respond by either pointing to or saying the number of the selected response option. If another verbal response is given, such as "The red block" or "The three blue balls," you should ask the examinee to show which option was the intended response. Generally, if an examinee does not respond after you have prompted them with "Do you have an answer?" when the time limit expires, you can proceed to the next item with "Let's try another one." Figure Weights provides two Demonstration Items plus one Sample Item to ensure that the examinee understands the task demands before the test items begin.

Lists of important Figure Weights rules are presented next. Important behaviors to watch for and note while administering the Figure Weights subtest are listed in Rapid Reference 2.15.

Start, Reverse, and Discontinue Rules
- Do not administer to examinees who are age 70 or older, except for clinical purposes; norms extend only to age 69.
- Start with the Demonstration Items A and B, the Sample Item, and then proceed to Item 4. However, if the examinee is suspected to have an intellectual disability, start with Item 1 after administering the Demonstration and Sample Items.
- If the examinee obtains a score of 0 on either Item 4 or 5, administer the preceding items in reverse order until two consecutive perfect scores are obtained.
- Discontinue after three consecutive scores of 0.

Other Rules
- There is a 20-second time limit for Items 1 to 12 and a 40-second time limit for Items 13 to 27.

- Provide a "warning" of the time elapsing by asking, "Do you have an answer?" after 10 seconds on Items 1 to 12 and after 30 seconds on Items 13 to 27.
- Timing should begin after the last word of the instructions is spoken or after the item is presented.
- Remember to point to the visual stimuli, each of the response options, and the question mark during administration.
- If examinees give multiple responses and it is unclear what their intended response is, ask for clarification of their intended response (e.g., "Which one did you mean?").
- Request that examinees clarify their response (either by pointing or by selecting the number of their response choice) if they provide an alternate verbalization as their response.
- Item 16 requires that the instructions be read verbatim.

Comprehension

This subtest requires only questions written in the *Manual* and the Record Form. Examinees may need a question repeated from time to time, and this is

---

≡ *Rapid Reference 2.15*

Behaviors to Note on Figure Weights

- Observe whether there is verbalization during problem solving.
- Observe whether the examinee calculates the correct answer with mathematical calculation (done by "writing" in the air or by "writing" on the table.)
- Note if the examinee touches the Stimulus Booklet to aid in the visualization process. Determine if this behavior is present for the higher-level items with three scales to compare (e.g., 16 to 27) versus the earlier, less complex two-scale items.
- Notice how the examinee handles frustration on this test. For example, a response such as "None of those responses is correct" may indicate defensiveness or avoidance. A repeated response of "I don't know" may indicate that the examinee is giving up when faced with frustration.
- Note any patterns in the errors. For example, do errors indicate that the examinee has begun erroneously matching colors or shapes rather than finding the equivalently weighted shapes?
- Note patterns of spontaneously correcting oneself. Examinees who jump to a response and then correct themselves may be impulsive or uncertain of themselves.

allowed. However, the question should be repeated in its entirety and should not be abbreviated in any way. Four of the Comprehension questions require responses from two of the general categories. It is important to remember to query for another response if an examinee spontaneously provides an answer from only one category. When requesting a second response, be sure to restate the question as indicated on pages 169–170 of the *WAIS-IV Administration and Scoring Manual*.

WRONG: "Tell me another reason."

RIGHT: "Tell me another reason why child labor laws are needed."

Whereas most items require the adult to demonstrate deductive reasoning in response to socially relevant questions, note that Items 11, 14, 15, and 18 require the adult to reason inductively in response to proverbs.

Lists of important Comprehension rules are presented next. Important behaviors to watch for and note while administering the Comprehension subtest are listed in Rapid Reference 2.16.

Start, Reverse, and Discontinue Rules
- Start with Item 3, unless the examinee is suspected of an intellectual disability, in which case begin with Item 1.
- If the examinee obtains a score of 0 or 1 on either Items 3 or 4, administer the preceding items in reverse order until two consecutive perfect scores are obtained. In addition, corrective feedback is given if the examinee does not give a 2-point response on either Item 3 or 4.
- Discontinue after three consecutive scores of 0.

General Rules
- You may repeat a question, but it must be repeated verbatim.
- Items 5, 8, 9, and 10 require two general concepts for a 2-point response; prompt for another response if only one general concept is given in the examinee's response.
- Query vague or incomplete responses.
- Do not explain the meaning of any words in the questions.

Cancellation

Administration of this subtest requires Response Booklet 2, a stopwatch, the *Administration and Scoring Manual,* the Record Form, and a #2 pencil without an eraser. The Cancellation subtest requires the examinee to both scan a structured arrangement of shapes and mark target shapes within a specified time

≡ Rapid Reference 2.16

Behaviors to Note on Comprehension

- Observe whether unusually long verbal responses are an attempt to cover up for not actually knowing the correct response or because the examinee tends to be obsessive about details.
- Some of the Comprehension questions have rather long verbal stimuli. Note whether inattention is impacting adults' responses to such items. For example, only part of the question may be answered.
- Note whether defensiveness is occurring in responses to some Comprehension items. For example, when asked the "democracy" item, if the adult's response does not really answer the question and is something like "We shouldn't have it at all," this may be defensive responding.
- Note whether the adults require consistent prompting for a second response or whether they spontaneously provide enough information in their answer.
- Observe the responses carefully to determine whether poor verbal ability is the cause of a low score or whether it is due more to poor social judgment.
- Note how subjects respond to queries. Some may be threatened or frustrated with the constant interruption, and others may seem quite comfortable with the extra structure. When asked for another reason, some people simply restate the first reason in different words or otherwise do not give a second "idea."

limit. Like the other Processing Speed subtests, the directions for Cancellation are lengthy. Be sure to be well rehearsed before attempting administration of this task.

Two items are contained in the Cancellation Response Booklet 2: Item A with red squares and yellow triangles and Item B with orange stars and blue circles. On each item, the goal is for the examinee to mark the target shapes within 45 seconds. If the examinee fails to mark a target or marks a distractor item during the Sample Items, the examiner should provide corrective feedback. It is important not to proceed to Item 1 until the examinee fully understands the task. Spontaneous corrections should not be discouraged, unless such corrections occur frequently enough to impede performance. Do not allow examinees to use an eraser, but if they want to self-correct, you can encourage them to make or scratch out their correction and move on (Raiford et al., 2010).

Lists of important Cancellation rules are presented next. Important behaviors to watch for and note while administering the Cancellation subtest are listed in Rapid Reference 2.17.

Start and Discontinue Rules

- All examinees begin with the Demonstration Items, the Sample Items, and then the Test Items.
- On each item, discontinue after 45 seconds. (There is no reverse rule.)

Other Rules

- Do not administer to examinees who are age 70 or older, except for clinical purposes; norms extend only to age 69.
- Try not to paraphrase the directions, yet do not lose rapport with the examinee by burying your head in the *Manual.*
- While the examinee is completing the Sample Items, correct any errors immediately as they are made.
- Only slash marks are allowed for marking the target shapes.
- If necessary, remind the examinee that he or she must start at the beginning of the row and not skip any items.
- Some examinees attempt to complete the left half of the 11-by-17 booklet (as you would if reading a book). In such cases, remind the examinee to work all the way across each of the 18 shapes in a row.

≡ Rapid Reference 2.17

Behaviors to Note on Cancellation

- Watch for shaking hands, a tight grip on the pencil, or pressure on the paper when writing. These behaviors may indicate anxiety.
- Note whether examinees have difficulty with or resistance to working quickly. This behavior may relate perfectionism.
- Observe attention and concentration. Is the examinee's focus consistent throughout the task, or does it wane as the task progresses?
- Observe signs of fatigue, boredom, or inattention as the subtest progresses. Noting the number of responses produced during 15-second item intervals within the 45-second limit may provide helpful behavioral information in this regard.
- Observe whether the examinee's response rate is consistent throughout the subtest.
- Note whether the examinee quickly but carelessly circles responses. This behavior may suggest impulsivity.
- Note the effect of distractors on the examinee's performance. Remember that the target items are identically placed on both the items.

Source: Adapted from D. P. Flanagan & A. S. Kaufman, *Essentials of WISC-IV Assessment.* Copyright © 2009 John Wiley & Sons, Inc. This material is used by permission of John Wiley & Sons, Inc.

Picture Completion

This subtest requires the use of the *Manual*, Stimulus Booklet 2 with incomplete drawings, a stopwatch, and the Record Form to record responses. This subtest is generally easy to administer and is viewed as fun and game-like by most adolescents and adults. The most common mistakes in administering Picture Completion concern the three queries that are each allowed to be given only *once* during the entire subtest, if needed:

- "Yes, but what is missing?"
- "A part is missing in the picture. What is missing?"
- "Yes, but what is the most important part that is missing?"

Although these prompts are listed on the Record Form, common examiner errors are to forget to use these queries or to use each one several times instead of the mandated "once." Other types of administration errors may occur if an adult or adolescent produces a verbal response that is unclear or ambiguous. If this type of response is given, it is necessary to query for clarification of the response. Responses may be verbal or nonverbal (pointing), as both are considered acceptable. It is important to keep in mind that this test's main focus is not on verbal ability but on visual perception, spatial ability, and holistic processing. However, important information about verbal ability may be gleaned in this last-administered test. Interestingly, although Picture Completion is intended as a nonverbal subtest, the Sample Item's instructions to the adult subtly encourage verbalization by instructing adults to "Look at each picture and TELL me what is missing." The word *tell* suggests a verbal response, whereas *show* would have prompted a nonverbal response. However, the directions for the remaining test items remove the word *tell* and simply state: "Look at this picture. What part is missing?"

Lists of important queries and other Picture Completion rules are present next. Important behaviors to watch for and note while administering the Picture Completion subtest are listed in Rapid Reference 2.18.

Start, Reverse, and Discontinue Rules
- Start with the Sample Item and then proceed to Item 4. However, if an individual is suspected of intellectual disability, start with Item 1 after the Sample is administered.
- If a score of 0 is obtained on either Item 4 or Item 5, administer the preceding items in reverse order until two consecutive perfect scores are obtained. If the examinee does not give a correct response on Item 4 or 5, provide corrective feedback.
- Discontinue after four consecutive scores of 0.

Queries

• Give each of the three queries only *once* for the entire administration of Picture Completion.

Other Rules

• The time limit for each item is 20 seconds. Begin timing after you have spoken the last word of the instruction or after the item itself has been presented.
• If verbal response is ambiguous, say, "Show me where you mean."
• On Items 8, 10, and 19, get clarification about where in the picture the examinee's verbal response is referring, if necessary.
• The Record Form provides a place to record the examinee's verbal response and the pointing response. Mark "PC" if the examinee pointed correctly and "PX" if the examinee pointed incorrectly in response to the item.
• Some verbal responses must be accompanied by a correct pointing response to earn credit. Those verbal responses are listed in the right-hand column of the table on pages 202–204 of the *Administration and Scoring Manual* and should be clarified by asking, "Show me where you mean."
• If the examinee points to the correct place but spoils the response by giving a clearly incorrect verbal response, the item is failed.

≡ *Rapid Reference 2.18*

Behaviors to Note on Picture Completion

• The speed at which an adult or adolescent responds is noteworthy. A reflective individual may take more time in responding (but most likely can respond within the 20-second time limit), whereas an impulsive individual may respond very quickly but incorrectly.
• Note whether the examinee is persistent in stating that nothing is missing from the picture (rather than responding "I don't know"), as it may reflect oppositionality or inflexibility.
• If nonverbal responses (pointing) are consistently observed, it may be evidence of a word retrieval problem in adults. Although it is acceptable to give a nonverbal response, it is far more common to give a verbal response.
• Verbal responses that are imprecise ("the connector") or overly elaborative ("the small piece of material that forms a connection between the two

sections of the eyeglasses which hold the lenses in place") are also noteworthy.

- Note whether adults give responses that consistently indicate a focus on details ("the grain" on the door, "the flakes on the pie crust" on the pie crust weave, or "the pollen" on the roses).
- After individuals have been redirected (i.e., "Yes, but what is the *most important* part that is missing?"), it is important to note whether they still continue to respond with the same quality of response. This persistence in approach may indicate not understanding the task or inflexibility in thinking.

Pitfalls of Subtest Administration

The basic rules of subtest administration have been reviewed in this chapter. Several areas are found to be continually problematic for most examiners when they administer the WAIS-IV. A list of such problems is shown in the Common Pitfalls of Subtest Administration Caution box. By reviewing this box, you can ensure that you are especially aware of the most prominent administration pitfalls, whether you are learning the WAIS-IV in a graduate-level assessment course or are starting with prior experience administering the WAIS-III and are now learning the WAIS-IV.

CAUTION
....
Common Pitfalls of Subtest Administration

1. **Block Design**
    - Neglecting to make sure that the proper variety of block faces are showing before the item is begun
    - Placing the model or Stimulus Booklet in an incorrect position
    - Correcting block rotations more than once during the subtest
    - Remembering to use the reverse rule when adults' score is 0 on Design 6, even if they earn 4 points on Design 5

2. **Similarities**
    - Forgetting to give an example of a 2-point response if the examinee's response to Item 4 or 5 is not perfect
    - Overquerying or underquerying vague responses

3. **Digit Span**
    - Reading the sequence of digits too quickly
    - Inadvertently chunking the numbers as they are read
    - Giving extra help on Digit Span Backward or Sequencing

(continued)

- Forgetting to administer Digit Span Backward to adults who score 0 on Digit Span Forward
- Forgetting to administer Digit Span Sequencing to adults who score 0 on Digit Span Backward

4. **Matrix Reasoning**
   - Not continuing on to Item 4 if Sample Items are incorrect
   - Moving to Item 1 after the Samples if the Samples were correct
   - Giving feedback on items beyond the Sample
   - Allowing examinees to guess randomly
   - Not allowing self-corrected responses after subsequent items have been administered (Raiford et al., 2010)

5. **Vocabulary**
   - Not recording exact verbal responses
   - Not querying vague responses appropriately
   - Forgetting to use the Stimulus Booklet to allow adults to see the words they are defining
   - Forgetting to provide corrective feedback if necessary on Item 5 or 6

6. **Arithmetic**
   - Repeating the questions more than one time
   - Stopping the stopwatch when a question is repeated
   - Allowing paper and pencil to be used if asked

7. **Symbol Search**
   - Proceeding with the task before the examinee clearly understands what is required
   - Burying your head in the *Manual* while reading directions
   - Teaching or permitting the examinee to use anything but a slash mark (/) to respond. Responding with an "X" can result in an artificially low estimate of processing speed (Raiford et al., 2010).

8. **Visual Puzzles**
   - Losing rapport with the examinee by burying your head in the *Manual* while reading long directions
   - Forgetting to start the stopwatch after the item is presented
   - Forgetting to prompt the examinee when 10 seconds remain in Items 1 to 7 with "Do you have an answer?" (or after 20 seconds for Items 8 to 26)
   - Forgetting that the time limit increases from 20 to 30 seconds at Item 8
   - Forgetting to tell examinees "Show me" what their selected response was if they verbalize a response other than the numbers of their selections
   - Forgetting to remind examinees to select three pieces if they select fewer than that in their response

9. **Information**
   - Defining words if asked by the examinee

- Forgetting to give required prompts (e.g., "What unit of distance?") to an incomplete answer
- Being unaware that it is permissible to give neutral queries (e.g., "Tell me more") to Information responses that are incomplete or ambiguous (Queries are not limited to responses on Similarities, Comprehension, and Vocabulary.)

10. Coding

- Losing rapport with the examinee by burying your head in the *Manual* while reading long directions
- Forgetting to start the stopwatch when the examinee begins
- Not paying attention to examinees and allowing them to skip over items
- Allowing a left-handed examinee to partially block the key with their left hand and forgetting to provide them with an extra Coding Key

11. Letter-Number Sequencing

- Reading items too slowly or too quickly
- Neglecting to correct an examinee on any missed practice item
- Repeating a trial of an item if the examinee asks for repetition
- Counting a response as an error if the letters are read in sequence before the numbers
- Forgetting to give corrective feedback on teaching Items 1 and 2 if the examinee responds incorrectly or does not respond within about 30 seconds
- Allowing more than 30 seconds for a response

12. Figure Weights

- Losing rapport with the examinee by burying your head in the *Manual* while reading long directions
- Forgetting to start the stopwatch after the item is presented
- Forgetting to prompt the examinee when 10 seconds remain in Items 1 to 12 with "Do you have an answer?" (or after 30 seconds for Items 13 to 27)
- Forgetting that the time limit increases from 20 to 40 seconds at Item 13
- Forgetting to tell examinees "Show me" what their selected response was if they verbalize a response such as "the two red stars"
- Forgetting to read the instructions verbatim on Item 16 to introduce the items with three scales

13. Comprehension

- Forgetting to give corrective feedback on Item 3 or 4 if the examinee does not obtain a perfect score
- Forgetting to query for a second response (Items 5, 8, 9, and 10) if necessary
- Querying a second time if a post-query response falls within the same general concept (Raiford et al., 2010)
- Explaining the meaning of a word if asked (No explanations or definitions are allowed to be given.)
- Neglecting to write down the exact verbal response

(continued)

14. Cancellation

- Forgetting to time the examinee
- Forgetting to discontinue after 45 seconds
- Forgetting to administer the second item
- Forgetting to provide corrective feedback when the examinee marks incorrect responses during the Sample Items
- Forgetting to carefully watch examinees during the test items and remind them to not skip any items or not to go back and mark a missed item

15. Picture Completion

- Forgetting to provide the correct answer to Item 4 or 5 if the examinee does not give correct response
- Giving the allowed queries too often
- Forgetting to time the Picture Completion items (20-second limit)
- Forgetting to administer in reverse sequence if a 0 score is obtained on either Item 4 or 5
- Forgetting to circle PC or PX to record a pointing response
- Forgetting to query when the examinee does not spontaneously point when providing a response from the right-hand-column items (that require pointing in addition to a verbal response)

🐟 TEST YOURSELF 🐟

1. **List the materials that are not included in the WAIS-IV kit that the examiner should be prepared to bring him- or herself.**

2. **TRUE or FALSE? The examiner must memorize all directions in order to administer the test appropriately.**

3. **In establishing rapport with the examinee during the administration of the WAIS-IV, you may tell him or her:**
   a. You got that answer correct, nice work.
   b. Most test takers find some questions easy and some questions quite difficult.
   c. We won't be able to complete the test unless you refrain from using the restroom during the evaluation.
   d. That wasn't quite right, let's do another one.

4. **TRUE or FALSE? If you find you need to adapt the test to accommodate an individual with special needs, it is better not to administer the test altogether.**

5. **List some modifications that may be made in the test administration procedures to accommodate individuals with special needs.**

6. **Which of these subtests do NOT use a "reverse rule"?**
   a. Block Design
   b. Similarities
   c. Digit Span
   d. Matrix Reasoning
   e. Vocabulary
   f. Arithmetic
   g. Symbol Search
   h. Visual Puzzles
   i. Information
   j. Coding
   k. Letter-Number Sequencing
   l. Figure Weights
   m. Comprehension
   n. Cancellation
   o. Picture Completion

7. **When applying the reverse rule, you must**
   a. Go back to Item I and administer all items sequentially until you get to where you started.
   b. Go back to administer items until one earlier item is correct.
   c. Go back to administer items until two consecutive items are correct, not including the item with which you initially started.
   d. Go back to administer items until two consecutive items are correct, including the item with which you initially started.

8. **Which is the only subtest in which all items must be administered?**

9. **TRUE or FALSE? If you are administering a subtest with subjective scoring and are unsure of what score an examinee's response should get, it is best to take a few minutes to carefully review that item's scoring rules and tell the examinee to wait quietly.**

10. **To preserve the balance of maintaining rapport and getting necessary clinical information, it is best to:**
    a. Record the examinee's score only if it can save some time and quicken the pace of the evaluation.
    b. Record the examinee's responses verbatim, but using abbreviations when possible.

(continued)

   c. Record only incorrect responses to analyze clinically.

   d. Tell the examinee to wait just a few minutes while you very carefully write down every single word that is said.

11. **Which subtests require the use of a stopwatch?**

   a. Block Design

   b. Similarities

   c. Digit Span

   d. Matrix Reasoning

   e. Vocabulary

   f. Arithmetic

   g. Symbol Search

   h. Visual Puzzles

   i. Information

   j. Coding

   k. Letter-Number Sequencing

   l. Figure Weights

   m. Comprehension

   n. Cancellation

   o. Picture Completion

12. **Give examples of queries that you may use to obtain more information about a vague, ambiguous, or incomplete response.**

13. **TRUE or FALSE? You may repeat questions or instructions only on Verbal Comprehension subtests and never on Perceptual Reasoning subtests.**

THOUGHT QUESTIONS

14. **Why was it wise for the test developers to include Sample Items and allow teaching the task on the first two items?**

15. **What are some of the benefits and weaknesses of using a standardized instrument?**

16. **What may cause a disruption in the rapport between examiner and examinee, and what might you do to preserve it?**

17. **What areas of administration are likely to cause the most difficulty for novice examiners?**

Answers: 1. two #2 pencils without erasers, stopwatch, clipboard, extra paper, and writing implements; 2. false; 3. b; 4. false; 5. administering the test in American Sign Language, adding printed words, administering only one scale, eliminating time limits, extending the testing over more than one session. 6. c, h, j, l, m, n;

7. d; 8. cancellation; 9. false; 10. b; 11. a, e, f, g, j, l, n, o; 12. "Tell me more about that." "Explain what you mean."; 13. false

Thought Question Answers

14. Allowing examiners to teach the task ensures that the examinee understands the task; therefore, allowing the examiner to determine when the examinee does not know the answer as opposed to when he or she does not understand the task.

15. Benefits of standardized instruments include being able to compare an individual to a similar group of people to gain an understanding of how he or she functions. You can obtain standardized scores, which are a common metric that is readily compared across many measures. A disadvantage of standardized instruments is that the normative sample may not always be appropriate to compare a particular individual to (i.e., if the ethnic background is very dissimilar to the normative group). Another disadvantage is that when testing patients with special needs, the standardized instruments do not offer flexibility in procedures, which are often needed with these groups. Not all standardized tests offer good reliability and validity, so the values obtained from these tests may not offer completely valuable information.

16. If the examinee is terribly shy, rapport may be difficult to establish. More time may need to be spent developing a relationship with the examinee before beginning testing. If the examinee is terribly frustrated with a particular subtest, he or she may become disinterested in the testing. The examiner may need to give the examinee extra encouragement or a break before continuing testing. If the examinee has a variable attention span, rapport may be disrupted as well. The examiner may have to be extra vigilant in keeping the subject on track and offer more frequent breaks, or extend the testing over more than one day.

17. Novice examiners are likely to have difficulty with scoring subjective subtests, such as Vocabulary, Similarities, and Comprehension. Difficulty with utilizing multiple testing materials during some Perceptual Reasoning subtests, such as Block Design, while accurately recording the time with the stopwatch is also problematic for novices. Subtests that have very lengthy directions, such as Visual Puzzles, Figure Weights, Coding, and Symbol Search, can often cause problems to those who are new to the WAIS-IV.

Three

HOW TO SCORE THE WAIS-IV

TYPES OF SCORES

The WAIS-IV provides three types of scores: raw scores, scaled scores, and IQ/index scores. The raw score is the first obtained and is simply the sum of points earned on a subtest. The raw score alone is meaningless, because it is not a norm-referenced score. To interpret an examinee's performance, you must translate the raw scores into standard scores (either scaled scores or IQ/ Indexes). Rapid Reference 3.1 lists the metrics for various types of standard scores. The subtest scaled scores have a mean of 10 and a standard deviation of 3 (ranging from 1 to a maximum of 19). The IQs and factor indexes have a mean of 100 and a standard deviation of 15 (ranging from 40 to 160 for Full Scale IQ [FSIQ] and from 50 to 150 for indexes).

Most individuals earn scores on the WAIS-IV that are within 1 standard deviation from the mean. Specifically, about two-thirds of the examinees earn IQs or Indexes between 85 and 115. The number of examinees whose scores

≡ Rapid Reference 3.1

Metrics for Standard Scores

Type of Standard Score	Mean	Standard Deviation	Range of Values
Scaled Score	10	3	1–19
FSIQ	100	15	40–160
Index	100	15	50–150

are 2 standard deviations from the mean (from 70–130) jumps up to about 95%. A very small number earn scores that are higher than 130 (about 2.2%) or lower than 70 (also about 2.2%). For the subtest scaled scores, corresponding values are: about 66% score between 7 and 13 and about 95% score between 4 and 16; the extreme 2.2% in each "tail" earn scaled scores of 1–3 (very low functioning) and 17–19 (very high functioning).

STEP-BY-STEP: HOW THE WAIS-IV IS SCORED

Raw Scores

The first step in the process of scoring is obtaining raw scores for each of the administered subtests. Much of the scoring for this test is straightforward and lacking in ambiguity, but there are a few subtests (mainly on the Verbal Comprehension Index) in which subjectivity presents constant thorns to examiners during the scoring process. Raiford et al. (2010) point out that "to facilitate accurate scoring, it is particularly critical to record the entire response verbatim on Verbal Comprehension subtests" (p. 26). Later in this chapter we review some suggestions on how to properly score the more tricky types of responses. For the most part, all that is necessary to calculate the subtests' raw scores is careful addition. The Caution box displays common errors in the process of calculating raw scores that you need to avoid.

CAUTION

Common Errors in Raw Score Calculation

- Neglecting to add points earned from the first few items that were not administered to the total raw score
- Neglecting to add the points recorded on one page of the Record Form to the points recorded on the next page (i.e., Digit Span, Vocabulary, Information, and Comprehension)
- Forgetting to subtract the number of incorrect responses from correct responses on Symbol Search and Cancellation
- Transferring total raw scores incorrectly from inside the Record Form to Score Conversion summary tables on the front page of the Record Form
- Miscalculating the raw score sum via an addition mistake
- Including points earned on items that were presented after the discontinue criterion was met

Scaled Scores

To determine an examinee's scaled scores, you will need: (1) the individual's chronological age; (2) his or her subtest raw scores from the Record Form; and (3) Table A.1 from the *WAIS-IV Administration and Scoring Manual*. The steps to convert raw scores into scaled scores are listed in the Rapid Reference 3.2. In addition to the 15 subtest scaled scores that can be calculated, the WAIS-IV yields scaled scores for four process tests: Block Design No Time Bonus (BDN), Digit Span Forward (DSF), Digit Span Backward (DSB), and Digit Span Sequencing (DSS). These process scores are calculated in a similar manner to the core and supplemental subtest scaled scores (see Rapid Reference 3.3), but they require referencing a different table in the *WAIS-IV Administration and Scoring Manual* (Table C.1; Wechsler, 2008). Four additional process scores yield only raw scores: Longest Digit Span Forward (LDSF), Longest Digit Span Backward (LSDB), Longest Digit Span Sequence (LDSS), and Longest Letter-Number Sequence (LLNS). Thus, for LDSF, LDSB, LDSS, and LNSS, the scoring process stops with raw scores, but the interpretation of these scores continues in Chapter 5 of this book.

The tables used to obtain the scaled scores are user-friendly and easy to find in the tabbed format of the *WAIS-IV Manual*. Examiners commonly make errors when they are rushed to look up scores or when they do not take the time to double-check their work.

CAUTION

Process Scores That Yield Only Raw Scores

Process Score	Raw Score Available	Scaled Score Available
Block Design No Time Bonus (BDN)	Yes	Yes
Digit Span Forward (DSF)	Yes	Yes
Digit Span Backward (DSB)	Yes	Yes
Digit Span Sequencing (DSS)	Yes	Yes
Longest Digit Span Forward (LDSF)	Yes	No
Longest Digit Span Backward (LSDB)	Yes	No
Longest Digit Span Sequence (LDSS)	Yes	No
Longest Letter-Number Sequence (LLNS)	Yes	No

≡ *Rapid Reference 3.2*

Converting Raw Scores to Scaled Scores

1. Transfer the total raw scores from the bottom right corner of each subtest on the Record Form to the appropriate spot on the Score Summary Page (page 11 of the Record Form).

2. For each subtest, find the scaled score equivalent to the obtained Raw Score. These scores should be obtained by looking in Table A.1 of the *Administration and Scoring Manual*, on the page that lists the appropriate norms group based on each examinee's chronological age.

3. Record each subtest's scaled score under all of the possible columns on the Record Form (VCI, PRI, WMI, PSI, and FSIQ).

4. Optional Step: If you wish to compare scores to the reference group of adults ages 20–34, obtain scaled scores from Table A.2 and record them in the right-hand column of the Score Summary Page. However, these optional scaled scores are not used to compute Indexes or FSIQ. They are primarily of interest to examiners who administered the WAIS or WAIS-R, which based scaled scores for individuals of all ages on the 20- to 34-year-old reference group. (IQ on those tests, however, was always based on the person's chronological age.)

≡ *Rapid Reference 3.3*

Process Scores: Converting Raw Scores to Scaled Scores

1. For the four process scores that yield scaled scores—Block Design No Time Bonus, Digit Span Forward, Digit Span Backward, and Digit Span Sequencing—transfer the total raw scores from the bottom right corner of each process subtest on the Record Form to the appropriate spot on the Process Analysis table (inside cover of the Record Form).

2. For each subtest's process score, find the scaled score equivalent to the obtained raw score. These scores should be obtained by looking in Table C.1 of the *Manual*, on the page that lists the examinee's age.

3. Record each subtest's scaled score beside the appropriate subtest's process score in the table.

4. To prepare for interpretation of the process scores, transfer the scaled scores from BDN, DSF, DSB, DSS, and Block Design onto the table labeled "Scaled Score Discrepancy Comparison." (Calculations for interpretation are discussed in Chapter 6 of this book.)

CAUTION

Common Errors in Obtaining Scaled Scores

- Miscalculating a sum when adding scores to obtain the Raw Score or the Sum of Scaled Scores
- Writing illegibly, leading to errors
- Using a score conversion table that references the wrong age group
- Misreading across the rows of the score conversion tables

IQs and Factor Indexes

Once the scaled scores have been obtained, you are ready to find the FSIQ and factor indexes. Care should be taken in the next steps to ensure that calculation errors are not made.

Converting Scaled Scores to IQ/Indexes

1. Calculate the sum of the scaled scores for the appropriate subtest scores for the four Indexes and the Full Scale IQ (see Figure 2.10 of the *WAIS-IV Administration and Scoring Manual*). NOTE: The supplemental subtests Letter-Number Sequencing, Figure Weights, Comprehension, Cancellation, and Picture Completion are not used in the Sums of Scaled Scores for the Indexes or the FSIQ *unless* they are replacing another subtest.
2. Record the sums of the scaled scores on the bottom row of the respective column for each of the indexes and the FSIQ on the Summary Page of the record form (i.e., the Record Form's front page). Rapid Reference 3.4 reviews the subtests that comprise each Composite.
3. Copy the Sums of Scaled Scores to the Sum of Scaled Scores to Composite Score Conversion table at the bottom of the first page of the Record Form, where it is labeled Sums of Scaled Scores.
4. For each index and the FSIQ, determine the appropriate composite score based on the Sum of Scaled Scores. (See Tables A.3–A.7 of the *Administration and Scoring Manual*.)
5. In addition, record the Percentiles and Confidence Intervals for each of the scales; they are also found in Tables A.3–A.7 of the Manual.

Raw Scores of Zero May Invalidate Composite

If an examinee obtains a total raw score of 0 (zero) on a subtest, you must make special considerations when converting that raw score to a scaled score,

≡ Rapid Reference 3.4

Subtests Comprising WAIS-IV Index Scores, FSIQ, and GAI

Subtest	Scale	FSIQ	GAI
Similarities	VCI	FSIQ	GAI
Vocabulary	VCI	FSIQ	GAI
Information	VCI	FSIQ	GAI
(Comprehension)	(VCI)		
Digit Span	WMI	FSIQ	
Arithmetic	WMI	FSIQ	
(Letter-Number Sequencing)	(WMI)		
Block Design	PRI	FSIQ	GAI
Matrix Reasoning	PRI	FSIQ	GAI
Visual Puzzles	PRI	FSIQ	GAI
(Figure Weights)	(PRI)		
(Picture Completion)	(PRI)		
Symbol Search	PSI	FSIQ	
Coding	PSI	FSIQ	
(Cancellation)	(PSI)		

Key: Verbal Comprehension Index (VCI); Perceptual Reasoning Index (PRI); Working Memory Index (WMI); Processing Speed Index (PSI), Full Scale IQ (FSIQ); General Ability Index (GAI).

Subtests in parentheses are supplemental and may be substituted for a core subtest on a scale if a core subtest is spoiled.

Index score, and FSIQ. The difficulty with a raw score of zero is that the score does not indicate the examinee's true ability; rather, it indicates that the examinee's ability cannot be determined by the particular set of subtest items. Ultimately, a raw score of zero indicates that the subtest did not have enough low-level (or easy) items ("floor items") to adequately assess the individual's skills. The Don't Forget box lists the situations in which raw scores of zero will invalidate a composite.

Prorating and Scoring Options

Options are available for calculating the Indexes or FSIQ if not all 10 core subtests were administered or if some of the subtests were spoiled during the administration. Some of the subtests may be replaced by others to calculate

DON'T FORGET

··

When Raw Scores of Zero Invalidate a Composite

Total Raw Scores of Zero	Effect on Composite
On two of the three subtests that contribute to the VCI (including potential substitutions)	No VCI, GAI, or FSIQ can be derived.
On two of the three subtests that contribute to the PRI (including potential substitutions)	No PRI, GAI, or FSIQ can be derived.
On both subtests that contribute to the WMI (including potential substitutions)	No WMI or FSIQ can be derived.
On both subtests that contribute to the PSI (including potential substitutions)	No PSI or FSIQ can be derived.

Key: Verbal Comprehension Index (VCI); General Ability Index (GAI); Full Scale IQ (FSIQ); Perceptual Reasoning Index (PRI); Working Memory Index (WMI); Processing Speed Index (PSI). *Note:* If a supplemental subtest score is available to replace the subtest on which a Raw Score of zero was earned, it would be appropriate to substitute the supplemental subtest in order to derive a composite (that otherwise would have been invalid because too many zero scores would not allow calculation of that composite).

the composite scores. Comprehension may substitute for Similarities, Vocabulary, or Information. Letter-Number Sequencing may substitute for Digit Span or Arithmetic. Picture Completion may substitute for Block Design, Matrix Reasoning, or Visual Puzzles. Figure Weights may also substitute for Block Design, Matrix Reasoning, or Visual Puzzles. For individuals age 70 or older, Figure Weights, Letter-Number Sequencing, and Cancellation are not administered, and therefore cannot be used to substitute for a core subtest at these older age ranges.

The choice to substitute one subtest for another is not one that can be made randomly. You certainly would not want to substitute one subtest for another because a client performed better (or worse) on one or the other. The decision to substitute one subtest for another must be based on solid reasons. For

CAUTION

··

Minimal Subtest Substitution Is Allowed

- Only one subtest substitution is allowed when deriving each Index score.
- No more than two substitutions from different Index scales are allowed when deriving the FSIQ.

example, if Digit Span was spoiled because of distracting noises that were present during the administration, this would be a valid reason to substitute Letter-Number Sequencing. An *a priori* decision to substitute Cancellation for Coding may be made if adults' fine motor control is so poor that it would be unreasonable for them to draw small symbols, but they could write simple slashes through the Cancellation responses. Picture Completion or Figure Weights may be substituted for Block Design, for example, if it was clear that the examinee had motor challenges that prevented him or her from manipulating the blocks. In this case, a decision may be made ahead of time to utilize Picture Completion or Figure Weights in the PRI score because they require no motor manipulation.

Prorating scores becomes necessary when only two PRI subtests or two VCI are available. In the prorating process, an estimated sum of the VCI or PRI scale is used to derive the composite score. The WMI and the PSI should never be prorated, because proration requires at least two valid subtest scaled scores, and these two Indexes each comprise only two subtests. The Full Scale IQ can be computed after either the VCI or the PRI (or both) have been prorated.

DON'T FORGET

Substituting Certain Subtests

VCI Subtest	↔	Replacement Subtest
Similarities	↔	Comprehension
Vocabulary	↔	Comprehension
Information	↔	Comprehension
WMI Subtest		
Digit Span	↔	Letter-Number Sequencing*
Arithmetic	↔	Letter-Number Sequencing*
PRI Subtest		
Block Design	↔	Figure Weights* or Picture Completion
Matrix Reasoning	↔	Figure Weights* or Picture Completion
Visual Puzzles	↔	Figure Weights* or Picture Completion
PSI Subtest		
Symbol Search	↔	Cancellation*
Coding	↔	Cancellation*

*Letter-Number Sequencing, Figure Weights, and Cancellation can be administered only to examinees under age 70.

The process of prorating the VCI or PRI can be easily undertaken by utilizing Table A.8 in the *WAIS-IV Administration and Scoring Manual*. Simply determine the prorated score by referencing the sum of the two subtests administered. If you would like to determine the prorated score manually, you may do so by using a simple formula. On the Verbal Scale, you multiply the sum of the scaled scores by 3/2 and round to the nearest whole number, which is then your prorated score. It is important to always indicate on the Record Form when a score has been prorated. You may do so by using the abbreviation "PRO."

There are special considerations for the FSIQ when proration is completed. If either the VCI or the PRI (or both) is prorated, then the FSIQ should be calculated using these newly prorated Sums of Scaled Scores. However, if only one subtest score is available for either the WMI and/or PSI, then the prorated FSIQ must be calculated differently. The prorated score for the FSIQ may be derived from Table A.9 of the *Administration and Scoring Manual* if nine subtest scores are available. The second section of Table A.9 is used to derive the FSIQ if eight subtests are available.

Scoring Subtests Requiring Judgment

The core and supplemental subtests of the Verbal Comprehension Index require some level of judgment in their scoring because of the nature of examinees' highly variable verbal responses. Most often Vocabulary, Similarities, and Comprehension require such judgment, but some responses to Information questions can also require prudence in scoring. Therefore, one of the most common scoring errors that examiners make is in assigning inaccurate point values on the VCI subtests (Raiford et al., 2010). For each of these four Verbal subtests, the *WAIS-IV Administration and Scoring Manual* provides sample responses in addition

---

CAUTION

....

Requirements When Simultaneously Substituting and Prorating

If you must use both substitution and proration when deriving the FSIQ or the GAI, be aware of these rules:

1. One substitution and one prorated sum of scaled scores are allowed.

2. The substitution and proration must occur on different index scores.

    Example: You can derive the FSIQ from a prorated VCI and a WMI calculated with Letter-Number Sequencing Substituting for Digit Span, plus a normally calculated PRI and PSI.

to scoring criteria. Because it is impossible to list every possible answer that an examinee may state, the *Manual* must be used only as a guide; each examiner must interpret the scoring system for each of the unique responses.

Verbal responses often seem to fall in a borderline area, fitting neither a 1- or 2-point response clearly. Indeed, some answers seem to be perfect 1.5-point responses. Because variable verbal responses occur commonly, it is important to be familiar with both the specific scoring examples and the general scoring criteria for these Verbal subtests. In general, the examinee's ability to express him- or herself properly should not be included in the scoring of a response. For example, if poor grammar or improper pronunciation is used, an examinee should not be penalized. The content of what is said is most important. For example, the response to the Vocabulary item *PLAGIARIZE* "to stole somebody's writin' and preten' like it yours" would earn full credit even though it contains poor grammar. For the Similarities item, *ACCEPTANCE and DE-NIAL*, the response "Reactivating to situations" uses poor grammar, but the content and thoughts behind it are correct, again earning full credit.

Some adults or adolescents may spontaneously give long responses that actually contain two or more responses in one. Examinees may also elaborate responses after being queried. When such elaboration occurs, a fundamental misconception about the item may be apparent in the response. This is termed a spoiled response, and the item is then scored 0 points. For example, if a response to the Similarities item *PIANO-DRUM* is "music," the examiner should then query (*Q*) the response. If the examinee elaborates by saying, "You make the rhythm by hitting the drum, but you make the melody by tapping on the piano keys," the response should be considered spoiled. Although the original response, "music," fell under the 1-point category, the examinee's elaboration clearly showed a misconception of how the two were *alike*. Therefore, the entire response is scored 0 because of spoilage.

Another case of elaboration or multiple responses to a Verbal subtest item may occur when an adult gives a series of responses in which the *second* or *third* response is intended be the actual response. If this is the case, the *final* answer should be scored. However, if multiple responses are given— some incorrect and some correct—but it is unclear which is the final answer, the examinee should be asked to clarify the intended final response. Then the only response scored should be whichever answer is indicated to be the designated final answer. Subtle cues in adults' responses must be used to determine which response is intended as the actual response. Usually if a string of responses is given, with the last phrase being the intended response, examinees will accentuate the last response by dropping their voice at the end of the last word or giving a nonverbal nod of the head. Other adults will give many responses, all equally accentuated and all separated by equal pauses, which tends to lead to a lack of clarity about which response was the intended final response. A helpful, but not leading, manner in which to prompt the examinee is by saying "You said —, —, and —. Which one was your answer?"

On other occasions, many responses may be given that vary greatly in their quality. For example, 0-, 1-, and 2-point responses may occur in one long answer. If this case occurs, and no spoiled responses are present, then simply score the best response. For example, if an examinee spontaneously responds "to build up . . . to start something . . . to create" to the Vocabulary item *GENERATE*, then each part of the response is worth different point values. In this response, "to build up" earns 0 points, "to start something" earns 1 point, and "to create" earns 2 points. None of these responses spoils another or reveals misconceptions about the word "generate," so the best response ("to create") should be scored; therefore, the examinee earns 2 points.

General Scoring Criteria for Verbal Subtests

Vocabulary, Similarities, and Comprehension all include a set of general scoring criteria, along with the specific examples listed in the manual. The fine points of each of the scoring guidelines are highlighted in Rapid References 3.5, 3.6, and 3.7.

Rapid Reference 3.5

Vocabulary Scoring Rules

2 points	• Shows a good understanding of the word
	• Good synonym
	• Major use
	• One or more definitive features of an object
	• General classification to which the word belongs
	• Correct figurative use of the word
	• Several less definitive but correct descriptive features that cumulatively indicate understanding of the word
	• For verbs, a definitive example of action or a causal relation
1 point	• Response is generally correct, but shows poverty of content
	• A vague or less pertinent synonym
	• A minor use, not elaborated
	• An attribute that is correct but not definitive or not a distinguishing feature

	• An example using the word itself, not elaborated
	• A concrete instance of the word, not elaborated
	• A correct definition of a related form of the word
0 points	• Obviously wrong responses
	• Verbalizations that show no real understanding even after query
	• A demonstration that is not elaborated with words
	• Not totally incorrect responses, but ones that, even after questioning, are vague or trivial or show a great poverty of content

≡ Rapid Reference 3.6

Similarities Scoring Rules

2 points	• A general, major classification of the pair
	• A universal property of the pair
	• A concept pertinent to both members of the pair
1 point	• A specific property common to both that is a minor or less pertinent similarity
	• A major classification that is less pertinent for both members of the item, but correct general classifications
0 points	• A property that is not pertinent to both members of the pair
	• A property that is too general in nature
	• Description of differences between members of the item pair
	• Clearly wrong responses

≡ Rapid Reference 3.7

Comprehension Scoring Rules

2 points	• Expression of the 2-point general concept indicated in the *Manual*
	• Expression of two general responses on items 5, 8, 9, and 10
1 point	• Expression of the 1-point general concept indicated in the *Manual*
	• For items that require two general concepts, 1 point is awarded if the examinee's queried response refers to the same general concept as the initial response
0 points	• In general, are vague or trivial responses, or not addressing the question

Subtest-by-Subtest Scoring Keys

Some subtests require 0- and 1-point scoring and others require 0-, 1-, and 2-point scoring. The overall scoring rules are consistent throughout the WAIS-IV, but there are also subtle nuances of which the examiner should be aware. The Don't Forget box includes important keys to remember for scoring each subtest.

DON'T FORGET

Scoring Keys

Subtest	Range of Item Scores	Scoring Pointers
1. Block Design	0–2 (items 1–4)	• For designs 1–4, successful completion within the time limit on the first Trial earns 2 points.
	0 or 4 (items 5–8)	• For designs 1–4, successful completion within the time limit on the second Trial earns 1 point.
	0 or 4–7 (items 9–14)	• For designs 5–8, successful completion within the time limit earns 4 points.
		• For designs 9–14, points ranging from 4–7 are awarded on the basis of completion time.
		• For items 1–14, designs completed correctly after the allowed time limit has expired are scored 0.
		• If designs 1–4 are not administered, then award 2 points for each of those items.
		• Partially correct responses are scored 0.
Process Score: Block Design No Time Bonus (BDN)	0–2 (items 1–4)	• For designs 1–4, successful completion within the time limit on the first trial earns 2 points.
	0 or 4 (items 5–14)	• For designs 5–14, successful completion within the time limit earns 4 points. (No bonus points are awarded.)
		• For items 1–14, designs completed correctly after the allowed time limit has expired are scored 0.

Subtest	Range of Item Scores	Scoring Pointers
2. Similarities	0–2	• Utilize the general 0–2-point scoring criteria and specific examples. • Score spontaneous improvement in responses. • Degree of abstraction is key in assigning credit to responses. • Add 2 points to the raw score for each of the unadministered reversal items.
3. Digit Span	0–2	• Exact correct repetition is given 1 point per trial (2 points per item possible). • Self-corrections are given credit. • Score 0 points if the examinee gives an incorrect response. • Score 0 points if the examinee does not respond within approximately 30 seconds. • The Raw Scores from Digits Forward, Digits Backward, and Sequencing are combined to create the Digit Span Raw Score. • Do not average the scores from Digits Forward and Digits backward to obtain an estimate of sequencing (Raiford et al., 2010).
Process Score: Digit Span Forward (DSF)	0–16	• Sum of the Forward item scores
Process Score: Digit Span Backward (DSB)	0–16	• Sum of the Backward item scores
Process Score: Digit Span Sequence (DSS)	0–16	• Sum of the Sequencing item scores
Process Score: Longest Digit Span Forward (LDSF)	0–9	• Number of digits recalled on the last Forward trial scored 1 point
Process Score: Longest Digit Span Backward (LDSB)	0–8	• Number of digits recalled on the last Backward trial scored 1 point

(continued)

Subtest	Range of Item Scores	Scoring Pointers
Process Score: Longest Digit Span Sequence (LDSS)	0–9	• Number of digits recalled on the last Sequencing trial scored 1 point
4. Matrix Reasoning	0–1	• Do not add score from Sample Items A or B into calculation of the Raw Score. • Examinees are not penalized due to speediness of responding. • Self-corrected responses (even after other items are administered) should be given credit (Raiford et al., 2010). • The correct answers are printed in bold blue font on the Record Form. Score 1 point for correct response.
5. Vocabulary	0–1 (items 1–3) 0–2 (items 4–30)	• For Picture Items 1–3, score 1 point for correct response. • For Picture Items 1–3, score 0 points for incorrect response or no response within approximately 30 seconds. • For Items 4–30, utilize the general 0- to 2-point scoring criteria and specific examples. • Slang or regionalisms not in the dictionary are scored 0. • Any meaning found in a standard dictionary is scored correct. • Poor grammar is not penalized in scoring. • Add 1 point to the raw score for each of the unadministered reversal items 1–3, and 2 points for item 4.
6. Arithmetic	0–1	• If subject gets the numeric value correct but does not give the unit, score 1 point. • If subject gives a correct response with an alternate unit (e.g., 1 hour = 60 seconds), score 1 point. • Problems completed correctly after the 30-second time limit has expired are scored 0.

(continued)

Subtest	Range of Item Scores	Scoring Pointers
		• Add 1 point to the raw score for each of the unadministered reversal items.
7. Symbol Search	0–60	• Use the Symbol Search Scoring Template to score responses.
		• If both a shape and NO are marked for the same item, the response is incorrect.
		• The Symbol Search Total Raw Score is calculated by subtracting the Number Incorrect from the Number Correct.
		• Any items left blank are not included in the score computation.
		• Any item completed after the 120-second time limit should not be counted in the score calculation.
8. Visual Puzzles	0–1	• Items completed after the time limit are scored 0 points.
		• The three correct responses for each item are printed in bold blue font on the Record Form.
		• All three responses for each item must be correct to earn 1 point.
		• If an examinee does not choose three correct responses or does not know the answer, score 0 points.
9. Information	0–1	• The list of possible responses in the *Manual* is not exhaustive. Give credit for any response that is of the same caliber as the samples.
		• Add 1 point to the raw score for each of the unadministered reversal items.
10. Coding	0–135	• Use the Coding scoring template to check the examinee's responses.
		• One point is given for each correctly drawn symbol (completed within 120 seconds).
		• Spontaneous correction of an incorrect symbol is scored 1.

(continued)

Subtest	Range of Item Scores	Scoring Pointers
		• A response that is imperfect but a clearly identifiable symbol is scored 1. • Skipped items are not counted.
11. Letter-Number Sequencing	0–3 (0 = fail all trials1 = pass one trial 2 = pass 2 trials 3 = pass all three trials)	• If a letter or number is omitted in the response, it is incorrect. • For items 1–2, there is only one correct response for each trial. • For items 3–10, credit is given if letters are given in the correct sequence and then numbers in the correct sequence. • Each of the three trials in an item is worth 1 point. • Practice items are not included in the Raw Score.
Process Score: Longest Letter-Number Sequence (LLNS)	0–8	• The number of letters and numbers recalled on the last trial are scored 1 point.
12. Figure Weights	0–1	• Responses completed after the time limit are scored 0. • Correct responses are printed in bold blue font in the Record Form. • Correct responses within the time limit are scored 1. • Incorrect responses or "I don't know" responses are scored 0.
13. Comprehension	0–2	• Utilize the general 0- to 2-point scoring criteria and specific examples. • The *Administration and Scoring Manual* is not all-inclusive and must be used only as a guide. • Score spontaneous improvement in responses. • Degree of understanding expressed by the examinee is scored. • For responses that require two general concepts, only 1 point is earned if both ideas stated by the (*continued*)

Subtest	Range of Item Scores	Scoring Pointers
		examinee are included in the same general concept.
		• Add 1 point to the Raw Score for each of the unadministered reversal items.
14. Cancellation	0–36 (items 1 & 2)	• Use the Cancellation scoring template to score the responses.
		• Marks on target shapes are correct, and marks on nontarget shapes are incorrect.
		• If a mark on one shape inadvertently extends through an adjacent shape, score only the originally marked shape.
		• Subtract the number incorrect from the number correct for each item score.
		• Total Raw Score is the sum of the scores from the two items
15. Picture Completion	0–1	• Score 0 if examinee responds after 20 seconds.
		• Correct verbal responses earn 1 point.
		• Certain verbal responses earn 1 point only if accompanied by a correct pointing response. Those verbal responses are listed in the right column of the Sample Responses table in the *Manual*.
		• If only a pointing response is given, 1 point is awarded for correctly pointing.
		• If examinee points to the correct place but gives an incorrect verbal response, score 0.
		• Correct description using a synonym or examinee's own words, score 1.
		• Add 1 point to the Raw Score for each of the unadministered reversal items.

Computer Scoring Procedures

Examiners can save time scoring and reporting results with the computerized WAIS-IV Scoring Assistant and Report Writer Software. The WAIS-IV Scoring Assistant is available for $289.00 on www.pearsonassess.com (price as of August 2012). The software program requires examiners to enter Raw Scores, and the software generates concise score reports and statistical reports with graphs and tables. It also provides the Raw to Scaled Score conversions and strength and weakness discrepancies. The WAIS-IV scores may also be integrated with other scoring applications, such as the WMS-IV and WIAT-II, and can produce cross-battery analysis of scores. The WAIS-IV Report Writer software includes all capabilities of the Scoring Assistant but also produces individualized, comprehensive reports that go beyond scores, tables, and graphs. For example, this Report Writer software provides a nontechnical client report, a comprehensive narrative report with narrative interpretations, and a clinical and background review. The WAIS-IV Report Writer software is available for $489.00 on www.pearsonassess.com. Rapid Reference 3.8 lists the minimum software requirements for WAIS-IV Scoring Assistant and Report Writer.

≡ Rapid Reference 3.8

System Requirements for WAIS- IV Scoring Assistant and Report Writer

Minimum System Requirements
- Windows Vista/XP/2000
- 400 MHz processor
- 256 MB RAM; more memory improves performance
- 2 MB video card capable of 800 × 600 resolution (16-bit color)
- 175 MB free hard disk space when installing PsychCorpCenter®–II for the first time
- Internet Explorer 6.0
- CD-ROM drive

Recommended System Requirements
- Windows Vista/XP (SP 2)/2000 (SP 4)
- 1 GHz processor
- 512 MB RAM; more memory improves performance

- 2 MB video card capable of 1024 x 768 resolution (32-bit color)
- 175 MB free hard disk space when installing PsychCorpCenter®–II for the first time
- Internet Explorer 6.0 or higher
- CD-ROM drive
- Microsoft Word

🪶 TEST YOURSELF 🪶

1. **TRUE or FALSE? Like earlier editions of Wechsler's adult tests, the WAIS-IV scaled scores are determined by comparing an individual's performance to that of the reference group of adults ages 20–34.**

2. **Unless replacing another subtest, none of the following subtests are used in the calculation of the FSIQ except**
   a. Letter-Number Sequencing
   b. Symbol Search
   c. Comprehension
   d. Figure Weights

3. **If Digit Span is a spoiled subtest, which of the following subtests can replace it?**
   a. Letter-Number Sequencing
   b. Symbol Search
   c. Cancellation
   d. Arithmetic

4. **At what age can Figure Weights no longer be substituted for other PRI subtests?**
   a. 50
   b. 60
   c. 65
   d. 70

5. **Which one of the following scales is NOT safe to prorate?**
   a. Full Scale IQ
   b. Perceptual Reasoning Index
   c. Verbal Comprehension Index
   d. Processing Speed Index

(continued)

6. **What is the mean and standard deviation of scaled scores?**
   a.   100 and 15
   b.   50 and 10
   c.   10 and 3
   d.   5 and 2
   e.   500 and 100

7. **Of the WAIS-IV process tasks, which ones yield a Scaled Score in addition to the Raw Score?**
   a.   Block Design No Time Bonus (BDN)
   b.   Digit Span Forward (DSF)
   c.   Digit Span Backward (DSB)
   d.   Digit Span Sequencing (DSS)
   e.   Longest Digit Span Forward (LDSF)
   f.   Longest Digit Span Backward (LSDB)
   g.   Longest Digit Span Sequence (LDSS)
   h.   Longest Letter-Number Sequence (LLNS)

8. **TRUE or FALSE? If you forget to administer the Digit Span Sequencing portion of the Digit Span subtest, you can simply calculate the Digit Span Scaled Score based on the Raw Score sum of Digit Span Forward and Digit Span Backward because that was how Digit Span was calculated on previous versions of the WAIS.**

9. **TRUE or FALSE? As long as an examinee points to the correct location of the missing object in Picture Completion, score the response "1," even if the verbal response is incorrect.**

Answers: 1. false; 2. b; 3. a; 4. d; 5. d; 6. c; 7. a–d; 8. false; 9. false

Four

HOW TO INTERPRET THE WAIS-IV: CONCEPTUAL AND CLINICAL FOUNDATIONS

Your philosophy toward the interpretation of individually administered clinical tests should be an intelligent one. The basic premise of test interpretation that we put forth in this book is one that we and others have advocated before (Kamphaus & Reynolds, 1987; Kaufman, 1979, 1990, 1994a; Kaufman & Lichtenberger, 1999, 2000, 2006; Kaufman, Lichtenberger, Fletcher-Janzen, & Kaufman, 2005; Reynolds & Fletcher-Janzen, 1989). We begin this chapter by clearly articulating the tenets of the intelligent testing philosophy. We then segue into a description of qualitative and clinical factors that may influence performance on the WAIS-IV and that should be considered when using an intelligent approach to test interpretation.

INTELLIGENT TESTING PHILOSOPHY

We believe it is critical that examiners use an intelligent approach to testing and understand our basic philosophy before proceeding with the specifics of test interpretation. Assessment should be of the individual and for the individual. The examiner's role in assessment is more than simply examining the scores; rather, he or she must bring together research knowledge, theoretical sophistication, and solid clinical skill when interpreting tests. The intelligent testing philosophy that we follow is five-fold, as shown in the Don't Forget box.

1. *Subtests measure what the individual has learned.* This concept comes directly from Wesman's (1968) introduction of the intelligent testing approach. The content of all tasks, whether verbal or nonverbal, is learned within a culture. The learning may take place formally in the school, casually in the home, or incidentally through everyday life. As a measure of past learning, the IQ test is best thought of as a kind of achievement test, not as a simple measure of aptitude. Plain and simple, cognitive tests

DON'T FORGET

Tenets of the Intelligent Testing Philosophy

1. Subtests measure what the individual has learned.
2. Subtests are samples of behavior and are not exhaustive.
3. Standardized, individually administered tests assess mental functioning under fixed experimental conditions.
4. Test batteries are optimally useful when interpreted from a theoretical model.
5. Hypotheses generated from the test profile should be supported with data from multiple sources.

measure prior learning. Thus, the strong relationships between cognitive tests and achievement measures are not surprising. However, even though the predictive validity of cognitive test scores is strong, the relationship between cognitive test scores and school achievement need not indicate a predetermined fate for an individual. That is, if results from a cognitive test are appropriately interpreted and translated into helpful recommendations, then positive change in academic achievement may occur, thereby changing one's IQ-determined "destiny."

The interaction between learning potential and availability of learning experiences is too complex to ponder for any given person, making the whole genetics–environment issue of theoretical value but impractical and irrelevant for the interpretation of that person's test profile. Issues of heredity versus environment and the validity of the IQ construct are meaningful for understanding the multifaceted intelligence construct; the accumulating research helps test developers, practitioners, and theoreticians appreciate the foundation of the tests used to measure intelligence; and the IQ tests, as vehicles for the research, are essential sources of group data for use in scientific study of these topics. But all of the controversy loses meaning for each specific person referred for evaluation when the clinician administers an IQ test to study and interpret just what the person has or has not learned and to help answer the practical referral questions.

2. *Subtests are samples of behavior and are not exhaustive.* This tenet is relevant to the generalizability of the test findings. Because test results usually are obtained within 1 or 2 hours and include samples of behavior from a select set of tasks, caution needs to be exercised in generalizing the results to other behaviors in different circumstances. The individual Wechsler subtests, or the subtests that compose the Woodcock-Johnson (third edition; WJ III), Kaufman tests, and other cognitive tests, do not reflect the essential ingredients of intelligence whose mastery implies

some type of ultimate life achievement. They, like tasks developed originally by Binet, are more or less arbitrary samples of behavior. Teaching people how to solve similarities, assemble blocks to match abstract designs, or repeat digits backward will not make them smarter in any broad or generalizable way. What we are able to infer from the person's success on the tasks and style of responding to them is important; the specific, unique aspect of intellect that each subtest measures is of minimal consequence.

Limitations in the selection of tasks necessarily mean that one should be cautious in generalizing the results to circumstances that are removed from the one-on-one assessment of a finite number of skills and processing strategies. Intelligence tests should, therefore, be routinely supplemented by other formal and informal measures of cognitive, clinical, and neuropsychological functioning to facilitate the assessment of mental functioning as part of a more thorough evaluation. In addition, theoretical models of intelligence should be used as a guide for selecting cognitive tasks to administer during an evaluation, and examiners should not be wedded to a single instrument, even one as popular as the WAIS-IV. Dawn Flanagan's cross-battery assessment provides a wonderful methodology for ensuring that any comprehensive evaluation of a person's intelligence measures a diversity of key broad and narrow Cattell-Horn-Carroll (CHC) abilities (Flanagan, Ortiz, & Alfonso, 2007).

To the degree that tasks are chosen to meet theoretical constructs, the array of cognitive subtests in a comprehensive test battery is systematic and not arbitrary. Nonetheless, even when using cross-battery assessment, neither a global IQ nor a thorough profile of CHC abilities should be interpreted as an estimate of a person's "total" or "complete" level of intellectual functioning. Examination of one's individual cognitive strengths and weaknesses obtained from IQ test data is more fruitful when combined with supportive data from other samples of behavior such as those data obtained from supplemental measures. These measures might include behavioral assessment, personality assessment, neuropsychological assessment, adaptive behavior assessment, and even informal assessment of abilities that are not easily tested by standardized instruments such as measures of the creative and practical intelligence components of Sternberg's triarchic theory of successful human intelligence (Sternberg, Kaufman, & Grigorenko, 2008).

3. *Standardized, individually administered tests assess mental functioning under fixed experimental conditions.* Strict adherence to the standardized procedures of

administration and scoring of standardized tests is important to ensure the comparability of obtained test results to those of the normative group. However, these same formal procedures for administration and scoring add to the artificial nature of the testing situation. Very infrequently in real life does someone sit across from you with an easel and stopwatch and ask you to perform a task while your every move is being observed, scrutinized, and recorded. Thus, awareness of the experimental nature of the testing process will help prevent over-interpreting a person's IQ as their maximum capacity.

Standardized administration and scoring means conducting an experiment with $N = 1$ every time an examiner tests someone on an intelligence test. For the results of this experiment to be meaningful, the experimenter-examiner must adhere precisely to the wording in the *Manual*, give appropriate probes as defined in the instructions, time each relevant response diligently, and score each item exactly the way comparable responses were scored during the normative procedure. Following these rules prevents examiners from applying a flexible clinical investigatory procedure during the administration (as Piaget always advocated with his *méthode clinique*), from giving feedback to a person who urgently desires it, or from cleverly dislodging from the crevices of a person's brain his or her maximum response to each test item.

It is necessary to be an exceptional clinician to establish and maintain rapport and to weave the standardized administration into a natural, pleasant interchange between examiner and subject. Clinical skills are also essential when observing and interpreting a person's myriad behaviors during the examination and when integrating all available information and data to interpret the profile of test scores. But it is vital for an examiner to follow the standardized procedures to the letter while administering the test; otherwise, the standard scores yielded for the person will be invalid and meaningless. To violate the rules is to negate the value of the meticulous set of norms obtained under experimental conditions by major test-publishing companies for their tests.

The testing situation has a certain built-in artificiality by virtue of the stopwatch, the precise words to be spoken, and the recording of almost everything spoken by the examinee. A person with excellent visual-spatial and manipulative skills might perform slowly and ineffectively on Block Design because of anxiety caused by the time pressure; or a person with a good common-sense understanding of social situations (coupled with limited word knowledge) may fail several Comprehension items because of a failure to understand some of the key words used in the questions. It is tempting to give credit to a design solved "just 2 or 3 seconds overtime" or to simplify the wording of a question that the person "certainly knows the answer to." But the good examiner will resist these temptations, knowing that the people in the reference group did not receive such help.

Testing the limits on a subtest often can give valuable insight into the reasons for failure or confusion, so long as this flexible, supplemental testing occurs *after* the score has been recorded under appropriate conditions. In an experiment, the empirical results are of limited value until they are interpreted and discussed in the context of pertinent research and theory by a knowledgeable researcher. By the same token, the empirical outcomes of an IQ test are often meaningless until put into context by the examiner. That is the time for a clinician's acumen and flexibility to be displayed. Interpreting test scores in the context of observed behaviors can aid in the appropriate interpretation of the scores. For example, when an adolescent's oppositionality during testing has led to a low level of motivation on timed tasks, this behavior is crucial to understanding that the obtained scores may be a gross underestimate of the adolescent's abilities. In addition, such observations can be useful in translating test results into practical recommendations. Kaufman (1990) states:

> The value of the scores increases when the examiner functions as a true experimenter and tries to determine *why* the child earned the particular profile revealed on the record form; the IQs become harmful when they are unquestioningly interpreted as valid indicators of intellectual functioning and are misconstrued as evidence of the [person's] maximum or even typical performance. (p. 9)

4. *Test batteries are optimally useful when interpreted from a theoretical model.* This tenet is an important notion to remember when attempting to organize test data in a meaningful way. Using the appropriate theoretical model is crucial when trying to understand the reasons underlying the peaks and valleys of a person's cognitive profile to facilitate the translation of the scores into pragmatic, fundamental, theoretically meaningful areas of deficit and strength. As will be discussed in Chapter 5, the WAIS-IV has foundations in cognitive neuroscience theory and research, and its scores can be interpreted from a variety of theoretical models, ranging from the CHC model (Flanagan et al., 2007) to neuropsychological approaches such as Luria's (1973, 1980).

Figure 4.1. Information Processing Model

In addition to these theoretical foundations, alternate models may be applied to interpret the profile of test scores. For example, an information-processing model that features input, integration, storage, and output (Silver, 1993) could be a helpful framework for test interpretation (see Figure 4.1). This model was used in the next section on Qualitative and Clinical Analyses of the WAIS-IV when developing the sections on Influences Affecting Subtest Scores and Clinical Considerations for each subtest. For example, consider Block Design, which is influenced by visual-perceptual problems (Input), the cognitive style of field dependence–field independence (Integration), and working under time pressure

(Output). Or consider some of the clinical considerations that pertain to Similarities: (a) creativity and visual imagery may be used to come up with the relationship between two concepts (Integration); (b) clinically rich information can be gleaned from the nature of the verbal response, such as overelaboration or overly general responses (Output); and (c) correct responses on the easier items may simply reflect overlearned, everyday associations rather than true abstract thought (Storage).

Whether test results are interpreted within a test's own theoretical model or by reorganizing the subtests to better fit another theoretical framework, the results will be best explained and translated into practical recommendations if presented within a theoretical framework.

The information-processing approach depicted in Figure 4.1 is a supplementary system for WAIS-IV interpretation, not at all the main thrust. Our primary interpretive approach is rooted in empirically validated CHC and neuropsychological theoretical foundations. We agree with Floyd and Kranzler (2012) that our information-processing model

is somewhat dated and does not reflect the complexity of processing in more contemporary models. As a result, it does not include an array of processing steps (e.g., memory retrieval) . . . It also tends to focus on general categories of processing (related to cognitive abilities) rather than specific processes. (p. 515)

To address the more sophisticated, contemporary approaches to processing we included an invited chapter by George McCloskey in the first edition of this book, which he updated for the new edition with two of his colleagues, Emily Hartz and Katherine Scipione (Chapter 6).

However, we continue to include the simple, straightforward information-processing model depicted in Figure 4.1 as a supplementary aspect of our theory-based interpretive approach because, as Floyd and Kranzler (2012) note, it "may sensitize those interpreting intelligence tests . . . to the construct-irrelevant influences related to input (e.g., visual acuity problems) and output (e.g., motor deficits)" (p. 515). Furthermore,

it seems to make practical sense to examine the influences associated with input of information into the cognitive system and the output via responses when clinicians are evaluating item-level performances; these influences are observable for the most part. Labeling of these steps is modeled well by the interpretive [approach] of Kaufman and Lichtenberger. (Floyd & Kranzler, 2012, p. 520)

5. *Hypotheses generated from the test profile should be supported with data from multiple sources.* This tenet is a key postulate to prevent misuse of test results, and is related to all of the previous four tenets of intelligent testing. Results from one instrument should not be interpreted alone as the gospel truth about an individual. Rather, when hypotheses are created from an individual's profile, supplemental information should be found that could confirm or disconfirm the hypotheses. Test score profiles are optimally meaningful when interpreted in the context of known background information, observed behaviors, and approach to each problem-solving task.

Virtually any examiner can deduce that the WAIS-IV Verbal Comprehension Index (VCI) is not a very good measure of the crystallized intelligence of a person raised in a foreign culture, a person who understands Spanish or Vietnamese far better than English, or a person with a hearing impairment, and that the WAIS-IV Processing Speed Index (PSI) does not measure speed of mental processing very well for a person with crippling arthritis or a visual handicap. The goal of the intelligent tester is to deduce when one or more subtests or indexes may be an invalid measure of a person's intellectual functioning for more subtle reasons: distractibility, poor arithmetic achievement in school, subcultural differences in language or custom, emotional content of the items, suspected or known lesions in specific regions of the brain, fatigue, boredom, extreme shyness, bizarre thought processes, inconsistent effort, and the like.

Being a great detective—able to follow up leads and hunches about peaks and valleys in a profile—is the hallmark of an intelligent tester. Such a tester will integrate IQ test profiles with background information, clinical observations of behaviors, and other tests administered in order to more fully understand the examinee's profile.

The importance of this fifth tenet is probably best explained through an example. Consider an adult female who is hypothesized to have a weak short-term memory based on her WAIS-IV profile that featured low scores on Digit Span, Arithmetic, and Letter-Number Sequencing. Her low scores on these subtests may be caused by poor short-term memory but may also be a result of anxiety, distractibility, lack of concentration, or other factors. What was the woman like during the evaluation? Did she appear focused and remain on task? Was she distractible? Did she seem nervous, fidgety, or exhibit other signs of anxiety? Was she observed to be distractible in other settings, for example, in the classroom or workplace, or perhaps in other environments as well? Did she score low on other tests of short-term memory, such as the Short-Term Memory Tests of the WJ III? Did her background include a history of difficulty remembering people's names or phone numbers or forgetting appointments? The answers to questions such as these will support or disconfirm the hypothesis of poor short-term memory. With multiple sources of data backing a hypothesis, you can feel much more confident in stating a person's abilities. Thus, in this book we present an interpretive approach to analyzing the WAIS-IV as part of a comprehensive battery that integrates many sources of data.

TYING TOGETHER THE TENETS OF INTELLIGENT TESTING

The principles discussed in the preceding sections direct our attention to one important point: *The focus of any assessment is the person being assessed, not the test.* Many psychological reports stress what the scales or subtests measure instead of what aspects of the person are particularly well developed or in need of improvement; many reports are so number-oriented that the reader loses sight of the person's uniqueness. The WAIS-IV enables psychologists to better understand a person's cognitive functioning, but other facets of an individual are also revealed during an assessment and should be fully integrated to represent that person as a whole. Although the section of an assessment report that systematically reports and interprets the FSIQ and index scores is valuable, the behavioral observations section of a case report is often more revealing, and ultimately of more value, if it helps explain how or why examinees arrived at the scores they did. The content of the responses and the person's style of responding to various types of tasks can be more important as a determinant of developmental level and intellectual maturity than the scores assigned to the items or tasks. When several tests are administered to a person (intelligence, language, achievement, personality, neuropsychological), the results must be integrated from one test battery to the other. Intelligent testing does not apply only to the interpretation of intelligence tests. The examiner's main role is to generate hypotheses that pertain mostly to assets and deficits within the CHC, neuropsychological, or other empirically based models, and then confirm or deny these hypotheses by exploring multiple sources of evidence. This integrative, flexible, clinical-empirical methodology and philosophy, as outlined in the preceding tenets, defines the approach taken in this book for the interpretation of the WAIS-IV.

Some researchers argue that the WAIS-IV should be interpreted as a one-score measure of g (e.g., Canivez & Watkins, 2010a, 2010b). We believe the opposite—

that Full Scale IQ is just the very beginning of test interpretation, not the endpoint. Diagnostic decisions should be based on test data, clinical observations during the testing session, background information, data from other assessments, and referral questions geared specifically to the person being evaluated. Without context, test scores are meaningless; without understanding a person's pattern of strengths and weaknesses, the Full Scale IQ is meaningless. The guidelines for interpreting WAIS-IV test profiles and the illustrative case reports in Chapter 10 rest solidly on the intelligent testing framework.

QUALITATIVE AND CLINICAL ANALYSES OF THE WAIS-IV

In order to maintain focus on the examinee, rather than on the test itself during test interpretation, as the examiner, you must consider the results in the context of what is observed during the testing. Test-taking behaviors may exert a negative or positive influence on WAIS-IV performance. Behavioral factors have the potential to affect the reliability and validity of test scores, although they are essentially unrelated to the test construct being measured (Sattler, 2008).

Qualitative analyses of performance on WAIS-IV tasks serve several functions during the interpretation process.

1. *Qualitative analyses provide a cross-check for you to evaluate the **reliability** of the person's test scores obtained during any test sessions.*

   Therefore, if the reliability of test-taking behavior is called into question in the initial session, you may want to schedule additional sessions at different times and places to see if maladaptive test-taking

DON'T FORGET
....
Summary of the Functions of Qualitative Analyses
- Provide a cross-check for you to evaluate the reliability of the person's test scores obtained during test sessions
- Provide a cross-check of the validity of the test scores obtained during test sessions
- Help determine definitions of standards of test performance
- Provide supplemental information for interpreting scores when test-taking behaviors systematically interfere with performance
- Help ensure that positive as well as negative influences of various test-taking behaviors are observed
- May assist with making decisions about abilities or constructs that should be investigated further

CAUTION

**Types of Questions That Concern the
Reliability of Observed Behaviors**

- Does the examinee act this way every time he or she is tested?
- Does the examinee act this way only when being tested in a standardized fashion, or is it in any testing situation?
- Does the examinee act this way when in other structured situations?
- Does the examinee exhibit these test-session behaviors with other examiners or authority figures?

behaviors are consistently present. If the behaviors are present during other testing sessions then the examiner will need to check for the same behaviors across settings. (Kaufman et al., 2005, pp. 143–144)

It is key to determine if the observed behaviors are *consistently present* during test sessions and alternate settings. The Caution box lists the types of questions that concern the reliability of behaviors examined in qualitative analyses.

Within a testing session, examiners need to determine whether a person exhibits different test-session behaviors when different modalities are required. For example, some people display poor attention and distractibility when subtests are presented with only auditory stimuli (e.g., Digit Span and Similarities) but are able to sustain attention and exhibit less distractibility with subtests that measure similar constructs with both visual and auditory cues (e.g., Vocabulary). If you notice such a pattern on these WAIS-IV subtests, you may want to verify the observation of the qualitative analyses of behaviors with other tests and with other personnel to see if the inattentive and distractible behaviors are consistently present. If the behaviors are indeed consistently present, then determine the validity of the behavior as it relates to the impact on test performance.

2. *Qualitative analyses of behaviors provide a cross-check of the **validity** of the test scores obtained during test sessions.* If you determine that the behavior is reliably present, then determine the impact of the behavior. For a behavior to be valid, it must exert a moderate to severe impact on test performance in a consistent way.

One of the implicit goals of any cognitive ability battery is to obtain results that are not unduly affected by a person's conduct during the

CAUTION

Types of Questions That Concern the Validity of Observed Behaviors

- Did the test-session behavior help or hurt the examinee's performance on a specific item or subtest?
- Did the test-session behavior appear to have a mild, moderate, or severe impact on test performance?

test session (Glutting & Oakland, 1993). In other words, qualitative analyses of behaviors help determine if the person's obtained (*quantitative*) scores reflect the intended cognitive constructs as opposed to the constructs within the context of other extraneous behavioral (*qualitative*) variables. (Kaufman et al., 2005, p. 145)

Hebben and Milberg (2002) suggest that an examiner "should try to document any behaviors that seem unusual or rare within his or her own typical experience, and then decide whether this information is relevant to clinical decision making" (p. 77). *Validity*, in this sense, is concerned with the *relevance* of the behavior, and relevance pertains especially to the question of whether behaviors observed during the test session *interfered* with test performance. The specific questions that concern the validity of qualitative analyses of behaviors are addressed in the Caution box.

3. *Qualitative analyses of behaviors "help ensure that the positive as well as negative influences of various test-taking behaviors are observed. These analyses also aid in understanding the process of the test situation as well as the products"* (Kaufman et al., 2005, p. 147). For example, many people who have poor visual-spatial skills will encounter great difficulty on the Block Design subtest of the WAIS-IV. Some people will become frustrated and give up easily; others will verbally mediate their way through the test; and others will simply stay with the task until it is finished regardless of how long it takes. All three of these approaches to working the designs on Block Design give valuable clues about what behaviors sustain eventual success for a given person. The luxury of large batteries like the WAIS-IV is that they provide multiple opportunities to observe not only a person's behavioral weaknesses and trouble areas but also the basic strengths of the person that contribute to good test scores and, it is hoped, to success in other environments as well.

4. *Qualitative analyses of behaviors may assist with making decisions about follow-up testing, including assessment of abilities or constructs that are not generally measured*

by a cognitive ability battery such as the WAIS-IV. As Kaufman et al. (2005) indicate, these difficulties suggest weaknesses in executive functioning: " (1) independently orienting and sustaining attention, (2) demonstrating impulsivity when reflection is needed, (3) staying still and orienting to test materials, (4) entertaining competing answers, (5) demonstrating rigidity when flexibility is needed, and (6) checking answers" (p. 147). If you observe these behaviors and believe that they are interfering with scores on the WAIS-IV, then investigate further or recommend further testing in the area of executive functioning. However, these same behaviors might be associated with excessive anxiety or depression rather than poor executive functioning.

The factors that we believe are most likely to influence performance on the WAIS-IV are listed in the pages that follow, but they are not exhaustive and are intended primarily to alert you to a diversity of possible behaviors to observe and interpret. In Chapter 6 of this book, McCloskey, Hartz, and Scipioni offer a detailed neuropsychological processing approach to WAIS-IV interpretation that provides many valuable and innovative insights into the qualitative analysis of test data. Be sure to make decisions about qualitative observations that are specific to the person being examined. The information must make sense in light of the person's background information, observations made by other professionals who work with the person on a daily basis, and other tests administered in the comprehensive assessment. Determining the validity of test scores in this context relies on your skillful clinical interpretation of behaviors as well as your willingness to form hypotheses about test-taking behaviors and to test those hypotheses.

In addition to the listing of possible influencing factors for the WAIS-IV are various clinical suggestions to aid in interpreting each subtest. These clinical points come from clinical experience (our own as well as generations of Wechsler lore and feedback from colleagues) and the literature (e.g., Kamphaus, 1993; Kaufman, 1990, 1994a; Raiford et al., 2010; Reitan & Wolfson, 1992; Sattler, 1998; Weiss, Saklofske, Coalson, & Raiford, 2010a, 2010b; Zimmerman & Woo-Sam, 1985).

The clinical considerations are meant to be suggestions of hypotheses to consider, not as definite causes for good or poor performance on particular subtests. Each psychologist must employ his or her own theoretical framework to provide the best interpretation of any particular clinical evidence.

Although many have suggested clinical hypotheses about Wechsler profiles, empirical research has not supported hypotheses initially proposed by Rapaport and other clinicians. This lack of validation is likely because of the very complicated nature of interpreting pieces of clinical information in isolation. Even two top-notch clinicians may not have exactly the same interpretation of clinical data after testing the same individual (Lipsitz, Dworkin, & Erlenmeyer-Kimling, 1993).

SUBTEST-BY-SUBTEST QUALITATIVE AND CLINICAL ANALYSES

BLOCK DESIGN: Influences Affecting Subtest Scores
- Cognitive style (field dependence-field independence)
- Visual-motor coordination
- Visual-perceptual problems
- Working under time pressure

BLOCK DESIGN: Clinical Considerations
- Scores may be substantially lowered by obsessive concern with detail or reflectivity. Bonus points can be earned for quick, perfect performance. The comparison between Block Design and Block Design No Time Bonus can help determine the influence that speed of performance had on the person's score.
- Visual-perceptual problems are often apparent on this subtest. If a low score occurs, the input of the visual material may be related to inaccurate perception rather than problem-solving ability or motor output. Testing the limits often can help determine whether the adult is having perceptual difficulties or other problems.
- Scores should be interpreted in light of problem-solving approaches that were observed. Some adults use a trial-and-error approach, some a systematic and planned approach. Factors such as rigidity, perseveration, speed of mental processing, carelessness, self-concept, cautiousness, and ability to benefit from feedback impact the test.
- Some individuals may have little motivation to try and give up easily; others learn as they take the test and sometimes catch on just when they discontinue. In such cases, testing the limits by administering further items can be of great clinical value (although any extra items administered beyond the discontinue rule cannot be counted in the score).
- Performance on this test is vulnerable to any kind of cerebral brain damage (especially right hemisphere). Lesions to the posterior region of the right hemisphere, especially the parietal lobes, can strongly impact Block Design.

SIMILARITIES: Influences Affecting Subtest Scores
- Flexibility
- Interests
- Negativism ("They're not alike")
- Overly concrete thinking
- Outside reading

SIMILARITIES: Clinical Considerations
- Degree of abstractness should be evaluated; responses may be *abstract* (table and chair are "furniture"), *concrete* (coat and suit are "made of cloth"), or *functional* (north and west "tell you where you are going").
- Clinically rich information can be gleaned from the nature of the verbal response: Overelaboration, overly general responses, overly inclusive responses, or self-references should be noted. Overelaboration may suggest obsessiveness. Overly inclusive responses may suggest a thought disorder. Self-references are unusual during Similarities and may be indicative of personal preoccupation.
- Obsessive adults may provide responses that vary in quality by embedding a 2-point response among 1- or 0-point responses. This may lead to unusually high scores, as long as no response spoils the answer.
- The pattern of responses should be examined. An adult who earns a raw score by accumulating several 1-point responses may differ substantially in potential from an adult who earns the same raw score with some 2-point and 0-point responses. The individual who mixes the 2s and 0s probably has a greater capacity for excellent performance.
- Creativity may be exhibited in trying to come up with the relationship between two concepts. Sometimes visual imagery may be used. The creativity does not invariably mean a wrong response.
- Correct responses on the easier items may simply reflect overlearned, everyday associations rather than true abstract thought. In general, though, Similarities items require fluid, abstract reasoning in addition to crystallized knowledge. "The two words are expected to be known, but their relationship is not usually taught directly in most educational settings and must be reasoned" (Weiss et al., 2010a, p. 64).
- Individuals who miss the first item administered provide the opportunity to see how they benefit from feedback. The examiner gives an example of a correct answer if the examinee does not provide a perfect answer to the first item administered. Adults who catch on quickly

to these prompts demonstrate flexibility and adaptability. Rigidity may be evident if the adult continues to insist that certain pairs are "not alike."
• Formal learning is less emphasized than new problem solving. The adult's task is to relate to verbal concepts, but the individual concepts tend to be simple and well known (table-chair).

DIGIT SPAN: Influences Affecting Subtest Scores
• Ability to receive stimuli passively
• Attention span
• Anxiety
• Distractibility
• Flexibility (when switching among forward, backward, and sequencing)
• Learning disabilities
• Attention-Deficit/Hyperactivity Disorder (ADHD)
• Negativism (refusal to try to reverse digits, to exert effort until the more challenging Backward or Sequencing items, or to take a "meaningless" task)

DIGIT SPAN: Clinical Considerations
• The Process-level scores of Digit Span Forward, Backward, and Sequencing will help to discern whether failure is caused by poor sequential ability (right numbers in wrong order) or by poor rote memory (forgetting digits, but otherwise correctly repeating the series). Problems with inattention, distractibility, or anxiety may be evident in responses that bear little relationship to the actual stimuli.
• After the task, testing the limits and questioning whether any strategy can be employed to help differentiate between poor strategy generation (e.g., chunking), low motivation, anxiety, distractibility, sequencing problems, or memory problems.
• Digit Span Backward and Sequencing, which require mental manipulation or visualization of the numbers (aspects of working memory), are more impacted by number ability than is Digits Forward. Thus, those who have better number ability may perform better on Digits Backward or Sequencing.
• Typically, adults and adolescents produce Forward spans that are one digit longer than sequencing spans. Longer sequencing than forward spans (by two or more digits) occurs relatively rarely within the normal population of adults and is therefore noteworthy: less than 5% of the time (averaging across all ages) (Wechsler, 2008, Table C.5). One explanation for a longer Sequencing span is that individuals may find it to be more challenging and worthy of sustaining effort, or individuals may

have better skill at representational (high-level) tasks than at automatic (overlearned) tasks such as Digits Forward.

- Conversely, most adults have longer sequencing spans than backward spans. Less than 5% of adults have a backward span that is longer than their sequencing span by 2 or more points. Although both the sequencing and backward tasks require working memory, the process of sequencing numbers is typically a more well-learned task than repeating numbers backward.

- Typically, adults and adolescents produce Forward spans that are one to two digits longer than backward spans. Longer Backward than Forward spans occur relatively rarely within the normal population of adults and are therefore noteworthy: less than 4% of the time (averaging across all ages) (Wechsler, 2008, Table C.5). One explanation for a longer Backward span is that individuals may find it to be more challenging and worthy of sustaining effort, or individuals may have better skill at representational (high-level) tasks than at automatic (overlearned) tasks such as Digits Forward.

- Less-than-ideal testing conditions may adversely affect performance on this subtest (visual or auditory distractions), and hearing impairment may make examinees vulnerable to failure.

- Repeating digits seems to be more impaired by state anxiety (or test anxiety) than by chronic (trait) anxiety.

- Impulsivity may be evident when adults begin to respond before the examiner has completed the series of digits, or when the examinee repeats the digits very rapidly.

- Learning ability may be evident when adults make errors on the first trial but then are able to pass the second trial. Look for this pattern in other subtests as well (Letter-Number Sequencing, Block Design).

MATRIX REASONING: Influences Affecting Subtest Scores
- Ability to respond when uncertain
- Cognitive style (field dependence–field independence)
- Color blindness (for some items, the use of several colors may confuse color-blind individuals)
- Flexibility
- Motivation level
- Negativism ("None of them go there")
- Overly concrete thinking
- Persistence
- Visual-perceptual problems

MATRIX REASONING: Clinical Considerations

- Because this subtest is not timed, response time may vary widely for adults. Those who are mentally retarded or neurologically impaired may take longer to respond. Impulsivity may be indicated by extremely quick, incorrect responses. Failure to respond within a reasonable amount of time (45 seconds) is of potential diagnostic value, as it may indicate reflective style, obsessiveness, or confusion.
- Some items have complex visual stimuli. Individuals with visual-perceptual problems may display stimulus overload in attempting to input the multicolored, spatially complex items.
- A holistic processing approach is most common in solving the matrices. Some individuals choose to answer the problem with a trial-and-error approach by testing each of the possible choices one by one. Others may use a more planful approach to the problem, first mentally creating a solution to fill in the answer and then searching the given responses to see if one matches the solution they had envisioned.
- Perseveration may be apparent on this subtest if an individual repeatedly chooses the same number response for each item (e.g., number 5).
- Color blindness must be ruled out as a potential cause for poor performance. If such information is not offered spontaneously by the examinee, consider probing for information on color blindness if there is less difficulty on items that depend on form versus those that depend on color.
- Indecisiveness (e.g., "It is either 1 or 3") may indicate insecurity or need for feedback.

VOCABULARY: Influences Affecting Subtest Scores

- Cultural opportunities at home
- Foreign language experience
- Intellectual curiosity and striving
- Interests
- Outside reading
- Richness of early environment
- School learning

VOCABULARY: Clinical Considerations

- Repression may lead to poor performance by pushing out of consciousness any word meanings that are even mildly conflict-laden. Repression may also impair the acquisition of new word meanings as well as recall of specific words on the Vocabulary subtest.

- Similar to Information, high scores relative to other Verbal subtests can reflect intellectual ambitiousness or stress for achievement in one's life.
- The content presented in an adult's or adolescent's response lends itself to analysis regarding the person's fears, guilt, preoccupations, feelings, interests, background, cultural milieu, bizarre thought processes, perseveration, and clang associations (ponder-yonder, remorse-of course). Themes in response content may occur also in conjunction with Comprehension or Similarities, as well as during spontaneous conversation during the assessment.
- Perseveration is sometimes evidenced when individuals give the same opening line for each response (*"Confide*, that's a hard one to define . . .").
- Responses that are overlearned, almost booklike definitions, should be distinguished from those that appear to be responses driven by intellectual vigor and personalization of the responses with current experiences.
- The open-ended nature of the Vocabulary responses make it possible to glean information about an individual's verbal fluency, not just word knowledge. Some words are easily defined by one-word synonyms, but some individuals may give excessive verbiage in their response or may give a response in a roundabout manner.
- Hearing difficulties may become apparent for those individuals who are illiterate (cannot read the visually presented word list) or for those who focus only on the auditory stimuli. Because the words are presented in isolation, the examinee has no context clues that could help him or her understand the word.
- Level of abstract thinking can also be evaluated in Vocabulary items. Some responses may be abstract (confide is "to entrust") or more concrete (confide is "talking to a person"). Nonetheless, little is required in terms of fluid, abstract reasoning. "There is no apparent demand for reason in this subtest; it is essentially the case that one 'knows' the word" (Weiss et al., 2010a, p. 63).

ARITHMETIC: Influences Affecting Subtest Scores
- Attention span
- Anxiety
- Concentration
- Distractibility
- Learning disabilities/ADHD
- School learning
- Working under time pressure

ARITHMETIC: Clinical Considerations

- Inferring the cause of the error is useful: whether it was computational, reasoning, failure to attend, or misunderstanding the meaning of a question. For example, in response to a question about the number of hours it takes to walk 25 miles at the rate of 5 miles per hour, the answer "7" reflects a computational error, while "30" reflects a reasoning error, and "5,000" is bizarre. This type of bizarre response may suggest inattention, lack of comprehension, or a thought disorder. Such an unusual response on Arithmetic should be explored further.

- Because Arithmetic has a strong factor loading (.77) on the Fluid Reasoning Cluster (T. Keith, personal communication, January 30, 2009), if difficulties with reasoning are suspected, consider comparing Arithmetic to the other fluid reasoning tasks of Matrix Reasoning and Figure Weights. If the scores are reasonably consistent, then reasoning ability is likely related to performance on Arithmetic.

- Testing the limits by removing the time limit and with paper and pencil is often helpful to help assess the roles of anxiety and concentration on test performance.

- For developmentally disabled adults, the subtest measures a portion of adaptive functioning, as items involve money, counting, and other real-life situations.

- Adolescents or adults who have struggled with mathematics in school may become anxious when asked to respond to school-like Arithmetic questions. Their response to the anxiety and frustration may be clinically interesting: Can they compose themselves? Do they respond with hostility? Do they reject the test?

- It is important to consider when individuals are able to respond correctly to the questions but failed to do so within the time limits. Those who tend to be reflective, compulsive, obsessive, or neurologically impaired may exhibit this pattern of responding.

- Observe for signs of trying to compensate for the auditory nature or memory requirements of the task: for example, finger writing on the table, or asking for a pencil and paper or a calculator.

- "A few users have commented that the use of names from other cultures that appear on two of the Arithmetic items may be distracting. . . . If it is thought that the use of one of these names has caused the examinee to respond incorrectly, it is acceptable to readminister the item following administration of all subtests using an alternate name to test the limits" (Raiford et al., 2010).

SYMBOL SEARCH: Influences Affecting Subtest Scores
- Anxiety
- Distractibility
- Learning disabilities/ADHD
- Motivation level
- Obsessive concern with accuracy and detail
- Persistence
- Visual-motor coordination
- Visual-perceptual problems
- Working under time pressure

SYMBOL SEARCH: Clinical Considerations
- Similar to most Processing Speed and Perceptual Reasoning subtests, visual impairment should be ruled out before interpreting a low Symbol Search score.
- As noted in Chapter 2, it is important to be an astute observer during this task, as many observed behaviors can help interpret the Symbol Search score. Concentration, distractibility, obsessive concern with detail, impulsiveness, reflectivity, motivation level, visual-perceptual problems, or anxiety are just some of the factors that may be inferred to be related to a person's performance on Symbol Search.
- A learning curve may be present on this test. Individuals who begin to answer later items more quickly may have developed a plan or strategy after completing earlier items. To note whether speed of responding is, in fact, increasing, you can track how many items were answered during each of the four 30-second intervals during the subtest.
- Visual memory ability sometimes can be inferred from observations on this task. Some adults may look at the Target symbols only once and then find the response in the Search Group, and others may look back and forth several times between the Target and Search groups before marking their response. The repeated referring back and forth between the symbols may indicate poor visual memory (or of insecurity).
- After the entire test has been administered, you may test the limits to help discern why certain responses were made. Point to some items answered correctly and some that were wrong, and ask the adult to explain why they choose their response.

VISUAL PUZZLES: Influences Affecting Subtest Scores
- Ability to respond when uncertain
- Flexibility

- Motivation level
- Negativism ("It's impossible. That design can't be made.")
- Overly concrete thinking
- Persistence
- Visual-perceptual problems
- Worries about time limits
- Impulsivity in responding
- Ability to self-correct

VISUAL PUZZLES: Clinical Considerations

- Response time may vary widely for adults on this task (although there is a time limit). Those who are developmentally disabled or neurologically impaired may take longer to respond. Impulsivity may be indicated by extremely quick, incorrect responses. Failure to respond within a reasonable amount of time (before the time limit) is of potential diagnostic value, as it may indicate reflective style, obsessiveness, or confusion.
- As with Matrix Reasoning, some items have complex visual stimuli. Individuals with visual-perceptual problems may display stimulus overload in attempting to input the multicolored, spatially complex items.
- A holistic processing approach is most common in solving the puzzles. Some individuals choose to answer the problem with a trial-and-error approach by testing each of the possible choices one by one before deciding which three work best. Others may use a more planful approach to the problem, first mentally creating a solution and then searching the given responses to see which triad matches the solution they had envisioned. "Successful performance requires the ability to maintain a visual image in mind temporarily while mentally rotating, inverting and otherwise manipulating that image and matching the resulting percept to a visual target" (Weiss et al., 2010a, p. 66).
- Perseveration may be apparent on this subtest if an individual repeatedly chooses the same number response for each item (e.g., responds with numbers 1, 2, 3 every time).
- Indecisiveness may indicate insecurity or need for feedback.

INFORMATION: Influences Affecting Subtest Scores

- Alertness to the environment
- Cultural opportunities at home
- Foreign language background
- Intellectual curiosity and striving
- Interests

- Outside reading
- Richness of early environment
- School learning

INFORMATION: Clinical Considerations

- Items are generally nonthreatening and emotionally neutral.
- Rationalizations and excuses may be produced in response to this test (i.e., "That isn't important").
- Effortless, automatic responding facilitates good performance. Adults or adolescents with chronic anxiety may suffer early failures and depressed scores in general.
- Retrieval difficulties may be revealed on this test when success on harder items is proceeded by failure on easy items.
- Alertness to the environment in addition to formal schooling together are the source of most of the factual knowledge needed for success.
- Unnecessary detail and trivial responses may suggest obsessiveness.
- Intellectual ambitiousness can be reflected in high scores and often is coupled with high Vocabulary scores.
- A perfectionistic approach may be evident when no response is preferred to an imperfect answer.
- An adolescent's or adult's pattern of responses may reflect cultural background. For example, questions pertaining to U.S. history or other famous leaders in America may pose more difficulty than those on general geography or science for individuals who are not originally from the United States.
- Bizarre or odd responses can shed light on an individual's mental state. For example, a response such as "There are 1,000 weeks in a year," or "Gandhi is the guy I saw at the supermarket" may indicate a need to explore mental functioning further.

CODING: Influences Affecting Subtest Scores

- Anxiety
- Distractibility
- Learning disabilities/ADHD
- Motivation level
- Obsessive concern with accuracy and detail
- Persistence
- Visual-motor coordination
- Visual-perceptual problems
- Working under time pressure

CODING: Clinical Considerations

- Visual or motor impairment must be ruled out before interpreting a low score.
- Individuals who have demonstrated perfectionistic or compulsive tendencies before Coding should be told *during the sample items* that they need to copy the symbols legibly but not perfectly.
- Changes in rate of responding during the subtest can be related to motivation, distraction, fatigue, boredom, and so forth. Thus, it is a good idea to note the number of symbols copied during each of the four 30-second periods within the 120-second limit.
- Astute observation is key to interpreting scores on this subtest. Include these points in your interpretation of the score: coordination (grip on the pencil), attention/concentration, distractibility, motivation level, visual perceptual problems (rotating or distorting symbols), perfectionistic tendencies, perseveration (copying the same symbol for a whole line), or anxiety.
- Some individuals appear to have to search for each number in the row of stimulus pairs, seemingly unaware that the "5" is always right before the "6." This behavior could indicate sequencing problems.
- Short-term visual memory deficits may be evident if adults keep referring back to the key before copying symbols (or these individuals may be insecure). Those who have memorized several pairs of symbols are likely to have a good visual memory (if they are not making errors in their response).

LETTER-NUMBER SEQUENCING: Influences Affecting Subtest Scores

- Ability to receive stimuli passively
- Attention span
- Anxiety
- Concentration
- Distractibility
- Flexibility
- Illiteracy or dyslexia (does not know letters and alphabet at an automatic level)
- Learning Disabilities
- Attention-Deficit/Hyperactivity Disorder (ADHD)
- Negativism (refusal to take a "meaningless" task)
- Persistence

LETTER-NUMBER SEQUENCING: Clinical Considerations

- Sequencing, poor short-term memory, inattention, distractibility, or anxiety may be causative factors for trouble on Letter-Number

Sequencing. Similar to Digit Span, sequencing problems can be evident from correctly remembering the numbers and letters but in the wrong sequence. Short-term memory may be implicated if part of the sequence is correct but some of the numbers or letters are forgotten.

- Observe the examinee for signs of stimulus overload, which can lead to frustration. Statements such as "That is too much to remember at once" or "How about just the numbers?" can indicate an examinee's being overwhelmed with the amount of auditory stimuli.

- Digit Span Backward and Digit Span Sequencing are more conceptually related to Letter-Number Sequencing (LNS) than Digits Forward. The backward and sequencing items, like LNS, require the examinee to mentally manipulate or visualize the stimuli. (Some examinees who rely on visualization strategies will close their eyes during the administration of the items and/or during their response.) If strategies were generated to respond to the Backward or Sequential items on Digit Span, the examinee may benefit from using those or similar strategies on LNS.

- As there are three trials for each item, subjects have an opportunity to develop and test strategies. Test the limits or question the examinee after the test is complete to gather information about any strategies that may have been generated to complete the task.

- Like Digit Span, the skills required for this test are impaired more by state (test) anxiety than by chronic anxiety.

- Whereas number sequences are automatic for most adolescents and adults, the precise alphabetic sequence has not been adequately "overlearned" for many individuals. Note whether some examinees consistently make errors on the letters but get all of the numbers right. Do these individuals have reading problems (e.g., illiteracy or dyslexia)?

- LNS is a novel task, not likely to be encountered in the real world, and requires a good, flexible approach to succeed. Adolescents and adults who do poorly may display problems on other tasks that depend on fluid ability (e.g., Matrix Reasoning) or flexibility (e.g., Similarities).

FIGURE WEIGHTS: Influences Affecting Subtest Scores
- Ability to respond when uncertain
- Flexibility
- Motivation level
- Negativism ("None of them go there")
- Overly concrete thinking
- Persistence

- Ability to shift sets
- Executive functioning problems
- Worries about time limits
- Impulsivity in responding
- Ability to self-correct
- Math anxiety

FIGURE WEIGHTS: Clinical Considerations

- Examinees who are mathematically minded or who are skilled in the concepts of algebra may be more likely to view this as a math-like test. Whereas the solution to each item "can be expressed with algebraic equations, there is no task requirement to do so—thus eliminating the demand for acquired knowledge of advanced mathematical equations" (Weiss et al., 2010a, p. 65).
- Response time may vary widely for adults on this task (although there is a time limit). Those who are developmentally disabled or neurologically impaired may take longer to respond. Impulsivity may be indicated by extremely quick, incorrect responses. Failure to respond within a reasonable amount of time (before the time limit) is of potential diagnostic value, as it may indicate reflective style, obsessiveness, or confusion.
- Figure Weights places a great demand on executive functioning skills because the examinee must sustain attention while using several different cognitive processes at the same time.

  Although Figure Weights involves working memory, it reduces this involvement relative to typical quantitative tasks (e.g., mental arithmetic) through the visual presentation of items in a stimulus book which allows the patient to continually refresh stimuli held in working memory while solving the problem. (Weiss et al., 2010a, p. 65)

- Individuals who have difficulty shifting sets may have trouble because the shapes represent different "weights" on every item, so this task requires continual set shifting. An increased difficulty may be noticed when the examinee is required to shift from examining two to three scales beginning with Item 16.
- A flexible problem-solving approach in which an individual examines the problem from left to right, but can also view it from right to left, can be beneficial on this task.
- Some individuals choose their answer to the problem with a trial-and-error approach by testing each of the possible choices one by one before

deciding which one works best. Others may use a more planful approach to the problem, first mentally creating a solution when examining the scales and then searching the given responses to see which response matches the solution they had envisioned.

- Perseveration may be apparent on this subtest if an individual repeatedly chooses the same number response for each item.
- Indecisiveness may indicate insecurity or need for feedback.

COMPREHENSION: Influences Affecting Subtest Scores
- Cultural opportunities at home
- Development of conscience or moral sense
- Flexibility (ability to shift from social reasoning to proverb items and ability to give a "second reason")
- Negativism ("We shouldn't have to pay taxes")
- Overly concrete thinking

COMPREHENSION: Clinical Considerations
- A stable and emotionally balanced attitude and orientation are necessary for success on this subtest. Any type of maladjustment may lower scores.
- A high score on Comprehension alone is not enough evidence to interpret strong social adjustment. Corroborating evidence must be obtained from clinical observations, background information, or adaptive behavior inventories.
- Responses offer clues about a disturbed individual's social-adaptive functioning in practical, social situations, but be cautious about generalizing from single-issue questions to the complexities of the real world.
- When responses appear overlearned, stereotypical, or parroted, test the limits to determine the level of real understanding and reasoning ability.
- Like responses to Similarities and Vocabulary, responses to Comprehension may vary in their degree of abstractness. This ability to reason may be especially evident in the explanation of the proverbs. Ability to think in abstract terms (*swallow* means "Don't generalize from a single instance") is distinct from more concrete types of responses (*brooks* means "if the brook is so shallow and you throw a rock in, it makes noise"). Like Similarities, this subtest depends on fluid reasoning as well as crystallized knowledge. Comprehension items usually "assume certain facts are known (e.g., cars must have license plates), but the reasons for these facts are typically not taught directly in school" (Weiss et al., 2010a, p. 64).

- Five of the Comprehension items require further questioning if only one response is given, and all questions allow querying for clarification of responses. Analyze how individuals respond to follow-up questioning. Do they become defensive? Are they inflexible and unable to move beyond their original response? Clinically relevant bits of information can be obtained from observing the difference between someone who is spontaneously able to produce two concise responses versus someone who needs constant structure and prodding.

CANCELLATION: Influences Affecting Subtest Scores
- Attention span
- Concentration
- Distractibility
- Visual acuity
- Visual-motor coordination
- Reflectivity/impulsivity
- Planning
- Ability to perform under time pressure

CANCELLATION: Clinical Considerations
- As this is one of the last subtests administered, fatigue and boredom should be ruled out as possible explanations for a low score.
- Anxiety may be notable on this subtest. Shaking hands, a tight pencil grip, or pressure on the paper when writing could be signs of nervousness.
- The pace at which an individual works may be related to impulsivity (quick, careless responding) or perfectionism (slower, more careful responding).
- Attention and concentration may impact this brief task. It is a monotonous task that requires sustained attention for success. Inconsistent responding (or an inconsistent response rate) across the two items may indicate difficulties sustaining attention or concentration. "The decision-making component requires patients to simultaneously discriminate both the color and shape of the stimuli, and inhibit responding when only one of these two features is present" (Weiss et al., 2010a, p. 73).
- Executive functioning can impact performance on this task. Along with maintaining attention, examinees must ignore distractor stimuli while marking the targets. In addition, examinees must shift sets from between Items 1 and 2 when the target items shift.

PICTURE COMPLETION: Influences Affecting Subtest Scores
- Ability to respond when uncertain
- Alertness to the environment
- Cognitive style (field dependence–field independence)
- Concentration
- Negativism ("Nothing is missing")
- Working under time pressure

PICTURE COMPLETION: Clinical Considerations
- Adults usually find this task nonthreatening and consider it enjoyable.
- Although this subtest is timed, the 20-second limit is usually ample time for adults who are neither mentally retarded nor neurologically impaired. Impulsivity may be indicated by extremely quick, incorrect responses. Failure to respond within the limit is of potential diagnostic value, as even reflective individuals typically respond within the limit.
- Verbal responses are far more common than nonverbal responses on this Performance task, especially since the directions explicitly say "TELL me what is missing." Although nonverbal responses are also considered correct, the frequency of such responses should be evaluated and may possibly indicate word retrieval problems. Verbal responses that are imprecise or vague may also indicate word retrieval problems.
- Negativity or hostility may be noted in persistent "Nothing is missing" responses.
- Obsessiveness or concentration problems may be evident in responses that are focused on trivial details of a picture (i.e., brand name on the glasses). Similarly, confabulatory responses (indicating that something not in the picture is missing—e.g., feet in the tennis shoes, blood on the knife) are of clinical interest. Giving trivial or confabulatory responses several times during the subtest is of potential diagnostic interest, especially because examiners are instructed to redirect individuals the first time they give a trivial response or a confabulatory response.
- This task appears to be relatively resilient to the impact of brain damage. It is not able to consistently or reliably indicate right cerebral damage, which perhaps may be related to the nature of verbal responding by most adults, and "it is entirely possible that the nature of the task is not as heavily demanding of adequate brain functions as are some of the other subtests" (Reitan & Wolfson, 1992, p. 107).

🐟 TEST YOURSELF 🐟

1. **All of the following are principles of the intelligent testing philosophy EXCEPT:**
   a. Subtests measure what the individual has learned.
   b. Subtests are samples of behavior and are not exhaustive.
   c. Behavioral observations and background information are of little importance in interpreting a person's test profile.
   d. Test batteries are optimally useful when interpreted from a theoretical model.
   e. IQ tests assess mental functioning under fixed experimental conditions.

2. **In the intelligent testing approach to test interpretation, the clinician is best thought of as a first-rate**
   a. Detective
   b. Physician
   c. Soldier
   d. Pilot
   e. Computer programmer

3. **Which one of the following WAIS-IV subtests is NOT especially vulnerable to distractibility?**
   a. Digit Span
   b. Symbol Search
   c. Picture Completion
   d. Coding
   e. Arithmetic

4. **Which WAIS-IV subtest is affected by a person's visual-perceptual problems and also has a long research history as being especially vulnerable to brain damage?**
   a. Vocabulary
   b. Block Design
   c. Visual Puzzles
   d. Arithmetic
   e. Digit Span Forward

5. **Which of the following WAIS-IV subtests best provides clinical information about a person's ability to express his or her ideas in words and to provide possible insight into the person's fears,**

guilt, preoccupations, feelings, interests, and cultural
background?

a. Information
b. Picture Completion
c. Letter-Number Sequencing
d. Vocabulary
e. Block Design

6. **Which WAIS-IV subtest (apart from Arithmetic) is most likely to be viewed as a math-like test by examinees who are "mathematically minded" or who are skilled in the concepts of algebra?**

a. Figure Weights
b. Block Design
c. Visual Puzzles
d. Symbol Search
e. Information

Answers: 1. c; 2. a; 3. c; 4. b; 5. d; 6. a

Five

HOW TO INTERPRET THE WAIS-IV: STEP-BY-STEP

INTRODUCTION TO INTERPRETATION

Examining and interpreting the 50-plus values on the Profile Page and Analysis Page of the WAIS-IV Record Form require a systematic plan. Just randomly grabbing interesting-looking scores is not a useful approach. In this chapter, we present an approach that guides you through the most global score to the most specific, to determine the most meaningful hypotheses about the examinee's abilities. Using this approach will set up a logical outline to follow when writing the Test Results and Interpretations sections of your WAIS-IV reports.

The steps of interpretation presented in this chapter begin with an analysis of the WAIS-IV indexes to determine the best way to summarize a person's overall intellectual ability. We offer examiners the choice of interpreting the four WAIS-IV Indexes or five alternate WAIS-IV factors derived from Cattell-Horn-Carroll (CHC) theory. Next, both Normative and Personal Strengths and Weaknesses among the indexes (or alternative factors) are identified. Interpretation of fluctuations in the person's Index or Factor profile offers the most reliable and meaningful information about WAIS-IV performance, because it identifies strong and weak areas of cognitive functioning relative to both same-age peers from the normal population (interindividual or normative approach) and the person's own overall ability level (intraindividual or ipsative approach). We also offer additional interpretive steps involving WAIS-IV composites (called clinical clusters) for examiners who choose to go beyond the FSIQ and index or factor profile in an attempt to uncover additional information about a person's cognitive capabilities, as well as generate potentially meaningful hypotheses about areas of integrity or dysfunction.

In the first edition of the book, we provided an empirically based and theory-supported interpretive system for individuals ages 16 to 69, but we fell far short concerning the elderly population. The five-factor CHC system that we proposed for WAIS-IV interpretation required the administration of two supplemental subtests that are not normed above age 69 (Figure Weights and Letter-Number Sequencing). Similarly, the step that permitted comparisons of clinical clusters required one or both of those supplemental subtests for *six* of the eight comparisons. In short, adults ages 70 to 90 were excluded from some of the best features that our interpretive system had to offer.

We have solved that problem in this second edition, thanks to the development of a new five-factor model that is applicable to all ages, 16 to 90 years, based on Confirmatory Factor Analysis (CFA) research conducted by Niileksela et al. (2012) and described in Chapter 1 (see Figure 1.3). This new set of factors also allows us to add an additional step of clinical cluster comparisons that *excludes* Figure Weights and Letter-Number Sequencing and, therefore, *includes* elderly individuals.

The end result is that we now offer examiners the choice of two alternate five-factor models derived from CHC theory: (a) the original model from the first edition of the book ("Keith" model), which requires Figure Weights and Letter-Number Sequencing, and applies to ages 16 to 69 only; and (b) the new approach ("Core" model) that depends only on the 10 core WAIS-IV subtests and applies to the full age range, 16 to 90 years. Analogously, we offer two steps, instead of one, for making the eight clinical cluster comparisons—one that depends on the administration of both Figure Weights and Letter-Number Sequencing (ages 16 to 69 only) and one that does not (ages 16 to 90). Our interpretive approach reflects numerous modifications of and enhancements to prior methods of Wechsler test interpretation, including our own (e.g., Flanagan & Kaufman, 2004; Kaufman, 1979; Kaufman & Lichtenberger, 2002). Previously, Kaufman (1979, 1994a; Kaufman & Lichtenberger, 1999, 2000, 2002) stressed ipsative analysis and an eclectic array of "shared abilities" for identifying areas of strength and weakness, whereas others emphasized normative CHC theory-based approaches (e.g., Flanagan & Ortiz, 2001; Flanagan, Ortiz, Alfonso, & Mascolo, 2002, 2006).

The Kaufman (or Kaufman-Lichtenberger) methodology has been the subject of much commentary (e.g., Flanagan & Harrison, 2012). It has been praised as advancing the field of test interpretation:

> Further evidence of the influence of measurement science on intelligence test interpretation and the problems associated with profile analysis can be found in an influential book by Kaufman (1979), *Intelligent Testing with the WISC-R*. He provided a logically appealing and systematic method for WISC-R interpretation that was rooted in sound measurement theory. . . .

Although such interpretive methods remained "clinical," . . . the reliance on measurement science for the interpretive process created new standards for assessment practice (Kamphaus, Winsor, Rowe, & Kim, 2012, p. 62).

However, that system became dated as the fields of test development and test interpretation embraced theory in every possible way. And, importantly, the shared-ability ipsative approach "was unable to conquer some lingering validity problems" (Kamphaus et al., 2012, p. 62), as spelled out by various researchers (Floyd & Kranzler, 2012; McDermott, Fantuzzo, Glutting, Watkins, & Baggaley, 1992; Watkins & Canivez, 2004).

In response to the changing field of assessment, most notably the increasing role played by CHC and Luria-based theory in test construction and interpretation, we modified our approach for the KABC-II (Kaufman et al., 2005) and WAIS-III (Kaufman & Lichtenberger, 2006). Indeed, our new approach for the WAIS-IV (Lichtenberger & Kaufman, 2009), which we refined and expanded in the present edition of the book, represents our biggest departure from the old system.

Like Flanagan and Kaufman's (2004, 2009) approach to WISC-IV interpretation and our approach to both KABC-II and WAIS-III interpretation (Kaufman & Lichtenberger, 2006; Kaufman et al., 2005), our method for WAIS-IV interpretation links ipsative analysis with normative analysis, rather than focusing exclusively on either one or the other. In addition, our method:

1. Emphasizes cluster scores and deemphasizes individual subtest scores in the interpretive steps
2. Uses base rate data to evaluate the clinical meaningfulness of cluster and index score variability
3. Grounds interpretation in theories of cognitive abilities (e.g., CHC theory and neuropsychological theory) and in the cognitive neuroscience research that forms the theoretical basis for the WAIS-IV
4. Provides guidance on the use of supplemental measures to test hypotheses about significant subtest variation or outlier scores
5. Permits thorough theory-based profile interpretation for elderly individuals (ages 70 to 90) as well as for individuals ages 16 to 69.

As discussed in Chapter 4, the step-by-step *quantitative* analysis of WAIS-IV profiles should be examined in the context of *qualitative* factors that may help explain a person's test performance. Qualitative information on each of the subtests was presented in Chapter 4 to aid in interpreting WAIS-IV performance, and additional information on qualitative analysis is presented in Chapter 6, which focuses on neuropsychological test interpretation. Qualitatively analyzing a person's performance can facilitate the selection of supplementary measures to augment the WAIS-IV when necessary. So, too, can basing test selection on a theoretical model such as Flanagan et al.'s (2007) cross-battery approach that is rooted in CHC theory. *All interpretations of test performance gain diagnostic meaning when they are corroborated by other data sources and when they are empirically or logically related to the area or areas of difficulty specified in the referral.*

The interpretive steps described here are illustrated using a WAIS-IV profile of Laura, a 17-year-old 12th grader who was referred for an assessment of her neurocognitive and psychological functioning. (Laura's full case report is included in Chapter 10.) In addition, a comprehensive WAIS-IV Interpretive Worksheet (included in Appendix A.1 on the CD-ROM in this book and designed to be completed by hand) walks the examiner through our interpretation method step by step. A software program, also included on the CD-ROM, called the WAIS-IV Data Management and Interpretive Assistant v2.0 (WAIS-IV DMIA), automates our interpretive system and is described alongside the worksheet. The WAIS-IV Interpretive Worksheet and the WAIS-IV DMIA have some stylistic differences but yield identical information. It is recommended that users of this book complete a few interpretive worksheets by hand in order to fully understand the interpretive steps before using the automated WAIS-IV DMIA. Also, while practicing the WAIS-IV interpretive steps, you can use the automated program to check the accuracy of the information you filled out by hand on the interpretive worksheet. Note that the WAIS-IV Interpretive Worksheet can be downloaded from the CD-ROM.

Administration Tips for Using the Step-by-Step Interpretive System

WAIS-IV examiners administer 10 subtests to obtain a person's FSIQ (assuming they do not opt to obtain a prorated FSIQ), and they have the option of administering five supplemental subtests to obtain further data. Of these five supplemental subtests, three are normed only for ages 16 to 69 and are not administered to adults ages 70 to 90 (except for clinical purposes): Figure Weights, Letter-Number Sequencing, and Cancellation. Only two of the supplemental tasks span the full 16–90 range: Comprehension and Picture Completion. The basic interpretive system presented here can be used for individuals of all ages who are administered the core group of 10 subtests. That system incorporates FSIQ, the four indexes, and two special scores (GAI and Cognitive Proficiency Index [CPI]). As mentioned, the system also includes two valuable theory-based interpretive options in Steps 4–10 that focus on five-factor scores instead of the four indexes. The first option, the five Keith factors, *requires the administration of two supplemental subtests that are normed for ages 16 to 69 but not for elderly individuals: Figure Weights and Letter-Number Sequencing.* The second five-factor option, designed especially for adults ages 70 to 90 (Niileksala, Reynolds, & Kaufman, 2012), relies only on the 10 core subtests. *This option also provides a backup five-factor interpretive option for adolescents and adults below age 70 who were not administered Figure Weights and Letter-Number Sequencing.* Importantly, both interpretive systems measure the same five CHC constructs; however, they use slightly different combinations of subtests for two of the factors.

Steps 11 and 12 involve a series of eight comparisons of pairs of clusters, many of which are theory based, to gain a deeper understanding of the person's WAIS-IV profile of strengths and weaknesses. All of the comparisons in Step 11 require the administration of at least one supplemental subtest. To be able to make all eight comparisons, four supplemental subtests must be administered: Figure Weights, Letter-Number Sequencing, Comprehension, and Picture Completion. Because the first two subtests listed are normed only for ages 16 to 69, Step 11 is intended only for that age range.

Step 12 has been added to our interpretive system, as noted in the introduction to this chapter, to let examiners make all eight comparisons for adults ages 70 to 90. However, five of the eight comparisons in Steps 11 and 12 require the administration of either Comprehension or Picture Completion, supplemental subtests that are normed for the entire WAIS-IV age range. If examiners administered at least one of these subtests to a given person, then the clinical cluster comparisons are probably worth conducting. If not, then the interpretive system should end with Step 10.

Examiners will choose *either* Step 11 *or* Step 12 for any given individual. Both Steps 11 and 12 make the same eight comparisons, but some of the clusters are made up of slightly different subtests. As is true for the new five-factor interpretive option, Step 12 *provides a backup series of cluster comparisons for adolescents and adults below age 70 who were not administered Figure Weights and Letter-Number Sequencing.* Similar to the two five-factor systems, Step 12 makes the same eight pair-wise comparisons of clusters as Step 11 (e.g., Visual-Motor Speed vs. Mental Manipulation), but most clusters differ in the subtests they comprise.

The supplemental Cancellation subtest is excluded from our interpretive system, although it may provide useful clinical information to examiners who opt to administer it.

DON'T FORGET

To make full use of our step-by-step interpretive system, we recommend that examiners routinely administer these supplemental subtests:

- Ages 16–69: Figure Weights, Letter-Number Sequencing, Comprehension, and Picture Completion
- Ages 70–90: Comprehension and Picture Completion

If it is not feasible to administer all four supplemental subtests, examiners who test individuals ages 16 to 69 should try to administer Figure Weights and Letter-Number Sequencing whenever possible, because these subtests were specifically designed to assess fluid reasoning and working memory, respectively, and are exceptionally good measures of their intended constructs. Examiners who routinely give these two supplements: (a) are able to interpret Keith's five-factor interpretation of the WAIS-IV, which we consider to be the primary and preferred approach, and (b) are able to use Step 11 (instead of Step 12) of our system, which utilizes the richest measures of fluid reasoning and working memory, two of the key theoretical constructs from cognitive neuroscience research that were used by the test publisher's scientists to develop the WAIS-IV. Examiners who want to follow up our step-by-step interpretive system with the neuropsychological analysis of subtests detailed in Chapter 6 should also make a special effort to administer Picture Completion because of its unique contributions to neuropsychological analysis of the WAIS-IV, as Dr. George McCloskey and colleagues explain in that chapter.

STEPS 1–3: ANALYZE THE FSIQ AND THE INDEX PROFILE

Step 1: Report the Person's WAIS-IV Standard Scores (FSIQ and Indexes) and Subtest Scaled Scores

For Step 1, create a table of the person's standard scores (FSIQ and four Wechsler indexes), as well as the person's scaled scores on all subtests administered. Report the name of each index and subtest along with the person's obtained score on each one. For the FSIQ and indexes *only*, report the confidence interval, percentile rank, and descriptive category associated with the person's obtained standard scores. For subtests, report the percentile associated with the person's obtained scaled scores (see Rapid Reference 5.1). Examiners need to select whether to use the 90% or 95% confidence interval for standard scores, namely the FSIQ and the four indexes. Examiners should always report standard scores with their associated confidence intervals. (Although most of the information obtained in Step 1 is found on the cover of the WAIS-IV Record Form, examiners may choose to create a similar table for inclusion in a psychological report.)

Traditional descriptive category systems consider Average functioning to be 90–109 and include other categories, such as Low Average (80–89) and Superior (120–129). A traditional category system is included in the *WAIS-IV Technical and Interpretive Manual* (Psychological Corporation, 2008, Table 6.3), and those descriptive labels appear frequently in case reports (see, e.g., Lichtenberger, Mather, Kaufman, & Kaufman, 2004). However, we suggest using an alternative category approach

≣ Rapid Reference 5.1

National Percentile Ranks Corresponding to Scaled Scores

Percentile Rank	Scaled Score	Corresponding IQ
99.9	19	145
99.6	18	140
99	17	135
98	16	130
95	15	125
91	14	120
84	13	115
75	12	110
63	11	105
50	10	100
37	9	95
25	8	90
16	7	85
9	6	80
5	5	75
2	4	70
1	3	65
0.4	2	60
0.1	1	55

known as the Normative Descriptive System (shown in Rapid Reference 5.2) that is based on the distance, in standard deviation (SD) units, from the mean. The Average Range in the Normative system is 85 to 115, which corresponds to 100 ±1 SD. Although either system may be used to classify a person's overall intellectual functioning on the WAIS-IV, Flanagan and Kaufman (2009) recommend the Normative Descriptive System, a general approach that "is commonly used by neuropsychologists and is becoming more widespread among clinical and school psychologists" (p. 137). Figure 5.1 shows an example of Step 1 using Laura's profile.

Step 2: Determine the Best Way to Summarize Overall Intellectual Ability

Two composites are available for the WAIS-IV—the traditional FSIQ and the General Ability Index (GAI)—composed only of the subtests that constitute the

≡ *Rapid Reference 5.2* ★

Alternative "Normative" Descriptive System for WAIS- IV

Standard Score Range	WAIS-IV Descriptive Classification	Alternative Description of Performance
140+ 139 135 131 130	Very Superior 130+	Upper Extreme/ Normative Strength 131+
129 125 120	Superior 120 to 129	Above Average/ Normative Strength 116 to 130
119 116 115 111 110	High Average 110 to 119	
109 105 100 99 95 90	Average 90 to 109	Average Range/ Normal Limits 85 to 115
89 85 84 80	Low Average 80 to 89	
79 75 70	Borderline 70 to 79	Below Average/ Normative Weakness 70 to 84
≤ 69	Extremely Low ≤ 69	Lower Extreme/ Normative Weakness ≤ 69

VCI and PRI (Psychological Corporation, 2008). The GAI, which excludes subtests associated with a person's working memory and processing speed, has also been used as an alternate measure of global intelligence for the WISC-III (Prifitera, Weiss, & Saklofske, 1998), WISC-IV (Flanagan & Kaufman, 2004, 2009;

Index/IQ Subtest	Score	Conf. Interval	Percentile Rank	Descriptive Category	Is Index/IQ/Cluster Interpretable?
Verbal Comprehension	96	91-101	39	Average/Within Normal Limits	Yes
Similarities	9		37		
Vocabulary	11		63		
Information	8		25		
(Comprehension)	10		50	Does not contribute to Index or IQ	
Perceptual Reasoning	79	74-84	8	Below Average/Normative Weakness	Yes
Block Design	5		5		
Matrix Reasoning	7		16		
Visual Puzzles	7		16		
(Figure Weights)*	4		2	Does not contribute to Index or IQ	
(Picture Completion)	6		9	Does not contribute to Index or IQ	
Working Memory	95	90-100	37	Average/Within Normal Limits	Yes
Digit Span	11		63		
Arithmetic	7		16		
(Letter-Number Sequencing)*	4		2	Does not contribute to Index or IQ	
Digit Span Backward	10		50	Does not contribute to Index or IQ	
Digit Span Sequencing	11		63	Does not contribute to Index or IQ	
Processing Speed	97	92-102	42	Average/Within Normal Limits	Yes
Symbol Search	10		50		
Coding	9		37		
(Cancellation)*	9		37	Does not contribute to Index or IQ	
Full Scale IQ	83	78-88	13	Below Average/Normative Weakness	Yes
GAI	86	82-93	18	Average/Within Normal Limits	Yes
CPI	96	90-102	39	Average/Within Normal Limits	Yes
Keith Factor	(roll cursor over the red triangle to see which subtests comprise each cluster)				
Crystallized Intelligence (Gc)	97	92-102	42	Average/Within Normal Limits	Yes
Short-Term Memory (Gsm)	86	81-93	18	Average/Within Normal Limits	No
Fluid Reasoning (Gf)	75	71-83	5	Below Average/Normative Weakness	Yes
Visual Processing (Gv)	78	73-86	7	Below Average/Normative Weakness	Yes
Processing Speed (Gs)	97	90-104	42	Average/Within Normal Limits	Yes

Figure 5.1. Illustration of Step 1 Using Laura's WAIS-IV Profile with the WAIS-IV Data Management and Interpretive Assistant (DMIA)

Prifitera, Saklofske, Weiss, & Rolfhus, 2005), and WAIS-III (Kaufman & Lichtenberger, 2006). The three VCI and three PRI subtests that compose the WAIS-IV GAI are usually the best measures of *g*, whereas the Working Memory and Processing Speed subtests are often among the worst measures (Tulsky, Saklofske, Wilkins, & Weiss, 2001). Because the GAI is composed of strong measures of general ability, it is especially useful for estimating general ability for individuals whose scores on memory and speed subtests deviate significantly from their scores on measures of verbal and nonverbal tasks (Psychological Corporation, 2008).

Steps 2a and 2b, described next, help determine whether the FSIQ or GAI provides the best measure of a person's global intellectual ability (or whether neither global score should be used).

Step 2a. Consider the person's four WAIS-IV Indexes. Subtract the lowest index from the highest index. Answer this question: *Is the size of the standard score difference less than 1.5 SDs (<23 points)?*

- If YES, then the FSIQ may be interpreted as a reliable and valid estimate of a person's global intellectual ability. Proceed directly to Step 3.
- If NO, then the variation in the indexes that compose the FSIQ is considered too great (i.e., ≥23 points) for the purpose of summarizing global intellectual ability in a single score (i.e., the FSIQ). Proceed to Step 2b.

Step 2b. When the FSIQ is not interpretable, determine whether the General Ability Index (GAI) may be used to describe overall intellectual ability. Answer this question: *Is the size of the standard score difference between the VCI and PRI less than 1.5 SDs (<23 points)?*

- If YES, then the GAI may be calculated and interpreted as a reliable and valid estimate of a person's general intellectual ability. To calculate the GAI and obtain its 90% or 95% confidence intervals, simply sum the scaled scores on the six subtests that compose the GAI (Similarities, Vocabulary, Information, Block Design, Matrix Reasoning, and Visual Puzzles) and enter this sum into the appropriate table (see Appendix C of the *WAIS-IV Technical and Interpretive Manual*). After calculating GAI, proceed to Step 3.
- If NO, then the variation in the indexes that compose the GAI is considered too great (i.e., ≥23 points) for the purpose of summarizing global ability in a single score (i.e., GAI). Therefore, neither FSIQ nor GAI is appropriate, suggesting that the person's global ability cannot be meaningfully conveyed as a single score. Proceed to Step 3.

As we explained in our interpretive system for the WAIS-III (Kaufman & Lichtenberger, 2006, Appendix A), the FSIQ, as originally conceptualized by Wechsler, should be the global score of choice, *unless it includes so much variability that it cannot be meaningfully interpreted.* In that instance, it is sensible to substitute the GAI for the FSIQ. But, again, we believe that the GAI should be interpreted as an estimate of a person's overall cognitive ability only if it does not contain too much variability. We therefore recommend that the GAI be interpreted only when two conditions are met: (a) there is too much variability among the four indexes to permit meaningful interpretation of FSIQ; *and* (b) standard scores on the two scales that compose GAI (VCI and PRI) differ by less than 1.5 SDs, indicating that GAI provides a meaningful summary of the person's global ability. Rapid References 5.3, 5.4, and 5.5 provide examples of how to describe the FSIQ and the GAI in a written report. Figure 5.2 shows an example of Step 2 using Laura's profile.

STEP 2. The Best Way to Summarize Overall Intellectual Ability is Determined

Step 2a. To determine whether the FS-IQ is interpretable, the lowest index is subtracted from the highest index.

$$\frac{97}{\text{Highest}} - \frac{79}{\text{Lowest}} = \frac{18}{\text{Difference}}$$

Index Standard
Scores:

Is the size of the difference less than 1.5 standard deviations (i.e., < 23 points)?
YES, FS-IQ may be interpreted as a reliable and valid estimate of a person's overall intellectual ability.

Step 2b. To determine whether the General Ability Index (GAI) may be used to summarize overall intellectual ability, the absolute difference between the VCI and PRI is calculated.

$$\frac{96}{\text{VCI}} - \frac{79}{\text{PRI}} = \frac{17}{\text{Absolute Difference}}$$

Index Standard
Scores:

Is the size of the difference less than 1.5 standard deviations (i.e., < 23 points)?
YES, GAI may be interpreted as a reliable and valid estimate of a person's overall intellectual ability.

Core VCI and PRI subtest scaled scores are summed, and the GAI that corresponds to this sum is located.

Scaled Scores:	9	+	11	+	8	+	5	+	7	+	7	=	47	=	**86**
	SI		VC		IN		BD		MR		VP		Sum		**GAI**

Figure 5.2. Illustration of Step 2 Using Laura's Profile With the WAIS-IV DMIA

There is, however, one exception to the guidelines for Step 2: Always interpret a person's overall score on the WAIS-IV—even if there is too much variability in *both* FSIQ and GAI—whenever a global score is essential for diagnosis (e.g., of intellectual disability) or placement (e.g., in a gifted program). The Caution Box preceding Step 3 reminds examiners about this particular instance.

≡ Rapid Reference 5.3

....

Example of How to Describe an Interpretable FSIQ in a Psychological Report

An interpretable FSIQ means that the size of the difference between the highest and lowest indexes does not equal or exceed 1.5 SDs (23 points). In the case of Laura, the difference between her highest index (97 on the PSI) and her lowest index (79 on the PRI) equals 18 points. This value is less than 23 points, so her FSIQ is interpretable.

Laura earned an FSIQ of 89, classifying her overall intellectual ability, as measured by the WAIS-IV, as Average Range/Within Normal Limits. The chances are good (95%) that Laura's true FSIQ is somewhere within the range of 85 to 93. Her FSIQ is ranked at the 23rd percentile, indicating that she scored higher than 23% of other individuals the same age in the standardization sample.

≡ Rapid Reference 5.4

Example of How to Describe the GAI in a Psychological Report

Miguel's WAIS-IV Full Scale IQ (FSIQ) could not be interpreted because he demonstrated too much variability in his performance across the four indexes that make up this score: the Verbal Comprehension, Perceptual Reasoning, Working Memory, and Processing Speed Indexes. However, because Miguel's performance on the Verbal Comprehension (98) and Perceptual Reasoning (90) Indexes was similar, these indexes can be combined to yield a General Ability Index (GAI). The GAI differs from the FSIQ in that it is not influenced directly by Miguel's performance on working memory and processing-speed tasks.

Miguel earned a GAI of 93, classifying his general level of intellectual ability as Average Range/Within Normal Limits. The chances are good (95%) that Miguel's true GAI is somewhere within the range of 87 to 99. His GAI is ranked at the 33rd percentile, indicating that he scored higher than 33% of other individuals of the same age in the standardization sample.

≡ Rapid Reference 5.5

Example of How to Describe in a Psychological Report the Finding of Both a Noninterpretable FSIQ and a Noninterpretable GAI

A noninterpretable FSIQ means that the size of the difference between the highest and lowest indexes equals or exceeds 1.5 SDs (23 points). A noninterpretable GAI means that the size of the difference between the VCI and PRI equals or exceeds 1.5 SDs (23 points). In the case of Susan, the difference between her highest index (98 on the VCI) and her lowest index (70 on the PSI) equals 28 points. This value is more than 23 points, so her FSIQ is noninterpretable. In addition, the difference of 25 points between Susan's VCI (98) and PRI (73) equals or exceeds 1.5 SDs (23 points). Consequently, her GAI is also noninterpretable.

Susan earned a Full Scale IQ (FSIQ) of 76, but this estimate of her overall intellectual ability cannot be interpreted meaningfully because she displayed too much variability in the four indexes that compose this full-scale score. Therefore, Susan's intelligence is best understood by her performance on the separate WAIS-IV indexes—namely, Verbal Comprehension, Perceptual Reasoning, Working Memory, and Processing Speed.

CAUTION

....

Exception to the Rule Regarding Interpretation of FSIQ and GAI

Always interpret a person's overall score on the WAIS-IV whenever a global score is essential for diagnosis (e.g., of intellectual disability) or placement (e.g., in a gifted program). Even if both the FSIQ and GAI are noninterpretable based on our empirical criteria, select the one that provides the most sensible overview of the examinee's intelligence for use in the diagnostic or placement process. Use clinical judgment to make this decision. For example, if the examinee was impulsive or distractible when administered the working memory and/or the processing speed subtests, then select the GAI (which excludes the WMI and PSI).

Step 3: Determine Whether the Difference Between the Person's GAI and Cognitive Proficiency Index Is Unusually Large

When the two Working Memory core subtests are combined with the two Processing Speed core subtests, a special index standard score may be computed and interpreted: the Cognitive Proficiency Index (CPI) (Dumont & Willis, 2001; Weiss, Saklofske, Schwartz, Prifitera, & Courville, 2006). The CPI, a term coined by Dr. Larry Weiss, reflects the person's proficiency for processing certain types of information. As Weiss and colleagues (2006) indicate, "Proficient processing, through quick visual speed and good mental control, facilitates fluid reasoning and the acquisition of new material by reducing the cognitive demands of novel tasks" (p. 170). Although the computation of the CPI is supported from a psychometric perspective, it has been questioned from a neuropsychological basis (Hebben, 2009).

This step uses sound psychometric procedures to compare the CPI and GAI. (See Table 5.1 for the reliability coefficients of these indexes.) The result of the comparison has practical and clinical benefits, especially for individuals with learning disabilities, traumatic brain injuries, and Asperger's disorder (Weiss et al., 2006); however, deficits in specific neurological substrates should not be inferred even when the person's GAI is unusually larger than his or her CPI.

As detailed in Step 2b, the GAI (composed of the core VCI and PRI subtests) sometimes serves as the best estimate of a person's global ability when the FSIQ is not interpretable. The CPI–GAI comparison is an especially useful interpretive step for those individuals whose global ability is best represented

Table 5.1. Internal Consistency Reliability Coefficients of WAIS-IV GAI and CPI by Age and Overall Sample

Age Group	GAI *SI+VC+IN+BD+MR+VP*	CPI *DS+AR+CD+SS*
6–17	.96	.93
18–19	.97	.94
20–24	.97	.94
25–29	.97	.94
30–34	.97	.93
35–44	.97	.94
45–54	.98	.94
55–64	.97	.94
65–69	.98	.95
70–74	.97	.95
75–79	.97	.95
80–84	.97	.95
85–90	.97	.95
All	.97	.94

Note: The subtest abbreviations underneath the GAI and CPI represent the subtests that comprise each index.

Source: Standardization data and analysis results from the Wechsler Adult Intelligence Scale—Fourth Edition (WAIS-IV). Copyright © 2008 by NCS Pearson, Inc. Used with permission. All rights reserved.

by GAI (based on Step 2a and 2b computations). However, examiners may compare the CPI and GAI (even when FSIQ is interpretable) so long as both the GAI and CPI are found to be interpretable.

Step 3a. Before conducting the GAI–CPI comparison, you must first determine whether the two indexes represent unitary abilities or processes.

For the GAI, answer this question: *Is the size of the difference between VCI and PRI less than 1.5 SDs (i.e., <23 points)?* (If this question has already been answered in Step 2b, use that result for Step 3a.)

- If YES, then the GAI can be calculated and interpreted as a reliable and valid estimate of the person's overall intellectual ability. Proceed

Table 5.2. Differences Between GAI and CPI Required for Statistical Significance (at p < .05 and p < .01) and to Be Considered Uncommon

	Difference Required for Significance		Difference Required for an Unusually Large or Uncommon Discrepancy			
	$p < .05$	$p < .01$	10% Base Rate	5% Base Rate	2% Base Rate	1% Base Rate
Difference between GAI & CPI	8.8	11.6	19	23	27	30

Source: Standardization data and analysis results from the Wechsler Adult Intelligence Scale—Fourth Edition (WAIS-IV). Copyright © 2008 by NCS Pearson, Inc. Used with permission. All rights reserved.

Note: "Unusually large or uncommon" denotes differences estimated to occur infrequently in the WAIS-IV standardization sample. We suggest using 10% of the normative population to denote uncommonly large discrepancies, but values are also shown for the 5%, 2%, and 1% levels for examiners who prefer a more stringent criterion. The uncommon differences in this table were estimated by the formula provided by Sattler (1982, Table C-11) for computing the percentage of a population obtaining discrepancies between two standard scores. This formula includes the correlation between GAI and CPI, which was kindly provided by Pearson Assessments (J. J. Wang, personal communication, March 23, 2009). The correlation used in the formula was the value for the total sample, ages 16–90 years.

to the next part of this step to determine whether the CPI can be interpreted.

• If NO, then the GAI–CPI comparison cannot be made.

For the CPI, answer this question: *Is the size of the difference between WMI and PSI less than 1.5 SDs (i.e., <23 points)?*

• If YES, then the CPI and GAI can both be calculated and interpreted as reliable and valid estimates of the person's functioning. Proceed to Step 3b.
• If NO, then the GAI–CPI comparison cannot be made.

Step 3b. Calculate the GAI and CPI. (If the GAI has already been calculated in Step 2b, use that value for Step 3 and calculate CPI.)

To compute GAI: (a) sum the person's scaled scores on the three core VCI and three core PRI subtests, and (b) enter this sum into Appendix C of the *WAIS-IV Technical and Interpretive Manual* to determine the GAI, percentile rank, and confidence interval (select either 90% or 95% confidence).

To compute CPI: (a) sum the person's scaled scores on the two core WMI and two core PSI subtests, and (b) enter this sum into Appendix A.2 (see the CD-ROM in this book) to determine the person's CPI, percentile rank, and confidence interval (select either 90% or 95% confidence).

Figure 5.3. Illustration of Step 3 Using Laura's Profile With the WAIS-IV DMIA

Step 3c. Determine whether the size of the difference between the GAI and CPI (regardless of direction) is significant. The difference needed for significance at the p < .05 level is 8.8 points, and the difference needed for significance at the p < .01 level is 11.6 points.

Step 3d. Determine whether the size of the difference between the GAI and CPI (regardless of direction) is unusually large or uncommon, occurring less than 10% of the time in the WAIS-IV standardization sample. If the difference is 19 points or more, it should be considered uncommonly large. Table 5.2 reviews the values necessary for GAI versus CPI differences to be considered significantly large and uncommonly large. Examiners who prefer a more stringent criterion than 10% for determining uncommonly large differences can select the 5%, 2%, or 1% levels, as reported in Table 5.2. Figure 5.3 shows an example of Step 3 using Laura's profile.

INTRODUCTION TO STEPS 4–10: TWO PATHS OF INTERPRETATION

In the next seven steps, examiners may choose to evaluate the WAIS-IV in one of three ways:

A. *(Ages 16–90)* Interpret the four indexes that the WAIS-IV yields (i.e., Wechsler four-index model).

B. *(Ages 16–69 Only)* Interpret the five-factor model of the WAIS-IV that requires the administration of the supplemental Figure Weights and Letter-Number Sequencing subtests. This model is referred to as the *Keith five-factor model.*

C. *(Ages 16–90)* Interpret a five-factor model of the WAIS-IV that is based only on the 10 core subtests. This model is referred to as the *Core five-factor model.*

The confirmatory factor-analytic data in the *WAIS-IV Technical and Interpretive Manual* support the validity of the four WAIS-IV indexes (i.e., VCI, PRI, WMI, and PSI), as does research reported in the literature (Benson, Hulac, & Kranzler, 2010; Canivez & Watkins, 2010a, 2010b; Ward, Bergman, & Hebert, 2012). However, WAIS-IV confirmatory factor analyses (CFAs) reported in Chapter 1 of this book also support the validity of the two five-factor models mentioned previously: the Keith five-factor model (Benson et al., 2010; T. Keith, personal communication, January 30, 2009; Ward et al., 2012) and the Core five-factor model (Niileksela et al., 2012). These CHC-based models support separate Fluid Reasoning and Visual Processing Factors, which makes the five-factor models especially good choices when there is variability in the person's scaled scores on the core and supplemental subtests associated with the PRI. The five-factor models that we have assembled for interpretation include the clusters shown as follows (supplemental subtests, for ages 16–69, are in italics):

Factor Name	Keith Five-Factor Model Subtests (ages 16–69 only)	Core Five-Factor Model Subtests (all ages 16–90)
Crystallized Intelligence (Gc)	Vocabulary + Information	Vocabulary + Information
Short-Term Memory (Gsm)	Digit Span + *Letter-Number Sequencing*	Digit Span Backward + Digit Span Sequencing
Fluid Reasoning (Gf)	Matrix Reasoning + *Figure Weights*	Matrix Reasoning + Arithmetic
Visual Processing (Gv)	Block Design + Visual Puzzles	Block Design + Visual Puzzles
Processing Speed (Gs)	Symbol Search + Coding	Symbol Search + Coding

We decided in advance to limit each factor to two subtests such that both the four-index Wechsler model and our alternate five-factor models are composed of 10 subtests. The *Gc*, *Gv*, and *Gs* factors are identical for both models. The *Gf* factor includes Matrix Reasoning in both models, but *Arithmetic* replaces Figure Weights in the Core five-factor model. Digit Span and Letter-Number Sequencing compose the *Gsm* factor in the Keith model; in the Core model *Gsm* is represented by Digits Sequencing and Digits Backward because of their strong loadings in the CFAs conducted by Niileksela et al. (2012).

Rapid Reference 5.6 explains how we determined which two subtests would represent each of the five Keith and Core factors. The internal consistency reliability coefficients for all factors in both models are shown in Table 5.3.

Note that although the names of the five Keith and Core factors reflect terminology consistent with CHC theory, there are alternate ways to interpret the two five-factor models in addition to CHC theory. For example, these five

≡ *Rapid Reference 5.6*

Development of the Five Two-Subtest Factors for the Keith and Core Models

In Chapter 1, Figure 1.2 displays the results of the Keith five-factor CFA for all ages, and Figure 1.3 shows the Core five-factor CFA for ages 70–90. The Core CFA for all ages is virtually identical to the data shown in Figure 1.3 (Niileksala et al., 2012), but we chose to focus on the elderly sample in that figure because they are the ones who were excluded from the Keith model that we featured in the first edition of this book. In both CHC solutions, the same five constructs resulted, with two to four subtests loading on each factor. We examined the subtest loadings, and considered each subtest both from a clinical and a CHC theoretical perspective to determine the best combination of subtests to compose each factor.

- In the Keith CFA, the *Gc* factor was defined by four subtests: Similarities (.83), Vocabulary (.89), Comprehension (.84), and Information (.80). We chose the combination of Vocabulary and Information to represent the *Gc* factor because, theoretically, they are exemplars of the *Gc* construct, are excellent measures of a person's knowledge base, and are less influenced by fluid reasoning than are Similarities and Comprehension. For simplicity, we opted to keep the same pair of subtests for the Core model. In any case, Comprehension, despite its .83 loading (Figure 1.3), was not an option because it is supplemental.

(continued)

- Three subtests—Picture Completion (.64), Block Design (.76), and Visual Puzzles (.73)—defined the Gv factor in the Keith model. We chose Visual Puzzles and Block Design to represent the Gv factor because of their strong factor loadings and their strong representation of the Gv construct. In addition, Picture Completion is a supplemental rather than a core subtest, and its items often elicit verbal (rather than nonverbal) responses. We kept the same dyad for the Core model.

- Matrix Reasoning (.72), Figure Weights (.77), and Arithmetic (.77) comprised the Gf factor in the Keith CFA. We chose Matrix Reasoning and Figure Weights to represent the Gf construct in the Keith model because of their strong factor loadings and strong representation of the Gf construct. Although Arithmetic also has a strong Gf factor loading, it has been shown to be influenced by other cognitive and behavioral variables, such as short-term memory, crystallized knowledge, distractibility, and anxiety. Nonetheless, Arithmetic proved to be an excellent measure of Gf in both the Keith and Core CFA, and was paired with Matrix Reasoning in the Core five-factor model to enable Gf to be measured in the elderly population. (Arithmetic and Matrix Reasoning loaded .73–.74 on Gf at ages 70–90.) Note that the Gf factors in both models correlated about 1.0 with general intelligence or g.

- The choice of subtests for the Gsm factor in the Keith model was easy, because it was defined by only two subtests—Digit Span (.85) and Letter-Number Sequencing (.81). For the Core model (Figure 1.3), we chose Digits Sequencing (.73) and Digits Backward (.72) because of their strong loadings. Both subtests are excellent measures of working memory (as is Letter-Number Sequencing), whereas Digits Forward (.56) is more a measure of memory span. Although the Gsm factors in both the Keith and Core solutions are assigned the label of Short-Term Memory (a CHC Broad Ability), they are more accurately described by the term Working Memory, a Narrow Ability.

- The Gs factor had two subtests that strongly loaded on it in the Keith solution—Coding (.81) and Symbol Search (.80)—and these two tasks are strong theoretical and clinical representations of the construct. Thus, those two tasks were chosen to represent this factor. Cancellation also loaded on the Gs Factor, but its loading (.56) was not as strong as that of the other two subtests. Because Cancellation is not administered above age 69 and is supplemental, Coding (.90) and Symbol Search (.78) naturally represented Gs in the Core model.

factors can be interpreted from a neuropsychological approach based on Luria's (1973, 1980) theory. This theoretical foundation for interpretation is similar to the bases for NEPSY-II (Korkman, Kirk, & Kemp, 2007), Cognitive Ability System (CAS; Naglieri & Das, 1997), and the KABC-II (Kaufman & Kaufman, 2004). Luria (1970) believed that the brain's basic functions can be represented by three main blocks (or functional systems), which form the framework of Naglieri and Das's (1997) PASS model. These three blocks are responsible for arousal and attention (Block 1); the use of one's senses to

Table 5.3. Internal Consistency Reliability Coefficients for the Keith Five Factors and the Core Five Factors, by Age and for Total Sample

	FACTOR						
Age Group	Keith & Core Crystallized Knowledge (Gc) VC + IN	Keith Short-Term Memory (Gsm) LN + DS	Core Short-Term Memory (Gsm) DBack + DSeq	Keith Fluid Reasoning (Gf) MR + FW	Core Fluid Reasoning (Gf) MR + A	Keith & Core Visual Processing (Gv) BD + VP	Keith & Core Processing Speed (Gs) CD + SS
16–17	.95	.94	.84	.93	.92	.93	.88
18–19	.95	.94	.86	.93	.91	.93	.90
20–24	.96	.93	.87	.92	.90	.92	.90
25–29	.95	.95	.89	.94	.93	.94	.90
30–34	.95	.96	.88	.95	.94	.94	.87
35–44	.96	.94	.90	.93	.93	.93	.87
45–54	.97	.95	.89	.94	.94	.95	.87
55–64	.97	.94	.87	.93	.93	.93	.91
65–69	.97	.94	.87	.94	.94	.94	.91
70–74	.97	—	.88	—	.92	.93	.91
75–79	.97	—	.89	—	.95	.91	.92
80–84	.97	—	.87	—	.92	.88	.92
85–90	.98	—	.91	—	.92	.89	.92
All	.96	.94	.88	.93	.93	.93	.90

Source: Standardization data and analysis results from the *Wechsler Adult Intelligence Scale—Fourth Edition* (WAIS-IV). Copyright © 2008 by NCS Pearson, Inc. Used with permission. All rights reserved.

Note: The subtest abbreviations underneath the factors represent the subtests that comprise each factor. The Processing Speed Factor (Gs) is identical to the WAIS-IV Processing Speed Index (PSI). Gc = Crystallized Knowledge; Gsm = Short-Term Memory; Gf = Fluid Reasoning; Gv = Visual Processing; and Gs = Processing Speed.

analyze, code, and store information (Block 2); and the application of executive functions for formulating plans and programming behavior (Block 3). Using Lurian theory, cognitive functions are viewed as complex capacities with interactive subcomponents that contribute to performance within and across functional domains. As Kemp, Kirk, and Korkman (2001) summarize:

> Cognitive functions, such as attention and executive functions, language, sensory perception, motor function, visuospatial abilities, and learning and memory are complex capacities in the Lurian tradition. They are composed of flexible and interactive subcomponents that are mediated by equally flexible, interactive, neural networks. (p. 6)

Rapid Reference 5.7 demonstrates how the Keith and Core five factors may be interpreted from either a CHC or Lurian-based neurological perspective, depending on one's personal theoretical focus. The Lurian complex capacities provide a theoretical explanation of the five-factor solutions that is no less defensible than CHC theory: Attention and Executive Functions (Gf), Language (Gc), Sensorimotor (Gs), Visuospatial Functions (Gv), and Memory and Learning (Gsm).

≡ *Rapid Reference 5.7*

Suggested Interpretation of the Keith and Core Five-Factor Models From CHC and Lurian-Based Neurological Perspectives

Lurian Neuropsychological Perspective	CHC Perspective
Short-Term Memory (Gsm) Factor	
Performing the complex capacities that involve conceptualizing, categorizing, and making associations (Memory and Learning). On the WAIS-IV, these capacities closely resemble Luria's Block 2 "successive" or sequential processing, namely arranging input in sequential or serial order to solve a problem, where each idea is linearly and temporally related to the preceding one.	Taking in and holding information, and then using it within a few seconds. The emphasis is on the CHC Narrow Ability of Working Memory, which demands mental manipulation and the ability to actively maintain pertinent information in one's conscious awareness.
Visual Processing (Gv) Factor	
Performing the complex capacities of integrating visuospatial and motor skills and using nonmotor visuospatial processing	Perceiving, storing, manipulating, and thinking with visual patterns

Lurian Neuropsychological Perspective	CHC Perspective

(Visuospatial Abilities). These capacities closely resemble Luria's Block 2 "simultaneous" processing, in which stimuli must be integrated and synthesized in holistic fashion to solve a complex visual-spatial problem.

Fluid Reasoning (Gf) Factor

Performing the high-level, decision-making, executive processes often associated with Block 3, where the emphasis is on the use of flexible strategies and planning, especially the ability to adopt and shift cognitive sets, monitor behavior, and maintain impulse control (Attention and Executive Functions). However, as Reitan (1988) states, "Block 3 is involved in no sensory, motor, perceptual, or speech functions and is devoted exclusively to analysis, planning, and organization of programs for behavior" (p. 335). Therefore, integration of the three blocks is especially important to solve these problems efficiently.	Solving novel problems by using abstract thinking abilities, such as inductive, deductive, and quantitative reasoning

Crystallized Ability (Gc) Factor

Performing complex linguistic capacities associated with speech and language that place special demands on both receptive and expressive functions (Language). On the WAIS-IV, the person must demonstrate his or her store of verbal-conceptual and factual knowledge as well as the ability to process the linguistic stimuli.	Demonstrating the breadth and depth of knowledge acquired from one's culture

Processing Speed (Gs) Factor

Performing complex perceptual and motor capacities that involve integrating visual perception and eye-hand coordination, most notably graphomotor precision and speed (Sensorimotor).	Fluently and automatically performing cognitive tasks, especially when under pressure to maintain focused attention and concentration

Note: The subtests that compose each Keith or Core factor can be interpreted in a manner parallel to certain scales and subtests on other tests, such as the NEPSY-II, CAS, and KABC-II. The Gsm Factor subtests are similar conceptually to NEPSY-II Memory and Learning, CAS Successive, and KABC-II Sequential/Gsm. The Gv Factor subtests are similar conceptually to NEPSY-II Visuospatial Abilities, CAS Simultaneous, and KABC-II Simultaneous/Gv. The Gf Factor subtests are similar conceptually to the NEPSY-II Animal Sorting and Clocks subtests in the Attention and Executive Functioning Domain, CAS Planning, and KABC-II Planning/Gf. The Gc Factor subtests are similar conceptually to NEPSY-II Language and KABC-II Knowledge/Gc. The Gs Factor subtests are similar conceptually to NEPSY-II Sensorimotor, except that the WAIS-IV subtests have a clear-cut cognitive component and the NEPSY-II subtests do not.

Examiners who prefer to interpret the four WAIS-IV Wechsler indexes, based on their personal theoretical and clinical orientations, need not use either five-factor system for any of the individuals they test; however, the five-factor approaches will be especially appealing to examiners who favor the CHC theory and enjoy using cross-battery assessment (Flanagan, Alfonso, & Ortiz, 2012; Flanagan, Ortiz, & Alfonso, 2007), as well as those who want to examine the profile from a Lurian neuropsychological perspective. The next steps will assist you in deciding which interpretive model to use. The text walks you through the steps to perform accurate and psychometrically sound interpretation of the data.

Step 4: Selecting the Wechsler Four-Index Model, the Keith Five-Factor Model, or the Core Five-Factor Model

This step is designed to help you decide whether to use the Wechsler four-index model or one of the five-factor models for interpretation. Answering the next three questions will help you select the appropriate model.

When making the decision, keep in mind that you do not have to be an advocate of CHC theory to select the five-factor model. For example, Larry Weiss (personal communication, November 10, 2011), one of the world's leading experts on IQ tests who oversees development and standardization of the Wechsler tests, does not see any conflict between the CHC five-factor approach and the Wechsler four-factor model:

> To me, this is only about pulling a fluid factor out of WAIS-IV—which has been an active research goal for the Wechsler team since 1997 with the addition of Matrix Reasoning (a fluid reasoning task) and carried forward into the 2008 revision with the addition of Figure Weights (another fluid reasoning task) and the item modifications made to force Arithmetic to pull more for working memory and fluid reasoning than numerical skill.

We agree fully with Weiss's notion that the two approaches are complementary and not at odds with each other.

Step 4a. Answer this question: *Considering your personal theoretical and clinical foundations, do you choose to interpret the WAIS-IV data with a five-factor model?*

- If definitely NO, proceed to Step 5 to interpret data with the Wechsler four-index model.
- If definitely YES, continue to Step 4b to choose the appropriate five-factor model.

- If you are *uncertain*, then consider the suggestion of Weiss et. al., (in press). They found empirical support for both four- and five-factor solutions in normal and clinical samples. They suggest beginning interpretation with the four indexes, but to consider switching to five factors if there are discrepant scores within one or more indexes. The most pertinent Indexes to examine are the PRI and WMI. Follow these steps:
  1. Compute the range of the scaled scores that compose the PRI (Block Design, Matrix Reasoning, Visual Puzzles). Subtract the lowest scaled score from the highest one. Is the size of the difference less than 5 points? *If NO, then the PRI includes discrepant scores.*
  2. Compute the difference between the scaled scores that compose the WMI (Digit Span, Arithmetic). Subtract the lower scaled score from the higher one. Is the size of the difference less than 5 points? *If NO, then the WMI includes discrepant scores.*
  3. If you answered YES to both questions, proceed to Step 5 to interpret data with the Wechsler four-index model.
  4. If you answered NO to one or both questions, continue to Step 4b to choose the appropriate five-factor model.

Step 4b. Answer this question: *Is the person you tested between the ages of 16 and 69?*

- If NO, proceed to Step 7 to interpret data with the Core five-factor model.
- If YES, go to Step 4c.

Step 4c. Answer this question: *Did you administer **both** Letter-Number Sequencing and Figure Weights (supplemental subtests)?*

- If NO, proceed to Step 7 to interpret data with the Core five-factor model.
- If YES, go to Step 6 to interpret data with the Keith five-factor model.

Note that even if you do choose to interpret the WAIS-IV profile from the perspective of a five-factor model, you should always report the scores from the four Wechsler indexes in your case report as well. This reporting of information should include the Index standard scores, confidence intervals, and percentile ranks. Professionals and organizations familiar with the Wechsler tests will want to be informed of those four index scores, even if your interpretation is based on a reorganization of the data into a five-factor model. Weiss et al. (2010a) make the following insightful comments about the indexes:

VCI: "The VCI reflects an individual's ability to comprehend verbal stimuli, reason with semantic material, and communicate thoughts and ideas with words. Such abilities are imperative for intelligent functioning in modern society" (p. 63).

PRI: "The construct measured by the PRI has changed from primarily perceptual organization with some fluid reasoning in WAIS-III to primarily fluid reasoning with some perceptual organization in WAIS-IV" (p. 65).

WMI: "The WMI measures attention, concentration, and working memory. . . . Working memory can be thought of as mental control (an executive process) involving reasonably higher-order tasks (rather than rote tasks), and it presumes attention and concentration" (p. 68).

PSI: "The PSI measures the speed of mental processing, using visual stimuli and graphomotor skills, and is importantly related to the efficient use of other cognitive abilities" (p. 72).

For a crisp understanding of the Keith and Core five-factor solutions from the vantage point of CHC theory, consult two recent exceptional state-of-the-art chapters on the theoretical bases and practical applications of the popular model (Flanagan, Alfonso, & Ortiz, 2012; Schneider & McGrew, 2012). The Broad and Narrow Abilities measured by the WAIS-IV are summarized in depth by Flanagan et al. (2012, pp. 470–471) in a table that permits direct comparison to the CHC abilities measured by other major intelligence tests. Schneider and McGrew (2012) provide a series of insightful figures that depict graphically (a) how the CHC Broad Abilities relate to each other conceptually and functionally (p. 135), (b) how the Broad Abilities serve as parameters of an information processing model (p. 136), and (c) how the Narrow Abilities associated with the acquisition of knowledge (e.g., Lexical Knowledge, Language Development, and General Information, all measured by the WAIS-IV) interface with each other (p. 137).

As a final note, it is acceptable to report standard scores for both the Wechsler four indexes and the five factors; however, you need to be mindful that these two sets of scores combine to yield many numbers. Be particularly careful with how you choose to write your report to clarify which scores you are writing about in the test results section. Many of the scores from the two models have similar labels, so it is important to emphasize the most salient aspects of the Wechsler indexes and five factors so that the reader is not overwhelmed with the information that you are presenting or confused by the wealth of data. Although we do not especially advise it, examiners certainly have the option of interpreting *both* the Wechsler index profile (Step 5) and a five-factor profile (Step 6 or 7) to see which result provides the richest source of hypotheses about the person's pattern of strengths and weaknesses. In that instance, it is absolutely essential to be prudent and concise when writing the case report. Sometimes less is more when conveying important highlights of a person's cognitive test profile. Figure 5.4 shows an example of Step 4 using Laura's profile.

DON'T FORGET

Recommendations for Report Writing When Using the Keith or Core Five-Factor Model

- When the Keith or Core five-factor model is used as the basis of your interpretation, always report the scores from the four Wechsler indexes in your case report as well.
- Include the index standard scores, confidence intervals, and percentile ranks.
- It is acceptable to report standard scores for both the Wechsler four indexes and the Core or Keith five factors.
- Be mindful to write with clarity, because many of the scores from the two models have similar labels.
- Emphasize the most salient aspects of the Wechsler indexes and Core or Keith factors to distinguish the differences between the scores.

Step 5: Determine Whether Each of the Four Wechsler Indexes Is Unitary and, Thus, Interpretable

Skip this step if you are interpreting the person's profile via the Keith or Core five-factor approach. Proceed to Step 6 for the Keith five-factor model. Proceed to Step 7 for the Core five-factor model.

When the variability among subtest scaled scores within an index is unusually large, then the standard score does not provide a good estimate of the ability it is intended to measure and, therefore, is not interpretable. In other words, when a substantial difference between the scaled scores composing an index is found, the index cannot be interpreted as representing a unitary ability. The notion of unitary abilities was also a guiding principle in our approach for interpreting other Wechsler scales as well (Flanagan & Kaufman, 2004, 2009; Kaufman, 1994a; Kaufman & Lichtenberger, 2000, 2006; Lichtenberger & Kaufman, 2004). Rapid Reference 5.8 shows an example of how to

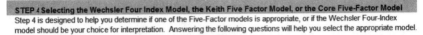

Figure 5.4. Illustration of Step 4 Using Laura's Profile With the WAIS-IV DMIA

interpret a unitary index (or factor) in a psychological report. Rapid Reference 5.9 shows an example of how to interpret a nonunitary index (or factor) in a psychological report. Binder and Binder's (2011) study of subtest variability on the WAIS-IV indicates that individuals whose highest scaled score is large (e.g., 17) will tend to have more subtest "scatter" than those whose best performance was more modest, such as a scaled score of 11. They observed correlations in the low .60s between a person's highest WAIS-IV scaled score and the person's scaled-score range (highest minus lowest scaled score). Therefore, expect a greater number of "uninterpretable" Indexes for people who earned high scores on at least one component subtest. That generalization applies as well when evaluating the unitary nature of the five factors in Steps 6 and 7 or the clinical clusters in Steps 11 and 12.

≡ *Rapid Reference 5.8*

Example of How to Interpret a Unitary Index in a Psychological Report

The Processing Speed Index (PSI), a measure of Processing Speed (Gs), represents Laura's ability to perform simple, clerical-type tasks quickly. Laura's Gs ability was assessed with two tasks: One required her to quickly copy symbols that were paired with numbers according to a key (37th percentile), and the other required her to identify the presence or absence of a target symbol in a row of symbols (50th percentile). The difference between Laura's performances on these two tasks was not unusually large, indicating that her PSI is a good estimate of her processing speed. Laura obtained a PSI of 97 (89–106), which is ranked at the 42nd percentile and is classified as in the Average Range/Within Normal Limits.

≡ *Rapid Reference 5.9*

Example of How to Interpret a Nonunitary Index in a Psychological Report

The Verbal Comprehension Index (VCI), a measure of Crystallized Intelligence (Gc), represents Stephan's ability to reason with previously learned information. Crystallized intelligence develops largely as a function of both formal and informal educational opportunities and experiences and is highly dependent on exposure to mainstream U.S. culture. Stephan's Gc was assessed by tasks that required him to define words (16th percentile), draw conceptual similarities between words (37th percentile), and answer general factual questions (84th percentile). The variability among Stephan's performances on these tasks was unusually large, indicating that his overall Crystallized knowledge or ability to reason with previously learned information cannot be summarized in a single score (i.e., the VCI).

Note: Subsequent steps of interpretation may be used to provide additional information about Stephan's Gc performance.

Step 5a. Determine whether the size of the difference among subtest scaled scores within the VCI (composed of three subtests) is too large. Subtract the lowest subtest scaled score from the highest subtest scaled score. Answer this question: *Is the size of the difference less than 1.5 SDs (<5 points)?*

- If YES, then the ability presumed to underlie the VCI is unitary and may be interpreted. (The Don't Forget box provides the definition of a unitary ability.)
- If NO, then the difference is too large (≥5 points), and the VCI cannot be interpreted as representing a unitary ability.

DON'T FORGET

Definition of a Unitary Ability

A unitary ability is an ability (such as Crystallized Intelligence or Processing Speed) that is represented by a cohesive set of scaled scores, each reflecting slightly different or unique aspects of the ability. Thus, when the variability among the subtest scaled scores that compose a WAIS-IV Index is not unusually large, the ability presumed to underlie the Index is considered unitary and may be interpreted. For example, a person obtaining scaled scores of 9, 5, and 8 on Similarities, Vocabulary, and Information, respectively, has a difference score of 4 associated with the VCI (9 − 5 = 4). A difference of less than 1.5 SDs (i.e., <5 points) between the highest and lowest subtest scaled score is needed for an index to be considered as representing a unitary ability. Therefore, in this example, the VCI represents a unitary ability and may be interpreted as a reliable and valid estimate of verbal reasoning, concept formation, and acquired knowledge, or Crystallized Intelligence (Gc).

Step 5b. Follow the same procedure as in Step 5a to determine the interpretability of the PRI (also composed of three subtests).

Step 5c. Determine whether the size of the difference between the subtest scaled scores that compose the two-subtest WMI is too large. Subtract the lower scaled score from the higher one. Answer this question: *Is the size of the difference less than 1.5 SDs (<5 points)?*

- If YES, then the ability presumed to underlie the WMI is unitary and may be interpreted.
- If NO, then the difference is too large (≥5 points), and the WMI cannot be interpreted as representing a unitary ability.

Step 5d. Follow the same procedure as in Step 5c to determine the interpretability of the PSI (also composed of two subtests).

Although an index is considered uninterpretable when the variability among the subtests that comprise it is too large, in some instances it makes sense to look at the normative classifications of the scaled scores to determine whether a general conclusion may be made about a person's range of observed functioning in the ability presumed to underlie the index (Flanagan & Kaufman, 2004, 2009). Specifically, when all subtest scaled scores within an index are consistently low (≤ 8) or consistently high (≥ 12), that fact should be noted and explained in a report. The Don't Forget box provides information on how to describe a notable integrity in the ability that the index represents. Figure 5.5 shows an example of Step 5 using Laura's profile.

DON'T FORGET

Subtests with Unusual Variability, But All ≥ 12

If the variability among subtest scaled scores composing an index is unusually large, and all scaled scores are 12 or greater, then describe the examinee's range of observed functioning in the ability presumed to underlie the index as a notable integrity in this way:

The Perceptual Reasoning Index (PRI), a measure of Fluid Reasoning and Visual Processing (Gf/Gv), represents Susan's ability to reason using visual stimuli. Susan's fluid reasoning and visual processing abilities were assessed by tasks that required her to recreate a series of modeled or pictured designs using blocks (84th percentile), identify the missing portion of an incomplete visual matrix from one of several response options (98th percentile), and select three puzzle pieces that would combine to recreate a puzzle (99.9th percentile). The variability among Susan's performances on these tasks was unusually large, indicating that her overall fluid reasoning and visual processing ability cannot be summarized in a single score (i.e., the PRI). However, it is clear that Susan's fluid reasoning and visual processing ability is a notable integrity for her because her performance on the tasks that compose the PRI ranged from Average Range/Within Normal Limits to Upper Extreme/Normative Strength.

Step 6: Determine Whether Each of the Five Keith Factors Is Unitary and, Thus, Interpretable (Ages 16–69 Only)

Skip this step if you interpreted the person's profile via the Wechsler four-index approach (Step 5). Proceed to Step 8.

Similar to examining variability within a Wechsler index, when the variability among subtest scaled scores within a Keith factor is unusually large, then the standard score does not provide a good estimate of the ability it is intended to measure and, therefore, is not interpretable. In other words, when a substantial difference between the scaled scores factor is found, the factor cannot be interpreted as representing a unitary ability.

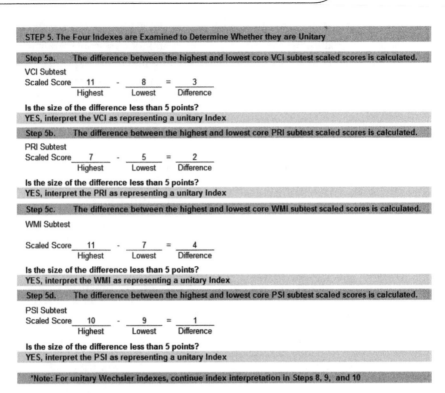

Figure 5.5. Illustration of Step 5 Using Laura's Profile With the WAIS-IV DMIA

Step 6a. Calculate the standard scores for the five Keith factors by summing the scaled scores for the two subtests that comprise each cluster and converting the sum to a standard score using the norms in Appendixes A.3–A.6 on the CD-ROM. (Note that the *Gs* Factor Standard Score is identical to PSI and should be obtained from Table A.6 on page 223 of the *WAIS-IV Administration and Scoring Manual*.)

Step 6b. Determine whether the size of the difference between the subtest scaled scores that compose the Crystallized Intelligence (*Gc*) factor (Vocabulary and Information) is too large. Subtract the lower subtest scaled score from the higher subtest scaled score. Answer this question: *Is the size of the difference less than 1.5 SDs (<5 points)?*

- If YES, then the ability presumed to underlie the *Gc* factor is unitary and may be interpreted.
- If NO, then the difference is too large (≥5 points), and the *Gc* factor cannot be interpreted as representing a unitary ability.

Step 6c. Follow the same procedure as in Step 6a to determine the interpretability of the Short-Term Memory (*Gsm*) factor (comprised of Digit Span and Letter-Number Sequencing).

Step 6d. Follow the same procedure as in Step 6a to determine the interpretability of the Fluid Reasoning (*Gf*) factor (comprised of Matrix Reasoning and Figure Weights).

Step 6e. Follow the same procedure as in Step 6a to determine the interpretability of the Visual Processing (*Gv*) factor (comprised of Block Design and Visual Puzzles).

Step 6f. Follow the same procedure as in Step 6a to determine the interpretability of the Processing Speed (*Gs*) factor (comprised of Symbol Search and Coding).

Step 6g. Determine how many of the Keith five factors are interpretable

DON'T FORGET

What Do I Do With a Noninterpretable Index or Factor?

When an index is found to be noninterpretable, the variability among the subtest scaled scores composing the index is too large to allow for the interpretation of a single ability. For example, when the variability among the VCI subtest scaled scores is unusually large, the VCI cannot be interpreted as representing the ability of Crystallized Intelligence (Gc). However, the subtests composing the noninterpretable index may be combined with other subtests in different ways to allow for meaningful interpretations of more specific abilities at later steps in the interpretive process (e.g., Step 8).

CAUTION

Three or More Keith or Core Factors Needed for Interpretation

Number of Interpretable Factors	Recommendation
5	Proceed with interpretation of Keith or Core five-factor model
4	Proceed with interpretation of Keith or Core five-factor model
3	Proceed with interpretation of Keith or Core five-factor model
2	Stop interpretation of five-factor model, and instead interpret Wechsler four-index model
1	Stop interpretation of five-factor model, and instead interpret Wechsler four-index model
0	Stop interpretation of five-factor model, and instead interpret Wechsler four-index model

by reviewing the results of Steps 6b–6f. If three or more of the factors are interpretable, proceed with your interpretation of the WAIS-IV data using the Keith five-factor model. However, if only one or two of Keith's five factors are interpretable, we strongly recommend using the Wechsler four-index model to interpret the WAIS-IV data. Thus, if only one or two of Keith's five factors are interpretable (i.e., three or more Keith factors are not unitary and cannot be meaningfully interpreted), go back to Step 5 and complete interpretation of the Wechsler four-index model. (However, remember that we do recommend always listing the four Wechsler index scores in your written report, even when you do interpret the profile from the perspective of a five-factor model.)

Similar to what we suggested with uninterpretable indexes, in some instances of an uninterpretable factor, it makes sense to look at the normative classifications of the subtest scaled scores to determine whether a general conclusion may be made about a person's range of observed functioning in the ability presumed to underlie the factor. Specifically, when all subtest scaled scores within a factor are consistently low ($\leq$8) or consistently high ($\geq$12), that fact should be noted and explained in a report. The Don't Forget box provides information on how to describe a notable limitation in the ability that the factor represents. Figure 5.6 shows an example of Step 6 using Laura's profile.

DON'T FORGET

Subtests With Unusual Variability, But All $\leq$8

If the variability among subtest scaled scores composing a factor is unusually large and all scaled scores are 8 or greater, then describe the examinee's range of observed functioning in the ability presumed to underlie the factor as a notable limitation:

The Short-Term Memory (Gsm) factor, a measure of the working memory aspect of short-term memory, represents Amy's ability to apprehend and hold information in immediate awareness, manipulate the information, and produce a result. Amy's working memory was assessed by tasks that required her to repeat numbers verbatim, to repeat numbers in reverse order, or to sequence numbers (9th percentile); and to listen to a sequence of numbers and letters and repeat the numbers in ascending order, followed by the letters in alphabetical order (0.1st percentile). The variability among Amy's performances on these tasks was unusually large, indicating that her overall short-term memory ability cannot be summarized in a single score. However, Amy's working memory ability is a notable limitation for her because her performance on the tasks that compose the Short-Term Memory Factor ranged from Below Average/Normative Weakness to Lower Extreme/Normative Weakness.

STEP 6.	The Five Keith Factors are Examined to Determine Whether they are Unitary								

Step 6a.　　　Calculate the standard scores for the five Keith Factors
Step 6b-f.　　Determine if the size of the difference between subtest scores is less than 1.5 SDs (< 5 points)

Keith Factor	Scaled Score 1		Scaled Score 2		Sum of Scaled Scores	Factor Standard Score	Absolute Difference between Scores 1 & 2	Is the difference < 5 points?	
Gc	VC	11	+ IN	8	= 19	97	3	Yes	The ability presumed to underlie the Factor is unitary & may be interpreted.
Gsm	DS	11	+ LN	4	= 15	86	7	No	Factor cannot be interpreted as representing a unitary ability.
Gf	MR	7	+ FW	4	= 11	75	3	Yes	The ability presumed to underlie the Factor is unitary & may be interpreted.
Gv	BD	5	+ VP	7	= 12	78	2	Yes	The ability presumed to underlie the Factor is unitary & may be interpreted.
Gs	SS	10	+ CD	9	= 19	97	1	Yes	The ability presumed to underlie the Factor is unitary & may be interpreted.

Step 6g.	Determine how many of Keith's Five Factors are interpretable

Number of interpretable Keith Factors = 4
Are fewer than 3 factors interpretable? = No　　Then proceed to Step 8 to interpret the Five Keith Factors.

*Note that the Keith Factors are only interpreted when the examinee is ages 16-69 and when both LN & FW were administered.

Figure 5.6. Illustration of Step 6 Using Laura's Profile With the WAIS-IV DMIA

Step 7: Determine Whether Each of the Five Core Factors Is Unitary and, Thus, Interpretable

Skip this step if you interpreted the person's profile via the Wechsler four-index approach (Step 5) or the Keith five-factor approach (Step 6). Proceed to Step 8.

Similar to examining variability within a Wechsler index, when the variability among subtest scaled scores within a Core factor is unusually large, then the standard score does not provide a good estimate of the ability it is intended to measure and, therefore, is not interpretable. In other words, when a substantial difference between the scaled scores factor is found, the factor cannot be interpreted as representing a unitary ability.

Step 7a. Calculate the standard scores for the five Core factors by summing the scaled scores for the two subtests that comprise each cluster and converting the sum to a standard score using the norms in Appendixes A.18–A.21 on the CD-ROM. (Note that the *Gs* Factor Standard Score is identical to PSI and should be obtained from Table A.6 on page 223 of the *WAIS-IV Administration and Scoring Manual.*)

Step 7b. Determine whether the size of the difference between subtest scaled scores that compose the Crystallized Intelligence (*Gc*) factor (Vocabulary and Information) is too large. Subtract the lower subtest scaled score from the higher subtest scaled score. Answer this question: *Is the size of the difference less than 1.5 SDs (<5 points)?*

- If YES, then the ability presumed to underlie the *Gc* factor is unitary and may be interpreted.
- If NO, then the difference is too large (≥5 points), and the *Gc* factor cannot be interpreted as representing a unitary ability.

Step 7c. Follow the same procedure as in Step 7a to determine the interpretability of the Short-Term Memory (*Gsm*) factor (comprised of Digit Span Backward and Digit Span Sequencing).

Step 7d. Follow the same procedure as in Step 7a to determine the interpretability of the Fluid Reasoning (*Gf*) factor (comprised of Matrix Reasoning and Arithmetic).

Step 7e. Follow the same procedure as in Step 7a to determine the interpretability of the Visual Processing (*Gv*) factor (comprised of Block Design and Visual Puzzles).

Step 7f. Follow the same procedure as in Step 7a to determine the interpretability of the Processing Speed (*Gs*) factor (comprised of Symbol Search and Coding).

Step 7g Determine how many of the Core five factors are interpretable by reviewing the results of Steps 7b–7f. If three or more of the factors are interpretable, proceed with your interpretation of the WAIS-IV data using the Core five-factor model. However, if only one or two of the Core five factors are interpretable, we strongly recommend using the Wechsler four-index model to interpret the WAIS-IV data. Thus, if only one or two of the Core five factors are interpretable (i.e., three or more Core factors are not unitary and cannot be meaningfully interpreted), go back to Step 5 and complete interpretation of the Wechsler four-index model. (However, remember that we do recommend always listing the four Wechsler index scores in your written report, even when you do interpret the profile from the perspective of a five-factor model.)

Similar to what we suggested with uninterpretable indexes, in some instances of an uninterpretable factor, it makes sense to look at the normative classifications of the subtest scaled scores to determine whether a general conclusion may be made about a person's range of observed functioning in the ability presumed to underlie the factor. Specifically, when all subtest scaled scores within a factor are consistently low (≤8) or consistently high (≥12), that fact should be noted and explained in a report. The Don't Forget box provides information on how to describe a notable limitation in the ability that the factor represents.

Step 8: Determine *Normative Strengths* and *Normative Weaknesses* in the Index (or Factor) Profile

Whether you have pursued the Wechsler four-index model (Step 5), the Keith five-factor model (Step 6), or the Core five-factor model (Step 7) to guide your analysis of the WAIS-IV data, you should complete Steps 8, 9, and 10. These steps provide a method for interpreting unitary Wechsler indexes and unitary factors.

STEP 8. *Normative Strengths* and *Normative Weaknesses* in the Index or Factor Profile are Determined

The standard score of each underlined Wechsler Index is entered in the table below.
An "X" is placed in the box corresponding to the appropriate normative category for each Index.

Wechsler Index	Standard Score	Normative Weakness <85	Within Normal Limits 85-115	Normative Strength >115
VCI	96		X	
PRI	79	X		
WMI	95		X	
PSI	97		X	

The standard score for each of the Five Factors that are underlined is entered in the table below.
An "X" is placed in the box corresponding to the appropriate normative category for each Index.

Keith or Core Factor	Standard Score	Normative Weakness <85	Within Normal Limits 85-115	Normative Strength >115
Gc	97		X	
Gsm				
Gf	75	X		
Gv	78	X		
Gs	97		X	

Figure 5.7. Illustration of Step 8 Using Laura's Profile With the WAIS-IV DMIA

Only unitary Wechsler indexes or unitary Core or Keith factors identified in the previous steps are included in this analysis. To determine Normative Strengths and Normative Weaknesses in a person's index or factor profile, review the exact value of the interpretable Indexes. If the index or factor standard score is greater than 115, the ability measured by the index or factor is a Normative Strength. If the index or factor standard score is less than 85, the ability measured by the index or factor is a Normative Weakness. If the index or factor standard score is between 85 and 115 (inclusive), the ability measured by the index or factor is Within Normal Limits. For example, a client's PRI of 123 is a Normative Strength. However, her WMI of 115 and PSI of 114 are both in the Average Range and, therefore, Within Normal Limits. Figure 5.7 shows an example of Step 8 using Laura's profile.

Step 9: Determine *Personal Strengths* and *Personal Weaknesses* in the Index (or Factor) Profile

The Normative Strengths and Normative Weaknesses discussed in Step 8 indicate a person's abilities relative to other individuals of about the same age. In contrast,

Personal Strengths and Personal Weaknesses, which are identified in Step 9, refer to indexes or factors that differ significantly from the person's own mean index or factor standard score. Rapid Reference 5.10 provides descriptions of these terms as well as other terms that are pertinent for understanding Step 9.

≡ *Rapid Reference 5.10*

Terms Used to Describe Fluctuations in a Person's WAIS-IV Index Profile

Term (Abbreviation)	Definition
Index	A standard score with a mean of 100 and standard deviation of 15
Normative Strength (NS)	An index that is above 115
Normative Weakness (NW)	An index that is below 85
Normal Limits (NL)	An index that is 85–115 (inclusive)
Personal Strength (PS)	An index that is significantly higher than the examinee's own mean index, using the .05 level of significance
Personal Weakness (PW)	An index that is significantly lower than the examinee's own mean index, using the .05 level of significance
Uncommon Personal Strength (PS/Uncommon)	A Personal Strength that is not only statistically significant but also substantially different from the examinee's own mean; that is, the size of the difference between the index and the examinee's mean of all four indexes is unusually large, occurring less than 10% of the time in the WAIS-IV standardization sample.
Uncommon Personal Weakness (PW/Uncommon)	A Personal Weakness that is not only statistically significant but also substantially different from the examinee's own mean; that is, the size of the difference between the index and the examinee's mean of all four indexes is unusually large, occurring less than 10% of the time in the WAIS-IV standardization sample.
Key Asset (KA)	An index that is an Uncommon Personal Strength and a Normative Strength
High Priority Concern (HPC)	An index that is an Uncommon Personal Weakness and a Normative Weakness

Source: Adapted from D. P. Flanagan & A. S. Kaufman, *Essentials of WISC-IV Assessment.* Copyright © 2009 John Wiley & Sons, Inc. This material is used by permission of John Wiley & Sons, Inc.

Step 9a. Compute the mean of the person's index or factor standard scores and round to the nearest tenth of a point. Note that all indexes or factors (interpretable and noninterpretable) are included in the computation of the mean for practical reasons. Excluding any index or factor would result in the need for numerous tables for determining both statistical significance and uncommon index/factor variation (i.e., mean indexes based on 2, 3, and 4 index combinations).

Step 9b. Subtract the mean of all index or factor standard scores from each *interpretable* index or factor standard score. Use the values reported in

> # DON'T FORGET
>
> ### Identifying Personal Strengths and Weaknesses
>
> When determining the examinee's Personal Strengths and Personal Weaknesses, compare only interpretable indexes (or factors) to the examinee's mean index (or factor). Noninterpretable indexes (or factors) *are* included in the computation of the examinee's mean index (or factor), but they *are not* compared to that mean or interpreted. Follow parallel processes when identifying personal strengths and weaknesses among the four indexes and five Keith or Core factors.

Table 5.4 to determine whether the size of the difference between an interpretable index and the mean of all indexes is significant. Use the values reported in Table 5.5 to determine whether the size of the difference between an interpretable Keith factor and the mean of all Keith factors is significant. Use the values reported in

Table 5.4. Differences Required for Statistical Significance (at p < .05 and p < .01) Between an Index and the Mean of All Four Indexes, by Age and Overall Sample

Age	p Value	VCI	PRI	WMI	PSI
16–17	.05	6.5	6.1	6.8	8.3
	.01	8.5	8.1	9.0	10.8
18–19	.05	5.6	6.3	6.3	7.6
	.01	7.4	8.3	8.3	9.9
20–24	.05	5.7	6.4	7.0	7.6
	.01	7.5	8.4	9.3	10.0
25–29	.05	5.5	5.5	5.8	7.5
	.01	7.2	7.2	7.7	9.8
30–34	.05	5.6	5.6	6.0	8.4
	.01	7.4	7.4	7.8	11.0
35–44	.05	5.6	6.0	6.0	8.4
	.01	7.4	7.9	7.9	11.1

(continued)

Table 5.4. (Continued)

Age	p Value	VCI	PRI	WMI	PSI
45–54	.05	5.1	5.5	5.9	8.3
	.01	6.8	7.3	7.8	11.0
55–64	.05	5.0	5.8	6.2	7.2
	.01	6.6	7.7	8.1	9.4
65–69	.05	5.0	5.8	6.2	7.2
	.01	6.6	7.7	8.1	9.4
70–74	.05	5.1	5.9	6.6	7.2
	.01	6.7	7.7	8.6	9.5
75–79	.05	5.5	6.2	5.8	6.9
	.01	7.2	8.1	7.7	9.0
80–84	.05	5.1	6.9	6.3	6.9
	.01	6.8	9.1	8.3	9.1
85–90	.05	4.6	6.6	6.6	6.9
	.01	6.1	8.6	8.6	9.1
All[a]	.05	5.5	5.9	6.3	7.5
	.01	7.3	7.8	8.3	9.9

Source: J. Naglieri (personal communication, January 25, 2009).

Note: Use this table only with interpretable indexes. To use this table, calculate the mean of all four indexes (rounded to the nearest 10th). Subtract this mean value from each interpretable Index and obtain difference scores. Select a significance level (.05 or .01). We recommend using .05 (the shaded portions of the table). Compare the difference score to the value in the appropriate row (.01 or .05) and the appropriate Index column. If the difference score is equal to or greater than this value, the difference is statistically significant. If the difference score is less than this value, the difference is not statistically significant. For example, if a 57-year-old obtained an interpretable WMI of 85 and the mean of all four Indexes was 93.2, you would subtract the mean of all four Indexes from the WMI. The difference score of 8.2 (85 − 93.2 = −8.2) is compared to the value for the WMI at the .05 level for a 57-year-old (i.e., 6.2). Because the difference score is equal to or greater than the value listed in the table, you would interpret the difference as statistically significant. Additionally, because the WMI was lower than the mean, it is considered a Personal Weakness.

[a]All = overall WAIS-IV standardization sample (ages 16–90).

Table 5.6 to determine whether the size of the difference between an interpretable Core factor and the mean of all Core factors is significant. These tables include differences required for statistical significance at both the .05 and .01 levels. We recommend using the .05 level that appears in the shaded rows of the appropriate table, but examiners may choose either the .05 or .01 level. Because some of the

Table 5.5. Differences Required for Statistical Significance (at p < .05 and p < .01) Between Each Keith Factor and the Mean of All Five Keith Factors, by Age and Overall Sample—Ages 16–69 Only

Age Group	p Value	Crystallized Knowledge (Gc) VC+IN	Fluid Reasoning (Gf) MR+FW	Visual Processing (Gv) BD+VP	Short-Term Memory (Gsm) DS+LN	Processing Speed (Gs) CD+SS
16–17	.05	6.2	7.0	7.0	6.6	8.7
	.01	8.2	9.2	9.2	8.7	11.4
18–19	.05	6.0	6.8	6.8	6.4	7.8
	.01	7.8	8.9	8.9	8.4	10.3
20–24	.05	5.6	7.2	7.2	6.8	7.9
	.01	7.3	9.4	9.4	9.0	10.3
25–29	.05	5.9	6.3	6.3	5.9	7.8
	.01	7.8	8.3	8.3	7.8	10.2
30–34	.05	5.9	5.9	6.4	5.5	8.8
	.01	7.8	7.8	8.4	7.2	11.5
35–44	.05	5.6	6.8	6.8	6.4	8.8
	.01	7.3	9.0	9.0	8.5	11.6
45–54	.05	5.0	6.4	5.9	5.9	8.8
	.01	6.6	8.4	7.8	7.8	11.5
55–64	.05	4.9	6.7	6.7	6.3	7.4
	.01	6.5	8.8	8.8	8.3	9.8
65–69	.05	4.9	6.3	6.3	6.3	7.4
	.01	6.4	8.2	8.2	8.2	9.7
All [a]	.05	5.6	6.6	6.6	6.2	8.2
	.01	7.3	8.7	8.7	8.2	10.7

Source: J. Naglieri (personal communication, February 10, 2009).

Note: Only examinees ages 16 to 69 can be administered the subtests necessary to calculate the five Keith factors. The subtest abbreviations underneath the factor names represent the subtests that comprise each Keith factor. Use this table only with interpretable Keith factors. To use this table, calculate the mean of all five factors (rounded to the nearest 10th). Subtract this mean value from each interpretable Keith factor and obtain difference scores. Select a significance level (.05 or .01). We recommend using .05 (the shaded portions of the table). Compare the difference score to the value in the appropriate row (.01 or .05) and the appropriate Keith factor column. If the difference score is equal to or greater than this value, the difference is statistically significant. If the difference score is less than this value, the difference is not statistically significant.

[a] All = WAIS-IV standardization sample (ages 16–69 only).

Table 5.6. Differences Required for Statistical Significance (at p < .05 and p < .01) Between Each Core CHC Factor and the Mean of All Five Core Factors, by Age and Overall Sample

Age Group	p Value	Crystallized Knowledge (Gc) VC+IN	Fluid Reasoning (Gf) MR+AR	Visual Processing (Gv) BD+VP	Short-Term Memory (Gsm) DS-Back+ DS-Seq	Processing Speed (Gs) CD+SS
16–17	.05	6.5	7.6	7.3	10.0	8.9
	.01	8.5	10.0	9.6	13.1	11.7
18–19	.05	6.4	7.9	7.2	9.4	8.2
	.01	8.4	10.4	9.5	12.4	10.8
20–24	.05	6.0	8.2	7.6	9.1	8.2
	.01	7.9	10.8	10.0	12.0	10.8
25–29	.05	6.3	7.1	6.7	8.4	8.1
	.01	8.3	9.3	8.8	11.0	10.6
30–34	.05	6.4	6.8	6.8	8.8	9.0
	.01	8.4	8.9	8.9	11.6	11.8
35–44	.05	5.9	7.1	7.1	8.1	9.0
	.01	7.8	9.3	9.3	10.6	11.8
45–54	.05	5.4	6.6	6.2	8.4	9.0
	.01	7.1	8.7	8.2	11.0	11.8
55–64	.05	5.4	7.1	7.1	9.0	7.8
	.01	7.1	9.3	9.3	11.8	10.2
65–69	.05	5.3	6.6	6.6	9.0	7.7
	.01	7.0	8.7	8.7	11.8	10.1
70–74	.05	5.4	7.4	7.1	8.7	7.8
	.01	7.1	9.7	9.3	11.4	10.2
75–79	.05	5.3	6.2	7.7	8.3	7.3
	.01	7.0	8.1	10.1	10.9	9.6
80–84	.05	5.6	7.5	8.8	9.1	7.5
	.01	7.4	9.9	11.6	12.0	9.9
85–90	.05	4.8	7.4	8.4	7.7	7.4
	.01	6.4	9.7	11.0	10.1	9.7

Table 5.6. (*Continued*)

Age Group	p Value	Crystallized Knowledge (*Gc*) VC+IN	Fluid Reasoning (*Gf*) MR+AR	Visual Processing (*Gv*) BD+VP	Short-Term Memory (*Gsm*) DS-Back+ DS-Seq	Processing Speed (*Gs*) CD+SS
All[a]	.05	5.9	7.1	7.1	8.7	8.1
	.01	7.8	9.3	9.3	11.4	10.6

Source: J. Naglieri (personal communication, January 19, 2012).

Note: The subtest abbreviations underneath the factor names represent the subtests that comprise each Core factor. Use this table only with interpretable indexes. To use this table, calculate the mean of all five Core factors (rounded to the nearest 10th). Subtract this mean value from each interpretable Core factor and obtain difference scores. Select a significance level (.05 or .01). We recommend using .05 (the shaded portions of the table). Compare the difference score to the value in the appropriate row (.01 or .05) and the appropriate Core factor column. If the difference score is equal to or greater than this value, the difference is statistically significant. If the difference score is less than this value, the difference is not statistically significant.

[a]All = overall WAIS-IV standardization sample (ages 16–90).

values for specific age levels differ from those reported for the total sample, we recommend using the differences reported by age. In order to be considered statistically significant, the difference must be equal to or greater than the value required for significance. Note that the Bonferroni correction has not been applied to values in Tables 5.4, 5.5, and 5.6 to be consistent with the method that we advocated for the WAIS-III (Kaufman & Lichtenberger, 2006, Appendix A), and that Flanagan and Kaufman (2004, 2009) advocate for the WISC-IV. Although others, such as Longman (2004), have applied the Bonferroni correction when conducting similar analyses, we prefer not to apply this conservative procedure for the same reason we prefer the .05 to the .01 level of significance—to permit the identification of more, rather than fewer, hypotheses to explore.

Use these criteria for identifying personal strengths and weaknesses:

i. If the difference is significant and the interpretable index or factor is higher than the mean, then the index or factor is a Personal Strength for the person.

ii. If the difference is significant and the interpretable index or factor is lower than the mean, than the index or factor is a Personal Weakness for the person.

Step 9c. Determine whether Personal Strengths and Personal Weaknesses are uncommon using the less than 10% base rate criterion. Because statistical significance means only that an observed difference is "real" (i.e., not due to chance), it is necessary to determine whether the difference is also unusually large or uncommon. Differences among indexes or factors that occur infrequently in the standardization sample may be valuable in making diagnoses and generating educational recommendations when corroborated by other data. *If the magnitude of the observed difference between an interpretable index and the mean of all indexes (or between a factor and the mean of all factors) is equal to or greater than 15 points, then the difference is uncommon.*

The WAIS-IV data needed to determine uncommon differences were not available for the Wechsler indexes, Keith factors, or Core factors. However, we estimated the size of an uncommon difference by examining pertinent WAIS-III and WISC-IV data; for both tests, the size of uncommon discrepancies between an index and the mean of all indexes (10% base rate) was consistently about 1 standard deviation (15 points).

Step 9d. Identify "Key Assets" and "High Priority Concerns" in the person's profile using the next criteria to identify personal strengths and weaknesses that are of greatest importance, diagnostically and educationally:

i. Significant Personal Strengths that are also uncommon and greater than 115 are labeled Key Assets.

ii. Significant Personal Weaknesses that are also uncommon and less than 85 are labeled *High Priority Concerns.*

Figure 5.8 shows an example of Step 9 using Laura's profile.

Step 9. Determine Personal Strengths and Personal Weaknesses in the Index or Factor Profile

Wechsler Index	Standard Score	Rounded Mean of All Indexes or Factors	Difference Score	Critical Value Needed for Significance (p<.05)	Personal Strength (PS) or Personal Weakness (PW)	Uncommon (U) or Not Uncommon (NU) (base rate <10%)	Normative Strength (NS) or Normative Weakness (NW)	Key Asset (KA) or High Priority Concern (HPC)
VCI	96	91.8	4.3	6.5		NU		
PRI	79	91.8	-12.8	6.1	PW	NU	NW	
WMI	95	91.8	3.3	6.8		NU		
PSI	97	91.8	5.3	8.3		NU		
Keith or Core Factor								
Gc	97	86.6	10.4	6.2	PS	NU		
Gsm		86.6		6.6				
Gf	75	86.6	-11.6	7.0	PW	NU	NW	
Gv	78	86.6	-8.6	7.0	PW	NU	NW	
Gs	97	86.6	10.4	8.7	PS	NU		

Note. PS = Personal Strength; PW = Personal Weakness; U = Uncommon; NU = Not Uncommon; NS = Normative Strength; NW = Normative Weakness; KA = Key Asset; HPC = High Priority Concern

Figure 5.8. Illustration of Step 9 Using Laura's Profile With the WAIS-IV DMIA

Step 10: Interpret Fluctuations in the Person's Index or Factor Profile

Reliable and useful information for making diagnostic and educational decisions can be obtained from interpreting a person's index or factor profile. To provide clarity about the meanings of the descriptive terms (e.

CAUTION
....

Interpretation of Scores

No single score, including an interpretable index or factor, should be used in isolation to make a diagnosis or to develop an individualized education program (IEP).

g., High Priority Concern, Key Asset) used in your psychological reports, you may include a section that defines these terms. Rapid Reference 5.10 provides a description of all the terms that are used to classify indexes or factors. Consult Flanagan and Kaufman (2009, pp. 165–168) for examples of how to describe indexes or factors that are classified as strengths or weaknesses. To properly interpret the person's profile using the interpretive system described here, it is important for examiners to understand theories related to cognitive assessment such as CHC theory or concepts of neuropsychological theory. The Broad Abilities and Narrow Abilities that form the essence of CHC theory are particularly useful concepts to understand. For an in-depth discussion of CHC theory, consult the writings of Flanagan and her colleagues (Flanagan et al., 2007; Flanagan et al., 2012; Flanagan & Kaufman, 2009; Flanagan, McGrew, & Ortiz, 2000). Basic definitions of CHC Broad and Narrow Abilities are also summarized in Appendix A.7 on the CD-ROM. An overview of neuropsychological theory and CHC theory related to the interpretation of the Core and Keith five-factor models was presented in Rapid Reference 5.7. The information in Rapid Reference 5.7 can also provide a useful outline for neuropsychologically based and CHC-based interpretation of the Wechsler four-index model: the VCI Index measures the CHC construct of *Gc*; PRI measures the CHC constructs of both *Gv* and *Gf*; WMI measures the CHC construct of *Gsm*; and PSI measures the CHC construct of *Gs*.

Before conducting Step 11 or 12 of the interpretive system, it is useful to summarize the results of Steps 4 through 10 and record your clinical impressions. In addition, you should specify which Planned Clinical Comparisons (conducted in Steps 11–12) might be most useful to gain a better understanding of the person's cognitive capabilities.

INTRODUCTION TO STEPS 11–12: ANALYZING PLANNED CLINICAL COMPARISONS

Based on the theoretical foundations of the WAIS-IV, knowledge of the abilities measured by the WAIS-IV, CHC theory, neuropsychological theory, and relevant research on the relationships between specific cognitive abilities and learning/achievement, a select number of additional comparisons may provide meaningful hypotheses about cognitive capabilities. Such information would go beyond that generated from the Index Profile Analysis or Factor Profile Analysis in the earlier interpretive steps. Flanagan and Kaufman (2004, 2009) developed eight theory-based clinical clusters, composed of two or three WISC-IV subtests, and Kaufman and Lichtenberger (2006) adapted those clusters for the WAIS-III.

We have adapted those WISC-IV and WAIS-III cluster comparisons to the WAIS-IV and created new cluster comparisons specifically focused on the WAIS-IV's theoretical underpinnings. Rapid References 5.11 and 5.12 list the clinical clusters that are needed to make the eight pair-wise comparisons in Steps 11–12. These Rapid References list the subtests that comprise each cluster in Steps 11 and 12; they also provide a brief definition of each cluster derived from the perspective of the WAIS-IV's theoretical foundations (see Rapid Reference 5.11) and from the perspective of CHC Theory (see Rapid Reference 5.12). Note that if you have conducted the analysis of the Keith or Core five factors in Steps 4 through 10, some of the clinical clusters described here in Steps 11–12 are the same as the factors analyzed in earlier steps.

≡ *Rapid Reference 5.11*

Clinical Clusters From WAIS-IV Theoretical Model

Clinical Cluster	Subtests Comprising Cluster
Visual-Motor Speed	*Steps 11 and 12: Block Design + Coding + Symbol Search*

Definition: The Visual-Motor Speed Cluster consists of three subtests, all of which require visual-motor speed and quick information processing. Coding and Symbol Search compose the Processing Speed Index. Block Design is the one Perceptual Reasoning subtest that also requires visual-motor coordination and speed of processing. Processing speed has been shown to be related to aging in adults (Finkel, Reynolds, McArdle, & Pederson, 2007) and has a dynamic relationship to mental capacity (Kail & Hall, 1994) and to other fluid reasoning tasks (Fry & Hale, 1996; Kail, 2000). "Many novel learning tasks involve information processing that is both routine (such as reading a policy memo at work) and complex (such as determining the impact of the memo on one's job function). When speed of processing information is at least in the average range or a relative strength for a patient, this may facilitate both reasoning and the acquisition of new information" (Weiss et al., 2010a, p. 74).

| **Problem-Solving without Visual Motor Speed** | **Step 11: Matrix Reasoning + Visual Puzzles + Picture Completion + Figure Weights** |
| | **Step 12: Matrix Reasoning + Visual Puzzles + Picture Completion** |

Definition: For Step 11, the Problem-Solving without Visual-Motor Speed Cluster includes the four Perceptual Reasoning tasks (two Core, two supplemental) that do not require a motor response. For Step 12, Figure Weights is not included because it is not normed for adults ages 70–90. The WAIS-IV increased the emphasis on the theoretical constructs of fluid reasoning and visual problem solving by adding two new subtests: Visual Puzzles and Figure Weights (Psychological Corporation, 2008). On the WAIS-III, most nonverbal Problem-Solving subtests required visual-motor coordination and speed. However, with Object Assembly and Picture Arrangement eliminated from the WAIS-IV, Block Design is now the only remaining PRI subtest that demands coordination and speed. Therefore, by excluding Block Design and considering the remaining PRI subtests as a cluster, it is possible to measure a person's fluid reasoning and visual-spatial problem solving without the "contamination" of either the person's motor coordination or speed.

| *Mental Manipulation* | **Step 11: Letter-Number Sequencing + Digit Span** |
| | **Step 12: Digit Span Backward + Digit Span Sequencing** |

Definition: The Mental Manipulation Cluster measures the ability to actively maintain information in conscious awareness and perform some operation or manipulation with it (an ability commonly referred to as working memory but labeled here as Mental Manipulation to avoid confusion with the WAIS-IV Working Memory Index). Letter-Number Sequencing, Digit Span Backward, and Digit Span Sequencing tap one's ability to temporarily store and perform a set of cognitive operations on information that requires divided attention and the management of the limited capacity of short-term memory. Digit Span Sequencing, an excellent measure of mental manipulation, was added to WAIS-IV Digit Span because of concern that Digit Span Forward "was a measure of short-term and not working memory" (Weiss et al., 2010a, p. 69). However, it is nonetheless suitable that Digit Span Forward is included as part of the Mental Manipulation cluster because it "requires initial registration of the verbal stimulia prerequisite for mental manipulation of the stimuli" (Weiss et al., 2010a, p. 69). Unlike the WMI, the Mental Manipulation Cluster does not include Arithmetic because of Arithmetic's additional demands on verbal comprehension, fluid reasoning, and mathematical knowledge. Research has shown that working memory is an essential component of higher order cognitive processes such as fluid reasoning (Psychological Corporation, 2008). "Employed adults with serious deficits in working memory may have considerable difficulties at work. A weakness in working memory may make the processing of complex information more time consuming and tax the patient's mental energies more quickly compared to co-workers" (Weiss et al., 2010a, p. 70). The Mental Manipulation Clusters in Step 11 and Step 12 are identical to the Keith and Core *Gsm* factors, respectively.

≡ Rapid Reference 5.12

Clinical Clusters From a CHC Theoretical Model

Clinical Cluster	Subtests Comprising Cluster
Fluid Reasoning (Gf) Cluster	**Step 11: Matrix Reasoning + Figure Weights** **Step 12: Matrix Reasoning + Arithmetic**

CHC Definition: The Fluid Reasoning (Gf) Cluster consists of subtests that measure the Broad Gf ability in CHC theory. Gf is defined as encompassing the mental operations that an individual uses when faced with a novel task that cannot be performed automatically. These mental operations include forming and recognizing concepts, perceiving relationships among patterns, drawing inferences, problem solving, and so forth. Matrix Reasoning measures the narrow Gf ability of General Sequential Reasoning (Deduction), which is defined as the ability to start with stated rules, premises, or conditions, and to engage in one or more steps to reach a solution to a novel problem. Figure Weights (Step 11) is primarily a measure of Quantitative Reasoning, and also involves the fluid reasoning abilities of induction and deduction (Psychological Corporation, 2008). Like Figure Weights, Arithmetic (Step 12) is primarily a measure of Quantitative Reasoning. The Fluid Reasoning (Gf) Clusters in Step 11 and Step 12 are identical to the Keith and Core Gf factors, respectively.

Visual Processing (Gv) Cluster	**Steps 11 & 12: Block Design + Visual Puzzles**

CHC Definition: The Visual Processing (Gv) Cluster consists of two subtests that measure the Broad Gv ability in CHC theory. Gv is defined as the ability to generate, perceive, analyze, synthesize, store, retrieve, manipulate, and transform visual patterns and stimuli. Block Design measures the narrow Gv ability of Spatial Relations, which is defined as the ability to perceive and manipulate visual patterns rapidly, or to maintain orientation with respect to objects in space. Visual Puzzles involves Gv—especially the narrow abilities of Visualization and Spatial Relations—and some aspects of Fluid Reasoning (Gf). Unlike Block Design, Visual Puzzles does not involve any motor manipulation. The Visual Processing (Gv) Cluster is identical to both the Keith and Core Gv factor.

Verbal Fluid Reasoning (Gf-Verbal) Cluster	**Steps 11 & 12: Similarities + Comprehension**

CHC Definition: The Verbal Fluid Reasoning (Gf-verbal) Cluster comprises two subtests that involve the Broad Gc ability in CHC theory. Gc is defined as the breadth and depth of a person's accumulated knowledge of a culture and the effective use of that knowledge. Notwithstanding their primary Gc classifications, Similarities and Comprehension, to some extent, both require the use of the narrow Gf ability of Induction. Because Similarities and Comprehension (although primarily verbal or Gc subtests) both require the ability to reason (inductively) with verbal stimuli, this cluster is labeled Verbal Fluid Reasoning. *This cluster requires administration of the supplemental Comprehension subtest.*

Lexical Knowledge (Gc-VL) Cluster **Steps 11 & 12: Vocabulary + Similarities**

CHC Definition: The Lexical Knowledge (Gc-VL) Cluster consists of two subtests that measure the Broad Gc ability in CHC theory. Gc is defined as the breadth and depth of a person's accumulated knowledge of culture and the effective use of that knowledge. Both Vocabulary and Similarities measure the narrow Gc ability of *Lexical Knowledge*, which is defined as the extent of vocabulary that can be understood in terms of correct word meanings. (Lexical Knowledge is a primary ability for Vocabulary and a secondary ability for Similarities.) Therefore, this cluster was labeled Lexical Knowledge.

General Information (Gc-K0) Cluster **Steps 11 & 12: Comprehension + Information**

CHC Definition: The General Information (Gc-VL) Cluster consists of two subtests that measure the Broad Gc ability in CHC theory. Gc is defined as the breadth and depth of a person's accumulated knowledge of culture and the effective use of that knowledge. These subtests, Comprehension and Information, primarily measure the narrow Gc ability of *General Information*, which is defined as an individual's range of general knowledge. Therefore, this cluster is labeled General Information. *This cluster requires administration of the supplemental Comprehension subtest.*

Long-Term Memory (Gc-LTM) Cluster **Steps 11 & 12: Vocabulary + Information**

CHC Definition: The Long-Term Memory (Gc-LTM) Cluster consists of two subtests that measure the Broad Gc ability in CHC theory. These subtests, Vocabulary and Information, measure to a greater or lesser extent the narrow Gc ability of *General Information*. Vocabulary also measures the narrow Gc ability of *Lexical Knowledge*. However, because both Vocabulary and Information represent knowledge that is typically stored in long-term memory, this cluster was labeled Long-Term Memory. Note that "Long-Term Memory" is not a CHC label per se and therefore should not be confused with the broad Long-Term Retrieval (Glr) ability in CHC theory. The Long-Term Memory (Gc-LTM) Cluster is identical to both the Keith and Core Gc factor.

Short-Term Memory (Gsm-MW) Cluster **Step 11: Letter-Number Sequencing + Digit Span**

Step 12: Digit Span Backward + Digit Span Sequencing

CHC Definition: The Short-Term Memory (Gsm-MW) Cluster consists of subtests that measure the Broad Gsm ability in CHC theory. Gsm is defined as the ability to apprehend and hold information in immediate awareness and to use it within a few seconds. Letter-Number Sequencing and Digit Span Backward, and Digit Span Sequencing measure the narrow Gsm ability of *Working Memory*, which is defined as the ability to temporarily store and perform a set of cognitive operations on information that requires divided attention and the management of the limited capacity of short-term memory. Digit Span also measures the narrow Gsm ability of *Memory Span*, which is defined as the ability to attend to and immediately recall temporally ordered elements in the correct order after a single presentation. The Short-Term Memory (Gsm-MW) Clusters in Step 11 and Step 12 are identical to the Keith and Core Gsm factors, respectively.

Choosing Step 11 or Step 12

Examiners will use *either* Step 11 *or* Step 12, not both. For Step 11, six of the eight comparisons include Letter-Number Sequencing, Figure Weights, or both. It is, therefore, applicable only to ages 16 to 69 and only if these supplemental subtests were administered. Step 12 has been added to the interpretive system to extend the clinical comparisons to ages 70 to 90. It is also useful for examiners who did not administer Letter-Number Sequencing or Figure Weights to a person between the ages of 16 and 69.

To choose the appropriate step, answer these questions:

> *Is the person you tested between the ages of 16 and 69?*
> - If NO, proceed to Step 12.
> - If YES, Answer this question: *Did you administer **both** Letter-Number Sequencing and Figure Weights (supplemental subtests)?*
> - If NO, proceed to Step 12.
> - If YES, proceed to Step 11.

Internal consistency reliability coefficients for most clinical clusters are presented in Table 5.7 for each age group and for the overall WAIS-IV standardization sample. The note to the table explains that the reliability coefficients for four of the clusters appear in Table 5.3 (because these four clusters are identical to four of the factors in the five-factor interpretive models).

Step 11: Conduct Clinical Comparisons (Ages 16–69 Only)

Eight pair-wise comparisons of clinical clusters are conducted in this step— three that are derived from the Wechsler theoretical model (see Rapid Reference 5.13) and five that are derived from the CHC theoretical model (see Rapid Reference 5.14). Six of these comparisons require administration of Letter-Number Sequencing and/or Figure Weights. *If you did not administer one or both of these subtests, then proceed to Step 12.*

The number of comparisons you will be able to make in Step 11 depends on whether you administered the supplemental subtests Picture Completion and Comprehension. Picture Completion is required for two of the three comparisons depicted in Rapid Reference 5.13; Comprehension is needed for three of the five comparisons shown in Rapid Reference 5.14. If you administered one or both of these supplemental subtests, then it is worth conducting this step. If you administered neither, then you will be unable to make five of the eight clinical cluster comparisons. Proceed only if the three remaining comparisons seem particularly important for the individual you tested.

Table 5.7. Internal Consistency Reliability Coefficients for the New WAIS-IV Clinical Clusters, by Age and Overall Sample

Age Group	Steps 11–12 Visual-Motor Speed BD+CD+SS	Step 11 Problem Solving Without Visual–Motor Speed MR+VP+PC+FW	Step 12 Problem Solving Without Visual–Motor Speed MR+VP+PC	Steps 11–12 Verbal Fluid Reasoning SI+CO	Steps 11–12 Lexical Knowledge VC+SI	Steps 11–12 General Information CO+IN
16–17	.91	.94	.93	.89	.92	.91
18–19	.92	.95	.93	.92	.94	.93
20–24	.91	.94	.92	.92	.94	.94
25–29	.93	.95	.94	.92	.94	.93
30–34	.91	.96	.94	.92	.94	.93
35–44	.90	.95	.94	.93	.95	.94
45–54	.91	.96	.94	.92	.95	.94
55–64	.93	.95	.94	.92	.94	.94
65–69	.93	.96	.95	.93	.95	.95
70–74	.93	—	.95	.92	.95	.94
75–79	.93	—	.95	.92	.94	.93
80–84	.92	—	.92	.92	.96	.94
85–90	.94	—	.92	.94	.96	.94
All	.92	.95	.94	.92	.95	.94

Source: Standardization data and analysis results from the *Wechsler Adult Intelligence Scale—Fourth Edition* (WAIS-IV). Copyright © 2008 by NCS Pearson, Inc. Used with permission. All rights reserved.

Note: The subtest abbreviations underneath the clinical clusters represent the subtests that comprise each cluster. Reliability coefficients for the Mental Manipulation, Short-Term Memory, Fluid Reasoning, and Visual Processing clusters are not shown in this table. The values for Visual Processing are the same as the ones shown for Core & Keith *Gv* in Table 5.3. The Mental Manipulation and Short-Term Memory clusters are identical in subtest content; their reliability coefficients are presented in Table 5.3 (Step 11 = Keith *Gsm*; Step 12 = Core *Gsm*). The reliability coefficients for Fluid Reasoning are likewise presented in Table 5.3 (Step 11 = Keith *Gf*; Step 12 = Core *Gf*). And the same is true for the reliability coefficients for Long-Term Memory, which is identical in content to *Gc* in both the Keith and Core models.

Step 11a Before conducting clinical comparisons, you must first determine whether the clusters in the comparison represent unitary abilities. To do this, compute the difference between the scaled scores of the two subtests that compose each clinical cluster. Subtract the lower scaled score from the higher one. Answer this question: *Is the size of the scaled-score difference less than 5?*

- If YES, the clinical cluster represents a unitary ability and the clinical comparison that includes this cluster may be made *only* if the other cluster in the comparison also represents a unitary ability. Proceed to Step 11b.
- If NO, the clinical cluster does not represent a unitary ability and the clinical comparisons that include this cluster should not be made.

Figure 5.9 shows an example of Step 11a using Laura's profile.

Step 11b Calculate the clinical cluster by summing the scaled scores for the two subtests that comprise the clinical cluster and converting the sum to a standard score using the norms in Appendixes A.8–A.17 on the CD-ROM. Figure 5.10 shows an example of Step 11b using Laura's profile.

≡ *Rapid Reference 5.13*

Step 11: Planned Clinical Cluster Comparisons From a Wechsler Theoretical Model

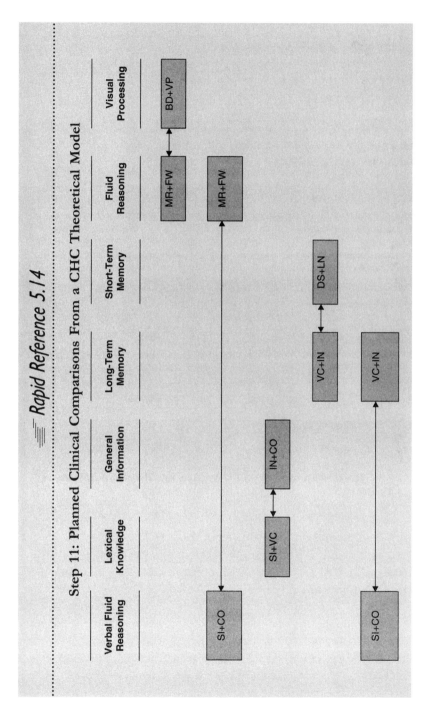

Rapid Reference 5.14

Step 11: Planned Clinical Comparisons From a CHC Theoretical Model

Step 11. Clinical comparisons are conducted.

The questions below determine whether to use the clinical comparisons in Step 11 or 12.

Question: Is the person you tested between the ages of 16-69?

Yes,   Age = 17

Answer the next question below.

Question: Did you administer both Letter-Number Sequencing & Figure Weights?

Yes, administered Letter-Number Sequencing.

Yes, administered Figure Weights.

Complete Step 11 below.

Step 11a. This step determines whether each clinical cluster is unitary and interpretable.

There are 8 possible clinical comparisons. You may evaluate all, or select the comparisons that are most appropriate for a given individual based on the referral questions and assessment results.

The difference between the highest and lowest subtest scaled scores in a cluster is calculated. *If the size of the difference is less than 5 points, then the clinical cluster is unitary.*

Cluster	Subtests	Highest Scaled Score		Lowest Scaled Score		Difference	Is Cluster Interpretable?
Visual Motor Speed	BD+CD+SS	10	-	5	=	5	No
Problem Solving without Visual Motor Speed	MR+VP+PC+FW	7	-	4	=	3	Yes
Mental Manipulation	LN+DS	11	-	4	=	7	No
Verbal Fluid Reasoning	SI+CO	10	-	9	=	1	Yes
Lexical Knowledge	VC+SI	11	-	9	=	2	Yes
General Information	CO+IN	10	-	8	=	2	Yes
Long-Term Memory	VC+IN	11	-	8	=	3	Yes
Short-Term Memory	LN+DS	11	-	4	=	7	No
Fluid Reasoning	MR+FW	7	-	4	=	3	Yes
Visual Processing	BD+VP	7	-	5	=	2	Yes

Figure 5.9. Illustration of Step 11a Using Laura's Profile With the WAIS-IV DMIA

Step 11c Determine whether the size of the difference between the clusters in the comparison is unusually large or uncommon, occurring less than 10% of the time in the WAIS-IV standardization sample (see Table 5.8). To do this, calculate the difference between the clusters in the comparison (consult Rapid Reference 5.13 and Rapid Reference 5.14). If the size of the difference is equal to or greater than the value reported for the comparison in Table 5.8, then the difference is uncommon. If the size of the difference between the two clusters in the comparison is less than the table value, then the difference is not uncommon. Specifically, a comparison between two interpretable clinical clusters can have either one of two outcomes:

Step 11b.	Clinical clusters that represent unitary abilities or processes are calculated by summing the scaled scores for the subtests that comprise the cluster and converting the sum to clinical cluster standard score.

*Note that only interpretable clusters are calculated below.

Subtest	Visual Motor Speed	Problem Solving without Visual Motor Speed	Mental Manipulation	Verbal Fluid Reasoning	Lexical Knowledge	General Information	Long-Term Memory	Short-Term Memory	Fluid Reasoning	Visual Processing
Block Design	5									5
Similarities				9	9					
Digit Span			11					11		
Matrix Reasoning		7							7	
Vocabulary					11		11			
Arithmetic										
Symbol Search	10									
Visual Puzzles		7								7
Information						8	8			
Coding	9									
Letter-Num. Seq.			4					4		
Figure Weights		4							4	
Comprehension				10		10				
Cancellation										
Picture Completion		6								
Sum of Scaled Scores		24		19	20	18	19		11	12
Cluster Standard Score		76		97	100	94	97		75	78
Percentile Rank		5		42	50	34	42		5	7
Confidence Interval		72-82		91-104	95-105	89-100	92-102		71-83	73-86
Subtest	Visual Motor Speed	Problem Solving without Visual Motor Speed	Mental Manipulation	Verbal Fluid Reasoning	Lexical Knowledge	General Information	Long-Term Memory	Short-Term Memory	Fluid Reasoning	Visual Processing

Figure 5.10. Illustration of Step 11b Using Laura's Profile With the WAIS-IV DMIA

1. The size of the difference between the two interpretable clinical clusters is uncommon in the normative population.
2. The size of the difference between the two interpretable clinical clusters is *not* uncommon in the normative population.

Figure 5.11 shows an example of Step 11c using Laura's profile.

Step 11d Regardless of the outcome of Step 11c, describe the results of the planned clinical comparisons. Keeping in mind the tenets of intelligent testing, all hypotheses that are derived from the post hoc planned clinical comparisons should be supported with additional sources of data (e.g., behavioral observations, other test results, referral concerns). In Chapter 10, based on the case reports of Laura O., age 17, and Jim W., age 64, we illustrate how to describe these comparisons and to use multiple data sources to interpret the results. Laura displayed an unusually large discrepancy between verbal and nonverbal fluid reasoning, and Mr. W. had an uncommonly large difference between his Lexical Knowledge and General Information. The discrepancies for both

Table 5.8. Step 11: Size of Difference Between Pairs of Clinical Clusters Needed to Be Considered Unusually Large or Uncommon

Cluster Comparison			Amount of Difference
Visual-Motor Speed (BD+CD+SS)	vs.	Problem Solving without Visual-Motor Speed (MR+VP+PC+FW)	20
Visual-Motor Speed (BD+CD+SS)	vs.	Mental Manipulation (LN+DS)	24
Mental Manipulation (LN+DS)	vs.	Problem Solving without Visual-Motor Speed (MR+VP+PC+FW)	22
Fluid Reasoning (MR+FW)	vs.	Visual Processing (BD+VP)	20
Verbal Fluid Reasoning (SI+CO)	vs.	Fluid Reasoning (MR+FW)	22
Lexical Knowledge (VC+SI)	vs.	General Information (CO+IN)	15
Long-Term Memory (VC+IN)	vs.	Short-Term Memory (LN+DS)	24
Verbal Fluid Reasoning (SI+CO)	vs.	Long-Term Memory (VC+IN)	16

Source: Standardization data and analysis results from the *Wechsler Adult Intelligence Scale—Fourth Edition* (WAIS-IV). Copyright © 2008 by NCS Pearson, Inc. Used with permission. All rights reserved.

Note: "Unusually large or uncommon" denotes differences estimated to occur less than 10% of the time in the WAIS-IV standardization sample. The differences in this table were estimated by the formula provided by Sattler (1982, Table C-11) for computing the percentage of a population obtaining discrepancies between two standard scores. This formula includes the correlations between the two standard scores for each comparison, which were kindly provided by Pearson Assessments (J. J. Wang, personal communication, March 23, 2009). Two comparisons are based on data for the total WAIS-IV standardization sample (ages 16–90): Lexical Knowledge vs. General Information and Verbal Fluid Reasoning vs. Long-Term Memory. All other comparisons are for ages 16–69 only and are based on correlations for ages 16–69.

clients provided key interpretive and diagnostic information. For additional examples of how to describe comparisons between a similar set of clinical clusters on the WISC-IV, see Flanagan and Kaufman (2009, pp. 176–178). Suggested hypotheses for the meanings of patterns of findings from the clinical comparisons are provided in Rapid Reference 5.15.

Index/IQ Subtest	Score	Conf. Interval	Percentile Rank	Descriptive Category	Is Index/IQ/Cluster Interpretable?
Verbal Comprehension	96	91-101	39	Average/Within Normal Limits	Yes
Similarities	9		37		
Vocabulary	11		63		
Information	8		25		
(Comprehension)	10		50	Does not contribute to Index or IQ	
Perceptual Reasoning	79	74-84	8	Below Average/Normative Weakness	Yes
Block Design	5		5		
Matrix Reasoning	7		16		
Visual Puzzles	7		16		
(Figure Weights)*	4		2	Does not contribute to Index or IQ	
(Picture Completion)	6		9	Does not contribute to Index or IQ	
Working Memory	95	90-100	37	Average/Within Normal Limits	Yes
Digit Span	11		63		
Arithmetic	7		16		
(Letter-Number Sequencing)*	4		2	Does not contribute to Index or IQ	
Digit Span Backward	10		50	Does not contribute to Index or IQ	
Digit Span Sequencing	11		63	Does not contribute to Index or IQ	
Processing Speed	97	92-102	42	Average/Within Normal Limits	Yes
Symbol Search	10		50		
Coding	9		37		
(Cancellation)*	9		37	Does not contribute to Index or IQ	
Full Scale IQ	83	78-88	13	Below Average/Normative Weakness	Yes
GAI	86	82-93	18	Average/Within Normal Limits	Yes
CPI	96	90-102	39	Average/Within Normal Limits	Yes
Keith Factor	(roll cursor over the red triangle to see which subtests comprise each cluster)				
Crystallized Intelligence (Gc)	97	92-102	42	Average/Within Normal Limits	Yes
Short-Term Memory (Gsm)	86	81-93	18	Average/Within Normal Limits	No
Fluid Reasoning (Gf)	75	71-83	5	Below Average/Normative Weakness	Yes
Visual Processing (Gv)	78	73-86	7	Below Average/Normative Weakness	Yes
Processing Speed (Gs)	97	90-104	42	Average/Within Normal Limits	Yes

Figure 5.11. Illustration of Step 11c Using Laura's Profile With the WAIS-IV DMIA

Rapid Reference 5.15

Hypotheses for Observed Differences Between Clinical Clusters

Fluid Reasoning (*Gf*) Cluster > Visual Processing (*Gv*) Cluster

Hypotheses: This difference may indicate that the individual's overall reasoning ability is good and that, despite difficulty with visual processing, the individual can solve problems by focusing on characteristics that are less visual in nature. For example, on Matrix Reasoning, the individual may not focus on the spatial aspects of the pattern to arrive at an answer (e.g., the pattern shifts from top to bottom, then left to right, then back to the top), but rather he or she may focus on the number of dots in a pattern to complete the matrix. Also, an individual with such a pattern of abilities may do well when he or she uses a strategy such as verbal mediation to solve problems with substantial visual information. That is, an individual may be able to solve a problem involving visual stimuli only after translating the visual information into verbal information.

(continued)

Visual Processing (*Gv*) Cluster > Fluid Reasoning (*Gf*) Cluster

Hypotheses: This difference may indicate that the individual has good concrete visual skills but experiences difficulty when asked to reason with visual information. Implications may include difficulty with mathematical application tasks, such as making predictions based on visual stimuli (e.g., graphs, charts). An individual with this pattern of performance may also have difficulty interpreting visual information. That is, an individual with higher visual processing skills than visual reasoning skills may be able to see specific details in visual information but may have difficulty integrating visual information to solve problems.

Fluid Reasoning (*Gf*) Cluster > Verbal Fluid Reasoning (*Gf*-verbal) Cluster

Hypotheses: This difference may indicate that the individual can reason better with visually based stimuli as compared to verbal stimuli. An individual with this pattern of performance may learn best when new information is presented visually.

Verbal Fluid Reasoning (*Gf*-verbal) Cluster > Fluid Reasoning (*Gf*) Cluster

Hypotheses: This difference may indicate that the individual can reason better with verbally based stimuli as compared to visual stimuli. An individual with this pattern of performance may learn best when new information is presented verbally. Moreover, an individual with this pattern of performance may do well with lecture formats that are primarily verbal in nature but may get lost when too many visual aids are used (e.g., graphs, diagrams) to teach a new concept.

Lexical Knowledge (*Gc*-VL) Cluster > General Information (*Gc*-K0) Cluster

Hypotheses: This difference may indicate that the individual has facility with words and can reason with words but has minimal knowledge of factual information or has difficulty applying knowledge in specific situations. An individual with this pattern of performance may have difficulty with written expression, in terms of breadth and depth of content, despite an appropriate vocabulary. On reading tasks, the individual may be able to read (decode) well and generally comprehend what he or she is reading but may not be able to make meaningful connections or draw inferences because of a lack of background knowledge.

General Information (*Gc*-K0) Cluster > Lexical Knowledge (*Gc*-VL) Cluster

Hypotheses: This difference may indicate that the individual has good knowledge of factual information but lacks facility with words and may have difficulty reasoning with words. On writing assignments, an individual with this pattern of performance may have good content but may be unable to communicate his or her thoughts well. That is, the individual's writing may appear poorly developed (e.g., writing is bland, lacks variety with regard to adjectives). On reading tasks, an individual with this pattern of performance may have good comprehension when reading about familiar topics, but he or she may have poor comprehension when reading about topics that are novel or that contain several

(continued)

unknown words. Thus, it is not unusual for an individual with this pattern of performance to be described as having inconsistent comprehension skills.

Long-Term Memory (*Gc*-LTM) Cluster > Short-Term Memory (*Gsm*-WM) Cluster

Hypotheses: This difference may indicate that the individual can retrieve information but has trouble encoding the information. In other words, the individual's stores of knowledge are likely the result of repeated practice using several meaningful associations. On reading and writing tasks, an individual with this pattern of performance may do well with known topics but poorly on new ones. Additionally, because of difficulty with holding information in immediate awareness long enough to use it, an individual with this pattern of performance may have difficulty efficiently copying information from written material or recording information from a lecture or from the board. Finally, an individual with this pattern of performance may have difficulty with a bottom-up learning approach in which the component parts of a general concept are presented separately and sequentially. This learning approach may cause particular difficulty for the individual primarily because he or she cannot hold the component parts in memory long enough to be able to synthesize them into the whole concept.

Short-Term Memory (*Gsm*-WM Cluster) > Long-Term Memory (*Gc*-LTM) Cluster

Hypotheses: This difference may indicate that the individual can encode information but has trouble retrieving it. Individuals with this pattern may do well with new topics in the short term, but if there is a delay between their learning of information and the need to demonstrate their knowledge, they may demonstrate a poor outcome. A classic example is when an employer or instructor indicates that the individual demonstrated an understanding of a particular topic while it was being presented but did not remember it later in the day. Also, an individual with this pattern of performance is often described as knowing information shortly after studying it but not being able to demonstrate that knowledge later (e.g., on a cumulative exam). These individuals are probably not forgetting information per se; rather, they are not encoding information at a level that is necessary for efficient retrieval.

Long-Term Memory (*Gc*-LTM) Cluster > Verbal Fluid Reasoning (*Gf*-verbal) Cluster

Hypotheses: This difference may indicate that the individual has an adequate fund of knowledge but cannot reason well with that knowledge.

Verbal Fluid Reasoning (*Gf*-verbal) Cluster > Long-Term Memory (*Gc*-LTM) Cluster

Hypotheses: This difference may indicate that the individual can reason well but that he or she has an insufficient amount of information with which to reason.

Visual-Motor Speed > Problem Solving Without Visual-Motor Speed

Hypotheses: This difference may indicate that an individual has a strong ability to quickly encode and respond to visually presented information by giving a motor

(continued)

response (e.g., either by manipulating blocks or writing with a pencil) but has more difficulty responding to visual information that requires processing through nonverbal reasoning when speed of responding is not a critical factor. Individuals with strong manual-motor dexterity or motor coordination may reveal a well-developed ability on the Visual-Motor Speed Cluster while not performing as well on the Problem Solving without Visual-Motor Speed Cluster. Such individuals may also perform well because they are highly motivated to beat the clock but may be overwhelmed with stimuli that is spatially complex or that requires a higher level of cognitive processing. Individuals who do not employ verbal mediation strategies when working may struggle more with tasks on the Problem Solving without Visual-Motor Speed Cluster while still being able to perform adequately on the Visual-Motor Speed Cluster.

Problem Solving Without Visual-Motor Speed > Visual-Motor Speed

Hypotheses: This difference may indicate that an individual has a strong ability to perceive and process visual information using nonverbal reasoning when speed of responding is not a critical factor, but he or she has more difficulty quickly encoding and responding to visually presented information by responding motorically (e.g., either by manipulating blocks or writing with a pencil). Individuals with weaker manual-motor dexterity or motor coordination may reveal a poorly developed ability on the Visual-Motor Speed Cluster while performing well on the Problem Solving without Visual-Motor Speed Cluster. Such an individual may also demonstrate signs of anxiety when required to beat the clock but may be less anxious and more motivated to work spatially complex stimuli or stimuli that require a higher level of cognitive processing. Individuals who employ verbal mediation strategies when working may show enhanced performance on tasks from the Problem Solving without Visual-Motor Speed Cluster while still struggling on the Visual-Motor Speed Cluster, which lends itself less to verbal mediation.

Visual-Motor Speed > Mental Manipulation

Hypotheses: This difference may indicate that the individual's attention to visual stimuli is better developed than his or her auditory attention abilities. The output required for the tasks on the Visual-Motor Speed Cluster differs greatly from that of the tasks on the Mental Manipulation Cluster. Specifically, an individual with such a difference may have a better ability to respond by using visual-motor coordination than by using expressive language skills. Although working memory is employed with both of these clinical clusters, an individual with higher visual-motor speed may have a better-developed ability to apply working memory to visual stimuli (Visual-Motor Speed Cluster) than to auditory stimuli (Mental Manipulation Cluster). If an individual has difficulty with auditory processing speed (or the speed at which auditory information is registered), he or she may display weaker performance on the Mental Manipulation Cluster than on the Visual-Motor Speed Cluster, which requires quick encoding of and response to visual stimuli.

Mental Manipulation > Visual-Motor Speed

Hypotheses: This difference may indicate that the individual's auditory attention abilities are better developed than his or her ability to attend to visual stimuli. The output required for the tasks on the Mental Manipulation Cluster differs greatly from that of the tasks on the Visual-Motor Speed Cluster. Specifically, an individual with such a difference may have a better ability to respond by using expressive

(continued)

language skills than by using visual-motor coordination. Although working memory is employed with both of these clinical clusters, an individual may have a more well-developed ability to apply working memory to auditory stimuli (Mental Manipulation Cluster) than to visual stimuli (Visual-Motor Speed Cluster). If an individual has difficulty with encoding and responding rapidly to visual stimuli, he or she may display weaker performance on the Visual-Motor Speed Cluster than on the Mental Manipulation Cluster, which benefits from speedy auditory processing (i.e., the speed at which auditory information is registered).

Problem Solving Without Visual-Motor Speed > Mental Manipulation

Hypotheses: This difference may indicate that the individual's attention to visual stimuli is better developed than his or her auditory attention abilities. Although working memory may enhance performance on both of these clinical clusters, an individual with poor auditory working memory (Mental Manipulation Cluster) will be more likely to show this pattern of performance. If an individual has difficulty with auditory processing speed (or the speed at which auditory information is registered), he or she may display weaker performance on the Mental Manipulation cluster than the Problem Solving without Visual-Motor Speed Cluster, which emphasizes reasoning more than processing speed.

Mental Manipulation > Problem Solving Without Visual-Motor Speed

Hypotheses: This difference may indicate that the individual's auditory attention abilities are better developed than their ability to attend to visual stimuli. Although working memory is employed with both of these clinical clusters, an individual with a strong auditory working memory (Mental Manipulation Cluster) may be more likely to display this pattern of performance. If an individual has difficulty with nonverbal reasoning (even without emphasizing speed), he or she may display weaker performance on the Problem Solving without Visual-Motor Speed Cluster than on the Mental Manipulation cluster, which benefits from speedy auditory processing (without requiring reasoning).

Source: Adapted from Flanagan & Kaufman (2004). Additional hypotheses may be developed from using a neuropsychological approach, which is described in Chapter 6.

Note: Per the intelligent testing approach that we advocate in this book, all hypotheses based on observed differences between clinical cluster scores should be validated with other sources of data.

Interpretation of the WAIS-IV profile (from the global ability, to the indexes, to these clinical clusters) must consider other variables than true differences in ability. Chapter 4 reviewed many of these clinical and behavioral variables that may elucidate an examinee's WAIS-IV profile. In addition, Chapter 6 provides detailed information from a neuropsychological approach to interpretation that can provide more insight into understanding peaks and valleys in a person's abilities. Interpretation of the process scores that the WAIS-IV offers is detailed in Chapter 6. Integration of all of these quantitative and qualitative aspects of the WAIS-IV profile will provide the most accurate portrait of an individual's cognitive abilities.

≡ *Rapid Reference 5.16*

Step 12: Planned Clinical Cluster Comparisons From a Wechsler Theoretical Model

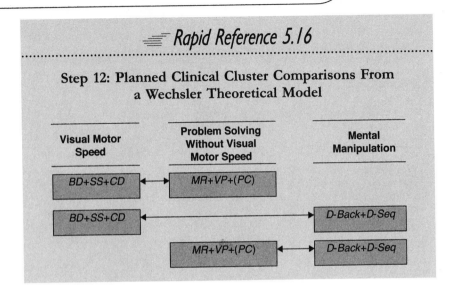

Step 12: Conduct Clinical Comparisons (Ages 16–90)

If you just completed Step 11, do not conduct this step. You have finished our interpretive system. Otherwise, proceed with this step.

Eight pair-wise comparisons of clinical clusters are conducted in this step—three that are derived from the Wechsler theoretical model (see Rapid Reference 5.16) and five that are derived from the CHC theoretical model (see Rapid Reference 5.17).

Step 12 excludes the two supplemental subtests that are normed for ages 16–69 only (Figure Weights, Letter-Number Sequencing). However, the number of comparisons you will be able to make in Step 12 does depend on whether you administered the supplemental Picture Completion and Comprehension subtests. Picture Completion is required for two of the three comparisons depicted in Rapid Reference 5.16; Comprehension is needed for three of the five comparisons shown in Rapid Reference 5.17. If you administered one or both of these supplemental subtests, then it is worth conducting this step. If you administered neither, then you will be unable to make five of the eight clinical cluster comparisons. Proceed only if the three remaining comparisons seem particularly important for the individual you tested.

Step 12a Before conducting clinical comparisons, you must first determine whether the clusters in the comparison represent unitary abilities. To do this, compute the difference between the scaled scores of the two subtests that compose each clinical cluster. Subtract the lower scaled score from the higher one. Answer this question: *Is the size of the scaled-score difference less than 5?*

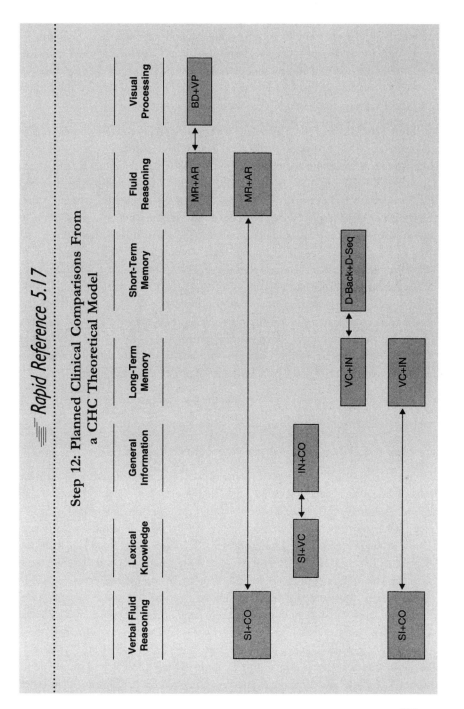

Rapid Reference 5.17

Step 12: Planned Clinical Comparisons From a CHC Theoretical Model

- If YES, the clinical cluster represents a unitary ability and the clinical comparison that includes this cluster may be made *only* if the other cluster in the comparison also represents a unitary ability. Proceed to Step 12b.
- If NO, the clinical cluster does not represent a unitary ability and the clinical comparisons that include this cluster should not be made.

Step 12b Calculate the clinical cluster by summing the scaled scores for the two subtests that comprise the clinical cluster and converting the sum to a standard score using the norms in Appendixes A.8, A.22, A.23, A.11, A.12, A.13, A.14, A.24, A.25, and A.17 on the CD-ROM. The *WAIS-IV Interpretive Worksheet* in Appendix A.1 also clearly shows how to obtain each cluster standard score.

Step 12c Determine whether the size of the difference between the clusters in the comparison is unusually large or uncommon, occurring less than 10% of the time in the WAIS-IV standardization sample (see Table 5.9). To do this, calculate the difference between the clusters in the comparison (consult Rapid Reference 5.16 and Rapid Reference 5.17).

If the size of the difference is equal to or greater than the value reported for the comparison in Table 5.9, then the difference is uncommon. If the size of the difference between the two clusters in the comparison is less than the table value, then the difference is not uncommon. Specifically, a comparison between two interpretable clinical clusters can have either one of two outcomes:

1. The size of the difference between the two interpretable clinical clusters is uncommon in the normative population.
2. The size of the difference between the two interpretable clinical clusters is *not* uncommon in the normative population.

Step 12d Regardless of the outcome of Step 12c, describe the results of the planned clinical comparisons. Keeping in mind the tenets of intelligent testing, all hypotheses that are derived from the post hoc planned clinical comparisons should be supported with additional sources of data (e.g., behavioral observations, other test results, referral concerns). In Chapter 10, based on the case reports of Laura O., age 17, and Jim W., age 64, we illustrate how to describe these comparisons and to use multiple data sources to interpret the results. Laura displayed an unusually large discrepancy between verbal and nonverbal fluid reasoning, and Mr. W. had an uncommonly large difference between his Lexical Knowledge and General Information. The discrepancies for both clients provided key interpretive and diagnostic information. (Although Step 11 was used for both illustrative cases, the examples apply to Step 12 as well.) For additional examples of how to describe and interpret comparisons between a similar set of clinical clusters, see Flanagan and Kaufman (2009, pp. 176–178). Suggested

Table 5.9. Step 12: Size of Difference Between Pairs of Clinical Clusters Needed to Be Considered Unusually Large or Uncommon

Cluster Comparison			Amount of Difference
Visual-Motor Speed (BD+CD+SS)	vs.	Problem Solving without Visual-Motor Speed (MR+VP+PC)	20
Visual-Motor Speed (BD+CD+SS)	vs.	Mental Manipulation (D-Back + D-Seq)	25
Mental Manipulation (D-Back + D-Seq)	vs.	Problem Solving without Visual-Motor Speed (MR+VP+PC)	24
Fluid Reasoning (MR+ A)	vs.	Visual Processing (BD+VP)	20
Verbal Fluid Reasoning (SI+CO)	vs.	Fluid Reasoning (MR+AR)	21
Lexical Knowledge (VC+SI)	vs.	General Information (CO+IN)	15
Long-Term Memory (VC+IN)	vs.	Short-Term Memory (D-Back + D-Seq)	24
Verbal Fluid Reasoning (SI+CO)	vs.	Long-Term Memory (VC+IN)	16

Source: Standardization data and analysis results from the *Wechsler Adult Intelligence Scale—Fourth Edition* (WAIS-IV). Copyright © 2008 by NCS Pearson, Inc. Used with permission. All rights reserved.

Note: "Unusually large or uncommon" denotes differences estimated to occur less than 10% of the time in the WAIS-IV standardization sample. The differences in this table were estimated by the formula provided by Sattler (1982, Table C-11) for computing the percentage of a population obtaining discrepancies between two standard scores. This formula includes the correlations between the two standard scores for each comparison, which were kindly provided by Pearson Assessments (J. J. Wang, personal communication, March 23, 2009, and J. J. Zhu, personal communication, November 7, 2011). All comparisons are based on data for the total WAIS-IV standardization sample (ages 16–90).

hypotheses for the meanings of patterns of findings from the clinical comparisons are provided in Rapid Reference 5.15; these hypotheses apply to Step 12 as well as Step 11.

Interpretation of the WAIS-IV profile (from the global ability, to the indexes, to these clinical clusters) must consider other variables than true differences in ability. Chapter 4 reviewed many of these clinical and behavioral variables that may elucidate an examinee's WAIS-IV profile. In addition, Chapter 6 provides detailed information from a neuropsychological approach to interpretation that can provide more insight into understanding peaks and valleys in a person's abilities. Interpretation of the process scores that the WAIS-IV offers is detailed in Chapter 6. Integration of all of these quantitative and qualitative aspects of the WAIS-IV profile will provide the most accurate portrait of an individual's cognitive abilities.

⚞ TEST YOURSELF ⚟

1. **If the FSIQ is not interpretable, then**
   a. The GAI should automatically be designated as the best representation of a person's general intellectual ability.
   b. Determine if the GAI can be calculated and interpreted as a reliable and valid estimate of a person's general intellectual ability.
   c. The WAIS-IV is not a good test to measure the person's IQ.
   d. The CPI should be considered as the best measure of the person's general intellectual ability.

2. **TRUE or FALSE? If the examinee is age 75, the Keith five-factor model is especially useful for profile interpretation.**

3. **A personal strength in visual processing ability may be evident from**
   a. A Visual Processing (Gv) Cluster score of 90 that is uncommonly higher than the mean factor score of 74
   b. A Visual Processing (Gv) Cluster score of 120 that is uncommonly higher than the mean factor score of 95
   c. A Visual Processing (Gv) Cluster score of 82 that is uncommonly higher than the mean factor score of 65
   d. All of the above

4. **Using the normative descriptive system to describe the WAIS-IV Index scores, a score of 84 should be described as**
   a. A Normative Strength
   b. Within normal limits
   c. A Normative Weakness
   d. None of the above

5. **Alex obtained a PRI of 79, which is significantly lower than his other indexes and is uncommon in the normal population. Alex's PRI is best described as a**
   a. Key Asset
   b. Personal Strength
   c. Personal Weakness
   d. High Priority Concern

6. **An abnormally large discrepancy between PRI and VCI means it is**
   a. Rare among the normal population
   b. Equivalent to a statistically significant discrepancy
   c. At least a 50-point discrepancy
   d. At least a 5-point discrepancy

7. **TRUE or FALSE? If the PRI is not a unitary ability for an 80-year-old person, then examiners may consider interpreting the profile from the Core five-factor model.**

8. **If an individual has a WMI less than 85, that person has a possible deficit in**
   a. Working memory
   b. Auditory attention
   c. Expressive language
   d. Speed of auditory processing
   e. Any or all of the above areas

9. **Wechsler indexes, Keith factors, Core factors, and clinical clusters**
   a. Must be interpreted from a CHC theoretical model
   b. Must be interpreted from a neuropsychological perspective
   c. Must be interpreted from the perspective of the test publishers
   d. Must consider theory, behavior, and the background of the client in interpretation

10. **A low score on the Keith or Core factor of Short-Term Memory (Gsm) may be interpreted as all of the following EXCEPT**
    a. Distractibility or attentional difficulties
    b. Difficulty with numbers
    c. Poor visual-motor ability
    d. Excessive anxiety

11. **A low score on the Processing Speed Index (PSI) is LEAST likely to be due to**
    a. Fine motor control difficulty
    b. Reflective processing style
    c. Poor visual memory
    d. Poor nonverbal reasoning

12. **TRUE or FALSE? In calculation of an individual's personal strengths and weaknesses in the index profile or the factor profiles, you compare each of their interpretable index or factor scores to the person's own mean index or factor score.**

Answers: 1. b; 2. false; 3. d; 4. c; 5. d; 6. a; 7. true; 8. e; 9. d; 10. c; 11. d; 12. true.

Six

CLINICAL APPLICATIONS I

A Neuropsychological Approach to Interpretation of the WAIS-IV and the Use of the WAIS-IV in Learning Disability Assessments

George McCloskey
Emily S. Hartz
Katherine Scipioni

INTRODUCTION

This chapter applies neuropsychological concepts to the interpretation of performance on the WAIS-IV. The approach described here is an extension of the process-oriented approach that has been applied in the interpretation of the WISC-IV (McCloskey, 2009; McCloskey & Maerlender, 2005) and reflects the clinical interpretation methods of Edith Kaplan and her colleagues (Kaplan, 1988; Kaplan, Fein, Morris, Kramer, & Delis, 1999). The approach described here is consistent with the intelligent testing approach described in Chapter 4 of this book and is also compatible with the cognitive hypothesis testing model offered by Hale and Fiorello (2004). The focus of this approach is on how examinees perform the items of each WAIS-IV subtest, as well as the scores they earn on each of those subtests. Therefore, the key to effective interpretation of test performance after administration is careful observation of test performance during administration. Integration of what was observed during administration with what is scored after administration enables the clinician to more accurately characterize the specific cognitive strengths and weaknesses of the examinee.

The approach presented in this chapter is best summarized through the Interpretive Levels Framework shown in Figure 6.1 and summarized in Rapid References 6.1 through 6.5. Interpretation of the WAIS-IV can occur on multiple levels. Each of these levels represents a particular degree of aggregation, or disaggregation, of the information gathered during administration and assembled after administration. Each successive level, from bottom to top, represents an aggregation of information that obscures the details revealed by the levels below it. The Full Scale IQ obscures variability that may be present at the index level. Each index score obscures the contribution of individual subtest scores to the index. Each subtest score obscures the contribution of individual item scores to the subtest. Each item score obscures the contribution of variability in task cognitive construct use that may be observed during item administration. Although interpretation at each level can be viewed from a neuropsychological perspective, some levels are more suited to the application of a wide range of neuropsychological concepts than others. Although there is merit in the interpretation of FSIQ, Wechsler's Index scores, Keith's five theory-based factors, the new Core five factors, and assorted clusters of subtests (as explained thoroughly in Chapter 5), the premise of this chapter is that the most effective neuropsychological interpretation of WAIS-IV performance will be found at the subtest, item, and task-specific cognitive constructs levels.[1]

This chapter focuses on WAIS-IV interpretation at the subtest, item, and task-specific cognitive construct levels, with some treatment of subtest clusters

---

1. From the perspective of the authors of this book, the tenets expressed in this chapter on neuropsychological interpretation are valuable as a follow-up to the step-by-step approach delineated in Chapter 5, not as a replacement for that approach. As such, the book authors consider this Kaplan-based approach to WAIS-IV interpretation as a key clinical and *qualitative* supplement to the Chapter 5 quantitative system (although much of the neuropsychological approach is data based). In particular, the book authors believe that interpretation of subtests and items should always be a second line of interpretation, following the first line—namely, the step-by-step analyses of FSIQ, GAI, CPI, the four Wechsler Indexes, the five Keith factors, the five Core factors, and the diverse clinical clusters. The authors of this chapter would undoubtedly reverse the order of the "first line" and "second line," which the book authors believe enriches the breadth and quality of the WAIS-IV interpretation system presented in this book.

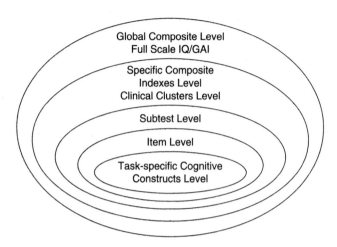

Global Composite Level
Full Scale IQ/GAI

Specific Composite
Indexes Level
Clinical Clusters Level

Subtest Level

Item Level

Task-specific Cognitive
Constructs Level

Figure 6.1. Interpretive Levels Framework Applied to the WAIS-IV

at the specific composite level. The final section of this chapter discusses a model for the assessment of learning disabilities and how the WAIS-IV interpreted from a neuropsychological perspective can be used in the assessment of adolescent and adult learning disabilities.

LEVELS OF INTERPRETATION

Global Composite Level of Interpretation

At the global composite level, all of the subtests from two or more indexes are summed together to yield a broader composite score. The WAIS-IV offers two such global-level composite scores: FSIQ and GAI. GAI and FSIQ interpretations assume that performance across the multiple indexes they encompass was relatively uniform and that a closely related group of cognitive constructs was used by the examinee while performing the index-specific tasks comprising the global composite. A GAI or FSIQ standard score is thought to be a homogeneous indication of the examinee's degree of capability, relative to a standardization sample comparison group, in using the cognitive constructs thought to be assessed by the index-specific tasks aggregated to form the global composite. Global composite-level interpretation obscures the contribution of the separate indexes to the global score, assuming that variations in index-level performance represent random fluctuations that are unimportant or impossible to interpret meaningfully in an empirically valid manner.

≡ *Rapid Reference 6.1*

Key Facts About the Global Composite Level of Interpretation

- All of the subtests from two or more indexes are summed together to yield a broader composite score.
- The WAIS-IV offers the FSIQ and GAI.
- When the differences between index scores are statistically significant and uncommonly large, the FSIQ and GAI are masking information that is critical to a neuropsychological interpretation of performance.

Although some psychologists might argue that the FSIQ or the GAI offer a neuropsychological perspective on overall level of cognitive functioning, even the most diehard globalist must admit that the FSIQ and GAI greatly obscure the contribution of various cognitive constructs to the overall level of performance. When these various sources are out of balance in a dramatic way (i.e., the differences between index scores are statistically significant and highly unusual relative to standardization sample performance), the FSIQ and GAI are masking information that is critical to a neuropsychological interpretation of performance. The only situation in which the FSIQ and/or GAI can be justified even marginally as a reflection of overall neuropsychological functioning is when index-level and subtest-level scores all cluster within a very restricted score range, showing minimal and nonsignificant variation. That approach to global scores is entirely consistent with the step-by-step interpretive approach spelled out in Chapter 5. Even cases where index and subtest scores do not vary significantly, however, significant variation at the item level may offer a much richer source of neuropsychological interpretation, especially in cases where some form of cognitive impairment is suspected. When significant variations in index- and/or subtest-level scores are present, neuropsychological interpretation must focus at levels below the global composite level.

Specific Composite (Index) Level of Interpretation

At the specific composite level, various subtest scaled score triads and dyads are aggregated to form composite scores called indexes that are represented normatively by standard scores. Each index standard score represents an aggregation of performance across multiple subtests. Index-level interpretation assumes that performance across the multiple subtests was relatively uniform and that a closely related group of cognitive constructs was used by the examinee while performing the subtests constituting the index. An index standard score is thought to be a homogeneous indication of the examinee's degree of capability, relative to a standardization sample comparison group, in using the cognitive constructs thought to be assessed by the cluster of subtests that form the index. Index-level interpretation obscures the contribution of individual subtests to the index, assuming that variations in subtest-level performance represent random fluctuations that are unimportant or impossible to interpret meaningfully in an empirically valid manner.

Index-level interpretation provides a more varied perspective on cognitive function than the FSIQ or GAI, acknowledging that performance is likely to vary across four (or two) general cognitive domains labeled Verbal Comprehension, Perceptual Reasoning, Working Memory, and Processing Speed. This is an improvement over FSIQ and GAI in that variations among the indexes can offer a richer source for neuropsychological interpretation when these variations are significant and unusually large. The index level of interpretation is likely to pick up on glaring imbalances that might be present among the four general domains represented on the WAIS-IV. Contrasting performance on the VCI and PRI with performance on the WMI and PSI is certainly a step in the right direction in acknowledging the need for a neuropsychological perspective on interpretation. Stopping at this level of analysis when significant and unusual differences among index scores are found, however, significantly limits the potential effectiveness of a neuropsychological approach to interpretation of WAIS-IV test performance.

Limiting interpretation to the index level is problematic, because more than just four broad cognitive constructs should be considered when applying a cognitive neuropsychological perspective to interpretation of the WAIS-IV. The seeming unitary nature of each of the four WAIS-IV indexes is not an accurate representation of the multiple cognitive constructs that are needed to perform the aggregated tasks of each of the indexes. This is especially apparent in cases where subtest scores within an Index differ significantly. Focusing interpretation at the index score level can result in erroneous neuropsychological interpretations of performance.

A more valid approach to aggregation of subtest score information at the specific composite level is the subtest cluster method, which combines scores from one or more subtests only after interpretive analysis supports the contention that the clustered subtests are measuring similar cognitive constructs at the level of specificity needed for effective interpretation.

Subtest Level of Interpretation

Individual subtest scores are obtained by summing performance across all items of the subtest, producing an aggregate raw score that is converted into a norm-referenced scaled score. Subtest-level interpretation assumes that performance across the multiple items of the subtest was relatively uniform and that the same set of task-specific cognitive constructs was used by the examinee while performing all of the items constituting the subtest. A subtest scaled score is thought to be a homogeneous indication of the examinee's degree of capability, relative to a standardization sample comparison group, in using the task-specific cognitive constructs thought to be assessed by the items of that subtest. Subtest-level interpretation obscures the contribution of item response patterns, item clusters, or individual items to subtest performance, assuming that variations in item-level performance represent random fluctuations that are unimportant or impossible to interpret meaningfully in an empirically valid manner.

Clinicians seeking to interpret WAIS-IV assessment from a neuropsychological perspective are on somewhat firmer ground when attention is focused at the subtest level. The need for subtest-level interpretation is clear when significantly large differences are present between or among the subtests that comprise an index. In these instances, a clear pattern of difference in the use of cognitive constructs might be readily apparent.

Although subtest-level interpretation can be more specific than index- or global-level interpretation, clinicians attempting to interpret the WAIS-IV from a neuropsychological perspective using the subtest scaled score profile are at

---

≡ *Rapid Reference 6.2*

···

Key Facts About the Specific Composite (Index) Level of Interpretation

- Subtest scaled score triads and dyads form composite scores called indexes that are represented normatively by Standard Scores.
- Index-level interpretation assumes that performance across the multiple subtests was relatively uniform.
- Interpretation at this level assumes that the examinee used a closely related group of cognitive constructs while performing the subtests constituting the index.
- An alternative to index-level interpretation is the subtest cluster method, which combines scores from subtests only after interpretive analysis indicates that subtests are measuring similar cognitive constructs.

≡ *Rapid Reference 6.3*

Key Facts About the Subtest Level of Interpretation

- Subtest scores are an aggregate raw score that is converted into a norm-referenced scaled score.
- Interpretation at the subtest level assumes that the same set of cognitive constructs was used by the examinee while performing the items constituting the subtest.
- The contribution of item response patterns, item clusters, or individual items to subtest performance is obscured at this level of interpretation.
- Subtest-level performance involves multiple cognitive constructs, so test hypotheses on a case-by-case basis in order to develop stronger inferences about how task-specific cognitive constructs are affecting subtest performance.

risk of missing important aspects of performance that would significantly alter the interpretation of a subtest score profile. In the majority of cases, interpretation of subtest differences is not particularly straightforward, because performance on each of the subtests of the WAIS-IV always involves the use of multiple cognitive constructs. Additionally, the multiple cognitive constructs used to perform a subtest can vary from one examinee to another. Because subtest-level performance involves multiple cognitive constructs, it is necessary to test hypotheses on a case-by-case basis in order to develop stronger inferences about how specific cognitive constructs are affecting subtest performance. If interpretation remains focused solely on the subtest score level, then the clinician must use additional subtests to test hypotheses about the contribution of various cognitive constructs to subtest performance. The greater the number of possible cognitive constructs required for subtest performance, the greater the number of competing hypotheses that require further testing.

Item Level of Interpretation

All WAIS-IV items are scored individually using predetermined criteria. Each item score represents an aggregate statement about the cognitive constructs used to perform the item. The methods used to assign scores to items assume that only the cognitive constructs thought to be required for item performance are being assessed as intended, and they are contributing equally to the performance of each item. A correct response indicates that the examinee demonstrated effective use of the cognitive constructs intended to be assessed with the item. An incorrect response indicates the ineffective use of the cognitive constructs intended to be assessed with the item. It is also assumed that examinee item responses will follow a specific pattern throughout the subtest, where consistently correct performance on a subset of items in the "easy range" will be followed by variable performance on a subset of items in the "challenging range," which will be followed by incorrect responses on a subset of items in the "too-difficult range."

Taken at face value, item scores obscure the possible differential contribution of multiple cognitive constructs to item success or item failure, and deviations from the expected pattern of item performance represent random fluctuations that are unimportant or impossible to interpret meaningfully in an empirically valid manner. Rather than taking an examinee's set of item-level scores at face value, item-level interpretation attempts to identify and understand unusual patterns of item performance, such as easy items answered incorrectly or difficult items answered with ease, or performance on a cluster of items that is inconsistent with the expected pattern. When performed effectively, item-level interpretation will draw on knowledge obtained at the task-specific cognitive constructs level to generate hypotheses about the cognitive constructs that are, or are not, being used in the performance of individual items or subsets of items.

Although subtest-level interpretation is much more likely to yield valuable information from a neuropsychological perspective than index scores, specific subtests that can be used to test hypotheses about the contribution of different cognitive constructs to WAIS-IV subtest performance are not always available and/or clinicians often cannot devote the time needed to thoroughly test every hypothesis using additional subtests. In these instances, neuropsychological interpretation of subtest performance can be greatly enhanced through careful inspection of item-level performance. Item-level analysis focused on item response patterns, item cluster performance, and individual item performance often will yield information that can be very useful in testing hypotheses about the specific cognitive construct likely to be involved in subtest performance.

Task-Specific Cognitive Constructs Level of Interpretation

The task-specific cognitive constructs level of interpretation acknowledges the fact that an examinee's attempt to complete any single item from any subtest of the WAIS-IV will require an attempt to use multiple cognitive constructs.

≡ *Rapid Reference 6.4*

Key Facts About the Item Level of Interpretation

- Item scores are aggregate statements about the cognitive constructs used to perform the item.
- An examinee's response indicates whether he or she effectively used the cognitive constructs intended to be assessed with the item.
- Item scores obscure the possible differential contribution of multiple cognitive constructs to item success or item failure.
- Deviations from the expected pattern of item performance represent random fluctuations that are unimportant or impossible to interpret meaningfully in an empirically valid manner.
- Analyzing item response patterns, item cluster performance, and individual item performance often will yield information that is useful in testing hypotheses about the specific cognitive constructs involved in subtest performance.

Although each item is constructed in a manner that assumes that the use of a specific cognitive construct, or set of constructs, will be the most efficient and effective way to perform the item, there is no guarantee that individual examinees will chose to use those specific cognitive constructs in their efforts to complete the item. Individual examinees will use their own decision-making processes to determine what cognitive constructs they draw on to perform an item. The cognitive constructs chosen by the examinee are likely to reflect inherent preferences or biases of the examinee, and they may not be consistent with the cognitive constructs the item was intended to assess. Careful observation of how the examinee performs an item is therefore critical to an accurate understanding of what cognitive constructs are actually being assessed by that item.

No matter what efforts are made to try to ensure that a specific task is assessing a specific cognitive construct, most examinees' specific neural capabilities will enable them to choose for themselves the cognitive constructs they wish to engage in their efforts with a task. This fact will continue to frustrate the efforts of researchers and clinicians who desire to identify and use tasks that are pure measures of a single cognitive construct. This fact also confounds the standard view of subtest reliability, in which all sources of unexplained variability in task performance are considered measurement error. Unfortunately, such misguided conceptions of reliability are used to support the argument against the use of subtest-level interpretation of test performance and to discourage clinicians from attempting to understand the individual variation observed in task performance. In many cases, careful clinical observation of task performance can identify and explain how examinees are using cognitive constructs, thereby increasing the interpretive validity as well as the reliability of the assessment process by explaining the unexplained sources of variability in performance that would have been identified only as measurement error.

A cognitive neuropsychological approach to WAIS-IV interpretation requires a solid understanding of the various cognitive constructs that could be involved in the performance of the individual items of each subtest and knowledge of the kinds of behaviors that are most likely to indicate the use of these cognitive constructs. This level of analysis requires more than simply looking for item response patterns, performance on item clusters, or knowing whether a specific item was scored as right or wrong. As noted earlier, examinees determine for themselves what cognitive constructs they choose to use to perform test items, necessitating careful observation of examinee performance and an understanding of how specific behaviors can reflect the use of specific cognitive constructs. Effective interpretation of the cognitive constructs used during individual items informs all subsequent levels of interpretation, thereby increasing the likelihood of an accurate characterization of the examinee from a neuropsychological perspective.

≡ Rapid Reference 6.5

Task-Specific Cognitive Constructs Level of Interpretation

- Individual examinees determine what cognitive constructs they draw on to perform an item.
- Careful observation of how the examinee performs an item is critical to the accurate understanding of what cognitive constructs are actually being assessed by that item.
- The interpretive validity and the reliability of the assessment process are increased by illuminating the unexplained sources of variability in performance that may be inferred from careful clinical observations of how examinees are using cognitive constructs.
- Effective interpretation of the cognitive constructs used during individual items informs all subsequent levels of interpretation, thereby increasing the likelihood of an accurate characterization of the examinee from a neuropsychological perspective.

NEUROPSYCHOLOGICAL INTERPRETATION OF WAIS-IV PERFORMANCE

To effectively use and interpret the WAIS-IV from a neuropsychological perspective, it is necessary to understand the multifactorial nature of the WAIS-IV subtests. Specifically, examiners should consider what cognitive constructs the subtests assess and how these cognitive constructs are reflected in item-level performance and subtest- and composite-level scores. (Because the neuropsychological interpretation of WAIS-IV performance is so complex, we warn against deriving hypotheses of neurological pathology by the simple presence of significant differences among scores.)

CAUTION

Overinterpretation of VCI-PRI Difference

Perhaps the most notable erroneous interpretation of index-level scores is the conception that significant and unusual differences between the VCI and PRI index scores (and comparable differences between VIQ-PIQ scale scores on the WAIS, WAIS-R, and WAIS-III) consistently represent a pathognomonic sign of some form of neuropsychological impairment or a general form of "hemispheric imbalance." The legitimate research studies that have reported the neuropsychological implications of VIQ-PIQ differences (and more recently on VCI-PRI differences) and hemispheric functioning imbalances typically offer caveats such as: "It is cautioned that these VIQ-PIQ discrepancies in isolation are ineffective indexes of cerebral dysfunction and that patterns of performance must be viewed in the context of a complete neuropsychological examination and relevant medical and educational historical data" (Bornstein, 1983, p. 779).

Despite such prudent cautionary statements, overstatement of the neuropsychological implications of VCI-PRI differences in either direction still occurs in many psychological reports and professional and popular literature sources. As shown in the following table, the WAIS-IV standardization data do not support a general interpretation of cognitive impairment based solely on VCI-PRI significant differences.

Percentage of the WAIS-IV Standardization Sample Displaying a VCI-PRI or PRI-VCI Discrepancy This Size or Larger for Various FSIQ Score Ranges

Size of Discrepancy	<79	80–89	90–109	110–120	>119
			FSIQ Score Range		
10	40.8	45.9	45.9	45.7	53.5
15	19.0	21.9	26.2	31.2	35.5
20	7.4	10.1	15.1	17.3	18.5
25	3.7	3.6	6.7	9.1	9.5

These data reveal a picture of cognitive functioning that is in direct contradiction to the well-entrenched myth that the greater the VCI-PRI difference, the greater the likelihood that some form of cerebral dysfunction is present. Applying the "VCI-PRI significant difference equals cognitive impairment" argument to the data from the WAIS-IV standardization sample leads one to the absurd conclusion that the more capable a person is (based on FSIQ), the more likely it is that he or she is demonstrating hemispheric imbalance and brain dysfunction, because the proportion of VCI-PRI differences rises as the FSIQ increases. Considering that most types of brain dysfunction tend to have the effect of lowering FSIQ, it is curious to note that the frequency of occurrence of VCI-PRI differences decreases proportionately with the drop in FSIQ level, therefore producing the situation where individuals in the general population most likely to be affected with some form of undetected neurological complications (i.e., those scoring below FSIQ 90) that would produce hemispheric imbalances or cognitive impairment actually display less variability in their score profile than those who are more often thought of as being neurologically intact (i.e., those scoring above FSIQ 120). Although it is certainly possible that a person with a high FSIQ and a large difference between VCI and PRI scores is suffering from a neurological disorder, the idea that a VCI-PRI difference of 10 points, or even 20 points, denotes pathology is unwarranted and unsupportable from the standardization data. It is important to note that the pattern of cumulative percentages of VCI-PRI differences shown in the WAIS-IV standardization data was also present in the WAIS-III and the WISC-IV standardization sample data.

Although some examiners choose to administer only the core 10 WAIS-IV subtests that constitute the four indexes, cognitive neuropsychological interpretation can be greatly enhanced when one or more of the five supplemental subtests are administered along with the core subtests, as the additional subtests offer a more varied perspective on the examinee's use of cognitive constructs. The next section discusses the subtests of the WAIS-IV from a neuropsychological perspective, organized by the four indexes. The goal will be to demonstrate how the index-level scores often mask important variations in test performance and how information from the levels of the subtest clusters, subtests, items, and cognitive constructs can be used to enhance test interpretation from a neuropsychological perspective.

WHAT DO THE VERBAL COMPREHENSION SUBTESTS MEASURE?

The Verbal Comprehension Index (VCI) subtests were designed primarily to assess the use of specific cognitive constructs applied with orally presented verbal content. These constructs are the primary focus of interpretation of the VCI, as well as each individual subtest, and include retrieval of verbal

DON'T FORGET

··

Cognitive Constructs Most Likely to Be Involved in Verbal Comprehension Tasks

Primary Constructs Targeted for Assessment

Retrieval of verbal information from long-term storage

Retrieval of word meanings (Vocabulary)

Retrieval of facts from various content areas (Information)

Reasoning with orally presented verbal information

Reasoning with conceptually related words (Similarities)

Reasoning with real-world cause-and-effect relationships (Comprehension)

Secondary Constructs Not Specifically Targeted for Assessment

Auditory Acuity

Auditory Attention

Auditory Discrimination

Auditory Comprehension (Receptive Language)

Auditory Processing Speed

Initial Registration of auditorily presented verbal information

Working Memory applied with auditorily presented verbal information

Expressive Language Production

Executive Function cueing and directing of receipt of input, internal processing of input, and production of responses

information from long-term storage and reasoning with verbal information. The roles of these primary cognitive constructs in task performance are described in Appendix B.1. Examiners who are interested in knowing as much as possible about the examinee's ability to reason with verbal information are strongly encouraged to administer the supplementary Comprehension subtest, even though it is not a core subtest of the VCI.[2]

Beyond the two primary cognitive constructs targeted for assessment with the VCI, the specific formats of each VCI subtest make demands on the examinee that require the engagement of additional cognitive constructs in order to achieve success. Although these constructs are required for effective

---

2. The book authors also recommend administering Comprehension (Chapter 5), because two of the comparisons that involve the clinical clusters depend on the person's performance on Comprehension.

subtest performance, they are not considered to be the primary target of the assessment (i.e., the intention of the subtest is not to quantitatively assess the examinee's use of these cognitive constructs). These secondary cognitive constructs include Auditory Attention, Auditory Discrimination, Auditory Comprehension, Auditory Processing Speed, Expressive Language, Working Memory applied to verbal content, and multiple Executive Functions applied to cue and direct the mental processing of language and working with verbal content. The roles of these secondary cognitive constructs in subtest performance are described in detail in Appendix B.2.

When VCI subtest scores are interpreted, either collectively using the VCI or individually, it is often assumed that the subtests are measuring the primary constructs intended to be assessed. The secondary constructs required for effective performance are either ignored or assumed to be intact and functioning as expected, allowing the focus of interpretation to be on the primary constructs. For example, if an examinee cannot respond effectively to Similarities and Comprehension items, then the assumption often is that the examinee has poor reasoning abilities; if the examinee cannot provide adequate responses to the Vocabulary and Information subtests, then the assumption is that the examinee does not know the meanings of the words or does not know the specific facts about which he or she is being asked. In many cases where low performance is observed, however, such assumptions are not necessarily warranted. To know if these assumptions about the primary constructs are valid, the role of the secondary cognitive constructs in task performance must be explored in detail. Secondary cognitive constructs can interfere with task performance to a significant degree when not accessed or when applied ineffectively. Thus, it is inappropriate to focus subtest score interpretation exclusively on the primary constructs that are thought to be assessed.

When low scores or scores that are not consistent with what is known about the examinee are obtained with one or more of the VCI subtests, careful analysis of the shared and/or unique contributions of secondary cognitive constructs and more detailed analysis of item responses and the ways in which the responses were delivered should be undertaken. As indicated in the earlier discussion, poor performance on the VCI subtests is thought to reflect a lack of reasoning and/or a lack of stored knowledge (i.e., a lack of verbal intelligence). Clinicians who appreciate that a low score on one or more VCI subtests could be caused by many different sources can draw on their knowledge of cognitive constructs shared by subtests and observations about the manner in which the responses were delivered to help obtain a better understanding of the cognitive constructs that are most likely to have contributed to the poor performance.

Appendix B.3 provides an interpretive summary table that can be used to assist with the analysis of VCI subtests in terms of cognitive constructs that could be contributing to performance on each subtest. Appendix B.5 provides a summary of the interpretations associated with behaviors observed during administration of the VCI subtests that can be used to enhance hypothesis testing about what cognitive constructs are, or are not, being used to perform subtests.

When VCI subtest scores vary greatly and/or when the examiner observes behaviors that suggest that secondary cognitive constructs are influencing task performance, subtest cluster analysis may be helpful in identifying specific strengths and weaknesses in the use of various cognitive constructs. Appendix B.5 outlines the general interpretation of subtest clusters and illustrates the application of the subtest cluster analysis method with the VCI subtests.

When you are engaged in subtest interpretation at the composite level with subtest cluster analysis or at the subtest level, subtest comparisons should include the determination of whether a statistically significant difference exists between the scores earned on the subtests being compared. Use a rounded value of 3 scaled score points to signify a statistically significant difference for any of the comparisons between pairs of VCI subtests or between subtest clusters. Appendix B.5 provides guidelines for interpreting comparisons between specific VCI subtests, and Appendix B.6 provides a worksheet to aid in the interpretation of VCI subtest scaled score comparisons. Appendix C.1 provides a case study example that illustrates the application of subtest cluster-, subtest-, item-, and task-specific cognitive construct–level interpretation of Verbal Comprehension subtest performance.

WHAT DO THE PERCEPTUAL REASONING SUBTESTS MEASURE?

The Perceptual Reasoning Index (PRI) subtests were designed primarily to assess the application of reasoning with nonverbal, visual stimuli including the ability to "analyze and synthesize abstract visual stimuli" (Wechsler, 2008, pp. 13–14). Assessment of these reasoning constructs is intended to be the primary focus of interpretation of the PRI as well as the individual PRI subtests. The role of the primary cognitive construct of reasoning in task performance is described in detail in Appendix B.7.

Beyond the primary cognitive construct targeted for assessment with the PRI subtests, the specific formats of each subtest make demands on the

DON'T FORGET

....

Cognitive Constructs Most Likely to Be Involved in Perceptual Reasoning Tasks

Primary Constructs Targeted for Assessment
   Reasoning with visually presented nonverbal stimuli
   Reasoning with visual quantitative information (Figure Weights)
   Reasoning with conceptually related concrete visual stimuli
   Reasoning with conceptually related abstract visual stimuli
   Reasoning about how to integrate visual elements to create a model
Secondary Constructs Not Specifically Targeted for Assessment
   Visual Acuity
   Visual Discrimination
   Visual Processing Speed
   Initial registration of nonverbal visual stimuli
   Working memory applied with nonverbal visual stimuli
   Executive Function cueing and directing of receipt of input, internal processing, and production of responses

examinee that require the engagement of additional cognitive constructs in order to achieve success. Although these constructs typically are required for effective subtest performance, they are not considered to be the primary target of the assessment (i.e., the intention of the subtest is not to quantitatively assess the examinee's use of these cognitive constructs). These secondary cognitive constructs include Visual Perception and Representation; Visual Discrimination; Visualization; Motor Dexterity; Visual, Motor, and Visuo-motor Processing Speed; Working Memory applied to visual nonverbal content; and multiple Executive Functions applied to cue and direct the mental processing of nonverbal visual stimuli. The roles of these secondary cognitive constructs in subtest performance are described in detail in Appendix B.7.

Contrary to the claim of the test publisher, the replacement of the Picture Completion subtest with the Visual Puzzles subtest did not increase the likelihood that the cognitive construct of primary concern (i.e., reasoning with visual stimuli) would be the cognitive construct having the greatest impact on performance of the PRI subtests. As noted in Appendix B.7, the constructs most likely to be assessed with the Visual Puzzles subtest focus on basic visual processing and visual processing speed constructs, rather than reasoning with visual stimuli.

The wording used here to describe the primary cognitive construct of the Perceptual Reasoning tasks (i.e., reasoning with nonverbal, visual stimuli) was very purposefully chosen. The phrase "Reasoning with nonverbal visual stimuli" is not synonymous with the term *nonverbal reasoning*. Placing nonverbal visual materials in front of an examinee is not a guarantee that the examinee will reason nonverbally with those materials, especially when clinicians use standardized directions that include verbal explanations of how to perform items when introducing PRI subtests. Although it may be advantageous to reason without engaging language abilities when attempting PRI subtests, it is not necessary to do so. Clinicians are likely to observe examinees who engage language abilities to "talk themselves through" some or all aspects of specific Matrix Reasoning, Figure Weights, or Picture Completion items. Such verbal mediation can be helpful, or even essential, to the success of the efforts of some examinees with these tasks. Less likely to be observed is the examinee who attempts to verbally mediate most or all of his or her work with the Block Design and/or Visual Puzzles subtests, but even such a mismatched allocation of mental constructs, though unusual, is not entirely without occurrence.

In contrast to the previous discussion, when PRI subtest scores are interpreted, either collectively using the PRI or individually, it is often assumed that scores reflect the primary construct of reasoning with nonverbal, visual material. In such cases, the secondary constructs required for effective performance are either ignored or assumed to be intact and functioning as expected, thereby allowing the focus of interpretation to be on reasoning construct. From this perspective, if an examinee cannot respond effectively to Visual Puzzles, Block Design, and/or Matrix Reasoning items, then the assumption is that the examinee has poor nonverbal reasoning ability. In many cases where low performance is observed, however, such an assumption is not necessarily warranted. To know if the assumption about the primary construct is valid, the role of the secondary cognitive constructs in task performance must be understood and explored in more detail. When not accessed, or when applied ineffectively, these secondary cognitive constructs can interfere with task performance to a significant degree, making it inappropriate to focus subtest score interpretation exclusively on the primary construct thought to be assessed.

Clinicians should take note of the variety of secondary cognitive constructs assessed with the Picture Completion and Figure Weights subtests. Knowing how an examinee performs with these two supplemental subtests can greatly enhance interpretation of Perceptual Reasoning performance. Examiners are strongly encouraged to include these two supplemental tasks as part of their standard administration of the WAIS-IV.[3]

When low scores or scores that are not consistent with what is known about the examinee are obtained with one or more of the PRI subtests, careful analysis of the shared and/or unique contributions of the secondary cognitive constructs and more detailed analysis of item responses and the ways in which responses were delivered should be undertaken. As indicated in the previous discussion, poor performance on the PRI subtests is thought to reflect a lack of reasoning with nonverbal visual material (i.e., a lack of nonverbal intelligence). Clinicians who appreciate that a low score on one or more PRI subtests could be caused by many different sources can draw on the subtest cluster-, item-, and task-specific cognitive construct–level analyses to help obtain a better understanding of why the examinee performed poorly and the implications of such poor performance.

Appendix B.8 provides an interpretive summary table that can be used to assist with the analysis of PRI subtests in terms of cognitive constructs thought to be assessed by each subtest. Appendix B.9 provides a summary of the interpretations associated with behaviors observed during administration of the PRI subtests that can be used to enhance hypothesis testing about what cognitive constructs are, or are not, being used to perform subtests.

The Block Design No Time Bonus Process Score (BDN) score offers a unique opportunity to contrast performance on the Block Design subtest with and without bonus points added for speed of completion of the final six most difficult items on the subtest. The BDN score is a formalized, norm-referenced application of the cognitive constructs level of interpretation applied to the items of the Block Design subtest. The BDN score acknowledges the fact that speed of performance is a construct unique from the constructs required for accurate solution of the more difficult items, and provides a quantitative means of testing the extent to which speed affected an examinee's overall level of subtest performance.

When engaged in subtest interpretation at the composite level with subtest cluster analysis or at the subtest level, subtest comparisons should include the determination of whether a statistically significant difference exists between the

---

3. The book authors strongly encourage administering Figure Weights and Letter-Number Sequencing (Chapter 5), because many aspects of the step-by-step system depend on the person's scores on these two supplemental subtests. They are less enthusiastic about administering Picture Completion. However, the book authors urge examiners to routinely administer Picture Completion if they plan to conduct the kind of neuropsychological interpretation advocated in this chapter.

scores earned on the subtests being compared. Use a rounded value of 3 scaled score points to signify a statistically significant difference for any of the comparisons between pairs of PRI subtests or between subtest clusters (see Appendix B.10).

When PRI subtest scores vary greatly and/or when the examiner observes behaviors that suggest that secondary cognitive constructs are influencing task performance, subtest cluster analysis may be helpful in identifying specific strengths and weaknesses in the use of various cognitive constructs. Appendix B.9 illustrates the application of the subtest cluster analysis method with the PRI subtests, and Appendix B.11 provides a worksheet to aid in the interpretation of Perceptual Reasoning task scaled-score comparisons. Appendix C.1 provides a case study example that illustrates the application of item- and task-specific cognitive construct–level procedures in the interpretations of PRI subtest performance.

WHAT DO THE WORKING MEMORY SUBTESTS MEASURE?

The Working Memory Index (WMI) subtests were designed primarily to assess the constructs involved in the initial registration and holding of information (sometimes referred to as short-term memory) and the mental manipulation of information that is being held in mind (often referred to as working memory). All three of the WMI subtests assess these constructs using auditorily presented verbal and verbal-quantitative stimuli. Assessment of these constructs is the primary focus of interpretation of the WMI, as well as the individual WMI subtests. The roles of these primary cognitive constructs in task performance are described in detail in Appendix B.12.

Beyond the primary cognitive constructs targeted for assessment with the WMI subtests, the specific formats of each subtest make demands on the examinee that require the engagement of additional cognitive constructs in order to achieve success. Although these constructs are required for effective subtest performance, they are not considered to be the primary target of the assessment (i.e., the intention of the subtest is not to quantitatively assess the examinee's use of these cognitive constructs). These secondary cognitive constructs include Auditory Acuity, Auditory Discrimination, Auditory Processing Speed, Attention to Auditorily Presented Verbal Information, Language Expression, and multiple Executive Functions applied to cue and direct the use of initial registration and working memory resources. The roles of these secondary cognitive constructs in subtest performance are described in detail in Appendix B.12.

DON'T FORGET

Cognitive Constructs Most Likely to Be Involved in Working Memory Tasks

Primary Constructs Targeted for Assessment
  Initial registration of stimuli
  Mental manipulation of stimuli

Secondary Constructs Not Specifically Targeted for Assessment
  Auditory discrimination
  Attention to auditory stimuli
  Auditory processing speed
  Mental processing speed
  Retrieval of verbal information from long-term storage
  Organization/sequencing ability
  Math skills
  Expressive language ability
  Executive Function cueing and directing of receipt of input, internal processing, and production of responses

In many cases where low performance is observed on one or both of the WMI core subtests, the generalized assumption of poor initial registration and/or poor working memory capacities is not necessarily warranted. To know if the assumption about these primary constructs is valid, the role of the secondary cognitive constructs in task performance and the effect of input and response formats must be understood and explored in more detail. When not accessed, or when applied ineffectively, secondary cognitive constructs can interfere with task performance to a significant degree, making it inappropriate to focus index or subtest score interpretation exclusively on the primary constructs that are thought to be assessed. Additionally, without knowing how the examinee performs when input and response formats are varied, the clinician is in danger of overinterpreting the generalizabiity of the WMI score.

When low scores or scores that are not consistent with what is known about the examinee are obtained from one or more of the WMI subtests, careful analysis of the shared and/or unique contributions of the secondary cognitive constructs and more detailed analysis of item responses and the ways in which responses were delivered should be undertaken. As indicated in the previous discussion, poor performance on WMI subtests is thought to reflect a lack of effective initial registration and manipulation of information in working memory. Clinicians who appreciate that a low score on one or more of the WMI subtests could be caused by many different sources can draw on the item- and cognitive construct–level analyses to help obtain a better understanding of why the examinee performed poorly and the implications of such poor performance.

Appendix B.13 provides an interpretive summary table that can be used to assist with the comparison of registration and mental manipulation tasks in terms of the cognitive constructs that may be involved in the performance of test items. Appendix B.14 provides a summary of the interpretations associated with behaviors observed during administration of the WMI subtests that can be used to enhance hypothesis testing about what cognitive constructs are, or are not, being used to perform subtests.

Meaningful interpretation of WMI subtest and Digit Span Process Task comparisons should include the determination of whether a statistically signifi- cant difference exists between the scores earned on the subtests and/or tasks being compared. Use a rounded value of 3 scaled score points to signify a statistically significant difference for any of the comparisons of the WMI subtests (see Appendix B.15).

When WMI subtest scores vary greatly and/or when the examiner observes behaviors that suggest that secondary cognitive constructs are influencing task performance, subtest cluster analysis may be helpful in identifying specific strengths and weaknesses in the use of various cognitive constructs. Appendix B.16 provides a worksheet to aid in the interpretation of Working Memory Domain task scaled-score comparisons. Appendix C.1 provides a case study example that includes the use of the interpretive worksheet and illustrates the application of the item and cognitive constructs levels in the interpretations of Working Memory task performance.

The addition of Digit Span Sequencing to the Digit Span subtest and the pairing of the Digit Span subtest with the Arithmetic subtest to form a two- subtest WMI substantially increased the likelihood that the primary cognitive construct of applying working memory with auditorily presented verbal and verbal/quantitative information would be reflected in the WMI score. Attempt- ing to assess an examinee's use of working memory solely through the lens of the WMI, however, still has several drawbacks. Interpretation can be strengthened to some degree with the addition of the supplemental Letter-Number Sequencing Subtest and the use of the Digit Span Process Task scaled scores for Digit Span Forward (DSF), Digit Span Backward (DSB), and Digit Span Sequencing (DSS).

Without an understanding of the role that secondary cognitive constructs play in task performance, clinicians frequently will have difficulty effectively interpreting an examinee's performance. For example, it is a neuropsychological fact that stimuli must be effectively registered before they can be manipulated in mind (i.e., no manipulation of information can occur if the information was not initially registered and/or is no longer being held in mind). How then does a clinician explain the performance of an examinee who repeats only four digits forward but is able to repeat six digits in reverse? The former result suggests a capacity for initially registering and holding only four digits, but in order to perform Digit Span Backward, the examinee first had to register and hold six digits and then mentally manipulate those six digits to provide a correct response. In such cases, although the examinee has the capacity to initially register and hold six digits, difficulties with the use of one or more secondary constructs reduced the examinee's ability to demonstrate that capacity in a consistent manner.

Clinicians interested in examining in more detail the relationship between performance on Digit Span Forward, Digit Span Backward, and Digit Span Sequencing will find cumulative frequency (Base Rates) tables comparing longest digit span values among these three digit span process tasks in Appendix C, Table C.6 of the *WAIS-IV Administration and Scoring Manual.*

When WMI subtest scores are interpreted either collectively using the WMI or individually, it is typically assumed that the WMI and the WMI subtest scores reflect a general level of working memory involvement. The secondary constructs required for effective performance are either ignored completely or are assumed to be intact and functioning as expected to allow for the focus of interpretation to be on the primary constructs of initial registration and mental manipulation of stimuli.

WHAT DO THE PROCESSING SPEED SUBTESTS MEASURE?

The Processing Speed Index (PSI) subtests were designed primarily to assess processing speed with nonverbal, visual stimuli. Assessment of processing speed therefore is the primary focus of interpretation of the PSI, as well as for the individual PSI subtests. The WAIS-IV includes a new supplementary subtest called Cancellation. The role of processing speed in PSI subtest performance is discussed in Appendix B.17.

Beyond the primary cognitive construct targeted for assessment with the PSI subtests, the specific formats of each subtest make demands on the examinee that require the engagement of additional cognitive constructs in order to achieve success. Although these constructs typically are required for effective subtest performance, they are not considered to be the primary target of the assessment (i.e., the intention of the subtest is not to quantitatively assess the examinee's use of these cognitive constructs). These secondary cognitive constructs include Visual Discrimination, Graphomotor abilities/skills, Attention to Visually Presented Information, and multiple Executive Functions applied to cue and direct the use of visual processing and processing speed resources. The roles of these secondary cognitive constructs in subtest performance are described in detail in Appendix B.17. Clinicians familiar with the WISC-IV Cancellation subtest should make note of the substantial difference in the kind of executive functions most likely to be involved in performance of the WAIS-IV Cancellation subtest compared to those involved with the WISC-IV Cancellation subtest.

It is important to recognize that the PSI comprising the Coding and Symbol Search subtests offers a fairly limited measure of processing speed. All three of the PSI subtests employ a visual presentation format that requires the processing of nonverbal visual stimuli and graphomotor responses. The WAIS-IV PSI subtests do not address processing speed directly applied to academic tasks such as the fluent reading or writing of words or the completion of math problems. As a result of this narrow focus of input, processing, and output demands, PSI

DON'T FORGET
···

Cognitive Constructs Most Likely to Be Involved in Processing Speed Tasks

Primary Constructs Targeted for Assessment
  Visual processing speed
  Motor processing speed
  Visual-motor processing speed
Secondary Constructs Not Specifically Targeted for Assessment
  Visual perception
  Visual discrimination
  Attention to visual details
  Multitasking
  Organization ability/skills
  Graphomotor ability/skill
  Use of working memory with visual stimuli
  Language representation of visual stimuli
  Executive Function cueing and directing of receipt of input, internal processing, and production of responses

scores have limited generalizability to academic settings or work settings involving these academic skills. Clinicians who wish to know about an examinee's processing speed for reading cannot infer this from the PSI score or the individual Symbol Search, Coding, or Cancellation subtest scores. Such information needs to be obtained from one or more specific measures of reading speed. From a process approach perspective, however, there is a link between performance on the Coding subtest and written expression production.

Because effective performance of both Coding and written expression tasks involves basic graphomotor ability or skills, an examinee who experiences extreme difficulties with graphomotor production on the Coding subtest is likely to experience somewhat similar difficulties with the graphomotor demands of written expression tasks. Additionally, the multitasking demands of the Coding subtest are similar to the multitasking demands of written expression tasks, and both require the effective use of executive function constructs to direct and coordinate such multitasking performance. When an examinee earns a low score on the Coding subtest, performance with written expression production should be assessed. Use of a testing-the-limits Coding Copy Process procedure can also offer important insights into how an examinee responds to reduced graphomotor and multitasking demands. Because of the increased complexity involved in producing words and sentences in writing, however, a high score on the Coding subtest is no guarantee that an examinee will not experience graphomotor or other kinds of difficulties with written expression tasks.

When PSI subtest scores are interpreted, either collectively using the PSI or individually, it is typically assumed that score levels reflect a general level of processing speed. The secondary constructs required for effective performance are often either ignored completely or assumed to be intact and functioning as expected to allow for the focus of interpretation to be on the primary construct. For example, if an examinee earns a low score on the Coding subtest, the assumption often is that the examinee's processing speed is slower than that of same-age peers.

In many cases where low performance is observed, such an assumption is not necessarily warranted. To know if the assumption about the primary construct is valid, the role of the secondary cognitive constructs in task performance must be understood and explored in detail. When not accessed, or when applied ineffectively, these secondary cognitive constructs can interfere with task performance to a significant degree, making it inappropriate to focus subtest score interpretation exclusively on the primary constructs thought to be assessed.

When low scores or scores that are not consistent with what is known about the examinee are obtained from one or more of the PSI subtests, careful analysis of the shared and/or unique contributions of the secondary cognitive constructs and more detailed analysis of item responses and the ways in which responses were delivered should be undertaken. As indicated in the prior discussion, poor performance on PSI subtests is thought to reflect a general lack of processing speed. Clinicians who appreciate that a low score on one or more of the PSI subtests could be caused by many different sources can draw on the item-and task-specific cognitive construct–level analyses to help obtain a better understanding of why the examinee performed poorly and the implications of such poor performance.

Appendix B.18 provides an interpretive summary table that can be used to assist with the comparison of PSI subtests in terms of the cognitive constructs that may be involved in the performance of test items. Appendix B.19 provides a summary of the interpretations associated with behaviors observed during administration of the PSI subtests that can be used to enhance hypothesis testing about what cognitive constructs are, or are not, being used to perform subtests.

Meaningful interpretation of PSI subtest comparisons should include the determination of whether a statistically significant difference exists between the scores earned on the subtests being compared. Use a rounded value of 3 scaled score points to signify a statistically significant difference for any of the comparisons of the Working Memory subtests (see Appendix B.20).

When PSI subtest scores vary greatly and/or when the examiner observes behaviors that suggest that secondary cognitive constructs are influencing task performance, subtest cluster analysis may be helpful in identifying specific strengths and weaknesses in the use of various cognitive constructs. Appendix B.21 provides a worksheet to aid in the interpretation of Processing Speed scaled-score comparisons. Appendix C.1 provides a case study example that includes the use of the interpretive worksheet and illustrates the application of the item and cognitive constructs levels in the interpretations of Processing Speed task performance.

LEARNING DISABILITY ASSESSMENT AND THE WAIS-IV

The long history of the controversies regarding exactly what constitutes a learning disability and whether intellectual assessments are relevant to the identification and classification of individuals with learning disabilities has been most recently summarized by Fletcher, Lyon, Fuchs, and Barnes (2007), and Flanagan, Kaufman, Kaufman, and Lichtenberger (2008). Much of the controversy appears to stem more from confusions about operational definitions of terms such as *intelligence, ability, process, reading, writing,* and *mathematics* than from actual evidence that does, or does not, link cognitive constructs with learning disabilities. When interpretation of cognitive constructs remains at the global composite level, is referred to as intelligence, and is operationally defined as the Full Scale IQ, it should come as no surprise that many researchers have found little or no relationship between this overgeneralized summation of cognitive constructs and specific skill-related learning disabilities (Fletcher et al., 2007). Discussion of current neuropsychologically oriented perspectives on learning disabilities can be found in Berninger and Richards (2002), Flanagan and Alfonso (2011), Mapou (2008), McCloskey, Whitaker, Murphy, and Rogers (2012), Pennington (2009), and Wolfe, Schreiber, and Wasserstein (2008).

Consistent with the rest of this chapter, this section focuses on a neuro-psychologically oriented interpretation of the WAIS-IV at the clinical cluster, subtest, item, and task-specific cognitive construct levels and attempts to show how information obtained from the WAIS-IV can be useful in the assessment of examinees thought to have a learning disability. To accomplish this goal, it is essential that a more specific set of operational definitions, such as those presented in Rapid Reference 6.6, be used when discussing the issue of learning disabilities.

CONSTRAINTS ON LEARNING AND PRODUCTION

The concepts presented in Rapid Reference 6.6 can be used to construct a model of learning and production such as that shown in Appendix B.22 for reading, Appendix B.23 for written expression, Appendix B.24 for math, and Appendix B.25 for listening and oral expression. Some cognitive constructs act as constraints on learning; that is, the amount of learning that takes place will be limited by the amount of the construct that is available for use. Other cognitive constructs are impediments that slow the rate of acquisition of new learning but do not necessarily limit learning and production in the same way as constraints.

Impediments to learning that result from the presence of process deficits are most likely to impact the acquisition of basic-level reading, writing, math, and oral communication skills. In the case of reading (Appendix B.22), phonological and orthographic process and oral-motor functioning deficits will make it difficult for a person to develop the reading skills of sight word recognition, word decoding, and fluency (rapid rate of reading). Development of these basic skills can also be impacted by executive function deficits that make it difficult to coordinate the use of the various processes involved in skill acquisition. Deficits in the ability to reason with verbal information, to use language to comprehend meaning, or to grasp the visuospatial implications of what is read will constrain the acquisition of the more complex reading comprehension skills.

Reading comprehension can also be constrained by inadequate access to, or availability of, working memory resources; difficulty with accessing, or lack of development of, various knowledge lexicons; executive function difficulties with the coordination of the use of multiple constructs during the reading process; and difficulties with the cueing and directing of mental resources needed for sustained attention to, and active engagement with, what is being read. In a manner similar to that described here for reading and illustrated in Appendixes B.23–B.25, cognitive constructs act as impediments or constraints on skill development in writing, mathematics, and oral communication.

Most models of learning disability, including those used to craft the definitions that appear in public law (Individuals with Disabilities Education Improvement Act of 2004) and professional practice references (American Psychiatric Association, 2000), posit an absence of ability constraints on learning (i.e., the ability to reason, to use language, and to grasp visuospatial relations is not interfering with learning, but the presence of deficits in cognitive constructs other than abilities [e. g., processes] that are contributing to problems with the acquisition of reading, writing, math, and oral communication skills).

An important goal of assessment with the WAIS-IV in cases where learning disabilities are suspected is to help identify cognitive constructs that are, or are not, likely to be impeding or constraining learning and/or production. The questions that clinicians using the WAIS-IV need to ask are:

- Do WAIS-IV results reflect the presence or the absence of ability constraints that would impact learning to read, write, calculate, and orally communicate?
- Do WAIS-IV results reflect the presence or the absence of process deficits or deficits in the use of cognitive constructs other than abilities that would impact learning to read, write, calculate, and orally communicate?

In order to answer these questions, the clinician must know what specific abilities could act as constraints on, or impediments to, academic skills acquisition and where in the WAIS-IV they are assessed. Likewise, the clinician must know what specific processes and cognitive constructs other than abilities could act as constraints on or impediments to academic skills acquisition and where in the WAIS-IV they are assessed.

Knowledge of cognitive constructs and their potentially impeding or constraining effects does not come from the FSIQ or even from each of the four index scores of the WAIS-IV. As shown in Appendix B.1 and discussed throughout this chapter, the WAIS-IV index scores each represent the possible use of an amalgam of various processes, abilities, skills, and lexicons, only some of which would act as constraints on learning to communicate orally, read, write, or calculate and solve math problems. If the WAIS-IV is to be used to provide indicators of cognitive constraints on or impediments to learning, then the accurate identification and description of these constraints will occur through interpretation at the subtest cluster, subtest item, and task-specific cognitive construct levels. Appendixes B.26–B.29 offer guidelines for how the WAIS-IV can be used to indicate the presence or absence of cognitive constraints or impediments.

CONCEPTIONS OF LEARNING DISABILITY

Using the concepts just introduced, a learning disability can be operationally defined in two different ways, which are discussed as follows.

Ability-Achievement Discrepancy Conception of Learning Disability

The first definition is more consistent with the original conception of a learning disability in that it reflects a discrepancy between levels of abilities and levels of achievement. The ability-achievement model represented here differs from the traditional conception in the consideration of the effects of other cognitive constructs on learning and in what the term *achievement* represents. The model, as shown in Figure 6.2, defines a *learning disability* as a condition wherein:

1. There is an absence of any specific ability constraints that would interfere with learning in a specific academic skill domain (i.e., at least average levels of abilities known to act as constraints on learning of that skill).
2. There is a presence of
   a. One or more processing deficits (i.e., there is a deficit in the engagement of one or more basic processes in conjunction with the necessary lexicons and the necessary executive functions) and/or
   b. Memory deficits (especially working memory deficits)
3. The processing and/or working memory deficits have a negative impact on basic skill development and acquisition (i.e., basic skills have not been acquired or are being acquired at a very slow rate).
4. The lack of basic skill development may be preventing, disrupting, or slowing the development of complex skills.
5. The lack of basic skill development is reflected in poor performance on measures of achievement.

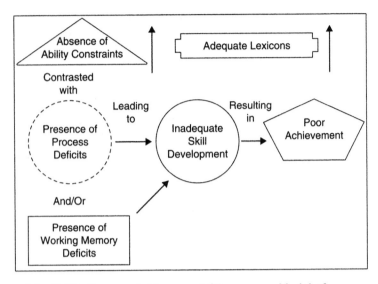

Figure 6.2. Ability-Process-Achievement Discrepancy Model of Learning Disability

Note that the ability constraints referred to in this model are skill specific (i.e., they refer only to those abilities that act as constraints on the specific academic skill domain). For example, reasoning with verbal information would be a direct constraint on the development of more complex reading and writing skills, but reasoning with nonverbal visual information would not be a direct constraint on reading and writing skills. The need for identifying direct ability constraints nullifies the use of the WAIS-IV Full Scale IQ and the Perceptual Reasoning Index standard scores as indicators of ability. Even use of the Verbal Comprehension Index score is somewhat problematic because the VCI is composed of subtests that assess retrieval of long-term storage (Vocabulary and Information) much more than reasoning with verbal information (Similarities). The best indicators of reasoning ability constraints related to the development of reading skills would be the Similarities and Comprehension subtest scores (provided item- and cognitive construct–level analysis confirmed that both of these tasks were assessing the use of reasoning ability).

An additional ability constraint on reading skill development would be the ability to understand language. Although the VCI could be used in this case as an indicator of the absence of a language constraint, the Comprehension, Information, and Arithmetic subtests are the best indicators of the ability to comprehend language, followed by the Similarities and Vocabulary subtests. A composite of these five subtests, with the greatest weight placed on the first three mentioned, would be a better indicator of receptive language ability than the VCI. Thus, the elements of the WAIS-IV that could be used most reasonably as indicators of ability constraints on applying reading skills are found at the subtest cluster level rather than the index level.

Appendixes B.26–B.29 offer guidelines for using information from the WAIS-IV to identify ability constraints and/or deficits in basic process and/or memory capacity use. Figure 6.2 shows how patterns of scores from the WAIS-IV and WIAT-III could be used to identify learning disabilities in reading.

ABILITY AND ACHIEVEMENT DEFICIT MODEL OF LEARNING DISABILITY

An alternate model for identifying a learning disability has emerged more recently. This newer model is based on the consistency of ability constraints and academic skill deficits (i.e., in the presence of ability constraints a person has difficulty learning new skills and achieving, regardless of whether process deficits are, or are not, present). Although now referred to as a model of learning disability, this conception traditionally has been referred to as the "slow learner" model, or in cases where the impairment of abilities such as reasoning is severe, as mental retardation (now referred to as intellectual disability).

The model, as shown in Figure 6.3, defines a learning disability as a condition wherein:

1. There is a presence of one or more specific ability constraints that would interfere with learning in a specific academic skill domain (i.e., below-average levels of abilities known to act as constraints on learning of that skill).
2. The ability constraints have a negative impact on basic, complex, and content domain skill development and acquisition (i.e., basic skills have not been acquired or are being acquired at a very slow rate).
3. The lack of basic, complex, and content domain skill development is reflected in poor performance on measures of achievement.

An example of this model for reading disability would involve poor reasoning and/or language abilities as reflected in low VCI scores or, more accurately, in low performance on the reasoning with verbal information and/or receptive language clusters mentioned in the first model combined with low scores on measures of reading skill.

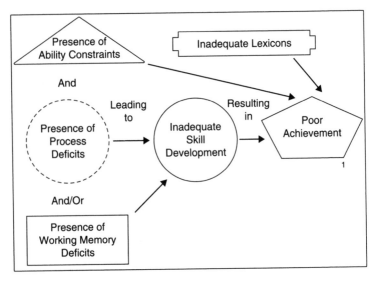

Figure 6.3. Ability-Process-Achievement Consistency Model of Learning Disability

REPORTING WAIS-IV RESULTS IN AN INTEGRATED REPORT FORMAT

Examiners interested in organizing their reports to reflect a neuropsychologically oriented approach to interpretation can use the case study in Appendix C as a model for structuring the various sections. The report format used in the case study has some notable features that clinicians may find very helpful in communicating results clearly to clients of various backgrounds. These include:

1. Front-loading the summary sections of the report. This makes it easier for the clients to get the big picture quickly without having to wade through details that may or may not make sense to them.
2. When constructing reports for minors, provide a recommendations section that is broken down into three subsections:
   a. What the child can do for himself or herself
   b. What the parents can do for the child
   c. What school staff can do for the child
3. Address classification issues in a separate section appropriately labeled to reflect the fact that administrative classifications are not always

consistent with the clinical information presented in your report; while administrative classifications and the specific professional addressing the client's needs may vary from state to state or by other geographic or administrative demarcations, your clinical impressions do not. For example, the reading problems that you identify in your report and what needs to be done to address those reading problems will not change from one state to another, although the school staff responsible for doing what needs to be done for the child might change from one state to another along with the classification label. It is essential that clinical findings remain independent from, but related to, the administrative issues of a case. This point applies to clinicians using the *Diagnostic and Statistical Manual* diagnostic categories as much as it does to professionals in school systems, especially in today's health care environment where diagnoses often are required for reimbursement for services much more than for guiding the development of an intervention plan.

4. Provide interpretive details in an appendix to the report. The amount of detail offered can depend on the nature of the case.

5. Organize interpretation of the WAIS-IV and other cognitive testing by the cognitive constructs assessed rather than by the tests administered. This enables a coherent picture of findings to emerge across assessment methods and allows interpretation to be focused effectively at the cluster, subtest, item, and task-specific cognitive construct levels consistent with the interpretive framework provided in this chapter.

≡ *Rapid Reference 6.6*

Operational Definitions for Understanding the Relationship Between Cognition and Learning

Cognitive constructs can be operationally defined as the general class of patterns of neural activation within various regions of the neocortex that are involved in the production of perception, thought, action, and the cognitive dimension of emotion. Cognitive constructs can be differentiated into separate conceptual categories: basic processing, processing, motor function, processing and motor function speed, abilities, lexicons, skills, strategies, executive functions, memory capacities, learning, and achievement.

(continued)

Basic Processes

- *Basic processes* are narrow-band cognitive constructs responsible for organization of input; they are responsible for the creation of basic mental representations.
- Basic processes enable and support learning and production.
- Basic process deficits obstruct learning and production but often can be bypassed or compensated for at least to some degree because of their narrow (i.e., relatively restricted) range of operation.
- In some instances, the effects of process deficits can be significantly reduced if the deficits are addressed during early developmental stages with a good intervention program (e.g., phonemic awareness training for young children). In these cases, the process deficit may have been caused more by underutilization of intact neural networks than by the presence of damaged neural connections. In the case of underutilization, instruction increases the frequency and effectiveness of use of the process.
- It is possible that basic process deficits resulting from damage to neural networks can be remediated through early childhood intervention as well.
- Severe basic process deficits can result in learning disabilities involving slowed and/or inconsistent learning and production.
- Basic processes include:
  - Auditory perception
  - Auditory discrimination
  - Auditory attention
  - Visual perception
  - Visual discrimination
  - Visual attention
  - Kinesthetic perception
  - Kinesthetic discrimination
  - Kinesthetic attention

Processing

Processing refers to neural activity involving the coordinated use of one or more basic processes, often in conjunction with the accessing of lexicons (described following) under the direction of executive functions (described following).

Basic Motor Functions

Basic motor functions are the fine motor capacities used in the performance of cognitive assessment tasks. All intellectual and cognitive assessment tasks require some form of motor output in order to judge the adequacy of task performance. Variations in the adequacy of motor functioning are important to observe and quantify in order to understand how strengths or weaknesses in motor functioning may be enhancing or impeding learning of academic skills and production with academic tasks.

Processing Speed and Basic Motor Functioning Speed

The term *processing speed* refers to the speed with which one or more processes can be coordinated and applied in the formation of mental representations, often in conjunction with the accessing of Lexicons and typically while under the direction of one or more Executive Functions. For all processing speed assessment tasks, processing speed is combined with some form of basic motor function in order to have an output that can be judged for adequacy of task performance. As a result, all measures of processing speed also are measures of basic motor functioning speed.

Abilities

• *Abilities* are broadband cognitive constructs that operate on mental representations initially formed through the use of basic processes.

• Abilities enable extended formulation and use of mental representations during learning and production.

• Ability deficits constrain learning and production; the degree of deficit places an upper limit on the quality (i.e., depth and complexity) of the learning and production; compensatory or bypass strategies typically are not very effective in countering ability deficits because of the broad range of influence of these more complex cognitive constructs.

• Severe ability deficits result in cognitive impairments that greatly constrain learning and production (e.g., severe language impairment, severe visuospatial impairment, mental retardation).

• Abilities include:
  ▪ Reasoning abilities
  ▪ Language abilities
  ▪ Visual and visuospatial abilities

Lexicons

Lexicons are stored knowledge bases from which information can be retrieved and used to inform learning or production. Lexicons can range from very basic, narrow forms of knowledge (e.g., the separate phonemes of the English language; how light strikes objects and creates shadows) to very complex forms of knowledge that vary greatly in depth and breadth (how to factor a polynomial; how to put a car engine [specific make and model] together; classical music influences on the early development of rock and roll).

Skills (Basic, Complex, Content specific)

• *Skills* are what are taught and learned through formal educational experiences. The term *skill* can be used in a temporal sense to represent what is being learned at the present time or to represent what was learned in the past or what will be learned in the future. Skills are a subclass of lexicons that specify the content of instructional lessons. Skills can be further delineated by content as basic, complex, or content domain.

(continued)

- The term *basic skills* refers to the skills that form the foundation for all other skill areas. The four broad basic skill domains include:
  a. Oral communication
  b. Reading
  c. Writing
  d. Mathematics
- Each of these broad skill domains consists of many subdomains or subskills:
  - Basic reading skills include sight word recognition, phonological awareness, word decoding, and rapid word recognition.
  - Basic writing skills include graphomotor letter, number, and word formation and copying; word spelling; written sentence structure and written sentence formation; and rapid text production.
  - Basic mathematics skills include computation procedures, basic quantity problem solutions, and rapid application of computation procedures.
  - Basic oral communication skills include reflective listening, diction and projection of voice, prosody, and rapid speech production.
- Basic skills are the focus of instruction and learning in early elementary school. Basic skill learning represents the building of a set of general lexicons that will enable the application of oral communication, reading, writing, and mathematics to a wide range of subject content areas and to the learning of more complex skills. Skill building is an intermediate state between the immediate experiencing of new information and retrieval of information from an established lexicon; an established skill forms its own lexicon. "Automaticity" refers to the speed and ease with which basic skill lexicons can be accessed, retrieved, and applied.
- Basic skill learning and use relies heavily on the use of basic processes under the direction of multiple executive functions. Basic skill learning and use, therefore, is most likely to be disrupted when process deficits are present.
- Complex skills are oral communication, reading, writing, and mathematics skills that enable a person to take the mental representations formed through the use of basic skills, add additional layers of representation, and manipulate all the information to produce relatively complex levels of meaning. The four complex skills include:
  a. Extended listening and/or speaking for meaning
  b. Reading comprehension
  c. Extended written text generation
  d. Applied mathematics problem solving
- Complex skills use the skill foundations built through basic skill learning and use. Complex skill development and use involves the application of one or more basic skills integrated with the use of one or more abilities and the accessing of one or more lexicons, all under the direction of multiple executive functions. For example, the skill of complex reading comprehension requires the application of the basic skills of word recognition and/or decoding and reading rate to form in the mind an accurate basic representation of the information that was on the page. The more complex the grammatic structure of the material that was read, the greater the need for

involvement of specific language abilities to enable meaningful representation at a deeper level.

- If the material read relates to a specific topic, lexicons representing that person's knowledge of the topic will need to be accessed, along with language ability to provide a context for what was read. If the ideas represented by the words are complex, reasoning abilities will need to be engaged to obtain the highest level of meaning possible from the material. The application of these skills, lexicons, and abilities requires extensive use of executive functions to coordinate the multitasking that must take place during such complex reading comprehension. In addition to the use of multiple basic skills, lexicons, and abilities, application of complex skills very often requires the direction and use of working memory capacities (described as follows).

- Complex skills are the focus of instruction and learning in the upper elementary grades. The development and use of complex skills can be disrupted by inadequate development and use of basic skills (resulting from the effects of process deficits or lack of direct instruction), by insufficient storage of information in lexicons, by constraints imposed by inadequate or underdeveloped abilities, by constraints imposed by inadequate or underutilized working memory capacity, and/or by constraints imposed by inadequate or underutilized executive functions.

- The term *content domain skills* refers to skills that are developed in specific subject domains and subdomains, such as the domain of science and the subdomains of biology, chemistry, and physics. Although basic and complex skills may be involved in learning in these content domains, the skills that are the focus of learning involve the building of lexicons related to the specific area of knowledge. The link between learning and lexicon building in these content areas is apparent in the language used to denote course and learning objectives. Educators speak of increasing a student's knowledge of biology rather than increasing or building a student's biology skills. Despite the emphasis on specific content knowledge storage, other lexicons that are acquired, such as how to use laboratory equipment, are more readily perceived as skills.

Strategies

- *Strategies* are learned and stored or newly generated routines that can be applied to increase the efficiency of the use of abilities, processes, and/or skills.

- Strategies are ways to chain together in a specific order a combination of one or more executive function cues, basic processes, abilities, skills, and retrieval from lexicons to enhance learning and production.

- Strategy development, storage, and use are cued by executive functions or by an external mediating source, such as a teacher or parent.

Executive Functions

- *Executive functions* are a unique category of mental construct delineated by their directive role. Executive functions cue and direct the use of other mental constructs and coordinate multitasking efforts.

(continued)

- Executive functions can be used to guide all aspects of mental activity. They are not the processes, abilities, lexicons, skills, strategies, or memory states but rather orchestrate the use of all of these other mental constructs.

Memory Capacities or Memory States
(Initial Registration, Manipulation, Retrieval)

- *Memory* represents a category of cognitive constructs that are distinct from processes, abilities, lexicons, skills, strategies, and executive functions.
- Memory represents a temporal state of mind; that is, memory is the essential mental manifestation of time and space; memory states provide the temporal and spatial contexts—a time signature—for all perception, emotion, cognition, and action.
- Memory constructs/states share some characteristics with abilities in that they are broadband and constrain learning and production.
- Memory constructs/states share some characteristics with basic processes in that while weak states/poor construct can obstruct learning and production, they often can be bypassed or compensated for at least to some degree.
- Memory constructs/states include:
  - Initial registration of information in the immediate moment; the experience of "now"
  - Retrieval from long-term storage; going back in time to recall previous "immediate" moments
  - Holding and manipulating information in mind; extending the immediate moment into the future, projecting possible immediate moments into the future, or creating scenarios for future immediate moments
- Lack of memory capacity can greatly obstruct learning.
- Poor initial registration constrains how much information can be represented in mind at one time.
- Poor retrieval capacity limits access to lexicons.
- Poor working memory capacity constrains how much information can be held in mind, how long that information can be held, and the extent to which the information being held in mind can be manipulated to enable extended states of learning, problem solving, and production.

Learning

Learning is the process of building new lexicons through the use of basic processes, basic and complex skills, and strategies, along with the accessing of lexicons and the application of abilities. Learning can occur on a continuum from being mediated extensively by others to being self-mediated. The greater the self-mediation, the greater the demand for executive function involvement in the learning process.

Achievement

Achievement is the end result (the product) of the use of basic processes, basic and complex skills and strategies, accessing of lexicons, and application of abilities to a contextually meaningful task.

It is important to note that the boundaries of these categories are somewhat amorphous and changeable. At least theoretically, processes, abilities, and executive functions can be taught and learned, thereby becoming skills. Skills can be stored and retrieved and applied in the immediate moment, making them lexicons. The interrelated and overlapping nature of the category definitions, however, should not deter clinicians from making the important distinctions represented by each of these cognitive construct categories.

 TEST YOURSELF

....

1. **The focus of a neuropsychological approach to WAIS-IV interpretation is on**
   a. How examinees perform the items of each WAIS-IV subtest, rather than the scores they earn on each of those subtests
   b. How examinees perform the items of each WAIS-IV subtest in addition to the scores they earn on each of those subtests
   c. The lowest scores in an examinee's profile

2. **TRUE or FALSE? A neuropsychologically based WAIS-IV interpretation deemphasizes global scores and focuses mainly on the subtests, items, and cognitive constructs.**

3. **TRUE or FALSE? The interpretive validity and the reliability of the assessment process are increased by illuminating the unexplained sources of variability in performance that may be inferred from careful clinical observations of how examinees are using cognitive constructs.**

4. **TRUE or FALSE? VCI-PRI discrepancies in isolation are effective indexes of cerebral dysfunction.**

5. **A child with a learning disability in the area of reading may have deficits in which of the following areas?**
   a. Phonology
   b. Orthography
   c. Oral-motor processes
   d. Executive function
   e. Any of the above

Answers: 1. b; 2. true; 3. true; 4. false; 5. e

Seven

CLINICAL APPLICATIONS II: AGE AND INTELLIGENCE ACROSS THE ADULT LIFE SPAN

Research on the relationships between aging and intelligence had its inception nearly 100 years ago in comparisons between adults and children (Kirkpatrick, 1903), and the topic has captivated researchers in theoretical and clinical disciplines for more than half a century (Willoughby, 1927). Whether intelligence declines with increasing age has long been the subject of research and debate by experts in the field (Baltes & Schaie, 1976; Horn & Donaldson, 1976). The nature of the complex relationship between aging and changes in intellectual functioning is of prime concern to clinicians who test clients across a wide age span, inasmuch as proper WAIS-IV interpretation demands understanding of normal, or expected, differential fluctuations in a person's ability spectrum from late adolescence and young adulthood to old age. Distinguishing between normal and pathological development is often the essence of competent diagnosis in clinical and neuropsychological assessment.

Probably the most comprehensive and cleverly conceived set of studies has been the life's work of K. Warner Schaie (1994), in collaboration with numerous colleagues (e.g., Hertzog & Schaie, 1988). His results have transformed the preconceptions of professionals throughout the world regarding the inevitability of declines in mental functioning along the path to old age. In particular, Schaie's clever sequential combination of cross-sectional and longitudinal research designs has shown the importance of considering cohort (generational) effects when conducting research on aging. Furthermore, Schaie's research program suggests that when declines in intelligence do occur with age, they do so at far later ages than was formerly believed. But Schaie consistently used the group-administered, speeded Primary Ability Tests (PMA; Thurstone & Thurstone, 1949), normed only through age 18. As valuable as his findings are, they cannot replace research results based directly on the WAIS-IV, its predecessors, and other intelligence tests for adults in helping clinicians understand the kinds of changes to anticipate during clinical and neuropsychological evaluations. Consequently, we focus on individually administered clinical tests of intelligence in this chapter, including recent studies of the WAIS-IV (Baxendale, 2011; Lichtenberger & Kaufman, 2009; Salthouse & Saklofske, 2010).

Analyses of previous Wechsler adult scales focused on Horn's (1989) expansion of the Cattell-Horn-Carroll (CHC) *Gf-Gc* theory, a natural fit for Wechsler's Verbal-Performance dichotomy. More recent analyses of the WAIS-III and WAIS-IV are rooted in CHC theory, which fits nicely with the organization of the subtests into four factor indexes. The main questions of interest are whether intelligence is maintained through old age or whether it declines; or whether some abilities maintain, and even increase, as we age, whereas other abilities decline, perhaps precipitously, across the life span.

DO COGNITIVE ABILITIES DECLINE WITH ADVANCING AGE? A CROSS-SECTIONAL APPROACH

To answer the crucial questions that pertain to the relationship between adults' IQs and the aging process, we have integrated the results of both cross-sectional and longitudinal investigations. These different types of studies are treated in the sections that follow, with emphases on the pros and cons of each style and on an integration of the findings from both kinds of empirical investigation. Brief descriptions of different types of aging studies are shown in Rapid Reference 7.1.

Cross-Sectional Investigations of Wechsler's Adult Scales

The existence of large-scale standardization data on Wechsler's scales has provided clinicians and researchers with an impressive body of Census-representative data on the intelligence of adult samples at a wide cross-section of chronological ages. However, inferring developmental changes from cross-sectional data is a risky business. Groups that differ in chronological age necessarily differ on other variables that may confound apparent age-related differences. A child born in 1940 had different educational and cultural opportunities from one born in 1970. When tested in 2007 as part of the WAIS-IV standardization sample, the former child was in the 65- to 69-year-old sample, while the latter individual was a member of the 35- to 44-year-old group. Differences in their test performance may be partially a function of their

≡ Rapid Reference 7.1

Types of Aging-IQ Studies

- **Cross-sectional:** Comparison of the test performance of different age groups at the same point in time (e.g., the adults tested during the standardization of an intelligence test, such as ages 20–24, 45–54, and 65–69)
- **Longitudinal:** Comparison of the test performance of the same groups of individuals at different points in time (e.g., when they are 25, 40, and 70 years)
- **Longitudinal using independent samples:** Comparison of the test performance of different samples of adults at different points in time, where the samples are from the same cohort (year of birth). For example, comparing the test scores of adults born between 1971 and 1975 when the WAIS-III was standardized in 1995 (at ages 20–24) and when the WAIS-IV was standardized 12 years later (at ages 32–36) in 2007. The samples are independent, but they are comparable on important variables, such as gender and socioeconomic status, and they are from the same cohort.
- **Cross-sequential:** A blend of cross-sectional and longitudinal research popularized by Schaie (1983b) in his Seattle Longitudinal Study. Cross-sectional age groups are tested at a single point in time, and many of these adults are also followed up years later.

chronological ages during the 2000s and partially a function of the generational or cohort differences that characterized their respective periods of growth from childhood to adulthood. Cohort differences, even seemingly obvious ones like the greater number of years of education enjoyed by adults born more recently, were mostly ignored by clinicians and researchers through the 1950s and even the 1960s. Wechsler (1958) inferred an early and rapid decline in intelligence by uncritically accepting changing mean scores across the adult age range as evidence of a developmental trend: "What is definitely established is . . . that the abilities by which intelligence is measured do in fact decline with age; and . . . that this decline is systematic and after age 30 more or less linear" (p. 142). Although such interpretations were prevalent a half century ago, researchers on aging are now thoroughly familiar with the impact of cultural change and cohort differences, including educational attainment, on apparent declines in intelligence with age, and have greatly revised the pessimism of Wechsler's conclusions.

When examining mean IQ test performance for different age groups across the adult life span, the results can be sobering. Table 7.1 presents mean IQs for various adult age groups on the W-B I, WAIS, WAIS-R, WAIS-III, and WAIS-IV[1]. Whereas mean IQs on Wechsler's scales are necessarily set at 100 for each age group, the data in Table 7.1 base the mean IQs on common yardsticks (see note to Table 7.1) to permit age-by-age comparisons. Overall, the striking apparent age-related changes in intelligence from the twenties through old age, especially in Performance IQ (P-IQ), are so overwhelming (and depressing, if taken at face value) that it is easy to understand why Wechsler and others concluded that the path to old age is paved by a steady, unrelenting loss of intellectual function. Also intriguing in Table 7.1 is the incredible similarity in the cross-sectional data for the four adult Wechsler batteries that were normed in 1937, 1953, 1978, 1995, and 2007. In particular, the mean P-IQs (relative to a common yardstick) for the WAIS, WAIS-R, WAIS-III, and WAIS-IV are uncannily similar for each age group between 20–24 and 65–69, never differing by more than 4 IQ points. Considering that each corresponding age group in the WAIS, WAIS-R, WAIS-III, and WAIS-IV samples was subject to huge generation or cohort effects, the similarities in the cross-sectional data seem quite remarkable. (Forty-year-olds in the WAIS sample, for example, were born just before World War I, whereas their age contemporaries in the WAIS-R sample were born just before World War II; those in the WAIS-III sample were born just after the Korean War, and those in the WAIS-IV sample were born in the turbulent 1960s.) Though the mean scores for adults over age 70 in the fourstandardization samples differ more substantially than the means for ages 20–69, the accumulated data over a 54-year span (1953–2007) indicate that adults who are in their 70s also earn mean Performance IQs in the 70s when they are compared to a common yardstick.

However, the data for separate age groups cannot be interpreted in isolation. Table 7.2 presents educational attainment data for the WAIS, WAIS-R, and WAIS-III standardization samples, showing the percent in each sample with 0–8 years of schooling and the percent with 13 or more years of schooling (at least

---

1. The WAIS-IV yields four Indexes and FS-IQ, but not V-IQ or P-IQ. For comparative purposes, however, V-IQ and P-IQ were computed for the WAIS-IV using estimated mean raw scores on separate subtests, by age, provided by Wisdom, Mignogna, and Collins (2012, Tables 14). We converted these raw scores to scaled scores, by age group, using the WAIS-IV norms table for ages 20–34 (Wechsler, 2008, Table A.2) for all groups. We then summed the scaled scores for the six traditional Verbal subtests and the five traditional Performance subtests (substituting Visual Puzzles for Object Assembly). We converted these sums to V-IQs and P-IQs using pertinent tables in the WAIS-III manual (Wechsler, 1997, Tables A.3 and A.4). WAIS-IV FS-IQs, also derived from Wisdom et al.'s data, are composed of the ten core WAIS-IV subtests; scaled scores were obtained for all age groups from the 20-34-year conversion table and sums were entered into the WAIS-IV Full Scale IQ norms table (Wechsler, 2008, Table A.7) to compute mean FS-IQs.

Table 7.1. Mean IQs across the Adult Life Span on the W- BI, WAIS, WAIS- R, WAIS- III, and WAIS-IV for Designated Cross-Sectional Age Groups

Age Group	Verbal IQ					Performance IQ					Full Scale IQ				
	W-BI	WAIS	WAIS-R	WAIS-III	WAIS-IV	W-BI	WAIS	WAIS-R	WAIS-III	WAIS-IV	W-BI	WAIS	WAIS-R	WAIS-III	WAIS-IV
20–24	100	98	96	97	(98)	105	102	101	99	(100)	103	100	97	98	100
25–34	100	100	98	100	(99)	100	100	99	99	(99)	103	100	97	100	99
35–44	98	99	94	102	(101)	93	95	93	97	(96)	95	98	94	100	99
45–54	95	97	95	104	(100)	86	89	89	92	(91)	91	93	92	99	97
55–64	93	95	93	99	(98)	83	84	84	86	(86)	88	90	88	94	94
65–69	—	91	91	98	(96)	—	80	79	81	(83)	—	86	84	90	90
70–74	—	85	90	97	(93)	—	72	76	79	(79)	—	78	82	89	86
75+	—	80	87	93	(88)	—	66	72	74	(72)	—	73	78	83	79

Note: W-B I data for ages 55–64 are based only on adults ages 55–59. All sums of scaled scores for all scales are based on scaled-score norms for ages 20–34. Mean IQs for the W-B I, WAIS, and WAIS-R are based on the IQ conversion table for ages 25–34; mean IQs for the WAIS-III are based on the IQ conversion table for ages 20–34. WAIS data for ages 65–69 through 75+ are for the stratified elderly sample tested by Doppelt and Wallace (1955). WAIS-R data for ages 20–74 are from Kaufman, Reynolds, and McLean (1989). WAIS-R data for ages 75+ are for the stratified elderly sample tested by Ryan, Paolo, and Brungardt (1990), and were kindly provided by Ryan (personal communication, March, 1998) for 115 individuals ages 75–89. WAIS-III data for all ages are from Kaufman (2001). Standardization data of the Wechsler Adult Intelligence Scale: Third Edition. Copyright © 1997 by The Psychological Corporation. Used by permission. All rights reserved. WAIS-IV data are based on mean subtest raw scores, by age group, estimated by Wisdom et al. (2012). *Mean WAIS-IV Verbal and Performance IQs are in parentheses to denote that V-IQ and P-IQ are not yielded by the WAIS-IV.* They were computed by entering relevant sums of scaled scores on six Verbal and five Performance subtests into V-IQ and P-IQ conversion tables in WAIS-III manual.

Table 7.2. Percents of the Standardization Samples of the WAIS, WAIS-R, and WAIS-III with 0–8 and 13+ Years of Schooling, by Age Group

Age Group	0–8 Years of Schooling				13+ Years of Schooling			
	WAIS (1953)	WAIS-R (1978)	WAIS-III (1995)	WAIS-IV (2007)	WAIS (1953)	WAIS-R (1978)	WAIS-III (1995)	WAIS-IV (2007)
20–24	22	4	4	3	20	40	51	56
25–34	25	5	4	4	20	44	51	59
35–44	40	10	4	4	18	32	56	58
45–54	54	16	8	4	14	26	49	57
55–64	66	28	14	6	11	19	36	55
65–69	—	38	18	9	—	19	30	45
70–74	—	45	16	11	—	16	29	39
75–79	—	—	19	15	—	—	29	36
80–89	—	—	32	18	—	—	22	33

Note: Data are from the manuals for the WAIS (Wechsler, 1955), WAIS-R (Wechsler, 1981), WAIS-III (Psychological Corporation, 1997), and WAIS-IV (Psychological Corporation, 2008).

1 year of college). This table reveals the folly of interpreting changes in mean scores from age to age as evidence of developmental change. Good standardization samples match the U.S. Census proportions on key background variables, and some variables, such as educational attainment, differ widely from age group to age group. With each passing decade, an increasing proportion of adults stay longer in elementary and high school, and more and more people attend college. Consequently, the younger-adult age groups will tend to be relatively more educated than the older-adult age groups. Similarly, any age group tested in the early 1950s on the WAIS will be considerably less educated than that same age group tested in the late 1970s on the WAIS-R, which, in turn, will be less educated than its age-mates in the mid-1990s WAIS-III sample (see Table 7.2).

When Tables 7.1 and 7.2 are viewed together, it is evident that the lower IQs earned by older adults, relative to younger adults, mirror the older adults' lower level of education. For example, for the WAIS-R sample, 45% of adults ages 70–74 had less than nine years of schooling, compared to only 5% of those ages 25–34; for the WAIS-III sample, the corresponding percentages were 16 and 4, and for the WAIS-IV the values were 11 and 4 (see Table 7.2). Maybe the entire "decline" in mean IQs across the adult life span is illusory, reflecting nothing more than the higher level of educational attainment for the younger age groups relative to the

CAUTION

Don't be fooled by declines in mean standard scores with increasing age in cross-sectional samples of adults. Remember that older samples tend to be less educated than younger samples. The declines in mean scores may result from differences in *education* more so than *age*.

older ones. That possibility was explored with WAIS standardization data about 40 years ago in the United States (Birren & Morrison, 1961) and about 30 years ago in Puerto Rico (Green, 1969). Interestingly, these two cross-sectional studies gave different answers to the question. However, subsequent studies with the WAIS-R (Kaufman, Reynolds, & McLean, 1989), WAIS-III (Kaufman, 2000a, 2001), and other tests (e.g., Kaufman & Horn, 1996) have provided more definitive data for answering the aging-IQ questions via cross-sectional methodology.

WAIS Studies

Birren and Morrison (1961) controlled education level statistically by parsing out years of education from the correlation of each WAIS subtest with chronological age, using standardization data for 933 Caucasian males and females aged 25–64. Scores on each of the 11 subtests initially correlated negatively with age, with all Performance subtests correlating more negatively ($-.28$ to $-.46$) than did the Verbal tasks ($-.02$ to $-.19$). After statistically removing the influence of educational attainment from the correlations, four of the six Verbal subtests produced *positive* correlations. On the Performance Scale, the removal of education level did not erase the negative correlations between IQ and age. Some of the partial correlations were strongly negative, even after the statistical removal of education, notably Digit Symbol ($-.38$) and Picture Arrangement ($-.27$). Birren and Morrison (1961) gave evidence that the decrease in verbal (but not nonverbal) abilities with age was an artifact of education level.

Green approached the problem differently in his analysis of the Puerto Rican standardization data for the Spanish WAIS. He added and subtracted subjects from each of four age groups (25–29, 35–39, 45–49, and 55–64) until they were balanced on educational attainment. Each sample comprised about 135 adults (total = 539), with mean years of education ranging from 7.6 to 7.8. Green's equated samples demonstrated an increase in Verbal sums of scaled scores and only a slight decrement in Performance scores. He concluded from his analyses that "[i]ntelligence as measured by the WAIS does not decline in the Puerto Rican population before about age 65. The same conclusion is almost certainly true for the United States" (Green, 1969, p. 626). Despite Birren and Morrison's (1961) contradictory finding with the WAIS Performance Scale, Green's assertions were accepted by writers such as Labouvie-Vief (1985), who praised his work as the "most careful study thus far of education-related effects on patterns of intellectual aging" (p. 515). However, Green's data had limited generalizability because his groups averaged fewer than eight years of education, with 43% having between none and five years of formal education. It made no sense to generalize these findings to more educated samples of adults.

WAIS-R Studies

Kaufman et al. (1989) analyzed the WAIS-R standardization data for ages 20–74 years ($N = 1,480$), a sample that was carefully stratified on gender, race (Caucasian–non-Caucasian), geographic region, educational attainment, and occupation. The researchers used both ANOVA and multiple regression methodology, controlled for educational attainment, and based norms for all adults on a reference group of 20- to 34-year-olds. The ANOVA results are depicted in Figures 7.1 and 7.2, which show the mean WAIS-R Verbal IQs

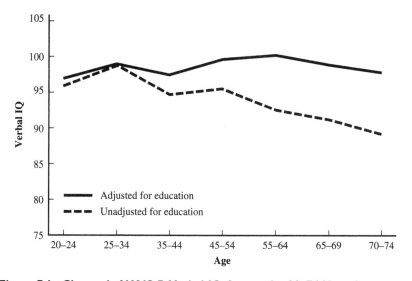

Figure 7.1. Change in WAIS-R Verbal IQ Across the 20–74-Year Age Range, Both With and Without a Control for Education; IQs Were Based on Norms for Ages 25–34

Source: Data are from Kaufman et al. (1989).

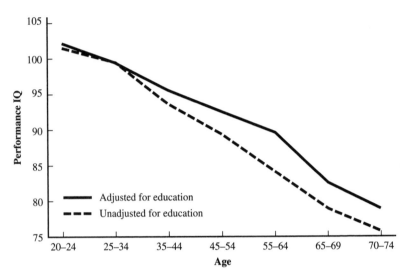

Figure 7.2. Change in WAIS-R Performance IQ Across the 20–74-Year Age Range, Both With and Without a Control for Education; IQs Were Based on Norms for Ages 25–34

Source: Data are from Kaufman et al. (1989).

(V-IQs) and P-IQs, respectively, for seven adult age groups, both with and without a control for education. After controlling for education, the decline in Verbal IQ disappeared, but the decline in P-IQ remained substantial. On the Verbal Scale, the peak IQ (99.8) occurred for ages 55–64 after equating for education level; even at ages 70–74, the weighted mean V-IQ was nearly 98. In contrast, education-controlled means in P-IQ dipped below 90 at ages 55–64 and below 80 for 70–74-year-olds.

The multiple regression analysis determined the percent of variance accounted for by age alone and by education alone differed substantially for WAIS-R V-IQ and P-IQ, as summarized in Rapid Reference 7.2. As shown, age alone accounted for 28% of the variance in P-IQ but only 3% in V-IQ—and that 3% is dwarfed by the 45% value for education alone.

All of these results are consistent with Birren and Morrison's (1961) WAIS data but not Green's (1969). These WAIS-R findings give support to Botwinick's (1977) classic intellectual aging pattern, which posits maintenance of performance on nontimed tasks versus decline on timed tasks. The results also support Horn's (1989) interpretation of the classic pattern from the *Gf-Gc* theory of intelligence and from the more contemporary CHC theory (McGrew, 2005):

≡ Rapid Reference 7.2

Relative Contributions of Age and Education to WAIS-R IQs for Ages 20–74

Percent of Variance

Accounted for by	Age Alone	Education Alone
Verbal IQ	3	45
Performance IQ	28	33

Source: Data are from Kaufman et al. (1989).

Crystallized abilities remain stable through old age ("maintained" abilities) while fluid abilities (and other abilities such as visualization and speed) decline steadily and rapidly, starting in young adulthood ("vulnerable" abilities).

The distinction in the adult development literature of fluid versus crystallized abilities was first made by Horn and Cattell (1966, 1967) in the 1960s. Fluid intelligence (*Gf*), manifested by the ability to solve novel problems, is presumed to increase with neurological maturation during childhood and adolescence and to decline throughout adulthood concomitantly with neurological degeneration. In contrast, crystallized intelligence (*Gc*, knowledge and skills dependent on education and experience) is expected to continue to increase during one's life, reflecting cultural assimilation.

The results of these cross-sectional analyses also accord well with Baltes's (1997) two-component (mechanics–pragmatics) life span theory of intellectual development. The pragmatics component resembles crystallized ability and is believed by Baltes to be maintained across the adult life span. The array of abilities that make up P-IQ corresponds closely to the broad "mechanics" component of cognition in Baltes's theory. In contrast to the pragmatics component, the mechanics component is vulnerable to the effects of normal aging and subsumes reasoning, spatial orientation, memory, and perceptual speed (Baltes, Staudinger, & Lindenberger, 1999). This computer analogy refers to the mind's hardware (mechanics) and software (cognitive pragmatics).

WAIS-III Studies

Kaufman (2000a, 2001) analyzed data from the WAIS-III standardization sample of 2,450 individuals at ages 16–89 years (basing all IQs on a reference group ages

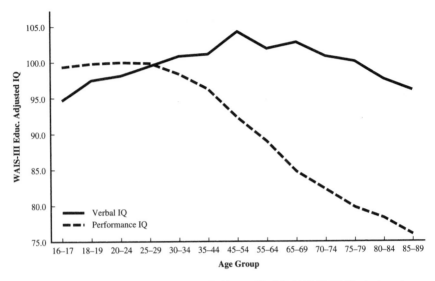

Figure 7.3. Mean "Reference Group" (Ages 20–34) WAIS-III Verbal and Performance IQs, by Age, for Adults Ages 16–17 to 85–89 Years, Adjusted for Educational Attainment (Values for Ages 16–19 are Unadjusted)

Source: Data Are From Kaufman (2001)

20–34). The increase in age range to almost 90 years made it clear that V-IQ is a maintained ability and remains robust well into the 70s, but it is decidedly *not* maintained through very old age (Kaufman, 2001). After age 79, *Gc* declined precipitously. In fact, V-IQ decreased just as much as P-IQ for people in their 80s, even with education controlled, as shown in Table 7.3 and depicted pictorially in Figure 7.3. P-IQ peaked in young adulthood, then declined steadily and dramatically across the age range (especially at ages 45 and above); education-adjusted mean P-IQs were below 80 for adults in their 80s.

The age-related patterns of mean V-IQ and P-IQ for the WAIS-III resemble closely the results for the WAIS and WAIS-R. Furthermore, similar patterns—including the decline in both *Gc* and *Gf* for the elderly—have been demonstrated for the Canadian WAIS-III (Lee, Gorsuch, Saklofske, & Patterson, 2008) and for a variety of batteries, such as the Kaufman tests (e.g., Kaufman & Horn, 1996; Kaufman, Johnson, & Liu, 2008) and the Woodcock-Johnson (McGrew, Woodcock, & Ford, 2006). And these differences are worldwide, emerging in Germany (Baltes & Lindenberger, 1997; Melchers, Schürmann, & Scholten, 2006), The Netherlands (Mulder, Dekker, & Dekker, 2004), the United Kingdom (Rabbitt, 1993), and many other countries as well. These findings are entirely consistent

Table 7.3. Education Level and Mean WAIS-III IQs of Each Standardization Age Group (Mean IQs Adjusted for Educational Attainment Are in Parentheses)

Age Group	Percent High School Dropout	Percent College Graduate	*Mean WAIS-III IQs*		
			Verbal	Performance	Full Scale
20–24	15.0	11.0	97.1 (98.1)	99.4 (100.0)	98.5 (99.4)
25–29	14.0	23.5	99.4 (99.5)	99.9 (99.9)	99.9 (100.0)
30–34	14.0	23.0	101.0 (100.9)	98.4 (98.4)	99.9 (99.9)
35–44	9.5	29.0	102.4 (101.2)	97.3 (96.3)	100.1 (98.9)
45–54	17.5	25.0	103.8 (104.4)	91.8 (92.4)	99.0 (99.7)
55–64	26.5	18.0	98.9 (102.1)	86.3 (89.0)	93.8 (97.0)
65–69	32.0	14.0	98.2 (102.9)	80.9 (84.8)	90.2 (94.9)
70–74	31.5	14.0	97.1 (101.1)	78.8 (82.3)	88.7 (92.8)
75–79	34.0	13.5	96.0 (100.3)	76.2 (79.7)	86.8 (91.1)
80–84	49.3	11.3	91.4 (97.8)	72.9 (78.2)	81.0 (87.4)
85–89	50.0	12.0	89.8 (96.3)	69.9 (75.9)	78.6 (85.3)

Note: Percentages of high school dropouts and college graduates for the WAIS-III standardization sample are from The Psychological Corporation (1997, Table 2.6). Mean WAIS-III IQs for all ages are based on sums of scaled scores for ages 20–34. Education-adjusted IQs (values in parentheses) are adjusted to match the educational attainment of adults ages 25–34. Mean IQs and adjusted IQs are from Kaufman (2001). Standardization data of the Wechsler Adult Intelligence Scale: Third Edition. Copyright © 1997 by The Psychological Corporation. Used by permission. All rights reserved.

with Horn's (1989) and Baltes's (1997) notions of maintained and vulnerable abilities during the adult aging process.

The familiar P-IQ decline is especially noteworthy in view of the exclusion from the standardization sample of many low-functioning adults. Eligibility requirements for the WAIS-III standardization samples were strict to ensure that the norms are truly based on "normal" people. For example, the sample excluded adults with sensory impairments (e.g., hearing loss) or coordination problems; those who took antidepressants, or antianxiety medication, or had more than occasional drinks of alcohol; and those with known or possible neurological impairment (including people who went to a professional for memory problems) (Psychological Corporation, 1997). The liberal exclusion of adults with suspected or known thinking impairments has an upside for aging research: Any observed declines in cognitive function are likely to be "real" declines, not artifacts of the inclusion of many cognitively impaired adults in the older age groups.

The four WAIS-III Indexes display patterns of age-by-age education-adjusted means that are decidedly different from each other (see Figure 7.4), with each one corresponding to different CHC abilities: VCI = *Gc*, POI = *Gf/Gv*,

Figure 7.4. Mean "Reference Group" Indexes on the Four WAIS-III Factors for Adults Ages 16–17 to 85–89 Years, Adjusted for Educational Attainment (Values for Ages 16–19 Are Unadjusted)

Source: Data are from Kaufman (2001).

WMI = (*Gsm*), PSI = *Gs* (Kaufman, 2000a). The four separate indexes foster better understanding of age changes in cognitive ability than is possible from the factorially complex V-IQ and P-IQ. As pictured, VCI (*Gc*) was maintained throughout most of the adult life span, whereas the other three Indexes were vulnerable to the effects of aging, consistent with predictions from theory (Horn & Hofer, 1992).

WMI (*Gsm*) was the least vulnerable of the three and PSI (*Gs*) was the most vulnerable, considerably more so than POI (now called PRI on the WAIS-IV). In Lee et al.'s (2008) study of the Canadian WAIS-III, the PSI was also considerably more vulnerable than the POI. Note in Figure 7.4 that the graphs for the U.S. sample converge prior to age 30 before following their distinct paths toward old age. Even at ages 45–54, when VCI peaks (mean = 105.9), the means for POI and PSI are already 12 to 14 points lower. In contrast, the V-IQs and P-IQs are complex. WAIS-III IQs correspond to unitary constructs from CHC theory, with P-IQ basically composed of two major components, nonverbal and spatial problem solving (*Gf* and *Gv*) and speed of problem solving (*Gs*). Examination of the age-by-age changes on POI and PSI (Figure 7.4), in conjunction with age patterns on P-IQ (Figure 7.3), offers insight into the nature of the well-known dramatic decline on P-IQ during adulthood with increasing age. Interestingly, the age-by-age pattern of education-adjusted mean IQs on the WAIS-III P-IQ is closely similar to the pattern of Indexes on the POI during its period of early stability (ages 16–44), but they overlap with the pattern for PSI during the period of rapid decline with increasing age (especially ages 55–74). The rapid decline of P-IQ with increasing age, therefore, is likely more a function of the highly speeded nature of some of its subtests than of their *Gf* or *Gv* component.

WAIS-IV Studies

Salthouse and Saklofske (2010) used WAIS-IV standardization data to compare the performance of individuals in two broad age groups: 16–64 ($n = 1,600$) vs. 65–90 ($n = 600$). Consistent with the WAIS-III research that examined age changes on the four Indexes, effect sizes were large for PSI (1.47 *SD*) and PRI (1.31 *SD*), moderate for WMI (0.63 *SD*), and small for VCI (0.22 *SD*). When educational level was controlled, effect sizes were as follows:

PSI   =   1.34
PRI   =   1.19
WMI =   0.47
VCI   = −0.03.

The effect size of -0.03 for VCI indicates that the two age groups performed about equally well. When Salthouse and Saklofske (2010) compared the two groups on the separate subtests, the education-controlled effect sizes for Vocabulary (-0.29) and Information (-0.20) indicated that the older sample outperformed the younger sample on these prototypical measures of Gc. In contrast, the younger group scored higher on the one VCI subtest that depends on Gf as well as Gc—Similarities (0.18). They also scored notably higher on the new Digit Span Sequencing task (0.57), an excellent measure of working memory. Two measures of Gs and one test of Gf had effect sizes greater than 1.0 even after education was controlled, namely Coding (1.25), Symbol Search (1.21), and Matrix Reasoning (1.09). All of these findings are entirely consistent with the results of previous Wechsler studies and, more generally, with the large body of cognitive literature (e.g., Craik & Salthouse, 2008; Salthouse, 2010).

Apart from observing the well-known finding of lower IQ test performance by older than younger adults, Salthouse and Saklofske (2010) examined—and identified—several key *similarities* between the two samples. The two groups had comparable factor structures, loadings on the general ability (g) factor, internal consistency reliability coefficients, stability coefficients, gender differences on cognitive abilities, and correlations with education level. Their primary research question was whether "the WAIS-IV tests measure the same aspect of functioning in adults under and over age 65" (Salthouse & Saklofske, 2010, p. 233), despite the wide gap in ability level. Their tentative answer was "yes."

Baxendale (2011) also used WAIS-IV standardization data to conduct a cross-sectional analysis in which she set ages 16–17 years as the reference group for all adults. First, she identified the raw score for each subtest that yielded a scaled score of 10 at ages 16–17. Then she entered that identical profile of raw scores into the scaled-score tables for each of 13 age groups between 16–17 and 85–90 and computed mean Indexes and Full Scale IQs for each age group. She repeated this procedure for scaled scores of 6 (IQ = 73) and 14 (IQ = 129) and graphed the results for the three different ability groups.

Baxendale's (2011) results were generally consistent with previous findings. At all three ability levels VCI was maintained for much of the life span before declining mildly. WMI showed notable decline relative to the VCI, but far less decline than the extremely vulnerable PRI and PSI. In that respect, her findings mirrored previous cross-sectional studies of WAIS-III and WAIS-IV indexes (e.g., Kaufman, 2001; Salthouse & Saklofske, 2010). However, Baxendale observed the atypical finding of greater decline on PRI than PSI, perhaps because of her choice of methodology and the ceiling effects of the PSI when older individuals are compared to adolescents. She noted that, "A performance that gives a Processing Speed Index of 122 in a 17-year-old would yield a score of more than 150 (the test ceiling) in anyone older than the age of 70 years" (Baxendale, 2011, p. 166). Another methodological issue of concern in her cross-sectional investigation is failure to adjust for educational differences across the wide span of age cohorts.

However, failure to control for educational attainment is less a concern for WAIS-IV than for previous editions of Wechsler's adult scale. Table 7.2 presented education differences for adult age cohorts between 20–24 and elderly adults for WAIS through WAIS-IV. The percentange of adults with 0–8 years of schooling differed widely from age group to age group in the 1950s when the WAIS was standardized, in the late 1970s when the WAIS-R was standardized, and even in the mid-1990s when the WAIS-III was standardized. That same kind of variability characterized the percents at each age with college experience (13 or more years of schooling). But, as evidenced in Table 7.2, the age groups have become more homogenized in educational attainment in 2007 when the WAIS-IV was standardized. Ages 20–24 through 55–64 had almost identical percents of individuals with less than nine years of schooling (3–6%) and with college experience (55–59%). Therefore, the *uncorrected* WAIS-IV Indexes and FS-IQ for cross-sectional age groups between 20 and 64 years provide a good estimate of intellectual changes with age even without controlling for educational attainment

Furthermore, *parents' education* for ages 16–19 (4% with 0–8 years; 59% with 13+ years; Psychological Corporation, 2007, Table 3.3) is entirely consistent with the values for self-education at 20–64; and the percents for ages 65–69 (9% and 45%; see table 7.2) are not far off either. Consequently, the means on the four Indexes for diverse age groups, presented below, provide a good estimate of changes in intellectual ability with increasing age for ages 16–69 years. Values for ages 70–90 require cautious interpretation because some of the decline shown in the mean scores is a result of educational differences. Likewise, mean WAIS-IV FS-IQs shown for various age groups between 20–24 and 75+ in Table 7.1 reflect good estimates of the decline of intelligence in adults between 20–24 and 65–69, even without the educational control.

Here are the mean Indexes for selected age groups on the WAIS-IV. They were computed by using the mean raw scores estimated by Wisdom et al. (2012) for separate age groups on the 10 core WAIS-IV subtests. These raw scores were entered into the WAIS-IV scaled-score conversion table for ages 20–34 (Wechsler, 2008, p. 219); then the VCI, PRI, WMI, and PSI sums of scaled scores were entered into the pertinent WAIS-IV Index conversion table (Wechsler, 2008, Tables A.3-A.6).

Age Group	WAIS-IV Index			
	VCI	PRI	WMI	PSI
16–19	96	101	100	100
20–24	98	101	100	100
25–34	100	100	100	99
35–44	102	97	101	97
45–54	104	92	99	93
55–64	103	88	97	88
65–69	102	84	96	84
70–79	100	80	92	78
80–90	95	72	86	69

These WAIS-IV cross-sectional data are entirely consistent with the results of previous cross-sectional Wechsler studies, including age changes on the four WAIS-III Indexes (Kaufman, 2000a). In that study, adjustment for education raised all four Indexes by 3–4 points for adults ages 65–79 and by 5–7 points for those in their 80s.

Cautions Associated With Cross-Sectional Investigations

Despite the careful experimental designs of the cross-sectional investigations conducted on large standardization samples, this type of study, which uses educational attainment as the only control, has a few built-in problems that must be considered:

- *Equating on educational attainment.* Matarazzo (1972) wondered whether years of formal education is "a variable with identical meaning across generations" (p. 115), and his concern has merit (Kaufman, 2001). Equating groups that differ substantially in age on educational attainment is an inexact science and must be considered as approximate correction for a changing society's inequalities. For example, schooling beyond high school, commonplace now, was enjoyed primarily by the elite in the 1950s. The meaning of "attended college" or "graduated college," therefore, is not a constant across generations; analogously, "high school dropout" has a far greater stigma for younger than for older adults in the 2000s than it did a half century earlier.

- *Cohort effects.* Regardless of consistencies across studies, instruments, and generations, inferences from cross-sectional studies about developmental (ontogenetic) changes in intelligence are speculative at best. When education level is controlled, one aspect of cohort differences is eliminated to some extent. However, numerous other variables associated with growing up at a given period of time are unknown, unmeasured, or unquantifiable. Yet such variables as motivation level, historical events, social customs and mores, the availability of television and personal computers, constant updates on current events, child-rearing techniques, nutrition, the quality and extent of prenatal care and knowledge, and the impact of mass media will affect apparent age-related changes in scores on mental tests.

- *Time-of-measurement effects.* In addition, time-of-measurement effects interact with performance on intelligence tests. Real changes either in mental ability or in test-taking ability could affect how every group of adults (regardless of cohort) performs on a given test. These sweeping cultural changes could affect individuals aging from 25 to 35 in much the same way that they affect others who age from 40 to 50 during the same time frame. For example, in the 1920s, tests were uncommon for everyone, and scores would likely be relatively low for a person of 20 or 40 or 60 tested on unfamiliar items like verbal or figure analogies; people of the same ages tested in the 1960s or 1970s would likely score relatively higher on these same tests because such tests had become a familiar part of U.S. culture. This type of control for cultural change was used by Owens (1966) in his landmark longitudinal study (discussed in the next section). Not all cultural changes relate to test-taking ability, however, as Flynn (1987) made abundantly clear by showing that whole societies have increased in IQ at a steady rate and continue to do so (Flynn, 2007; 2009b). Flynn has probably come as close as anyone to quantifying these cultural or time-of-measurement effects by using cross-sectional data to show systematic IQ gains across generations. That these gains differ dramatically from country to country stresses their cultural-environmental origin. Because differences in IQs earned in different eras by individuals of the same age reflect both time-of-measurement and cohort effects,

Kausler (1982, 1991) prefers to use the term *time lag* to denote these changes in intelligence scores.

• *Internal and external validity.* By controlling for education level in various cross-sectional studies, the investigators have conducted studies high in *internal validity*, permitting both the identification of causative factors and the generalization of these causative factors to other similar samples (Kausler, 1982, 1991). The downside of the high internal validity of the cross-sectional aging-IQ studies is low *external validity*, meaning poor generalization of the "adjusted" age differences to the population at large. In fact, in the real world, older individuals are less well educated than younger adults. Consequently, the actual, unadjusted values come closer to describing true differences in the mean scores of different age groups. With the WAIS-III, though, even the unadjusted values may not validly describe true differences in the population at large in view of the unusual number of exclusionary criteria applied to the selection of the standardization sample (criteria that were used for the WAIS-IV as well). However, unadjusted values cannot be used to infer causality of the differences, and they have limited value for implying developmental change. Because of the very nature of the limitations of cross-sectional research, it is essential that any conclusions about aging and IQ be buttressed by the results of longitudinal research.

DOES IQ DECLINE WITH ADVANCING AGE? A LONGITUDINAL APPROACH

Inferring developmental trends from cross-sectional data is risky, partly because of cohort effects and partly because of the failure to test the same individuals more than once. Longitudinal investigations of aging and intelligence solve both problems by holding constant cohort variance (each individual is, in effect, his or her own cohort control) and by observing developmental changes within the same person over time. In fact, longitudinal investigations of the Wechsler-Bellevue (Berkowitz & Green, 1963) and WAIS (Eisdorfer & Wilkie, 1973) have generally shown little age-related decline in ability, far less than has been revealed by cross-sectional analysis. Unfortunately, longitudinal studies of intelligence and aging are beset by problems different from the disadvantages of cross-sectional studies but nonetheless potentially debilitating.

In the next sections we discuss some of these pitfalls, especially in studies using Wechsler's adult tests. We then treat two of the best-designed and most influential longitudinal studies: Owens's (1953) Army Alpha investigation of adults tested originally in 1919 as Iowa State freshmen; and Schaie's (1983b) 21-year Seattle longitudinal study with the PMA that utilized sophisticated cohort-sequential methodology. We conclude this section with Kaufman's (1990, 2001; Lichtenberger & Kaufman, 2009) longitudinal investigations of Wechsler's scales (including the WAIS-IV) using independent samples.

Problems in Investigating Aging Longitudinally

Ideally, the alleged early and rapid decline in P-IQ—and other measures of Gf, Gv, and Gs—with increasing age could be verified or disproved by the continual retesting of the same individuals. Some excellent longitudinal investigations using the WAIS, or a portion of it, have been conducted (Schaie, 1983a), but the results have not answered the question. The main difficulty lies less with the research studies than with the WAIS itself.

Practice Effects and Progressive Error on Wechsler's Performance Scale

With all tests, the effects of using the same instrument repeatedly introduce unwanted error into the analysis, a confounding known as progressive error (Kausler, 1982, 1991). This type of error is important for any studies involving Wechsler's Performance Scale because of the nature of the items and the enormous practice effect associated with them. Adults who are retested on the WAIS or WAIS-R after about a month will gain only about 2 to 3 points on the Verbal Scale versus 8 to 9 points on the Performance Scale (Kaufman, 1994b). This profound practice effect on P-IQ extends for at least four months (Catron & Thompson, 1979). On the WAIS-III, the P-IQ practice effect was about 8 points for ages 16–54 years, 6 points for ages 55–74, and 4 points for 75–89 (Kaufman & Lichtenberger, 1999). For the WAIS-IV, practice effects for the PRI and PSI are about 4 to 5 points (Psychological Corporation, 2008, Table 4.5; see Rapid Reference 8.15).

Even if the practice effect dissipates after a year or two, this variable still looms large in longitudinal investigations. The practice effect may not impede the results of the first retest in a longitudinal study, but it surely will not disappear by the third, fourth, or fifth retest and may be quite large even for elderly individuals. In the first of two Duke longitudinal studies, comprising an initial sample of 267 adult volunteers between the ages of 59 and 94 from North Carolina, 42 "survivors" were tested up to 11 times on the WAIS between 1955 and 1976. The second Duke study involved a four-subtest WAIS short form administered to an initial sample of 502 adults, ages 46–70, from the same general area; the 331 survivors were given the short form four times between 1970 and 1976 (Siegler, 1983). The two Duke longitudinal investigations were exceptional studies, uncovering fascinating relationships among the cognitive, memory, personality, sensory, and motor variables administered repeatedly to the subjects. But it is impossible to make inferences about changes in P-IQ over time for samples that are so overexposed to the five Performance subtests.

These tasks are new the first time they are given, but the novelty wears off quickly. When people are retested after a few weeks or months, they seem to remember only a few specific nonverbal items; even if they recall many of the puzzles or pictures, no feedback for correctness is given either during or after the test. What people do tend to remember is the type of items they faced and the kinds of strategies and attack modes that seemed successful. When individuals are tested repeatedly on Wechsler's Performance tasks, the tests no longer measure the kind of intelligence that thrives on novel problem-solving tasks with visual-spatial stimuli, and it becomes questionable whether they are effective measures of intelligence the third or fourth time around.

Failure to account for the effects of practice when evaluating changes in intelligence with increasing age challenges the findings of a variety of longitudinal studies, such as the excellent Bonn longitudinal study that tested two cohorts of adults (ages 60–65 and 70–75) on the Hamburg-Wechsler (German WAIS) as many as six times between 1965 and 1980 (Schmitz-Scherzer & Thomae, 1983). The younger cohort performed fairly constantly on the Verbal Scale over the 12-year period, whereas the older cohort dropped significantly as they aged from the 70s to mid-80s. On the Performance Scale, both cohorts either maintained or improved their scores between the 1965 and 1972 testings (four administrations) before showing a sizable drop in 1976–1977. The Verbal changes are consistent with the results of other investigations. The Performance changes imply virtually no loss of function for the older cohort between the ages of about 72 to 79 and small gains in Performance scores for the younger cohort between ages 62 and 66. However, such interpretations of Performance abilities are fanciful, based on the problem of progressive error. It should be noted, however, that not everyone interprets practice effects as an artifact. Flynn (1998) suggested that

> decline after age 50 for fluid intelligence is less than we once believed; the elderly show a surprisingly robust gain from practice effects, which may not boost our estimate of their IQs but does show a lively ability to learn in old age. (p. 106)

Selective Attrition

A second major problem of longitudinal aging research is selective attrition of subjects. When using volunteer subjects, "at all ages in adulthood, those who do not volunteer initially and those who do not show up in retesting tend to be lower scorers on ability tests than those who do cooperate" (Horn & Donaldson, 1976, p. 717). The first Duke longitudinal study was especially valuable in generating research to help quantify this effect. Analysis of data from the first 10 years of the study (Eisdorfer & Wilkie, 1973) revealed "a substantial loss of *S*s, with the lowest IQ group sustaining a loss of 72 percent; the middle IQ group, a loss of 51.4 percent; and the high IQ group, a loss of only 36.8 percent" (p. 28). Even more dramatic evidence of the selective attrition factor came from Siegler and Botwinick's (1979) analysis of data from all 11 "waves" of the first Duke study. Individuals who continue to be retested over time are more intelligent than those who drop out early.

Among 60- to 74-year-olds in the Duke study, the relationship is nearly linear between IQ at the initial assessment and the number of times the person returned to be tested, as depicted in Figure 7.5. Of the 179 individuals tested on the WAIS in the first wave, only 18 returned to be tested at all 10 subsequent

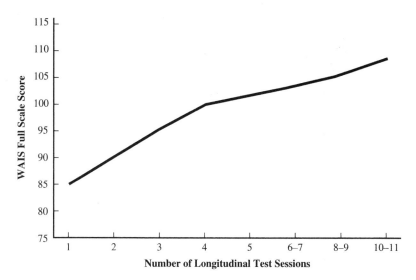

Figure 7.5. Mean WAIS Full Scale Scores Earned by Adults (Aged 60–74 years) on the Initial Assessment, Shown as a Function of the Number of Longitudinal Test Sessions in Which the Subjects Participated

Source: Data are from Siegler & Botwinick (1979).

assessments. Overall, the 60- to 74-year-olds who came once or twice earned mean sums of scaled scores on the Full Scale of 85 to 90, compared to means of close to 110 for those who came to be tested 10 or all 11 times. Obviously some of the elderly subjects died or were too ill to be tested, but many simply chose not to be retested for whatever reason; the selective attrition factor occurs as well for younger adults, although the effect seems to increase with age (Horn & Donaldson, 1976).

Hence, generalizations from longitudinal studies must be made quite cautiously because of the considerable selective attrition factor. At the very least, it is essential for researchers to partly compensate for this problem by following Eisdorfer and Wilkie's (1973) advice: "The appropriate analysis of longitudinal data should use data only from the same subjects across time, whether *S*s are lost secondary to death or drop out" (p. 28).

TWO GROUNDBREAKING LONGITUDINAL INVESTIGATIONS OF IQ AND AGING

We now turn to two of the most influential and well-designed investigations of IQ and aging: Owens's Iowa State Army Alpha Study and Schaie's 21-Year Seattle Cohort-Sequential Study.

Iowa State Army Alpha Study

Owens (1953) administered the Army Alpha test in 1950 to 127 men, age 50, who had previously been among 363 Iowa State University freshmen who had been administered the same test in 1919 at age 19. These initial results "were important in stimulating a critical reexamination of the inevitability of intellectual decline in adulthood" (Schaie, 1983c, pp. 13, 15); the study "ushered in an era of new ideas in research on adult development and intelligence" (Cunningham & Owens, 1983, p. 20). The study continued in 1961, when 96 of these men were tested once more, at age 61 (Owens, 1966); Owens also tested a random sample of 19-year-old Iowa State freshmen on the Army Alpha in 1961–1962 to permit a time-lag comparison, thereby estimating the impact of cultural change on the obtained test scores. The Army Alpha, one of Wechsler's primary sources for selecting Verbal subtests, comprises eight tasks, including tests of Information, Practical Judgment (Comprehension), Arithmetical Problems, and Synonyms–Antonyms (Vocabulary).

Results of the Iowa State longitudinal investigation for the 96 men tested three times on the Army Alpha reveal improvement in Verbal and Total scores between ages 19 and 50, followed by a slight decline from age 50 to 61. Reasoning displayed small increments from one testing occasion to the next, while Numerical evidenced the opposite profile. The most noteworthy changes were the improvement in Verbal scores from age 19 to 50 and the sudden decrease in Numerical scores from age 50 to 61. Owens then corrected the data for cultural change, based on the better performance (especially in Reasoning) by the 19-year-olds tested in the early 1960s compared to the 19-year-olds tested in 1919. Following this time-lag correction, what had appeared to be slight increments in Reasoning were actually steady decrements in performance. Despite the correction for cultural change, Verbal Factor scores continued to show gains between ages 19 and 61; numerical scores showed a loss across this same age span, but a smaller loss than was observed for Reasoning.

Cunningham and Owens's (1983) overall conclusion from the Iowa State study was that:

> The results suggest peak performance and the beginning of declines of overall intellectual functioning roughly in the decade of the 50s for this elite sample. The losses appear to be small and probably are not of much practical significance until at least age 60. (p. 34)

The decline in Reasoning is especially noteworthy because the tasks that measured it included a heavy dose of *Gc*. Although Reasoning was interpreted by Owens (1966) as a measure of fluid ability, the scale was defined by *verbal* tests such as Analogies (e.g., *fear* is to *anticipation* as *regret* is to?).

Schaie's 21-Year Seattle Cohort-Sequential Study

Schaie's (1983b) sophisticated combination of cross-sectional and longitudinal designs was predicated on the contributions of three variables to the scores obtained by adults on intelligence tests: chronological age, cohort (year of birth), and time of measurement (the year the tests were administered). He conducted four independent cross-sectional studies with the group-administered PMA test in 1956 ($N = 500$, ages 25–67); in 1963 ($N = 996$, ages 25–74); in 1970 ($N = 705$, ages 25–81); and in 1977 ($N = 609$, ages 25–81). All samples comprised approximately equal numbers of men and women, with the groups tending to be relatively well educated for the 1960s and 1970s (about 50% with one or more years of college).

Coinciding with the last three cross-sectional studies were longitudinal investigations ranging from 7 to 21 years. Three 7-year studies included the retesting of as many subjects as possible from the 1956 ($N = 303$), 1963 ($N = 420$), and 1970

(N = 340) cross-sectional investigations. In addition, Schaie conducted two 14-year studies and one with a 21-year interval between testings. These rigorous cross-sequential, cohort-sequential, and longitudinal designs permitted Schaie and his colleagues to identify cohort and time-of-measurement variation in an attempt to understand "true" intelligence differences due to aging.

His 1968 investigation (Schaie & Strother, 1968) was widely publicized in popular texts at that time (Cronbach, 1970; Matarazzo, 1972) because it showed dramatic differences in the aging-IQ growth curve from cross-sectional data alone (his 1956 sample of 500) and the curve obtained from his first 7-year longitudinal study. The cross-sectional data for ages 20–70 revealed the same type of plunge in abilities with age that characterized the WAIS, WAIS-R, or WAIS-III Full Scale IQ before an adjustment for education (see Table 7.1); the mix of cross-sectional and longitudinal data for the smaller sample (a sequential analysis) demonstrated growth curves showing virtually no decline across the age range. These findings applied to the separate components of the PMA, whether measuring verbal ability or skills akin to Wechsler's Performance subtests, especially tasks like Block Design with a strong Gv component (Space, a measure of spatial orientation).

These data became the subject of controversy, with Horn and Donaldson (1976) and Botwinick (1977), for example, citing variables such as selective attrition to account for the apparent maintenance of both fluid and crystallized abilities through old age. Regardless of the arguments and counterarguments (Baltes & Schaie, 1976; Horn & Donaldson, 1977), the early Schaie data show both consistency and inconsistency with Wechsler cross-sectional results. In Schaie's findings, scores on the nonverbal, Gf/Gv tasks (Space and a measure of inductive reasoning) clearly began a decline much later in life than was found for Wechsler's Performance subtests. Yet, like the Wechsler findings, scores on Space and Reasoning peaked far earlier than the more crystallized PMA subtests (Verbal Meaning and Number).

Subsequent analyses (e.g., Schaie & Hertzog, 1983) revealed Schaie's responsiveness to the criticisms and the concomitant efforts by his research team to refine their methodologies and analyses. Schaie and Hertzog (1983) admitted that their original cross-sequential design was ill suited to evaluate age changes; furthermore, the results of the two 14-year longitudinal studies they reported indicated earlier declines in intelligence (i.e., before age 60) than were previously observed in Schaie's laboratory. The best integration of the numerous analyses appears in Schaie's (1983b) thorough treatment of the 21-year Seattle project. Figure 7.6 depicts Schaie's results for Verbal Meaning (Gc), Space (Gv), and Reasoning (Gf). Gc increases steadily until age 53, with a notable decline occurring between ages 67

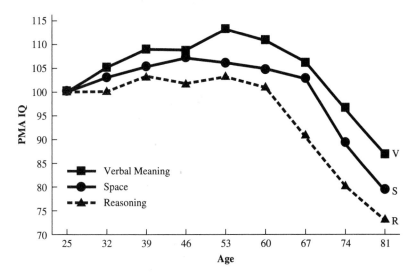

Figure 7.6. Performance on Three Primary Mental Abilities (PMA) Subtests at Ages 25–81 as a Proportion of Age 25 Performance (Set at 100), Corrected for Time of Measurement, Attrition, and Cohort Efforts

Source: From Schaie (Schaie, 1983b, Table 4.18), based on 7-year longitudinal data.

and 74. *Gv* peaks earlier than *Gc* (age 46) but has its first sizable decline between the same 67- to 74-year period. Nonetheless, its decline is more dramatic than that of the *Gc* test. *Gf* declines substantially after age 60, plunging to 73 by age 81.

These results are basically in agreement with the differential results for the measures of maintained abilities (*Gc*, *Gq*) versus vulnerable abilities (*Gf*, *Gv*, *Gs*, *Gsm*) described by Horn (1989) and observed on Wechsler's scales. Unlike the popular interpretations of the initial findings reported by Schaie and his colleagues, intelligence does decline with chronological age, and that decline becomes precipitous in old age. However, the use of longitudinal data juxtaposed with cross-sectional results on the PMA suggest that the decrements may not begin until relatively late in life.

LONGITUDINAL INVESTIGATIONS OF WECHSLER'S SCALES USING INDEPENDENT SAMPLES

The key question that remains unanswered from cross-sectional investigations of Wechsler's series of scales is whether the rapid decline on Wechsler's *Gf*, *Gv*, *Gs*, and working memory scales, even after control for years of formal education, is an artifact of other unknown cohort variables. Another important question is whether the substantial decline in *Gc* in old age is an artifact of uncontrolled cohort variables.

While writing the aging chapter in the first edition of this book, Kaufman (1990, Chapter 7) was troubled by the lack of an answer to the important question about P-IQ decline and conducted a study that was inspired by the methodologies of Owens (1966), Schaie (1983b), and Parker (1986), and by Kausler's (1982) detailed discussions of the pros and cons of diverse methodologies. Parker (1986) had the clever idea of examining the comparative performance of year-of-birth cohorts by equating the standardization samples of the Wechsler-Bellevue I, WAIS, and WAIS-R. However, he focused solely on the Full Scale IQ, when it was the separate V-IQs and P-IQs that were of the greatest theoretical interest for analyses of aging. But Parker's article made Kaufman (1990) realize the analogy between the WAIS and WAIS-R standardization samples and Schaie's repeated cross-sectional analyses between 1956 and 1977.

For example, people born in 1905 would have been 48 years old in 1953, when the WAIS was standardized, and 73 years old when the WAIS-R was standardized 25 years later in 1978. By comparing the performance of people born in the same year (i.e., from the same cohort) at two points in time, it was suddenly possible to easily conduct a longitudinal study of aging and IQ with cohort effects controlled.

The use of independent samples, or "cohort substitution" (Kausler, 1982), if they are truly comparable and random, makes it "possible to compute age-change estimates that are controlled for the effects of testing and experimental mortality" (Schaie, 1983b, p. 106). Kaufman (1990) used the cohort substitution method with the WAIS and WAIS-R normative samples serving as the data source, primarily to determine whether longitudinal data would replicate the cross-sectional finding of rapidly declining P-IQ across most of the life span. He then used the same method with the WAIS-R and WAIS-III standardization samples (Kaufman, 2001), and recently did it again with the WAIS-III and WAIS-IV samples (Lichtenberger & Kaufman, 2009), thanks to the kindness of Pearson Assessments for making the pertinent WAIS-IV data available. In the WAIS-IV study, it was possible to compare age changes on the four indexes between 1995, when the WAIS-III was standardized, and 2007, when the WAIS-IV was normed.

Longitudinal Studies of WAIS, WAIS-R, and WAIS-III Verbal and Performance IQs

The WAIS and WAIS-R standardization samples are quite similar to each other, each matching relevant Census data on numerous key variables. They differ in

Table 7.4. The Four Adult Age Cohorts Represented in the WAIS and WAIS-R Standardization Samples

Cohort (Year of Birth)	Age in 1953 (WAIS Standardization)	Age in 1978 (WAIS-R Standardization)
1924–1933	20–29	45–54
1914–1923	30–39	55–64
1909–1913	40–44	65–69
1904–1908	45–49	70–74

Source: Data are from Kaufman (1990, 2001).

that the data were collected 25 years apart, in approximately 1953 and 1978. Thus, several cohorts in the WAIS sample are also represented in the WAIS-R sample. For example, adults born in the 1909–1913 cohort were tested at ages 40–44 in 1953 (on the WAIS) and again at ages 65–69 in 1978 (on the WAIS-R). To the degree that the two samples are comparable, a comparison of the test perform-ance of 40- to 44-year-olds on the WAIS with that of the 65- to 69-year-olds 25 years later on the WAIS-R represents a longitudinal comparison of adults from the same cohort.

Four adult cohorts are represented within both the WAIS and WAIS-R standardization samples, as shown in Table 7.4. In essence, Kaufman (1990) followed each of four cohorts longitudinally from 1953 to 1978 to see if individuals born in the same era gained or lost IQ points over the course of a generation. Before making the comparisons, he had to perform some essential empirical steps:

- Verify that the independent samples were extremely well matched and comparable within each of the four cohorts on the important variables of gender, ethnicity, geographic region, and educational attainment.
- Convert sums of scaled scores on the WAIS and WAIS-R to a common yardstick to permit age-by-age comparisons. (Kaufman chose to use the norms for ages 25–34.)
- Control for the fact that different tests (WAIS versus WAIS-R) were administered at the two points in time. He added 6 to 6.5 points to each WAIS-R IQ (the median IQ differences from 20 studies totaling over 1,300 subjects) (Kaufman, 1990, Table 3.13) to convert these IQs to WAIS IQs. These "corrections" to the WAIS-R IQs helped answer the

crucial question: How many IQ points higher would adults have scored had they been administered the WAIS instead of the WAIS-R?

• Apply a time-lag correction to control for cultural change during the 25-year span, just as Owens (1966) did in his Iowa State study. Adjustment for cultural change requires a comparison of the IQs earned by each cohort in 1953 with the IQs earned by adults of the same age in 1978. The 1909–1913 cohort, for example, was 40–44 years old in 1953. This group was compared to adults aged 40–44 in 1978 to determine how cultural changes have affected test scores for this age group. Similar time-lag comparisons were conducted for each of the other three cohorts who, in 1953, were ages 20–29, 30–39, and 45–49. The analyses showed that cultural change affected each of the four cohorts about equally, producing about a 3-point IQ gain on the Verbal and Scale and about a 5-point gain on the Performance Scale, presumably because of some type of culture-related change between 1953 and 1978 that affected all adults who were between the ages of 20 and 49 in 1953. Kaufman (1990) adjusted the estimated WAIS IQs earned by each cohort in 1978 for these time-lag effects to remove the influence of cultural change.

Kaufman (2001) repeated this same procedure a decade later, using data from the WAIS-R and WAIS-III standardization samples. The methodology was virtually identical with only slight variations—for example, the reference group was based on ages 20–34 instead of 25–34. In this study, Kaufman examined changes on the V-IQ and P-IQ for seven cohorts over the 17-year span from 1978 to 1995. These cohorts, summarized in Table 7.5, range from individuals born between 1954 and 1958 (tested at age 22 and again at 39) to adults born between 1904 and 1908, who were 72 during the WAIS-R standardization and 89 when the WAIS-III was normed.

Table 7.5 presents the four age cohorts from the first study (WAIS/WAIS-R) alongside the seven cohorts from the second study. As shown, the four cohorts from the initial study were also in the follow-up study, so in actuality these four cohorts were tested at three different points in time, spanning a total of 42 years. For example, individuals born between 1909 and 1913 were tested on the WAIS at ages 40–44, on the WAIS-R at ages 65–69, and on the WAIS-III at ages 82–86.

The results of both longitudinal studies are summarized in Table 7.6 (changes in V-IQ over time) and Table 7.7 (changes in P-IQ over time). The changes in IQ shown in the tables have been adjusted for instrument

Table 7.5. Age Cohorts (Independent Samples) Tested on the WAIS in 1953, on the WAIS-R in 1978, and on the WAIS-III in 1995

Cohort (Year of Birth)	Age in 1953 (WAIS)	Age in 1978 (WAIS-R)	Age in 1995 (WAIS-III)
1954–1958	—	**22** (20–24)	**39** (37–41)
1944–1953	—	**29.5** (25–34)	**46.5** (42–51)
1934–1943	—	**39.5** (35–44)	**56.5** (52–61)
1924–1933	**24.5** (20–29)	**49.5** (45–54)	**66.5** (62–71)
1914–1923	**34.5** (30–39)	**59.5** (55–64)	**76.5** (72–81)
1909–1913	**42** (40–44)	**67** (65–69)	**84** (82–86)
1904–1908	**47** (45–49)	**72** (70–74)	**89** (87–91)

Source: Data are from Kaufman (1990, 2001). Standardization data of the *Wechsler Adult Intelligence Scale: Third Edition* Copyright © 1997 by The Psychological Corporation. Used by permission. All rights reserved. "Wechsler Adult Intelligence Scale" and "WAIS" are trademarks, in the United States and/or other countries, of Pearson Education, Inc. or its affiliate(s).

Table 7.6. Adjusted Age Changes in Wechsler's Verbal IQ for Adult Cohorts (Independent Samples) Tested Two or Three Times between 1953 and 1995

Cohort (Year of Birth)	Median Age			Adjusted Verbal IQ Change		
	WAIS 1953	WAIS-R 1978	WAIS-III 1995	1953–1978 (25-yr interval)	1978–1995 (17-yr interval)	1953–1995 (42-yr interval)
1954–1958	—	22	39	—	+6.3	—
1944–1953	—	29.5	46.5	—	+3.2	—
1934–1943	—	39.5	56.5	—	−1.0	—
1924–1933	24.5	49.5	66.5	−1.5	−5.6	−7.1
1914–1923	34.5	59.5	76.5	−3.3	−2.9	−6.2
1909–1913	42	67	84	−3.9	−7.4	−11.3
1904–1908	47	72	89	−5.5	−8.3	−13.8

Note: Changes in Wechsler's Verbal IQ are adjusted for instrument and time lag.
Source: Data are from Kaufman (1990, 2001). Standardization data of the *Wechsler Adult Intelligence Scale: Third Edition* Copyright © 1997 by The Psychological Corporation. Used by permission. All rights reserved. "Wechsler Adult Intelligence Scale" and "WAIS" are trademarks, in the United States and/or other countries, of Pearson Education, Inc. or its affiliate(s).

Table 7.7. Adjusted Age Changes in Wechsler's Performance IQ for Adult Cohorts (Independent Samples) Tested Two or Three Times between 1953 and 1995

Cohort (Year of Birth)	Median Age			Adjusted Performance IQ Change		
	WAIS 1953	WAIS-R 1978	WAIS-III 1995	1953–1978 (25-yr interval)	1978–1995 (17-yr interval)	1953–1995 (42-yr interval)
1954–1958	—	22	39	—	−2.1	—
1944–1953	—	29.5	46.5	—	−5.8	—
1934–1943	—	39.5	56.5	—	−9.3	—
1924–1933	24.5	49.5	66.5	−11.6	−10.9	−22.5
1914–1923	34.5	59.5	76.5	−12.5	−10.1	−22.6
1909–1913	42	67	84	−12.9	−9.2	−22.1
1904–1908	47	72	89	−13.5	−10.1	−23.6

Note: Changes in Wechsler's Performance IQ are adjusted for instrument and time lag.

Source: Data are from Kaufman (1990, 2001). Standardization data of the *Wechsler Adult Intelligence Scale: Third Edition* Copyright © 1997 by The Psychological Corporation. Used by permission. All rights reserved. "Wechsler Adult Intelligence Scale" and "WAIS" are trademarks, in the United States and/or other countries, of Pearson Education, Inc. or its affiliate(s).

(whether WAIS versus WAIS-R or WAIS-R versus WAIS-III) and time lag. The tables show the median age of each cohort at each point in time (1953, 1978, and 1995) and the number of IQ points that each cohort either increased or decreased as they got older. For example, consider again the 1909–1913 cohort. As shown in Table 7.7, their mean Verbal IQs decreased by 3.9 points between ages 42 and 67 and decreased by 7.4 points between ages 67 and 84. Overall, the decrease over the 42-year span was 11.3 points.

Consider first the results of the 1990 study. The most striking finding in the data is the difference between the Verbal and Performance Scales. The mean Verbal IQs for the four cohorts (see Table 7.6) decreased by a few points over the 25-year span between 1953 and 1978, ranging from 1.5 points for the 1924–1933 cohort to 5.5 points for the oldest cohort (1904–1908). In contrast, the decreases in mean Performance IQs for same four cohorts (see Table 7.7) are huge, ranging from 11.6 to 13.5 IQ points (an average decrease of 12.6 points, or .84 standard deviations [SDs]). Substantial decreases in P-IQ occurred for each cohort, whether they advanced in age from 24.5 to 49.5 (on the average) or from 47 to 72.

The results of the WAIS-R/WAIS-III longitudinal study, also summarized in Tables 7.6 and 7.7, reinforce the findings from the first study and expand those findings by including more cohorts. The two youngest cohorts had higher mean V-IQs in their 40s than in their 20s. Otherwise, each cohort lost IQ points on each scale. The decreases in mean Verbal IQ are small in magnitude, except for the two oldest cohorts. By contrast, the Performance IQ decreases were substantial in magnitude, and similar in value, for the five oldest cohorts. Over the 17-year period, adults born before 1944 lost 10 points (±1) of Performance IQ, or about two-thirds of a SD, whether they were about 60, 70, 80, or 90 years of age in 1995.

When the changes in Performance IQ are examined for the four cohorts that were tested at all three points in time, spanning 42 years, the results are remarkable in their consistency from cohort to cohort (Table 7.7). Each cohort lost 22 to 23 points (mean = 22.7), or 1.5 SDs over that interval, whether they aged from about 25 to 65 or from about 45 to 85. The changes in 42 years on Verbal IQ are substantial for the two oldest cohorts, averaging 12.6 points (.84 SD). Taken together, the results of the two longitudinal investigations of independent samples support the maintenance of Verbal IQ, except for a loss of verbal skills for adults in their 80s, and the vulnerability of Performance IQ across the life span. These findings are entirely consistent with the cross-sectional analyses of Wechsler's scales, with or without a control for education.

LONGITUDINAL STUDY OF WAIS-III AND WAIS-IV FACTOR INDEXES

As soon as the WAIS-IV was published, Pearson Assessments kindly agreed to make the pertinent data available to permit Lichtenberger and Kaufman (2009) to continue the series of longitudinal investigations of independent samples. This analysis focused on the four indexes that had appeared on the WAIS-III alongside V-IQ and P-IQ, and that replaced those IQs on the WAIS-IV. Once again, Lichtenberger and Kaufman (2009) applied Kaufman's familiar methodology to the 11 cohorts who were administered the WAIS-III and WAIS-IV during their respective standardizations (see Table 7.8). This time the interval was 12 years between the 1995–1996 standardization of the WAIS-III and the 2007–2008 standardization of the WAIS-IV. (The first WAIS-IV standardization case was received in March 2007, and the last case was received in April 2008; D. L. Coalson, personal communication, October 6, 2008.)

Table 7.8. Eleven Age Cohorts Tested on the WAIS-III in 1995 and on the WAIS-IV in 2007

Cohort (Year of Birth)	Age in 1995 (WAIS-III)	Age in 2007 (WAIS-IV)
1978–1979	16–17	28–29
1976–1977	18–19	30–31
1971–1975	20–24	32–36
1966–1970	25–29	37–41
1961–1965	30–34	42–46
1951–1960	35–44	47–56
1941–1950	45–54	57–66
1931–1940	55–64	67–76
1926–1930	65–69	77–81
1921–1925	70–74	82–86
1916–1920	75–79	87–90

Source: Data are from Lichtenberger and Kaufman (2009). Analysis results from the *Wechsler Adult Intelligence Scale—Fourth Edition* (WAIS-IV). Copyright © 2008 by NCS Pearson, Inc. Reproduced with permission. All rights reserved. "Wechsler Adult Intelligence Scale" and "WAIS" are trademarks, in the United States and/or other countries, of Pearson Education, Inc. or its affiliate(s).

Two of the indexes comprised identical subtests on the WAIS-III and WAIS-IV (VCI and PSI) and two were modified. For WMI, Kaufman and Lichtenberger used the two-subtest WAIS-IV scale (Digit Span-Arithmetic) rather than the three-subtest WAIS-III scale, because Letter-Number Sequencing was not administered above age 69. The WAIS-III POI, renamed PRI on the WAIS-IV, overlapped on two subtests (Block Design and Matrix Reasoning). The third POI subtest was Picture Completion, which is supplemental on the WAIS-IV. Lichtenberger and Kaufman (2009) recomputed WAIS-IV PRI with Picture Completion instead of Visual Puzzles to ensure that the cohort changes in mean scores from the WAIS-III to WAIS-IV were based on the identical set of subtests. They then adjusted the cohort changes on the four indexes for instrument effects, using the mean differences obtained in the counterbalanced WAIS-III/WAIS-IV study of 240 adults reported in the *WAIS-IV Manual* (Psychological Corporation, 2008, Table 5.5). And, again, they adjusted the changes for time lag to determine age changes over time on the four indexes.

The results of this study, summarized in Table 7.9, are remarkably similar to the results of Kaufman's previous longitudinal studies, especially the WAIS-R/WAIS-III comparisons. VCI and WMI displayed the same curvilinear pattern of increases in mean scores for the younger cohorts and decreases for the older cohorts that characterized V-IQ (Table 7.6). PRI and PSI dropped substantially for most cohorts, particularly for adults born between 1916 and

Table 7.9. Twelve-Year Changes in WAIS-III/WAIS-IV Factor Indexes for 11 Age Cohorts

Cohort (Year of Birth)	Median Age 1995	Median Age 2007	12-Year Change in Standard Score Points			
			VCI	PRI (POI)	WMI	PSI
1978–1979	16.5	28.5	+7.0	−1.2	+4.3	+2.2
1976–1977	18.5	30.5	+3.4	−1.4	+0.6	+2.7
1971–1975	22	34	+1.6	2.0	+0.4	−5.0
1966–1970	27	39	+1.0	−4.0	+1.2	−1.1
1961–1965	32	44	+1.5	−3.4	−1.9	−4.5
1951–1960	39.5	51.5	+2.4	−4.6	−3.0	−4.8
1941–1950	49.5	61.5	−0.8	−5.4	−3.4	−6.2
1931–1940	59.5	71.5	−3.2	−6.3	−3.5	−7.0
1926–1930	67	79	−5.0	−9.6	−4.8	−10.5
1921–1925	72	84	−6.4	−7.2	−7.2	−8.6
1916–1920	77	89	−8.8	−8.4	−8.3	−7.3

Note: All scaled scores are based on the norms for ages 20–34 years. All Indexes are based on WAIS-III norms for both WAIS-III and WAIS-IV (exception—WMI is based on WAIS-IV norms for both instruments because two-subtest norms are not available for the WAIS-III). Twelve-year standard-score change is adjusted for Instrument Effects (WAIS-III versus WAIS-IV) and for Time Lag Effects (cultural change). VCI = Verbal Comprehension Index; PRI = Perceptual Reasoning Index; POI = Perceptual Organization Index (includes Picture Completion instead of Visual Puzzles); WMI = Working Memory Index; PSI = Processing Speed Index. PRI is composed of Block Design, Matrix Analogies, and Picture Completion to be comparable to WAIS-III POI.

Source: Data are from Lichtenberger and Kaufman (2009). Analysis results from the *Wechsler Adult Intelligence Scale—Fourth Edition* (WAIS-IV). Copyright © 2008 by NCS Pearson, Inc. Reproduced with permission. All rights reserved. "Wechsler Adult Intelligence Scale" and "WAIS" are trademarks, in the United States and/or other countries, of Pearson Education, Inc. or its affiliate(s).

1960. Decreases in function were especially large for the four cohorts who were at least 70 years of age in 2007, with mean decrements in index scores averaging 8.0 for PRI and 8.4 points for PSI. Loss of cognitive function was also substantial on the VCI and WMI for the two cohorts who were at least 80 years of age (mean decreases of 7.6 and 7.8 points, respectively).

Technically, it is methodologically incorrect to construct age gradients from a combination of longitudinal and cross-sectional data: "the use of cross-sequential results to evaluate age changes [is] ill considered" (Schaie & Hertzog, 1983, p. 532). Nonetheless, we believe that the best way to show differences across the life span on the abilities that are measured by the four WAIS-IV Indexes is to do just that. In Figure 7.7 we present smoothed trend lines based on polynomial regression to represent the age gradients for each of the four Indexes. Data points

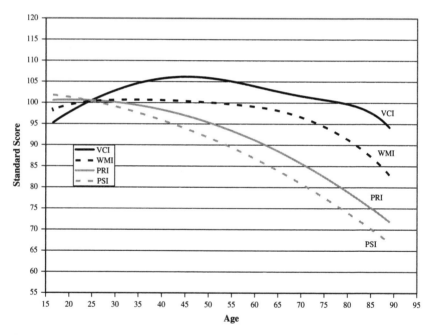

Figure 7.7. Age Gradients for the Four WAIS-IV Indexes Based on Mean Scores Earned by the 11 Cohorts when Tested in 1995 on the WAIS-III and in 2007 on the WAIS-IV

Source: Data are from Lichtenberger and Kaufman (2009). Analysis results from the *Wechsler Adult Intelligence Scale—Fourth Edition* (WAIS-IV). Copyright © 2008 by NCS Pearson, Inc. Reproduced with permission. All rights reserved. "Wechsler Adult Intelligence Scale" and "WAIS" are trademarks, in the United States and/or other countries, of Pearson Education, Inc. or its affiliate(s).

are the two standard scores on each index for each cohort (i.e., the WAIS-III Index earned in 1995 and the WAIS-IV Index, adjusted for instrument effects). Hence, Figure 7.7 shows the polynomial curve of best fit for the 22 data points for each Index.

VCI (*Gc*) is a maintained ability for most of the adult life span, increasing into the 50s before declining substantially in old age. Both PRI (*Gf/Gv*) and PSI (*Gs*) are vulnerable across the entire age span, with *Gs* the most vulnerable ability of all. WMI (*Gs*) too is vulnerable to the aging process, but it is maintained longer than *Gs*, *Gv*, or *Gf* and is clearly less vulnerable than PRI and PSI. The age gradients for the four Indexes are extremely similar to the gradients of these same Indexes in the cross-sectional investigation of the WAIS-III (see Figure 7.4), and the aging curves for VCI and PRI mirror the cross-sectional age gradients for V-IQ and P-IQ, respectively (see Figure 7.3). Additionally, the key findings of this WAIS-IV longitudinal investigation are generally consistent with the results of cross-sectional studies of the WAIS-IV (Baxendale, 2011; Salthouse & Saklofske, 2010), including the WAIS-IV cross-sectional data we presented earlier for the four Indexes, which we based on estimates of subtest raw score means (Wisdom et al., 2012).

OVERVIEW OF THE WECHSLER LONGITUDINAL INVESTIGATIONS WITH INDEPENDENT SAMPLES

The three Wechsler cohort-substitution studies provide results that agree remarkably well with the cross-sectional data for Wechsler's adult scales and for other adult scales, such as the Kaufman Adolescent and Adult Intelligence Test (KAIT; Kaufman & Kaufman, 1993). Combining cross-sectional and longitudinal data suggests a loss of about 0.5 points per year in Performance IQ, or 5 points per decade, which is precisely Horn's (1985; Horn, Donaldson, & Engstrom, 1981) best estimate of the adult decline in fluid intelligence based on his reviews and results of numerous studies.

Taken together, the three cohort-substitution studies offer broad support to the developmental reality of a loss in nonverbal intellectual function (*Gf*, *Gv*, *Gs*) across virtually the entire adult life span; a loss in *Gsm*, especially working memory, as adults enter old age, and even a considerable loss in verbal function (primarily *Gc*) during the decade of the 80s. These meaningful declines on the WAIS-III and WAIS-IV, in particular, are dramatic in view of the systematic exclusion of so many potentially low-functioning adults from their normative samples. On the WAIS-IV, adults were excluded from the sample for many different reasons—for example, being diagnosed with a learning disorder or

ADHD, currently taking medication that might impact test performance (e.g., some antidepressants), or being previously diagnosed with substance dependence (Psychological Corporation, 2008, Table 3.1).

The consistency in the P-IQ, PRI, PSI, and WMI decrease with increasing age for U.S. men and women born during the first 80 years of the 20th century—from cross-sectional and longitudinal data on the WAIS, WAIS-R, WAIS-III, and WAIS-IV—is simply phenomenal.

INTERPRETATION OF COGNITIVE DECLINE: SPEED OR PROBLEM SOLVING

The accumulated cross-sectional and longitudinal data obtained on several versions of Wechsler's adult scales, including cross-sectional data on the Canadian WAIS-III (Lee et al., 2008) and Kaufman tests (e.g., Kaufman & Horn, 1996; Kaufman et al., 2008) and longitudinal data on the Woodcock-Johnson (McArdle, Ferrer-Caja, Hamagami, & Woodcock, 2002), provide a compelling picture of aging and cognition. This picture extends worldwide, as similar findings have occurred in the United Kingdom (Rabbitt, Donlan, Watson, McInnes, & Bent 1995), Germany (Baltes & Lindenberger, 1997; Melchers et al., 2006; Zimprich & Martin, 2002), and The Netherlands (Mulder, Dekker, & Dekker 2004). Adults' performance on tests of crystallized ability (Horn) or pragmatics (Baltes) is maintained during much of the life span and does not decline appreciably until the mid-70s or 80s; in contrast, their performance on tests of fluid–visualization–speed abilities (Horn) or mechanics (Baltes) declines early in the life span and continues the steady descent throughout middle and old age. This pattern of maintenance and decline applies to academic skills. Adults maintained their ability to read words from their early 20s to late 80s, with no decline evident even in old age, but they declined substantially with age on academic skills that are dependent on reasoning ability: reading comprehension, math, and written expression (Kaufman et al., 2008).

On the WAIS-IV, this dichotomy is depicted by the maintenance of V-IQ and VCI and the vulnerability of P-IQ, PRI, and PSI. The Horn and Baltes theoretical explanations of the "classic aging pattern" stand in opposition to Botwinick's (1977) speeded-unspeeded rationale for the tasks that decline with normal aging versus those that are maintained throughout most of the adult life span. In this section we examine the evidence for these competing hypotheses, especially to evaluate whether the age-related decline on PRI and PSI are primarily a function of diminished cognitive capacity or of diminished speed.

Numerous investigators have interpreted the classical pattern from Botwinick's perspective: for example, Jarvik and Bank (1983) in their longitudinal analysis of aging among elderly twins. The decline in speed with advancing age is a fact. This slowing

> is not only an acknowledged laboratory result but also of considerable practical importance. Age-related slowness is evident in tasks of daily living such as zipping a garment, dialing a telephone, picking up coins, unwrapping a band-aid, cutting with a knife, and even putting on a shirt. (Salthouse, 1985, p. 400)

It is also evident from the WAIS-III cross-sectional data and the WAIS-IV longitudinal data that the tests that depend the most on visual-motor speed—the ones that comprise the PSI—show declines with aging that are steeper than the declines for vulnerable subtests that are less speed-dependent (Figures 7.4 and 7.7).

The decline in speed is clearly crucial and accounts for a portion of the variance in the decline in *Gf* and *Gv*, and in working memory as well. Botwinick (1977) argued that decreased processing speed with age was *the* cause of decreasing performance ability. Salthouse (1985) has also emphasized that the decline in *Gf* is partly a function of the well-known age-related decrease in virtually all tasks that require speed of performance. Probably the best integration of the wealth of accumulated data suggests that processing speed plays a moderate to substantial role in accounting for the decline in *Gf* across the adult life span (Berg, 2000). In general, the results of cross-sectional studies often suggest that processing speed accounts for much of the age-related decline on *Gf* (Verhaeghen & Salthouse, 1997), whereas longitudinal data suggest a more modest role for processing speed and age-related decline (Sliwinski & Buschke, 1999; Zimprich & Martin, 2002). Nonetheless, Salthouse (2004) maintains that a decline in processing speed is the main culprit to account for most of the age-related declines in cognitive function, regardless of the specific abilities measured by the tasks. Hartley (2006) believes that the main cause of cognitive decline is not the processing speed per se but the greatly reduced ability to process the *symbols* used in the various tests of processing speed (which, more broadly, may reflect multidimensional physiological decline).

Even though processing speed, or the processing of symbols, may underlie cognitive decline in all aspects of functioning, evidence does show that problem-solving ability suffers even when speed of performance is not a factor in determining test scores. Some of this evidence is summarized briefly here:

- Doppelt and Wallace (1955) administered WAIS Arithmetic and all Performance subtests to an "old age" sample aged 60 and older under standard conditions and also under "irregular" conditions, when elderly adults were allowed to solve each item with unlimited time. (Bonus points were not considered in their analysis.) The subjects improved their scores only trivially on all tasks except Block Design. Storandt (1977), in a similar investigation with 40 young and 40 elderly adults matched on verbal ability, supported Doppelt and Wallace's results. The elderly group improved their raw scores significantly on only one of the five WAIS subtests, this time Picture Arrangement, while the younger subjects (ages 20–30) failed to improve their scores significantly on any of the tasks. The 20-second time limit for Picture Completion items was adequate in both studies because none of the groups of subjects improved their Picture Completion raw scores significantly with unlimited time. In fact, trivial gains of less than one-half point were observed for all subsamples in the two studies.

- The aging pattern for the untimed WAIS-III Matrix Reasoning subtest is virtually identical to highly speeded subtests such as Block Design and Object Assembly (Kaufman, 2000a), a finding that is also supported by the results of Salthouse and Saklofske's (2010, Table 8.1) analysis of WAIS-IV PRI subtests. Similarly, the nonspeeded Kaufman tests of Matrices and Gestalt Closure subtests display the same vulnerability as tests that place a premium on response speed (Kaufman et al., 2008; Kaufman, Kaufman, Chen, & Kaufman, 1996; Wang & Kaufman, 1993).

- Visual-motor speed, rather than mental processing speed per se, seems to be the most vulnerable to normal aging. In fact, when vocal answers are required rather than motor responses, the relationship between speed and aging no longer holds (Salthouse, 1985). This consistent research finding was supported by the age trends for the WAIS-R and WAIS-III Arithmetic (Kaufman, 2000a; McLean, Kaufman, & Reynolds, 1988). On the WAIS-R, when education was controlled, each adult age group between 20–24 and 70–74 earned a mean scaled score of about 10 (range of 9.9 to 10.4). Yet all WAIS-R Arithmetic items are timed (the first nine items allow only 15–30 seconds apiece), and the last five items award one bonus point apiece for quick, perfect performance. On the WAIS-III, mean values ranged from 9.9 to 10.8 at ages 20–24 to 70–74; not until ages 85–89 did the education-adjusted mean Arithmetic scaled score dip below 9.6. And processing speed is rewarded even more on WAIS-III than WAIS-R Arithmetic, as the final two WAIS-III items award two possible bonus points for rapid solutions. (WAIS-IV Arithmetic allots no bonus points for any Arithmetic items.) Clearly, the speeded component of Arithmetic did not impair the performance of elderly adults on this Wechsler subtest.

• Zimprich (1998) used a statistical technique called *latent growth curve methodology* to investigate the contention that the loss of speed during aging leads directly to decrements in fluid ability. Using data from the Bonn Longitudinal Study of aging ($N = 127$; mean age $= 67$) at four measurement points, Zimprich analyzed data on two markers of mental speed (WAIS Digit Symbol and a simple psychomotor task) and two measures of *Gf* (WAIS Object Assembly and Block Design, both of which actually measure *Gf* and *Gv*). After analyzing separate and combined Latent Growth Curve Models for speed and *Gf*, Zimprich concluded that the results were not supportive of the speed hypothesis as changes in *Gf* within each individual did not relate to change in mental speed.

• On Wechsler's adult scales, the PSI produces the most dramatic age declines. However, cognitive research suggests that poor Digit Symbol–Coding performance is not just a function of speed of responding. Storandt (1976) examined the speed and cognitive components of this Performance subtest. First, Storandt tested the pure motor speed of young and elderly adults by simply having them copy symbols as rapidly as possible without the matched pairs. Younger adults far outstripped the elderly in this task. However, when these groups were also given the standard WAIS Digit Symbol subtest, a clear-cut cognitive differential was evident as well; the superior performance by the younger subjects could not be explained by the speed differential alone. In fact, the cognitive and speed components contributed about equally to the differential. And as Hartley (2006) suggests, the processing of symbols may underlie all cognitive decline.

• Rabbitt et al.'s (2007) cranial magnetic resonance imaging (MRI) study with 40 men and 25 women ages 64 to 85 years found that increases in "white matter lesion prevalence" accounted for all of the age-related variance on tests of speed but none of the age-related variance on tests of *Gf*. Ultimately, however, declines in processing speed, processing symbols, and fluid reasoning are only three of many variables that contribute to lower scores by older than younger adults on cognitive tests. Volumes have been written about other possible variables that play a considerable role in cognitive decline and that indoubtedly interact with *Gf* and *Gs*—for example, *sensory acuity* (Baltes &

Lindenberger, 1997), *working memory* (Salthouse, 1992), *executive functions and frontal lobe functioning* (Raz, 2000), and *physical health* (Backman, Small, Wahlin, & Larsson, 2000).

CAN COGNITIVE DECLINE BE SLOWED OR PREDICTED IN ADVANCE?

Data from a five-year longitudinal study that compared the intelligence and memory of 69 eminent academics (aged 70 and older) with 30 elderly blue-collar workers led the researchers to reach two sobering conclusions: (1) slower rates of decline are *not* associated with high ability, and (2) cognitive deterioration on nonverbal IQ tests is *universal* (Christensen, Henderson, Griffiths, & Levings, 1997). Although the authors of another study of eminent adults, University of California at Berkeley professors, included the optimistic phrase "evidence for successful aging" in their title (Shimamura, Berry, Mangels, Rusting, & Jurica, 1995), their results belie their optimism. Their oldest sample of professors, who averaged only 64.7 years of age, performed about equally to middle-aged and young professors in their ability to recall factual passages that were read to them (*Gc*). On all other tasks in the study, however, the elderly professors scored significantly and substantially lower than the other professors.

If elderly professors in these two studies show basically characteristic patterns of age-related decline on measures of *Gf*, speed, and memory, are these losses in cognitive functioning inevitable, or can they be slowed down?

Engagement in Cognitive Activities and Maintenance of Intelligence

Evidence does exist that lifestyle is related to decline in intellectual functioning. Much of the research on participation in diverse activities and cognitive performance has been cross-sectional; hence, one cannot attribute causality to these relationships, because they tend to be reciprocal. How can one distinguish whether engagement in the activities helped maintain intelligence or whether the more intelligent people sought out the stimulating activities? Nonetheless, in summarizing the findings from many cross-sectional investigations, Hultsch, Hertzog, Small, and Dixon (1999) concluded that, generally, "these studies have reported that greater participation in physical, social, and intellectual activities is associated with higher levels of cognitive performance on a wide range of cognitive tasks" (p. 246). In addition, cross-sectional data from Hultsch, Hammer, and Small (1993) suggest that the relationship between engagement and cognitive performance may become stronger in old age.

Longitudinal data from the Seattle Longitudinal Study (Schaie, 1984, 1994) suggest that people who pursue much environmental stimulation and who continue their formal and informal educations throughout their life spans tend to display strong mental functioning in later years (Gribbin, Schaie, & Parham, 1980). Being involved in a stimulating early work experience has also been associated with IQ maintenance (Willis, 1985), as has coming from high socioeconomic status and remaining fully engaged with the environment (Schaie, 1984). In contrast, the largest declines tend to be shown by older adults (most notably by intelligent females) who have faced family dissolution or personal disengagement (Willis, 1985); widowed women who were never in the workforce and who were disengaged were particularly vulnerable to cognitive decline (Schaie, 1984). Additionally, longitudinal data obtained on World War II veterans tested twice (40-year interval) revealed significant relationships between participation in cognitive activities (and health, and education) and maintenance of intelligence (Arbuckle, Gold, Andres, Schwartzman, & Chaikelson, 1992).

However, as Hultsch et al. (1999) pointed out, both the Schaie and Arbuckle data used lifestyle criteria that are confounded with numerous factors, such as socioeconomic status and education, raising the possibility that differences in initial ability level were largely responsible for producing the apparent maintenance of intellectual ability in old age. Consequently, many of the longitudinal findings, like the cross-sectional findings, prevent a clear understanding of cause versus effect. Probably the best data for addressing the causality issue are provided by the Victoria Longitudinal Study of 250 middle-aged and older adults tested three times in six years (the initial sample at time 1 comprised 487 adults ages 55–86) (Hultsch et al., 1999). The investigators administered a battery of tests that measured nine hypothesized latent variables, three of which involved crystallized intelligence (vocabulary, story recall, reading comprehension), with the rest emphasizing memory or processing speed. In a well-designed and well-controlled study, they assessed activity lifestyle in a variety of areas such as physical fitness, social activities, and novel information processing activities (e.g., playing bridge, learning a language), while also measuring the self-reported health and personality of the subjects.

They identified a significant relationship between intellectually related activities (but not social and physical activities) and change in cognitive functioning, but overall their hypotheses involving health, personality, and lifestyle were not supported. Furthermore, the results of Hultsch et al.'s (1999) structural equation modeling were just as supportive of the hypothesis that intelligent people lead intellectually stimulating lives as vice versa. In addition, their failure to include *Gf* tasks in their design prevented a possible understanding of differences in the maintenance of *Gf* versus *Gc*. Overall, the data from the Victoria study are inconclusive.

Despite Hultsch et al's (1999) findings that physical activity, *per se*, did not correlate with cognitive functioning, Hertzog (2011) notes that, "Over the last decade compelling evidence has emerged that aerobic exercise in middle age and old age promotes enhanced cognitive function in older adults" (p. 184). Short-term intervention studies with samples of elderly adults have shown the benefit of aerobic exercise in substantially improving performance on tests of executive functioning and controlled attention (akin to *Gf*) (see the meta-analysis conducted by Colcombe & Kramer, 2003). Also, several innovative intervention studies with elderly adults have produced optimistic results regarding the short-term benefits of (a) participating in a complex videogame environment (Basak, Boot, Voss, & Kramer, 2008) and (b) engaging in a training program that emphasizes "executive control" rather than teaching a specific problem-solving strategy (Hertzog, Kramer, Wilson, & Lindenberger, 2009). Simply encouraging elderly adults to participate in stimulating tasks may enhance cognitive functioning (Tranter & Koutstaal, 2008), but results of the diverse intervention studies remain controversial and open to debate (Hertzog, 2011).

Prediction of Declining Cognitive Ability

It might, however, be possible to predict which elderly adults will decline most in their cognitive ability (Gregory, Nettelbeck, Howard, & Wilson, 2008). Gregory et al. (2008) administered a computerized measure of *inspection time* (IT) to a sample of 124 adults (79 women, 45 men; mean age = 77 years) from an Australian study of aging. The IT task required the adults to respond rapidly, using a keyboard, to stimuli presented on the screen for a brief time. The stimuli were two vertical lines (one about twice the length of the other) connected at the top by a vertical line. Many stimuli were presented, one after the other, separated by a warning sign (a small cross). The task was to indicate, using a keyboard, whether the shorter of the two vertical lines was on the right or left. This measure of IT was administered to the sample of elderly adults on three occasions (Time 1 in 2003, Time 2 six months later in 2004, and Time 3 one year after that in 2005). People with slow ITs in 2003 performed relatively poorly in 2005 on measures of *Gf*, *Gs*, and working memory but not on measures of *Gc*. Elderly adults whose IT slowed down after 2003 (the ones who became slower at processing information as they aged) performed relatively poorly in 2005 on *Gf* and *Gs*. However, changes in IT were *not* directly associated with analogous changes in *Gf*, *Gs*, or other cognitive abilities. "Thus, there is evidence that IT level is associated with cognitive decline but no evidence that declines in IT are accompanied by concurrent changes in cognitive abilities" (Gregory et al., 2008, p. 669).

 TEST YOURSELF

1. **Which of the following abilities is considered a maintained ability?**
   a. Crystallized ability (*Gc*)
   b. Fluid reasoning (*Gf*)
   c. Processing speed (*Gs*)
   d. Visual processing (*Gv*)
   e. Short-term memory (*Gsm*)

2. **What major variable, if left uncontrolled, tends to confound the results of cross-sectional analyses of aging and intelligence (and, therefore, has been controlled in most studies)?**
   a. Educational attainment
   b. Physical health
   c. Home environment
   d. Emotional intelligence
   e. Gender

3. **TRUE or FALSE? Schaie and his colleagues believe that their research supports the notion that intelligence is basically maintained through old age or, at most, declines late in the adult life span.**

4. **What kind of abilities are fluid reasoning (*Gf*) and processing speed (*Gs*) concerning changes in cognitive ability across the life span?**
   a. Maintained
   b. Responsive to intervention
   c. Vulnerable
   d. Static
   e. Unreliable

5. **The biggest threats to the conclusions that can be drawn from longitudinal studies of aging and intelligence are progressive error (the effects of practice) and**
   a. Boredom
   b. Verbal expression

(continued)

   c. Short-term memory
   d. Selective attrition
   e. All of the above

6. **TRUE or FALSE? Most researchers on aging and intelligence have documented empirically that speed is responsible for all of the decline that Horn and others have attributed to diminished fluid intelligence.**

7. **TRUE or FALSE? Kaufman's longitudinal studies of aging and intelligence on Wechsler's scales, using independent samples, yielded results that contradicted the results of previous cross-sectional investigations of Verbal IQ and Performance IQ.**

8. **Which Wechsler scale shows the greatest declines between young adulthood in both cross-sectional and longitudinal studies of aging and intelligence?**
   a. Perceptual Reasoning Index (PRI)
   b. Processing Speed Index (PSI)
   c. Working Memory Index (WMI)
   d. Verbal Comprehension Index (VCI)
   e. Verbal IQ

9. **TRUE or FALSE? Research studies on elderly samples have consistently shown that if time limits are removed on Wechsler's Performance subtests, then elderly adults improve their scores significantly on virtually all subtests.**

10. **According to the Victoria Longitudinal Study, what activity in old age has been *most* associated with maintenance of intelligence in old age?**
   a. Engaging in intellectual activities (e.g., playing Scrabble)
   b. Engaging in social activities (e.g., hosting parties)
   c. Engaging in physical activities (e.g., jogging)
   d. Engaging in restful activities (e.g., getting 8 hours of sleep each night)
   e. All of the above

Answers: 1. a; 2. a; 3. true; 4. c; 5. d; 6. false; 7. false; 8. b; 9. false; 10. a

Eight

CLINICAL APPLICATIONS III: WAIS-IV USE WITH SPECIAL GROUPS, PRACTICE EFFECTS, AND GENDER DIFFERENCES

I n this chapter, we focus on the application of the WAIS-IV with special clinical groups as well as two topics that concern normal samples—practice effects and gender differences. The *WAIS-IV Technical and Interpretive Manual* (Psychological Corporation, 2008) provided data on relatively small samples of individuals in these clinical groups: intellectually gifted, major depressive disorder, autistic and Asperger's disorder, Attention-Deficit/Hyperactivity Disorder (ADHD), mild cognitive impairment, reading and mathematics disorders, traumatic brain injury, probable Alzheimer's dementia, borderline intellectual functioning, and mild and moderate intellectual disability.

Several WAIS-IV clinical studies have appeared in the literature since the publication of the first edition of this book (e.g., Goldstein and Saklofske (2010; Holdnack, Goldstein, and Drozdick, 2011), but these studies are based on samples that were already included in the WAIS-IV manual, not on new clinical data. The results of these studies are included in pertinent sections of this chapter to extend our understanding of the cognitive profiles of these samples, but the crux of the research-based information provided in this chapter on clinical samples is limited to the specific samples tested as part of the initial standardization and validation of the WAIS-IV (Psychological Corporation, 2008).

In addition to the extended discussion of the WAIS-IV test profiles of clinical populations, this chapter includes an analysis of the practice effects and gender differences observed for normal samples on FSIQ, Indexes, and scaled scores.

The data on WAIS-IV practice effects in normal samples provide a baseline reference for evaluating the gains observed for clinical patients who are tested more than once on the WAIS-IV. Gender data for normal individuals are provided to determine whether this key background variable needs to be taken into account when interpreting the WAIS-IV profiles of males and females referred for evaluation. The related topic of ethnic differences, interpreted within the context of socioeconomic status, was discussed in Chapter 1.

As the *WAIS-IV Technical and Interpretive Manual* (Psychological Corporation, 2008) aptly points out, the data obtained on the clinical samples should be interpreted with caution for several reasons. The studies' samples were not randomly selected and typically were based on small numbers (mean sample size = 38, ranging from as few as 16 to as many as 73 subjects). In most cases, data are included from several independent clinical settings that did not guarantee that the same criteria and procedures were used for diagnosis. In some cases, the groups consisted of participants with a heterogeneous set of diagnoses and treatments. For example, the individuals with ADHD and major depression consisted of some who were taking medication for the treatment of symptoms and some who were not. The group of individuals with traumatic brain injuries did not differentiate patients with open versus closed head injuries, and included different causes and severities of brain injury (although all were recent injuries, occurring in the past 6–18 months). Because of the time frame in which the data were collected, the individuals with "probable Alzheimer's-type dementia" were not diagnosed with the scientific and technological advancements in imaging that the most recent studies employ (Dubois et al., 2007).

Although these group data are useful for beginning to develop a preliminary understanding of how certain clinical populations perform on the WAIS-IV, these data should not be used to make differential diagnoses. In addition to the variables just mentioned, which limit generalizability, it is important to note that these clinical groups are not necessarily representative of a whole diagnostic class and do not reflect the individual differences within a diagnostic class. For each individual within a diagnostic group, many variables interact and affect performance on a test battery such as the WAIS-IV. These individual variables, including academic, developmental, medical, and family history; behavioral observations; and other test data must be integrated to properly interpret the results of any individual assessment battery. Thus, use caution when applying the results of these group data to the interpretation of any individual test results. A summary of these group data for the clinical samples is provided in Rapid Reference 8.1.

INDIVIDUALS WITH AUTISTIC DISORDER AND ASPERGER'S DISORDER

Rapid Reference 8.2 details the highest and lowest mean WAIS-IV subtest scaled scores for individuals with autistic disorder and Asperger's disorder.

⇒ Rapid Reference 8.1

Mean Indexes and Full Scale IQs for Clinical Samples

	N	VCI	PRI	WMI	PSI	FSIQ
Intellectually Gifted	34	127.2	119.6	123.3	**112.4**	126.5
Major Depressive Disorder	41	101.8	97.8	99.5	**95.8**	98.6
Asperger's Disorder	40	104.5	100.0	96.0	**88.4**	97.5
ADHD	44	100.9	98.6	94.7	**94.0**	96.9
Mild Cognitive Impairment	53	99.0	**93.9**	96.6	94.9	94.8
Reading Disorder	34	89.5	91.1	**88.9**	94.5	88.7
Mathematics Disorder	41	91.2	86.8	**84.1**	93.2	86.2
Traumatic Brain Injury	22	92.1	86.1	85.3	**80.5**	83.9
Probable Alzheimer's Dementia—Mild	44	86.2	85.8	84.3	**76.6**	81.2
Autistic Disorder	16	80.9	89.7	85.7	**75.1**	79.8
Borderline Intellectual Functioning	27	77.3	75.8	**74.2**	80.9	72.7
Intellectual Disability—Mild	73	65.9	65.4	**61.5**	63.8	58.5
Intellectual Disability—Moderate	31	56.8	55.0	**53.1**	53.8	48.2

Source: Data are from The Psychological Corporation (2008), Tables 5.21 to 5.32.

Note: Clinical samples are ordered by their mean FSIQ. The lowest index for each sample is in **bold**.

Given that individuals with Asperger's disorder are unlike individuals with autistic disorder because they do not show clinically significant delays in language, it is not surprising that two of three of their highest scores are on tasks dependent on language (i.e., Information and Vocabulary). In contrast, for individuals with autistic disorder, whose difficulties include language disorders, one of their three lowest scores was on a language-based task (e.g., Comprehension), and their three highest scores were on nonverbal tasks.

In a separate study using data collected during the WAIS-IV standardization, Holdnack et al. (2011) reported similar findings for the group of high-functioning individuals with autistic disorder; that group scored lowest on Verbal Comprehension and Processing Speed. Like many of the special groups, the lowest performances for both autism-spectrum groups were on subtests

≡ Rapid Reference 8.2

Highest and Lowest Mean WAIS-IV Scaled Scores of Adults With Autistic Disorder or Asperger's Disorder

Autistic Disorder (N = 16)
(Ages 16–28, M = 20.3 yrs)
(FSIQ = 79.8; 93.7% Male)

Asperger's Disorder (N = 40)
(Ages 16–40, M = 22.5 yrs)
(FSIQ = 97.5; 77.5% Male)

Highest Subtests	Scaled Score	Highest Subtests	Scaled Score
Matrix Reasoning	8.6	Information	11.6
Visual Puzzles	8.3	Vocabulary	10.9
Block Design	7.9	Block Design	10.2
Lowest Subtests	**Scaled Score**	**Lowest Subtests**	**Scaled Score**
Comprehension	5.7	Symbol Search	8.4
Symbol Search	5.6	Cancellation	7.7
Coding	5.1	Coding	7.3

Sources: WAIS-IV data are from The Psychological Corporation (2008), Tables 5.19, 5.28, and 5.29. WISC-IV data are from The Psychological Corporation (2003) and Flanagan & Kaufman (2009).

Note: Both of these clinical samples performed remarkably similar to comparable samples tested on the WISC-IV. The three lowest subtests on the WISC-IV and WAIS-IV for children with autistic disorder were identical and ranked in the same order (e.g., Coding was the most difficult). This exact finding held true for the sample of children with Asperger's disorder as well. Strengths for both samples were similar (not identical) for the WISC-IV and WAIS-IV. On the WISC-IV, the children with autistic disorder did best on Block Design and Matrix Reasoning; the children with Asperger's disorder did best on Similarities and Information.

that make up the PSI, which likely reflects the sensitivity of these measures to generalized cognitive impairment. However, in Holdnack et al.'s (2011) sample, they found that there was an absence of a significant difference between the Asperger's syndrome group and the control samples across multiple comparisons, with both doing better than the individuals with high-functioning autism.

Individuals with autistic disorder and Asperger's disorder often obtain lower FSIQs than GAIs (Flanagan & Kaufman, 2009). According to the *WAIS-IV Technical and Interpretive Manual* (Psychological Corporation, 2008), more than 55% of the individuals in the WAIS-IV special group studies with diagnoses of Asperger's disorder and 38% of the individuals with diagnoses of autism showed GAIs five or more points greater than their FSIQs. This finding suggests that their WMIs or PSIs (or both) negatively influenced the expression of their general intellectual abilities measured by their VCIs and PRIs. However, looking deeper into the performance on WAIS-IV Working Memory tests is helpful, because significant differences were *not* found on either Digit Span Forward or Backward between normal controls and those with high-functioning autism (Holdnack et al., 2011). The average scores in their sample for Digits Forward and Backward were 8.0 and 9.0, respectively, in contrast to the Digit Span Sequencing score of 6.4. Therefore, even though no Working Memory subtest (including Digit Span) emerged as a weak area for individuals with autistic disorder (see Rapid Reference 8.2), it is feasible that Digit Span Sequencing should be linked with measures of processing speed and verbal expression (like Comprehension) as having possible diagnostic value.

The general pattern of lower PSI and WMI scores paired with higher VCI and PRI scores has also been reported on the WISC-IV (Mayes & Calhoun, 2008), which provides cross-validation for these findings on the WAIS-IV.

INDIVIDUALS WHO ARE INTELLECTUALLY GIFTED

Rapid Reference 8.3 indicates that the sample of 34 intellectually gifted adults performed best on tasks involving crystallized knowledge and short-term memory, but, consistent with previous research, they showed relatively weaker performance on tasks dependent on speeded processing. This finding is particularly important because clinicians are sometimes tempted to infer the presence of acquired deficits in bright individuals who do not show above average or better performances across all subtest scores. With average-level performance on speeded tasks, individuals with intellectual giftedness may show superior conceptual ability or skills with acquired knowledge. This pattern of performance in individuals who are intellectually gifted reveals a response set reflecting that they are more interested in optimal performance that may entail reflective processing and accuracy than speed.

DON'T FORGET

Strong Digit Span Performance Is Unique to Gifted Sample

- Digit Span was the second-highest scaled score earned by intellectually gifted individuals.

- Otherwise, no working memory subtest was among the top three scaled scores for any clinical sample.

≡ Rapid Reference 8.3

Highest and Lowest Mean WAIS-IV Scaled Scores of Individuals Who Are Intellectually Gifted

Intellectually Gifted (N = 34)
(Ages 17–64, M = 34.4 yrs)
(FSIQ = 126.5; 38.2% Male)

Highest Subtests	Scaled Score
Vocabulary	15.2
Digit Span	14.7
Information	14.6
Lowest Subtests	**Scaled Score**
Picture Completion	12.5
Symbol Search	11.9
Cancellation	11.6

Sources: WAIS-IV data are from The Psychological Corporation (2008), Tables 5.19 and 5.20. WISC-IV data are from The Psychological Corporation (2003) and Flanagan & Kaufman (2009).

Note: On the WISC-IV, intellectually gifted children scored highest on Vocabulary and lowest on Cancellation, but otherwise the WISC-IV and WAIS-IV strengths and weaknesses did not correspond to each other. In fact, Digit Span—a strength on the WAIS-IV—was a relative weakness on the WISC-IV.

INDIVIDUALS WITH INTELLECTUAL DISABILITY OR BORDERLINE INTELLECTUAL FUNCTIONING

Data from individuals with intellectual disabilities (mental retardation) are often difficult to interpret, because this group combines multiple etiologies. Intellectual disability may result from acquired brain damage as well as a variety of genetic and congenital conditions, each potentially affecting the brain and the development of intelligence in a different way. Rapid Reference 8.4 presents the highlights of the subtest profiles for 73 adolescents and adults with mild disability and 31 individuals with moderate disability. In two samples from the *WAIS-IV Technical and Interpretative Manual* (Psychological Corporation, 2008), the pattern weaknesses for individuals with mild or moderate intellectual disability consistently include poorest performances on those tasks that rely heavily on processing speed. In contrast, the pattern of strengths included Visual Puzzles and Information for individuals with mild and moderate intellectual disability. For individuals with mild intellectual disability, Picture Completion was also among the highest subtest scores. For individuals with moderate intellectual disability, Vocabulary was among the highest subtest scores.

≋ Rapid Reference 8.4

Highest and Lowest Mean WAIS-IV Scaled Scores of Individuals Who Have Mild or Moderate Intellectual Disability

Mild Intellectual Disability (N = 73) (Ages 16–63, M = 32.0 yrs) (FSIQ = 58.5; 45.2% Male)		Moderate Intellectual Disability (N = 31) (Ages 16–63, M = 30.5 yrs) (FSIQ = 48.2; 61.3% Male)	
Highest Subtests	**Scaled Score**	**Highest Subtests**	**Scaled Score**
Visual Puzzles	4.7	Visual Puzzles	3.4
Information	4.3	Vocabulary	3.1
Picture Completion	4.2	Information	3.0
Lowest Subtests	**Scaled Score**	**Lowest Subtests**	**Scaled Score**
Coding	3.2	Coding	1.6
Letter-Number Sequencing	3.1	Digit Span	1.3
Digit Span	2.8	Letter-Number Sequencing	1.2

Sources: WAIS-IV data are from The Psychological Corporation (2008), Tables 5.19, 5.21, and 5.22. WISC-IV data are from The Psychological Corporation (2003) and Flanagan & Kaufman (2009).

Note: Individuals with mild or moderate intellectual disability displayed slightly different patterns of subtest strengths and weaknesses on the WISC-IV and WAIS-IV. For example, Vocabulary, a strength on the WAIS-IV for individuals with moderate intellectual disability, was a weakness for that clinical sample on the WISC-IV.

Contrary to results on the WISC-IV (Flanagan & Kaufman, 2009), both groups of individuals with intellectual disability more often showed higher WAIS-IV VCI and PRI scores than WMI and PSI scores, because they appeared to do better on the more complex tasks emphasizing reasoning and acquired knowledge that compose the VCI and PRI than on the speed- and memory-based tasks that make up the PSI and WMI. In the group of individuals with moderate intellectual disability, mean WAIS-IV scores on PSI and WMI were nearly identical (53.8 and 53.1, respectively), and these indexes were quite similar for the mild group as well (63.8 vs. 61.5). In contrast, on the WISC-IV, the sample with mild intellectual disability showed a 6.2 point higher score on the PSI than WMI. These inconsistencies between data on these WISC-IV and WAIS-IV samples of intellectual disability support the fact that the patterns of low and high subtests or indexes in and of themselves should not be considered indicative of a diagnostic category.

Rapid Reference 8.5 shows the highest and lowest scores for a sample of 27 adolescents and adults with borderline intellectual disability. Individuals with borderline intellectual functioning (with an average FSIQ of 72.2) showed a different pattern of performance than those with mild intellectual disabilities (with an average FSIQ of 58.9). For example, in the group with borderline intellectual functioning, Symbol Search was among one of the highest subtest scores, while it was among the lowest for those with mild intellectual disabilities. Also, three of the PRI subtests were among the lowest for the borderline intellectual functioning group, but these were not among the lowest for those who were in the Mildly Impaired range.

≡ Rapid Reference 8.5

Highest and Lowest Mean WAIS-IV Scaled Scores of Individuals With Borderline Intellectual Functioning or Attention-Deficit/Hyperactivity Disorder

Borderline Intellectual Functioning (N = 27) (Ages 16–65, M = 30.1 yrs) (FSIQ = 72.7; 37.0% Male)		ADHD (N = 44) (Ages 18–31, M = 23.1 yrs) (FSIQ = 96.9; 63.6% Male)	
Highest Subtests	**Scaled Score**	**Highest Subtests**	**Scaled Score**
Symbol Search	6.7	Picture Completion	10.4
Cancellation	6.7	Vocabulary	10.4
Picture Completion	6.7	Information	10.3
		Comprehension	10.3
Lowest Subtests	**Scaled Score**	**Lowest Subtests**	**Scaled Score**
Vocabulary	5.6	Matrix Reasoning	9.3
Matrix Reasoning	5.6	Arithmetic	8.6
Block Design	5.6	Coding	8.4
Figure Weights	5.4		
Arithmetic	5.1		

Sources: WAIS-IV data are from The Psychological Corporation (2008), Tables 5.19, 5.23 and 5.26. WISC-IV data are from The Psychological Corporation (2003) and Flanagan & Kaufman (2009).

Note: On the WISC-IV and WAIS-IV, individuals with ADHD displayed similar subtest profiles. As on the WAIS-IV, children with ADHD were strong in WISC-IV Picture Completion and weak on both Arithmetic and Coding.

INDIVIDUALS WITH ATTENTION-DEFICIT/ HYPERACTIVITY DISORDER

Rapid Reference 8.5 summarizes the profiles of a sample of 44 young adults diagnosed with ADHD. Individuals with ADHD would be expected to show strengths in verbal and perceptual reasoning areas (as long as their attentional problems are not so great as to interfere with test taking itself). Poor performance on WMI and PSI tasks would likely be related to the premium these tasks place on attention, concentration, and speed—all critical areas of concern in this population. Somewhat supportive of this pattern were the facts that among the lowest subtests for this ADHD sample were one PSI task (Coding), one WMI task (Arithmetic), and one PRI task (Matrix Reasoning). The highest performances for the ADHD sample were on Picture Completion and Vocabulary. Flanagan and Kaufman (2009) reported a similar pattern in the WISC-IV data for individuals with ADHD.

Individuals with ADHD tend to have difficulties with working memory and processing speed, which may result in lower FSIQs (Weiss et al., 2010a). The data presented in the *WAIS-IV Technical and Interpretive Manual* (Psychological Corporation, 2008) indicate that more than 30% of individuals with ADHD obtained GAIs five or more points greater than their FSIQs. Individuals with ADHD tended to perform relatively poorly on the subtests comprising the WMI and PSI, accounting for their lower FSIQs than GAIs (Mayes & Calhoun, 2007; Weiss et al., 2010a).

INDIVIDUALS WITH LEARNING DISABILITIES IN READING OR MATHEMATICS

Rapid Reference 8.6 presents the highest and lowest subtest scores for 34 individuals with learning disabilities in reading (mean age = 18.1) and 41 individuals with learning disabilities in mathematics (mean age = 17.8). These groups show similar patterns of strengths but different patterns of weaknesses. Both groups of individuals with learning disabilities had their strongest performance on tasks that required processing speed (Symbol Search) or that required simple verbal responses (Picture Completion). Not surprisingly, individuals who have mathematics disorders struggled more with Figure Weights, likely because of the quantitative reasoning skill that is required to solve the problems. The Arithmetic subtest is among the lowest scores for the individuals with both types of learning disorder as well, suggesting that this subtest measures a wider range of processes than arithmetic ability alone.

≡ Rapid Reference 8.6

Highest and Lowest Mean WAIS-IV Scaled Scores of Individuals With Learning Disabilities in Reading or Math

Reading Disorder (N = 34) (Ages 16–24, M = 18.1 yrs) (FSIQ = 88.7; 50.0% Male)		Math Disorder (N = 41) (Ages 16–24, M = 17.8 yrs) (FSIQ = 86.2; 46.3% Male)	
Highest Subtests	**Scaled Score**	**Highest Subtests**	**Scaled Score**
Symbol Search	9.9	Symbol Search	9.5
Picture Completion	9.2	Picture Completion	9.4
Figure Weights	8.8	Similarities	8.7
		Comprehension	8.7
Lowest Subtests	**Scaled Score**	**Lowest Subtests**	**Scaled Score**
Coding	8.2	Visual Puzzles	7.5
Comprehension	8.2	Figure Weights	7.3
Arithmetic	7.5	Arithmetic	6.6
Vocabulary	7.5		

Sources: WAIS-IV data are from The Psychological Corporation (2008), Tables 5.19, 5.24 and 5.25. WISC-IV data are from The Psychological Corporation (2003) and Flanagan & Kaufman (2009).

Note: On the WISC-IV, children with reading disorders scored high on Symbol Search and low on Arithmetic, but their other strengths and weaknesses did not correspond to their high and low scaled scores on the WAIS-IV. Children with math disorders scored lowest on WISC-IV Arithmetic (consistent with their specific learning disability), but otherwise their WISC-IV and WAIS-IV subtest profiles were inconsistent.

INDIVIDUALS WITH TRAUMATIC BRAIN INJURY

In factor-analytic analysis of WAIS-IV data of 31 adults with traumatic brain injury (TBI) that was gathered as part of the development of the WAIS-IV, Goldstein and Saklofske (2010) found a four-factor solution that was similar to the factor structure for the general population. Their analysis yielded fairly clear Verbal Comprehension, Perceptual Reasoning, Processing Speed, and Working Memory factors. One notable difference, however, was that Matrix Reasoning loaded more strongly on the Working Memory Factor (0.74) than on the Perceptual Reasoning factor (0.49) for the TBI sample. However, as Goldstein and Saklofske (2010) point out, these data are just "preliminary efforts . . . with exploratory analysis" (p. 207), and the four-factor solution similar to the general population's solution may be the best-fitting model.

⩵ Rapid Reference 8.7

Highest and Lowest Mean WAIS-IV Scaled Scores of Adults With Traumatic Brain Injury or Major Depression

Traumatic Brain Injury (N = 22) (Ages 20–44, M = 29.0 yrs) (FSIQ = 83.9; 72.7% Male)		Major Depression (N = 41) (Ages 50–86, M = 62.8 yrs) (FSIQ = 98.6; 26.8% Male)	
Highest Subtests	**Scaled Score**	**Highest Subtests**	**Scaled Score**
Vocabulary	8.9	Vocabulary	10.6
Information	8.8	Matrix Reasoning	10.4
Picture Completion	8.5	Information	10.4
Lowest Subtests	**Scaled Score**	**Lowest Subtests**	**Scaled Score**
Cancellation	7.1	Visual Puzzles	9.2
Matrix Reasoning	7.1	Figure Weights	9.2
Symbol Search	6.1	Coding	9.0

Sources: WAIS-IV data are from The Psychological Corporation (2008), Tables 5.19, 5.27 and 5.30. WISC-IV data are from The Psychological Corporation (2003) and Flanagan & Kaufman (2009).

Note: On the WISC-IV, the clinical sample with closed head injuries displayed similar subtest profiles to the ones displayed by the TBI clinical sample on the WAIS-IV. Like the TBI sample, the group with closed head injuries had strengths in Picture Completion and Information and weaknesses in Cancellation and Symbol Search. The WISC-IV clinical sample with open head injuries had a weakness in Symbol Search but otherwise had a different pattern of high and low scores than the WAIS-IV TBI clinical sample.

Rapid Reference 8.7 contains the highest and lowest subtest scores for 22 adults ages 20–44 with TBI. This TBI group is heterogeneous with respect to the localization and severity of their brain damage. The highest subtest scores are in verbal areas known to be fairly well preserved in TBI, while the lowest would be consistent with the conventional wisdom that traumatic brain injuries impact speed of processing (Lezak, Howieson, & Loring, 2004). However, expected pattern of low performance on all the WMI subtests was not present. This pattern likely reflects the diffuse cortical and subcortical pathology in many traumatic brain injuries rather than focal or localized damage (Hebben, 2009). As expected, a large effect size was noted for individuals with TBI when compared to matched control groups on a speeded paper-and-pencil task (Symbol Search) and on a mental math test (Arithmetic). However, several perceptual reasoning tasks also showed relatively large effect sizes when compared to matched controls: Matrix Reasoning, Visual Puzzles, and Figure Weights. Examination of the Digit Span process scores is informative for this TBI population. The group with TBI showed a larger effect size compared to matched controls for Digit Span Sequencing than Digit Span Backward. The TBI group's average scores were 7.1 for Digit Span Sequencing versus 8.6 on Digit Span Backward. According to the test publisher, the Digit Span Sequencing task "appears to increase the sensitivity of Digit Span to TBI" (Psychological Corporation, 2008, p. 112).

In clinical interpretation of WAIS-IV profiles with patients with TBI, it is important to consider not only which scores are low and which are intact, but also how the patient's scores compare to the base rates of low scores in healthy people (Brooks, Holdnack, & Iverson, 2011). It is common for healthy people to obtain some low scores on the WAIS-IV. However, when comparing healthy adults to TBI patients with similar predicted levels of premorbid functioning, Brooks et al. (2011) found that TBI patients were 13 times more likely to be identified as having a low cognitive profile. We agree that considering base rate data is an important piece of accurate interpretation of low WAIS-IV scores for patients with TBI.

INDIVIDUALS WITH MAJOR DEPRESSION

Rapid Reference 8.7 presents strengths and weaknesses for a clinical sample of 41 older adults ages 50–86 diagnosed with major depressive disorder. It is important to evaluate the WAIS-IV results in light of the fact that a significant number (78%) were taking medication for their depression symptoms at the time of the testing. Therefore, it is likely that fewer depressive symptoms, and an atypical cognitive profile for depression, may have characterized this sample. There was a relatively small effect size for the PSI compared to a matched control group and for two of the three Processing Speed subtests. Overall, the lowest subtest scaled scores were on Coding and two Perceptual Reasoning subtests (Visual Puzzles and Figure Weights). Although there was little variability overall in the profile of individuals with depression (the lowest scaled score was 9.0 and the highest was 10.6), there were some consistencies with previous findings on cognitive tests for individuals with major depression— namely, individuals with major depressive disorder consistently show lower performance on processing speed tasks compared to other cognitive tasks (Gorlyn et al., 2006). Likewise, some studies (e.g., Naismith et al., 2003) have shown that compared to normal controls, individuals with major depression show poorer performance on timed tests (Visual Puzzles and Figure Weights have time limits).

INDIVIDUALS WITH PROBABLE ALZHEIMER'S-TYPE DEMENTIA AND MILD COGNITIVE IMPAIRMENT

Rapid Reference 8.8 shows the highest and lowest mean WAIS-IV scaled scores of 44 elderly adults with probable Alzheimer's dementia (mean age = 77.2) and 53 elderly adults with mild cognitive impairment (mean age = 73.7). By definition, individuals in the WAIS-IV clinical sample who met the criteria for probable dementia of the Alzheimer's type showed "deficits in two or more areas of cognition, and progressive decline in memory and other cognitive functions" (Psychological Corporation, 2008, p. 120). For this clinical sample, the lowest subtest scaled scores were obtained for Symbol Search, Coding, and Information, and this trio of subtests also showed the largest effect sizes, when comparing the clinical group to matched controls. The Digit Span process scores for this clinical group also revealed that the lowest score was on Digit Span Sequencing. Digit ordering tasks have been shown to be sensitive to the cognitive declines noted in individuals with probable dementia of the Alzheimer's type (MacDonald, Almor, Henderson, Kempler, & Andersen, 2001). In contrast to these areas of weaker

≡ Rapid Reference 8.8

Highest and Lowest Mean WAIS-IV Scaled Scores of Elderly Adults With Probable Alzheimer's Dementia—Mild or Mild Cognitive Impairment

Probable Alzheimer's Dementia—Mild (N = 44) (Ages 58–90, M = 77.2 yrs) (FSIQ = 81.2; 25.0% Male)		Mild Cognitive Impairment (N = 53) (Ages 59–90, M = 73.7 yrs) (FSIQ = 94.8; 52.8% Male)	
Highest Subtests	**Scaled Score**	**Highest Subtests**	**Scaled Score**
Vocabulary	8.4	Vocabulary	10.1
Comprehension	7.8	Similarities	9.9
Block Design	7.8	Information	9.8
Lowest Subtests	**Scaled Score**	**Lowest Subtests**	**Scaled Score**
Information	6.5	Block Design	8.9
Coding	6.1	Visual Puzzles	8.6
Symbol Search	5.3	Picture Completion	8.5

Source: Data are from The Psychological Corporation (2008), Tables 5.19, 5.31 and 5.32.

Note: The elderly adults with mild cognitive impairment earned among their lowest scaled scores on Cancellation (7.9), Letter-Number Sequencing (8.0), and Figure Weights (8.9), but these subtests—which are not administered to adults above age 69—were given to only N = 14.

performance, the highest subtests for this group were Vocabulary, Comprehension, and Block Design. These relatively stronger scores on two of the VCI subtests may indicate more preserved functioning in the cognitive domains that require crystallized abilities or acquired knowledge.

In contrast to individuals with probable dementia of the Alzheimer's type, one of the criteria for the clinical group with mild cognitive impairment (MCI) was that they could not meet the diagnostic criteria for dementia. The diagnostic criteria for the MCI group yielded a heterogeneous group of individuals who exhibited memory impairment or impairment in another cognitive domain, along with preserved basic daily living functioning. This MCI sample was also unique because it contained a higher number of college-educated individuals than is typically seen in a normal population. The lowest subtests for the MCI group were the PRI subtests of Picture Completion, Visual Puzzles, and Block Design. In contrast, the verbal tasks appeared relatively preserved. The highest subtest scaled scores were noted for Vocabulary, Similarities, and Information. Because of the heterogeneity of this MCI sample and the relatively small sample size, additional research is needed to determine if this pattern of strong verbal and weak perceptual is replicable and generalizable in other samples.

One of the identified risk factors for progression from mild cognitive impairment to dementia is *functional impairment or decline* (Drozdick & Cullum, 2011). Functional ability refers to the skills required to live independently, such as physical self-care, management of finances, and completion of everyday tasks. In clinical use of the WAIS-IV for assessment of probable dementia or mild cognitive impairment, it is important to evaluate functional abilities within the context of cognitive and memory abilities. In the clinical sample of patients with probable Alzheimer's disease tested during the WAIS-IV

DON'T FORGET

....

Abilities Measured by Vocabulary Are Maintained in Aging

- Vocabulary was among the three highest scaled scores for 8 of the 13 samples and was the very highest for 5 samples. It was a weakness for only two groups: individuals with reading disorders or borderline intellectual functioning.

- This finding reinforces Vocabulary's niche as an ability that is maintained in the face of aging or brain damage and that is commonly used as an estimate of premorbid mental functioning.

- Information, likewise, was a strength for 8 clinical samples; it was a weakness only for elderly individuals with probable Alzheimer's-type dementia.

standardization, Drozdick and Cullum (2011) found a moderate to strong relationship between the WAIS-IV indexes and a measure of functional abilities. Specifically, they reported that PSI (.81) and WMI (.65) had the strongest correlations with functional abilities. The strength of the relationships between these variables may be helpful in understanding the likely impact that the level of cognitive impairment shown on WAIS-IV indexes has on a patient's day-to-day adaptive functioning.

COMPARISON OF THE VERBAL COMPREHENSION INDEX AND THE PERCEPTUAL REASONING INDEX FOR THE CLINICAL SAMPLES

Historically, many researchers have examined the Wechsler verbal-performance profiles of clinical samples to determine if patterns existed for certain groups (Kaufman & Lichtenberger, 2006). With the removal of the VIQ and PIQ from the WAIS-IV, the focus of interpretation has now shifted from the verbal-performance dichotomy to the patterns among the four Factor Indexes. However, clinicians and researchers alike may still be interested in studying patterns between the verbal (VCI) and nonverbal (PRI) indexes of the WAIS-IV or patterns within these separate WAIS-IV index subtests. Those interested in a thorough review of research on verbal-performance patterns on earlier editions of Wechsler's adult scales are directed to Kaufman and Lichtenberger (2006). Our interpretive approach for the WAIS-IV, presented in Chapter 5, suggests examining patterns among the indexes, and the *WAIS-IV Technical and Interpretive Manual* (Psychological Corporation, 2008) also suggests beginning basic profile analysis with an evaluation of discrepancies among the indexes, to "help the practitioner identify potentially meaningful patterns of strengths and weaknesses" (pp. 126).

Rapid Reference 8.9 lists the differences between the VCI and PRI composite scores for the special study groups. Although group data cannot be evaluated by the same criteria as those employed in individual profile analysis, it is useful to note that a significant VCI-PRI discrepancy at the .05 level is 8.82 points. Just over half of the clinical groups displayed a VCI-PRI difference of 4 or more points, with the largest difference of 8.8 points for the individuals with autism (PRI > VCI) and the second largest (7.6 points in favor of VCI) for the intellectually gifted sample. Except for the reading disorder group and the autism group, all groups displayed a VCI > PRI pattern, although only the samples of gifted, TBI, and MCI had discrepancies of 5 or more points. Note that such small differences between Indexes do not reflect functional or clinically significant differences in individuals.

≡ Rapid Reference 8.9

Differences Between the VCI and PRI for the Clinical Groups

Clinical Group	VCI	PRI	VCI–PRI Discrepancy
Intellectually Gifted	127.2	119.6	7.6
Traumatic Brain Injury	92.1	86.1	6.0
Mild Cognitive Impairment	99.0	93.9	5.1
Asperger's Disorder	104.5	100.0	4.5
Mathematics Disorder	91.2	86.8	4.4
Major Depressive Disorder	101.8	97.8	4.0
ADHD	100.9	98.6	2.3
Intellectual Disability—Moderate	56.8	55.0	1.8
Borderline Intellectual Functioning	77.3	75.8	1.5
Intellectual Disability—Mild	65.9	65.4	0.5
Probable Alzheimer's Dementia—Mild	86.2	85.8	0.4
Reading Disorder	89.5	91.1	−1.6
Autistic Disorder	80.9	89.7	−8.8

Source: Data are from The Psychological Corporation (2008), Tables 5.21 to 5.32.
Note: Data are sorted from highest to lowest VCI > PRI discrepancy.

COMPARISONS INVOLVING THE FSIQ, GAI, AND CPI FOR THE CLINICAL SAMPLES

The GAI, first introduced for the WISC-III (Prifitera et al., 1998) and utilized in our WAIS-IV interpretive system presented in Chapter 5 of this book, eliminates the contribution of the subtests comprising measures of working memory and processing speed that are included in the FSIQ. The GAI may be particularly useful for individuals in those special groups for whom there are frequently significant and abnormally large discrepancies between the scales that reflect verbal comprehension, crystallized knowledge, fluid reasoning, and visual processing (VCI/PRI) and the scales that measure attentional abilities and processing speed (WMI/PSI). There are multiple special populations for whom this is true, including individuals with intellectual giftedness (VCI and PRI > WMI and PSI), individuals with intellectual disability (WMI and PSI > VCI and PRI), and individuals sustaining head injuries (lower PSI than other indexes) (Strauss, Sherman, & Spreen, 2006).

If deficiencies in working memory and processing speed have lowered the FSIQ, Saklofske, Weiss, Raiford, and Prifitera (2006) suggest examining the difference between the FSIQ and GAI to determine "the impact of reducing the emphasis on working memory and processing speed on the estimate of general cognitive ability for individuals with difficulty in those areas due to traumatic brain injury or other neuropsychological difficulties" (p. 116). Thus, use of the GAI may be clinically informative in ways that the FSIQ is not. The *WAIS-IV Technical and Interpretive Manual* (Psychological Corporation, 2008, pp. 165–179) provides a table summarizing the distribution of the FSIQ-GAI discrepancies for the special groups included in the *Manual*. Use of this table allows examiners to compare the magnitude of an individual's discrepancy with the percentage of adults who obtained similar or greater levels of discrepancies (for both the standardization sample and special clinical samples).

In addition to the GAI, our interpretive system in Chapter 5 incorporates the Cognitive Proficiency Index (CPI), a combination of WMI and PSI. The tasks that constitute this new composite represent an individual's ability to proficiently process certain types of cognitive information using visual speed and mental control (Dumont & Willis, 2001; Weiss, Saklofske, Prifitera, & Holdnack, 2006; Weiss et al., 2010b). In our interpretive system, we suggest interpreting the CPI only when it is psychometrically sound, meaning that there are not uncommonly large differences between the WMI and the PSI. It is especially important to consider the differences between clinical groups on these indexes because interpretation of the CPI has been proposed as being valuable for such clinical groups (Hebben, 2009). Weiss and colleagues (2006, 2010b) have noted that comparing the GAI and CPI from the fourth edition of the Wechsler scales to each other (along with school achievement) is potentially useful in the identification of psychological processing deficits for certain clients with learning disabilities.

Rapid Reference 8.10 provides the mean FSIQ, GAI, and CPI obtained by the clinical samples. Mean FSIQs are provided in the *Manual* (Psychological Corporation, 2008). We calculated the mean GAI and CPI by summing each clinical sample's mean score on the pertinent WAIS-IV subtests and entering that sum into the appropriate conversion table. Upon examination of these data and the data presented in the *Manual*'s base rate tables, on average, most of the clinical groups showed a pattern of FSIQ < GAI performance. However, the magnitude of these differences is consistently small (4 points or less) and of little or no clinical significance. The FSIQ-GAI discrepancy should not be used to establish a diagnosis or distinguish among the individuals in these special groups, but analysis of the discrepancy and its direction can provide evidence of whether an

≡ Rapid Reference 8.10

Mean Standard Scores on GAI, CPI, and FSIQ for the Clinical Groups

Group	FSIQ	GAI	CPI	GAI-CPI Discrepancy	FSIQ-GAI Discrepancy
Asperger's Disorder	98	102	91	11	−4
Traumatic Brain Injury	84	88	80	8	−4
Intellectual Disability—Moderate	48	52	45	7	−4
Intellectual Disability—Mild	59	63	57	6	−4
ADHD	98	100	94	6	−2
Autistic Disorder	80	83	78	5	−3
Probable Alzheimer's Dementia—Mild	81	83	78	5	−2
Intellectually Gifted	127	126	121	5	1
Major Depressive Disorder	99	100	98	2	−1
Mathematics Disorder	86	88	87	1	−2
Mild Cognitive Impairment	97	97	96	1	0
Borderline Intellectual Functioning	73	74	75	−1	−1
Reading Disorder	89	89	91	−2	0

Source: Data are from The Psychological Corporation (2008), Tables 5.21 to 5.32.

Note: GAI and CPI were calculated by obtaining the average subtest scaled score for each clinical group, then calculating the rounded sums of scaled scores for the appropriate subtests that comprise each Index. These sums of scaled scores were finally converted to a standard score by using the appropriate conversion table in the *Manual* or this book. Data are sorted from highest to lowest GAI-CPI discrepancy.

individual is similar to others in the diagnostic group under consideration and help identify strengths and weaknesses to target in a treatment program.

The differences for clinical samples were much more dramatic for GAI versus CPI. Most groups displayed a GAI > CPI profile, with differences for eight of the samples ranging from 5 to 11 points. The huge 11-point difference emerged for the sample of individuals diagnosed with Asperger's disorder, and the difference for the sample with TBI (8 points) also exceeded 1/2 SD. The remaining samples with a substantial GAI > CPI difference (5–7 points) included people diagnosed with ADHD and those at the extremes of the FSIQ distribution: individuals identified as intellectually disabled (mild and moderate), as having probable Alzheimer's disorder, and as intellectually gifted. For the sample of intellectually gifted individuals, the pattern of GAI > CPI is consistent with the g loadings of the tasks (GAI subtests tend to be "high g" and CPI subtests tend to be "low g"). Gifted individuals perform better on tasks that are strong measures of general intelligence. For the other clinical samples with a notable GAI > CPI profile, it is likely that the disorder (e.g., Asperger's, Alzheimer's, TBI) directly affected the adults' working memory and processing speed. For all of these samples, including the gifted, the GAI probably reflects a better estimate of their global intelligence than does the FSIQ (because the latter composite includes all of the CPI subtests).

The group data for these clinical samples indicate that, in many cases, it may be psychometrically justified to combine the WMI and PSI into a single CPI index, and the GAI > CPI profile is surely meaningful in a clinical, practical sense. But that does not mean that either the CPI or discrepancies involving the CPI are meaningful from a *neuropsychological* perspective. As Hebben (2009) explains:

> There is a great deal of evidence linking various aspects of working memory to different parts of the frontal cortex (i.e., prefrontal, dorsomedial, and dorsolateral all seem to make some contribution). This is not the case for processing speed, which involves a wider array of cortical and subcortical areas; though it is possible the frontal cortex has some role in modulating processing speed. Other brain structures that might contribute to processing speed include the entire cortex itself, the basal ganglia, the various brainstem nuclei that factor into arousal, and the cerebellum. Even if both domains were impaired or limited in a single individual, there is no scientific basis to conclude this was caused by a compromise within the same area of the brain, even though this might be the case. (p. 220)

COMPARISON OF THE WORKING MEMORY INDEX AND THE PROCESSING SPEED INDEX FOR THE CLINICAL SAMPLES

In examining the differences between the WMI and the PSI in the clinical samples from the *WAIS-IV Manual*, some trends are apparent. Notably, all of the clinical samples showed a pattern of WMI > PSI. In the overall WAIS-IV standardization sample, a pattern of WMI > PSI was equally as common as a PSI > WMI pattern. The three clinical groups with the largest WMI > PSI patterns were the

≋ Rapid Reference 8.11

Discrepancies Between the WMI and PSI for Clinical Groups

Clinical Group	WMI	PSI	WMI-PSI Discrepancy
Intellectual Disability—Moderate	**53.1**	53.8	0.7
ADHD	94.7	**94.0**	0.7
Mild Cognitive Impairment	96.6	94.9	1.7
Intellectual Disability—Mild	**61.5**	63.8	2.3
Major Depressive Disorder	99.5	**95.8**	3.7
Traumatic Brain Injury	85.3	**80.5**	4.8
Reading Disorder	**88.9**	94.5	5.6
Borderline Intellectual Functioning	**74.2**	80.9	6.7
Asperger's Disorder	96.0	**88.4**	7.6
Probable Alzheimer's Dementia—Mild	84.3	**76.6**	7.7
Mathematics Disorder	**84.1**	93.2	9.1
Autistic Disorder	85.7	**75.1**	10.6
Intellectually Gifted	123.3	**112.4**	10.9

Source: Data are from The Psychological Corporation (2008), Tables 5.21 to 5.32.
Note: Data are sorted from lowest to highest WMI > PSI discrepancy.

intellectually gifted sample (10.9-point difference), the autistic disorder sample (10.6-point difference), and the mathematics disorder sample (9.1-point difference). Conversely, the groups with the smallest WMI-PSI discrepancies were the intellectual disability–moderate group (.7 point), the ADHD group (.7 point), and the mild cognitive impairment group (1.7 points). Rapid Reference 8.11 lists the WMI-PSI discrepancies for each of the clinical samples.

CLINICAL SAMPLES WITH RELATIVELY LOW SCORES ON THE PROCESSING SPEED INDEX

Rapid Reference 8.12 compares the PSI composite scores relative to the combined mean of the VCI, PRI, and WMI composite scores for the special study groups. In interpreting individual WAIS-IV profiles, a significant discrepancy between the PSI and the mean of all indexes is a difference of 7.5 standard

≡ *Rapid Reference 8.12*

Key Role of the Processing Speed Index: Clinical Samples That Scored Lowest or Highest on the *PSI*

	Mean of the Other 3 Indexes	PSI	Difference
PSI Is the LOWEST Index			
Asperger's Disorder	100.2	88.4	+11.8
Intellectually Gifted	123.4	112.4	+11.0
Autistic Disorder	85.4	75.1	+10.3
Probable Alzheimer's Dementia—Mild	85.4	76.6	+8.8
Traumatic Brain Injury	87.8	80.5	+7.3
ADHD	98.1	94.0	+4.1
Major Depressive Disorder	99.7	95.8	+3.9
PSI Is the HIGHEST Index			
Mathematics Disorder	87.4	93.2	−5.8
Borderline Intellectual Functioning	75.8	80.9	−5.1
Reading Disorder	89.8	94.5	−4.7

Source: Data are from The Psychological Corporation (2008), Tables 5.21 to 5.32.

Note: Difference equals the mean of the "other" three indexes (VCI, PRI, WMI) minus the PSI. Clinical samples are ordered by the magnitude of the difference.

score points between the two scores. (However, as mentioned, group data cannot be evaluated by the same criteria as those employed in individual profile analysis.) It is important to notice that all groups except for three displayed a *deficit* on the PSI relative to the mean index on the VCI, PRI, and WMI. Thus, a pattern of lower performance on the PSI does not provide adequate evidence for differential diagnosis. The individuals with mathematics disorders, reading disorders, and borderline intellectual functioning had a PSI that was higher than the mean of their other three Indexes. (All were about 5–6 points higher.) This finding of higher PSI scores in groups with learning disabilities is in contrast to results reported on the WISC-IV (Flanagan & Kaufman, 2009), which show a more typical pattern of weaker performance on the PSI in such samples. In contrast, groups of individuals with Asperger's and autistic disorder or those who were intellectually gifted showed WAIS-IV PSIs that were lower (by 10–11 points) than the mean of their other three indexes. These data may provide evidence that those

DON'T FORGET

....

Coding Is a Vulnerable Test in Clinical Samples

- Coding was a weakness for 8 of the 13 samples and a strength for none, reinforcing a wealth of research and clinical findings that show it to be vulnerable to aging and brain damage to both hemispheres and susceptible to distractibility, depression, and poor attention span.
- Symbol Search, however, was a strength as often as it was a weakness (three times).
- Eleven of the 13 samples had a low score on one or more processing speed subtests (all except individuals with major depression or borderline intellectual functioning).

who are intellectually gifted will not necessarily also have superior processing speed. Likewise, individuals who have autistic or Asperger's disorder may show deficits in their processing speed relative to their other intellectual abilities.

UTILITY OF THE PROCESS APPROACH

The *WAIS-IV Technical and Interpretive Manual* (Psychological Corporation, 2008) advises the clinician that "the final step in a profile analysis is the qualitative analysis of individual responses" (p. 131). Similarly, we suggest that using a process analysis such as that described in Chapter 6 of this volume may provide useful interpretive information. The focus of the *process approach* (Kaplan, 1988) is on the various processes an individual uses to solve a problem correctly and the processes that might lead to the failure to solve a problem (Hebben & Milberg, 2002).

Hebben (2009) points out some of the weaknesses of the process approach:

Though the process approach is intellectually and intuitively appealing, with its emphasis on breaking performance down into elements with potential relevance to rehabilitation and education, its empirical basis is not sufficiently well developed to allow for scientifically supportable clinical predictions by all clinicians. Without precise norms and a clearly spelled-out blueprint of how and when these procedures should be used, there is likely to be tremendous variation in the skill and accuracy with which this approach is applied. (p. 237)

Process scores in the *WAIS-IV Administration and Scoring Manual* (Wechsler, 2008) for the Block Design, Digit Span, and Letter-Number Sequencing tasks provide a quantitative picture of some of the processes that may be involved in the performance of these subtests. However, as with other data derived from the clinical samples, these analyses cannot be used routinely for differential diagnosis.

CLINICAL SAMPLES WITH NOTABLE DIFFERENCES BETWEEN SCALED SCORES ON DIGITS FORWARD AND DIGITS BACKWARD

The scaled score differences between Digits Forward and Digits Backward shown in Rapid Reference 8.13 range from 0.6 to 1.4. The small differences obtained by most of the clinical groups are not likely to be clinically significant and may not even be specific to the clinical samples. Table C.2 in the *WAIS-IV Administration and Scoring Manual* (Wechsler, 2008) indicates that individuals must show a greater than 3.65 scaled-score difference between Digits Forward and Digits Backward for the difference to be statistically significant at the .05 level. Digit Span Backward is more difficult than Digit Span Forward, so it is not surprising that Digits Forward is better than Digits Backward for the groups with Alzheimer's dementia, major depressive disorder, and mild cognitive impairment.

It is difficult to explain why some groups paradoxically seemed to have more difficulty with Digits Forward than Digits Backward; however, these data are derived from a single small sample of individuals and may not be generalizable to

≡ Rapid Reference 8.13

WAIS-IV Process Scores: Clinical Samples With Notable Differences Between Scaled Scores on Digits Forward and Digits Backward That Scored Lowest or Highest on the PSI

	Mean Digits Forward	Mean Digits Backward	Difference
Forward > Backward			
Probable Alzheimer's Dementia—Mild	8.8	7.8	+1.0
Major Depressive Disorder	10.8	10.0	+0.8
Mild Cognitive Impairment	10.2	9.5	+0.7
Backward > Forward			
Intellectually Gifted	13.3	14.7	−1.4
Reading Disorder	7.8	8.9	−1.1
Autistic Disorder	7.9	8.7	−0.8
Asperger's Disorder	9.0	9.7	−0.7
Traumatic Brain Injury	8.0	8.6	−0.6

Source: Data are from The Psychological Corporation (2008), Tables 5.21 to 5.32.

Note: Difference equals Mean Digits Forward minus Mean Digits Backward. Clinical samples are ordered by the magnitude of the difference.

other patients with similar diagnostic labels. As suggested in Chapter 6, one explanation for this finding is that it is possible that the requirement to actively manipulate numbers in the backward condition may have engaged these individuals more than passively reciting them in the forward condition, but a hypothesis such as this requires testing before it can be applied to clinical practice.

INTERPRETATION OF GAIN SCORES FOR NORMAL SAMPLES

Wechsler's scales for children and adults have long been known to produce substantial gains from test to retest, with this practice effect especially large for nonverbal tasks, such as those on the Performance IQ or Perceptual Reasoning and Processing Speed Indexes. On earlier editions of Wechsler's adult test, gain scores over an interval of several weeks or months have averaged about 2–3 points for V-IQ, 9 to 10 points for P-IQ, and 6 to 7 points for FSIQ (Kaufman, 1990, 1994b; Matarazzo & Herman, 1984). The larger gains on the Performance Scale probably reflect the fact that these tasks are novel only the first time they are administered. On subsequent administrations, the tasks are more familiar, and many examinees undoubtedly remember the strategies they used to solve the items (such as arranging the Block Design cubes to match the target stimuli), even if they do not recall specific items.

The impact of this practice effect on interpretation is to anticipate higher IQs on a retest simply because of the effects of practice and not real gains in intellectual functioning. Or, at least, an individual's gains should be substantially higher than "normal" or "baseline" gains before inferring improved intelligence. Another by-product of the gains concerns the differential practice effects for verbal versus nonverbal tasks (i.e., VCI and WMI versus PRI and PSI). Because the PRI and PSI usually will improve much more than the VCI on a retest, examiners can easily be misled by the magnitude of a person's VCI-PRI discrepancy on a retest. On the WAIS-R, for example, adults improved by about 8.5 points on P-IQ and 3 points on V-IQ (Wechsler, 1981), for a net P > V gain of 5 to 6 points. On the WAIS-III, adults improved by 7 points on the P-IQ and about 2 points on the V-IQ.

Examination of the WAIS-III indexes showed a similar pattern for the verbal versus nonverbal tasks with median test-retest gains of 2.3 and 2.6 points for the VCI and WMI, respectively, in contrast to the 5.6- and 4.2-point gains for the PRI and PSI, respectively (Psychological Corporation, 2008). On the WISC-IV, the differential is similar. PRI improved by 5.2 points and PSI improved by 7.1 points, compared to just 2.1 points for VCI and 2.6 points for WMI (*WISC-IV Technical and Interpretive Manual*, Psychological Corporation, 2003). Clinically, WISC-IV examiners might see a nonsignificant 7-point PRI > VCI profile on the first test jump to a significantly different 12 points on the second test, or a jump from an 18-point PRI > VCI discrepancy to an uncommonly large 23-point discrepancy. Conversely, a significant VCI > PRI profile of 12 points on Test 1 might diminish to a trivial 3 points on Test 2. In both instances, the changes in the VCI-PRI discrepancy on the retest is totally misleading and does not accurately portray the person's true difference between verbal and nonverbal abilities.

For the WAIS-IV, 298 retest subjects were obtained (interval averaging about five weeks; see Psychological Corporation, 2008, pp. 47–52), with four age groups represented (16–29, 30–54, 55–69, and 70–90). Rapid Reference 8.15 summarizes the gain scores for the 15 subtests, FSIQ, and four-factor indexes. The inclusion of a substantial sample of retest cases across the entire WAIS-IV age range permitted an analysis of gain scores by age. The two youngest age groups did not differ notably in their gain scores, mirroring the results of the two similarly aged retest samples for the WAIS-R and WAIS-III. However, there are interesting differences between the 30–54 group and the 55–69 group. Specifically, the overall gains in FSIQ, VCI, and WMI continued to increase from one age group to another, but there was a decrease in gain scores on the PRI. The PSI gain remained steady between ages 30–54 and 55–69.

When data for the two oldest WAIS-IV retest groups (ages 55–69 and 70–90) are analyzed alongside each other, other age trends are apparent. After age 69, the gain scores drop steadily for every index except PRI (which already showed a precipitous drop at age 55). The most notable decrease in gain scores was on the PSI in the 70–90 age group, which decreased from a gain of 5.4 to a gain of only 3.2. As discussed in Chapter 7 of this book, tasks that depend the most on visual-motor speed—the ones that comprise the PSI—show declines with aging that are steeper than the declines for vulnerable subtests that are less speed-dependent. Whatever the reason, the increase in FSIQs from the first to second testing shows this age-related pattern on both the WAIS-III and the WAIS-IV:

GAIN SCORES ON FSIQ

Age Group	WAIS-III	WAIS-IV
16–29	5.7 points	4.6 points
30–54	5.1 points	4.4 points
55–69*	3.9 points	5.0 points
70–90*	3.2 points	3.9 points

*Note that the last two age groups for the WAIS-III and WAIS-IV are slightly different. The WAIS-IV age groups are reported in the table, but the last two WAIS-III age groups were 55–74 and 75–89.

Furthermore, the notable nonverbal > verbal gain that has been axiomatic for Wechsler retests applies only to individuals ages 16–54 on the WAIS-IV. At those ages, expect a nonverbal > verbal (i.e., when nonverbal is PRI+PSI and verbal is VCI+WMI) gain of about 5 points. For ages 55–90, the nonverbal > verbal gain is about 1.5 points. These age-related differences need to be internalized by WAIS-IV examiners. When retesting elderly individuals (ages 70+) especially, do not expect the substantial gains that have long been associated with Wechsler's scales. Expect increases of only about 2 to 4 points on the individual Factor Indexes. However, gains of 7 or 8 points (about 1/2 SD) in FSIQ on a retest are noteworthy for an adult of any age, because they are substantially higher than the average gain of 4 to 4.5 points for most adults. In contrast, gains of 4 or fewer points (less than 1/3 SD) on the Full Scale are probably nothing more than a reflection of the practice effect.

Typically, decreases in IQs on a retest are considered a cause for some concern, because such losses have been shown to be rare within the normal population (Kaufman, 1990; Matarazzo & Herman, 1984). That axiom requires modification in view of the WAIS-IV data. When a person age 70 or older scores lower on FSIQ or any Index on a retest, such a decrease may reflect normal variability around the relatively small average gain scores found for these individuals. As a rule of thumb for examiners, losses in IQs or Index scores on a retest for adults ages 70–90 years should be at least 1/2 SD (7 or 8 points) below the initial value before inferring loss of function. For adults below age 70, decreases of about 5 points on a retest are likely to denote loss of function, a generalization that is consistent with the data for the WAIS-III (Kaufman & Lichtenberger, 1999).

Rapid Reference 8.14 lists the subtests in order of their average gain score across the age span. Largest gains were found for the Picture Completion subtest (1.8 scaled-score points). Four subtests had average gains of 0.8–0.9: Visual Puzzles, Symbol Search, Block Design, and Figure Weights. For the total retest sample, the smallest gains (0.1–0.2 point) were for two Verbal subtests (Vocabulary and Comprehension). In addition to these small gains, the untimed Matrix Reasoning subtest had a small 0.4-point gain, as did Letter-Number Sequencing. As on the WAIS-III, the very small gains on WAIS-IV's Matrix Reasoning are undoubtedly partially responsible for the smaller PRI gains, in general, for the WAIS-IV relative to the older WAIS, WAIS-R, and other Wechsler scales that did not include this subtest on the nonverbal scales.

One final point is worth noting. Although practice effects are present on the WAIS-IV, these gain scores are relatively small (typically 1/2 to 1/3 of an SD). Thus, these practice effects do not detract from the fact that the WAIS-IV is quite a stable test battery. Test-retest reliability coefficients for all ages combined were

≋ Rapid Reference 8.14

WAIS-IV Test-Retest Gains Across the Age Range

Point Gain From First to Second Testing

Subtest/Scale	Ages 16–29	Ages 30–54	Ages 55–69	Ages 70–90	Total
Picture Completion	2.4	2.2	1.7	1.2	1.8
Visual Puzzles	1.2	1.1	0.4	1.1	0.9
Symbol Search	1.1	1.0	1.1	0.2	0.9
Block Design	1.2	1.0	0.6	0.5	0.8
Figure Weights	0.9	1.0	0.4	—	0.8
Information	0.7	0.8	0.8	0.6	0.7
Coding	0.5	1.0	0.6	0.7	0.7
Cancellation	1.0	0.5	0.2	—	0.6
Digit Span	0.6	0.5	0.8	0.7	0.6
Similarities	0.4	0.7	0.8	0.5	0.5
Arithmetic	0.5	0.3	0.9	0.4	0.5
Letter-Number Sequencing	0.7	0.5	0.1	—	0.4
Matrix Reasoning	0.2	0.1	0.8	0.3	0.4
Comprehension	0.0	0.2	0.0	0.4	0.2
Vocabulary	0.2	0.1	0.2	0.0	0.1
VCI	2.2	3.0	3.4	2.1	2.6
PRI	5.0	4.4	3.9	3.8	4.2
WMI	2.7	2.0	4.6	3.4	3.3
PSI	4.6	5.6	5.4	3.2	4.6
FSIQ	4.6	4.4	5.0	3.9	4.5

Source: Data are from The Psychological Corporation (2008), Table 4.5. The gain scores are based on the Standard Difference column reported in Table 4.5 of the WAIS-IV Technical Manual.

Note: Subtests are ordered by the size off the practice effect for the total sample. The Standard Difference is the difference of the two test means divided by the square root of the pooled variance, computed using Cohen's (1996) Formula 10.4. This method yields slightly different values than a simple subtraction of Test 1 from Test 2 mean, but it provides a more accurate indication of the exact practice effect for each scale and subtest.

excellent: FSIQ = .96, VCI = .96, PRI = .87. WMI = .88, and PRI = .87 (Psychological Corporation, 2008, Table 4.5).

INTERPRETATION OF GENDER DIFFERENCES FOR NORMAL SAMPLES

WAIS-IV Indexes

Salthouse and Saklofske (2010) used correlational analysis (males coded as 0, females as 1) to explore gender differences on the four WAIS-IV Indexes, separately for two broad standardization age groups: 16–64 (n = 1,600) and 65–90 (n = 600). Females scored significantly higher than males ($p < .01$) on PSI for ages 16–64 (r = 0.20) and 65–90 (r = 0.10), though effect sizes were small. Males scored significantly higher than females on PRI (r = −0.12 for younger sample and −0.13 for older sample), VCI (−0.09/−0.07), and WMI (r = −0.07) at ages 16–64. The genders did not differ significantly on WMI in the elderly sample.

Rapid Reference 8.15 provides a summary of these results. Even though seven of the eight gender comparisons reached statistical significance, all effect sizes were quite small (no larger than 0.2 SD). When effect sizes are based on standard deviation (SD) units, "An effect size of less than 0.50 is small and suggests that the difference is probably not meaningful" (McLean, 1995, p. 39). Nonetheless, the differences of .10–.20 SD on PSI (favoring females) and PRI (favoring males) are likely to be interpretable because they accord well with a considerable body of literature on gender differences.

☰ Rapid Reference 8.15

....

Gender Differences on WAIS-IV Indexes

Scale	Age Group Ages 16–64	Ages 65–90
VCI	♂ > ♀	♂ > ♀
PRI	♂ > ♀	♂ > ♀
WMI	♂ > ♀	No difference
PSI	♀ > ♂	♀ > ♂

Note: ♂ > ♀ indicates that males scored significantly higher than females and ♀ > ♂ indicates that females scored significantly higher than males.

WAIS-III Indexes

Heaton, Taylor, and Manly (2003) examined WAIS-III gender differences at ages 20–89 years on the VCI, POI (Perceptual *Organization* Index), and PSI for a normal sample of 1,075 males and 1,237 females (analyses for WMI were based on 503 males and 570 females). They computed age-corrected and education-corrected z scores and observed the following gender differences: Females scored higher on PSI (.36 *SD*); males scored higher on VCI (.25 *SD*), POI (.17 *SD*), and WMI (.15 *SD*). The VCI difference on the WAIS-III favoring males is larger than the corresponding difference on the WAIS-IV, but is of no consequence because it is contrary to the bulk of literature on the topic:

> One set of findings that has been replicated many times is that females, on average, score higher on some tests of verbal abilities, especially those that require rapid access to and use of phonological and semantic information in long-term memory. (Halpern, Beninger, & Straight, 2011, p. 254)

The verbal abilities that females excel at resemble the abilities needed to perform well on Wechsler's VCI subtests.

Furthermore, the results of gender differences on verbal subtests included in major intelligence tests are contaminated because test developers have consistently tried to avoid gender bias during the test development phase, both in the selection of subtests for the batteries and in the choice of items for each subtest. Matarazzo (1972) pointed out:

> From the very beginning developers of the best known individual intelligence scales (Binet, Terman, and Wechsler) took great care to counterbalance or eliminate from their final scale any items or subtests which *empirically* were found to result in a higher score for one sex over the other. (p. 352; italics in original)

According to Wechsler (1958): "The principal reason for adopting such a procedure is that it avoids the necessity of separate norms for men and women" (p. 144). The counterbalancing or eliminating of gender-biased items primarily affects verbal subtests such as Information or Comprehension (and the WMI subtest Arithmetic), where the content of the item might favor one gender over the other. In contrast, subtests like Block Design, Matrix Reasoning, Symbol Search, and Coding are composed of "content-free" items that are not likely to be biased in any way. Therefore, interpreting gender differences on the PSI and PRI is reasonable from a scientific perspective.

CAUTION

....

Results of Gender Differences in IQ are Contaminated

Test developers for major intelligence tests have consistently tried to avoid gender bias during the test development phase, both in the selection of subtests for the batteries and in the choice of items for each subtest.

GENDER DIFFERENCES ON PROCESSING SPEED

The female advantage in processing speed, demonstrated across the entire adult age range on the WAIS-III and WAIS-IV, is well documented in the literature, although the reason for this female superiority is less apparent. Numerous experimental psychologists have systematically explored explanations for this persistent gender difference. Estes (1974) hypothesized that females outperform males on these psychomotor tasks because of a greater ability to verbally encode the abstract symbols. This hypothesis has received support from Royer (1978), who devised three forms of the symbol-digit substitution task. One form used the easily encoded WAIS symbols, while the others used symbols of greater spatial and orientational complexity (ones not readily encoded verbally). Females outperformed males significantly on the WAIS symbols, as expected, but males significantly outscored females on the most complex symbol set. Additional support for the Estes verbal encoding hypothesis comes from Majeres's (1983) experiment indicating female superiority on matching and symbol-digit tasks that utilize verbal material, contrasted with male superiority on symbol-digit substitution tasks employing spatial stimuli. However, some research results dispute the Estes hypothesis (e.g., Delaney, Norman, & Miller, 1981; Laux & Lane, 1985).

Although the female advantage in Digit Symbol and other tests of clerical speed has emerged in numerous investigations of children (e.g., Jensen & Reynolds, 1983) as well as adults, including cross-culturally, Feingold (1988) noted that the size of the discrepancy had fallen substantially from the mid-1940s to mid-1980s. Contrary to Feingold's (1988) observations, the WAIS-III versus WAIS-R data do not support a decrease in the female superiority in clerical speed through the mid-1990s, when the WAIS-III was normed. If anything, the discrepancy increased during the almost two decades that separated the standardizations. On the WAIS-R, females earned scaled scores that averaged 0.92 points higher than males, across four age groups between 16–19 and 55–74 years (Kaufman, McLean, & Reynolds, 1988), a discrepancy of 0.31 SD; that gender difference is not nearly as large as the discrepancy of 0.50 SD observed on

WAIS-III Digit Symbol-Coding (0.50 SD). However, Feingold's (1988) assertion is supported by comparing the female advantage on the PSI for the WAIS-III (0.36 *SD*) versus the WAIS-IV (0.20 *SD* for ages 16–64 and 0.10 *SD* for ages 65–90), which was standardized in 2007–2008.

GENDER DIFFERENCES IN SPATIAL VISUALIZATION

The higher scores by males than females on WAIS-III POI and WAIS-IV PRI undoubtedly reflect the well-documented male advantage in visuospatial ability, or *Gv* from CHC theory, a skill that is measured well by Block Design, Object Assembly (WAIS-III only), and Visual Puzzles (WAIS-IV only). Although Matrix Reasoning is primarily a measure of *Gf*, many of its items depend to some extent on orientation, mental rotation, and spatial visualization. A male advantage has been observed on a variety of other visuospatial tasks from other individual tests of intelligence for adolescents and adults, such as Memory for Block Designs (Kaufman & Horn, 1996) and Gestalt Closure (Kaufman, Chen, & Kaufman, 1995).

Jensen (1980) stated:

> The largest and most consistently found sex difference is spatial visualization ability, especially on spatial tests that require analysis, that is mentally breaking up a gestalt into smaller units in ways that facilitate spatial problem solving (e.g., the Block Designs test) . . . [;] the sex difference in spatial ability is not established consistently until puberty, and it persists thereafter. Generally, in studies of adolescents and adults, only about one-fourth of the females exceed the male median on various tests of spatial visualization. (p. 626)

Hyde (1981) calculated that about 4% of the variation in visuospatial abilities is attributed to gender differences, versus only about 1% each for verbal ability and quantitative ability. According to Deaux (1984), similar small effect sizes for the variable of gender have been identified for noncognitive factors as well, such as aggression and social influence. She states that, "although additional evidence remains to be gathered, 5% may approximate the upper boundary for the explanatory power of subject-sex main effects in specific social and cognitive behaviors" (p. 108).

Halpern et al. (2011) note that spatial abilities are grouped into three categories: spatial perception, spatial visualization, and mental rotation. Males outperform females in all three domains, with the largest differences on mental rotation. The male advantage in spatial abilities is evident at 3 to 5 months of age (Quinn & Liben, 2008), consistently appears in studies of preschool children (Levine, Huttenlocher, Taylor, & Langrock, 1999), and is characteristic across the entire age range (Halpern et al., 2011). A review of a wide array of mental rotation studies indicates that the male advantage is substantial at all ages and seems to increase slightly across the life span (Geiser, Lehmann, & Eid, 2008).

Related to this topic, Chastain and Joe (1987) performed a canonical correlation analysis using data from the entire WAIS-R standardization sample. They entered the 11 subtests and a variety of background variables into the analysis, interpreting as meaningful three canonical factors, one of which, labeled Manual Dexterity, included a .72 loading by Gender (males were coded as 1, females as zero). Block Design (.49) and being in a skilled occupation such as carpentry (.38) also related substantially to this dimension; other tasks with moderate loadings were Picture Completion, Object Assembly, Picture Arrangement, and Arithmetic. This canonical factor, defined primarily by "maleness," reiterates other findings of men outperforming women on visuospatial tasks.

CLINICAL IMPLICATIONS OF GENDER DIFFERENCES ON MENTAL TASKS

Effect sizes for the female processing speed advantage and the male spatial advantage are sometimes found to be moderate or large in the vast cognitive literature (Halpern et al., 2011); that magnitude of gender differences would be clinically meaningful. However, the effect sizes for the WAIS-IV Indexes are uniformly small, peaking at 0.20 for the female superiority on PSI. For the most part, effect sizes are trivial, and even though the male advantage on PRI and the female advantage on PSI are both "real" (and therefore interpretable) for groups of adults, they are of no clinical value for the interpretation of the WAIS-IV for individuals referred for evaluation. Similarly, the finding of a larger Flynn effect for females than males on the WISC, WAIS-R, and WAIS-III (Zhou, Gregoire, & Zhu, 2010, Figure 5.2) is an interesting group difference but has no practical or clinical value for clinical assessment.

🐟 TEST YOURSELF 🐟

....

I. **TRUE or FALSE?** Although a percentage of the clinical samples that had ADHD or major depression were on medication during the assessment of the **WAIS-IV**, it is not important to consider that factor in interpreting the results of these clinical group studies.

2. **TRUE or FALSE?** Digit Span Sequencing is one of the process tests that is sensitive to the cognitive impairment typical for individuals with probable Alzheimer's-type dementia.

3. Individuals who are gifted would likely perform the best on which of the following subtests?
   a. Symbol Search
   b. Cancellation
   c. Vocabulary
   d. Coding

4. Individuals with Asperger's disorder and autistic disorder performed poorest on which of the following **WISC-IV** indexes?
   a. VCI
   b. PSI
   c. WMI
   d. PRI

5. **TRUE or FALSE?** Except for the reading disorder group and the autistic disorder groups, all groups displayed a **VCI > PRI** pattern.

6. Practice effects evidenced by the gain scores from one testing to the next are strongest on average for which indexes?
   a. VCI and PRI
   b. PSI and WMI
   c. VCI and PSI
   d. PRI and PSI

7. For which one of the clinical samples was Digit Span (a Working Memory subtest) among the top three scaled scores?
   a. Asperger's Disorder
   b. Intellectually Gifted
   c. Probable Alzheimer's Dementia
   d. ADHD

8. **TRUE or FALSE?** When the WMI and the PSI are not uncommonly different from one another, the subtests from these two indexes may be combined to yield the Cognitive Proficiency Index (CPI).

9. **TRUE or FALSE?** Females tend to earn higher scores than males on Block Design and other measures of visuospatial ability.

Answers: 1. false; 2. true; 3. c; 4. b; 5. true; 6. d; 7. b; 8. true. 9. false.

Nine

STRENGTHS AND WEAKNESSES OF THE WAIS-IV

Ron Dumont
John O. Willis

T he authors of this chapter still believe, as we did when the first edition of
this volume was published, that, on balance, the WAIS-IV is a very good
instrument. We think enough of it and of other Wechsler scales to use
them in our own practices, to teach them to our captive audiences of graduate
students, and to write this chapter. Both of us have had extensive experience
with many other cognitive assessment instruments long before the WAIS-IV was
published. Since its publication in 2008, several test reviews (e.g., Climie &
Rostad, 2011; Hartman, 2009; Loring & Bauer, 2010; Schraw, 2010), independent
analyses (e.g., Benson, Hulac, & Kanzler, 2010; Canivez & Watkins, 2010a,
2010b), and book-length interpretive guides (e.g., Lichtenberger & Kaufman,
2009; Weiss et al., 2010b) suggest that, overall, the WAIS-IV is generally
regarded positively and described as a well-developed and significantly
improved instrument. Since the publication of the first edition of this
volume, these authors have continued to use the WAIS-IV many times in
real assessment cases and have further developed opinions, both positive and
negative, about it. Although we find the test to be overall a vast improvement
over the prior edition and have welcomed many of the changes in the update,
we still find several aspects of the test annoying or problematic. (Admittedly, we
are easily annoyed.)

The WAIS-IV provides an efficient, thorough, reasonable, and statistically
reliable and valid assessment of cognitive abilities. It is designed with features that
enhance useful interpretation.

STRENGTHS OF THE WAIS-IV

This chapter first presents the strengths of the WAIS-IV, followed by a section on the test's weaknesses. Within these two dichotomous sections, we have organized the test's pros and cons in these categories: test development, administration and scoring, reliability and validity, standardization, and interpretation. This list of assets and detriments is by no means exhaustive, but it does reflect what we view as the key positive and negative aspects. A summary of these points is provided at the end of this chapter.

Test Development

In the process of developing the WAIS-IV, many positive changes were made to Wechsler's adult test. The key assets that we describe include updating of the theoretical foundations; adding new strong measures of fluid reasoning, working memory, and visual processing; and adding normed process scores. The test materials were also improved during the process of test development.

Update of Theoretical Foundations
One of the revision goals for the WAIS-IV was to "update theoretical foundations" (Psychological Corporation, 2008, p. 17). As we note, the important goal of enhancing measurement of fluid reasoning was at least partially met by the valuable addition of the Figure Weights subtest, although we would have liked to have normative scores for fluid reasoning included in the test norms with a differentiation between visual/spatial ability and fluid reasoning. The issue is complicated by the fact that, whereas almost all theorists and researchers would agree that Figure Weights and Matrix Reasoning measure fluid reasoning, there would be differing opinions about the Similarities subtest. Additionally, Benson et al.'s (2010) evaluation of the WAIS-IV structure found that Figure Weights and Matrix Reasoning *and* Arithmetic "can be interpreted as measures of Gf." Canivez and Watkins (2010a, 2010b), using several factor-analytic techniques, found support for the four Composite Scores, but cautioned that the Full Scale IQ accounted for most of the variance and that most methods recommended extraction of only one or two factors. Canivez and Watkins recommend that test interpretation be done primarily at the level of the Full Scale IQ.

Also, as will be noted, assessment of working memory has been considerably increased. Finally, the increased measurement of processing speed is also in line with current theory and research. All three areas are especially critical for assessment of cognitive changes over the adult life span.

As will be discussed at length, the lack of explicit adherence to Cattell-Horn-Carroll (CHC) categories disappoints those of us who lean on that particular taxonomy and use it to compare results of different tests with the same examinee, but the WAIS-IV was never intended to conform to the CHC ability structure. The explicit goals of updating theoretical foundations, increasing developmental appropriateness, increasing user-friendliness, enhancing clinical utility, and improving psychometric properties were, in our opinion, all met, despite our quibbles.

Addition of Figure Weights: Adds Another Strong Gf Measure

When the WAIS-III was released in 1997, we were especially excited about the inclusion of the then-new Matrix Reasoning subtest, because the Wechsler scales had, since their creation, lacked any clear measure of fluid reasoning. Our excitement was short-lived when we realized that the Matrix Reasoning subtest was not sufficient by itself for examiners to feel confident in explaining a person's fluid reasoning abilities. Usually at least two subtests in the same broad ability (in this case fluid reasoning, or Gf)[1] are necessary to compute a score for that broad ability (Flanagan et al., 2007). With the current addition of the Figure Weights subtest, a fluid reasoning subtest that appears to be measuring the narrow ability of Quantitative Reasoning, examiners can interpret a person's fluid reasoning skills and do so with more confidence, although there is no separate normative score for fluid reasoning provided in the test manual (see Chapter 5 for ways of computing fluid reasoning standard scores).

Addition of Digit Sequencing: A Measure of WM to Accompany DB and LNS

We also believed that the WAIS-III had problems with the interpretability of Short-term Memory (Gsm) ability. On the WAIS-III, short-term memory, called "Working Memory," was composed of two subtests (Digit Span and Arithmetic). Although both subtests might be considered measures of Gsm, Digit Span, with both a digit-forward and a digit-backward task, was, in our opinion, a mixture of memory span (Gsm-MS) and working memory (Gsm-MW) (see, e.g., Hale, Hoeppner, & Fiorello, 2002; Reynolds, 1997), whereas Arithmetic was a measure of both working memory (Gsm-MW) and quantitative ability (Gq). This combination of different narrow abilities often made the interpretation of the Working Memory Index problematic.

---

1. We are using names and notations for Cattell-Horn-Carroll (CHC) Broad and Narrow abilities taken from Carroll (1997); Flanagan & McGrew (1997); Flanagan et al. (2007); Flanagan et al. (2006); and Horn & Blankson (2005).

With the addition of the new Digit Sequencing task to the Digit Span subtest, a stronger measure of working memory has been added to the test. The Digit Span subtest now includes three tasks: Forward, Backward, and Sequencing. Comparing a person's results from the Digits Forward task (Memory Span) to those of the Digits Backward task, Digit Sequencing task, and Letter-Number Sequencing subtest (all measures of Working Memory) with the aid of the interpretive tables in Appendixes B and C of the *Administration and Scoring Manual* (Wechsler, 2008, pp. 229–253) may allow for a clearer interpretation of the different short-term memory abilities measured by the WAIS-IV.

Addition of Visual Puzzles: Enhances Measures of Gv

The addition of the new Visual Puzzles subtest to the WAIS-IV has increased the interpretability of Visual Spatial (*Gv*) abilities. When Visual Puzzles is combined with Block Design, there are two strong measures of *Gv*, with Visual Puzzles measuring the narrow ability of visualization (VZ) and Block Design measuring spatial relations (SR). The supplemental subtest, Picture Completion, is also a *Gv* measure and, according to Benson et al. (2010), can be grouped together with Visual Puzzles and Block Design and used as a measure of *Gv*, again, though, without a separate normative score for *Gv* (again, see Chapter 5 for methods of computing a *Gv* standard score).

Block Design: Process Score for No Time Bonus (BDN)

Like the WISC-IV (Wechsler, 2003), the WAIS-IV provides norms for pass-fail scoring of Block Design. Time limits still apply, but time-bonus points are not used. Although the BDN may not be substituted for the regular Block Design score, the additional Process Score still provides useful information for examinees who have slow motor responses, slow decision speed, poor motor coordination, or a tendency toward high levels of uncertainty. Appendix C in Wechsler (2008, pp. 242–248) provides scaled scores for BDN as well as critical values and base rates for differences between Block Design and Block Design No Time Bonus.

Update of Materials, Artwork, and Record Form

The materials for the WAIS-IV have been updated to include new artwork, a revised Record Form, and enlarged Symbol Search and Coding subtest materials. We are especially happy with the revised Record Form, as there is now much more room for recording an examinee's responses. For just one example, the section of the form for recording the responses to the Digit Span subtest has been enlarged so that the examiner can now record verbatim the numbers given as a response. On the WAIS-III, there was very little room in the space provided to fit the actual responses.

Administration and Scoring

There are several positive aspects to the WAIS-IV's administration and scoring procedures. The key points on which we elaborate include the generally easy procedures for administration and scoring, streamlining of starting and stopping points, and improved scoring for Vocabulary.

Fairly Easy Administration

The WAIS-IV is not effortless to administer, but—despite Hartman's (2009) frequent comparisons with the shorter and tightly focused Reynolds Intellectual Assessment Scales (RIAS; Reynolds & Kamphaus, 2003)—it is not unduly or unnecessarily difficult. With the elimination of both the Object Assembly and Picture Arrangement subtests, the WAIS-IV has become less cumbersome with its manipulatives. Only Block Design requires anything other than the Stimulus Booklets for administration. No more fumbling for Object Assembly boxes and pieces, no more shield to hide the placement of the puzzle parts, and no more Picture Arrangement cards to shuffle, deal, and drop on the floor. Examiners do need to use both the *Administration Manual* and the Record Form, along with a Stimulus Booklet and a stopwatch for some subtests, especially Block Design, but this divided-attention task is not difficult to master.

Generally Easy Scoring

Difficult judgments and subjectivity in scoring rules cause interexaminer variation and errors in scores. Some mistakes are frequent, and some result in serious errors in subtest and total test scores (e.g., Alfonso & Pratt, 1997; Belk, LoBello, Ray, & Zachar, 2002; Kuentzel, Hetterscheidt, & Barnett, 2011; Willis, 2001). With the exception of three Verbal Comprehension subtests (Similarities, Vocabulary, and Comprehension), on which items can be scored as 2, 1, or 0, the scoring rules for all other subtest items (with some minor exceptions noted as follows) strike us as generally clear and unequivocal.

Streamlining of Discontinue Rules, Entry Points

The administration of the WAIS-IV seems to flow a bit more efficiently, and one reason for this may be the revised discontinue rules, which have been shortened for the most part. Many subtest discontinuations have been reduced by at least one item (e.g., from four consecutive failures to three), and two subtests (Vocabulary and Information) have been reduced from six to three consecutive failures. Entry points and other essential information generally have been made clear and user-friendly on the Record Form.

Scoring of Vocabulary

Unlike some vocabulary tests, the WAIS-IV Vocabulary instructions (Wechsler, 2008) state: "All word meanings recognized by standard dictionaries are acceptable and are scored according to the quality of the definition" (p. 101). Although "regionalisms or slang" are not acceptable, the examiner is instructed to query such responses and other responses when the examiner is "unsure about the acceptability of a response." Subjectively, there do not appear to be enough difficult words for examinees with college or postgraduate education, but scaled scores of 19 are available at all ages, requiring perfect raw scores at ages 35:0 to 84:11.

Start Points

All subtests except for Digit Span, Symbol Search, Coding, Letter-Number Sequencing, and Cancellation have starting points (after any sample items) higher than Item 1. There are clear rules for dropping back from the starting item when necessary, and examinees who are believed to have intellectual disabilities "should always begin with Item 1." These rules should minimize both boredom and frustration.

Reliability and Validity

With the state-of-the art procedures for test development and standardization, it is no surprise that the psychometric qualities of the WAIS-IV are strong. Canivez (2010) offers qualified approval, with some concerns, of the technical characteristics of the WAIS-IV. Schraw (2010) generally approves of the standardization, reliability, and validity evidence. We detail the assets of the test's reliability and validity next.

Reliability

The WAIS-IV Composite, Indexes, and subtests generally have strong reliability. This topic is discussed at length in Chapter 4 of the *Technical and Interpretive Manual* (Psychological Corporation, 2008). Test scores cannot be trusted unless the tests are internally consistent and likely to yield very similar scores for the same person under similar circumstances, so reliability is an essential foundation for any responsible use of test scores. It is a necessary, but not sufficient, basis for application of test scores. A test can be reliable but still not valid for a particular purpose; without reliability, however, it cannot be valid for any purpose.

It is still too early to be able to measure long-term stability of WAIS-IV scores, and long-term stability statistics are depressed by genuine changes in the abilities of the persons being retested. Short-term stability coefficients for all subtests (including process scores) at all tested ages (Psychological Corporation, 2008, p. 48), ranged from .71 (adequate) to .90 (reliable). For the core subtests, short-term stability coefficients were .74 to .90, with a median of .82.

Evidence of Validity

Validity data for the WAIS-IV are discussed in Chapter 1 and in the WAIS-IV *Technical and Interpretive Manual* (Psychological Corporation, 2008, pp. 57–122). Validity evidence from comparisons with tests of cognitive abilities and tests of academic achievement supports the use of the WAIS-IV for cognitive assessment and prediction of achievement. Independent analyses (e.g., Benson et al., 2010; Canivez & Watkins, 2010a, 2010b) provide some support for the factor structure of the WAIS-IV.

Evidence of Validity With Special Groups

Although the WAIS-IV is not normed on individuals with severe disabilities or disabilities that are likely to invalidate test scores, studies were done with 13 special groups (Psychological Corporation, 2008, pp. 98–122). When assessing individuals with special characteristics, that information in the *Manual* is extremely helpful. Additional analyses of these data are discussed by Lichtenberger and Kaufman in Chapter 8.

The *Administration and Scoring Manual* (Wechsler, 2008, pp. 10–19) provides some brief, helpful considerations for testing individuals with special needs and detailed recommendations for testing examinees who are deaf or hard of hearing; additional information is available in the *Technical and Interpretive Manual* (Psychological Corporation, 2008, Appendix D, pp. 185–187) adapted from Hardy (1993) and Hardy-Braz (2003).

Standardization

Normative samples are important for tests, just as for opinion polls. If the normative sample does not resemble the population to whom examinees will be compared, scores will be misleading. The normative sample of the WAIS-IV is described in Chapter 3 of the *Technical and Interpretive Manual* (Psychological Corporation, 2008). We consider it to meet or exceed good current practice and to provide a trustworthy basis for an individual's scores.

Examinee candidates for the normative sample were screened extensively for potentially confounding issues that presumably might impair the validity of test performance. A complete list of the exclusionary criteria for the normative sample is presented in Table 3.1 (p. 31) of the *Technical and Interpretive Manual*

(Psychological Corporation, 2008). Special consideration was given to the trend for increased prescription medication use in older adults. Procedures were established to evaluate individuals' medication use, particularly those medications that could potentially affect cognitive test performance.

Interpretation

The newest version of the WAIS has made interpretation easier, and the test publishers have provided additional interpretive information for clinicians in the test kit. We describe these assets and additional strengths related to the topic of interpretation next.

Easier Interpretation

The WAIS-III (Wechsler, 1997) subtest scores were shuffled into confusing combinations. Three subtests contributed to the Verbal Comprehension Index (VCI), Verbal IQ (VIQ), and Full Scale IQ (FSIQ). A fourth Verbal subtest contributed to the VIQ and FSIQ but not to the VCI or any other index score. Two other Verbal subtests contributed to the VIQ and FSIQ but to the Working Memory Index (WMI) rather than to the VCI. The remaining Verbal subtest was included in the WMI but not in the VIQ and PIQ.

Three Performance subtests were included in the WAIS-III: Performance IQ (PIQ), FSIQ, and Perceptual Organization Index (POI). One was included in the PIQ and FSIQ, but in the Processing Speed Index (PSI) rather than in the POI. Another Performance subtest was included in the PIQ and FSIQ scores, but in none of the Index scores. Yet another was part of the PSI score but not of the PIQ or FSIQ. Finally, one Performance subtest (Object Assembly) was not included in any index or IQ scores.

Coherent explanations of the composition of the various WAIS-III IQ and Index scores were elusive for both evaluators and readers of our reports. The composition of the WAIS-IV components is much easier to understand, as shown in Table 9.1. Each subtest either contributes to both an Index Scale and the FSIQ or serves as a supplementary subtest.

Additional Interpretive Information

As with the WISC-IV (Wechsler, 2003), the WAIS-IV provides valuable "Critical Value and Base Rates Tables for Discrepancy Comparisons" (Wechsler, 2008, pp. 229–240) and "Process Analysis Tables" (pp. 241–253) for the Block Design with no time-bonus points and for the various Digit Span tasks. Critical values are given for .15 and .05 but not .10 significance levels. Tables for comparing WAIS-IV and Wechsler Individual Achievement Test (2nd ed.;

Table 9.1. Comparison of WISC-IV, WAIS-III, and WAIS-IV Index and Full Scale IQ Composition

Subtest	WISC-IV	WAIS-III*	WAIS-IV
Information	*supplemental*	VCI + FSIQ	VCI + FSIQ
Comprehension	VCI + FSIQ	FSIQ	*supplemental*
Similarities	VCI + FSIQ	VCI + FSIQ	VCI + FSIQ
Vocabulary	VCI + FSIQ	VCI + FSIQ	VCI + FSIQ
Word Reasoning	*supplemental*	—	—
Picture Completion	*supplemental*	POI + FSIQ	*supplemental*
Block Design	PRI + FSIQ	POI + FSIQ	PRI + FSIQ
Matrix Reasoning	PRI + FSIQ	POI + FSIQ	PRI + FSIQ
Picture Concepts	PRI + FSIQ	—	—
Visual Puzzles	—	—	PRI + FSIQ
Figure Weights	—	—	*supplemental*
Picture Arrangement	—	FSIQ	—
Object Assembly	—	*supplemental*	—
Arithmetic	*supplemental*	WMI + FSIQ	WMI + FSIQ
Digit Span	WMI + FSIQ	WMI + FSIQ	WMI + FSIQ
Letter—Number Sequencing	WMI + FSIQ	WMI	*supplemental*
Coding	PSI + FSIQ	PSI + FSIQ	PSI + FSIQ
Symbol Search	PSI + FSIQ	PSI	PSI + FSIQ
Cancellation	*supplemental*	—	*supplemental*

*WAIS-III FSIQ subtests are also included in the Verbal IQ (VIQ) or Performance IQ (PIQ). VCI = Verbal Comprehension Index, PRI = Perceptual Reasoning Index, WMI = Working memory Index, PSI = Processing Speed Index, FSIQ = Full Scale IQ.

WIAT-II) scores are provided in the WAIS-IV *Technical and Interpretive Manual* (Psychological Corporation, 2008, Appendix B, pp. 151–163). These WIAT-II comparisons appear to be based on correlational data from 93 high school students, which suggests cautious interpretation. Tables B.4 and B.8 (Psychological Corporation, 2008, pp. 158, 161) include the limitation "for

Ages 16:0–19:11." Examiners who wish to use the WIAT-II college norms with the WAIS-IV need to exercise caution.

The Wechsler Individual Achievement Test—Third Edition (WIAT-III; Pearson, 2009) *Technical Manual* (Breaux, 2009) provides WIAT-II correlations with the WAIS-IV FSIQ, GAI, VCI, and PRI; and predicted WIAT-III achievement scores, critical values for significant differences, and base rates for discrepancies for the same WAIS-IV scores. There are also data for simple-difference comparisons. These norms are offered for ages 16 through 19 and appear to be based on a study with 59 participants of ages 16 and 17. The *Technical Manual with Adult Norms* (Breaux, 2010) *provides the same data for ages 20:0 through 50:11, apparently based on scores of 79 adults in that age range.*

Aligning the Indexes to Be Compatible With WISC-IV

As the Wechsler Scales have developed over the years, they have each gradually shifted from the original Wechsler Verbal/Performance dichotomy to the current utilization of a Full Scale IQ and four index scores. We are happy to find that the WAIS-IV has totally replaced the Verbal-Performance IQ designations with terminology and labels that are much more in alignment with the *Wechsler Intelligence Scale for Children, Fourth Edition* (Wechsler, 2003; WISC-IV), as well as with the newly released *Wechsler Abbreviated Scale of Intelligence, Second Edition* (Wechsler, 2011; WASI-II). Evaluators providing reevaluations will find better (albeit not perfect) alignment with the WISC-IV, but loss of alignment with the examinee's previous WAIS-III scores.

However, we are not entirely comfortable with the assertion *"The terms VCI and PRI should be substituted for the terms VIQ and PIQ in clinical decision-making and other situations where VIQ and PIQ were previously used"* (Wechsler, 2008, p. 5, emphasis in the original). The old VIQ included both VCI and WMI subtests, and the old PIQ contained both PRI and PSI subtests. Table 9.1 shows the subtest composition for the Full Scale IQ and the four indexes of the WISC-IV, the WAIS-III, and the WAIS-IV. As can be seen, the tests derive their respective FSIQs and indexes from different combinations of subtests, with only the Processing Speed Index having a direct subtest match between the WISC-IV and WAIS-IV. Although specific differences still remain between the two tests, and some of those differences may be developmentally appropriate, the alignment of the WAIS-IV into the four indexes will, we hope, lead to easier understanding and interpretation across the two tests, particularly for those individuals who have been administered the WISC-IV and then, later, the WAIS-IV.

WEAKNESSES OF THE WAIS-IV

Although our overall impression of the WAIS-IV is a positive one, we did find some negative aspects that we discuss next in categories that parallel those discussed in the section on the test's strengths.

Test Development

The goals of the test publisher's development team led them to develop a stronger test when they revised the WAIS-III. Thus, only one detriment to the WAIS-IV's test development is described.

Loss of Object Assembly and Picture Arrangement

Although, as noted, removal of Object Assembly and Picture Arrangement has greatly simplified administration and clarified interpretation of the WAIS-IV and has removed two subtests of questionable reliability and validity, a few old practitioners will miss those venerable subtests, which were, for many decades, integral parts of the Wechsler scales. We are left with only one hands-on constructional subtest, Block Design. Some examiners believed we gained useful information by being able to watch the examinee work on the items of those subtests. The vast majority of examiners, most of whom did not administer those subtests on the WAIS-III and never saw the WAIS-R, WAIS, or Wechsler-Bellevue, will not agree with this opinion.

Loring and Bauer (2010), in their review of the WAIS-IV, opine that the change in composition of the WAIS-IV subtests, especially with the deemphasis on rapid solutions and the reduction in speed bonus points, may result in fewer FSIQ scores of 70 or below in certain clinical populations. This situation, if it holds true, could "decrease the number of individuals qualifying for special education or disability services using FSIQ cutoff criteria" (p. 268). Loring and Bauer predict that fewer examinees will qualify for rehabilitation services (probably true) and special education (probably the opposite). They add that the change in subtest composition has also created a "mismatch" with groups tested on previous Wechsler versions, and will "lead to differences in epidemiologic estimates describing prevalence of individuals with FSIQs in the impaired range" (p. 268).

Administration and Scoring

The administration and scoring procedures of the WAIS-IV have a few little quirks that we view as detriments. We elaborate on these issues: problems related to substitutions and prorating, poor instructions for certain tests, and questionable scoring rules for certain subtests.

Substitutions and Prorating
Although we agree that it is better to allow subtest substitutions and prorating than to invalidate an entire test, be unable to compute a FSIQ score, or have to report results that are obviously biased against an examinee's disability, we do have concerns about the potential for IQ roulette when substitutions are allowed. The *Administration and Scoring Manual* (Wechsler, 2008, pp. 29–30, 51–54) discusses substitutions and prorating and limits substitutions to no more than one per index scale and two for the entire test. Those rules still allow a tremendous number of different versions of the WAIS-IV composed of different subtests with varying reliabilities and different correlations with their index scales and the FSIQ. We would have preferred to see even stronger cautions about substitutions and prorating.

Poor Instructions for Scoring Certain Tasks
Although the instructions provided in the *Administration and Scoring Manual* (Wechsler, 2008) are typically clear and unambiguous, there remain, in our opinion, several aspects of administration and scoring that need clarification. (Some of these concerns apply to other Wechsler tests as well.)

Picture Completion—20-Second Rule
For the Picture Completion subtest, there is an explicit 20-second time limit for each item and, additionally, the *Manual* states: "If an examinee does not respond to an item within 20 seconds or if the examinee responds incorrectly in less than 20 seconds, proceed to the next appropriate item if the discontinuation criterion has not been met" (Wechsler, 2008, p. 199). Although this may seem straightforward, how does one define "respond"? Does it refer to the onset of the examinee's utterance (e.g., the "Well" in "Well . . . um . . . I think . . . maybe . . . it could be . . . uh . . . I guess . . . maybe . . . missing . . . that thing over there . . . where it comes together like the other one.") or the words that specify the missing part ("that thing") or the end of the examinee's comment ("other one")? For example, what is an examiner to do if the person being tested starts to respond to an item at the 18-second mark but correctly completes the response at 25 seconds? Is this scored as a 0 because the response was not given "within 20 seconds," or do we score it as a passed item because the person began his or her response within the 20 seconds? Or what of the case where a person responds incorrectly within the 20 seconds and then spontaneously self-corrects his or her answer, but the

corrected response runs over the 20-second time limit? How strict are we to be with the 20-second rule? Unfortunately, there is no clear guidance in the *Manual* or from the test company.

Figure Weights—Time Pressure

The older coauthor of this chapter had no difficulty with any of the Figure Weights items but was unable to solve some of the problems within the 20- and 40-second time limits. The constant interruption with the examiner's "Do you have an answer?" on every item 10 seconds before the time limit elapsed was not only a severe annoyance but a significant distraction. After the first few items, anticipation of the inevitable interruption developed into a distraction in its own right, making the subtest an unnecessarily unpleasant experience. Ineligibility for Figure Weights (and Letter-Number Sequencing) may be a welcome 70th birthday present for examinees.

Block Design—Rotations

Block Design (Wechsler, 2008, pp. 66–68) still counts as an error any rotation of 30 degrees or more of the design. Many evaluators would consider this rule proper and a strength of the test. We have come to prefer the approach taken by Elliott (2007) on the Differential Ability Scales of simply not penalizing rotations. Precisely distinguishing between 29 and 30 degrees can be challenging, and there seem to be many reasons for rotating designs, including an effort to turn them so the examiner can see them correctly. Even if such a benign error is not repeated after a single correction, as prescribed in the *Manual*, the examinee has still lost 2 or, more likely, 4 points.

Comprehension—What Is a Response?

Similar to our concerns regarding what constitutes a response on the Picture Completion subtest, we also have problems with the Comprehension subtest. Several items are flagged (§) as a reminder to the examiner that, for maximum points, the item requires distinct answers from at least two separate categories designated in the *Manual*. It is noted that if the "first response" to an item is clearly incorrect, the examiner does not query at all for a second response. However, the instructions also note that if the examinee's answer contains information from only one general concept, the examiner is to query using the specific wording provided in the *Manual* to obtain an additional response. If the additional response refers to the same general category, then the examiner does not ask for an additional response. Confusion comes from just what constitutes a "response." What if the person's first answer (response) contains two parts, both descriptions from one general concept? Is that answer considered to be one response or two? For example, for item 5, a person responds with "To kill germs so you don't get sick." In the *Manual*, the responses "To kill germs" and "So you don't get sick" are both correct, acceptable responses from one general concept. Is that specific response therefore referring to only one general concept, or is this actually two responses, both from the same general concept? If the person had simply said "To kill germs," that would clearly be one response from one general category, and we would query the response. If after the query the person says "So you don't get sick," we would have two clear responses, the second from the same general concept, and therefore would not ask for any additional response to the item. But if, as in our example, we consider that the answer as a whole was one response, we would then be required to query for a second response.

Information—Questionable Scoring Rules
We noticed only two items on the Information subtest that may cause scoring difficulty for the examiner. Although we cannot put the specific test item questions or the responses from the *Manual* in this volume, we do note that the examples given in the *Administration and Scoring Manual* (Wechsler, 2008) call for queries (Q) to some, but not other, responses for reasons that we simply cannot fathom. These seemingly minor quibbles about queries are very perplexing to student examiners and lead to interscorer unreliability among even experienced evaluators.

Although these issues in scoring responses may seem minor, with the reduction in consecutive items scored as zero needed for discontinuation, ambiguity in scoring may affect the overall scaled score. What if one of the items just given as examples were the last in the short discontinuation series? Scoring the item as a failure would end the subtest, whereas scoring it as a passed item would allow the examiner to continue and potentially increase the examinee's chances of passing more items, thus possibly increasing the scaled score for the subtest.

Cancellation
The WISC-IV (Wechsler, 2003) Cancellation subtest includes two tasks requiring speeded marking of animal pictures among various other pictures. The examinee is free to work in any direction(s) she or he might wish. The two tasks differ only in the arrangement of the pictures—aligned in straight rows or scattered randomly about the page—and examiners are encouraged to observe the examinee's approach to the task. In contrast, the WAIS-IV Cancellation subtest has two tasks that appear to be very similar to each other, and a left-to-right progression with no going back is strictly enforced. The rationale for these changes eludes us.

Interpretation

The interpretation process has been helped by some changes on the WAIS-IV but hindered by others. Next we discuss some of the challenges: the paucity of interpretive materials, not enough information about including supplementary subtests in interpretation, missing data for Cognitive Proficiency Index (CPI) calculations, and a lack of adequate CHC structure and taxonomy.

Paucity of Interpretive Materials: New Tests and New Procedures but an Apparent Lack of Any Interpretive Information to Aid Examiners Unfamiliar With the Tasks

Although the Wechsler scales have been prominent in cognitive assessments for years and have extensive research backing, the inclusion on the WAIS-IV of new subtests (Visual Puzzles, Figure Weights, and Cancellation) has left examiners with new interpretive possibilities. Unfortunately, the *WAIS-IV Interpretive Manual* lacks explanations or examples of just how an examiner might interpret WAIS-IV results. For example, what would be the correct interpretation for or implications of a significant difference between the Block Design and Visual Puzzles subtests or differences between the three aspects of the Digit Span subtest (DSF, DSB, and DSS)? Appendixes B and C of the *Administration and Scoring Manual* (Wechsler, 2008, pp. 229–253) provide useful normative data but no information about the implications of those data. Canivez (2010), in his review of the WAIS-IV, specifically noted "the absence of critical analyses and data to aid the clinician in adequately determining how best to interpret the different available scores." Loring and Bauer (2010) caution, among other things, that the VCI and PRI scales are not equivalent in content to the WAIS-III VIQ and PIQ: "WAIS-IV composite scores reflect more narrow and, in the case of the Verbal Comprehension Index (VCI) and Perceptual Reasoning Index (PRI), less neurologically sensitive measures than VIQ or PIQ to brain impairment, at least on the context of nonfocal brain disease" (p. 686).

The Pearson Assessment website Support and Resources Home Sample and Technical Reports pages (2009a, 2009b) provides one sample WAIS-IV/WMS-IV report at http://www.pearsonassessments.com/NR/rdonlyres/96186F86-E497-412C-B1A0-34945C06D10B/0/WAISIV_WMSIV_Writer_Report_21yrMale.pdf.

Pearson Assessment now offers a WAIS-IV supplementary instrument: *Advanced Clinical Solutions for the WAIS-IV and WMS-IV* (Wechsler, 2009) with new scores, new tests, and demographically adjusted norms. The interpretive scope of the WAIS-IV is considerably expanded, at the cost of another purchase by the examiner.

Determining S and W Based on Only the Core Subtests

The *Administration and Scoring Manual* (Wechsler, 2008, p. 239, Table B.5) provides examiners with critical values that can be used to determine if a subtest differs significantly from the overall mean of 10 subtests or the mean of 3 Verbal Comprehension or of 3 Perceptual Reasoning subtests. Unfortunately, this information, typically used to determine strengths and weaknesses, is incomplete. If an examiner administers the supplemental subtests (e.g., administering all 15 subtests) to gain additional information about the person, the *Manual* provides no way of determining if those additional subtests differ significantly from the person's mean subtest score. This information could easily have been provided, as was done for the WISC-IV by Sattler and Dumont (2004, Table A-4, pp. 291–302).

GAI but No CPI in the Manual

The WAIS-IV *Technical and Interpretative Manual* (Psychological Corporation, 2008, pp. 165–183) provides examiners with information regarding the use of the General Ability Index (GAI). The GAI is derived from the three subtests that enter the VCI and the three subtests that enter the PRI. (The table of significant differences between FSIQ and GAI [Psychological Corporation, 2008, p. 170] has been corrected by Pearson Assessment [2009c, 2009d].) No information is provided in the *Manual* about how examiners might calculate a CPI, which would be derived from the two subtests that comprise the WMI and the two subtests that compose the PSI. Weiss et al. (2010, pp. 80–89) provide a clear discussion of GAI and CPI, norms for CPI scores, critical values for significant differences between CPI and GAI scores, and base rates for CPI-GAI differences for the total norming sample and for five selected levels of FSIQ. The four CPI subtests (Digit Span, Arithmetic, Symbol Search, and Coding) are not as highly correlated with verbal and nonverbal intelligence as are the six other Verbal and Perceptual subtests and load on independent factors in the four-factor solution of the WAIS-IV. [Weiss et al. (p. 81) very generously credit us (Dumont & Willis, 2001) with having "first suggested" "creating a new composite of WMI and PSI," but we were merely following in the footsteps of Kaufman's (1979a, 1994a) "Third Factor" and "SCAD," Kaufman and Lichtenberger's (1999) "SCALD," and the Freedom from Distractibility or Sequential Factor (Bannatyne, 1974; Cohen, 1959; Rugel, 1974a, 1974b)].

We wish that the publisher had included the CPI and CPI-GAI normative data in the *Manual*. It is annoying to have to purchase additional books to obtain basic normative data on an expensive test [although, of course, we cheerfully purchase books such as the one you are reading and Weiss et al. (2010) for interpretive information, guidelines, and insights].

Lichtenberger and Kaufman also provide information for the calculation and interpretation of the CPI in Chapter 5 of this volume. Estimates of overall abilities calculated in this way should always be clearly identified as GAI and CPI scores in both text and tables of reports. These scores must not be confused with the Full Scale IQ, although they may be more useful estimates of intellectual ability in some cases, for example, for some gifted children and for some children with relative weaknesses in working memory and/or processing speed. For the latter group, the GAI and CPI may help avoid Dumont and Willis's Mark Penalty (Willis & Dumont, 2002, pp. 131–132), the depression of a measure of intelligence by a low score on a measure of a student's specific weakness. Other children may score significantly higher on the WMI and PSI indices than on the VCI and PSI indices, which may mask important difficulties with conceptual thinking if the FSIQ is used without the GAI and CPI.

Lack of Adequate Cattell-Horn-Carroll Structure and Taxonomy

Cattell-Horn-Carroll (CHC) theory has become a common language—a periodic table of cognitive ability elements—for evaluators (e.g., Carroll, 1997; Horn & Blankson, 2005). CHC theory allows evaluators to compare and contrast different measures of cognitive ability and achievement for research and for the McGrew, Flanagan, and Ortiz Integrated Cross-Battery Assessment (e.g., Flanagan & McGrew, 1997; Flanagan et al., 2007; Flanagan et al., 2006).

Like most recently published tests of cognitive abilities, the WAIS-IV can be organized by CHC broad and narrow abilities. However, although the test acknowledges the historical changes in the conception of intelligence and the contributions made by the CHC taxonomy, the test does not explicitly utilize the CHC categories. It instead uses labels and groupings that, while based on current theoretical models and research results in cognition and neuroscience (see, e.g., Psychological Corporation, 2008, pp. 1–5, 17–20, 57–122), do not facilitate interpretation within the CHC Cross-Battery model (e.g., Flanagan & McGrew, 1997; Flanagan et al., 2006, 2007). This problem—for examiners who wish to use the CHC structure—is particularly evident with the Perceptual Reasoning Index. Although the technical *Manual* makes it clear that certain subtests were added to the new WAIS in order to enhance the measurement of specific domains (e.g., Visual Puzzles to enhance Visual Spatial abilities and Figure Weights to enhance Fluid Reasoning), the Perceptual Reasoning Index remains, within the CHC taxonomy, a mixed measure of both Visual Spatial

Reasoning (Gv) (Block Design and Visual Puzzles) and Fluid Reasoning (Gf) (Matrix Reasoning). Figure Weights remains a supplemental subtest that may, unfortunately, not be administered, leaving the examiner with only one measure of CHC Gf and a loss of potentially valuable information. We wish that the test had made Figure Weights a core subtest and then clearly divided the Perceptual Reasoning Index into two indices, Visual Spatial Thinking and Fluid Reasoning. This would have, in our opinion, increased the overall interpretability of the WAIS-IV within the CHC framework and avoided the need to estimate the individual domains of Gv and Gf.

Benson et al. (2010), in their independent examination of the WAIS-IV factor structure, suggest that the "Cattell-Horn-Carroll (CHC)-inspired structure provides a better description of test performance than the published scoring structure does." To aid the practitioners, formulae are provided for computing what they consider to be composites of Gv, Gf (with and without Arithmetic), and Gq. (In Chapter 5, Lichtenberger and Kaufman provide alternate models by which to interpret the WAIS-IV data that allows for a separate calculation of Gv and Gf factors.)

Similar issues are evident with the Working Memory Index. When the index is interpreted, care must be taken to analyze whether the two abilities being measured are different from each other, thus reducing the overall interpretability of the index. The availability on the Record Form of "Process" scaled scores for Digit Span Forward, Digit Span Backward, and Digit Span Sequencing; critical values and base rates for differences among those scaled scores; and base rates for the greatest number of digits recalled in each condition and the differences among those spans would all allow the examiner to take some of that necessary care. The *Administration and Scoring Manual* (Wechsler, 2008, Table B.3, p. 237) also provides critical values for differences among scaled scores for Digit Span, Arithmetic, and Letter-Number Sequencing and (Table B.4, p. 238) base rates for differences between Digit Span and Arithmetic.

Final Comment

Although we have identified some concerns with the new WAIS-IV, we definitely consider it to be a significant improvement over the WAIS-III and, on balance, find it to be a valuable instrument with significant strengths. Rapid Reference 9.1 provides a summary of the WAIS-IV's strengths and weaknesses.

≡ Rapid Reference 9.1

Summary of Strengths and Weaknesses of the WAIS-IV

Strengths	Weaknesses

Test Development

Strengths	Weaknesses
• Developed new subtests to improve measurement of fluid reasoning, working memory, and visual processing. • Simplified composition of the WAIS-IV indexes and better alignment with the WISC-IV. • Process scores and new subtests strengthen interpretation of specific cognitive skills.	• New Figure Weights subtest was not included as a Core PRI subtest.

Administration and Scoring

Strengths	Weaknesses
• Easier to administer because of fewer manipulatives. • Much more user-friendly Record Form. • Improvement in artwork and response forms. • Scoring rules generally clear and unequivocal. • Streamlined discontinuation rules.	• Ambiguity regarding some scoring criteria. • Annoying instructions on one subtest. • Some questionable scoring rules.

Reliability and Validity

Strengths	Weaknesses
• Generally strong reliability. • Generally strong validity evidence for cognitive assessment and prediction of achievement. • Validity demonstrated for 13 special groups.	• WIAT-II predicted achievement scores based on 93 high school students.

Standardization

Strengths	Weaknesses
• Normative sample meets or exceeds current psychometric practice. • Normative sample provides a trustworthy basis for an individual's scores. • Special consideration for increased prescription medication use in older adults and other confounding issues.	

Strengths	Weaknesses
Interpretation	
• Subtests and indices based on both theory and research in cognitive abilities.	• Paucity of interpretive materials.
• Alignment of the WAIS-IV into the four indexes.	• Substitution and prorating flexibility.
• Composition of the WAIS-IV components much easier to understand.	• Determination of Strengths and Weaknesses based on only the core subtests.
• Useful information on testing examinees who are deaf or hard of hearing.	• No information provided for calculation of a Cognitive Processing Index.
	• Lack of complete Cattell-Horn-Carroll structure and taxonomy for examiners who prefer that structure.

 TEST YOURSELF

1. **TRUE or FALSE? One of the weaknesses of the WAIS-IV is that the new battery barely resembles the WISC-IV in content or structure.**

2. **One notable strength of the WAIS-IV is its improved measurement of visual processing, working memory, and**
   a. Verbal comprehension
   b. Creativity
   c. Fluid reasoning
   d. Verbal expression
   e. Arithmetic skills

3. **TRUE or FALSE? A strength of the WAIS-IV is inclusion in the test manual of numerous validity studies with clinical samples.**

4. **TRUE or FALSE? An advantage of the WAIS-IV over previous Wechsler adult scales is easier administration because of fewer concrete materials to manipulate.**

5. **Strengths of the WAIS-IV include**
   a. Generally strong reliability
   b. A much more user-friendly Record Form

(continued)

c. A high-quality standardization sample
d. Subtests and indices guided by theory and research in cognitive abilities
e. All of the above

6. TRUE or FALSE? One weakness of the WAIS-IV is the paucity of interpretive materials provided in the manual.

Answers: 1. false; 2. c; 3. true; 4. true; 5. e; 6. true

Ten

ILLUSTRATIVE CASE REPORTS

This chapter includes the case studies of one adolescent and one adult who were referred for neuropsychological and psychological evaluation. The WAIS-IV profile of Laura O. was presented in Chapter 5 to exemplify how to progress through the steps of interpretation; here the culmination of her case is presented in the first case report. The second case report examines the profile of a 64-year-old male, Jim W., who was referred for the evaluation of possible dementia.

Chapters 1 through 9 of this book have reviewed the key features of the WAIS-IV and how to administer, score, and interpret the instrument. The goal of this chapter is to bring all of these other facets of the book together and illustrate how the WAIS-IV may be utilized as part of a comprehensive test battery. Specifically, the case reports demonstrate how hypotheses are cross-validated with behavioral observations, background information, and supplemental tests. Throughout the first case report, Rapid Reference boxes provide information on what data should be included in each section of the report; the Don't Forget box details the basic outline for the reports we present. Final portions of the reports demonstrate how to translate results of the tests into effective recommendations.

For all cases presented in this book, the names and other pertinent identifying information have been changed to protect confidentiality of clients.

DON'T FORGET

Outline of Report

1. Identifying Information
2. Reason for Referral
3. Background Information
4. Appearance and Behavioral Observations
5. Tests Administered
6. Test Results and Interpretations
7. Summary (or Summary and Conclusions; Summary and Diagnostic Impression)
8. Recommendations
9. Signature
10. Psychometric Summary of Scores

≡ Rapid Reference 10.1

Pertinent Information to Include in Identifying Information Section

- Name
- Date of birth
- Age
- Grade in school (if applicable)
- Date(s) of testing
- Date of report
- Examiner's name

  For all cases presented in this book, the names and other pertinent identifying information have been changed to protect confidentiality of clients.

CASE REPORT: LAURA O., AGE 17, IMPAIRED SOCIAL SKILLS, POOR MOTIVATION, AND WEAK ATTENTION ABILITIES

Reason for Evaluation

Laura O. is a 17-year-old young woman who lives with her parents and her sisters, ages 15 and 13. Laura attends the 12th grade at her local high school. Her parents are both physicians. This evaluation was initiated by her mother, Dr. O., because of concerns regarding Laura's impaired social skills, her lack of motivation in all areas, poor attention abilities, and her "sluggishness." The aim of this neuropsychological assessment is to assess Laura's neurocognitive and psychological functioning to determine whether any deficits in this regard are impairing her performance. Furthermore, appropriate academic modifications will be recommended, along with other necessary treatment recommendations.

Background Information

Developmental History and Health

Laura was raised in a small town in the southern United States. According to Dr. O., Laura is the product of a normal, full-term pregnancy. However, at 35 weeks' gestation, Dr. O. was involved in a severe car accident and was very seriously injured. Laura did not apparently sustain any damage during this accident. She was delivered 11 days after her due date via a normal labor and delivery. Laura weighed 7 lbs. 7 oz. at birth, and no health problems were reported. She was described as an easygoing baby who ate and slept well. All developmental milestones were reached within appropriate limits.

≡ Rapid Reference 10.2

Pertinent Information to Include in Reason for Referral Section of Report

A. Who referred the client:
  1. Name and position of referral source.
  2. Questions of referral source.
B. Specific symptoms and concerns:
  1. Summarize current behaviors and relevant past behaviors.
  2. List any separate concerns that the client has him-/herself.

≡ Rapid Reference 10.3

Pertinent Information to Include in Background Information

Present in paragraph form the information you have obtained from all sources, including referral source, client, family members, social worker, teachers, medical records, and so on. State pertinent information only, not needless details.

The following information may be included:

• Current family situation (spouse, children, siblings, etc.). NO gossip.
• Other symptoms
• Medical history (including emotional disorders)
• Developmental history
• Educational history
• Employment history
• Previous treatment (educational or psychological)
• New or recent developments. Include stressors.
• Review of collateral documents (past evaluations)

Dr. O. described Laura as having no sensory sensitivities but noted that Laura has a "strange gait when walking." Laura tends to be a healthy young woman who does not have many somatic complaints and sleeps well at night. No surgeries or hospitalizations were reported, and Laura has not had any head injuries, although she did suffer an abrasion on her head when a dresser fell on top of her as a toddler. Laura wears corrective lenses for a visual acuity deficit. No hearing problems were reported. She takes allergy medications and uses an inhaler as needed for mild reactive airway disease.

According to Dr. O., there is no reported paternal family history of any psychological or neurocognitive problems. A maternal uncle committed suicide and a maternal cousin is described as evidencing Asperger-like traits. No other notable maternal family history was reported.

Academic History

Laura attended a mother's day-out program twice a week from age 18 months, and she was cared for at home by her parents and nanny during the remainder of the week. When she transitioned to a half-day kindergarten program, no problems were noted. School records indicated that Laura never excelled academically but obtained a B average throughout elementary school, and generally she was able to complete her homework without any difficulty. During these years, Laura's teachers did not note any significant concerns about her academic or social functioning.

During her middle school years, her mother reported that Laura's sluggishness—her tendency to do as little as possible to get by—and obstinacy were more evident. These problems continued throughout high school. Her mother indicated that Laura also began to demonstrate some notable struggles with math and science, and she failed a state standardized math test three times. Tutoring through Kumon Math Center was ineffective, according to Laura and her parents. Although Laura had no problems learning to read, her comprehension has always been poor, and she has struggled to grasp more abstract concepts when reading. She is reluctant to read for pleasure. She does not have good note-taking skills and will sit patiently rewriting the text from a page rather than summarizing major points. However, Laura tends to be a good speller. Laura's school counselor indicated that

> Laura has always wanted to be a high-achieving student and has tried very hard to achieve her goals . . . unfortunately, many times her expectations do not match the outcome and when this happens she becomes depressed and loses concentration in her academics and has feelings of not being worthy. . . . She had the same types of experiences in extracurricular activities.

Despite her difficulties, Laura independently completed and submitted applications to four colleges. However, her parents have some concerns about Laura's abilities to live away from home, and Laura may take classes through a local community college after graduating high school.

Emotional and Social Development

Laura's parents described her as a young woman who is "reliant" and has a strong musical ability. In addition, they said, "she is not easily beaten down by life, despite encountering frequent rejection." Her counselor described Laura as "a very polite young lady" who is very personable. However, Dr. O. indicated that Laura has many difficulties, and she appears to her mother to be somewhat depressed. Laura's apparent "laziness and her reluctance to exert effort in any area" is of concern to her parents. Laura loves singing and is a talented piano player. However, her parents stated that she is inconsistent in terms of the effort she exerts in this regard and cannot motivate herself to practice her piano exercises. Her parents said that they are concerned because "she tends to lie about completing her homework and will do the bare minimum in order to get by." Laura also indicated to the examiner that she does tend to be lazy and that she often lies but "is working on this."

According to her parents, Laura tends to be socially awkward, and she has some notable difficulty maintaining friendships. She is often mistreated and teased by her peers, and she is not included in many social activities. She has an odd sense of humor and is a very concrete, literal thinker. Laura tends to be short-tempered with her sisters, who are described as high-achieving young women. Laura had a boyfriend for a period of time, but she terminated this relationship because of her discomfort with his public displays of affection. Her parents have set limits on the Internet access available to Laura after noting that she had made some inappropriate choices in this regard.

Her mother noted that Laura does not demonstrate good personal hygiene. She would rather lose privileges, such as her allowance or cell phone, than complete her chores (i.e., clean her room and bathroom). Her mother indicated further concern that Laura does not appear to learn from the consequences of her actions and "demonstrates a lack of realism in some regard."

Behavioral Observations

Laura presented as a polite and pleasant young woman. She appeared comfortable interacting with the examiner, and rapport was easily established. Laura was extremely verbal throughout the testing; however, at times she appeared to be verbally uninhibited and notably impulsive. Laura was never inappropriate in her behavior, but she clearly did not always pick up on social cues. Her mood and affect were normal. Laura did not appear reactive or notably sensitive to the nature of the tasks or the levels of difficulty of the tasks.

Laura was not noted to be distractible or inattentive. She did not seem to have difficulty with restlessness during the testing, although some impulsivity was evident. No problems with initiation and persistence were observed. Both Laura's receptive language and her expressive language appeared intact. However, she did

≡ Rapid Reference 10.4

Pertinent Information to Include in Appearance and Behavioral Characteristics

- Talk about significant patterns or themes you see going on during testing.
- Sequence information in order of importance rather than in order of occurrence. (Do not just do a chronological list.)
- Describe the behavioral referents to your hypotheses. (Use specific examples.)
- Describe what makes this client unique. (Paint a picture for the reader.)

Suggested areas to review: (Note only significant behavior.)

Appearance
- Size: height and weight
- Facial characteristics
- Grooming and cleanliness
- Posture
- Clothing style
- Maturity: Does the person look his or her age?

Behavior
- Speech articulation, language patterns
- Activity level (foot wiggling, excessive talking, nail biting, tension, etc.)
- Attention span/distractibility
- Cooperativeness or resistance
- Interest in doing well
- How does the individual go about solving problems? (Trial and error? Quickly or reflectively? Check answers?)
- Reactions to failure or challenge:
  - Does client continue to work until time is up?
  - Does client ask for direction or help?
  - Did failure reduce interest in the task or working on other tasks?
  - When frustrated, is the client aggressive or dependent?
- Attitude toward self:
  - Regards self with confidence? Superior attitude? Inadequate? Defeated?
  - How did client strive to get approval? Response to your praise of effort?

Validity of Test Results
- For example, state: "On the basis of John's above behaviors, the results of this assessment are considered a valid indication of his current level of cognitive and academic ability."
- Or if not, state why.

not always focus on the essential factors in a situation, and when giving a verbal answer to a question, she tended to overgeneralize or focus on less relevant details. As a result, her responses were often long-winded, somewhat confusing, and less meaningful than a more concise and integrated response might be. During informal discussion, Laura seemed to be reciting "the correct response" but did not demonstrate the associated affective import that would be expected.

Laura worked diligently throughout the testing and persevered with all tasks. On the basis of these behavior observations, this assessment appears to be a valid measure of Laura's functioning at this time.

Assessment Procedures

- Clinical interview with Laura and her parents
- Wechsler Adult Intelligence Scale—Fourth Edition (WAIS-IV)
- Wechsler Individual Achievement Test—Third Edition (WIAT-III)
- IVA + Plus Continuous Performance Test (IVA + Plus)
- The Beery-Buktenica Developmental Test of Visual-Motor Integration (Beery VMI)
- California Verbal Learning Test—Second Edition (CVLT-II)
- Delis-Kaplan Executive Function System (D-KEFS): Selected Subtests
- Wisconsin Card Sort Test-64 Computer Version 2 (WCST-64)
- Beck Youth Inventory—Second Edition (BYI)
- Millon Adolescent Clinical Inventory (MACI)
- Thematic Apperception Test (TAT): Selected Cards
- Gilliam Asperger's Disorder Scale (GADS)
- Clinical Assessment of Interpersonal Relationships (CAIR)
- Adaptive Behavior Assessment System—Second Edition (ABAS-II)
- Achenbach Youth Self Report (YSR)
- Conners Comprehensive Behavior Rating Scales—Parent & Teacher Forms
- Conners Third Edition: Self Report & Parent Short Forms

Test Results

Intellectual Abilities

In order to assess Laura's intellectual ability, she was administered the *Wechsler Adult Intelligence Scale—Fourth Edition* (WAIS-IV), which is an individually administered test of an individual's intellectual ability and cognitive strengths and

≡ Rapid Reference 10.5

Pertinent Information to Include in Test Results and Interpretation

- Use paragraph form.
- Put numbers in this section, including IQs and index scores with confidence intervals and percentile ranks. When discussing performance on subtests, use *percentile ranks*. (Most people are not familiar with a mean of 10 and standard deviation of 3.) Do *not* include Raw Scores.
- *Tie in behaviors* with results to serve as logical explanations or reminders wherever appropriate.
- With more than one test, *find similarities* in performances and differences (discrepancies) and try to hypothesize if you have enough information to do so.
- Support hypotheses with *multiple sources* of data, including observed behaviors.
- Do not contradict yourself.
- Be sure that you are *describing the subtests*, not just naming them. Remember, the reader has no idea what "Picture Completion" means.
- Describe the underlying abilities that the task is tapping.
- Talk about the *person's abilities*, not the test.
- Be *straightforward* in your writing, not too literary; do not use metaphors.

weaknesses (see Table 10.1 for her score summary). This test yields five composite scores: Verbal Comprehension Index, Perceptual Reasoning Index, Working Memory Index, Processing Speed Index, and Full Scale IQ. In addition, this test also yields a General Ability Index, which is less sensitive to the influence of working memory and processing speed. Laura's general cognitive ability is in the Average Range/Within Normal Limits, as indicated by both her Full Scale IQ (FSIQ standard score of 89; 78–88 with 90% confidence; 13th percentile) and her General Ability Index (GAI standard score of 86; 82–93 with 90% confidence; 18th percentile). However, there are notable strengths and weaknesses in her cognitive profile, so it is informative to understand these specific abilities in addition to her global measures of functioning.

Laura's verbal reasoning abilities, as measured by the Verbal Comprehension Index, are in the Average range and above those of approximately 39% of her peers (VCI = 96). The Verbal Comprehension Index is designed to measure verbal reasoning and concept formation. When examining clinical clusters of scores within the Verbal Comprehension scale, Laura's consistent abilities in this domain are evident. For example, her facility with words and her

Table 10.1. Psychometric Summary of WAIS-IV Profile for Laura O

Index/IQ Subtest	Score	90% Confidence Interval	Percentile Rank	Descriptive Category
Verbal Comprehension	96	91–101	39	Average Range/Within Normal Limits
Similarities	9		37	
Vocabulary	11		63	
Information	8		25	
(Comprehension)	10		50	*Does not contribute to Index or IQ*
Perceptual Reasoning	79	74–84	8	Below Average/Normative Weakness
Block Design	5		5	
Matrix Reasoning	7		16	
Visual Puzzles	7		16	
(Figure Weights)	4		2	*Does not contribute to Index or IQ*
(Picture Completion)	6		9	*Does not contribute to Index or IQ*
Working Memory	95	90–100	37	Average Range/Within Normal Limits
Digit Span	11		63	
Arithmetic	7		16	
(Letter-Number Sequencing)	4		2	*Does not contribute to Index or IQ*
Processing Speed	97	92–102	42	Average Range/Within Normal Limits
Symbol Search	10		50	
Coding	9		37	
(Cancellation)	9		37	*Does not contribute to Index or IQ*
Full Scale IQ	83	78–88	13	Below Average/Normative Weakness
GAI	86	82–93	18	Average Range/Within Normal Limits

(continued)

Table 10.1. (continued)

Index/IQ Subtest	Score	90% Confidence Interval	Percentile Rank	Descriptive Category
CPI	96	90–102	39	Average Range/Within Normal Limits
Clinical Cluster				
Verbal Fluid Reasoning	97	91–104	42	Average Range/Within Normal Limits
Lexical Knowledge	100	95–105	50	Average Range/Within Normal Limits
General Information	94	89–100	34	Average Range/Within Normal Limits
Long-Term Memory	97	92–102	42	Average Range/Within Normal Limits
Short-Term Memory	86	81–93	18	Average Range/Within Normal Limits
Fluid Reasoning	75	71–83	5	Below Average/Normative Weakness
Visual Processing	78	73–86	7	Below Average/Normative Weakness

knowledge of factual information are equally well developed and both in the Average Range/Within Normal Limits. These similar skills were evident from her Lexical Knowledge Cluster (50th percentile) and her General Information Cluster (34th percentile). Additionally, her ability to reason with verbal information was comparable to her long-term memory of verbally encoded information. Her skills in these domains were also in the Average range (both the Verbal Fluid Reasoning Cluster and Long-Term Memory Cluster were in the 42nd percentile).

Similar to her Average skills noted on the Verbal Comprehension scale of the WAIS-IV, Laura's expressive language ability was intact on a separate measure of verbal fluency. Both her semantic and phonemic fluency were Average to High Average (63rd and 75th percentiles, respectively). However, Laura's basic word retrieval was mildly impaired on a measure of dysnomia.

In contrast to her Average Range abilities in the areas of verbal reasoning, lexical knowledge, general information, and verbal fluency, Laura's nonverbal reasoning abilities are in the Below Average Range. This weaker area of ability was evident from her score on the Perceptual Reasoning Index that was above those of only 8% of her peers (PRI standard score of 79). Compared to her other abilities, her equally impaired visual processing and nonverbal fluid reasoning skills are personal weaknesses and are also Normative Weaknesses when compared with others her age. These deficits were noted from her Fluid Reasoning Cluster (5th percentile) and her Visual Processing Cluster (7th percentile), which were both Below Average and considered Normative Weaknesses. Her ability to reason *verbally* is notably stronger than her ability to reason with *visual* material. In fact, the difference between her Verbal Fluid Reasoning Cluster (42nd percentile) and her Fluid Reasoning Cluster (5th percentile) is uncommonly large and occurs less than 10% of the time in the normative population.

Laura's impaired nonverbal problem-solving and spatial planning abilities were further supported by her Below Average performance on a challenging executive-function task requiring her to build a designated tower in the fewest number of moves possible by moving disks of varying size (9th percentile). Also consistent with her areas of personal weakness on the WAIS-IV Perceptual Reasoning scale was her visual-motor integration ability. When required to copy a series of geometric figures with paper and pencil, Laura's skills were in the Below Average range (10th percentile on the Developmental Test of Visual Motor Integration). Overall, Laura's notable personal and normative weaknesses in the areas of visual processing and nonverbal fluid reasoning indicate that she has a disorder in these basic psychological processes, which is a finding that should play an essential role in developing specialized interventions.

Despite her deficits in visual processing and nonverbal fluid reasoning, Laura demonstrated Average ability to quickly process simple or routine visual material without making errors (Processing Speed Index = 97; 42nd percentile). Laura's difficulties with visual stimuli may be mitigated when the stimuli are less spatially complex or when a lower level of cognitive processing is demanded, such as on the WAIS-IV Processing Speed tasks.

Laura also demonstrated Average Range abilities in her short-term memory. This Within Normal Limits performance was evident from her Working Memory Index standard score of 95 (37th percentile). Although Laura scored in the Average range on a measure of digit span recall, reversal, and sequencing (63rd percentile) and on a measure of her ability to mentally solve a series of arithmetic problems (16th percentile), she struggled on a supplementary task that required her to sequence a string of letters and numbers (2nd percentile).

A higher level of attention and cognitive shifting are needed on the letter-number sequencing task, which may have caused the inconsistency in her performance on these memory tasks.

Laura's memory skills were further assessed with the *California Verbal Learning Test—Second Edition* (CVLT-II) and the *Wechsler Memory Scale—Fourth Edition* (WMS-IV). She demonstrated intact performance on a demanding task of verbal list-learning memory. Her overall immediate recall was generally Average, and her short delay and long delay free and cued recall was within the normal range. Her number of repetition errors and intrusion errors was within normal limits. Laura's performance was intact on recognition testing. Similarly, her performance was intact on a measure assessing memory for organized verbal material (63rd percentile on both immediate and delayed recall trials). Consistent with her verbal memory skills, on a simple measure of visual recall, Laura demonstrated Average performance both on immediate and on delayed recall trials (50th and 63rd percentiles, respectively).

Attention and Executive Functioning

Sustained Visual and Auditory Attention. Laura's performance on WAIS-IV and WMS-IV tests of memory required sustained attention and concentration for successful completion. Her sustained attention was further assessed by means of the IVA + Plus Continuous Performance Test (IVA + Plus). This task is intended to be mildly boring and demanding of sustained attention over a 13-minute period of time. On this task Laura was required to respond to target stimuli (the number "1" presented in either an auditory or visual format on the computer) and refrain from responding to nontarget stimuli (the number "2" presented in the same formats). A diagnosis of Attention-Deficit/Hyperactivity Disorder, Predominantly Hyperactive-Impulsive Type was supported by the IVA + Plus test data. Laura was mildly impaired in her ability to inhibit responses to nontarget auditory stimuli; she exhibited some problems with auditory response control. In addition, Laura's Visual Prudence was extremely impaired. That is, Laura clicked impulsively numerous times to the nontarget visual stimuli. This weakness in response control suggests that Laura is likely to be overreactive and easily distracted in her daily life by any changes in her visual environment. Problems were noted in impulse control, particularly under high-demand conditions. Laura was intact in her ability to be consistent in her responses to both visual and auditory stimuli. Her stamina was strong, and her response time to auditory stimuli became faster over the course of the test. She was also able to maintain her mental processing speed in the visual domain during the test.

Laura did not show any problems with her general auditory and visual attentional functioning under low-demand or high-demand conditions. However, her Auditory Focus fell in the moderately to severely impaired range. At times Laura showed difficulty due to delays in her response to auditory test stimuli. Her pattern of responding indicated that her attention frequently "drifted off." Similarly, Laura's Visual Focus fell in the slightly impaired range. Most of the time she was able to process and stay focused on visual stimuli. Occasionally, momentary lapses in visual response times were found. These lapses in visual processing may be caused by slight fatigue or by her preoccupation with distracting thoughts.

Laura did not show any problems with her overall auditory or visual processing speed. Her recognition reaction time falls within the Average range. Similarly, she demonstrated no relative difference between her visual and auditory mental processing speeds. Thus, she has a balanced ability to process information in these two different sensory modalities. Laura's recognition response time to stimuli under low-demand conditions was much quicker than it was under high-demand conditions. In other words, her response times are clearly slower when she is required to make rapid, repeated responses.

In addition to the IVA, Laura and her parents completed various rating scales to give more information about Laura's attentional functioning. Laura's parents indicated some concerns regarding her attentional functioning, and she was rated as demonstrating mild to moderate deficits with inattention, hyperactivity, and impulsivity. In contrast, Laura described herself as functioning within the normal range on measures of attention and hyperactivity/impulsivity.

Cognitive Flexibility. Laura was administered the Trails, Verbal Fluency, Design Fluency, and Color-Word subtests from the D-KEFS in order to assess her cognitive flexibility. Notable variability in her performances was observed. Laura struggled on the Trails measure requiring her to shift between connecting numbers and letters in sequence (0.1 percentile). This indicates a deficit in cognitive flexibility on nonverbal tasks, although some definite problems with inhibition did impair Laura's performance on this task (i.e., she was distracted by two letters or two numbers close together). In contrast, Laura did not evidence this deficit on the Design Fluency task, and her nonverbal cognitive flexibility was intact on this measure (63rd percentile). Similarly, Laura's verbal fluency was also intact (37th–50th percentile). However, mild impairment in Laura's inhibition and cognitive flexibility were evident on the Color-Word task (16th–25th percentile).

Concept Formation. Laura's verbal-semantic and visual-perceptual concept formation skills were assessed by means of the D-KEFS Sorting Test. Her overall scores were in the Average range (50th percentile) on measures of free sorting, indicating an intact ability to perceive and form conceptual relationships and to express these relationships in abstract terms. However, Laura struggled on the component of this subtest requiring her to recognize those sorts made by the examiner (16th percentile). Frequently, people who demonstrate this deficit are especially vulnerable to distraction and become mentally derailed by the sorts generated by the examiner.

Laura demonstrated intact performance on a computerized assessment of her concept formation skills (WCST-64; 47th percentile), reflecting intact conceptual reasoning.

Academic Skills

In addition to her cognitive and neuropsychological abilities, Laura's academic skills were measured with the *Wechsler Individual Achievement Test—Third Edition* (WIAT-III). Laura's overall academic skills were in the Average range.

Reading. Laura presented consistent skills on different aspects of reading. Her strongest performance was on tasks that assessed her capability to correctly apply phonetic decoding rules when reading a series of nonsense words (79th percentile). Similarly, Laura scored in the High Average range on tasks that assessed her capability to read sentences and paragraphs and answer questions about what was read (77th percentile). Her reading speed was normal. She had Average performance on tasks that required her to correctly read a series of printed words (61st percentile).

Mathematics. Laura's skills in mathematics varied slightly. She performed in the Average range on tasks that evaluated her ability to add, subtract, multiply, and divide one- to three-digit numbers, fractions, and decimals, and to solve simple linear equations (53rd percentile). In contrast, Laura's performance was Low Average on tasks that required her to understand number, consumer math concepts, geometric measurement, basic graphs, and solve single-step and multistep word problems (18th percentile). When considering the 90% confidence interval, her Mathematical Reasoning abilities fall between the Below Average and Average range. The relative difficulty that Laura had on the WIAT-III Mathematical Reasoning is consistent with her academic history (which includes failing math tests) as well as her cognitive profile (which showed she has a disorder in these basic psychological processes of fluid reasoning). Taken together, these results indicate that she has a learning disorder in the area of mathematics reasoning.

Written Language. On tasks that required her to correctly spell verbally presented words, Laura performed in the Average range. Her skills in this area exceed those of approximately 73% of students her age. Laura also demonstrated Average performance on tasks that required her to generate words within a category, generate sentences to describe visual cues, combine sentences, and compose an organized, persuasive essay on a named topic (45th percentile).

Emotional Functioning

On various rating scales, Laura's parents rated Laura as demonstrating notable emotional distress and very significant social problems. On the GADS, Laura was rated by her parents as being borderline for a diagnosis of Asperger's disorder. In contrast, Laura did not rate herself as having difficulties in any area.

Laura's parents indicated some concerns regarding her adaptive functioning. Adaptive skills are practical everyday skills required to function and meet environmental demands, including effectively taking care of oneself and interacting with other people. The categories of adaptive behaviors assessed by the ABAS-II include Conceptual (communication and academic skills), Social (interpersonal and social competence skills), and Practical (independent living and daily living skills). Laura's parents rated her as demonstrating Below Average adaptive functioning overall. Laura's Conceptual Skills were rated as Below Average, and her Social Skills were rated as Extremely Low. Her Practical Skills were rated as Average. Laura was rated by her parents as demonstrating relative weaknesses in the "Social" and "Self-Care" skill areas. She was rated as demonstrating a strength in "Community Use" and "Health and Safety."

Family and Peer Relationships. When asked to draw a picture of herself with her family doing something together, Laura drew her family in the swimming pool. She drew herself as significantly smaller than her siblings, almost in an infantile manner, and she was inserted close to her mother in the picture. Laura described herself as a "mama's girl" and indicated that "I have to be close to my mother, I love my mom so much, she is my best friend, she has done so much for me." On other tests, Laura indicated a desire to spend more time alone with her mother and not to share her as much with her siblings. However, on the TAT, Laura told a story about a young woman who had different aspirations from her family, and the mother in the story asked, "Why isn't my daughter like me or the family?" Therefore, it is likely that although Laura is clearly seeking intense closeness with her mother, she continues to see herself as dissimilar from the other family members.

On the CAIR, Laura rated her relationship with her mother as a strength and rated her relationship with her father as Average. Laura further noted close

☰ Rapid Reference 10.6

Pertinent Information to Include in Summary and Diagnostic Impressions

- Summary information should already be stated earlier in the body of the report.
- Include summary of referral, key background, or behavioral observation points.
- Summarize the most important interpretations of global scores and strengths and weaknesses.
- Defend your diagnosis if one is made.

relationships with her sisters, along with close friendships with peers. She rated her relationships with her female peers and her teachers as Average. However, she rated her relationships with male peers as a weakness.

Personality Profile. Laura identified "schoolwork" as the problem that is troubling her the most. A tendency toward avoiding self-disclosure is evident in her response style. There is the likelihood of deficits in introspectiveness and psychological mindedness. What is most noticeable about Laura is her anxious conformity to the expectations of others, particularly family and authority, her overcontrol of emerging impulses, and her defensiveness about admitting psychological problems. Beneath her controlled facade and pseudo-poise are marked feelings of personal insecurity that are evident in a tendency to downgrade herself and to keep a comfortable emotional distance from others and an anticipation of rejection if she acts inappropriately. Her major defense against such events is an excessive conformity and the inhibition of any affect that might evoke ridicule or contempt from others. Notable also is her focus on minor irrelevancies that distract her attention from growing sexual feelings. Her facade of conformity may also hide repressed resentments felt toward those who may have humiliated her in the past. However, surges of anger will only rarely break through the surface restraint.

Laura's self-doubts and low self-esteem may have led her to seek the quiet conformity of a supportive institution such as her church or other social or school organizations. In this way, she hopes to gain a measure of security and may be able to identify with others, especially those in authority, whose actions cannot possibly be met with disfavor. A consistent and rigid behavioral pattern is maintained, in which all signs of autonomy are restrained and conformity to the rules of others is emphasized.

Summary

Laura is a 17-year-old girl who was referred for a neuropsychological evaluation because of difficulties with motivation, attention, and social skills. Her behavior during the testing revealed a tendency to be verbally uninhibited and impulsive as well as somewhat insensitive to social cues. Laura's general cognitive ability was in the Average range (WAIS-IV FSIQ of 89). However, there were notable areas of weakness in addition to her many cognitive abilities that were Within Normal Limits. Laura's cognitive abilities that were intact and in the Average range included verbal reasoning, lexical knowledge, general information, verbal fluency, short-term memory (verbal and visual), and processing speed. In contrast, Laura had personal and normative weaknesses in visual processing and nonverbal fluid reasoning, which indicate that she has a disorder in these basic psychological processes (evident from her WAIS-IV Perceptual Reasoning Index—8th percentile; VMI—10th percentile; and Tower Test—9th percentile).

On academic testing, Laura demonstrated a relative weakness in her math reasoning skills (WIAT-III Math Problem Solving score of 86). This difficulty with math reasoning is consistent with her educational history as well as her disorder in the basic psychological process of fluid reasoning. In contrast, her other academic abilities were in the Average range. As a whole, these academic and cognitive test results, paired with her academic history, indicate that she has a learning disorder in the area of mathematics reasoning.

Laura demonstrated variable performances on measures of attention and executive functioning. On a continuous performance test, Laura's response control was poor and was consistent with impaired inhibition noted on other measures. Her performance indicated a diagnosis of ADHD, Predominately Hyperactive-Impulsive Type. Parent rating scales further confirmed problems in this regard. Although Laura did not rate herself as demonstrating problems with response control, she did indicate on numerous occasions during informal conversation that she fails to think before she acts and speaks, and she tends to be highly impulsive. Laura demonstrated very impaired cognitive flexibility on one measure of higher-level cognitive functioning. In addition, her spatial planning and problem solving was mildly impaired on another measure.

Laura's neuropsychological profile is consistent with a nonverbal learning disability. This is a disorder in which the core deficit resides in the capacity to process nonlinguistic perceptual information and is primarily a right-hemisphere disorder. The Personal Weakness and Normative Weakness on her WAIS-IV

Perceptual Reasoning Index is suggestive of this diagnosis when coupled with other factors. Specifically, Laura's difficulties with visual-spatial organization, her variable nonverbal problem solving, attentional problems, and variable executive functions, along with her history of social-emotional difficulties, are consistent with a nonverbal learning disability.

From a psychological perspective, it is apparent that Laura is functioning below age expectancy. She appears to be struggling to separate from her mother and has a wish to be in the infantile stage, bound closely with her mother. Laura fears criticism and derogation and is inclined toward self-blame and self-punishment. There is a hesitation about expressing emotions, particularly hostility or sexuality. Laura demonstrates excessive conformity and the inhibition of any affect that might evoke rejection. Strong defensiveness, along with guilt and self-condemnation, appear to be prominent.

Diagnostic Impressions

314.01 Attention-Deficit/Hyperactivity Disorder, Predominantly Hyper-active-Impulsive Type

315.9 Learning Disability Not Otherwise Specified (i.e., Nonverbal Learning Disability)

315.1 Mathematics Disorder

V313.82 Identity Problem

Recommendations

As a result of Laura's diagnosis of ADHD, nonverbal learning disability, and a mathematics disorder, she would benefit from some interventions in a college setting. It is strongly recommended that Laura seek out services through the learning center at any college she might attend and request these modifications:

- Laura will benefit from extended time on all written tests.
- *Preferential seating* in all classes is strongly recommended. Whenever possible, minimize distractions in Laura's study area.
- *Reduce the amount of note taking required.* It is likely that Laura will benefit from having *instructor handouts* and *lecture outlines* available before the lecture for her to review. She would benefit from a *note taker.*
- *A private room for testing* should be available upon request.

- *A certified educational consultant* might be helpful in terms of assisting Laura in making appropriate choices regarding college choices. I am happy to provide a referral in this regard.

Stimulant medication to address symptoms of ADHD should be considered. In addition, Laura would clearly benefit from **psychotherapy** in order to help foster her emotional growth. I am happy to make an appropriate recommendation upon request.

Books on nonverbal-learning-disabled youth and appropriate interventions might be helpful for Laura and her parents to read, as well as those that provide academic support or tutoring. For example, *Nonverbal Learning Disabilities: A Clinical Perspective* by Joseph Palombo and *Syndrome of Nonverbal Learning Disabilities: Neurodevelopmental Manifestations* by Byron P. Rourke.

Michelle Lurie, PsyD
Clinical Neuropsychologist

Table 10.2. Psychometric Summary of Additional Tests for Laura O

Wechsler Memory Scale—Fourth Edition
(WMS-IV Selected Subtests)

Subtest	Scaled Score	Percentile Rank
Logical Memory I	11	63
Logical Memory II	11	63
Designs I	10	50
Designs II	11	63

Beery-Buktenica Developmental Test of Visual-Motor Integration (VMI)

Standard Scores	Percentile
81	10

Delis-Kaplan Executive Function System (D-KEFS)

Trail Making Test	Primary Measure: Completion Times	Scaled Score	Percentile Rank
	Visual Scanning	7	16
	Number Sequencing	11	63

(continued)

Table 10.2. *Continued*

Trail Making Test	Primary Measure: Completion Times	Scaled Score	Percentile Rank
	Letter Sequencing	8	25
	Number-Letter Switching	1	0.1
Verbal Fluency	**Primary Measure**	**Scaled Score**	**Percentile Rank**
	Letter Fluency	12	75
	Category Fluency	11	63
	Category Switching: Responses	9	37
	Category Switching: Accuracy	10	50
Design Fluency	**Primary Measure**	**Scaled Score**	**Percentile Rank**
	Filled Dots: Total Correct	11	63
Design Fluency	**Primary Measure**	**Scaled Score**	**Percentile Rank**
	Empty Dots Only: Correct	10	50
	Switching: Total	11	63
Color-Word Interference Test	**Primary Measures: Completion Times**	**Scaled Score**	**Percentile Rank**
	Color Naming	10	50
	Word Reading	11	63
	Inhibition	8	25
	Inhibition/Switching	7	16
Sorting Test	**Primary Measures: Completion Times**	**Scaled Score**	**Percentile Rank**
	Confirmed Correct Sorts	10	50
	Free Sorting Description Score	10	50
	Sort Recognition Description Score	7	16
Tower Test	**Primary Measures**	**Scaled Score**	**Percentile Rank**
	Total Achievement Score	6	9

Gilliam Asperger's Disorder Scale (GADS)

Subscale	Scaled Score	Probability of Asperger's Disorder
Social Interaction	4	
Restricted Patterns of Behavior	6	
Cognitive Patterns	6	
Pragmatic Skills	10	
Asperger's Disorder Quotient	77	**Borderline**

Adaptive Behavior Assessment System—Second Edition (ABAS-II)

Composite	Composite Score	Percentile Rank	Qualitative Range
GAC	82	12	Below Average
Conceptual	85	16	Below Average
Social	68	2	Extremely Low
Practical	90	25	Average

Wisconsin Card Sort Test-64 Computer Version 2

WCST Scores	Standard Scores	Percentile
Perseverative Errors	99	47

CASE REPORT: JIM W., AGE 64, POSSIBLE DEMENTIA

Reason for Referral

Mr. W. has a history of memory problems that began 37 years ago following a motorcycle accident that resulted in a severe coma. He also reported increased depression and irritability within the last year following an accident at work. He was referred for neuropsychological evaluation in order to assess his current level of cognitive and personality functioning, to assist in making a diagnosis, and to make recommendations regarding his treatment needs. Specifically, assessing for the presence of dementia is of concern.

CAUTION

Common Errors to Avoid in Report Writing

- Inappropriate detail
- Unnecessary jargon or technical terms
- Vague language
- Abstract statements
- Not supporting hypotheses with adequate data
- Gross generalizations from isolated information
- Inserting value judgments
- Discussing the test rather than the person's abilities
- Poor grammar
- Presenting behaviors or test scores without interpreting them
- Failure to adequately address reasons for referral
- Failure to provide confidence intervals or otherwise denote that all obtained test scores include a band of error
- Giving test results prematurely (e.g., in the section on "Appearance and Behavioral Characteristics")

Background Information

Mr. W. is a married, Caucasian male. He completed eight years of education and later earned his high school diploma. He is currently employed as a janitor and lives with his wife of 40 years, and has two adult children. English is his primary language, and he is right-handed.

Mr. W. was born and raised in an intact family on the East Coast. To his knowledge, there were no complications with his mother's pregnancy, labor, or delivery. He denied any history of developmental, emotional, or behavioral problems while growing up. Both his parents had a sixth-grade education. His father worked as a carpenter and died from a stroke. His mother worked as a waitress and died from throat cancer. He has three siblings who live out of state. He denied that his siblings have any significant health issues.

In his educational history, Mr. W. identified math as his best subject and reading and spelling as his worst. He noted that he had difficulty learning to read, that he had to repeat third grade, and that he was placed in a special program to help him learn to read in ninth grade. He dropped out of high school and enlisted in the Marine Corps at the age of 16. However, he indicated that later he attended an adult education program through the Veteran's Association and received his high school diploma.

In a review of his employment history, Mr. W. stated that he served more than 10 years in the Marine Corps. However, following his accident, he was no longer able to perform his duties effectively and was honorably discharged as a result of his disability. He then worked as a forklift operator for 28 years and has worked part time as a janitor for the last 2 years.

Medical History

According to Mr. W., he was involved in a motorcycle accident 37 years ago in which he apparently drove off the road and may have then hit his head on a rock. He stated that he does not remember the incident but that he has been told that someone found him the next morning and he was then taken to the hospital. Mrs. W. confirmed that her husband was comatose for two weeks, following which he was "semiconscious" for a period of time. She noted that he continued to be "not coherent and confused" for approximately six months and that he remained in the hospital for one year. Mr. W. stated that he was subsequently diagnosed with "organic brain syndrome secondary to trauma" but that he has never undergone a neuropsychological evaluation.

More recently, Mr. W. reported being involved in an accident at work last summer that caused serious injury to his back, along with his right knee and foot. His injury required surgery to place a steel rod in his back, and he has had two surgeries on his right foot. Mr. W. noted that he is taking Hydrocodone 5/500 mg and Percocet 5 mg for back pain as well as vitamin supplements. He reported that since the injury, he has been increasingly depressed and irritable, indicating that he can become very angry and explosive. Mrs. W. also noted that her husband experiences "stress from the injury on the job." Other than these injuries and medical issues in his adult history, Mr. W. reported that he had measles as a child and that he has had pneumonia.

A thorough review of neuropsychological symptoms was conducted with Mr. W. during his interview:

Sensory-Perceptual. Mr. W. reported that he wears glasses for both reading and distance. He also reported experiencing a change in his sense of taste and being overly sensitive to noise since his head injury. As a result of his injury last year, he indicated that he experiences pain in his back, knee, and foot, along with numbness, loss of feeling, and the feeling of pins and needles in his foot. He also noted that he experienced problems with loss of vision, blurred and double vision, and seeing unusual things following the first accident. He denied experiencing these problems more recently. He reported having "infrequent" headaches but denied having any other sensory-perceptual difficulties or pain-related problems.

Cognition-Thinking. Mr. W. and his wife reported that he experiences numerous cognitive difficulties. These difficulties include trouble with common sense, problem solving, judgment, mathematics, and thinking quickly. Also identified were difficulties concentrating, being easily distracted, inconsistent performance on tasks, disorganization, and experiencing periods where he loses time. Mr. W. also reported being inflexible, getting stuck on a problem, and having a hard time doing more than one thing at a time, while also finding it hard to stay on task.

Communication. Mr. W. reported experiencing several problems related to written and verbal communication. He indicated that he had difficulties with spelling, writing, and reading. He also reported having trouble understanding others and following the story in a movie or television show, as well as having difficulty remembering words and naming common objects. Fluctuations in talkativeness are also reported, noting both times of talking too much as well as talking too little.

Memory. The patient reported having numerous problems with his memory, including both short- and long-term memory. These problems include forgetting what he is doing, where he is, people's names and faces, and recent events. He also noted difficulty learning new things, being told that he repeats himself, memory loss around the time of his accident, and forgetting things from long ago. He commented, "My memory's been shot for a long time."

Motor Functioning. Mr. W. reported that he has difficulties with balance and coordination, muscle weakness, and trouble walking because of his accident and the resulting injuries from last year. He denied experiencing any such difficulties before his accident or experiencing any other problems with motor functioning.

Social. Mr. W. and his wife reported that he experiences difficulties in most interpersonal relationships, including with his wife, children, friends, coworkers, and employer. They also reported that he lacks tact and can be insensitive and aggressive. He reported a tendency to isolate himself at times. Mrs. W. stated that her husband became "a jerk and hotheaded" following the accident. She reported that he has frequent problems with anger and irritability, noting that there was frequent yelling in their relationship and that more recently her husband was unable to keep a job because of his argumentativeness and yelling.

Psychological. Mr. W. reported having symptoms of depression and anxiety. He also admitted experiencing mood swings, irritability, restlessness and agitation, anger outbursts, paranoia, intrusive thoughts, and difficulty handling stress. He noted that he can be impatient and impulsive but also experiences a lack of energy and passivity at times. Changes in sleep, appetite, weight, and sex drive were also reported.

Adaptive Behavior. Currently, Mr. W. is employed as a janitor. He reported that his wife does most of the work around the house (e.g., preparing meals, cleaning, yardwork, and paying bills), but that he takes out the trash and also collects cans and bottles for recycling as a hobby. He reported watching approximately three hours of television per day. He visits with friends and family and has people over to visit. However, his wife indicated that Mr. W. has a general lack of planning and engagement in leisure activities, particularly those of a social nature. She also noted that he has a "lack of social awareness of others' needs and appropriate social reciprocity." Conversely, Mr. W. denied any problems with self-care and is able to drive. However, he indicated that he needs clear and detailed instructions on how to reach the desired location or he will become lost.

Psychiatric History

Mr. W. denied experiencing any mental health symptoms outside of those identified previously in relation to his accidents: primarily depression, irritability, anxiety, lability, and impulsivity. His wife reported that they had been in marriage counseling previously and that they have again recently begun marriage counseling. Mr. W. denied having ever been diagnosed with a psychiatric illness besides organic brain syndrome. He reported taking lorazepam 1 mg for anxiety. The family psychiatric history is unremarkable.

Behavioral Observations

Mr. W. arrived on time for his appointments, having driven himself. He was a well-groomed man of average height and weight who was casually and appropriately dressed. He has a tattoo on his left upper arm of the Marine Corps bulldog. His posture and gait were unremarkable. He was initially irritable during his second appointment, noting confusion and frustration with having to come to the appointment by himself. However, he was cooperative and made good eye contact. His behavior and level of activity were initially appropriate. As the evaluation progressed, Mr. W. became increasingly tired and his impulse control diminished: He became playful, joking, and expansive in his behavior. There was no evidence of any tics or tremor.

During the administration of the various testing procedures, Mr. W. demonstrated adequate frustration tolerance and persistence on tasks that he found difficult. His response style was initially normal but became increasingly impulsive as he tired. He appeared to try his best on tasks presented to him. His work pace was slow, and he evidenced difficulties focusing his attention. He engaged in self-talk that was helpful to him in completing tasks.

Mr. W.'s speech was fluent and of normal rate, volume, and prosody. There was no evidence of any paraphasias or errors of articulation. He initiated conversation spontaneously and appropriately. He had somewhat limited comprehension and required frequent clarification of questions and directions. Associations were typically logical and goal-directed, although he occasionally became tangential in his thinking.

When asked to describe his usual mood during the past month, Mr. W. stated: "Irritable. I get upset over nothing." He also reported having feelings of depression and low self-esteem and stated: "I have no future, no friends, no brain power." He also described himself as "restless" and "always in fifth gear." He said he is quick to become irritable and angry, during which times he becomes explosive and yells. He appeared depressed with labile affect during the interview.

Thought content was negative for hallucinations, delusions, paranoid ideation, obsessions, compulsions, phobias, and suicidal or homicidal ideation. He denied any history of suicidal thoughts or behaviors.

During his interview, Mr. W. reported his symptoms and history in a consistent manner. There was no indication that he attempted to either minimize or exaggerate his reported symptoms. He put forth adequate effort on the tasks presented to him. What follows is judged to be an accurate assessment of both Mr. W.'s current cognitive and personality functioning.

Means of Assessment

Clinical interview with Mr. and Mrs. W.

Mental Status Examination

Wechsler Adult Intelligence Scale—Fourth Edition (WAIS-IV)

Wechsler Test of Adult Reading (WTAR)

Wechsler Memory Scale—Fourth Edition (WMS-IV)

Minnesota Multiphasic Personality Inventory-2-Restructured Form (MMPI-2-RF)

Test Results and Interpretation

Mr. W. was administered the *Wechsler Adult Intelligence Scale—Fourth Edition* (WAIS-IV), which is an individually administered test of intellectual functioning and cognitive abilities (see Table 10.3 for his complete score summary). The WAIS-IV comprises 15 separate subtests, which can be grouped into five global areas or factors[1]: (1) Crystallized Intelligence, which measures the depth of

---

1. Note that these five global areas are a different reorganization of the WAIS-IV subtests from the traditional Wechsler indexes: the Verbal Comprehension Index, Perceptual Reasoning Index, Working Memory Index, and Processing Speed Index. The scores for these four Wechsler indexes are reported in the Psychometric Summary, but the interpretation of the client's WAIS-IV profile is based on the five global factors just described.

knowledge acquired from one's culture; (2) Fluid Reasoning, which involves solving problems nonverbally; (3) Visual Processing, which requires perceiving, storing, and manipulating visual patterns; (4) Short-Term Memory, which involves taking in and holding information to use within seconds; and (5) Processing Speed, which measures cognitive processing efficiency. On the WAIS-IV, Mr. W. earned a Full Scale IQ (FSIQ) of 83, which indicates that his general intellectual ability is in the Below Average Range when compared to other adults his age. This overall level of performance ranked him at the 13th percentile, indicating that he scored higher than 13% of other adults of the same age in the standardized sample. The chances are good (90%) that Mr. W.'s true FSIQ is somewhere within the range of 78–88. Mr. W.'s general ability is considered a normative weakness as compared to others his age in the normal population.

Mr. W.'s cognitive profile showed both areas of relative strength and weakness. For example, within the nonverbal realm, his abilities ranged from the Average range to the Below Average range. Specifically, on tasks that demanded visual-spatial processing, Mr. W. scored in the Average range, earning a standard score of 100 (50th percentile) on the Visual Processing Factor. Mr. W.'s ability to process visual information is a significant relative strength compared to his abilities in other areas. In contrast, his ability to reason with visual information was significantly weaker. This weaker ability was evident from his standard score of 75 (5th percentile) on the Fluid Reasoning Factor. His performance on these problem-solving tasks was Below Average/Normative Weakness compared to others his age, and the underlying abilities are considered a personal weakness for him. The discrepancy between his stronger visual processing skills and his weaker visual reasoning skills is uncommonly large (occurring in less than 10% of the time in the normal population). Due to this difference, Mr. W. may be able to see specific details in visual information but may have difficulty integrating visual information to solve problems. He is challenged when tasks require a dynamic, flexible approach to problem solving and involve the capacity to discern the most salient aspects of a problem-solving situation, respond, and monitor the effectiveness of the response and change strategies as needed. Mr. W. has difficulty using the feedback provided to him and systematically testing possible solutions when problem solving.

Another related cognitive domain that was challenging for Mr. W. was processing speed. Like his personal weakness with processing visual information, when he was required to quickly respond to visual stimuli and use fine-motor coordination to deliver a response, he had difficulty relative to others his age. Mr. W. demonstrated Below Average abilities on the Processing Speed Factor with his standard

Table 10.3. Psychometric Summary of WAIS-IV Profile for Mr. W

Index/IQ Subtest	Score	90% Confidence Interval	Percentile Rank	Descriptive Category
Verbal Comprehension	**85**	**80–90**	**16**	**Average Range/Within Normal Limits**
Similarities	9		37	
Vocabulary	8		25	[Contributes to Keith Gc Factor]
Information	5		5	[Contributes to Keith Gc Factor]
(Comprehension)	4		2	
Perceptual Reasoning	90	85–95	25	Average Range/Within Normal Limits
Block Design	9		37	[Contributes to Keith Gv Factor]
Matrix Reasoning	5		5	[Contributes to Keith Gf Factor]
Visual Puzzles	11		63	[Contributes to Keith Gv Factor]
(Figure Weights)	6		69	[Contributes to Keith Gf Factor]
(Picture Completion)	8		25	
Working Memory	92	87–97	30	Average Range/Within Normal Limits
Digit Span	8		25	[Contributes to Keith Gsm Factor]
Arithmetic	9		37	
(Letter-Number Sequencing)	8		25	[Contributes to Keith Gsm Factor]
Processing Speed	**79**	**74–84**	**8**	**Below Average/ Normative Weakness**
Symbol Search	6		9	[Contributes to Keith Gs Factor]
Coding	6		9	[Contributes to Keith Gs Factor]
(Cancellation)	5		5	

Table 10.3. (continued)

Index/IQ Subtest	Score	90% Confidence Interval	Percentile Rank	Descriptive Category
Full Scale IQ	83	78–88	13	Below Average/Normative Weakness
GAI	86	82–93	18	Average Range/Within Normal Limits
CPI	82	77–89	12	Below Average/Normative Weakness
Keith Factor				
Crystallized Intelligence (Gc)	81	77–86	10	Below Average/Normative Weakness
Short–Term Memory (Gsm)	89	84–95	23	Average Range/Within Normal Limits
Fluid Reasoning (Gf)	75	71–83	5	Below Average/Normative Weakness
Visual Processing (Gv)	100	94–106	50	Average Range/Within Normal Limits
Processing Speed (Gs)	79	74–88	8	Below Average/Normative Weakness

score of 79 (8th percentile). Thus, his ability to fluently and automatically perform cognitive tasks, especially when under pressure to maintain focused attention and concentration, is a Normative Weakness. His difficulties in both the domains of visual processing and speed of processing are consistent with his self-reported difficulties with motor functioning and vision since his motorcycle accident.

Mr. W.'s ability to focus and sustain his concentration was not only required for processing speed tasks but was also required on specific tasks designed to measure his memory skill. Short-term memory is the ability to hold information in immediate awareness and then use it within a few seconds. Mr. W.'s short-term memory skills were variable, ranging from the Average range to the Below Average range, compared to others his age. On the Short-Term Memory Factor of the WAIS-IV, his abilities were Within Normal Limits, as he earned a standard score of 89 (23rd percentile) on that factor.

However, when examining separate areas of his memory functioning on the *Wechsler Memory Scale—Fourth Edition* (WMS-IV), some areas of weakness are also evident. On measures of immediate memory from the WMS-IV, Mr. W. demonstrated mild to moderate impairment overall (4th percentile). However, this overall score does not reflect the significantly discrepant scores on measures of auditory and visual immediate memory. He performed in the Average range on visual tasks involving recalling the details and spatial information about abstract visual designs (34th percentile), while demonstrating a moderate degree of impairment on auditory tasks involving the recall of stories and word pairs (1st percentile). On another measure of immediate verbal memory in which Mr. W. was asked to recall a list of unrelated words he had learned over several trials following a distracter task, he again demonstrated moderate to severely impaired range performance (below 1st percentile). On a measure of visual immediate memory in which he was asked to recall a complex abstract figure he had copied 3 minutes earlier, he scored in the mild range of impairment (10th percentile).

In contrast to short-term memory, long-term memory is the ability to store and fluently retrieve new or previously acquired information. Mr. W.'s ability to retrieve remote information from long-term memory lies within the mild to moderately impaired range (5th percentile). The 23-point difference between his actual and predicted score on this measure is significant and unusual, as less than 4% of the standardization sample demonstrates a discrepancy of this magnitude. His retrieval fluency lies in the average range (47th percentile).

In regard to overall *auditory memory* ability, Mr. W. demonstrated moderately impaired range performance overall (2nd percentile). When asked to recall a list of unrelated words he had previously learned following a half-hour delay, he scored in the moderate to severely impaired range (below 1st percentile). On other measures of auditory long-term memory involving meaningful stimuli from the WMS-IV, he performed in the mild to moderately impaired range (3rd percentile). He also demonstrated mild to moderate impairment on a measure involving the recall of stories, as well as on a measure involving the recall of word pairs (both 5th percentile). The 22-point discrepancy between his actual and predicted score on measures of auditory long-term memory is significant and unusual, as less than 4% of the standardization sample demonstrates a discrepancy of this magnitude. He performed in the moderately impaired range when presented with auditory information in a recognition format (1st percentile). The 29-point discrepancy between his actual and predicted score is significant and unusual, as less than 2% of the standardization sample demonstrates a discrepancy of this magnitude.

On overall *visual memory* ability, Mr. W. demonstrated Average-range performance (19th percentile). When asked to recall a complex abstract drawing he had copied following a half-hour delay, he scored in the mild to moderately impaired range (6th percentile). His performance was in the mildly impaired range when presented with this information in a recognition format (13th percentile). On measures of visual long-term memory from the WMS-IV, he performed within the Below Average range (14th percentile). There is not a significant difference between his actual and predicted scores on these measures. He performed in the mildly impaired range on a long-term memory measure of recalling visual detail and spatial location of abstract figures (9th percentile).

Like the variability noted in both his nonverbal skills and memory skills, Mr. W.'s abilities in the verbal domain also showed relative strengths and weaknesses. On verbal tasks that required Mr. W. to demonstrate the breadth and depth of his knowledge acquired from his culture, his abilities were in the Below Average range. These abilities were evident from his standard score of 81 (10th percentile) on the Crystallized Intelligence Factor of the WAIS-IV. However, when specific clinical clusters of scores were examined on the WAIS-IV verbal tasks, discrepancies in his abilities were noted. For example, his lexical knowledge (or word knowledge) was significantly stronger than his knowledge of factual information. In fact, the WAIS-IV revealed that his Lexical Knowledge Cluster standard score of 91 (27th percentile) was uncommonly larger than his General Information Cluster standard score of 71 (3rd percentile). Discrepancies as large as Mr. W.'s occur less than 10% of the time in the normal population. This pattern of performance indicates that Mr. W. has facility with words and can reason with words (Average Range abilities) but may have difficulty applying his knowledge in specific situations because of his lack of background knowledge (Below Average range). His eighth-grade education (and later GED) likely contribute to his Below Average range of factual information.

On measures of academic functioning related to language, Mr. W. scored in the Below Average range on a measure of his ability to read a list of words (2nd percentile). There is a 24-point discrepancy between his actual score and his predicted score based on his overall level of intellectual functioning. This difference is both significant and unusual, as only 2% of the standardization sample demonstrates a discrepancy of this magnitude. He also demonstrated moderately impaired range performance on a measure of his ability to spell to dictation (1st percentile). The 27-point discrepancy between his actual and predicted score is both significant and unusual, as less than 1% of the standardization sample demonstrates a discrepancy of this magnitude. His level of academic performance is consistent with the level of formal education that he acquired and with his areas of deficit in his cognitive profile on the WAIS-IV.

Personality Functioning

Mr. W. was administered a measure of general personality functioning, the MMPI-2-RF. Mr. W. reported several clinical concerns on this measure. He reported that he is experiencing poor health and feels weak and tired. He is likely to complain of sleep disturbance, fatigue, low energy, and sexual dysfunction, as well as multiple other somatic complaints. His responses indicate that he is also experiencing significant and pervasive emotional distress. He reported feeling sad, unhappy, hopeless, and depressed. He also reported being dissatisfied with his current life circumstances and is likely to feel overwhelmed, stressed, and worried. He lacks confidence, feels useless, and is prone to ruminate, be self-doubting, and feel insecure and inferior. He indicates that there is a lack of positive emotional experiences in his life and that he is generally pessimistic about life. He also reported being anger-prone and is likely to have problems with anger, irritability, and low frustration tolerance and to hold grudges, have temper tantrums, and be argumentative and abusive toward others. He reported having cynical beliefs, a hostile worldview, and being distrustful of others. He is likely to feel alienated and to have negative interpersonal experiences because of his cynicism.

Diagnostic Impression

Axis I: Dementia Due to Head Trauma (294.1)
   Major Depressive Disorder, moderate, recurrent (296.23)
   Reading Disorder (315.00)
Axis II: No diagnosis (V71.09)
Axis III: Head injury and chronic pain per client report
Axis IV: Inadequate social support
Axis V: Current GAF—53 (symptoms of moderate severity that interfere with social and adaptive functioning)

Summary and Conclusions

Mr. W. is a 64-year-old man who was referred for an evaluation of his cognitive functioning to assist in making a diagnosis and to assess for the presence of dementia. He has a history of memory problems that arose following a motorcycle accident and subsequent severe coma. Mr. W.'s overall level of intellectual ability is in the Below Average range (FSIQ of 83; 13th percentile). This level of overall functioning is generally consistent with what would be expected, given premorbid indicators of functioning. However, specific areas of impairment and strength were evident upon examination of his results on individual measures of cognitive and neuropsychological functioning.

Mr. W. generally demonstrates Average range functioning in the areas of visual processing, lexical knowledge, and certain parts of short-term memory. In contrast, he has Below Average abilities in these global areas: fluid reasoning, processing speed, and general information, as well as parts of his short- and long-term memory. He also evidences moderate impairment on academic measures of reading and spelling. Mr. W.'s performance on measures of memory is significantly varied. He evidences visual short-term memory within the Average range; however, his performance declines to the mildly impaired range when asked to remember an abstract design. Visual long-term memory is in the low average to mildly impaired range, while verbal short- and long-term memory lie in the moderately impaired range. This varied pattern of scores on the various memory tasks would suggest that Mr. W.'s memory deficits are the result of specific injury, as opposed to being a more global dementia, such as Alzheimer's disease. However, his longstanding memory impairment may be particularly troublesome to him at this time because of his recent injury and the resulting stress and chronic pain, which he indicates is generally in the mild to moderate range.

In regard to personality functioning, Mr. W. reported feeling tired, over-whelmed, and stressed. He indicates that he is sad and unhappy and feels hopeless and useless, which he likely ruminates about a great deal. He also reported feeling overly frustrated, irritable, and angry, which may result in explosive behavior. Mr. W. also reported symptoms that are typical of posttraumatic stress disorder; however, some of these symptoms appear to be related more to brain injury and cognitive impairment. Once immediate concerns regarding his level of stress and current functioning are addressed, trauma history and possible symptoms may be addressed more specifically.

In general, most of Mr. W.'s current problems appear related more to his depressive disorder, which is complicated by pain, and to the cognitive dys-function related to his brain injury from 37 years ago. There is no evidence of dementia of a more recent onset. His current cognitive functioning is worsened by his mood disorder and pain symptoms. Improvement in these areas should also result in improved cognitive functioning.

Recommendations

1. Mr. W. could benefit from individual therapy to address his depression, help him develop techniques to assist with memory deficits, and increase resiliency. It will be important to address stress and anger management as well as feelings of hopelessness and despair, and feelings of cynicism and distrust. Continued participation in couples therapy is also indicated to help his wife understand his deficits as well as to improve the patient's interpersonal functioning.

2. The patient is also likely to benefit from participation in a brain injury group, such as the one at Mesa College, to provide further assistance with cognitive impairments and life functioning.

3. Mr. W. should undergo a psychiatric reevaluation to determine if changes in his psychiatric medications are warranted in light of the current evaluation.

4. Mr. W. should be referred to a pain management specialist for an evaluation of his current medication regime and to provide psychological interventions.

5. In working with Mr. W., it will be important to be cognizant of his deficits in memory (particularly verbal memory), slower processing speed, and limited reading ability. For example, whenever possible, he should be given information in writing to decrease his reliance on verbal memory; however, the material must be written at an appropriate level and may need to use diagrams as well.

6. It will also be important to revisit topics and issues in subsequent sessions, given Mr. W.'s limited memory and slower processing speed. He will need more time to learn new material and will be slower in gaining new skills.

7. He will likely have difficulty understanding and following new instructions and should be assisted with clarifications, visual cues, and written reminders.

8. Given his varied attention, it will also be important to actively engage him and take steps to verify his attentiveness (e.g., asking him to summarize what has been said in his own words). Learning and utilizing other memory aids will also be important.

9. In situations where there are high demands on his concentration, he may have more problems functioning and have difficulty thinking things through before doing them; therefore, minimizing these demands will be important to decreasing impulsive and inappropriate behaviors.

10. Mr. W. also tires quickly, which contributes to impulsive and inappropriate behavior, and he should be encouraged to take breaks from demanding tasks and naps to help him revitalize. Helping him recognize when these breaks are needed will also be important.

Clark R. Clipson, PhD
Licensed Psychologist

🐾 TEST YOURSELF 🐾

1. **In the referral section of the report, you should be sure to include all of the following EXCEPT**
   a. Name and position of the person who referred the client for testing
   b. Specific referral question
   c. Previous test scores
   d. A summary of current behaviors/problems relevant to the referral concern

2. **TRUE or FALSE? It is especially important to include the details that you have heard from gossip in the Background section of the report.**

3. **The information in the Appearance and Behavioral Characteristics section of the report should be sequenced in**
   a. The order of occurrence of the behaviors
   b. Order of importance
   c. Alphabetical order
   d. Reverse chronological order

4. **In addition to describing important features of the subject's appearance and pertinent behaviors, the Appearance and Behavioral Characteristics section of the report should include**
   a. Test results
   b. A statement about the validity of the test results
   c. Brief recommendations
   d. Summary of the referral question

5. **It is good practice to mention any of these types of scores in the Test Results and Interpretation section of the report EXCEPT**
   a. Percentile ranks
   b. Confidence intervals

(continued)

    c. Raw scores

    d. Standard scores

6. **TRUE or FALSE? It is often a good idea to include in the Summary and Diagnostic Impressions section of the report test results that were not mentioned previously in the report.**

7. **List four common errors that examiners typically make in report writing:**

    a. _____

    b. _____

    c. _____

    d. _____

Answers: 1. c; 2. false; 3. b; 4. b; 5. c; 6. false; 7.

Chapter Eleven

THE INITIAL DIGITAL ADAPTATION OF THE WAIS-IV[1]

Tommie G. Cayton
Dustin Wahlstrom
Mark H. Daniel

Pearson Clinical Assessment

Investigations and prototype development to digitize aspects of the Wechsler intelligence scales have been ongoing for nearly a decade. These efforts recently came to fruition in the 2012 release of the initial digital adaptation of the *Wechsler Adult Intelligence Scale—Fourth Edition* (WAIS-IV; Wechsler, 2008, 2012) on Pearson's Q-interactive™ assessment platform. Q-interactive is a system for computer-assisted administration of individually administered tests using two Bluetooth-connected digital tablets—one for the practitioner (examiner) and one for the client (examinee).

One of the goals of this release was to adapt the WAIS-IV in a way in which the volumes of prior research would still be relevant. In order to do this, the adaptation included replacing the administration manual, technical manual, stimulus book, and record form with digital functionality, while retaining the manipulatives and response booklets with which the WAIS-IV was standardized. This approach, supported by empirical evidence of equivalence, allows the scores

---

1. The authors would like to thank Thomas Hanagan, David McGivney, and Eric Saperstein for helping improve previous versions of this document.

obtained from the digital administration to be treated as interchangeable with those in the original standardization so that the existing norms can be used.

Another goal was to make administration and scoring easier, more convenient, and more accurate so that the practitioner can focus attention on the examinee. This aim was accomplished in several ways. In addition to freeing the practitioner from transporting administration and technical manuals and maintaining inventories of record forms, the digital version eliminates the need to memorize start points, reversal rules, basal rules, and discontinue rules. It also eliminates the need to calculate raw score totals or find the right table to convert raw scores to scaled scores or index scores. Also, practitioners have the option of making audio recordings of oral responses to verbal items so that they can flag and return directly to an item that needs additional review before an accurate score can be assigned. The adaptation keeps the practitioner in control, increases the accuracy of administration, and makes scoring easier and more consistent with standardization. After becoming familiar with the digital system, it generally reduces the burden on practitioners so that they may observe the client more carefully and spend less time scoring and looking up values in tables. School beta testers estimated that using Q-interactive saved 15% to 20% in total time required from beginning the assessment to completion of reporting the results.

This chapter will describe how to use Q-interactive to administer the WAIS-IV, briefly summarize efforts and results to ensure that scores obtained with the digital administration are comparable to those obtained through a traditional administration, and describe the basic actions required on the Q-interactive platform before the actual administration session. It is designed to be an overview and general description of Q-interactive, not a step-by-step tutorial or users' manual. It assumes that readers are at least casually familiar with computers and specifically with the use of Internet browsers and the iPad. The focus is on the examiner/practitioner user, not on the requirements of a systems administrator.

Finally, the chapter is also not an in-depth description of the robust functionality of the full Q-interactive assessment platform. Readers who need additional information are referred to the following sources: www.HelloQ.com (Q-interactive's official website for information) and www.Apple.com (for information about iTunes or iPads). We will use the terms *examiner* and *practitioner* as equivalent. iPads are used in the examples throughout the chapter as they are the only tablet on which Q-interactive is available at publication, although other devices may be added in the future.

As the WAIS-IV (Wechsler, 2008, 2012) is only one of many assessments to be added to the Q-interactive platform, and in recognition that development of the platform will continue to refine current capabilities and add functions, this chapter will cover only the essentials of how a practitioner (a) uses the basic functions of the platform to add a client, (b) selects the WAIS-IV or combinations of the subtests of WAIS-IV, (c) synchronizes the information with the two iPads, and (d) administers and scores the WAIS-IV subtests. Importantly, this chapter was written before the release of the Q-interactive platform. Because this platform will continue to be improved and enhanced, some of the screenshots provided in figures throughout this chapter may not look or function exactly like the final version of the product.

OVERVIEW

The Q-interactive platform comprises two different components. The first is a browser-based set of functions called Central for:

- Creating client records
- Creating batteries of combinations of tests or subtests
- Creating *assessments*, which in Q-interactive refer to unique combinations of the client; the test or battery; and the date, time, and location
- Reporting and sharing the information obtained from conducting the assessments

The second component, Assess, is an application that allows a battery of tests to be administered via pairs of iPads (an Examiner Device and a Client Device).

The Examiner Device presents administration instructions to the practitioner and allows the practitioner to (a) control what is presented on the Client Device, (b) document or capture the responses by the client, (c) temporarily audio-record oral responses for follow-up scoring review, (d) assign scores to item responses, (e) document any observations or make notes, (f) start and stop timers, and, as appropriate, (g) view on the practitioner screen which responses the client has made on his or her screen. The Client Device replaces the stimulus book. It presents visual stimuli to clients and captures their touch responses (option selections).

Data about the clients and their test performance are maintained on the Examiner Device only until the practitioner has resolved all scoring issues, made any proration or substitution decisions, and synchronized the assessment session with the Central website, www.Qiactive.com. Once synced, all client-related data are removed from the Examiner Device, and the assessment record is moved to a cloud server, where it can be accessed via Central only. All audio recordings are deleted when the session information is removed from the Examiner Device.

ADMINISTERING WAIS-IV IN Q-INTERACTIVE ASSESS

Before reading this section, study Rapid Reference 11.1, which describes much of the terminology used throughout Q-interactive. Familiarity with these terms will facilitate an understanding of (a) the general workflow within Assess, (b) the major features that characterize the system, and (c) a step-by-step description of how to administer the WAIS-IV (Wechsler, 2008, 2012) subtests.

Description of Assess Workflow

As a general principle, the test-administration portion of Q-interactive was designed to enable examiners to do everything they can do in a standard administration. All subtests within Q-interactive follow a consistent workflow on the Examiner Device. This workflow is intended to increase usability by promoting a unified user experience, regardless of the subtest content. This

=== *Rapid Reference 11.1*

Commonly Used Q-interactive Terms

- *Assessment:* Unique combination of a client, a battery (collection of tests or subtests), a date, and a time
- *Instructions Screen:* First of two examiner screens for each item, from which instructions are read, stimuli shown, and the timer started
- *Capture Screen:* Second of two examiner screens for each item, on which responses are recorded and scored
- *Client Device:* Tablet on which stimuli are shown to the individual taking the test
- *Examiner Device:* Tablet used by the examiner to administer assessments; it may also be used to set up assessments.
- *Information (I) Pop-over:* Pop-over containing critical information regarding how a subtest is administered and scored
- *Instructions Pop-over:* Pop-over containing subtest-specific prompts
- *Event Buttons:* Buttons on the capture screen that contain item-specific information and can be used to document behavioral observations or other responses
- *Item Sidebar:* Screen section from which all subtests and items within the battery can be accessed
- *Global Bar:* Bar at the top of every screen that contains icons for the home screen, test side bar, and information (I) pop-over, among others
- *Item Bar:* Bar below the global bar that contains Speech bubble icon, item title (e.g., Matrix Reasoning Item 9), as well as the instructions pop-over and item flag

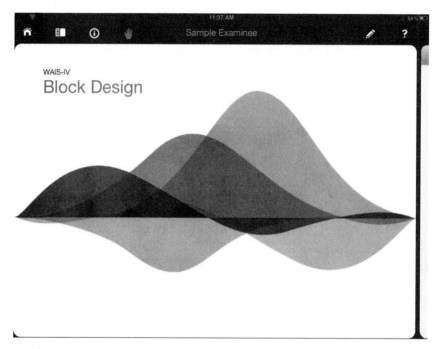

Figure 11.1. Subtest Cover Card

consistency is reflected both in structure (the content and sequence of the screens) and in functionality—for example, how the system applies the administration rules.

Structure

The standard subtest structure has four sections.

1. A *subtest cover card* (see Figure 11.1), which signals that a new subtest is about to be administered.
2. An *instructions screen*, which contains all required verbatim instructions for an item, as well as the item content itself for verbal subtests (e.g., "What does CONCEIVE mean?"). In addition, it contains a button that allows the examiner to display images on the Client Device, and it is where examiners begin timing subtests that require recording of response times.
3. A *capture screen*, which provides a means for the examiner to record the examinee's responses and score each item. WAIS-IV subtests vary

widely in their capture and scoring demands. Examiners log responses by selecting buttons or images, writing with a stylus or fingertip within a handwriting capture area, or making an audio-recording of verbal responses. Item scoring within the WAIS-IV on Q-interactive is manual, keeping the examiner in control. On most items, the examiner selects a button that represents either a point value or a correct/incorrect response. If examiners are unsure of the score or want to review it later, they can attach a red flag to an item by touching the flag icon on the capture screen. There are numerous other features of the capture screen, described later in this chapter.

4. An *End of Subtest section* (see Figure 11.2), which displays both raw and scaled scores for subtests on which scoring is complete. (The fields remain empty if any administered items have not been scored or still have flags.) The *End of Subtest* section also includes item-level scores, as well as any qualitative observations and subtest notes. From here, examiners can access all of the results for the entire battery by selecting the *Results* button in the upper-right corner of the screen.

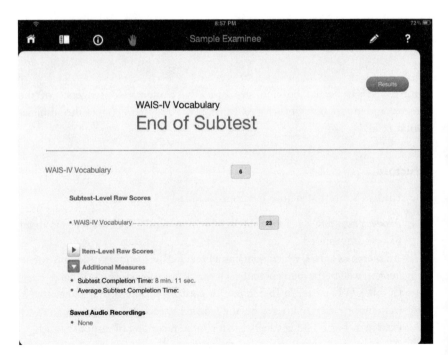

Figure 11.2. End of Subtest Screen

Administration Rules

For all subtests, start, reversal, and discontinue rules are programmed into the system; by swiping to the next screen, the examiner is taken to the appropriate next item within a subtest, so long as scores have been entered correctly. Whereas making these rules fully automatic might reduce errors and improve usability, cognitive assessment requires flexibility. In acknowledgment of that need for flexibility, several features have been implemented that provide examiners with control over the testing session. For example, discontinue rules can be overridden in order to test the limits, a manual discontinue function allows subtests to be exited before reaching a discontinue point, and the examiner can override an age-based start point if that start point is not appropriate for a given client (e.g., evaluation of suspected intellectual disability). Also, the examiner can edit an erroneously entered score for a previous item in order to prevent an incorrect application of a discontinue or reversal rule.

System Features

Q-interactive contains several system-level features. These fall into two categories: (1) modules that are used across instructions and capture screens to administer, record, or score; and (2) systemwide features intended to supplement the information provided on the instructions and capture screens. This second set of features is available from any instruction or capture screen and is designed to provide examiners with information necessary to follow standardized assessment procedures, as well as allow for efficient navigation within Q-interactive. Some of the more important features are described in the following sections.

Timer

A standard timer is used for all Q-interactive subtests. It is present at the bottom of the instruction screen and the upper right-hand corner of the capture screen for all timed items. Press the *Start* button within the timer to begin timing. Once the timer is running, that same button will say *Stop*. When it is tapped again to stop timing, it will say *Resume* (for instances where the timer was stopped too quickly, such as a client's self-corrections). Timing can be resumed and stopped as many times as necessary. The timer must be started from the instructions screen but can be stopped from either the instructions or the capture screen. *For items that require an image to be shown on the Client Device, the timer cannot be started until the image is shown on screen.*

There are several additional timer features. First, the timer will count up from 0 seconds or count down from the item's time limit (listed at the top of the timer for each item). The default state is to count up, which is indicated by the blue clock icon with an upward-facing arrow within it. To set the timer to count down, select the clock icon with the downward-facing arrow. When counting up, the timer will continue running until the examiner stops it, even if the time exceeds the item's time limit (for cases in which the examiner grants the examinee additional time to finish working). However, the downward-counting timer stops at 0 seconds. In both count-down and count-up modes, the digits within the timer turn red when there are 10 seconds or less remaining in the item's allowed completion time. This serves as a visual cue to the examiner that the time limit is about to be reached.

Once the time limit is exceeded, the timer will read *Time elapsed!* To accommodate unexpected events, the recorded completion time can be adjusted. Touching the time opens a pop-over containing up and down arrows that the examiner can use to correct inaccurate recordings (see Figure 11.3). While the timer is counting, touching the time will reveal a pop-over that allows for the

Figure 11.3. The Adjust Timer Function as Seen From the Coding Capture Screen

timer to be restarted if necessary. On items with time limits or time-based bonus points, the timer does not control how the item is scored. Rather, the timer's role is the same as that of a manual stopwatch, which is to give information that the examiner uses when assigning an item score.

Event Buttons

Capture screens contain event buttons on the right-hand side of the screen that serve the following purposes:

- The *WAIS-IV Manual* advises examiners to record when prompts, queries, or repetitions are provided, as well as when the examinee does not respond or responds "I don't know" to an item. Q-interactive provides buttons that allow each of these observations to be recorded as appropriate (DK, NR, P, R, and Q).
- Many subtests contain items that require specific examiner feedback (e.g., items on Information that require verbatim queries in response to specific examinee responses). On these items, the specific feedback is contained in pop-overs that appear when the appropriate event button is selected. Response options that require special actions are indicated with superscript characters that are linked to specific event buttons: An asterisk indicates that the corresponding event button tells the examiner what specific feedback to provide, and a superscript "†" attached to a 0-point response to a teaching item indicates that the event button displays the teaching instructions.
- The final use of event buttons is to record information that is important to scoring. For example, on Block Design the examiner can capture the response if it conforms to the 2 x 1, 2 x 2, or 3 x 3 configuration of the correct design, but if it has gaps between blocks that would result in a score of 0, the examiner records this by touching the *Gap > 1/4"* event button.

Notes

Selecting the pencil icon on the right side of the toolbar opens a screen overlay that can be used to write notes about an assessment session. Practitioners often write behavioral observations or other notes in the margins of the paper Record Forms. The Notes functionality is intended to address that need in Q-interactive. At the top of each note is a toolbar that allows the note to be linked to the item, the subtest, or generally applied to the test as a whole. This procedure allows the notes to be easily accessed and organized after the testing session, when writing reports or providing feedback to clients

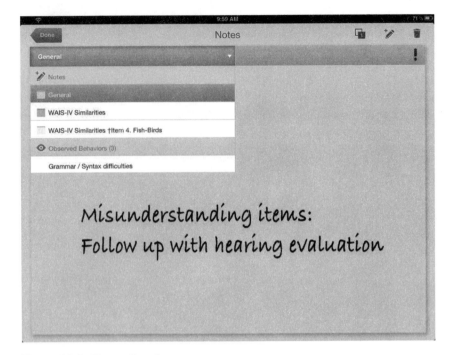

Figure 11.4. Notes Overlay

(see Figure 11.4). In addition, an exclamation point in the upper-right portion of the notes section allows the most important notes to be flagged. Overall, these features improve the examiner's ability to efficiently access and use the observations recorded during the test session.

Information (I) Pop-Over

Selecting the information (I) button, which is found in the left-hand section of the *global bar* (the bar across the top of every screen that contains icons for high-level functions), opens a pop-over box that provides basic information regarding the subtest that is currently being administered (see Figure 11.5). The intent of this pop-over is to provide information that is critical for standardized administration in a format that allows it to be accessed quickly and efficiently during the assessment session. It is not intended to replace the manual and does not include all information required for administration and scoring; rather, it was modeled after the headers that appear above each subtest in the paper Record Form and provides information about materials, start points, discontinue rules, timing, and so on. The (I) pop-over is organized into the

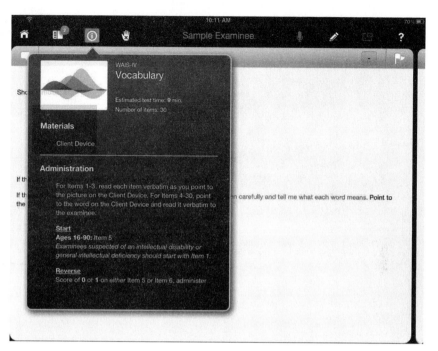

Figure 11.5. Information (I) Pop-Over

following sections: (a) Materials, (b) Administration, (c) Recording, (d) Timing, and (e) Scoring, with the contents generally following what is provided in the Record Form.

The Materials section lists all of the materials that the examiner needs to administer a subtest. If the Examiner Device is the only material required, the section is omitted from the (I) pop-over. The Administration section contains information about start points, reversal rules, and discontinue rules, as well as any other critical instructions that aren't found elsewhere in the platform. The Recording section may be the most important portion of the (I) pop-over and is critical for even the most seasoned WAIS-IV examiners, as it describes the unique way that Q-interactive uses event buttons to capture information that is traditionally written on paper Record Forms. The Timing section provides information about time limits, when to begin and stop timing items, and other pertinent information to ensure proper adherence to standardized timing procedures. Finally, the scoring section provides very brief information about the scores that are available for each item.

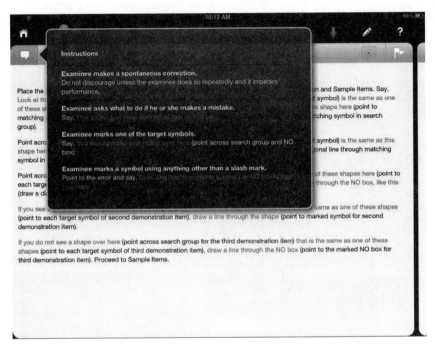

Figure 11.6. Instructions Pop-Over

Instructions Pop-over

Most WAIS-IV (Wechsler, 2008, 2012) subtests require the examiner to provide prompts in response to particular examinee behaviors. The Instructions pop-over (accessed by selecting the speech bubble icon in the upper left-hand portion of instructions and capture screens) provides examiners with all subtest-specific prompts with a single click (see Figure 11.6). In addition, it contains information about querying examinee responses and indicates when providing repetitions is appropriate. Note that for some subtests, such as Digit Span, the contents of the Instructions pop-over are divided by condition because some prompts apply to only a portion of the subtest. If a prompt, repetition, or query from this pop-over is provided, the examiner has the option of recording that behavior using event buttons located on the capture screen.

Test Sidebar

Digital testing in Q-interactive introduces numerous changes to the examiner's experience relative to traditional assessment. One of the biggest changes is the fact that examiners see only one item on the screen at a time. With a paper

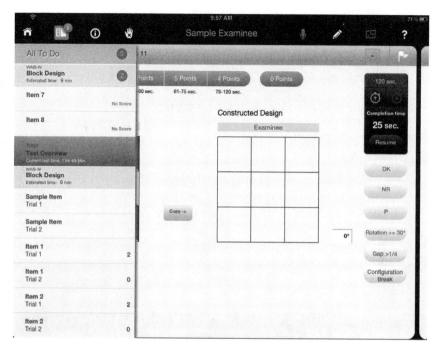

Figure 11.7. Test Sidebar With Open To-Do Section

Record Form, an entire subtest (and sometimes multiple subtests) is visible on a page. The Q-interactive test sidebar provides comparable information. To display the item sidebar, select the icon on the left-hand side of the global bar that looks like a list. Q-interactive will then display a column on the left side of the screen that contains all of the subtests in the current battery and their estimated testing times (see Figure 11.7). Selecting a subtest within this list reveals its items (including scores, discontinue points, and flags for previously administered items). Selecting an item opens an overlay depicting that item's capture screen.

When the capture screen for an administered item is opened via the sidebar, much of the functionality is preserved: scores, responses, and event buttons can all be modified, and the timer can be adjusted. (Although the capture screens for unadministered items can also be accessed through the test sidebar, none of the buttons are functional.) The primary use of the test sidebar is to resolve scores on previously administered items. This function allows clinicians to resolve the scores on several items at once by grouping flagged and unscored items in the "All To-Do" tab. When accessed through this section, the capture screens for all unscored and flagged items can be navigated by selecting forward and backward arrows on the upper right-hand corner of each capture screen. This procedure can significantly increase scoring efficiency after the assessment session.

OVERVIEW OF WAIS-IV SUBTEST DESIGNS

Verbal Comprehension Subtests

All of the WAIS-IV Verbal Comprehension subtests (Wechsler, 2008, 2012) utilize a similar design within Q-interactive. The examiner reads aloud the text presented on the instructions screen and on the capture screen, and scoring rules from the manual are organized into columns of sample responses that correspond to each point value (2-1-0 or 1-0, depending on subtest) (see Figure 11.8 for an example from Information). Sample responses are displayed on *picklist* buttons (e.g., "Soviet Union; USSR" and "Europe" in

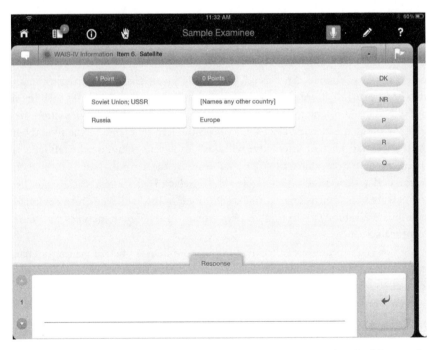

Figure 11.8. Example of a Capture Screen for Vocabulary, Similarities, and Information

Figure 11.8). Picklist buttons are utilized on all Verbal Comprehension subtests and Picture Completion. In addition to presenting the scoring rules, picklist buttons can be pressed to record that a particular response was given. For examiners who prefer to capture verbal responses verbatim, there is a *Response* capture area at the bottom of verbal response capture screens in which examiners can write.

On subtests that are often characterized by more verbose responses (e.g., Comprehension), this area may be insufficient to capture the entire response. A button on the right side of the *Response* area opens new panes that can be used to record additional information, and examiners can toggle between panes. Audio capture is also available and can be turned on or off in the system settings. It begins automatically when the examiner swipes to the capture screen and stops when the examiner swipes to the next screen. The respective verbal recording is then associated with the item being administered when the response was recorded. This approach prevents the examiner from having to wade through a lengthy audio recording to find the verbalizations associated with a particular item.

All items on Verbal Comprehension subtests are scored manually by selecting the button containing the point value that corresponds with the examinee's verbal response. Selecting one of the picklist options does not assign a score to the item; assigning a score requires examiner judgment. For example, an examinee can "spoil" previously given answers with comments indicating they did not really understand the concept being assessed. In such a case, the picklist button would be selected, a score *not* associated with the picklist item could be selected, and the "spoiling" response written in the Response capture area.

Items 5, 8, 9, and 10 on Comprehension required a unique design (see Figure 11.9). For these items, examinees must provide a verbal response that refers to at least two general concepts in order to receive full credit. This scoring procedure prevents the creation of sample response columns that correspond to point values; instead, picklist buttons reflect general concepts rather than the sample responses themselves, and the sample responses for each general concept are listed within pop-overs that appear any time a general concept picklist button is selected. Examiners still have the ability to write verbatim responses, although they must touch a picklist button if they need to verify that the examinee's response matches the samples associated with that general concept.

It is worth noting that Vocabulary also differs from the other Verbal Comprehension subtests in that it requires the use of the Client Device.

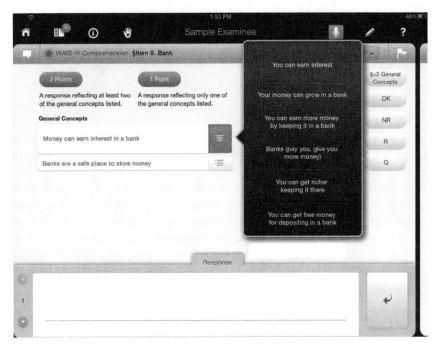

Figure 11.9. Example of a Capture Screen for a Multiple Concepts Item on Comprehension

For Items 1–3, images are shown on the screen and the examinee is required to name them. For Items 4–30, words are shown on the screen and the examiner points to the appropriate word while reading it aloud. Similar to other subtests that require the Client Device, the examiner controls what image is being shown by selecting a button on the instructions screen for the appropriate item.

Perceptual Reasoning Subtests

The WAIS-IV Perceptual Reasoning subtests (Wechsler, 2008, 2012) vary widely in their designs. All require the examinee to interact with stimuli on the Client Device, but the nature of that interaction and the tools available to the examiner to record it differ. On Block Design, examinees view the design on the Client Device and recreate it using the traditional block set. Examiners initiate the display of the image to be copied and begin the timer. The examiner records the constructed designs on the capture screen using an interactive

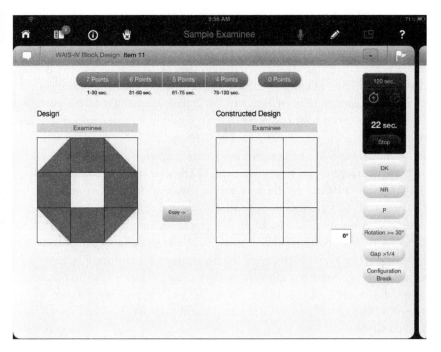

Figure 11.10. Example of a Capture Screen for Block Design

empty block grid (see Figure 11.10). The completed design on the left-hand side of the screen represents the correct design from the examiner's view, and the blank design on the right can be populated using one of two methods. First, for correct designs, the examiner can select the *Copy* button, which populates the empty grid in exactly the same manner as the correct design. For incorrect designs, individual boxes within the grid can be populated with different patterns. Double-tapping a block "cycles" it between all white and all red, and single tapping near a corner of a block turns that diagonal half of the block red. If the examinee's response is rotated, this can be captured by rotating the constructed design on the capture screen using two fingers on opposite edges of the design. The angle of rotation is indicated in a box to the lower right of the design.

The functions of the block design screen do not allow the capture of wrong designs that violate the standard 2 x 1, 2 x 2, or 3 x 3 block configurations. Two buttons are available on the right side of the capture screen to help record these design types. The first is the *Configuration Break* button, which indicates that the examinee created a design that did not adhere to the correct overall block structure. The second is the *Gap >1/4″* button, which indicates that the constructed pattern contains gaps between the blocks greater than 1/4 inch (resulting in a score of 0 points even though the block pattern may be constructed correctly). The *Notes* section can be used to draw any designs that the examiner would like to view for subsequent qualitative analysis.

All Block Design items require manual scoring on the part of the examiner. Each capture screen has buttons on the top of the screen that reflect the various point values available for a particular item, and the examiner selects the appropriate score based on the constructed design and elapsed completion time.

Matrix Reasoning and Figure Weights use a different kind of design. For each, examiners use a button on the instructions screen to display the stimulus image on the Client Device. Examinees can provide a verbal response or touch the desired response on the Client Device. When an option is selected on the Client Device, the box becomes momentarily highlighted in order to provide the examinee with a visual cue that the response was registered. It does not stay highlighted, however, in order to more closely resemble the task demands of the traditional versions of these subtests (in which there is no record on the Stimulus Book of what selection the examinee made). When an examinee selects a response on the Client Device, that selection is automatically registered on the capture screen of the Examiner Device as a blue box below the selection.

As shown in Figure 11.11, the row of response options on the Client Device is replicated on the capture screen, with the correct answer identified visually by a green box around the correct response. If an examinee self-corrects or selects more than one option, these selections are registered for the examiner to view. After clarifying the intended response, examiners can override the examinee's selections to represent the clarification by toggling responses on and off. The response can then be scored using the *1 Point* or *0 Points* buttons on the top of the screen.

Visual Puzzles functions similarly, except correct answers require three selections instead of just one. Similar to Matrix Reasoning and Figure Weights, all of the examinee's selections are registered by the system, and the examiner can override those responses in cases of self-corrections. Both Figure Weights and Visual Puzzles require the use of a timer. The timer is started on the instructions screen and can be stopped on either the instructions or capture screen. These two subtests require the examiner to prompt the examinee when 10 seconds are remaining in an item. To remind the examiner of this prompt, a message tray will drop down from the top of the screen when the timer indicates the examinee has 10 seconds remaining. The message tray contains the verbatim text required for the examiner's prompt (see Figure 11.12).

Figure 11.11. Example of a Capture Screen for Matrix Reasoning and Figure Weights

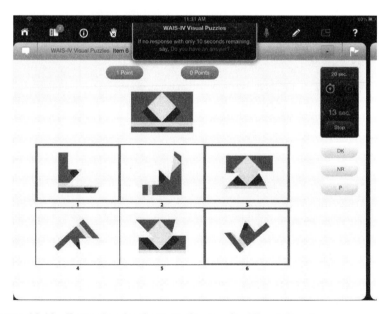

Figure 11.12. Example of a Capture Screen for Visual Puzzles

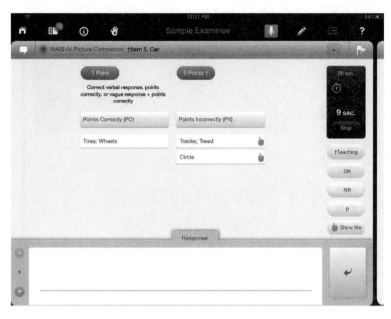

Figure 11.13. Example of a Capture Screen for Picture Completion

Picture Completion utilizes a design that is a unique mixture of components from Verbal Comprehension and Perceptual Reasoning subtests. The examiner uses a button on the instructions screen to display the stimulus on the Client Device; similar to the traditional version, examinees make a selection by stating the missing part of the picture or pointing to it on the screen. Picklist buttons on the capture screen indicate verbal responses that receive credit, as well as those that require the examinee to point to the correct location on the image to receive credit (see Figure 11.13). Similar to Verbal Comprehension subtests, verbatim responses can be captured either by selecting picklist buttons or by writing them in the *Response* box at the bottom of the screen. There are two unique features of Picture Completion:

- There is a special hand icon on all of the picklist responses that requires the examinee to also point in order to receive credit, to remind the examiner to prompt the examinee to point. This same hand icon is located on a button on the right side of the screen that contains the verbatim prompt text (as well as additional scoring information). Early prototyping of this design indicated it facilitated proper adherence to standardized administration rules.

- A feature called Picture-in-Picture allows the examiner to open a pop-over box on the capture screen that shows the examinee's screen, as well as a fingerprint indicating where on the screen the examinee pointed. This pop-over box can be activated by touching a small icon on the right side of the global bar and is intended to facilitate scoring. Scoring is done manually by selecting the *1 Point* or *0 Points* buttons at the top of the screen.

Working Memory Subtests

Digit Span and Letter-Number Sequencing use nearly identical design frameworks (see Figure 11.14). These two subtests are the only ones on WAIS-IV (Wechsler, 2008, 2012) that do not have instructions screens; rather, each trial is presented from a capture screen that has the sequence in the upper left-hand corner of the screen and the correct response(s) listed below the *1 Point* and *0 Points* buttons (note that for Digit Span Forward, the sequence read to the

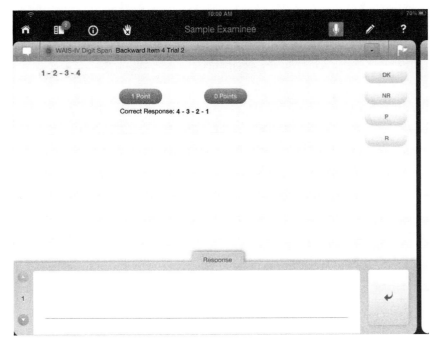

Figure 11.14. Example of a Capture Screen for Digit Span, Arithmetic, and Letter-Number Sequencing

examinee and the correct answer are identical). As on the Verbal Comprehension subtests, verbatim responses can be captured via the *Response* box at the bottom of the screen.

The response capture requirements for Arithmetic are very similar to Digit Span and Letter-Number Sequencing. The correct response is shown on the screen, and examiners select the point value associated with the examinee's response. Examiners can record verbatim responses if desired. However, Arithmetic differs from the other Working Memory subtests in that it has an instructions screen for every item. From this screen, examiners can read the verbatim text for each item and show images on the Client Device for Items 1–5. Arithmetic also requires the use of a timer, accessible from both the instructions and capture screens.

Processing Speed Subtests

The initial digital adaptation of WAIS-IV (Wechsler, 2008, 2012) was conservative in order to enable the use of preexisting normative data; as a result, a decision was made to have examinees complete Symbol Search, Coding, and Cancellation on the traditional paper response booklets. For each of these subtests, the examiner reads instructions from the instructions screen and begins timing the examinee. The examinee's performance is scored using templates after the testing session, and the total numbers of correct and incorrect (if necessary) responses are entered into the appropriate boxes on the capture screen (see Figure 11.15).

EVALUATING THE QUALITY OF THE Q-INTERACTIVE WAIS-IV

The adaptations described in this chapter to provide a computer-assisted administration of the WAIS-IV (Wechsler, 2008, 2012) were well received by examiners at beta sites. *A critical question, however, is whether the results of the digital version are comparable to those of the paper version.*

After the design process for all of the subtests was completed, the entire WAIS-IV battery went through two evaluation phases: equivalency testing and beta testing. As mentioned earlier, one of the primary design goals for the Q-interactive version of WAIS-IV was to be equivalent to the standard version, meaning that scores on the two versions would be interchangeable. If it were found that the digital format had no effect on scores, then the existing norms and reliability and validity information could be used. For the purpose of this research, a criterion of equivalence was set as an effect size no greater than

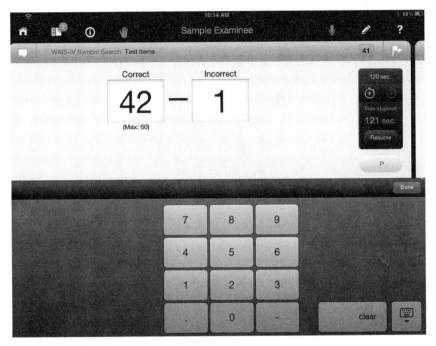

Figure 11.15. Example of a Capture Screen for Symbol Search, Coding, and Cancellation With Keypad for Entering Scores Open

0.2—that is, no more than one-fifth of a standard deviation. In order to achieve this goal, great care was taken to avoid any changes in examinees' test-taking experience that might substantially affect their performance.

A series of equivalence studies was conducted in the fall of 2011 (see Daniel, 2012, for a full description). In most of these studies, examinees took each subtest only once, in the digital format, and their performance was compared with the performance that was predicted on the basis of a set of covariate tests (other WAIS-IV subtests that had been administered using the standard format). One of the studies, a follow-up study of the Processing Speed subtests, used a retest design in which each examinee took the subtest in both formats, in counterbalanced sequence.

The initial study found that 12 of the 15 subtests met the equivalence criterion. Picture Completion was a more difficult task in the digital format, and this was attributed to insufficient clarity in the stimulus picture and a nonintuitive arrangement of the capture screen. A subsequent version in which these issues were corrected (i.e., the version described earlier in this chapter) passed the equivalence criterion in a follow-up study. Scores on Coding were higher in the digital format, and this was traced to a two-second delay in the initiation of timing because of a feature of the programming (which was corrected). Finally, Information yielded lower scores in the digital format, but a subsequent study found that most of this effect also showed up on the standard administration of this subtest, leaving a small effect (similar to that for the other verbal subtests) that could be attributed to the digital format. Table 11.1 shows the final results of the equivalence studies of WAIS-IV, in which no format effects reach the preestablished threshold for equivalence.

Table 11.1. WAIS-IV Equivalence Effect Sizes

Index/Subtest	N	Effect Size
VERBAL COMPREHENSION		
Information	99	−0.12
Similarities	36	−0.11
Vocabulary	40	−0.05
(Comprehension)	39	−0.12
PERCEPTUAL REASONING		
Block Design	36	−0.16
Matrix Reasoning	40	0.10
Visual Puzzles	40	0.18
(Figure Weights)	36	−0.02
(Picture Completion)	99	−0.17[*]
WORKING MEMORY		
Arithmetic	39	0.04
Digit Span	36	−0.08
(Letter-Number Sequencing)	36	−0.04
PROCESSING SPEED[a]		
Coding	30	0.07
Symbol Search	30	0.13
(Cancellation)	30	0.13

[*]$p < .05$
[a]Retest design, 15 matched pairs of examinees

The Q-interactive WAIS-IV (Wechsler, 2008, 2012) then went through two months of beta testing by psychologists and psychometrists at three locations: a forensic psychology practice in the Northeast, and a large neuropsychology clinic and an urban high school, both in the Midwest. Following on-site training, the professionals used the digital version of WAIS-IV with their clients and provided continuous feedback to the development team. This information led to technical improvements, such as strengthening the Bluetooth connection between the tablets, and to some functionality enhancements, such as changing from a button-press to a swipe as the method of moving to the next screen. The administration, capture, and scoring procedures were found by the beta testers to work well and save time.

Important lessons were learned in the equivalence studies and beta tests about the nature and amount of training needed to become proficient with the digital administration format. The examiners had a wide range of digital experience, ranging from those who already owned a tablet and smartphone to several who had never used either device. For the latter, learning the basic functions of the iPad took little time. In general, it took examiners about half a day to feel that they had a good understanding of how the Q-interactive interfaces work and another day of supervised practice for them to feel confident in their ability to administer WAIS-IV using the digital format. However, when they did a full practice administration on their own, they discovered that although they knew what to do, they could not conduct the administration smoothly because the procedures had not yet become habitual and automatic for them. Similar to learning to administer a test in traditional format, *it takes at least five to ten practice administrations to reach the point where the examiner can focus attention on the examinee rather than on the mechanics of administration.*

Before one can administer the WAIS-IV on Q-interactive effectively, however, several things need to be done (in addition to the indicated need for practice with the interface). The final section describes these requirements.

GETTING STARTED WITH Q-INTERACTIVE

Here is an overview of the equipment, software, and procedures required to be able to administer the WAIS-IV using Q-interactive (see Rapid Reference 11.2). More detailed instructions are provided to users when they purchase the system or through www.HelloQ.com. A user needs the following:

- A computer with access to the Internet through the latest versions of a certified browser (such as the latest version of Safari, MS Internet Explorer, FireFox, or Chrome) and with iTunes installed (contact www. HelloQ.com for a list of currently certified browsers)

≡ *Rapid Reference 11.2*

What Is Required to Administer a WAIS-IV Using Q-Interactive

1. Call Pearson Customer Service and set up a Q-interactive account and establish credentials to administer WAIS-IV.
2. Download the Q-interactive application from iTunes (the Q-icon with a black background).
3. Two iPads with at least 32 G memory, with Q-interactive application installed with appropriate setup options entered
4. Computer with one of the following browsers (or later): MS Explorer 7.0, Safari, Chrome, or Firefox
5. Creation of client record on www.Qiactive.com cloud server site (the Q-icon with the blue-green background), with assignment of WAIS-IV, a date, a time, and a location
6. Downloading of assigned assessments to iPads (will need wireless access to accomplish)

- Two tablets (iPads) that have Wi-Fi capability with at least 32 G of memory
- The Q-interactive software installed on each iPad

The user then takes the following steps to prepare to use Q-interactive to administer the WAIS-IV (Wechsler, 2008, 2012):

1. Configure the iPads for Q-interactive and link them through Bluetooth (see Rapid Reference 11.3).
2. Contact Pearson Customer Service to establish a Q-interactive account with access to the WAIS-IV (which requires meeting the user qualifications for administering, scoring, and interpreting the WAIS-IV).
3. Log in to Q-interactive Central (www.Qiactive.com) and create a client record.
4. Assign a battery of tests that includes the WAIS-IV to the client with a date, time, and location.
5. Log in to Q-interactive Assess on the Examiner Device to download the *assessment* (i.e., the unique combination of client, battery, date/time, and location).

Because Q-interactive uses browser-based software for all functions except actual test administration, most modern computers should be able to use Central without difficulty.

Figure 11.16. Q-Interactive Assess App Icon

Install Q-interactive Software

You will download the Q-interactive software (that will later be installed on the two iPads) to your computer from iTunes. (If iTunes is not already installed on your computer or if you have questions about installing applications on your computer or syncing them with your iPad, you may obtain the iTunes program and information from http://www.apple.com/itunes/.) To find the Q-interactive application, search the iTunes store using "Pearson" or "Q-interactive" and look for the icon shown in Figure 11.16.

Configure the iPads

Next, you will need to configure each of the iPads to prepare them for Q-interactive. The configuration is accomplished through clicking on the iPad's Settings icon. Consult your iPad user's manual for instructions on using the iPads Settings function. The options that are significant for the effective functioning of Q-interactive are described in Rapid Reference 11.3.

Creating Client Profiles, Batteries, and Assessments in Central

The Central website can be accessed from www.Qiactive.com with a username and password provided by Pearson Customer Service. You may create client

≡ *Rapid Reference 11.3*

Optimal Setup Options for Your iPad for Test Administration

1. Brightness & Wallpaper	Maximum brightness
2. Brightness & Wallpaper—Auto-Brightness	Off
3. General—Bluetooth	On
4. General—Auto-Lock	15 Minutes
5. General—Passcode Lock—Passcode	On
6. General—Passcode Lock—Require Passcode	Immediately
7. General—Passcode Lock—Simple Passcode	Off
8. General—Multitasking Gestures	Off
9. Assess—Application Mode	Practitioner (for one iPad)
10. Assess—Application Mode	Client (for one iPad)
11. Assess—Bluetooth™ Name	[Same entry for both iPads]
12. Assess—Enable Bluetooth Bypass	Off
13. Assess—Error Reporting	On
14. Assess—Host	Production

profiles, batteries, and assessments from your computer or the iPad on the Central (and they can be edited within Q-interactive Assess). Because of the amount of information that must be keyed, using the computer may often be more convenient. At login, practitioners will see a *Dashboard* screen (see Figure 11.17) that lists recently accessed clients or assessments. In addition to *Dashboard*, examiners can use three primary tabs to navigate the site: *Clients*, *Batteries*, and *Assessments*.

The website was designed to be flexible and address an array of user needs; as such, the process of setting up an assessment can begin at any of the three tabs. For simplicity, this chapter describes the process of creating an assessment from the perspective of a practitioner who is setting up a client for the first time. Note, however, that the same action can be accomplished through multiple paths.

Selecting or Creating a Client Record

Accessing the *Clients* tab reveals a list of all clients created by an individual practitioner, as well as a button that allows new clients to be created. When creating a new client, practitioners will be presented with a screen similar to Figure 11.18. (If you scroll or swipe up the screen, you will see the types of

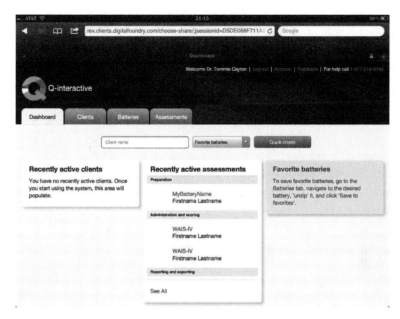

Figure 11.17. Central Dashboard Screen

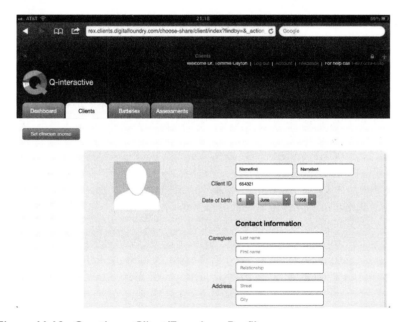

Figure 11.18. Creating a Client/Examinee Profile

information you may enter for each client. There are too many options to be presented on a single screen. The user will need to swipe up or down to access the full list.) In order for the system to function correctly, you must enter the client's first and last name, a Client ID number, date of birth, and gender. (If there is a potential for linking any of the assessment data directly with data from other systems, the ID you enter will need to be the same as the Client ID on the system with which the information will be linked.) The other information categories can be used as required by your local policies/needs. Once the desired and required information has been entered, scroll to the bottom of the screen to click the Save button. The information is saved, and a new client record will be created. (Client information can be edited after the record is created within Central as well as within Assess.)

Selecting or Creating a Test Battery

When a new client record has been saved, or when a client record is selected from the list, the presented screen (see Figure 11.19) has a drop-down menu at the bottom left with the label "Favorite Batteries" on the button. (Figure 11.19 is presented in portrait orientation in order to display all of its content; if you are using landscape orientation, you will have to scroll down to see the button.)

In Q-interactive, a *battery* is a set of tests and subtests that will be administered to an examinee during a test session. Click the down arrow on the right side of the Favorite Batteries button and a list of all the batteries that you have classified as "Favorites" is displayed for selection. If the desired battery is among those listed, click its name and then click the "Create Assessment" button.

If the combination of subtests or tests you would like to administer is not among those in the drop-down battery list, you will need to create a battery. Select "Favorite batteries" from the list and then click "Create assessment" (see Figure 11.19). This will take you to the Choose Battery screen that displays the lists of tests and batteries you are authorized to administer (see Figure 11.20). Note that you may need to scroll down the list to find a specific battery or test. Note also that if the list of available batteries or tests becomes too long, there are search functions at the top of the list.

To select an existing battery (which may consist of one or several tests or subtests), select the open circle next to the battery name. If the battery you want to administer is not listed, click the "Create Custom" button at the top right of the screen. The screen will split in half and an "Add" button will appear next to each test or battery. If you wish to include only some of the subtests within a test, click on the triangle between the selection circle and the battery/test icon and it will

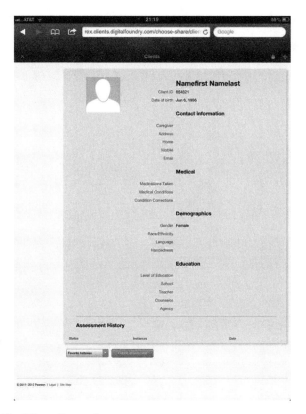

Figure 11.19. Client Record

expand to list all subtests included. Alternatively, you may click on "Expand all" at the top of the list and all subtests will be visible. Notice that an "Add" button now appears next to each subtest. Click "Add" for each test or subtest you want to include. The names of the selected tests and subtests now appear in the bottom of the window in the order you selected them (see Figure 11.21). The administration order can be changed once you have selected all the tests or subtests you want to include in your battery. Once you have completed your subtest selection, click on the "Configure and save" button.

The Configure Battery screen (see Figure 11.22) allows you to "Drag and drop" to put the selected tests and subtests in the order you would like to administer them. (If you make a mistake, you can use the "Back" button at the top of each screen.) Once the order is as desired, click the "Next" button at the top right of the screen. You will then be provided with a screen by which you can name the battery you have created and describe its directed population or

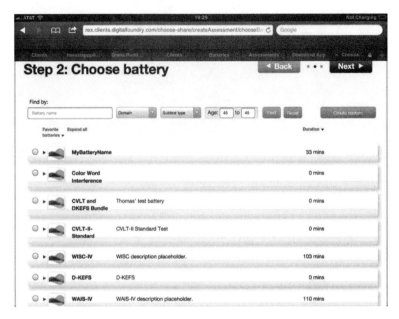

Figure 11.20. Choose Battery Screen

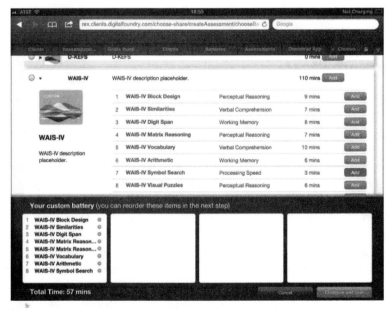

Figure 11.21. Creating a Custom Battery

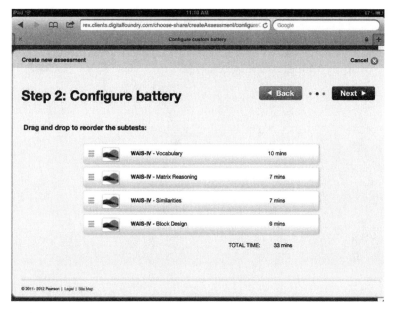

Figure 11.22. Configuring a Custom Battery

appropriate use. In the future this battery will appear in the Favorite Batteries list so that you and your colleagues can use it without having to recreate it each time. (If you do not assign a name to the battery, you can administer it, but it will not be saved as a Favorite Battery.)

It is important to note that Central can be configured so that groups (e.g., practices, clinics) can share access. If configured this way, individuals within a group can choose to share access to client profiles or custom batteries, which can be valuable in clinics where standard protocols are used or where clients are seen by psychometrists, trainees, and psychologists over the course of more than one visit.

Click Next, and the Assessment Information screen (see Figure 11.23) will be presented.

Creating an Assessment

On the Assessment Information Screen, enter the desired relevant information (Date, Time, and Location are required; the current date and time will be recorded as the scheduled assessment time if you do not change them). Then click "Finish" to move to the Assessment Tab summary screen (see Figure 11.24). If all is correct, click "Send to iPad." If the information is not correct, click "Edit"

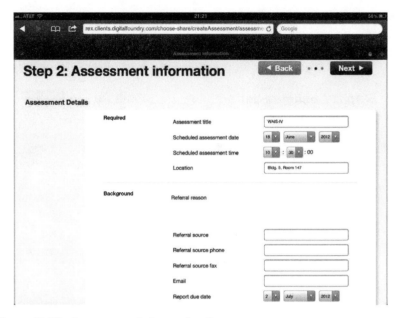

Figure 11.23. Assessment Information Screen

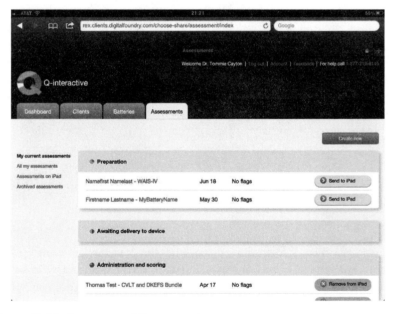

Figure 11.24. Summary of Assessments

≡ *Rapid Reference 11.4*

What to Do Before You Start Assessing

1. Make sure both iPads have an adequate charge.
2. Set up the assessment batteries that you use repeatedly.
3. Practice four to five administrations using Q-interactive before actual administration that counts.
4. Make sure your assigned assessment has been downloaded onto your iPads.
5. Make sure your Bluetooth link between the iPads is working well.
6. If you have been using your iPad to access the Qiactive server site, open the Safari app on your iPad and close all tabs that are still open (click on the "x" in the left side of the tab you want to close). Otherwise. the number of open tabs continues to increase with each usage.

just below "Send to iPad" and make corrections, save, and click "Send to iPad." Whenever an examiner uses an iPad to log into Assess, or selects the Sync button on the Assess home screen, all information required for the assessment will be downloaded to the iPad.

To Sync the iPad to Download Assessments

To sync your iPad so that it contains the information needed for all added assessments, simply launch the Q-interactive Assess application. If you have access to Wi-Fi, the system will search for and download any assessments for which you have clicked "Send to iPad" but you have not yet transferred to your device. You are now ready to administer the tests you have assigned. See Rapid Reference 11.4 for additional considerations. Also, when you are accessing Central on the iPad, by clicking the Assessments Tab you will be able to view assessments that have been downloaded below the Administration and Scoring header. This procedure allows examiners to track the progress of all assessments from Central.

Completing the Assessment

Once an assessment is complete, you will sync the data back to Central from the Examiner Device by selecting the Sync button at the top of the Assess home screen. This moves data to Central and permanently deletes it from the Examiner Device. There are three important points to note regarding Syncing:

- In the initial Q-interactive release, proration and substitution decisions can only be made within Assess and should thus be done before syncing.
- Audio recordings are not synced, so examiners must listen to any important recordings to resolve scores or document critical behaviors before syncing.
- Assessments cannot be synced until all item scores have been resolved. If there are any red flags associated with an assessment, resolve the tagged items before syncing.

Once synced, an assessment will appear within the Assessments tab underneath the Reporting and Exporting header. Selecting the assessment name will reveal an Overview screen that contains basic information about the assessment session (e.g., client name, date, examiner). From there, links on the left side of the screen allow examiners to access test results, notes, and all handwritten responses from each item's *Response* capture screen. Assessment information and results can be exported to a rich text file by selecting the Export button on the upper right-hand portion of the screen, and they can also be archived by selecting the Archive button located above the Export button. All data are maintained when an assessment is archived, but the assessment can no longer be accessed from the Assessment tab. To access archived assessments, select the Archived assessments link that is on the left side of the Assessment tab home screen, which will pull up a screen with all archived assessments. To locate past assessments from that list, search by client name using the search function at the top of the screen or sort the list of archived assessments by assessment name or date.

CONCLUSION

Adaptation of the WAIS-IV into Q-interactive (Wechsler, 2008, 2012) represents an initial attempt at converting traditional paper-and-pencil clinical assessments into a digital format. As described within this chapter, this initial adaptation was conservative in order to allow for the use of preexisting normative information. However, Q-interactive and the tests within it will continue to evolve rapidly. Designs will change in response to customer feedback, new technologies will result in updated functionalities, and more complex features that were outside the scope of the initial release will be added.

There are several benefits of the program in its current state (e.g., improved usability, better accuracy, increased efficiency), but the true promise of Q-interactive and digital assessment in general lies in what can be provided in the future as these changes come to fruition. As tests become digitally native, they will likely no longer rely on traditional norms, and more cutting-edge designs and scores will be developed. New constructs for understanding cognition, emotion, and behavior will be developed, and as a result clinicians will have available to them new ways of understanding their clients. In this respect, the digital WAIS-IV shares something in common with the initial Wechsler-Bellevue Intelligence Scale developed by David Wechsler: It is paving the way for a new era in assessment.

 TEST YOURSELF

1. **The name of the new digital administration platform for the WAIS-IV is**
   a. Apple-plus
   b. Q-interactive
   c. Computer-C
   d. Internet-Q

2. **TRUE OR FALSE? The new digital WAIS-IV administration is entirely automated; examiners are virtually redundant.**

3. **The digital WAIS-IV comprises two different components, namely, a browser-based set of functions called "Central" and**
   a. "Notate"—a software program that video records the entire test session
   b. "Persona"—a new methodology that interprets verbal responses from a clinical perspective
   c. "Assess"—an application that allows a battery of tests to be administered via pairs of iPads
   d. "Regulate"—an Internet device that evaluates the examinee's motivation throughout the test session

4. **TRUE OR FALSE? Digital administration of the WAIS-IV requires examinees to manipulate the cubes for Block Design when solving design items.**

5. **Which of the following is NOT a component of the standard subtest structure for the digitalized WAIS-IV?**
   a. Subtest Cover Card
   b. Instructions Screen
   c. Capture Screen
   d. Adaptive Testing Card
   e. End of Subtest Section

(continued)

6. **TRUE OR FALSE? The WAIS-IV digital administration has a feature that permits examiners to record the client's responses to verbal items.**

7. **In the digital WAIS-IV, which Perceptual Reasoning subtest utilizes a design that is a unique mixture of components from Verbal Comprehension and Perceptual Reasoning subtests?**
   a. Picture Completion
   b. Block Design
   c. Visual Puzzles
   d. Matrix Reasoning
   e. Figure Weights

8. **TRUE OR FALSE? The digital WAIS-IV requires examinees to complete Symbol Search, Coding, and Cancellation on the Client Device screen using a specialized stylus.**

9. **TRUE OR FALSE? Equivalence studies conducted by the test publisher demonstrate that the norms previously gathered for the traditional WAIS-IV subtests are also valid for the digitalized WAIS-IV subtests.**

10. **TRUE OR FALSE? When using the *TIMER*, the correct sequence is: (a) first display the stimulus screen and (b) then start the timer.**

Answers: 1. c; 2. false; 3. c; 4. true; 5. d; 6. true; 7. a; 8. false; 9. true; 10. true.

References

Alfonso, V. C., LaRocca, R., Oakland, T., & Spanakos, A. (2000). The course on individual cognitive assessment. *School Psychology Review, 29*, 52–64.

Alfonso, V. C., & Pratt, S. I. (1997). Issues and suggestions for training professionals in assessing intelligence. In D. P. Flanagan, J. L. Genshaft, & P. L. Harrison (Eds.), *Contemporary intellectual assessment: Theories, tests, and issues* (pp. 326–344). New York, NY: Guilford Press.

American Psychiatric Association. (2000). *Diagnostic and statistical manual of mental disorders* (4th ed., text rev.). Washington, DC: Author.

Anastasi, A., & Urbina, S. (1997). *Psychological testing* (7th ed.). Upper Saddle River, NJ: Prentice-Hall.

Arbuckle, T. Y., Gold, D., Andres, D., Schwartzman, A. E., & Chaikelson, J. (1992). The role of psychosocial context, age, and intelligence in memory performance of older men. *Psychology and Aging, 7*, 25–36.

Archer, R. P., Buffington-Vollum, J. K., Stredny, R. V., & Handel, R. W. (2006). A survey of test use patterns among forensic psychologists. *Journal of Personality Assessment, 87*, 64–94.

Archer, R. P., & Newsom, C. R. (2000). Psychological test usage with adolescent clients: Survey update. *Assessment, 7*, 227–236.

Atkins v. Virginia. (2002). 536 U.S. 304, 122 S.CT 2242.

Atkinson, L. (1992). Mental retardation and WAIS-R scatter analysis. *Journal of Intellectual Disability Research, 36*, 443–448.

Backman, L., Small, B. J., Wahlin, A., & Larsson, M. (2000). Cognitive functioning in very old age. In F. I. M. Craik & T. A. Salthouse (Eds.), *The handbook of aging and cognition* (2nd ed., pp. 499–558). Mahwah, NJ: Erlbaum.

Baltes, P. B. (1997). On the incomplete architecture of human ontogeny: Selection, optimization, and compensation as foundation of developmental theory. *American Psychologist, 52*, 366–380.

Baltes, P. B., & Lindenberger, U. (1997). Emergence of a powerful connection between sensory and cognitive functions across the adult life span: A new window to the study of cognitive aging? *Psychology and Aging, 12*, 12–21.

Baltes, P. B., & Schaie, K. W. (1976). On the plasticity of adult and gerontological intelligence: Where Horn and Donaldson fail. *American Psychologist, 31*, 720–725.

Baltes, P. B., Staudinger, U. M., & Lindenberger, U. (1999). Lifespan psychology: Theory and application to intellectual functioning. *Annual Review of Psychology, 50*, 471–507.

Bannatyne, A. (1974). Diagnosis: A note on recategorization of the WISC scaled scores. *Journal of Learning Disabilities, 7*, 272–274.

Basak, C., Boot, W. R., Voss, M. W., & Kramer, A. F. (2008). Can training in a real-time strategy videogame attenuate cognitive decline in older adults? *Psychology and Aging, 23*, 765–777.

Baxendale, S. (2011). IQ and ability across the adult life span. *Applied Neuropsychology, 18*, 164–167.

Belk, M. S., LoBello, S. G., Ray, G. E., & Zachar, P. (2002). WISC-III administration, clerical, and scoring errors make by student examiners. *Journal of Psychoeducational Assessment, 20*, 290–300.

Belter, R. W., & Piotrowski, C. (2001). Current status of doctoral-level training in psychological testing. *Journal of Clinical Psychology, 57*, 717–726.

Benson, N., Hulac, D. M., & Kranzler, J. H. (2010). Independent examination of the Wechsler Adult Intelligence Scale—Fourth Edition (WAIS-IV): What does the WAIS-IV measure? *Psychological Assessment, 22,* 121–130.

Berg, C. A. (2000). Intellectual development in adulthood. In R. J. Sternberg (Ed.), *Handbook of intelligence* (pp. 117–137). New York, NY: Cambridge University Press.

Berninger, V. W., & Richards, T. L. (2002). *Brain literacy for educators and psychologists.* New York, NY: Academic Press.

Berkowitz, B., & Green, R. F. (1963). Changes in intellect with age: I. Longitudinal study of Wechsler-Bellevue scores. *Journal of Genetic Psychology, 103,* 3–21.

Beuhner, M., Krumm, S., Ziegler, M., & Pluecken, T. (2006). Cognitive abilities and their interplay: Reasoning, crystallized intelligence, working memory components, and sustained attention. *Journal of Individual Differences, 27,* 57–72.

Binder, L. M., & Binder, A. L. (2011). Relative subtest scatter in the WAIS-IV standardization sample. *The Clinical Neuropsychologist, 25,* 62–71.

Binet, A. (1890a). Recherches sur les mouvements de quelques jeunes enfants. *La Revue Philosophique, 29,* 297–309.

Binet, A. (1890b). Perceptions d'enfants. *La Revue Philosophique, 30,* 582–611.

Binet, A. (1911). Nouvelle recherches sur la mesure du niveau intellectual chez les enfants d'école. *L'Année Psychologique, 17,* 145–210.

Binet, A., & Henri, V. (1895). La psychologie individuelle. *L'Année Psychologique, 2,* 411–465.

Binet, A., & Simon, T. (1905). Méthodes nouvelles pour le diagnostic du niveau intéllectuel des anormaux. *L'Année Psychologique, 11,* 191–244.

Binet, A., & Simon, T. (1908). Le développement de l'intelligence chez les enfants. *L'Année Psychologique, 14,* 1–94.

Birren, J. E., & Morrison, D. F. (1961). Analysis of the WAIS subtests in relation to age and education. *Journal of Gerontology, 16,* 363–369.

Bornstein, R. A. (1983). Verbal IQ-Performance IQ discrepancies on the Wechsler Adult Intelligence Scale—Revised in patients with unilateral or bilateral cerebral dysfunction. *Journal of Consulting and Clinical Psychology, 51,* 779–780.

Botwinick, J. (1977). Intellectual abilities. In J. E. Birren & K. W. Schaie (Eds.), *Handbook of the psychology of aging* (pp. 580–605). New York, NY: Van Nostrand Reinhold.

Breaux, K. C. (2009). *Wechsler Individual Achievement Test-Third Edition technical manual.* San Antonio, TX: Pearson.

Breaux, K. C. (2010). *Wechsler Individual Achievement Test-Third Edition technical manual with adult norms.* San Antonio, TX: Pearson.

Brooks, B. L., Holdnack, J. A., & Iverson, G. L. (2011). Advanced clinical interpretation of the WAIS-IV and WMS-IV: Prevalence of low scores varies by level of intelligence and years of education. *Assessment, 18,* 156–167.

Camara, W. J., Nathan, J. S., & Puente, A. E. (2000). Psychological test usage: Implications in professional psychology. *Professional Psychology: Research and Practice, 31,* 141–154.

Canivez, G. L. (2010). Review of the Wechsler Adult Intelligence Scale-Fourth Edition. In R. A. Spies, J. F. Carlson, and K. F. Geisinger (Eds.), *The eighteenth mental measurements yearbook* (pp. 684–688). Lincoln, NE: Buros Institute of Mental Measurements, University of Nebraska.

Canivez, G. L., & Watkins, M. W. (2010a). Exploratory and higher-order factor analyses of the Wechsler Adult Intelligence Scale-Fourth Edition (WAIS-IV) adolescent subsample. *School Psychology Quarterly, 25,* 223–235. doi: 10.1037/a0022046

Canivez, G. L., & Watkins, M. W. (2010b). Investigation of the factor structure of the Wechsler Adult Intelligence Scale-Fourth Edition (WAIS-IV): Exploratory and higher-order factor analyses. *Psychological Assessment, 22,* 827–836. doi: 10.1037/a0020429

Carroll, J. B. (1993). *Human cognitive abilities: A survey of factor-analytic studies.* Cambridge, England: Cambridge University Press.

Carroll, J. B. (1997). The three-stratum theory of cognitive abilities. In D. P. Flanagan, J. L. Genshaft, & P. L. Harrison (Eds.), *Contemporary intellectual assessment: Theories, tests, and issues* (pp. 122–130). New York, NY: Guilford Press.

Catron, D. W., & Thompson, C. C. (1979). Test-retest gains in WAIS scores after four retest intervals. *Journal of Clinical Psychology, 35,* 352–357.

Cattell, R. B. (1943). The measurement of adult intelligence. *Psychological Bulletin, 40,* 153–193.

Cattell, R. B. (1963). Theory of fluid and crystallized intelligence: A critical experiment. *Journal of Educational Psychology, 54,* 1–22.

Cattell, R. B., & Horn, J. L. (1978). A check on the theory of fluid and crystallized intelligence with description of new subtest designs. *Journal of Educational Measurement, 15,* 139–164.

Ceci, S. J., & Kanaya, T. (2010). "Apples and oranges are both round": Furthering the discussion on the Flynn effect. *Journal of Psychoeducational Assessment, 28,* 441–447.

Chastain, R., & Joe, G. W. (1987). Multidimensional relations between intellectual abilities and demographic variables. *Journal of Educational Psychology, 79,* 323–325.

Christensen, H., Henderson, A. S., Griffiths, K., & Levings, C. (1997). Does aging inevitably lead to declines in cognitive performance? A longitudinal study of elite academics. *Personality and Individual Differences, 23,* 67–78.

Climie, E. A., & Rostad, K. (2011). Test review: Wechsler Adult Intelligence Scale (4th ed.). *Journal of Psychoeducational Assessment, 29,* 581–586. doi: 10.1177/0734282911408707

Cohen, B. H. (1996). *Explaining psychological statistics.* Pacific Grove, CA: Brooks & Cole.

Cohen, J. (1959). The factorial structure of the WISC at ages 7-6, 10-6, and 13-6. *Journal of Consulting Psychology, 23,* 285–299.

Colcombe, S., & Kramer, A. F. (2003). Fitness effects on the cognitive function of older adults: A meta-analytic study. *Psychological Science, 14,* 125–130.

Colom, R., Lluis-Font, J. M., & Andres-Pueyo, A. (2005). The generational intelligence gains are caused by decreasing variance in the lower half of the distribution: Supporting evidence for the nutrition hypothesis. *Intelligence, 33,* 83–91.

Colom, R., Rebollo, I., Palacios, A., Juan-Espinosa, M., & Kyllonen, P. C. (2004). Working memory is (almost) perfectly predicted by *g. Intelligence, 32,* 277–296.

Cornell, E. L., & Coxe, W. W. (1934). *A performance ability scale: Examination manual.* New York, NY: World Book.

Costa, L. D. (1975). The relation of visuospatial dysfunction to digit span performance in patients with cerebral lesions. *Cortex, 11,* 31–36.

Craik, F. I. M., & Salthouse, T. A. (Eds.). (2008). *Handbook of aging and cognition* (3rd ed.). New York, NY: Psychology Press.

Cronbach, L. J. (1970). *Essentials of psychological testing* (3rd ed.) New York: Harper & Row.

Cunningham, W. R., & Owens, W. A. (1983). The Iowa State study of the adult development of intellectual abilities. In K. W. Schaie (Ed.), *Longitudinal studies of adult psychological development* (pp. 20–39). New York, NY: Guilford Press.

Daniel, M. (2012). Equivalence of Q-interactive™-administered cognitive tasks: WAIS-IV (Q-interactive™ Technical Report No. 1). Bloomington, MN: Pearson.

Deaux, K. (1984). From individual differences to social categories: Analysis of a decade's research on gender. *American Psychologist, 39,* 105–116.

Delaney, H. D., Norman, R. D., & Miller, D. A. (1981). An exploration of the verbal encodability hypothesis for sex differences in the Digit-Symbol (symbol-digit) test. *Intelligence, 5,* 199–208.

Diller, L., Ben-Yishay, Y., Gerstman, L. J., Goodkin, R., Gordon, W., & Weinberg, J. (1974). *Studies in cognitive and rehabilitation in hemiplegia,* Rehabilitation Monograph No. 50. New York, NY: New York University Medical Center Institute of Rehabilitation Medicine.

Doppelt, J. E., & Wallace, W. L. (1955). Standardization of the Wechsler Adult Intelligence Scale for older persons. *Journal of Abnormal and Social Psychology, 51*, 312–330.

Drozdick, L. W., & Cullum, C. M. (2011). Expanding the ecological validity of WAIS-IV and WMS-IV with the Texas Functional Living Scale. *Assessment, 18*, 141–155.

Drozdick, L. W., & Holdnack, J. A., Hilsabeck, R. C. (2011). *Essentials of WMS-IV Assessment.* Hoboken, NJ: Wiley.

Drozdick, L. W., Wahlstrom, D., Zhu, J., & Weiss, L. W. (2012). The Wechsler Adult Intelligence Scale—Fourth Edition. In D. P. Flanagan & P. L. Harrison (Eds.), *Contemporary intellectual assessment: Theories, tests, and issues* (3rd ed., pp. 197–223). New York, NY: Guilford Press.

Dubois, B., Feldman, H. H., Jacova, C., DeKosky, S. T., Barberger-Gateau, P., Cummings, J., . . . Scheltens, P. (2007). Research criteria for the diagnosis of Alzheimer's disease: Revising the NINCDS-ADRA criteria. *Lancet Neurology, 6*, 734–746.

Dubois, P. H. (1970). *A history of psychological testing.* Boston, MA: Allyn & Bacon.

Dumont, R., & Willis, J. O. (2001). Use of the Tellegen & Briggs formula to determine the Dumont-Willis Indexes (DWI-1 and DWI-2) for the WISC-III. Online. Available at http://alpha.fdu.edu/~dumont/psychology

Eisdorfer, C., & Wilkie, F. (1973). Intellectual changes with advancing age. In L. E. Jarvik, C. Eisdorfer, & J. E. Blum (Eds.), *Intellectual functioning in adults.* New York, NY: Springer.

Elliott, C. D. (2007). *Differential Ability Scales (DAS-II) 2nd ed., Administration and scoring manual.* San Antonio, TX: The Psychological Corporation.

Estes, W. K. (1974). Learning theory and intelligence. *American Psychologist, 29*, 740–749.

Feingold, A. (1988). Cognitive gender differences are disappearing. *American Psychologist, 43*, 95–103.

Finkel, D., Reynolds, C. A., McArdle, J. J., & Pederson, N. L. (2007). Age changes in processing speed as a leading indicator of cognitive aging. *Psychology and Aging, 22*, 558–568.

Flanagan, D. P. (2000). Wechsler-based CHC cross-battery assessment and reading achievement: Strengthening the validity of interpretations drawn from Wechsler test scores. *School Psychology Quarterly, 15*, 295–329.

Flanagan, D. P. & Alfonso, V.C. (2011). *Essentials of specific learning disability identification.* Hoboken, NJ: Wiley.

Flanagan, D. P., Alfonso, V. C., & Ortiz, S. O. (Eds.) (2012). The cross-battery assessment approach: An overview, historical perspective, and current directions. In D. P. Flanagan & P. L. Harrison (Eds.), *Contemporary intellectual assessment: Theories, tests, and issues* (3rd ed., pp. 459–483). New York, NY: Guilford Press.

Flanagan, D. P., & Harrison, P. L. (Eds.) (2012). *Contemporary intellectual assessment: Theories, tests, and issues* (3rd ed.). New York, NY: Guilford Press.

Flanagan, D. P., & Kaufman, A. S. (2004). *Essentials of WISC-IV assessment.* Hoboken, NJ: Wiley.

Flanagan, D. P., & Kaufman, A. S. (2009). *Essentials of WISC-IV assessment* (2nd ed.). Hoboken, NJ: Wiley.

Flanagan, D. P., Kaufman, A. S., Kaufman, N. L. & Lichtenberger, E.O. (2008). *Agora: The marketplace of ideas. Best practices: Applying response to intervention (RTI) and comprehensive assessment for the identification of learning disabilities* [Motion picture]. San Antonio, TX: Pearson.

Flanagan, D. P., & McGrew, K. S. (1997). A cross-battery approach to assessing and interpreting cognitive abilities: Narrowing the gap between practice and cognitive science. In D. P. Flanagan, J. L. Genshaft, & P. L. Harrison (Eds.), *Contemporary intellectual assessment* (pp. 314–325). New York, NY: Guilford Press.

Flanagan, D. P., McGrew, K. S., & Ortiz, S. O. (2000). *The Wechsler intelligence scales and Gf-Gc theory: A contemporary approach to interpretation.* Boston, MA: Allyn & Bacon.

Flanagan, D. P., & Ortiz, S. O. (2001). *Essentials of cross-battery assessment.* New York, NY: Wiley.

Flanagan, D. P., Ortiz, S. O., & Alfonso, V. C. (2007). *Essentials of cross-battery assessment* (2nd ed.). Hoboken, NJ: Wiley. See also the official site of the CHC Cross-Battery Approach by Dawn P. Flanagan and Samuel O. Ortiz, retrieved from http://facpub.stjohns.edu/~ortiz/cross-battery

Flanagan, D. P., Ortiz, S. O., Alfonso, V. C., & Mascolo, J. (2002). *The achievement test desk reference (ATDR): Comprehensive assessment and learning disabilities.* Boston, MA: Allyn & Bacon.

Flanagan, D. P., Ortiz, S. O., Alfonso, V., & Mascolo, J. T. (2006). *The achievement test desk reference (ATDR-II): A guide to learning disability identification* (2nd ed.). Hoboken, NJ: Wiley.

Fletcher, J. M., Lyon, G. R., Fuchs, L. S., & Barnes, M. A. (2007). *Learning disabilities: From identification to intervention.* New York, NY: Guilford Press.

Fletcher, J. M., Stuebing, K. K., & Hughes, L. C. (2010). IQ scores should be corrected for the Flynn effect in high-stakes decisions. *Journal of Psychoeducational Assessment, 28,* 469–473.

Floyd, R. G., & Kranzler, J. H. (2012). Processing approaches to interpretation of information from cognitive ability tests. In D. P. Flanagan & P. L. Harrison (Eds.), *Contemporary intellectual assessment: Theories, tests, and issues* (3rd ed., pp. 497–525). New York, NY: Guilford Press.

Flynn, J. R. (1987). Massive IQ gains in 14 nations: What IQ tests really measure. *Psychological Bulletin, 101,* 171–191.

Flynn, J. R. (1998). Rising IQ scores: Implications for the elderly. *Australian Journal on Ageing, 17,* 106–107.

Flynn, J. R. (2006). Tethering the elephant: Capital cases, IQ, and the Flynn effect. *Psychology, Public Policy, and Law, 12,* 170–178.

Flynn, J. R. (2007). *What is intelligence?* New York, NY: Cambridge University Press.

Flynn, J. R. (2009a). Requiem for nutrition as the cause of IQ gains: Raven's gains in Britain 1938–2008. *Economics and Human Biology, 7,* 18–27.

Flynn, J. R. (2009b). *What is intelligence?* (expanded ed.). New York, NY: Cambridge University Press.

Flynn, J. R. (2010). Problems with IQ gains: The huge vocabulary gap. *Journal of Psychoeducational Assessment, 28,* 412–433.

Flynn, J. R., & Weiss, L. (2007). American IQ gains from 1932 to 2002: The WISC subtests and educational progress. *International Journal of Testing, 7,* 209–224.

Frazier, T. W. (2011). Introduction to the special section on advancing WAIS-IV and WMS-IV clinical interpretation. *Assessment, 18,* 131–132.

Fry, A. F., & Hale, S. (1996). Processing speed, working memory, and fluid intelligence: Evidence for a developmental cascade. *Psychological Science, 7,* 237–241.

Gallagher, R. W., Somwaru, D. P., & Ben-Porath, Y. S. (1999). Current usage of psychological tests in state correctional settings. *Corrections Compendium, 24*(7), 1–20.

Galton, F. (1869). *Hereditary genius: An inquiry into its laws and consequences.* London, UK: Macmillan.

Galton, F. (1883). *Inquiries into human faculty and its development.* London, UK: Macmillan.

Geiser, C., Lehmann, W., & Eid, M. (2008). A note on sex differences in mental rotation in different age groups. *Intelligence, 36,* 556–563.

Glutting, J. J., & Oakland, T. (1993). *The guide to the assessment of test session behavior.* San Antonio, TX: The Psychological Corporation.

Goddard, H. H. (1911). A revision of the Binet scale. *Training School, 8,* 56–62.

Gold, J. M., Carpenter, C., Randolph, C., Goldberg, T. E., & Weinberger, D. R. (1997). Auditory working memory and Wisconsin Card Sorting test performance in schizophrenia. *Archives of General Psychiatry, 54,* 159–165.

Goldstein, K. (1948). *Language and language disturbances.* New York, NY: Grune & Stratton.

Goldstein, G., & Saklofske, D. H. (2010). The Wechsler intelligence scales in the assessment of psychopathology. In L. G. Weiss, D. H. Saklofske, D. L. Coalson, & S. E. Raiford (Eds.), *WAIS-IV clinical use and interpretation* (pp. 189–216). San Diego, CA: Academic Press.

Gorlyn, M., Keilp, J. G., Oquendo, M. A., Burke, A. K., Sackeim, H. A., & Mann, J. J. (2006). The WAIS-III and major depression: Absence of VIQ/PIQ differences. *Journal of Clinical and Experimental Neuropsychology, 28,* 1145–1157.

Green, R. F. (1969). Age-intelligence relationship between ages sixteen and sixty-four: A rising trend. *Developmental Psychology, 1,* 618–627.

Gregory, T., Nettelbeck, T., Howard, S., & Wilson, C. (2008). Inspection time: A biomarker for cognitive decline. *Intelligence, 36,* 664–671.

Gribbin, K., Schaie, K. W., & Parham, I. (1980). Complexity of life style and maintenance of intellectual abilities. *Journal of Social Issues, 36,* 47–61.

Groth-Marnat, G. (2009). *Handbook of psychological assessment* (5th ed.). Hoboken, NJ: Wiley.

Guilford, J. P. (1967). *The nature of human intelligence.* New York, NY: McGraw-Hill.

Guilford, J. P., & Fruchter, B. (1978). *Fundamental statistics in psychology and education* (6th ed.). New York, NY: McGraw-Hill.

Hagan, L. D., Drogin, E. Y., & Guilmette, T. J. (2010). IQ scores should not be adjusted for the Flynn effect in capital punishment cases. *Journal of Psychoeducational Assessment, 28,* 474–476.

Hale, J. B., & Fiorello, C. A. (2004). *School neuropsychology: A practitioner's handbook.* New York, NY: Guilford Press.

Hale, J. B., Hoeppner, J. B., & Fiorello, C. A. (2002). Analyzing Digit Span components to assessment of attention processes. *Journal of Psychoeducational Assessment, 20,* 128–143.

Halpern, D. F., Beninger, A. S., & Straight, C. A. (2011). Sex differences in intelligence. In R. J. Sternberg & S. B. Kaufman (Eds.), *Cambridge handbook of intelligence* (pp. 253–272). New York, NY: Cambridge University Press.

Hardy, S. T. (1993). Proper and effective use of sign language interpreters by school psychologists. Workshop presented at the meeting of the National Association of School Psychologists, Washington, DC.

Hardy-Braz, S. T. (2003). Enhancing school-based psychological services: Assessments and interventions with students who are deaf or hard of hearing. Workshop presented at the meeting of the National Association of School Psychologists, Toronto, Canada.

Harrison, P. L., Kaufman, A. S., Hickman, J. A., & Kaufman, N. L. (1988). A survey of tests used for adult assessment. *Journal of Psychoeducational Assessment, 6,* 188–198.

Hartley, A. (2006). Changing roles of the speed of processing construct in the cognitive psychology of human aging. In J. E. Birren & K. W. Schaie (Eds.), *Handbook of the psychology of aging* (6th ed., pp. 183–208). San Diego, CA: Academic Press.

Hartman, D. E. (2009). Test review Wechsler Adult Intelligence Scale IV (WAIS IV): Return of the gold standard. *Applied Neuropsychology, 16,* 85–87. doi: 10.1080/09084280802644466

Hauser, R. M. (1998). Trends in Black-White test-score differentials I: Uses and misuses of NAEP/SAT data. In U. Neisser (Ed.), *The rising curve: Long-term gains in IQ and related measures* (pp. 219–250). Washington, DC: American Psychological Association.

Heaton, R. K., Taylor, M. J., & Manly, J. (2003). Demographic effects and use of demographically corrected norms with the WAIS-III and WMS-III. In D. S. Tulsky, D. H. Saklofske, G. J. Chelune, R. K. Heaton, R. J. Ivnik, R. Bornstein, A. Prifitera, & M. F. Ledbetter (Eds.), *Clinical interpretation of the WAIS-III and WMS-III* (pp. 183–210). San Diego, CA: Academic Press.

Hebben, N. (2009). Review of special group studies and utility of the process approach with the WISC-IV. In D. P. Flanagan & A. S. Kaufman, *Essentials of WISC-IV Assessment* (2nd ed., pp. 216–242). Hoboken, NJ: Wiley.

Hebben, N., & Milberg, W. (2002). *Essentials of neuropsychological assessment.* New York, NY: Wiley.

Herring, J. P. (1922). *Herring revision of the Binet-Simon tests: Examination manual—Form A.* London, UK: World Book.

Hertzog, C. (2011). Intelligence in adulthood. In R. J. Sternberg & S. B. Kaufman (Eds.), *Cambridge handbook of intelligence* (pp. 174–190). New York, NY: Cambridge University Press.

Hertzog, C., Kramer, A. F., Wilson, R. S., & Lindenberger, U. (2009). Enrichment effects on adult cognitive development: Can the functional capacity of older adults be preserved and enhanced? *Psychological Science in the Public Interest* (9, Whole No. 1). Washington, DC: Association for Psychological Science.

Hertzog, C., & Schaie, K. W. (1988). Stability and change in adult intelligence: Simultaneous analysis of longitudinal means and covariance structures. *Psychology and Aging, 3*, 122–130.

Holdnack, J. A., & Drozdick, L. W. (2010). Using WAIS-IV and WMS-IV. In L. G. Weiss, D. H. Saklofske, D. L. Coalson, & S. E. Raiford (Eds.), *WAIS-IV clinical use and interpretation* (pp. 237–283). San Diego, CA: Academic Press.

Holdnack, J., Goldstein, G., & Drozdick, L. (2011). Social perception and WAIS-IV performance in adolescents and adults diagnosed With Asperger's Syndrome and Autism. *Assessment, 18*, 192–200.

Holdnack, J. A., Zhou, X., Larrabee, G. J., Millis, S. R., & Salthouse, T. A. (2011). Confirmatory Factor Analysis of the WAIS-IV/WMS-IV, *Assessment, 18*, 178–191.

Horn, J. L. (1985). Remodeling old model in intelligence. In B. B. Wolman (Ed.), *Handbook of intelligence: Theories, measurements, and applications* (pp. 267–300). New York, NY: Wiley.

Horn, J. L. (1989). Cognitive diversity: A framework of learning. In P. L. Ackerman, R. J. Sternberg, & R. Glaser (Eds.), *Learning and individual differences* (pp. 61–116). New York, NY: Freeman.

Horn, J. L., & Blankson, B. (2005). Foundations for better understanding of cognitive abilities. In D. P. Flanagan & P. L. Harrison (Eds.), *Contemporary intellectual assessment* (2nd ed., pp. 41–68). New York, NY: Guilford Press.

Horn, J. L., & Cattell, R. B. (1966). Refinement and test of theory of fluid and crystallized intelligence. *Journal of Educational Psychology, 57*, 253–270.

Horn, J. L., & Cattell, R. B. (1967). Age differences in fluid and crystallized intelligence. *Acta Psychologica, 26*, 107–129.

Horn, J. L., & Donaldson, G. (1976). On the myth of intellectual decline in adulthood. *American Psychologist, 31*, 701–719.

Horn, J. L., & Donaldson, G. (1977). Faith is not enough: A response to the Baltes-Schaie claim that intelligence will not wane. *American Psychologist, 32*, 369–373.

Horn, J. L., Donaldson, G., & Engstrom, R. (1981). Apprehension, memory, and fluid intelligence decline in adulthood. *Research on Aging, 3*, 33–84.

Horn, J. L., & Hofer, S. M. (1992). Major abilities and development in the adult period. In R. J. Sternberg & C. A. Berg (Eds.), *Intellectual development* (pp. 44–99). New York, NY: Cambridge University Press.

Hultsch, D. F., Hammer, M., & Small, B. (1993). Age differences in cognitive performance in later life: Relationships to self-reported health and activity life style. *Journal of Gerontology: Psychological Sciences, 48*, 1–11.

Hultsch, D. F., Hertzog, C., Small, B. J., & Dixon, R. A. (1999). Use it or lose it: Engaged lifestyle as a buffer of cognitive decline in aging? *Psychology and Aging, 14*, 245–263.

Hyde, J. S. (1981). How large are cognitive gender differences? A meta-analysis using w2 and d. *American Psychologist, 36*, 892–901.

Individuals with Disabilities Education Improvement Act of 2004, 20 U.S.C. §§ 407 *et seq.* (2004).

Jarvik, L. F., & Bank, L. (1983). Aging twins: Longitudinal psychometric data. In K. W. Schaie (Ed.), *Longitudinal studies of adult psychological development* (pp. 40–63). New York, NY: Guilford Press.

Jensen, A. R. (1980). *Bias in mental testing*. New York, NY: The Free Press.

Jensen, A. R. (1998). *The g factor: The science of mental ability*. Westport, CT: Praeger.

Jensen, A. R., & Figueroa, R. A. (1975). Forward and backward digit-span interaction with race and IQ. *Journal of Educational Psychology, 67*, 882–893.

Jensen, A. R., & Reynolds, C. R. (1983). Sex differences on the WISC-R. *Personality and Individual Differences, 4*, 223–226.

Kail, R. (2000). Speed of information processing: Developmental changes and links to intelligence. *Journal of School Psychology, 38*, 51–61.

Kail, R., & Hall, L. K. (1994). Processing speed, naming speed, and reading. *Developmental Psychology, 30*, 949–954.

Kail, R., & Salthouse, T. A. (1994). Processing speed, naming speed, and reading. *Developmental Psychology, 30*, 949–954.

Kamphaus, R. W. (1993). *Clinical assessment of children's intelligence*. Boston, MA: Allyn & Bacon.

Kamphaus, R. W., & Reynolds, C. R. (1987). *Clinical and research applications of the K-ABC*. Circle Pines, MN: American Guidance Service.

Kamphaus, R. W., Winsor, A. P., Rowe, E. W., & Kim, S. (2012). A history of intelligence test interpretation. In D. P. Flanagan & P. L. Harrison (Eds.), *Contemporary intellectual assessment: Theories, tests, and issues* (3rd ed.) (pp. 56–70). New York: Guilford Press.

Kane, M. J., Hambrick, D. Z., Tuholski, S. W., Wilhelm, O., Payne, T. W., & Engle, R. W. (2004). The generality of working memory capacity: A latent variable approach to verbal and visuospatial memory span and reasoning. *Journal of Experimental Psychology: General, 133*, 189–217.

Kaplan, E. (1988). A process approach to neuropsychological assessment. In T. Boll and B. K. Bryant (Eds.), *Clinical neuropsychology and brain function: Research, measurement, and practice* (pp. 125–167). Washington, DC: American Psychological Association.

Kaplan, E., Fein, D., Morris, R., Kramer, J. H., & Delis, D. C. (1999). *The WISC-III as a processing instrument*. San Antonio, TX: The Psychological Corporation.

Kaufman, A. S. (1979). *Intelligent testing with the WISC-R*. New York, NY: Wiley.

Kaufman, A. S. (1983). Intelligence: Old concepts-new perspectives. In G. W. Hynd (Ed.), *The school psychologist: An introduction* (pp. 95–117). Syracuse, NY: Syracuse University Press.

Kaufman, A. S. (1985). Review of Wechsler Adult Intelligence Scale-Revised. In J. V. Mitchell (Ed.), *The ninth mental measurements yearbook* (pp. 1699–1703). Lincoln, NE: University of Nebraska Press.

Kaufman, A. S. (1990). *Assessing adolescent and adult intelligence*. Boston, MA: Allyn & Bacon.

Kaufman, A. S. (1994a). *Intelligent testing with the WISC-III*. New York, NY: Wiley.

Kaufman, A. S. (1994b). Practice effects. In R. J. Sternberg (Ed.), *Encyclopedia of intelligence: Vol. 2* (pp. 828–833). New York, NY: Macmillan.

Kaufman, A. S. (2000a). Seven questions about the WAIS-III regarding differences in abilities across the 16 to 89 year life span. *School Psychology Quarterly, 15*, 3–29.

Kaufman, A. S. (2000b). Tests of intelligence. In R. J. Sternberg (Ed.), *Handbook of intelligence* (pp. 445–476). New York, NY: Cambridge University Press.

Kaufman, A. S. (2001). WAIS-III IQs, Horn's theory, and generational changes from young adulthood to old age. *Intelligence, 29*, 131–167.

Kaufman, A. S. (2009). *IQ testing 101*. New York, NY: Springer.

Kaufman, A. S. (2010a). Foreword. In L. G. Weiss, D. H. Saklofske, D. L. Coalson, & S. E. Raiford (Eds.), *WAIS-IV clinical use and interpretation* (pp. xiii–xxi). San Diego, CA: Academic Press.

Kaufman, A. S. (2010b). "In what way are apples and oranges alike?": A critique of Flynn's interpretation of the Flynn effect. *Journal of Psychoeducational Assessment, 28*, 382–398.

Kaufman, A. S. (2010c). Looking through Flynn's rose-colored spectacles. *Journal of Psychoeducational Assessment, 28*, 494–505.

Kaufman, A. S. (in press). Biography of David Wechsler. In F. Volkmar (Ed.), *Encyclopedia of autistic spectrum disorders*. New York, NY: Springer.

Kaufman, A. S., & Horn, J. L. (1996). Age changes on tests of fluid and crystallized intelligence for females and males on the Kaufman Adolescent and Adult Intelligence Test (KAIT) at ages 17 to 94 years. *Archives of Clinical Neuropsychology, 11,* 97–121.

Kaufman, A. S., Johnson, C. K., & Liu, X. (2008). A CHC theory-based analysis of age differences on cognitive abilities and academic skills at ages 22 to 90 years. *Journal of Psychoeducational Assessment, 26,* 350–381.

Kaufman, A. S., Kaufman, J. C., Chen, T., & Kaufman, N. L. (1996). Differences on six Horn abilities for fourteen age groups between 15–16 and 75–94 years. *Psychological Assessment, 8,* 161–171.

Kaufman, A. S., & Kaufman, N. L. (1990). *Administration and scoring manual for Kaufman Brief Intelligence Test (K-BIT)*. Circle Pines, MN: American Guidance Service.

Kaufman, A. S., & Kaufman, N. L. (1993). *Manual for Kaufman Adolescent & Adult Intelligence Test (KAIT)*. Circle Pines, MN: American Guidance Service.

Kaufman, A. S., & Kaufman, N. L. (2004). *Kaufman Assessment Battery for Children* (2nd ed.). Circle Pines, MN: American Guidance Service.

Kaufman, A. S., & Lichtenberger, E. O. (1999). *Essentials of WAIS-III assessment*. New York, NY: Wiley.

Kaufman, A. S., & Lichtenberger, E. O. (2000). *Essentials of WISC-III and WPPSI-R assessment.* New York, NY: Wiley.

Kaufman, A. S., & Lichtenberger, E. O. (2002). *Assessing adolescent and adult intelligence* (2nd ed.). Boston, MA: Allyn & Bacon.

Kaufman, A. S., & Lichtenberger, E. O. (2006). *Assessing adolescent and adult intelligence* (3rd ed.) Hoboken, NJ: Wiley.

Kaufman, A. S., Lichtenberger, E. O., Fletcher-Janzen, E., & Kaufman, N. L. (2005). *Essentials of KABC-II assessment*. Hoboken, NJ: Wiley.

Kaufman, A. S., McLean, J. E., & Reynolds, C. R. (1988). Sex, race, residence, region, and education differences on the WAIS-R subtests. *Journal of Clinical Psychology, 44,* 231–248.

Kaufman, A. S., Reynolds, C. R., & McLean, J. E. (1989). Age and WAIS-R intelligence in a national sample of adults in the 20- to 74-year age range: A cross-sectional analysis with educational level controlled. *Intelligence, 13,* 235–253.

Kaufman, A. S., & Weiss, L. G. (2010a). Introduction to the Special Issue of JPA on the Flynn Effect. *Journal of Psychoeducational Assessment, 28,* 379–381.

Kaufman, A. S., & Weiss, L. G. (Eds.) (2010b). Special issue on the Flynn Effect. *Journal of Psychoeducational Assessment* (28, Whole No. 5) Thousand Oaks, CA: Sage.

Kaufman, J. C., Chen, T., & Kaufman, A. S. (1995). Ethnic group, education, and gender differences on six Horn abilities for adolescents and adults. *Journal of Psychoeducational Assessment, 13,* 49–65.

Kaufman, S. B., Reynolds, M. R., Liu, X., Kaufman, A. S., & McGrew, K. (2012). Are cognitive g and academic g one and the same g?: An exploration on the Woodcock-Johnson and Kaufman tests. *Intelligence, 40,* 123–138.

Kausler, D. H. (1982). *Experimental psychology and human aging*. New York, NY: Wiley.

Kausler, D. H. (1991). *Experimental psychology, cognition, and human aging*. New York, NY: Springer-Verlag.

Keith, T. Z., & Reynolds, M. R. (2012). Using confirmatory factor analysis to aid in understanding the constructs measured by intelligence tests. In D. P. Flanagan & P. L. Harrison (Eds.), *Contemporary intellectual assessment: Theories, tests, and issues* (3rd ed., pp. 758–799). New York, NY: Guilford Press.

Kemp, S. L., Kirk, U., & Korkman, M. (2001). *Essentials of NEPSY assessment*. New York, NY: Wiley.

Kirkpatrick, E. A. (1903). *Fundamentals of child study: A discussion of instincts and other factors in human development with practical applications*. New York, NY: Macmillan.

Kite, E. S. (1916). *Translation of A. Binet and T. Simon*, The development of intelligence in children. Baltimore, MD: Williams & Wilkins.

Kohs, S. C. (1923). *Intelligence measurement*. New York, NY: Macmillan.

Korkman, M., Kirk, U., & Kemp, S. L. (2007). *The NEPSY Second Edition (NEPSY-II)*. San Antonio, TX: The Psychological Corporation.

Krach, S. K. (2010). Review of Essentials of WAIS-IV Assessment. *Journal of Psychoeducational Assessment, 28*, 276–279.

Kuentzel, J. G., Hetterscheidt, L. A., & Barnett, D. (2011). Testing intelligently includes double-checking Wechsler IQ scores. *Journal of Psychoeducational Assessment, 29*, 39–46. doi: 10.1177/0734282910362048

Laux, L. F., Lane, D. M. (1985). Information processing components of substitution test performance. *Intelligence, 9*, 111–136.

Lee, H. F., Gorsuch, R. L., Saklofske, D. H., & Patterson, C. A. (2008). Cognitive differences for ages 16 to 89 (Canadian WAIS-III): Curvilinear with Flynn and processing speed corrections. *Journal of Psychoeducational Assessment, 26*, 382–394.

Levine, S. C., Huttenlocher, J., Taylor, A., & Langrock, A. (1999). Early sex differences in spatial skill. *Developmental Psychology, 35*, 940–949.

Lezak, M. D., Howieson, D. B., & Loring, D. W. (Eds.). (2004). *Neuropsychological assessment* (4th ed.). New York, NY: Oxford University Press.

Lichtenberger, E. O., Broadbooks, D. Y., & Kaufman, A. S. (2000). *Essentials of cognitive assessment with KAIT and other Kaufman measures*. New York, NY: Wiley.

Lichtenberger, E. O., & Kaufman, A. S. (2004). *Essentials of WPPSI-III assessment*. Hoboken, NJ: Wiley.

Lichtenberger, E. O., & Kaufman, A. S. (2009). *Essentials of WAIS-IV assessment*. Hoboken, NJ: Wiley.

Lichtenberger, E. O., Mather, N., Kaufman, N. L., & Kaufman, A. S. (2004). *Essentials of assessment report writing*. Hoboken, NJ: Wiley.

Lipsitz, J. D., Dworkin, R. H., & Erlenmeyer-Kimling, L. (1993). Wechsler Comprehension and Picture Arrangement subtests and social adjustment. *Psychological Assessment, 5*, 430–473.

Longman, R. S. (2004). Values for comparison of WAIS-III index scores with overall means. *Psychological Assessment, 16*, 323–325.

Loring, D. W., & Bauer, R. M. (2010). Testing the limits: Cautions and concerns regarding the new Wechsler IQ and Memory scales. *Neurology, 74*, 685–690. Retrieved from http://www.neurology.org/cgi/content/full/74/8/685

Luria, A. R. (1973). *The working brain: An introduction to neuropsychology*. New York, NY: Basic Books.

Luria, A. R. (1980). *Higher cortical functions in man* (2nd ed.). New York, NY: Basic Books.

MacDonald, M. C., Almor, A., Henderson, V. W., Kempler, D., & Andersen, E. S. (2001). Assessing working memory and language comprehension in Alzheimer's disease. *Brain and Language, 78*, 17–42.

Majeres, R. L. (1983). Sex differences in symbol-digit substitution and speeded matching. *Intelligence, 7*, 313–327.

Mapou, R. L. (2008). *Adult learning disabilities and ADHD: Research-informed assessment*. New York, NY: Oxford University Press.

Matarazzo, J. D. (1972). *Wechsler's measurement and appraisal of adult intelligence* (5th ed.). New York, NY: Oxford University Press.

Matarazzo, J. D. (1981). Obituary: David Wechsler (1896–1981). *American Psychologist, 36,* 1542–1543.

Matarazzo, J. D., & Herman, D. O. (1984). Base rate data for the WAIS-R: Test-retest stability and VIQ-PIQ differences. *Journal of Clinical Neuropsychology, 6,* 351–366.

Mayes, S. D., & Calhoun, S. L. (2008). WISC-IV and WIAT-II profiles in children with high-functioning autism. *Journal of Autism and Developmental Disorders, 38,* 428–439.

McArdle, J. J., Ferrer-Caja, E., Hamagami, F., & Woodcock, R. W. (2002). Comparative longitudinal structural analyses of the growth and decline of multiple intellectual abilities over the life span. *Developmental Psychology, 38,* 113–142.

McCloskey, G. (2009). The WISC-IV Integrated. In D. P. Flanagan & A. S. Kaufman (Eds.), *Essentials of WISC-IV Assessment* (2nd ed., pp. 310–467). Hoboken, NJ: Wiley.

McCloskey, G., & Maerlender, A. (2005). The WISC-IV Integrated. In A. Prifitera, D. H. Saklofske, & L. G. Weiss (Eds.), *WISC-IV clinical use and interpretation: Scientist-practitioner perspectives* (pp. 101–149). Burlington, MA: Elsevier.

McCloskey, G., Whitaker, J., Murphy, R., & Rogers, J. (2012). Intellectual, cognitive, and neuropsychological assessment in three-tier service delivery systems in school. In D. P. Flanagan & P. L. Harrison (Eds.), *Contemporary intellectual assessment: Theories, tests and issues* (pp. 852–882). New York, NY: Guilford Press.

McDermott, P. A., Fantuzzo, J. W., Glutting, J. J., Watkins, M. W., & Baggaley, A. R. (1992). Illusions of meaning in the ipsative assessment of children's ability. *Journal of Special Education, 25,* 504–526.

McGrew, K. S. (2005). The Cattell-Horn-Carroll theory of cognitive abilities: Past, present, and future. In D. P. Flanagan & P. L. Harrison (Eds.), *Contemporary intellectual assessment: Theories, tests, and issues* (2nd ed., pp. 136–181). New York, NY: Guilford Press.

McGrew, K. S. (2010). The Flynn effect and its critics: Rusty linchpins and "lookin' for g and Gf in some of the wrong places." *Journal of Psychoeducational Assessment, 28,* 448–468.

McGrew, K. S., Woodcock, R., & Ford, L. (2006). The Woodcock-Johnson Battery, Third Edition. In A. S. Kaufman & E. O. Lichtenberger (Eds.), *Assessing adolescent and adult intelligence* (3rd ed., pp. 561–628). Hoboken, NJ: Wiley.

McLean, J. E. (1995). *Improving education through action research.* Thousand Oaks, CA: Corwin Press.

McLean, J. E., Kaufman, A. S., & Reynolds, C. R. (1988, November). What role does formal education play in the IQ-age relationships across the adult life-span? *Mid-South Educational Researcher, 17*(1), 6–8, 13–18.

Melchers, P., Schürmann, S., & Scholten, S. (2006). *Kaufman Test zur Intelligenzmessung für Jugendliche und Erwachsene handbuch* [Kaufman test for intelligence measurement for young people and adults manual]. Leiden, The Netherlands: PITS.

Moran, J. L., & Mefford, R. B. Jr. (1959). Repetitive psychometric measures. *Psychological Reports, 5,* 269–275.

Morris, R. D., Stuebing, K. K., Fletcher, J. M., Shaywitz, S. E., Lyon, G. R., Shankweiler, D. P., . . . Shaywitz, B. A. (1998). Subtypes of reading disability: Variability around a phonological core. *Journal of Educational Psychology, 90,* 347–373.

Mulder, J. L., Dekker, R., & Dekker, P. H. (2004). *Kaufman Intelligentietest voor Adolescenten en Volwassenen* [Kaufman intelligence test for adolescents and adults]. Leiden, The Netherlands: PITS.

Murphy, G. (1968). Psychological views of personality and contributions to its study. In E. Norbeck, D. Price-Williams, & W. M. McCord (Eds.), *The study of personality* (pp. 15–40). New York, NY: Holt, Rinehart & Winston.

Naglieri, J. A., & Das, J. P. (1997). *Cognitive Assessment System.* Chicago, IL: Riverside.

Naglieri, J. A., & Goldstein, S. (Eds.). (2009). *A practitioner's guide to assessment of intelligence and achievement.* Hoboken, NJ: Wiley.

Naismith, S. L., Hickie, I. B., Turner, K., Little, C. L., Winter, V., Ward, P. B., . . . Parker, G. (2003). Neuropsychological performance in patients with depression is associated with clinical, etiological, and genetic risk factors. *Journal of Clinical and Experimental Neuropsychology, 25*, 866–877.

Niileksela, C. R., Reynolds, M. R., & Kaufman, A. S. (2012). An alternative Cattell-Horn-Carroll (CHC) factor structure of the WAIS-IV: Age invariance of an alternative model for ages 70–90. Manuscript submitted for publication.

Nisbett, R. E. (2009). *Intelligence and how to get it: Why schools and culture count.* New York, NY: Norton.

Owens, W. A. (1953). Age and mental abilities: A longitudinal study. *Genetic Psychology Monographs, 48*, 3–54.

Owens, W. A. (1966). Age and mental ability: A second adult follow-up. *Journal of Educational Psychology, 57*, 311–325.

Parker, K. C. H. (1986). Changes with age, year-of-birth cohort, age by year-of-birth interaction, and standardization of the Wechsler adult intelligence tests. *Human Development, 29*, 209–222.

Pearson. (2009). *Wechsler Individual Achievement Test–Third Edition.* San Antonio, TX: Author.

Pearson Assessments. (2009a). Support and resources home sample reports. Retrieved from http://www.pearsonassessments.com/pai/ca/research/publications/samplerpts/reslist.htm

Pearson Assessments. (2009b). Support and resources home technical reports. Retrieved from http://www.pearsonassessments.com/pai/ca/research/publications/techrpts/reslist.htm

Pearson Assessments. (2009c). WAIS-IV corrected table. Retrieved from http://www.pearsonassessments.com/NR/rdonlyres/76496E27-0B90-478B-B7D5-CF05983EBCD8/0/WAISIVTechManual_TableC2.pdf

Pearson Assessments. (2009d). WAIS-IV correction letter. Retrieved from http://www.pearsonassessments.com/NR/rdonlyres/9663B2CF-529C-4B61-A289-9472728BF7E3/0/WAISIVTechManual_Letter.pdf

Pennington, B. F. (2009). *Diagnosing learning disorders: A neuropsychological framework.* New York, NY: Guilford Press.

Pintner, R., & Paterson, D. D. (1925). *A scale of performance tests.* New York, NY: Appleton & Co.

Prifitera, A., Saklofske, D. H., Weiss, L. G., & Rolfhus, E. (Eds.). (2005). *WISC-IV clinical use and interpretation: Scientist-practitioner perspectives.* San Diego, CA: Academic Press.

Prifitera, A., Weiss, L. G., & Saklofske, D. H. (1998). The WISC-III in context. In A. Prifitera & D. H. Saklofske (Eds.), *WISC-III clinical use and interpretation* (pp. 1–39). San Diego, CA: Academic Press.

Psychological Corporation, The. (1997). *WAIS-III and WMS-III technical manual.* San Antonio, TX: Author.

Psychological Corporation, The. (2003). *WISC-IV technical and interpretive manual.* San Antonio, TX: Author.

Psychological Corporation, The. (2008). *WAIS-IV technical and interpretive manual.* San Antonio, TX: Author.

Quinn, P. C., & Liben, L. S. (2008). A sex difference in mental rotation in young infants. *Psychological Science, 19*, 1067–1070.

Rabbitt, P. (1993). Baseline changes in cognitive performance with age. In R. Levy & R. Howard (Eds.), *Treatment and care in old age psychiatry* (pp. 11–30). Petersfield, UK: Wrightson Biomedical.

Rabbitt, P., Donlan, C., Watson, P., McInnes, L., & Bent, N. (1995). Unique and interactive effects of depression, age, socioeconomic advantage, and gender on cognitive performance of normal healthy older people. *Psychology and Aging, 10*, 307–313.

Rabin, L. A., Barr, W. B., & Burton, L. A. (2005). Assessment practices of clinical neuropsychologists in the United States and Canada: A survey of INS, NAN, and APA division 40 members. *Archives of Clinical Psychology, 20*, 33–65.

Raiford, S. E., Coalson, D., Saklofske, D. H., & Weiss, L. W. (2010). Practical issues in WAIS-IV administration and scoring. In L. G. Weiss, D. H. Saklofske, D. Coalson, & S. E. Raiford (Eds.), *WAIS-IV clinical use and interpretation: Scientist-practitioner perspectives* (pp. 25–59). San Diego, CA: Academic Press.

Raven, J. C. (1938). *Progressive matrices*. London, UK: Lewis.

Raz, N. (2000). Aging of the brain and its impact on cognitive performance: Integration of structural and functional findings. In F. I. M. Craik & T. A. Salthouse (Eds.), *The handbook of aging and cognition* (2nd ed., pp. 1–90). Mahwah, NJ: Erlbaum.

Reitan, R. M. (1988). Integration of neuropsychological theory, assessment, and application. *The Clinical Neuropsychologist, 2*, 331–349.

Reitan, R. M., & Wolfson, D. (1992). *Neuropsychological evaluation of older children*. South Tucson, AZ: Neuropsychology Press.

Reynolds, C. R. (1997). Forward and backward memory span should not be combined for clinical analysis. *Archives of Clinical Neuropsychology, 12*, 29–40.

Reynolds, C. R., & Fletcher-Janzen, E. (1989). *Handbook of clinical child neuropsychology*. New York, NY: Plenum Press.

Reynolds, C. R., & Kamphaus, R. W. (2003). *Reynolds Intellectual Assessment Scales*. Lutz, FL: Psychological Assessment Resources.

Reynolds, C. R., & Lowe, P. A. (2009). The problem of bias in psychological assessment. In T. B. Gutkin & C. R. Reynolds (Eds.), *The handbook of school psychology* (4th ed., pp. 332–374). Hoboken, NJ: Wiley.

Reynolds, C. R., Niland, J., Wright, J. E., & Rosenn, M. (2010). Failure to apply the Flynn correction in death penalty litigation: Standard practice of today maybe, but certainly malpractice of tomorrow. *Journal of Psychoeducational Assessment, 28*, 477–481.

Rodgers, J. L., & Wanstrom, L. (2007). Identification of a Flynn effect in the NLSY: Moving from the center to the boundaries. *Intelligence, 35*, 187–196.

Roid, G. (2003). *Stanford-Binet Intelligence Scales* (5th ed.). Itasca, IL: Riverside.

Roszkowski, M. J. (2001). Review of the Revised Minnesota Paper Form Board Test (2nd ed.). In J. C. Impara & B. S. Plake (Eds.), *Buros' fourteenth mental measurements yearbook* (pp. 1012–1015). Lincoln, NE: Buros Institute, University of Nebraska.

Royer, F. L. (1978). Sex differences in symbol-digit substitution task performance. *Intelligence, 2*, 145–151.

Rugel, R. (1974a). WISC subtest scores of disabled readers: A review with respect to Bannatyne's recategorization. *Journal of Learning Disabilities, 7*, 48–55.

Rugel, R. (1974b). WISC subtest scores of disabled readers: The factor structure of the WISC in two populations of disabled readers. *Journal of Learning Disabilities, 7*, 581–585.

Ryan, J. J., Paolo, A. M., & Brungardt, T. M. (1990). Standardization of the Wechsler Adult Intelligence ScaleRevised for persons 75 years and older. *Psychological Assessment, 2*, 404–411.

Saklofske, D. H., Weiss, L. G., Raiford, S. E., & Prifitera, A. (2006). Advanced interpretive issues with the WISC-IV full-scale IQ and general ability index scores. In L. G. Weiss, D. H. Saklofske, A. Prifitera, & J. Holdnack (Eds.), *WISC-IV advanced clinical interpretation* (pp. 99–138). New York, NY: Elsevier.

Salthouse, T. A. (1985). Speed of behavior and its implications for cognition. In J. E. Birren & K. W. Schaie (Eds.), *Handbook of the psychology of aging* (2nd ed., pp. 400–426). New York, NY: Van Nostrand Reinhold.

Salthouse, T. A. (1992). *Mechanisms of age–cognition relations in adulthood.* Hillsdale, NJ: Erlbaum.

Salthouse, T. A. (2004). Localizing age-related individual differences in a hierarchical structure. *Intelligence, 32,* 541–561.

Salthouse, T. A. (2010). *Major issues in cognitive aging.* New York, NY: Oxford University Press.

Salthouse, T. A., & Saklofske, D. H. (2010). Do the WAIS-IV tests measure the same aspects of cognitive functioning in adults under and over age 65? In L. G. Weiss, D. H. Saklofske, D. L. Coalson, & S. E. Raiford (Eds.), *WAIS-IV clinical use and interpretation* (pp. 217–235). San Diego, CA: Academic Press.

Sattler, J. M. (1982). *Assessment of children* (2nd ed.). La Mesa, CA: Author.

Sattler, J. M. (1998). *WAIS-III supplement.* San Diego, CA: Author.

Sattler, J. M. (2001). *Assessment of children: Cognitive applications* (4th ed.). La Mesa, CA: Author.

Sattler, J. M. (2008). *Assessment of children: Cognitive foundations* (5th ed.). San Diego, CA: Author.

Sattler, J. M., & Dumont, R. (2004). *Assessment of children: WISC-IV and WPPSI-III supplement.* San Diego, CA: Authors.

Sattler, J. M., & Ryan, J. (2009). *Assessment with the WAIS-IV.* San Diego, CA: Author.

Schaie, K. W. (Ed.). (1983a). *Longitudinal studies of adult psychological development.* New York, NY: Guilford Press.

Schaie, K. W. (1983b). The Seattle Longitudinal Study: A 21-year exploration of psychometric intelligence in adulthood. In K. W. Schaie (Ed.), *Longitudinal studies of adult psychological development* (pp. 64–135). New York, NY: Guilford Press.

Schaie, K. W. (1983c). What can we learn from the longitudinal study of adult psychological development? In K. W. Schaie (Ed.), *Longitudinal studies of adult psychological development* (pp. 1–19). New York, NY: Guilford Press.

Schaie, K. W. (1984). Midlife influences upon intellectual functioning in old age. *International Journal of Behavior Development, 7,* 463–478.

Schaie, K. W. (1994). The course of adult intellectual development. *American Psychologist, 49,* 304–313.

Schaie, K. W., & Hertzog, C. (1983). Fourteen-year cohort sequential analyses of adult intellectual development. *Developmental Psychology, 19,* 531–543.

Schaie, K. W., & Strother, C. R. (1968). The cross-sequential study of age changes in cognitive behavior. *Psychological Bulletin, 70,* 671–680.

Schmitz-Sherzer, R., & Thomae, H. (1983). Constancy and change of behavior in old age: Findings from the Bonn Longitudinal Study on Aging. In K. W. Schaie (Ed.), *Longitudinal studies of adult psychological development* (pp. 191–221). New York, NY: Guilford Press.

Schneider, W. J., and McGrew, K. S. (2012). The Cattell-Horn-Carroll model of intelligence. In D. P. Flanagan & P. L. Harrison (Eds.), *Contemporary intellectual assessment: Theories, tests, and issues* (3rd ed., pp. 99–144). New York, NY: Guilford Press.

Schraw, G. (2010). Review of the Wechsler Adult Intelligence Scale-Fourth Edition. In R. A. Spies, J. F. Carlson, & K. F. Geisinger (Eds.), *The eighteenth mental measurements yearbook* (pp. 688–690). Lincoln, NE: Buros Institute of Mental Measurements, University of Nebraska.

Sharp, S. E. (1898–1899). Individual psychology: A study in psychological method. *American Journal of Psychology, 10,* 329–391.

Shiffrin, R. M., & Schneider, W. (1977). Controlled and automatic human information processing: II. Perceptual learning, automatic attending, and a general theory. *Psychological Review, 84,* 127–190.

Shimamura, A. P., Berry, J. M., Mangels, J. A., Rusting, C. L., & Jurica, P. J. (1995). Memory and cognitive abilities in university professors: Evidence for successful aging. *Psychological Science, 6*, 271–277.

Shouksmith, G. (1970). *Intelligence, creativity and cognitive style*. New York, NY: Wiley.

Siegler, I. (1983). Psychological aspects of the Duke Longitudinal studies. In K. W. Schaie (Ed.), *Longitudinal studies of adult psychological development* (pp. 136–190). New York, NY: Guilford Press.

Siegler, I., & Botwinick, J. (1979). A long-term longitudinal study of intellectual ability of older adults: The matter of selective subject attrition. *Journal of Gerontology, 34*, 242–245.

Silver, L. B. (Ed.). (1993). *Child and adolescent psychiatric clinics of North America, 2*, 181–353.

Sliwinski, M., & Buschke, H. (1999). Cross-sectional and longitudinal relationships among age, cognition, and processing speed. *Psychology and Aging, 14*, 18–33.

Spearman, C. E. (1904). "General Intelligence," objectively determined and measured. *American Journal of Psychiatry, 15*, 201–293.

Spearman, C. E. (1927). *The abilities of man*. New York, NY: Macmillan.

Steen, R. G. (2009). *Human intelligence and medical illness: Assessing the Flynn effect*. New York, NY: Springer.

Sternberg, R. J. (1995). *In search of the human mind*. Fort Worth, TX: Harcourt Brace College.

Sternberg, R. J. (2010). The Flynn effect: So what? *Journal of Psychoeducational Assessment, 28*, 434–440.

Sternberg, R. J., Kaufman, J. C., & Grigorenko, E. L. (2008). *Applied intelligence*. New York, NY: Cambridge University Press.

Sternberg, R. J., & Kaufman, S. B. (Eds.). (2011). *Cambridge handbook of intelligence*. New York, NY: Cambridge University Press.

Sternberg, S. (1966). High-speed scanning in human memory. *Science, 153*, 652–654.

Storandt, M. (1976). Speed and coding effects in relation to age and ability level. *Developmental Psychology, 12*, 177–178.

Storandt, M. (1977). Age, ability level, and method of administering and scoring the WAIS. *Journal of Gerontology, 32*, 175–178.

Strauss, E., Sherman, E. M. S., & Spreen, O. (2006). *A compendium of neuropsychological tests: Administration, norms, and commentary* (3rd ed.). New York, NY: Oxford University Press.

Sundet, J. M., Barlaug, D. F., & Torjussen, T. M. (2004). The end of the Flynn effect? A study of secular trends in mean intelligence test scores of Norwegian conscripts during half a century. *Intelligence, 32*, 349–362.

Suzuki, L. A., Short, E. L., & Lee, C. S. (2011). Social and ethnic group differences in intelligence in the United States: Multicultural perspectives. *Cambridge handbook of intelligence* (pp. 273–292). New York, NY: Cambridge University Press.

Talland, G. A., & Schwab, R. S. (1964). Performance with multiple sets in Parkinson's disease. *Neuropsychologia, 2*, 45–57.

Teasdale, T. W., & Owen, D. R. (2005). A long-term rise and recent decline in intelligence test performance: The Flynn Effect in reverse. *Personality & Individual Differences, 39*, 837–843.

Teasdale, T. W., & Owen, D. R. (2008). Secular declines in cognitive test scores: A reversal of the Flynn Effect. *Intelligence, 36*, 121–126.

Terman, L. M. (1916). *The measurement of intelligence*. Boston, MA: Houghton-Mifflin.

Terman, L. M., & Childs, H. G. (1912). A tentative revision and extension of the Binet-Simon measuring scale of intelligence. *Journal of Educational Psychology, 3*, 61–74, 133–143, 198–208, 277–289.

Terman, L. M., & Merrill, M. A. (1937). *Measuring intelligence*. Boston, MA: Houghton-Mifflin.

Terman, L. M., & Merrill, M. A. (1960). *Stanford-Binet Intelligence Scale.* Boston, MA: Houghton-Mifflin.

Terman, L. M., & Merrill, M. A. (1973). *Stanford-Binet Intelligence Scale: 1972 Norms edition.* Boston, MA: Houghton Mifflin.

Thorndike, R. L., Hagen, E. P., & Sattler, J. M. (1986). *Stanford-Binet Intelligence Scale* (4th ed.). Chicago, IL: Riverside Press.

Thurstone, L. L., & Thurstone, T. G. (1949). *Examiner's manual for the SRA Primary Mental Abilities Test.* Chicago, IL: Science Research Associates.

Tranter, L. J., & Koutstaal, W. (2008). Age and flexible thinking: An experimental demonstration of the beneficial effects of the increased cognitively stimulating activity on fluid intelligence in healthy older adults. *Aging, Neuropsychology, and Cognition, 15,* 184–207.

Tulsky, D. S., Saklofske, D. H., Wilkins, C., & Weiss, L. G. (2001). Development of a General Ability Index for the Wechsler Adult Intelligence Scale—Third Edition. *Psychological Assessment, 13,* 566–571.

Unsworth, N., & Engle, R. W. (2007). On the division of short-term and working memory: An examination of simple and complex span and their relation to higher order abilities. *Psychological Bulletin, 133,* 1038–1066.

Vane, J. R., & Motta, R. W. (1984). Group intelligence tests. In G. Goldstein & M. Hersen (Eds.), *Handbook of psychological assessment* (pp. 100–116). New York, NY: Pergamon Press.

Verhaeghen, P., & Salthouse, T. A. (1997). Meta-analyses of age-cognition relations in adulthood: Estimates of linear and nonlinear age effects and structural models. *Psychological Bulletin, 122,* 231–249.

Wang, J., & Kaufman, A. S. (1993). Changes in fluid and crystallized intelligence across the 20- to 90-year age range on the K-BIT. *Journal of Psychoeducational Assessment, 11,* 29–37.

Ward, L. C., Bergman, M. A., & Hebert, K. R. (2012). WAIS-IV subtest covariance structure: Conceptual and statistical considerations. *Psychological Assessment, 24,* 328–340.

Wasserman, J. D. (2012). A history of intelligence assessment: The unfinished tapestry. In D. P. Flanagan & P. L. Harrison (Eds.), *Contemporary intellectual assessment: Theories, tests, and issues* (3rd ed., pp. 3–70). New York, NY: Guilford Press.

Watkins, M. W., & Canivez, G. L. (2004). Temporal stability of WISC-III subtest composite strengths and weaknesses. *Psychological Assessment, 16,* 133–138.

Wechsler, D. (1939). *The measurement of adult intelligence.* Baltimore, MD: Williams & Wilkins.

Wechsler, D. (1944). *The measurement of adult intelligence* (3rd ed.) Baltimore, MD: Williams & Wilkins.

Wechsler, D. (1946). *The Wechsler-Bellevue Intelligence Scale, Form II.* New York, NY: The Psychological Corporation.

Wechsler, D. (1949). *Manual for the Wechsler Intelligence Scale for Children (WISC).* New York, NY: The Psychological Corporation.

Wechsler, D. (1955). *Manual for the Wechsler Adult Intelligence Scale (WAIS).* San Antonio, TX: The Psychological Corporation.

Wechsler, D. (1958). *Measurement and appraisal of adult intelligence* (4th ed.). Baltimore, MD: Williams & Wilkins.

Wechsler, D. (1974). *Manual for the Wechsler Intelligence Scale for Children-Revised (WISC-R).* San Antonio, TX: The Psychological Corporation.

Wechsler, D. (1981). *Manual for the Wechsler Adult Intelligence Scale-Revised (WAIS-R).* San Antonio, TX: The Psychological Corporation.

Wechsler, D. (1997). *Wechsler Adult Intelligence Scale—Third Edition (WAIS-III) administration and scoring manual.* San Antonio, TX: The Psychological Corporation.

Wechsler, D. (2003). *Wechsler Intelligence Scale for Children (WISC-IV)* (4th ed.). San Antonio, TX: The Psychological Corporation.

Wechsler, D. (2008). *Wechsler Adult Intelligence Scale (WAIS-IV)* (4th ed.). San Antonio, TX: Pearson.

Wechsler, D. (2008, 2012). *Wechsler Adult Intelligence Scale (WAIS-IV)* (4th Ed.) [Digital]. Bloomington, MN: Pearson.

Wechsler, D. (2009a). *Advanced Clinical Solutions for the WAIS-IV and WMS-IV.* San Antonio, TX: Pearson Assessments.

Wechsler, D. (2009b). *Wechsler Memory Scale (WMS-IV)* (4th ed.). San Antonio, TX: Pearson.

Wechsler, D. (2011). *Wechsler Abbreviated Scale of Intelligence (2nd ed.) (WASI-II).* San Antonio, TX: Pearson, Inc.

Wechsler, D., & Naglieri, J. A. (2006). *Wechsler Nonverbal Scale of Ability (WNV).* San Antonio, TX: Harcourt Assessment.

Weiss, L. G. (2010). Considerations on the Flynn effect. *Journal of Psychoeducational Assessment, 28,* 482–493.

Weiss, L. G., Chen, H., Harris, J. G., Holdnack, J. A., & Saklofske, D. H. (2010). WAIS-IV use in a societal context. In L. G. Weiss, D. H. Saklofske, D. L. Coalson, & S. E. Raiford (Eds.), *WAIS-IV clinical use and interpretation* (pp. 97–139). San Diego, CA: Academic Press.

Weiss, L. G., Keith, T., Zhu, J., & Chen, H. (in press). WAIS-IV and clinical validation of the four- and five- factor interpretative approaches. Journal of Psychoeducational Assessment.

Weiss, L. G., Keith, T., Zhu, J., & Chen, H. (in press). WAIS-IV and clinical validation of the four- and five-factor interpretative approaches. Journal of Psychoeducational Assessment.

Weiss, L. G., Saklofske, D. H., Coalson, D., & Raiford, S. E. (2010a). Theoretical, empirical and clinical foundations of the WAIS-IV index scores. In L. G. Weiss, D. H. Saklofske, D. Coalson, & S. E. Raiford (Eds.), *WAIS-IV clinical use and interpretation: Scientist-practitioner perspectives* (pp. 61–94). San Diego, CA: Academic Press.

Weiss, L. G., Saklofske, D. H., Coalson, D., & Raiford, S. E. (Eds.). (2010b). *WAIS-IV clinical use and interpretation: Scientist-practitioner perspectives.* San Diego, CA: Academic Press.

Weiss, L. G., Saklofske, D. H., Schwartz, D. M., Prifitera, A., & Courville, T. (2006). Advanced clinical interpretation of WISC-IV index scores. In L. G. Weiss, D. H. Saklofske, A. Prifitera, & J. Holdnack (Eds.), *WISC-IV advanced clinical interpretation* (pp. 99–138). San Diego, CA: Elsevier.

Weiss, L. G., Saklofske, D., Prifitera, A., & Holdnack, J. (2006). *WISC-IV advanced clinical interpretation.* San Diego, CA: Academic Press.

Wesman, A. G. (1968). Intelligent testing. *American Psychologist, 23,* 267–274.

Willis, J. O. (2001). Scoring errors necessitate double-checking protocols. *Today's School Psychologist, 4,* 7.

Willis, J. O., & Dumont, R. P. (2002). *Guide to identification of learning disabilities* (3rd ed.) Peterborough, NH: Author.

Willis, S. L. (1985). Towards an educational psychology of the older adult learner: Intellectual and cognitive bases. In J. E. Birren and K. W. Schaie (Eds.), *Handbook of the psychology of aging* (2nd ed., pp. 818–847). New York, NY: Van Nostrand Reinhold.

Willoughby, R. R. (1927). Family similarities in mental-test abilities. *Genetic Psychology Monographs, 2,* 239–277.

Wisdom, N. M., Mignogna, J., & Collins, R. L. (2012). Variability in Wechsler Adult Intelligence Scale—IV subtest performance across age. *Archives of Clinical Neuropsychology, 27,* 389–397.

Wissler, C. (1901). The correlation of mental and physical tests. *Psychological Review, 3* (Monograph Supplement 16).

Wolf, L. E., Schreiber, H. E. & Wasserstein, J. (2008). *Adult learning disorders: Contemporary issues, a neuropsychologists handbook.* New York, NY: Psychology Press.

Yerkes, R. M. (1917). The Binet versus the point scale method of measuring intelligence. *Journal of Applied Psychology*, *1*, 111–122.

Yoakum, C. S., & Yerkes, R. M. (1920). *Army mental tests*. New York, NY: Henry Holt.

Zhou, X., Gregoire, J., & Zhu, J., (2010). The Flynn effect and the Wechsler scales. In L. G. Weiss, D. H. Saklofske, D. L. Coalson, & S. E. Raiford (Eds.), *WAIS-IV clinical use and interpretation* (pp. 141–166). San Diego, CA: Academic Press.

Zhou, X., Zhu, J., & Weiss, L. G. (2010). Peeking inside the "black box" of the Flynn effect: Evidence from three Wechsler instruments. *Journal of Psychoeducational Assessment*, *28*, 399–411.

Zimmerman, I. L., & Woo-Sam, J. M. (1985). Clinical applications. In B. B. Wolman (Ed.), *Handbook of intelligence* (pp. 873–898). New York, NY: Wiley.

Zimprich, D. (1998). Geschwindigkeit der Informationsverarbeitung und fluide Intelligenz im hoeheren Erwachsenenalter: Eine Sekundaeranalyse des Datenmaterials der Bonner Laengsschnittstudie des Alterns anhand von "Latent Growth Curve Models." [Speed of information processing and fluid intelligence in the elderly.] *Zeitschrift Fuer Gerontologie und Geriatrie*, *31*, 89–96.

Zimprich, D., & Martin, M. (2002). Can longitudinal changes in processing speed explain longitudinal age changes in fluid intelligence? *Psychology and Aging*, *17*, 690–695.

Annotated Bibliography

Drozdick, L. W., & Holdnack, J. A. (2011). *Essentials of WMS-IV assessment*. Hoboken, NJ: Wiley.

This book, which is devoted to the most recent version of Wechsler's Memory Scale (the Fourth Edition, WMS-IV), offers authoritative information from the developers of the test on its proper administration, scoring, and interpretation. The WMS-IV is a widely used measure of memory functioning that is particularly useful in the assessment of individuals with dementia, traumatic brain injury, and substance abuse problems, among other disorders. Written by experts on the WMS-IV, this book is a good source of information for dynamically integrating WMS-IV data with the WAIS-IV profile and scores on other measures of cognitive and memory functioning. The authors also offer expert assessment of the test's relative strengths and weaknesses, valuable advice on its clinical applications, and several illuminating case studies.

Flanagan, D. P., & Harrison, P. L. (Eds.). (2012). *Contemporary intellectual assessment: Theories, tests, and issues* (3rd ed.). New York, NY: Guilford Press.

This authoritative and state-of-the-art reference presents a comprehensive overview of intellectual and cognitive assessment, with a focus on clinical and practical applications, all steeped in a theoretical base. International experts and acknowledged leaders in this multidisciplinary field describe major theories of intelligence and provide the knowledge needed to use the latest measures of cognitive abilities with individuals of all ages. Evidence-based approaches to test interpretation, and their relevance for intervention, are described. For WAIS-IV users, the book addresses relevant issues in assessment, including topics such as culturally and linguistically diverse clients, gifted individuals, and those with learning difficulties and disabilities. In addition to treating the WAIS-IV with its own chapter, the book includes separate chapters on all major cognitive tests.

Flanagan, D. P., & Kaufman, A. S. (2009). *Essentials of WISC-IV assessment* (2nd ed.). Hoboken, NJ: Wiley.

This text, written primarily from an empirically based CHC foundation, provides details on administration, scoring, and interpretation of the WISC-IV. It details a theory-based approach to interpretation and includes step-by-step guidelines for applying this interpretive approach. The book also includes a CD-ROM containing software that automates the interpretive system for the WISC-IV. In addition, it provides information on many clinical populations and on the WISC-IV Integrated, as well as sample case reports.

Flanagan, D. P., Ortiz, S. O., & Alfonso, V. C. (2007). *Essentials of cross-battery assessment* (2nd ed.). Hoboken, NJ: Wiley.

This second edition provides a comprehensive set of guidelines and procedures for organizing assessments based on contemporary CHC theory and research. The authors integrate test results from different batteries in a psychometrically defensible way and interpret test results within the context of research on the relations between cognitive and academic abilities and processes. It also includes guidelines for assessing culturally and linguistically diverse populations and individuals suspected of having a specific learning disability. This book includes a CD-ROM containing three software programs for assisting in data management and interpretation, making decisions regarding the diagnosis of a specific learning disability, and discerning difference from disability in individuals whose cultural and linguistic backgrounds differ from the mainstream.

Frazier, T. W. (2011). Introduction to the special section on advancing WAIS-IV and WMS-IV clinical interpretation. *Assessment, 18,* 131–132.

This special section in an issue of the journal Assessment is a collection of work that highlights the major innovations and enhancements in the latest versions of the Wechsler Adult Intelligence Scale and Wechsler Memory Scale and provides clinically valuable information for clinicians who administer and interpret the WAIS-IV and WMS-IV as part of a comprehensive battery. The articles that comprise the special section of the journal bring important conceptual, technical, and clinically meaningful information to (a) clinicians who regularly use tests of cognitive ability and memory, (b) researchers who study and strive to improve assessment instruments, and (c) all professionals who endeavor to understand the cognitive underpinnings of disease.

Groth-Marnat, G. (2009). *Handbook of psychological assessment* (5th ed.). Hoboken, NJ: Wiley.

This revision of this resource on psychological assessment features thorough coverage of the principles of assessment, evaluation, referral, treatment planning, and report writing. Material is presented in a practical, skills-based manner (e.g., how to integrate test data into treatment plans and how to write psychological reports) and offers coverage of the most widely used assessment instruments (including the WAIS-IV, WMS-IV, WISC-IV, Rorschach, Thematic Apperception Test, neuropsychological screening tests, behavioral measures, CPI, MCMI-III, and MMPI-2/MMPI-A). This reference provides clinical psychologists, therapists, school psychologists, and counselors with step-by-step, expert guidance on how to conduct a comprehensive psychological evaluation.

Kaufman, A. S., & Lichtenberger, E. O. (2006). *Assessing adolescent and adult intelligence* (3rd ed.). Hoboken, NJ: Wiley.

This book on the WAIS-III provides in-depth discussion of topics that pertain to adult assessment in general. The review of research studies conducted on the Wechsler-Bellevue, WAIS, WAIS-R, and WAIS-III is especially relevant to the WAIS-IV. Topics include relationship of IQ to background variables (occupation, race/ethnicity, education, gender), as well as empirical research with patients diagnosed as having unilateral brain damage, Alzheimer's disease, Huntington's disease, dyslexia, alcoholism, mental retardation (intellectual disability), multiple sclerosis, learning disabilities, and other disorders. The book presents a discussion of the scales from a theoretical perspective, along with numerous hypothesized explanations for patterns of typical performance on the Wechsler scales. The philosophy of the intelligent testing approach is woven throughout the text and is exemplified in several case studies. The history of the Wechsler scales is also presented.

Psychological Corporation. (2008). *WAIS-IV technical and interpretive manual.* San Antonio, TX: Author.

This manual comes as part of the WAIS-IV kit and provides introductory information on the WAIS-IV. The text details development of the norms and the standardization procedures. Reliability and validity studies are presented. The WAIS-IV is compared to other measures of cognitive ability, memory functioning, language functioning, and motor speed. Studies on groups with neurological disorders such as Alzheimer's disease, Huntington's disease, Parkinson's disease, traumatic brain injury, multiple sclerosis, and temporal lobe epilepsy are reviewed. In addition, studies of mental retardation, attention-deficit/hyperactivity disorder, learning disabilities, and other disorders are addressed. Global information on interpretation is provided, along with a plethora of statistical tables for clinicians and researchers.

Sattler, J. M., & Ryan, J. (2009). *Assessment with the WAIS-IV.* San Diego, CA: Authors.

This book provides coverage of the rationale, psychometrics, administrative and scoring guidelines, and interpretative considerations for the WAIS-IV. For both students and professionals, the format of the chapters organizes the material in a practical manner (using examples, step-by-step instructions, and tables). General recommendations for assessment and report writing are presented, as well as information on specific populations, including individuals with sensory and physical impairments, the aging population, and individuals with cognitive disorders.

Wechsler, D. (2008). *WAIS-IV administration and scoring manual.* San Antonio, TX: The Psychological Corporation.

This manual comes as part of the WAIS-IV kit. It provides a basic description of the WAIS-IV scales and subtests. Revisions from the WAIS-III to the fourth edition are reviewed subtest by subtest. WAIS-IV examiners can gather important information about administration from this manual. For each WAIS-IV subtest, the starting, discontinue, and timing rules are articulated. Examiners are provided with a basic script and detailed directions for how to administer each subtest in a standardized manner. Subtest norms tables are provided in the back of the manual along with supplementary tables for determining the size of differences needed for significance.

Weiss, L. G., Saklofske, D. H., Coalson, D., & Raiford, S. E. (Eds.) (2010). *WAIS-IV clinical use and interpretation: Scientist-practitioner perspectives.* San Diego, CA: Academic Press.

Written by the creators of the WAIS-IV, this book discusses the changes made between the third and fourth editions of the WAIS along with common questions and answers about use and interpretation. Supplemental information is given about the General Ability Index (GAI) and the Cognitive Proficiency Index (CPI) that doesn't appear in the test manual. Advanced analyses and information beyond what is offered in the WAIS-IV manual are also detailed to help clinicians interpret data for special clinical populations, including patients from multicultural backgrounds, those evaluated in neuropsychological settings, those who are experiencing psychological disorders, and those who are elderly. Useful information is provided about using the WAIS-IV alongside the WMS-IV, and several innovative research investigations on ethnicity, socioeconomic status (SES), and aging are incorporated into diverse chapters.

About the Authors

Elizabeth O. Lichtenberger, PhD, is a licensed clinical psychologist in California and an author whose works have focused on psychological assessment. In addition to her current professional roles, she has worked as an adjunct faculty member at Alliant International University in San Diego and a researcher at the Laboratory for Cognitive Neuroscience at the Salk Institute for Biological Studies in La Jolla, California. Her work at the Salk Institute focused on the cognitive and neuropsychological patterns in children with genetic developmental disorders. Because of her expertise in psychological, psychoeducational, and neuropsychological assessment, she also serves as a psychoeducational test/measurement consultant and trainer for organizations and provides consultation to individual psychologists.

Dr. Lichtenberger is a published author of numerous books, book chapters, and articles on assessment and assessment instruments, including *Assessing Adolescent and Adult Intelligence* (3rd ed.), *Essentials of Assessment Report Writing*, *Essentials of KABC-II Assessment*, *Essentials of WIAT-II® and KTEA-II Assessment*, *Essentials of Cognitive Assessment with KAIT and Other Kaufman Measures*, *Essentials of WAIS-III Assessment*, *Essentials of WMS-III Assessment*, *Essentials of WPPSI-III Assessment*, and *Essentials of WISC-III and WPPSI-R Assessment*. In addition, she has served in an editorial capacity for books and journals. For example, she served as a consulting editor of the second edition of the *Encyclopedia of Special Education: A Reference for the Education of the Handicapped and Other Exceptional Children and Adults* and is currently on the editorial board of the journal *Psychology in the Schools*.

Alan S. Kaufman, PhD, a leading expert on intelligence testing, is Clinical Professor of Psychology at the Child Study Center at the Yale University School of Medicine. His books, tests, and intelligent testing approach have had worldwide impact on clinical assessment. Mentored by David Wechsler and Robert Thorndike, Dr. Kaufman's tests with his wife Nadeen (e.g., KABC-II and KTEA-II) and his approach to test interpretation reflect an integration of psychometric, theoretical, and clinical perspectives. Alan and Nadeen are the Series Editors of Wiley's *Essentials of Psychological Assessment* series.

Author Index

Subject Index

455

About the CD-ROM

INTRODUCTION

This appendix provides you with information on the contents of the CD that accompanies this book. For the latest information, please refer to the ReadMe file located at the root of the CD.

System Requirements

Make sure that your computer meets the minimum system requirements listed in this section. If your computer doesn't match up to most of these requirements, you may have a problem using the contents of the CD.

- A computer with a processor running at 120 Mhz or faster.
- At least 32 MB of total RAM installed on your computer; for best performance, we recommend at least 64 MB.
- A CD-ROM drive.
- Adobe Flash Player 9 or later (free download from Adobe.com).

NOTE: Many popular spreadsheet programs are capable of reading Microsoft Excel files. However, users should be aware that formatting might be lost when using a program other than Microsoft Excel.

Using the CD With Windows

To access the content from the CD follow these steps:

1. Insert the CD into your computer's CD-ROM drive. The license agreement appears (Windows 7 > Select Start.exe from the AutoPlay window or follow the same steps for Windows Vista.)
2. The interface won't launch if you have autorun disabled. In that case, click Start > Run (for Windows Vista, Start > All Programs > Accessories > Run). In the dialog box that appears, type D:\Start.exe. (Replace D with the proper letter if your CD drive uses a different letter. If you don't know the letter, see how your CD drive is listed under My Computer.) Click OK.

3. Read through the license agreement, and then click the Accept button if you want to use the CD. The CD interface appears. Simply select the material you want to view.

Using the CD on a Mac

To install the items from the CD to your hard drive, follow these steps:

1. Insert the CD into your computer's CD-ROM drive.
2. The CD icon will display on your desktop; double-click to open it.
3. Double-click the Start button.
4. Read the license agreement, and then click the Accept button to use the CD.
5. The CD interface will display. The interface provides a simple point-and-click way to explore the contents of the CD.

Note for Mac users: the content menus may not function as expected in newer versions of Safari and Firefox; however, the documents are available by navigating to the Author Files folder.

WHAT'S ON THE CD

The following sections provide a summary of the software and other materials you'll find on the CD.

Content

The accompanying CD-ROM contains worksheet files written and programmed in Microsoft Excel that allow readers to enter WAIS-IV data along with other specific test data and have it analyzed following the steps outlined in Chapter 5 of this book. The Excel program called *WAIS-IV Data Management and Interpretive Assistant* (WAIS-IV DMIA) v2.0 was programmed by Elizabeth Lichtenberger. Note that the WAIS-IV steps from Chapter 5 may be completed by hand, following the WAIS-IV Interpretive Worksheet included in Appendix A.1 (found in the "Contents" folder), or may be performed automatically using the WAIS-IV DMIA v2.0.

Examples of the Excel worksheets on the CD are presented as figures in the book. These automated worksheets are provided on the CD for your convenience in using, applying, and understanding the interpretive method described in this book. The WAIS-IV DMIA v2.0 is meant to expedite analysis and interpretation of WAIS-IV data.

It is important to note that the WAIS-IV DMIA does not convert WAIS-IV *raw scores* to any metric. Users of this program are responsible for following the test publisher's administration and scoring guidelines. That is, all WAIS-IV scores entered into this program must be derived from the norms and procedures provided by the test publisher. Note that the WAIS-IV clinical clusters created by Elizabeth Lichtenberger and Alan Kaufman are automatically computed by the WAIS-IV DMIA v2.0 based on actual norms provided to them by the test publisher. See Chapter 5 for details.

Also included on the CD-ROM are all the appendices mentioned throughout the book. These appendices may be found in a folder marked "Appendices." The following appendices are included:

Appendix A.1	WAIS-IV Interpretive Worksheet
Appendix A.2	CPI Equivalents of Sums of Scaled Scores
Appendix A.3	Crystallized Intelligence (Gc) Factor Equivalents of Sums of Scaled Scores for Keith Model
Appendix A.4	Short-Term Memory (Gsm) Factor Equivalents of Sums of Scaled Scores for Keith Model
Appendix A.5	Fluid Intelligence Reasoning (Gf) Factor Equivalents of Sums of Scaled Scores for Keith Model
Appendix A.6	Visual Processing (Gv) Factor Equivalents of Sums of Scaled Scores for Keith Model
Appendix A.7	Definitions of CHC Abilities and Processes
Appendix A.8	Visual Motor Speed Cluster Equivalents of Sums of Scaled Scores for Steps 11a and 12b
Appendix A.9	Problem Solving without Visual-Motor Speed Cluster Equivalents of Sums of Scaled Scores for Step 11a
Appendix A.10	Mental Manipulation Cluster Equivalents of Sums of Scaled Scores for Step 11a
Appendix A.11	Verbal Fluid Reasoning Cluster Equivalents of Sums of Scaled Scores for Steps 11a and 12b
Appendix A.12	Lexical Knowledge Cluster Equivalents of Sums of Scaled Scores for Steps 11a and 12b
Appendix A.13	General Information Cluster Equivalents of Sums of Scaled Scores for Steps 11a and 12b
Appendix A.14	Long-Term Memory Cluster Equivalents of Sums of Scaled Scores for Steps 11a and 12b
Appendix A.15	Short-Term Memory Cluster Equivalents of Sums of Scaled Scores for Step 11a
Appendix A.16	Fluid Reasoning Cluster Equivalents of Sums of Scaled Scores for Step 11a

Applications

Adobe Reader

Included on this CD is a link to download Adobe Acrobat Reader for viewing PDF files. For more information and system requirements, please go to www.adobe.com.

OpenOffice.org

Included on this CD is a link to download OpenOffice.org for viewing spreadsheet files. For more information and system requirements, please go to www.openoffice.org.

OpenOffice.org is a free multiplatform office productivity suite. It is similar to Microsoft Office or Lotus SmartSuite, but OpenOffice.org is absolutely free. It includes word processing, spreadsheet, presentation, and drawing applications that enable you to create professional documents, newsletters, reports, and presentations. It supports most file formats of other office software. You should be able to edit and view any files created with other office solutions.

Shareware programs are fully functional, trial versions of copyrighted programs. If you like particular programs, register with their authors for a nominal fee and receive licenses, enhanced versions, and technical support.

Freeware programs are copyrighted games, applications, and utilities that are free for personal use. Unlike shareware, these programs do not require a fee or provide technical support.

GNU software is governed by its own license, which is included inside the folder of the GNU product. See the GNU license for more details.

Trial, demo, or evaluation versions are usually limited either by time or by functionality (such as being unable to save projects). Some trial versions are very sensitive to system date changes. If you alter your computer's date, the programs will time out and no longer be functional.

TROUBLESHOOTING

If you have difficulty installing or using any of the materials on the companion CD, try the following solutions:

- *Turn off any anti-virus software that you may have running.* Installers sometimes mimic virus activity and can make your computer incorrectly believe that it is being infected by a virus. (Be sure to turn the anti-virus software back on later.)
- *Close all running programs.* The more programs you're running, the less memory is available to other programs. Installers also typically update files and programs; if you keep other programs running, installation may not work properly.
- *Reboot if necessary.* If all else fails, rebooting your machine can often clear any conflicts in the system.

CUSTOMER CARE

If you have trouble with the CD-ROM, please call the Wiley Product Technical Support phone number at (800) 762-2974. Outside the United States, call 1(317) 572–3994. You can also contact Wiley Product Technical Support at http:// support.wiley.com. Wiley will provide technical support only for installation and other general quality control items. For technical support on the applications themselves, consult the program's vendor or author.

To place additional orders or to request information about other Wiley products, please call (877) 762-2974.

CUSTOMER NOTE: IF THIS BOOK IS ACCOMPANIED BY SOFTWARE, PLEASE READ THE FOLLOWING BEFORE OPENING THE PACKAGE

This software contains files to help you utilize the models described in the accompanying book. By opening the package, you are agreeing to be bound by the following agreement.

This software product is protected by copyright and all rights are reserved by the author, John Wiley & Sons, Inc., or their licensors. You are licensed to use this software on a single computer. Copying the software to another medium or format for use on a single computer does not violate the U.S. Copyright Law. Copying the software for any other purpose is a violation of the U.S. Copyright Law.

This software product is sold as is without warranty of any kind, either express or implied, including but not limited to the implied warranty of merchantability and fitness for a particular purpose. Neither Wiley nor its dealers or distributors assumes any liability for any alleged or actual damages arising from the use of or the inability to use this software. (Some states do not allow the exclusion of implied warranties, so the exclusion may not apply to you.)